I0836654

GUIDE

TO

SOCIAL HAPPINESS,

BY

Mrs. Ellis

"My earliest and my best friend."

GUIDE

TO

SOCIAL HAPPINESS.

BY

MRS ELLIS,

AUTHOR OF WOMEN, DAUGHTERS, WIVES AND MOTHERS OF ENGLAND,

&c. &c.

New-York

EDWARD WALKER, 114 FULTON-STREET

CONTENTS.

PREFACE

In offering to the attention of the public, two volumes on the poetry of life, some apology seems necessary for prefixing to my book a title of such indefinite signification. If poetry be understood to mean mere versification, and life mere vitality, it would be difficult indeed to establish their connection with each other. The design of the present work is to treat of poetic feeling, rather than poetry; and this feeling I have endeavoured to describe as the great connecting link between our intellects and our affections; while the customs of society, as well as the license of modern literature, afford me sufficient authority for the use of the word life in its widely extended sense, as comprehending all the functions, attributes, and capabilities peculiar to sentient beings.

Whatever may be the opinion of the public respecting the manner in which my task has been executed, the enjoyment it has afforded to the writer, in being the means of a renewed acquaintance with the principles of intellectual happiness, is already in possession; and I have only to wish that the reader may be induced to seek the same enjoyment, in a more spiritual intercourse with nature, and a more profound admiration of the beauty and harmony of the creation.

THE

POETRY OF LIFE.

CHARACTERISTICS OF POETRY.

THAT the quality of modern Poetry is a subject of general complaint with those who would purchase—that the price affixed to it by the judgment of the public is equally complained of by those who would sell—in short, that Poetry is at present "a drug in the market," is a phrase too hackneyed, too vulgar and too frequently assented too, to need repetition here; except as an established fact, the nature, cause, and consequence of which, I propose endeavouring to point out in the following pages.

Wherever a taste for Poetry exists, there will be a desire to read as well as to write; to receive as well as to impart that enjoyment which poetic feeling affords. In other cases of marketable produce, the supply is found to keep pace with the demand, except when physical causes operate against it. If the poets of the present day have "written themselves out," as the common and unmeaning expression is, what, with a rapidly increasing population, should hinder the springing up of fresh poets to delight the world? The fact is, that most of the living poets have betaken themselves to Prose as a more lucrative employment, thus proving, that the taste for Poetry is lamentably decreasing in the public mind; and while on one hand, genius is weeping over her harvest "whitening in the sun," without hope of profit to repay the toil of gathering in the golden store; on the other, criticism is in arms against less sordid adventurers, and calls in no measured terms upon the mighty minstrels of past ages to avenge Parnassus of her wrongs.

Three different motives operate in stimulating men to write Poetry: the love of fame, the want of money, and an internal restlessness of feeling, which is too indiscriminately called genius. The first of these ceases with the second, for without the means of circulation there can be no hope of fame. The third alone operates in the present day, and small, indeed, is the recompense bestowed in these ungrateful times upon the poets who write because they cannot help it. Yet after all, is not this the true and legitimate method by which the genuine coin of genius is moulded? The love of fame is a high and soul-stirring principle, but still it is degraded with the stigma of selfish aggrandizement, and who does not feel that a shade is cast upon those expression of noble sentiment, which bear the impress of having been prepared and set forth solely for public approbation. The want of money is, indeed, a potent stimulus. How potent let the midnight labours of the starving poet testify. The want of money may it is true, urge onward towards the same goal as the love of fame, but the one operates, as it were, from behind, by the painful application of a goad; while the other attracts, and fascinates by the brightness of some object before, which too often proves to be an ignis fatuus in the distance. But there is within the human mind an active and powerful principle, that awakens the dormant faculties, lights up the brain, and launches forth imagination to gather up from the wide realm of nature the very essence of what every human bosom pines for, when it aspires to a higher state of existence, and feels the insufficiency of this. It is this heaven-born and ethereal principle, not inaptly personified as the Spirit of Poesy, that weaves a garland of the flowers which imagination has culled; and from the fervency of its own passion, to impart as well as to receive enjoyment, casts this garland at the feet of the sordid and busy multitude, who pause, not to admire, but trample its vivid beauty in the dust. It is this principle that will not let the intellectual faculties remain inactive, but is for ever working in the laboratory of the brain, combining, sublimating, and purifying. It is this principle, when under the government of right reason, which is properly called genius. It is this principle when perverted from its high purpose, and made the minister of base passions, which produces the most splendid and most melancholy ruin. It is this principle, when devoted to the cause of holiness, which scatters over the path of desolation flowers of unfading loveliness: pours floods of light upon our distant prospects of the celestial city; and inspires the harps of heaven-taught minstrels with undying melody.

This principle, in less figurative phraseology, I would describe as the Poetry of Life; because it pervades all things either seen, felt, or understood, where the associations are sublime, beautiful and tender, or refined. In short, where the ideas which naturally connect themselves with our contemplation of such subjects are most exclusively intellectual, and separate from sense.

That there is much Poetry in real life, with all its sorrows, and pains, and sordid anxieties, and that "all is not vanity and vexation of spirit under the sun," to him who can honestly and innocently enjoy the commonest blessings of Providence," has been already proved by one in whose steps I feel that I am unworthy to walk; but since, in his admirable lectures on Poetry, he has treated the subject as a science, rather than a principle; I am imboldened to take up the theme, to which he, above all men (more especially above all women) would have done justice, had he chosen to launch forth into more abstruse and speculative notions respecting the nature and influence of poetic feeling.

That the poetry of the present times is an unsaleable article needs then no farther proof than the observation and experience of every day, and since it is as difficult to believe that the human mind with all the advantages afforded by the most enlightened state of civilization should have become more base and degenerate, as that the treasury of nature should be exhausted, it becomes a subject of curious and interesting investigation to search out the cause, and ascertain whether it may not be in some measure attributable to our present system of education being one of words rather than of ideas, of the head rather than of the heart, of calculation rather than moral feeling.

While the full and free tide of knowledge is daily pouring from the press, while books and book makers appear before us in every possible situation, and under all imaginable circumstances, so that to have written a volume, is no less a distinction than to have read one through; while cheap and popular publications fraught with all manner of interesting details are accessible to the poorest classes of the community, it is impossible to believe that there is not sufficient talent concentrated or afloat to constitute a poet. And while the blue sky bends over all—while that sky is studded with the same bright host of stars, amongst which the philosopher is perpetually discovering fresh worlds of glory; while the seasons with their infinite variety still continue to bring forth, to vivify, and to perfect the produce of the earth; while the woods are vocal with melody, and the air is peopled with myriads of ephemeral beings whose busy wings are dipped in gold, or bathed in azure, or light and fragile as the gossomer, yet ever bearing them on through a region of delight, from the snowy bosom of the lily, to the scented atmosphere of the rose; while the mountain stream rushes down from the hills, or the rivers roll onward to the sea; and above all, while there exists in the heart of man a deep sense of these enjoyments—a mirror in which beauty is reflected—an echo to the voice of music; while he is capable of feeling admiration for that which is noble or sublime, tenderness for the weak, sympathy for the suffering, and affection for all things lovely, it is impossible to believe that true poetry should cease to please, or fail to awaken a response in the human heart. And that man is capable of all this, and more, and more capable in proportion as he cultivates and cherishes the noblest faculties of his nature, we have to thank the Giver of all our enjoyments, the Creator of all our capabilities.

How are these faculties now cultivated? "Knowledge is power." But neither is knowledge all that we live for, nor power all that we enjoy. There are deep mysteries in the book of nature which all can feel, but none will ever understand until the veil of mortality shall be withdrawn. There are stirrings in the soul of man which constitute the very essence of his being, and which power can neither satisfy nor subdue. Yet this mystery reveals more truly than the clearest proofs or mightiest deductions of science, that a master hand has been for ages, and is still at work, above, beneath, and around us; and this moving principle is for ever reminding us that in our nature we inherit the germs of a future existence over which time has no influence, and the grave no victory.

Far be it from every liberal mind to maintain the superiority of feeling over the other faculties of our nature. In forming a correct opinion on any subject of taste, it is necessary to examine, compare, and criticise, with an eye familiarized to what is most admirable, and a judgment controlled by a strict adherence to the rules of art. No argument is required to prove that were feeling allowed to be the sole impulse of our actions, we should become as culpable in morals, as absurd in our pursuits; or that the man gifted with the quickest perceptions and keenest sensibility, yet untutored in scientific rules, would expose himself to well-merited ridicule, should he attempt in a poem or a picture, to delineate his own conceptions of grandeur or beauty. Even were he able to throw into his performance the force of the most daring genius, or the most inextinguishable enthusiasm, it would prove in the end, no better than a mockery of art, and remain a memorial of his own madness and folly. Nor, on the other hand, will he who is by nature destitute of sensibility, or he who has spent the spring-time of existence in the crowded city, and expended all the fresh energies of his mind in the bustle and hurry of sordid occupations, having laid up no secret store of associations with what is noble, lovely or refined in nature, be able to produce a poem or a picture that will please the imagination or warm the heart, even though in his laboured performance, the critic should find no fault with the harmony of his numbers, the choice of his colouring, or the subjects of both.

The qualifications of a true poet are, in the first place, natural capacity, and favourable opportunity for receiving impressions; and in the second, ability to arrange, compare, and select from these impressions. Without the former, he must be deficient in materials for his work; without the latter, he must want the power to make a rational use of any materials whatever. It is the former alone that we can suppose to be wanting in the present day; for though the human mind unquestionably retains the same capabilities it possessed in the last century, it is possible that opportunities for imbibing strong impressions from external nature may not now be afforded with the same facility; and that in the present rapid march of intellect, the muse of poesy may be so hurried out of breath, as not to find time to chant her charmed lays.

The same causes which tend to destroy that taste, which would ensure to the works of our poets a welcome reception in refined and intellectual circles of society, necessarily operate against the production of poetry; and thus, while we refuse to feast our minds with ideas of the sublime and beautiful, we must naturally lose the higher sensibilities and finer perceptions of our nature. To awaken these sensibilities, and quicken these perceptions, by pointing out what it is which constitutes the poetry of life, will be the task of the writer through the following pages; to prove, that in order to see, think, or write poetically, it is necessary that we should at some period of our lives, have had time and opportunity to receive deep and lasting impressions; and that out of these impressions is woven the interminable chain of association which connects our perceptions of things present, with our ideas or conceptions of those which are remote.

In commencing a serious and arduous task, it would ill become an accountable agent to neglect the important inquiry of what may be the moral good of such an undertaking; and here the question will naturally occur to many, whether poetry is of any real value in promoting the happiness of man. England is a commercial country, and we know that poetry has little to do with increasing the facilities of commerce, as little as with the better regulation of the poor laws, or with the settlement of any of those leading questions which at present agitate the political world. But poetry has a world of its own—a world in which, if sordid calculations have no place, the noble, the immortal part of our nature is cherished, invigorated and refined.

In touching upon this inspiring theme, it is impossible not to feel the inadequacy of moderate powers when compared with those of perhaps the most luminous writers of the present day, whose review of Milton's works contains in direct relation to this subject, the following eloquent and inimitable appeal to the highest feelings of human nature. I quote at great length, because I would not break the charm of the whole passage by garbled extracts; and I risk the quotation at the peril of having the rest of my book contrasted with these pages, like a chaplet of mock gems, in which is one true diamond.

"Milton's fame rests chiefly on his poetry, and to this we naturally give our first attention. By those who are apt to speak of poety as light reading, Milton's eminence in this sphere may be considered as only giving him a high rank among the contributors to public amusement. Not so thought Milton. Of all God's gifts of intellect, he esteemed poetical genius the most transcendant. He esteemed it in himself as a kind of inspiration, and wrote his great works with something of the conscious dignity of a prophet. We agree with Milton in his estimate of poetry. It seems to us the divinest of all arts; for it is the breathing or expression of that principle or sentiment, which is deepest and sublimest in human nature; we mean of that thirst or aspiration, to which no mind is wholly a stranger, for something purer and lovelier, something more powerful, lofty, and thrilling than ordinary and real life affords. No doctrine is more common among Christians than that of man's immortality, but it is not so generally understood, that the germs or principles of his whole future being are *now* wrapped up in his soul, as the rudiments of the future plant in the seed. As a necessary result of this constitution, the soul, possessed and moved by these mighty, though infant energies, is perpetually stretching beyond what is present and visible, struggling against the bounds of its earthly prison-house, and seeking relief and joy in imaginings of unseen and ideal being.

This view of our nature which has never been fully developed, and which goes farther towards explaining the contradictions of human life than all others, carries us to the very foundation and sources of poetry. He, who cannot interpret by his own consciousness what we have now said, wants the true key to works of genius. He has not penetrated those sacred recesses of the soul, where poetry is born and nourished, and inhales immortal vigour, and wings herself for her heavenward flight. In an intellectual nature, framed for progress, and for higher modes of being, there must be creative energies, powers of original, and ever-growing thought; and poetry is the form in which these energies are chiefly manifested. It is the glorious prerogative of this art, that it makes 'all things new' for the gratification of a divine instinct. It indeed finds its elements in what it actually sees and experiences, in the worlds of matter and mind, but it combines and blends these into new forms, and according to new affinities; breaks down, if we may so say, the distinctions and bounds of nature; imparts to material objects life, and sentiment, and emotion, and invests the mind with the powers and splendours of the outward creation; describes the surrounding universe in the colours which the passions throw over it, and depicts the mind in those modes of repose or agitation, of tenderness or sublime emotion, which manifest its thirst for a more powerful and joyful existence. To a man of a literal and prosaic character, the mind may seem lawless in these workings; but it observes higher laws than it transgresses, the laws of the immortal intellect; it is trying and developing its best faculties; and in the objects which it describes, or in the emotions which it awakens, anticipates those states of progressive power, splendour, beauty and happiness, for which it was created.

"We accordingly believe that poetry, so far from injuring society, is one of the great instruments of its refinement and exaltation. It lifts the mind above ordinary life; gives it a respite from depressing cares, and awakens the consciousness of its affinity with what is pure and noble. In its legitimate and highest efforts, it has the same tendency and aim with Christianity; that is, to spiritualize our nature. True, poetry has been made the instrument of vice, the pander of bad passions; but when genius thus stoops, it dims its fires, and parts with much of its power; and even when poetry is enslaved to licentiousness or misanthropy, she cannot wholly forget her true vocation. Strains of pure feeling, touches of tenderness, images of innocent happiness, sympathies with suffering virtue, bursts of scorn or indignation at the hollowness of the world, passages true to our moral nature, often escape in an immoral work, and show us how hard it is for a gifted spirit to divorce itself wholly from what is good. Poetry has a natural alliance with our best affections. It delights in the beauty and sublimity of the outward creation and of the soul. It indeed portrays with terrible energy the excesses of the passions; but they are passions which show a mighty nature, which are full of power, which command awe, and excite a deep, though shuddering sympathy. Its great tendency and purpose is, to carry the mind beyond and above the beaten, dusty, weary walks of ordinary life; to lift it into a purer element; and to breathe into it more profound and generous emotion. It reveals to us the loveliness of nature, brings back the freshness of youthful feeling, revives the relish of simple pleasures, keeps unquenched the enthusiasm which warmed the springtime of our being, refines youthful love, strengthens our interest in human nature by vivid delineations of its tenderest and loftiest feeling, knits us by new ties with universal being, and through the brightness of its prophetic visions, helps faith to lay hold on the future life.

"We are aware that it is objected to poetry, that it gives wrong views, and excites false expectations of life; peoples the mind with shadows and illusions, and builds up imagination on the ruins of wisdom. That there is a wisdom against which poetry wars, the wisdom of the senses, which makes physical comfort and gratification the supreme good, and wealth the chief interest of life, we do not deny; nor do we deem it the least service which poetry renders to mankind, that it redeems them from the thraldom of this earth-born prudence. But passing over this topic, we would observe, that the complaint against poetry as abounding in illusion and deception, is in the main, groundless. In many poems, there is more truth than in many histories and philosophic theories. The fictions of genius are often the vehicles of the sublimest verities, and its flashes often open new regions of thought, and throw new light on the mysteries of our being. In poetry, the letter is falsehood, but the spirit is often profoundest wisdom. And if truth thus dwells in the boldest fictions of the poet, much more may it be expected in his delineations of life; for the present life, which is the first stage of the immortal mind, abounds in the materials of poetry; and it is the high office of the bard to detect this divine element among the grosser labours and pleasures of our earthly being. The present life is not wholly prosaic, precise, tame, and finite. To the gifted eye, it abounds in the poetic. The affections which spread beyond ourselves, and stretch far into futurity; the workings of mighty passions, which seem to arm the soul with almost super-human energy; the innocent and irrepressible joy of infancy; the bloom, and buoyancy, and dazzling hopes of youth; the throbbings of the heart, when it first wakes to love, and dreams of a happiness too vast for earth; woman, with her beauty, and grace, and gentleness, and fulness of feeling, and depth of affection, and her blushes of purity, and the tones and looks which only a mother's heart can inspire;—these are all poetical. It is not true that the poet paints a life which does not exist; he only extracts and concentrates, as it were, life's ethereal essence; arrests and condenses its volatile fragrance, brings together its scattered beauties, and prolongs its more refined but evanescent joys; and in this he does well; for it is good to feel that life is not wholly usurped by cares for subsistence, and physical gratifications, but admits, in measures which may be indefinitely enlarged, sentiments, and delights worthy of a higher being. This power of poetry to refine our views of life and happiness, is more and more needed as society advances. It is needed to withstand the encroachments of heartless and artificial manners, which make civilization so tame and uninteresting. It is needed to counteract the tendency of physical science, which being now sought, not as formerly for intellectual gratification, but for multiplying bodily comforts, requires a new development of imagination, taste, and poetry, to preserve men from sinking into an earthly, material, Epicurean life."

WHY CERTAIN OBJECTS ARE, OR ARE NOT, POETICAL.

That a book, a picture and sometimes a very worthy man, are without Poetry, is a fact almost as deeply felt, and as well understood, as the memorable anathema of Shakspeare against the man who had not music in his soul. In many books this is no defect; in all pictures it is a striking and important one; while in men it can only be a defect proportioned to the high standing they may choose to take in the scale of intellect or feeling. The spirit of Poetry has little to do with the labours of the artisan, nor would our tables be more plentifully supplied, were they furnished under the direction of the muses. But who would feel even the slightest gratification in reading Wordsworth's Excursion, with a companion, who could not feel poetically? or who would choose to explore the wild and magnificent beauties of mountain scenery, with one whose ideas were bounded by the limits of the Bank of England?

When our nature is elevated above the mere objects of sense, there is a want created in us of something, which the business of the world, nay, even science itself, is unable to supply; for not only is the bustling man of business an unwelcome associate in the wilderness of untrodden beauty, but even he becomes wearisome at last, who applies his noisy hammer to every projection of rock, and peeps into every crevice, and up the side of every precipice with eyes, thoughts, and memory for nothing but strata; precisely as it is presented to his vision then and there, without once giving himself time to draw deductions from what he discovers, to make an extended survey of the distant scenery, or to drink in the enjoyment of the magnificent whole.

In the general contemplation of external nature, we feel the influence of Poetry, though chiefly and almost exclusively in objects which are, in themselves or their associations, beautiful or sublime. Thus, we are pleased with a widely extended view, even over a level country, purely because the sublime idea of space is connected with it; but let this expanse be travelled over, closely inspected, and regarded in its minutia, and it becomes indescribably wearisome and monotonous. The fact is, the idea of space is lost, while the attention is arrested and absorbed by immediate and minor circumstances. The mind is incapable of feeling two opposite sensations at the same time, and all impressions made upon the senses being so much more quick and sudden than those made through them upon the imagination, they have the power to attract and carry away the attention in the most peremptory and vexatious manner. All subjects intended to inspire admiration or reverence, must therefore be treated with the most scrupulous regard to refinement. It is so easy for the vulgar touch to

> "Turn what was once romantic to burlesque."

A tone of ridicule may at once dispel the charm of tenderness, and a senseless parody may for awhile destroy the sublimity of a splendid poem.

Among the works of art, the influence of poetic feeling is most perceptible in painting and sculpture. A picture sometimes pleases from a secret charm which cannot well be defined, and which arises not so much from the proper adjustment of colour and outline according to the rules of art, as from the sudden, mysterious, and combined emotions which the sight of it awakens in the soul. But let any striking departure from these rules arrest the attention, let the eye be offended by the colouring, and the taste chocked by the grouping or perspective—the illusion is destroyed, and the poet awakes from his dream. It is precisely the same with sculpture, that most sublime production of the hand of man, which, by its cold, still, marble beauty, unawakened by the shocks of time, unmoved by the revolutions of the world, has power to charm the wandering thoughts, and inspire sensations of deep reverence and awe. But let us suppose the enthusiast returning to gaze upon the statue, which has been, through years of wandering, little less than an idol to his enraptured fancy, and that hands profane (for such things are) have presumed to colour the pupils of the up-turned eyes—let any other sensation whatever, directly at variance with what the figure itself is calculated to inspire, be made to strike the attention of the beholder, and he is plunged at once down that fatal and irrevocable step, which leads from the sublime to the ridiculous.

The human face, the most familiar object to our eyes, since they first opened upon the world, may be, and often is, highly poetical. Who has not seen amidst the multitude some countenance to which he turns, and turns again, with strange wonder and delight, assigning to it an appropriate character and place in scenes even the most remote from the present, and following up, in idea, the different trains of thought by which its expression is varied, and its intelligence communicated? Yet this face may not be in itself, or strictly speaking, beautiful; but, like the painting or the statue, it has the power to awaken the most pleasing associations. With such power there can be combined no mixture of the grotesque or vulgar; for, though poetry may be ridiculous, it is impossible for the ridiculous to be poetical.

There is Poetry in an infant's sleep. How much, let abler words than mine describe.

"So motionless in its slumbers, that, in watching it, we tremble, and become impatient for some stir or sound, that may assure us of its life; yet is the fancy of the little sleeper busy, and every artery and every pulse of its frame engaged in the work and growth of secretion, though his breath would not stir the smallest insect that sported on his lips—though his pulse would not lift the flower leaf of which he dreamed from his bosom: yet, following this emblem of tranquillity into after life, we see him exposed to every climate—contending with every obstacle—agitated by every passion; and under these various circumstances, how different is the power and the degree of the heart's action, which has not only to beat, but to beat time through every moment of a long and troubled life."*

We feel in reading this passage, even if we have never felt before, that there is poetry in an infant's sleep. Its waking moments are less poetical, because of the many little cares and vexations they force upon us; and no power on earth could convince us that there was poetry in an infant's cry. Yet is it neither softness nor sweetness which always constitutes the poetry of sound; for what can be more discordant in itself than the caw of the rook, the scream of the sea-gull, or the bleating of the lamb?

There is poetry in the low-roofed cottage standing on the skirts of the wood, beneath the overshadowing oak, around which the children of many generations have gambolled, while the wreathing smoke coils up amongst the dark green foliage, and the gray thatch is contrasted with golden moss and glittering ivy. We stand and gaze, delighted with this picture of rural peace, and privileged seclusion. We long to shake off the shackles of artificial society, the wearying cares of life, the imperative control of fashion, or the toil and traffic of the busy world, and to dwell for the remainder of our days in a quiet spot like this, where affection, that is too often lost in the game of life, might unfold her store of fire-side comforts, and where we and ours might constitute one unbroken chain of social fellowship, under the shelter of security and peace. But let us enter this privileged abode. Our ears are first saluted by the sharp voice of the matron, calling in her tattered rebels from the common. They are dragged in by violence, and a scene of wrath and contention ensues. The fragments of the last meal are scattered on the floor. That beautifully curling smoke, before it found a way to escape so gracefully, has made many a circuit round the dark and crumbling walls of the

* Dr. James Willson.

apartment; and smoke within the house is any thing but poetical, whatever it may be without. Need I say the charm is broken? Even after having made good our retreat, if we turn and look again, the low-roofed cottage does not appear the same as when we first beheld it. The associations are changed—the charm is indeed broken. May not this be the reason why fine ladies and gentlemen talk so much more about the poetry of a cottage, than those who know no other home comforts than a cottage affords? Even poverty itself may be poetical to those who merely regard it from a distance, or as a picture; but the vision is dispelled for ever by the first gripe of that iron hand, that spares neither the young, the helpless, nor the old.

There is poetry in the mouldering pile, upon which the alternate suns and storms of a thousand years have smiled and spent their fury—the old gray ruin hung over with festoons of ivy, while around its broken turrets a garland of wild plants is growing, from seeds which the wandering winds have scattered. We behold the imperishable materials of the natural world collected together, shaped out and formed by the art of man into that beautiful and majestic edifice; but where are the ready hands that laboured in that work of time and patience? The busy feet that trod those stately courts—the laughter that echoed through those halls—the sighs that were breathed in those secret cells—the many generations that came and went without leaving a record or a name—where are they? Scarcely can there be found an imagination so dull, but the contemplation of a ruin will awaken it to some dim and dreamy associations with past ages—scarcely a heart so callous, but it will feel, in connexion with such a scene, some touch of that melancholy which inspired the memorable exclamation "All is vanity and vexation of spirit!"

But let the ingenuity of man erect a modern ruin, or mock monastery, arch for arch, and pillar for pillar—nay, let him, if possible, plant weed for weed. The fancy will not be cheated into illusion—this mushroom toy of yesterday will remain a mockery still.

Amongst the labours of man's ingenuity and skill, there are few things more poetical than the aspect of a ship at sea, whether she goes forth with swelling sails before the wind, or lies becalmed upon a quiet shore. Even the simplest or rudest vessels floating on the surface of the water—from the lazy barge that glides along the smooth canal, to the light gondola that sports among the glowing waters of more classic shores—from the simple craft that ply upon our own rivers, to the rude canoe of the savage darting among reefs of coral; afford choice subjects for the painter's pencil, and the poet's song. Who has not watched with intense interest a little speck upon the ocean, that neared, and neared, until human forms at length were visible, and then the splash of the oar was heard at regular intervals, and, at last, on the crest of a foaming wave, the boat seemed to bound triumphant on the shore, where a little band of the long-tried and the faithful, amongst whom woman is never found wanting, welcome the mariners home, safe from the storms and the dangers of the sea? Who has not stood upon the beach, a silent, but deeply interested spectator, while a crew of hardy and weather-beaten sailors launched forth their little bark amongst the roaring breakers, battling their way through foam and surge, now dipping into the dark hollows between every swell, and then rising unharmed upon the snowy crest of the raging billows. A few moments more of determined struggle, and the difficulty is overcome; and now they have hoisted sail and are gone bounding over the dark blue waters, perhaps never to return. Who has not marked, while gazing on the surface of the silent lake when the moon was shining, that long line of trembling light that looks like a pathway to a better world, suddenly broken by the intervention of some object that proves to be a boat, in which human forms are discernible, though distant, yet marked out with a momentary distinctness, which affords imagination a fund of associations, connecting those unknown objects so quickly seen, and then lost for ever, with vague speculations about what they are or have been, from whence they have so suddenly emerged, to what unseen point of illimitable space they may be destined, and what may be the darkness, or the radiance of their future course. Or who has ever witnessed the departure of a gallant vessel under favouring skies, bound on a distant and uncertain voyage, her sails all trim, her rigging tight, her deck well manned, her cargo secure as human skill and foresight can make it, while she stoops one moment with unabated majesty, to rise more proudly the next, bursting through the ruffled waters, and dashing from her sides the feathery foam; without thinking of a proud and reckless spirit rushing forth on its adventurous career, unconscious of the rocks and shoals, the rude gales and the raging tempests, that await its onward course. Or who, without a thrill of something more than earthly feeling, can gaze over the unruffled surface of the sea when the winds are sleeping, and the waves at rest, except on the near voyage of the blue expanse, where a gentle murmur, with regular ebb and flow of soothing and monotonsus sound marks the intervals at which a line of sleepy waves rise, and fall, and follow each other, without pause or intermission, far up along the sparkling shore, and then recede into the depths of the smooth and shining waters.

The sun is high in the heavens—the air is clear and buoyant—now and then a white cloud sails along the field of azure, its misty form marked out in momentary darkness on the sea below, like the passing shadow of an angel's wings; while far, far in the distance, and gliding on towards the horizon, are those wandering messengers of the deep that bear tidings from shore to shore, their swelling sails now glancing white in the sunbeams, now darkened by the passing cloud. Musing on such a scene, we forget our own identity—our own earthly, bodily existence; we live in a world of spirits, and are lost in exquisite imaginings, in memories and hopes that belong not to the things of clay; every thing we behold is personified and gifted with intelligence; the rugged cliffs possess a terrible majesty, and seem to threaten while they frown upon the slumbering shore; the deep and boundless sea, represented at all times as acting or suffering by its own will or power, is now more than ever endued with the thoughts and passions of spiritual existence, and seems to speak to us in its own solemn and most intelligible language of terror in motion, and sublimity in repose: but more than all, the ships that go forth upon its bosom convey to our fancy the idea of being influenced by an instinct of their own; so well ordered are all their movements, so perfect appears the harmony of their construction and design, yet so hidden by the obscurity of the distance is the moving principle within, that by their own faith they seem to trust themselves where the foot of man dare not tread, and by their own hope they seem to be lured on to some distant point which the eye of man is unable to discern.

In a widely extended sea view there is unquestionably poetry enough to inspire the happiest lays, but the converse of this picture is easily drawn—and fatal to the poet's song would be the first view of the interior of any one of those gallant and stately ships about which we have been dreaming. The moving principle within, respecting which we have had such refined imaginings, is now imbodied in a company of hardy sailors, whose rude laughter, and ruder oaths, are no less discordant to our ear, than offensive to our taste. It is true, that a certain kind of order and discipline prevails amongst them, but the wretched passengers below are lost for a time to all mental sensations, and suffering or sympathizing with them, we soon forget the poetry of life.

There is poetry in the gush of sparkling waters that burst forth from the hill-side in some lonely and sequestered spot, and flow on in circling eddies amongst the rocks and fern, and tendrils of wild plants; on, on for ever—unexhausted, and yet perpetually losing themselves in the bosom of the silent and majestic river, where the hurry and murmur of their course is lost, like the restless passions that agitate the breast of man in the ocean of eternity: and there is poetry in the burst of the cataract that comes over the brow of the precipice with a seeming consciousness of its own power to bear down, and to subdue.

It is related of Richard Wilson, that when he first beheld the celebrated falls of Terni, he exclaimed "Well done, water!" Here, indeed, was no poetry—no association. His mind was too full of that mighty object as it first struck upon his senses, to admit at the moment of any relative idea; his exclamation was one of mere animal surprise, such as his dog might have uttered, had he possessed the organs of speech. And yet the same man, when he seized his pencil, and gave up his imagination to the full force of those impressions which, if we may judge by his works, few have felt more intensely, was able to portray nature, not merely seen as it is in any given section of the earth's surface, but to group together, and embody in one scene, all that is most harmonious in the quickly changing and diversified beauties of wood and water—hill and valley—sombre shade and glowing sunshine—deep solitudes, and resplendent heavens.

There is poetry in the hum of bees, when the orchards are in bloom, and the sun is shining in unclouded spendour upon the waving meadows, and the garden is richly spangled with spring flowers. There is poetry in the hum of the bee, because it brings back to us, as in a dream, the memory of bygone days, when our hearts were alive to the happiness of childhood—the time when we could lie down upon the green bank and enjoy the stillness of summer's noon, when our hopes were in the blossoms of the orchard, our delight in the sun-shine, our untiring rambles in the meadows, and our perpetual amusement in the scented flowers. Since these days, time has rolled over us with such a diversity of incident, bringing so many changes in our modes of living and thinking, that we have learned, perhaps at some cost, to analyze our feelings, and to say, rather than feel, that there is poetry in the hum of bees.

But let one of these honey-laden wanderers find his way into our apartment, and while he struggles with frantic efforts to escape through the closed window, we cease to find pleasure in his busy hum.

There is poetry in the flowers that grow in sweet profusion upon wild and uncultivated spots of earth, exposing their delicate eaves to the tread of the rude inhabitants of the wilderness, and spreading forth their scented charms to the careless mountain wind—in the thousand, thousand little stars of beauty looking forth like eyes, with no eye to look again; or cups that seem formed to catch the dew drops; or spiral pyramids of varied hue shooting up from leafy beds, and pointing faithfully to the shining sky; or crowns of golden splendour mounted upon fragile stems; or purple wreaths that never touched a human brow; all bursting forth, blooming and then fading, with endless succession in the midst of untrodden wilds;—in rain and sunshine, in silent night, and glowing day, with an end and purpose in their brief existence inscrutable to the mind of man.

The flowers of the garden, though possessing more richness and gorgeous beauty, are less poetical, because we see too clearly in their arrangement and culture, the art and labour of man; we are reminded at every group of the work of the spade, and perceive at once and without mystery, why they have been planted in the exact spot where they now grow.

There is poetry in the first contemplation of those numerous islands which gem the southern ocean—poetry in the majestic hills that rise one above another, their varied peaks and precipices clear and bright in unclouded sunshine, and their very summits clothed with unfading verdure; while bursting from amongst their deep recesses are innumerable streams that glide down their rugged sides, now glancing out like threads of silver, now hidden in shade and darkness, until they find their way into the broad and silent lagoon, where the angry surf subsides, and the mountains, woods, and streams, are seen again reflected in the glassy mirror of the unruffled water—unruffled, save by the rapid gliding of the light canoe, that darts among the coral rocks, and then lies moored in still water beneath some stately tree, whose leafy boughs form a welcome canopy of shade for the luxuriant revellers in that sunny clime.

Time was when those who had rejoiced over the first contemplation of this scene were compelled to mourn over the contrast which ignorance and barbarism presented on a nearer view, but now, blessed be the power that can harmonize the heart of man with all that is grateful and genial in the external world, the traveller approaching, and beholding this lovely picture, need no longer shrink from the horrors which a closer inspection formerly revealed.

If external nature abounds with poetry, how much more forcibly does it pervade the faculties and sentiments of the human mind. Consider only three—love, hope, and memory. What power even in the visions of the alchemist was ever able to transform like the passion of love? Investing what is real with all that we desire, converting deformity into loveliness, exchanging discord for harmony, giving to the eye the exquisite faculty of beautifying whatever it beholds, and to the ear a secret charm that turns every sound to music. And hope would be hope no longer if it did not paint the future in the colours we most admire. Its very existence depends upon the power it possesses to sweeten to the latest dregs, the otherwise bitter cup of life. Yet love and hope may be degraded by the false estimate we sometimes form of what is worthy of our admiration. Passion too often asserts her mastery over both, compelling her blind and willing slaves to call evil good, and good evil; while memory, if not always faithful to her trust, is at least disposed to hold it charitably, and thus preserves in their genuine distinctness, the fairest passages of life, but kindly obscures those which are most revolting in remembrance. In looking back upon the past, how little that is sordid, mean, or selfish, appears conspicuous now. Past hours of simple, every-day enjoyment, are invested with a charm they knew not at the time. A veil is thrown over the petty cares of bygone years—passion is disarmed of its earth-born violence, and sorrow looks so lovely in the distance, that we almost persuade ourselves it was better to weep such tears as we wept then, than to smile as we smile now.

But why pursue this theme? It is evident that neither sounds, objects, nor subjects of contemplation are poetical in themselves, but in their associations; and that they are so just in proportion as these associations are intellectual and refined. Nature is full of poetry, from the high mountain to the sheltered valley, from the bleak promontory to the myrtle grove, from the star-lit heavens to the slumbering earth; and the mind that can most divest itself of ideas and sensations belonging exclusively to matter, will be able to expatiate in the realms of nature with the most perfect fruition of delight.

INDIVIDUAL ASSOCIATIONS.

The difference of taste not unfrequently found in persons whose station and habits of life are similar may be attributed both to individual conformation, and to those instances of early bias received from local circumstances which none can remember, and which, consequently, no pen can record. That variety of taste is chiefly owing to the influence of association, is shown by those minor preferences or antipathies which certain individuals evince for things possessing no quality inherent in themselves to justify such peculiar choice or rejection, and which have no corresponding value in the opinion of mankind in general.

Without returning to the days of infancy, when the first impressions were made upon our senses, when our eyes were first able to see, and our ears to hear, it would be impossible to trace to their origin all our peculiarities of taste and feeling, or to assign the precise reason why we are subject to sensations of pleasure or disgust from causes which do not influence the rest of mankind in a similar manner—sensations which, from their singularity, and, to others, apparent absurdity, necessarily fall under the stigma of caprice.

Who can say how far his peculiar ideas of beauty and melody may have been derived from the countenance of the kind nurse who first smiled upon him in his cradle, and the sweet voice that first sung him to sleep; or of deformity and discord from the harsh brow whose frowns he first learned to dread, and the voice whose threatening tones were followed by punishment and pain.

If the taste of one individual is gratified by a picture upon which a strong and vivid light is thrown, and another prefers that which exhibits the cool tints of a cloudy atmosphere, it is attributed to some peculiarity in their several organs of sight; but is it not equally possible to be in some measure owing to one having been too much confined to darkness in his infancy, and the other painfully exposed to the glare of too much light?

These may appear but idle speculations, since we are, and ever must remain in want of that master key to the human understanding—the knowledge of the state of the infant mind, its degree of susceptibility, and the manner in which it first receives impressions through the organs of sense. So far as we can recollect, however, it is clear to all who will take the trouble to examine the subject, that strong partialities and prejudices are imbibed in very early life, before we are capable of reasoning, and that these sometimes remain with us to the last.

There are seldom two persons who agree exactly in their admiration of the proper names of individuals. One approves what the other rejects, and scarcely one instance in twenty occurs in which their feelings are the same: nor is it merely the harmony or discord of the sound which occasions their preference or dislike. Each attaches to the name in question a distinct character, most probably owing to some association of ideas between that name and a certain individual known in early life; and though they may have both known and lived amongs the same individuals, it is hardly probable that two minds should have regarded them precisely in the same manner. Hence from different associations arises a difference of taste.

In the present state of society there are few persons who have not, in the course of their reading, become familiarized with Scripture names earlier than with any other; and this, one would suppose, should lead to their being generally preferred and adopted. Yet so far from this being the case, they are many of them regarded with a degree of ridicule and disgust, which can only be accounted for by our first becoming acquainted with them before we have been inspired with love, gratitude, or reverence for the Record in which they are found. Nor is it easy to account for the perversion of the fine, full-sounding Roman names, in their usual application to our dogs, and other animals; and next to them to those miserable outcasts from human fellowship, which a professedly Christian world has deemed unworthy of a Christian nomenclature—the negro slaves; unless that schoolboys have generally enjoyed the honour of naming their fathers' dogs, when they were more familiar with Cæsar's Commentaries, than with the character of the illustrious Roman. Why are we not able for many years after our emancipation, to perceive and relish the beauties of those selections from the ablest poets, which we were compelled to learn by heart, as punishments at school? It is because our first acquaintance with them was formed under sensations of pain and compulsion, which time is long in wearing out.

If, by the mere sound of a name, such different sensations are excited in different minds, how much more extensive must be the variety of those called up by words of more comprehensive signification! Let us suppose four individuals—a newly elected member of parliament, a tradesman, a pauper, and a poet—each at liberty to pursue his own reflections, when the word *winter* is suddenly introduced to his mind. The statesman immediately thinks of the next convocation of the representatives of the people, when he shall stand forth to make his maiden speech; of the important subjects that will, probably, be laid before the consideration of the house, of the part he shall feel himself called upon to take in the discussion of these, and how he may be able to act so as to satisfy the claims of his constituents, and his conscience, without offending either. The tradesman thinks of his bills, and his bad debts; of the price of coals, and the winter fashions. The pauper thinks—and shivers while he thinks—of the cold blasts of that inclement season, of the various signs and prophecies that fortell a hard winter, and of how much, or rather how little the parish overseers will be likely to allow to his necessities for clothing, food, and fire. By a slight, and almost instantaneous transition of thought, one of these thinkers has already arrived at the idea of conscience, another at that of fashion, and a third at that of fire. But the poet (provided he be not identified with the pauper) passing over subjects of merely local interest, knows no bounds to his associations. His lively and unshackled fancy first carries him northward, to those frozen regions which man has visited but in thought. Here he floats through the thin and piercing air, then glides upon a sea of ice, or looks down from hills of everlasting snow; until wearied with the voiceless solitude, he seeks the abodes of man, and follows the fur-clad Laplander with his faithful reindeer over trackless and uncultivated wastes. But the poet, though a wanderer by profession, yet still faithful to home and early attachments, returns after every wayward excursion to drink of his native well, and to enjoy the peace of his paternal hearth. Here, in the clime he loves best, he beholds a scene of picturesque and familiar beauty—a still and cloudless morning, when the hoar frost is glittering upon every spray, and the trees, laden with a fleecy burden, cast their deep shadows here and there upon the silvery and unsullied bosom of the sheeted earth. He sees the solitary robin perched upon the leafless thorn, and hears its winter song of melancholy sweetness—that plaintive touching strain to which every human bosom echoes with a sad response. But quickly comes the roaring blast, like a torrent rushing down from the hills. The light snow is tossed like foam upon the waves of the wind; and the mountain pine, shaking off the frosty spangles from his boughs, for one moment quails before the fury of the thundering tempest, and then stands erect again upon the craggy steep, where his forefathers have stood for ages. Night gathers in with darkness and dismay, and while the moaning of the venerable oak resounds through the forest like the voice of a mighty and unseen spirit, and the bellowing of the blast seems mingled with the wilder shrieks of bewildered travellers, or seamen perishing on the deep, the poet beholds in the distance the glimmering lights of some hospitable mansion, and in an instant he is transported to a scene of happiness, glowing with social comforts, festivity, and glee; where the affrighted wanderer finds safety, the weary are welcomed to repose, and the wretched exchange their tears for joy.

Impressions made upon our minds by local circumstances, are frequently of so deep and durable a nature, as to outlive all the accidents of chance and change which occure to us in after life. Should the poet, or the painter in his study, endeavour to place before his mind's eye the picture of a brilliant sunset, he insensibly recalls that scenery in the midst of which his youthful imagination was first warmed into poetic life by the "golden day's decline." He sees, bright and gorgeous with sunbeams, the distant hill, which his boyish fancy taught him to believe it would be the height of happiness to climb;—the sombre woods that skirt the horizon—the valley, misty and indistinct below—the wandering river, whose glancing waters are here and there touched as they gleam out, with the radiance of the resplendent west—and while memory paints again the long deep shadows of the trees that grew around his father's dwelling, he feels the calm of that peaceful hour mingling with the thousand associations that combine to form his most vivid and poetical idea of sunset.

In this manner we not unfrequently single out from the works of art some favorite object, upon which we bestow an interest so deep, a regard so earnest, that they wear the character of admiration which no perceptible quality in the object itself can justify, and which other beholders are unable to understand. In a collection of paintings we look around for those which are most worthy of general notice, when suddenly our attention is struck with one little unpretending picture, almost concealed in an obscure corner, and totally unobserved by any one beside. It is the representation of a village church—the very church where we first learned to feel, and, in part, to understand the solemnity of the Sabbath. Beside its venerable walls are the last habitations of our kindred; and beneath that dark and mournful yew is the ancient pastor's grave. Here is the winding path so familiar to our steps, when we trod the earth more lightly than we do now—the stile on which the little orphan girl used to sit, while her brothers were at play—and the low bench beside the cottage-door, where the ancient dame used to pore over her Bible in the bright sunshine. Perhaps the wheels of Time have rolled over us with no gentle pressure since we last beheld that scene,—perhaps the darkness of our present lot makes the brightness of the past more bright. Whatever the cause may be, our gaze is fixed and fascinated, and we turn away from the more wonderful productions of art, to muse upon that little picture again, and again, when all but ourselves have passed it by without a thought.

It is not, however, the earliest impressions made upon the mind which are always the most lasting or vivid. We are all subject to the influence of strong and overpowering associations with circumstances which occur in after life, and of which we retain a clear recollection. We are apt to be deeply, yet differently affected by certain kinds of music. In the same apartment, and while the same air is sung or played by a minstrel unconscious of its secret power, and some of the audience will be thrown into raptures of delight, applauding and calling forth the strain again with unabated enjoyment; while one, in whose sad heart the springs of memory are opened, will turn away unnoticed in that happy crowd, to hide the tears which the thoughts of home and early days, when that strain was first heard, have called forth from the eyes of a stranger in a strange land. "If I might always listen to that tune," exclaims one, "I should never know unhappiness again!" "Spare me that song of mirth," is the secret prayer of the stranger; "it belongs to my own country. It tells me of the beauty and gladness of my native land. Spare me that song of mirth; for my heart is sorrowful, and I am alone."

Innumerable are the instances of daily, and almost hourly occurrence, in which we perceive that some particular tone of feeling is excited, but know not whence it takes its rise; as we listen to the wild music of the Æolian harp, that varies perpetually from one melody to another. We see the thrilling chords, we hear the sweet and plaintive sound, but we know not with all our wisdom what particular note the unseen minstrel will next produce, nor can we calculate the vibrations caused by his powerful but invisible hand.

When we hear the tender and affectionate expression, "I love this book because it was my mother's," we know at once why a book approved by a mother's judgment should be valued by a child; but when we hear any one say, "I prefer this room, this table, or this chair, to all others, because they belonged to my mother," the expression though quite as common, and equally natural, is not so generally understood. The room may be the least commodious in the house, the table the least convenient, the chair the least easy, yet they are valued not the less, because they are associated with the image of one who was more dear, perhaps more dear than any one will ever be again.

I have known the first wild rose of summer gathered with such faithful recollections, such deep and earnest love, such yearnings of the heart for by-gone pleasures, that for a moment its beauty was obscured by falling tears. The tolling of a bell after it has been heard for a departed friend, has a tone of peculiar and painful solemnity. The face of one whom we have met with comparative indifference in a season of happiness, is afterwards hailed with delight when it is all that remains to us of the past. The pebble that was gathered on a distant shore, becomes valuable as a gem when we know that we shall visit that land no more. There is no sound, however simple or sweet, that may not be converted into discord when it calls up jarring sensations in the mind; nor is there any melody in nature comparable to the tones of the voice that has once spoken to the heart.

Rosseau wept on beholding the little common flower that we call periwinkle. He wept because he was alone, and it reminded him of the beloved friend at whose feet it had been gathered. I remember being affected by this circumstance at a very early age, and the association has become so powerful, that, in looking at this flower, I always feel a sensation of melancholy, and persuade myself that the pale blue star, half concealed beneath the dark green leaves, is like a soft blue eye that scarcely ventures to look up from beneath the gloom of sorrow.

The crowing of the cock is generally considered a lively and cheering sound; yet I knew one, who for many years could not hear a cock crow at midnight without sensations of anguish and horror, because it had once been painfully forced upon her notice while she was watching the dead.

A gentleman of my acquaintance, in speaking to me of his mother's death, which was sudden and unexpected, described the day on which this event took place, as one of those periods in our existence when the mind seems incapable of *feeling* what it knows to be a painful truth. He had retired to rest, with an indistinct idea of what had occurred, but remained unable to realize the extent of his calamity. It had been his mother's custom to take away his candle every night—perhaps to breathe a prayer at his bed side. As he laid his head upon the pillow, he saw the light standing as usual, but no gentle form approached, and in an instant he felt the full force of his bereavement. He was setting off in life with brighter hopes than fall to the lot of many; but that first and purest of earth's blessings —a mother's love, was lost to him for ever.

Associations of this kind, however, are not such as constitute the fittest subjects for the poet; because, from their local or particular nature, they excite no general interest. They may be powerful in the mind of the writer, but will fail to awaken in other minds a proportionate degree of feeling; except when the sensible object, or particular fact described, is introduced merely as a medium for subjects of a nature to be generally felt and understood, such as memory, hope, or love. Thus, the Poet may properly address an object of which he alone perceives the beauty, or describe a circumstance of which he alone feels the pathos, provided he does not dwell too long upon the object or circumstance, merely as such, but carries the mind onward, by some ingenious association, to recollections which they naturally recall, hopes which were then cherished, or love, whose illimitable nature may be connected with all things lovely. By dwelling exclusively upon one subject of merely local interest, and neglecting such relative ideas as are common to all, the most egregious blunders, in matters of taste, are every day committed. Witticisms are uttered, which, however entertaining to those who know to what circumstances they owe their value, excite no corresponding risibility in the wondering or insensible hearers. Anecdotes are related, which, from being out of place or ill-timed, seem to fall from the lips of the speaker as a wearisome and empty sound. Subjects of conversation are introduced in mixed society, perhaps, intensely interesting to one or two, but from which all others are shut out. Books are selected, and read aloud to those who will not listen. Pictures are exhibited to those who cannot see their beauty. Pleasures are proposed, which from their want of adaptation, are converted into pain. Kind intentions are frustrated; and the best endeavours to be agreeable, rewarded with disappointment and ingratitude. In short, for want of that discriminating, versatile, and most valuable quality which mankind have agreed to call *tact*, and which might be fancifully described as the *nerve* of human society, many opportunities of enjoyment are wasted, many good people are neglected, and many good things are irrevocably lost.

It would be hard indeed if we might not indulge our individual fancies, by each mounting the hobby we like best. The absurdity consists in compelling others to ride with us, in forcing our favourites upon their regard, and expecting from them the same tribute of admiration which we ourselves bestow. There is no moral law to prevent our being delighted with what is repulsive to others; but it is an essential part of good manners, to keep back from the notice of society such particular preferences—a great proof of good taste, so to discipline our feelings, that we derive the most enjoyment from what is generally pleasing.

GENERAL ASSOCIATIONS.

In turning our attention to the subject of general associations, we enter upon a field so wide and fertile, that to select suitable materials for examination appears the only difficulty. All our most powerful and sublime ideas are common to mankind in a civilized state, and arise in the minds of countless multitudes from the same causes. By the stupendous phenomena of nature, as well as by the magnificent productions of art, we are all affected according to our various degrees of capability in precisely the same manner. We all agree in the impressions we receive from extreme cases, whether they belong to the majestic or the minute;

and no one who retained the possession of his reason would be excited to laughter by a thunder storm, or to awe and reverence by the tricks of a merry-andrew. But there are medium cases of a minor and more dubious nature, in which the poet's discriminating eye can best distinguish what is exalted or refined, puerile or base; and consequently what is most worthy of his genius. Nor let him who has openly committed himself in verse, believe that such distinction entitles him to make laws for his own accommodation, and observe or transgress the established rules of taste just as his own fancy may dictate. The same celestial fire which prompts his lay is warming humbler blossoms unmarked amongst the crowd; and mingled with the dense multitude which he disdains are countless poets uncommitted, who constitute a tribunal from which there is no appeal; who must eventually sit in judgment upon his works, give the tone to public opinion, and pronouncing his irrevocable doom, consign him to oblivion or to fame.

Those who have taken little pains to inquire into the nature and origin of their mental sensations, often express instantaneously a correct judgment of works of art, from what they would be very likely to call a kind of instinct or intuitive perception of what is right or wrong; but which might more philosophically be referred to combinations of ideas derived from certain impressions associated, compared, and established by a process of the mind which they took no note of at the time, and with which they have never made themselves acquainted. Of such is a great proportion of the multitude composed; and it is this fact which gives to public opinion that overpowering weight against which no single critic, or even select body of critics, can prevail.

The poet who is not a blind enthusiast, will learn by experience, if he know not without, that the public taste must be consulted in order to recommend himself to public approbation. He therefore gives himself up to the study of what is universally regarded as most ennobling, touching, or sublime. He endeavors to forget himself, and setting aside the pains and pleasures of his own limited experience as a little private store to draw upon when occasion may require, or as a secret lamp from which he may sometimes borrow light to rekindle his imagination, launches forth into the world of thought, and extracts from all existing or imaginable things that ethereal essense, which beautifies the aspect of nature, elevates the soul of man, and gives even to his every day existence such intensity of enjoyment, as those who look at facts only as they are recorded, and study matter merely as it is, can never know.

General associations must therefore occupy an important place in the consideration of all who would study the poetry of life; nor will such deem their time misspent in following up a close examination of some particular subjects with reference to this essential point.

Let us first consider that well known and familiar object, the human face, of which even single and distinct features have frequently been thought sufficiently important to inspire the poet's lay. From the earliest times, the forehead has been dignified with a kind of personality, and regarded as an index to the character of man, whether bold or bland, threatening or benign, disturbed or serene: nor is it in language peculiar to the poets only, that we speak of a man confronting his enemies with undaunted brow—or that he receives his sentence of punishment with a forehead undisturbed—that we are encouraged to hope for mercy by the bland or benign forehead of the judge—or bear adversity with a brow serene. Physiognomists profess to read the natural character of man chiefly from the form of his forehead; but whether studied scientifically or not, we all know in an instant what is indicated by the simultaneous contraction and lowering of the brow; we know also, without much assistance from study of any kind, when the nature of the forehead is noble or mean, harsh or mild; we naturally look to the upper part of the face, in order to form those instantaneous opinions of our fellow-creatures at first sight, which are not unfrequently a near approach to truth; and we may, with some degree of certainty, read in the forehead, when at rest, what are the principal elements of character in those with whom we associate. But scarcely can a feeling be excited, or a passion stirred, than the muscles of the forehead are agitated by a corresponding movement. How suddenly and strongly is the forehead affected by astonishment! and even in listening attentively to a common story, the eyebrows are occasionally elevated, and thus afford a sure indication that the hearer is interested, and that the narrator may proceed. How striking is the contraction of the forehead in deep and earnest thought! How unspeakably mournful under the gloom of sorrow! How frightfully distorted by the violence of rage! How solemn and yet how lovely in its character of intellectual beauty! It is difficult to connect one idea of a gross or corporeal nature with the forehead; all its indications are those of mind, and most of them of a powerful, refined, or elevated character; from the Madonna, whom no painter has thought worthy of a high degree of intellectual grace, yet whose forehead invariably indicates a character mild, delicate, and pure, to the dying gladiator, whose expiring anguish is less of the body than of the mind.

The forehead, therefore, is a subject well fitted for the poet's pen, and he may sing of its various qualifications without fear of transgressing the rules of good taste.

The eye is poetical in a still higher degree, because it possesses a greater facility in adapting itself to present circumstances, and reveals in greater minuteness and variety the passions and affections of the mind. Indeed, so perfect is the eye as an organ of intelligence, that it is more frequently spoken of in its figurative sense than in any other; and there is scarcely a writer, however grave, whose pages are not embellished by frequent poetical expressions in which the eye is the principal agent; such as,—the language of the eye—the eye of the mind—the eye of omnipotence and a countless multitude of figures, without which we should find it difficult to express our ideas, and which sufficiently prove how intimate and familiar is our acquaintance with the eye as a medium of intelligence, no less than as an organ of sense. With the universally intelligible expression of the eye, are associated our first ideas of pain or pleasure, fear or confidence: the infant naturally looks up into its mother's eye to read there the confirmation of her strange tones of anger or reproof, and if there is no condemnation in that oracle of truth, he feels that her words are but empty threats, returns to his gambols, and laughs again. The lover knows that his earnest suit is rejected if the eye of his mistress has no relenting in its glance; and the criminal who pleads for some mitigation of his sentence, looks for mercy in the eye of the judge.

It would be a fruitless expenditure of words to set about establishing the fact, that the eye is poetical. Every poet capable of stringing a rhyme has proved it to the world; every heart capable of feeling has acknowledged it to be true.

But while thousands and tens of thousands are poetizing about the eye, no one dares venture upon the nose; a fact which can only be accounted for by our having no intellectual associations with this member, and being accustomed to regard it merely for its sense of smell or as an essential ornament to the face. The nose is incapable of expressing any emotion of mind, except those which are vulgar or grotesque—such as laughter or gross impertinence. It is true, the nostrils are distended by any effort of daring, but it is rather with animal than moral courage, such as might animate a barbarian or a horse. It is indeed a curious, but incontrovertible fact, that while the enraptured slave of beauty is at liberty to expend his poetic fire in composing sonnets to his lady's eye, no sooner does he descend to the adjoining feature, than the poetry of his lay is converted into burlesque, and he is himself dismissed as a profaner of love and the muses.

The mouth, though frequently spoken of in a figurative sense, is less poetical than the eye, most probably because of its immediate connexion with the functions of the body. In the language of poetry, the lips and the tongue are generally substituted for the mouth; the one being associated with the more refined idea of a smile, and the other with the organs of speech.

Every one sees at the first glance that the chin is not a subject for poetry; for though its peculiar formation may be strongly indicative of boldness or timidity, as well as some meaner traits of character, it is so incapable of changing with the changing emotions of the mind, that the chin must remain to be considered merely as a feature of the face, and nothing more.

These notions, derived from the study of the human countenance, may appear to give to the subject a greater degree of importance than it really deserves; for there are many individuals not aware that they have ever bestowed more physiognomical study upon the face of man, than upon the plate from which they dine. But let one of these relate his favourite story to a stranger, who neither raises his eyes nor his eyebrows while he is speaking, whose mouth never for one moment relaxes into a smile, and who gives no sign that he is interested by any other motion of the head or face; the teller of the story how little soever he may think he has studied the subject, will perceive that he has wasted his words upon one who could not, or would not appreciate their value. This fact he knows with certainty, and without being told; because from childhood he has always been accustomed to see earnest attention accompanied by certain movements, or positions of the face; and has observed, that the same face would be very differently affected by weariness or absence of mind. Thus, we gather knowledge from experience every day without being aware of it, and are satisfied with the possession of our gain without inquiring from whence it was obtained.

The sentiments upon which mankind are generally agreed respecting the beauty or deformity of the human countenance, originate more frequently in association, than, without examination of the subject, we should be disposed to allow. How often are we struck with a similarity between certain faces and certain animals of the brute creation; and just in proportion as the resemblance is gross and brutal, we regard it with disgust and horror. The ancients established for themselves a standard of beauty, as far removed from such resemblance as the form of the human countenance would allow; and sometimes, in their contempt for the rude expression of animal life, they rushed into the opposite extreme, and extinguished all apparent capability of living—in their anxiety to avoid the mark of the beast, they lost sight of the characteristics of the man. The Egyptians appear to have imbodied in their sculpture the first, or rather the embryo idea of the sublime; and their huge, massive, and unmeaning heads, scarcely chisselled into form, are as far removed in their expression from what is gross, as what is human. The Grecians knew better what was requsite to the gratification of a refined and intellectual taste. They knew, that in order to ennoble their representations of the countenance of man, it must not only be divested of all resemblance to the brute, but that, to rouse the human bosom to sensations of admiration and delight, it must be enlivened with the expression of human intelligence. Had they proceeded but one step farther in their imitation of nature as it is—had they consulted the sympathies and affections of humanity, they might have immortalized the genius of the times by productions equally sublime, but infinitely more touching and beautiful.

As the Grecians reasoned and acted in the early stage of civilization, so we, in forming our earliest notions of the abstract nature of beauty, reason, perhaps unconsciously, to ourselves. We see that a low and rapidly retreating forehead, sunken eyes, short nose, distended and elevated at the tip, wide mouth, and scarcely perceptible chin, are common to animals of the most repulsive character; and we loathe the image of a human animal in any way resembling these. With that propensity inherent in our nature to rush towards the opposite of every thing which excites dislike or pain, we create a false taste, and affect to admire what is not to be found in real life. And as most living faces have some faint touch of resemblance to the animal creation, we are more enraptured than the rules of physiognomy would warrant, with the cold sublime of Grecian statuary. Nor is this taste likely to be corrected, because we study these marble beauties as statues only, and consequently find in them all that is required for loveliness in repose; but could a Grecian divinity step down from her pedestal, and come to visit our couch in sorrow, bend over us in sickness, or meet us at the door of our home after long absence and weary travel; we should then perceive the harsh coldness of what are called celestial brows, but which were certainly never intended to relax into the expression of affability, kindness, or sympathy.

The faces which are universally considered most interesting, are those which vary with every emotion of the soul; which seldom fail to please in general society, by keeping up a sort of corresponding indication with the feelings excited by different subjects under discussion. Yet these variations must not be too rapid, they must not correspond with every trifling change, or the expression will become puerile; because we are sure that so many different emotions felt in quick succession must neutralize each other, and we consequently doubt whether any feeling in connexion with such a countenance can be deep or lasting.

There is, however, beyond this charm of the human face, another of a more abstruse and intellectual character, one which more properly entitles it to be called poetical; and here it may not be improper to remark, that a certain degree of mystery enhances the value of almost all our mental enjoyments. The human mind is so constituted, that it feels peculiar gratification in being occasionally thrown upon its own resources. Instead of being constantly supplied with food selected and prepared for its use, it delights in being sometimes permitted to issue forth on an excursion of discovery, and is satisfied on such occasions with very uncertain aliment. Mystery offers to the mind this kind of liberty. We dwell the longest upon that face which reveals a great deal, but not all of what the thoughts are engaged with; we recur with redoubled interest to those subjects which we do not, on first examination, fully understand.

But to return to the human countenance. We meet with many faces animated, lively, and quickly affected by the topics or events of the moment. We remark of such, that they are pleasing, and our admiration ends here. But if, amongst the crowd, we distinguish one possessed of this capability in the extreme, not always using it, however, but sometimes looking grave and abstracted, retiring, as it were, from the confusion or the folly of the passing scene, to listen for awhile to the inner voice—the voice of the spirit, while the "tablet of unutterable thoughts is traced" upon it; we immediately begin to ponder upon what may be the secret springs from whence flow the thoughts, feelings, and affections of such a character. We bestow upon it much of what is closely interwoven with our own. We invest it with imaginary powers, and believe it to be possessed of resources from which the mind may draw as from unfailing wells, until at last we seem to have established an ideal intercourse with the mysterious unknown, and to have made a friend by no other agency than the sympathy of the soul.

What is most generally esteemed in society, might be easily discovered by what the greatest number of individuals are disposed to affect. Thus, while the affectation of attention is often substituted for attention itself, while dull faces are compelled to brighten into smiles without the animation of joy, while brows are stretched into a mockery of good humour when good humour is wanting; there are deeper practitioners playing off the art of being mysterious, dealing in half-revealed secrets, concealing their own names, looking abstracted by design, and forming plans for their own dignity, mimicking the Corsair, and fancying they resemble Lord Byron; with a hundred absurdities besides, too gross or to contemptible to enumerate, yet all tending to prove that there is a disposition prevailing amongst mankind, to admire and delight in what is mysterious.

If we are generally agreed in our notions of the beauty or deformity of the human face, we are still more unanimous in our estimate of that of animal form in general. Some, it is true, may prefer a tall or a broad figure, and others may choose exactly the opposite, but we are all of one opinion on the subject of symmetry and proportion; because our associations are the same, and we bestow the highest degree of admiration on the bodies, both of men and animals, when they posssss the combined qualities of firmness, flexibility, and adaptation.

All who have bestowed any attention upon the horse, must regard this noble animal with feelings of admiration and delight. It needs not the aid of scientific study to perceive in what perfection he possesses the combined qualities of strength and swiftness, endurance and facility of motion. Had one of these qualities been wanting—had he been feeble or inactive, had his power or his patience been soon expended, had he moved with awkwardness or difficulty, our admiration would have been considerably less, and we should probably now look with as little pleasure on the horse as on the rhinoceros. Again, every one thinks the stag a beautiful animal, perhaps the most beautiful in nature; but the stag wants the majestic power of the horse to give him an aspect of nobility, and, therefore, our admiration of him is of a qualified and secondary nature. In the same manner, it would not be difficult to trace the correspondence of our ideas through the whole extent of animal creation, except only where the chain of association is broken by accidental or local circumstances; and happy is it for the human race, that they are so constituted as to be disposed unanimously to avoid what is repulsive, and are able to partake, in social concord, of the exquisite enjoyment of admiring what is beautiful.

Had the mind of man been composed of heterogeneous or discordant elements, he must have wanted the grand principle of happiness—sympathy with his fellow-creatures. He might unquestionably have possessed his own enjoyments, but he must have been a selfish and isolated being. His intellectual powers might possibly have been cultivated, but without the stimulus of social affection, their growth must have been without grace, and their fruit without value. To compute the distance of the planets, to measure the surface of the earth, and penetrate into its secret mines, are occupations which might be carried on by man in his solitary and unconnected character; but in order that he might enjoy the benefit of a high tone of moral feeling, and thus be fitted for a state of existence where knowledge is only less supreme than love, it was necessary that the general current of his feelings should be softened and refined, by innumerable springs of tenderness and affection, flowing through the finer sensibilities of his nature, and filling that ocean of enjoyment, of which the human family have drank together in unity since the world began, and may continue to drink for generations yet to come, without fear that the fountains should be sealed, or the waters should become less pure.

THE POETRY OF FLOWERS.

There are few natural objects more poetical in their general associations than flowers; nor has there ever been a poet, simple or sublime, who has not adorned his verse with these specimens of nature's cunning workmanship. From the majestic sunflower, towering above her sisters of the garden, and faithfully turning to welcome the god of day, to the little humble and well-known weed that is said to close its crimson eye before impending showers, there is scarcely one flower which may not from its loveliness, its perfume, its natural situation, or its classical association, be considered highly poetical.

As the welcome messenger of spring, the snowdrop claims our first regard; and countless are the lays in which the praises of this little modest flower are sung. The contrast it presents of green and white, (ever the most pleasing of contrasts to the human eye,) may be one reason why mankind agree in their admiration of its simple beauties; but a far more powerful reason is the delightful association by which it is connected with the idea of returning spring; the conviction that the vegetable world through the tedious winter months has not been dead, but sleeping; and that long nights, fearful storms, and chilling blasts, have a limitation and a bound assigned them, and must in their appointed time give place to the fructifying and genial influence of spring. Perhaps we have murmured (for what is there in the ordinations of Providence at which man will not dare to murmur?) at the dreariness of winter. Perhaps we have felt the rough blast too piercing to accord with our artificial habits. Perhaps we have thought long of the melting of the snow that impeded our noon-day walk. But it vanishes at last; and there, beneath its white coverlet, lies the delicate snowdrop, so pure and pale, so true an emblem of hope, and trust, and confidence, that it might teach a lesson to the desponding, and show the useless and inactive how invaluable are the stirrings of that energy that can work out its purpose in secret, and under oppression, and be ready in the fulness of time to make that purpose manifest and complete. The snowdrop teaches also another lesson. It marks out the progress of time. We cannot behold it without feeling that another spring has come, and immediately our thoughts recur to the events which have occurred since last its fairy bells were expanded. We think of those who were near and dear to us then. It is possible they may never be near again; it is equally possible they may be dear no longer. Memory is busy with the past; until anticipation takes up the chain of thought, and we conjure up, and at last shape out in characters of hope, a long succession of chances and changes to fill up the revolving seasons which must come and go before that little flower shall burst forth in its loveliness again. Happy is it for those who have so counted the cost of the coming year, that they shall not find at the end they have expended either hope or desire in fruitless speculations.

It is of little consequence what flower comes next under consideration. A few specimens will serve the purpose of proving, that these lovely productions of nature are, in their general associations, highly poetical. The primrose is one upon which we dwell with pleasure proportioned to our taste for rural scenery, and the estimate we have previously formed of the advantages of a peaceful and secluded life. In connexion with this flower, imagination pictures a thatched cottage standing on the slope of the hill, and a little woody dell, whose green banks are spangled all over with yellow stars, while a troop of rosy children are gambolling on the same bank, gathering the flowers, as we used to gather them ourselves, before the toils and struggles of mortal conflict had worn us down to what we are now; and thus presenting to the mind the combined ideas of natural enjoyment, innocence, and rural peace—the more vivid, because we can remember the time when something like this was mingled with the cup of which we drank—the more touching, because we doubt whether, if such pure drops were still there, they would not to our taste have lost their sweetness.

The violet, while it pleases by its modest, retiring beauty, possesses the additional charm of the most exquisite of all perfumes, which, inhaled with the pure and invigorating breezes of spring, always brings back in remembrance a lively conception of that delightful season. Thus, in the language of poetry, "the violet-scented gale" is synonymous with those accumulated and sweetly-blended gratifications which we derive from odours, flowers, and balmy breezes; and above all, from the contemplation of renovated nature, once more bursting forth into beauty and perfection.

The jessamine, also, with its dark green leaves, and little silver stars, saluting us with its delicious scent through the open casement, and impregnating the whole atmosphere of the garden with its sweetness, has been sung and celebrated by so many poets, that our associations are with their numbers, rather than with any intrinsic quality in the flower itself. Indeed, whatever may have first established the rank of flowers in the poetical world, they have become to us like notes of music, passed on from lyre to lyre; and whenever a chord is thrilled with the harmony of song, these lovely images present themselves, neither impaired in their beauty, nor exhausted of their sweetness, for having been the medium of poetic feeling ever since the world began.

It is impossible to expend a moment's thought upon the lily, without recurring to that memorable passage in the sacred volume: "Consider the lilies of the field, how they grow. They toil not, neither do they spin; and yet I say unto you, that Solomon in all his glory was not arrayed like one of these." From the little common flower called heart's ease, we turn to that well known passage of Shakspeare, were the fairy king so beautifully describes the "little western flower." And the forget-me-not has a thousand associations tender and touching, but unfortunately, like many other sweet things, rude hands have almost robbed it of its charm. Who can behold the pale Narcissus, standing by the silent brook, its stately form reflected in the glassy mirror, without losing themselves in that most fanciful of all poetical conceptions, in which the graceful youth is described as gazing upon his own beauty, until he becomes lost in admiration, and finally enamoured of himself: while hopeless echo sighs herself away into a sound, for the love, which having centred in such an object, was never to be bought by her caresses, nor won by her despair.

Through gardens, fields, forests, and even over rugged mountains, we might wander on in this fanciful quest after remote ideas of pleasurable sensation connected with present beauty and enjoyment; nor would our search be fruitless so long as the bosom of the earth afforded a receptacle for the germinating seed, so long as the gentle gales of summer continued to waft them from the parent stem, or so long as the welcome sun looked forth upon the ever-blooming garden of nature.

One instance more, and we have done. The "lady rose," as poets have designated this queen o beauty, claims the latest, though not the least consideration in speaking of the poetry of flowers. In the poetic world, the first honors have been awarded to the rose, for what reason it is not easy to define; unless from its exquisite combination of perfume, form, and colour, which have entitled this sovereign of flowers in one country to be mated with the nightingale, in another, to be chosen with the distinction of red and white, as the badge of two honourable and royal houses. It would be difficult to trace the supremacy of the rose to its origin; but mankind have so generally agreed in paying homage to her charms, that our associations in the present day are chiefly with the poetic strains in which they are celebrated. The beauty of the rose is exhibited under so many different forms, that it would be impossible to say which had the greatest claim upon the regard of the poet; but certainly those kinds which have been recently introduced, or those which are reared by unnatural means, with care and difficulty, are to us the least poetical, because our associations with them are comparatively few, and those few relate chiefly to garden culture.

After all the pains that have been taken to procure, transplant, and propagate the rose, there is one kind perpetually blooming around us through the summer months, without the aid or interference of man, which seems to defy his art to introduce a rival to his own unparalleled beauty—the common wild rose; so luxuriant, that it bursts spontaneously into blushing life, sometimes crowning the hoary rock with a blooming garland, and sometimes struggling with the matted weeds of the wilderness, yet ever finding its way to the open day, that it may bask and smile, and look up with thankfulness to the bright sun, without whose rays its cheek would know no beauty so tender, that the wild bee which had nestled in its scented bosom when that sun went down, returns in the morning and beholds the colour faded from its cheek, while by its side an infant rose is rising with the blush of a cherub, unfolding its petals to live its little day, and then, having expended its sweetness, to die like its fair sisters, without murmur or regret. Blooming in the sterile waste, this lovely flower is seen unfolding its fair leaves where there is no beauty to reflect its own, and thus calling back the heart of the weary traveller to thoughts of peace and joy—reminding him that the wilderness of human life, though rugged and barren to the discontented beholder, has also its sweet flowers, not the less welcome for being unlooked for, nor the less lovely for being cherished by a hand unseen.

There is one circumstance connected with the rose, which renders it a more true and striking emblem of earthly pleasure than any other flower—*it bears a thorn.* While its odorous breath is floating on the summer gale, and its blushing cheek, half hid amongst the sheltering leaves, seems to woo and yet shrink from the beholder's gaze, touch but with adventurous hand the garden queen, and you are pierced with her protecting thorns: would you pluck the rose and weave it into a garland for the brow you love best, that brow will be wounded: or place the sweet blossom in your bosom, the thorn will be there. This real or ideal mingling of pain and sorrow, with the exquisite beauty of the rose, affords a never-ending theme to those who are best acquainted with the inevitable blending of clouds and sunshine, hope and fear, wea and wo, in this our earthly inheritance.

With every thing fair, or sweet, or exquisite in this world, it has seemed meet to that wisdom which appoints our sorrows, and sets a bound to our enjoyments, to affix some stain, some bitterness, or some alloy, which may not inaptly be called, in figurative language, a thorn. St. Paul emphatically speaks of a "thorn in the flesh," and from this expression, as well as from his earnestness in having prayed thrice that it might be removed, we conclude it must have been something particularly galling to the natural man. We hear of the thorn of ingratitude, the thorn of envy, the thorn of unrequited love—indeed of thorns as numerous as our pleasures; and few there are who can look back upon the experience of life, without acknowledging that every earthly good they have desired, pursued, or attained, has had its peculiar thorn. Who has ever cast himself into the lap of luxury, without finding that his couch was strewed with thorns? Who has reached the summit of his ambition without feeling on that exalted pinnacle that he stood on thorns? Who has placed the diadem upon his brow, without perceiving that thorns were thickly set within the royal circlet? Who has folded to his bosom all that he desired of earth's treasures, without feeling that bosom pierced with thorns? All that we enjoy in this world, or yearn to possess, has this accompaniment. The more intense the enjoyment, the sharper the thorn; and those who have described most feelingly the inner workings of the human heart, have unfailingly touched upon this fact with the melancholy sadness of truth.

Far be it from one who would not willingly fall under the stigma of ingratitude, to disparage the nature, or the number of earthly pleasures—pleasures which are spread before us without price or limitation, in our daily walk, and in our nightly rest—pleasures which lie scattered around our path when we go forth upon the hills, or wander in the valley, when we look up to the starry sky, or down to the fruitful earth—pleasures which unite the human family in one bond of fellowship, surround us at our board, cheer us at our fire-side, smooth the couch on which we slumber, and even follow our wandering steps long—long after we have ceased to regard them with gratitude or joy. I speak of the thorn which accompanies these pleasures not with murmuring or complaint. I speak of the wounds inflicted by this thorn with a living consciousness of their poignancy and anguish; because exquisite and dear as mere earthly pleasures may sometimes be, I would still contrast them with such as are not earthly. I would contrast the thorn and the wound, the disappointment and the pain which accompany all such pleasures as are merely temporal, with the fulness of happiness, the peace, and the crown, accompanying those which are eternal.

THE POETRY OF TREES.

In contemplating the external aspect of nature, trees, in their infinite variety of form and foliage, appear most important and conspicuous; yet so many are the changes which they undergo from the influence of the sun and the atmosphere, that it would be useless to attempt to speak of the associations belonging to this class of natural productions abstractedly, and detached from collateral circumstances. What poet, for instance, would describe the rich foliage of the summer woods, without the radiance of the summer sun; the wandering gale that waves their leafy boughs; the mountain side to which their knotted roots are clinging; the green valley where they live and flourish, safe from raging storms; and the murmuring stream, over which their branches bend and meet. There is, however, a marked distinction in the character of different trees, and a general agreement amongst mankind in the relative ideas connected with each particular species.

It is scarcely necessary to repeat how essential to our notions of perfection is the beauty of *fitness*—that neither colour, form, nor symmetry, nor all combined in one object, can command our unqualified admiration without *adaptation;* and that the mind, by a sort of involuntary process, and frequently unconsciously to itself, takes note of the right application of means, and the relation of certain causes with their natural effects. Thus, we admire the stately pine upon the mountain, not merely because the eye is gratified by a correspondence between its spiral form pointing upward towards the sky, and the high projecting pinnacles of rock, unbroken by the steps of time; but because we know that in consequence of this particular form, it is peculiarly adapted to sustain without injury the tempestuous gales which prevail in those inhospitable regions where it chiefly grows. There is something fierce, bristling, and defensive, in the very aspect of the pine; as if it set at naught the hollow roar of the tempest through its scanty foliage, and around its firm unshaken stem, while it stands like a guardian of the mountain wilds, armed at all points, and proudly looking down upon the flight of the eagle, and the wreaths of wandering clouds that flit across the wilderness of untrodden snow. But plant a single pine upon the gentle slope of a green lawn, amongst lilachs, and laburnums, and tender flowering shrubs, the charm of association is broken, and the veteran of the rugged mountainous waste is shorn of his honours; like a patriot chief, submitting himself to the polished chains of society at the court of his tyrant conqueror.

The oak, the monarch of the woods, presents to the contemplative beholder innumerable associations by which his mind is plunged into the profound ideas of grandeur, space, and time. We are first struck with the majestic form and character of this tree—the mass of its foliage, the depth and extent of its shadow, and the tremendous power of resistance bodied forth in its gnarled and twisted boughs; but above all other considerations connected with it, we are affected almost with reverence by the lapse of time required to bring those prodigious branches to perfection, and the many, many tides of human feeling that must ebb and flow, before those firmly knotted roots shall yield to the process of decay. In the natural course of meditation to which such a subject leads, we consider the striking truth, tha while nations have bowed and trembled beneath successive tyrants until by the wonted course of nature, the terrors of the oppressed have given place to the reckless desperation that works its way, by the overthrow of empires, the destruction of thrones, and the scattering of multitudes—while the laws and religion of half the world have been revolutionized, and what was once deemed a virtue has gradually become punishable as a crime—while sterile wastes have been reclaimed, and fertilized, and made fruitful, by the power and industry of successive generations of men, and arts and commerce have wrought wonders which our unsophisticated forefathers would have pronounced miraculous—the same oak has stood, perhaps at one time the witness of Druidical rites, at another affording shelter to the simple and unlettered peasant tending the herds of swine that fed upon its falling acorns: until, years rolling on, revolving summers crowning its brow with verdant beauty, and hoary winter scattering that beauty to the winds, have left it for our warning, an emblem of fallen majesty—its once sturdy boughs no sooner attacked by the worm of destruction within, than assailed, and torn, and broken by the merciless blast without.

Striking and magnificent as the oak unquestionably is in its peculiar attitude and growth, presenting at one view the combined ideas of ability to resist the strong, and power to defend the weak, it is yet scarcely less majestic than beautiful. What a combination of gorgeous hues its autumnal foliage displays! The eye of the painter revels in its sombre glory, its burnished hue, and its wild fantastic garniture of green and gold, contrasted with its own hoary stem, and the depth of shadow that is thrown by the rays of the declining sun in lengthening gloom over the quiet earth.

Nor is it merely with the outward aspect of this tree that our most powerful associations are connected. In a nation perpetually exulting in her maratime supremacy, we have learned to regard the oak as forming a sort of bulwark for the defence of our liberties. Thus, the British sailor calls upon his comrades by the proud title of "hearts of oak," and England is not unfrequently described as being protected by her "oaken walls."

There are, besides these, many other characters or points of consideration, in which we regard the oak with feelings of respect, and sometimes with poetical interest. Perhaps it is not least in the scale of importance, that many ancient and stately apartments, dedicated to solemn or religious purposes, are lined with panels of the wood of this tree. The same wood, beautifully carved and deepened into gloomy magnificence by the sombre influence of time, forms one of the principal ornaments in many religious houses; and when we look back to the customs of our ancestors, and the station which they occupied, with that respect which we naturally feel for their boasted hospitality, good cheer, and substantial magnificence, we seldom fail to surround them in imagination with goodly wainscoting of oak, to place a log of the same wood upon the blazing hearth, and to endow them with powers both mental and bodily, firm, stable, and unbending as this sturdy tree.

Amongst the trees of the forest, the elm may very properly be placed next in rank to the oak, from its majestic size and importance. Yet the elm has a very different character, and consequently excites in the contemplative mind a different train of associations and ideas. The massive and umbrageous boughs, or rather arms of the elm, stretching forth at right angles with its stately stem, present to the imagination a picture of calm dignity rather than defensive power. From the superficial manner in which the roots of this tree are connected with the earth, it is ill calculated to sustain the force of the tempest, and is frequently torn from its hold and laid prostrate on the ground by the gale, whose violence appears to be unheeded by its brethren of the forest. In painting, or in ideal picture-making, we plant the elm upon the village green, a sort of feudal lord of that little peopled territory; or in stately rows skirting the confines of the dead, where the deep shadow from its dark green foliage falls upon the quiet graves, and the long rank grass, and on the village church, when from her gray sides and arched windows she reflects the rays of the setting sun, and looks, in her silence and solemnity, like a sister to those venerable trees. There are no gorgeous hues in the foliage of the elm, no light waving, dancing or glistening amongst its heavy boughs. All is grave majesty; and when we see the smoke of the cottage slowly ascending, and clearly revealed against the sombre darkness of the elm, we think of the labourer returning to his evening meal, the birds folding their weary wings, the coo of the wood pigeon, the gentle fall of evening dew, the lull of winds and waves, the universal calm of nature, and a thousand associations rush upon us, connecting that lovely and untroubled scene with vast and profound ideas of solemnity and repose.

To the willow belongs a character peculiarly its own. It has no stateliness, or majesty, or depth of shadow, to strike the senses and set the imagination afloat; but this mournful tree possesses a claim upon our attention, as having become the universal badge of sorrow, fancifully adopted by the victims of despair, and worn as a garland by the broken-hearted. It has also a beauty and a charm of its own. It carries us in idea to green pastures, and peaceful herds that browse in deep meadows by the side of some peaceful river, whose sleepy waters, silently gliding over their weedy bed, seem to bear away our anxious and conflicting thoughts along with them. Seated by the rude and ancient-looking stem of this tree, we listen to the soft whispering of the wind among its silvery leaves, and gaze upon the glassy surface of the slowly moving stream, just rippled here and there by a stray branch projecting from the flowery bank, or a fairy forest of reeds springing up in spite of the ceaseless and invincible flow of that unfailing tide. We gaze, until the precise distinctions of past, present, and future fade away—the ocean of time flows past us like that silent river (would it were as unruffled in its real course;) and while retaining a dim and mysterious consciousness of our own existence, we lose all remembrance of its rough passages, all perception of its present bitterness, and all apprehension of its future perils. From such unprofitable musings, if too frequently indulged, we awake to a melancholy state of feeling, of which the willow has by the common consent of mankind become emblematical. Morbid, listless, and inactive, we shrink from the stirring necessities of life; we behold the happy flocks still feeding, and almost wish, that like them we could be content with a rich pasture, as the bound of our ambition—like them live, die, and be forgotten. The dreamy silence of those low damp fields increases our melancholy, and the pale and mournful aspect of the willow, prematurely hoary, becomes an emblem of our own fate and condition. It grows not erec: and stately like the stern elm, or bold and free like the waving ash, but stooping obliquely over the stream, or, shrinking from its companions with distorted limbs, tells to the morbid and imaginative beholder, a sad tale of early blight, or the rough dealing of rude and adverse winds. The loiterer still lingers, loath to leave a spot where one bitter root may yet remain unappropriated. He listens while he lingers, and thinks he hears the willow whispering its sorrows to the passing gale. The gale blows more freshly, and the willow then seems to sigh and shiver with the newly awakened agonies of despair.

Thus can the distorted eye of melancholy look on every object with a glass of its own colouring, and thus it is possible one of our most common and unimportant trees, naturally growing in the familiar walks of man, in the small enclosure near his door, the green paddock or the luxuriant meadow, may have acquired by the sanction of feeling, not of reason, its peculiar character as an emblem of sorrow and gloom.

The weeping willow, as being more gracefully mournful, might very properly have claimed that attention which has been given to the common and plebeian members of its family; but the weeping willow, while it has in this country fewer natural associations, is burdened and robbed of its poetic character by a great number of such as are neither natural nor pleasing. Could we think of this elegant and picturesque tree only in its most appropriate situation, drooping over the tomb of Napoleon, or could we have beheld this tomb itself, without its infinitely multiplied representations in poonah and every other kind of painting, we might then have enjoyed ideas and sensations connected with it of the most touching and exquisite nature. But, alas! our first failure in drawing has been upon the dangling boughs of the weeping willow; our first sonnet has been addressed to this pathetic tree; our first flourish in fancy needle-work has depicted a white urn delicately stitched with shining silk, and long green threads suspended over it, in mockery of its drooping branches. But above all, we have seen in the square ells of garden fronting those tall thin dwellings about town, where a squeezed and narrow neighbour jostles up on each side, leaving just room enough for a tin verandah, but no space to breathe or move, still less to think or feel;—we have seen, laden with a summer's dust, the countless little stunted weeping willows that throw aloft, as if in search of purer air, their slender, helpless arms, and would weep, if they could, yea, cry aloud, at this merciless malappropriation of their defenceless beauty.

These impressions must therefore necessarily be obliterated, and others, less vulgar and profane, be deeply impressed upon the mind, before the weeping willow can be established in that rank which it deserves to hold amongst objects whose general associations are poetical.*

Turning from the consideration of such trees as belong to the forest, the field, or the grove, to those which are reared and cultivated for domestic purposes; we find, even here, a world of ideas and associations, which, if not highly poetical, are fraught with the satisfaction of home comforts, and the interest of local attachments. In travelling through a fertile country, thickly peopled, not with the haggard, rude, or careless-looking labourers at the loom, but with a quiet and peaceful peasantry, whose delight is in the gardens, the fields, and the flocks which their fathers tended before them, how beautiful, in the season of their blossom, are the numerous orchards, neatly fenced in, and studding the landscape all over with little islands of rich promise, where the brightest tints of the rose, and the fairest of the lily, mingle with odorous perfume in all the luxuriant profusion of nature! Again, when the harvest is over, and the golden fruit, perfected by a summer's sun, is suspended in variegated clusters from every bough, how delightful is the contemplation

* It is a fact now generally known, that the first weeping willow grown in England, was planted in Pope's garden at Twickenham, and is said to have been sent from Turkey, with a present from his friend, Lady Mary Wortley Montague.

of that rural and picturesque scene!—how sweetly the ideas it presents to the mind are blended with our love of nature and natural enjoyments, and our gratitude for the bounty and goodness of a gracious Providence.

Descending to the class of inferior trees, or rather plants, our poetical associations increase in proportion as these are more picturesque, graceful, or parasitical; and consequently, are more easily woven into the landscape, either real or imaginary, which forms the subject of contemplation. Amongst such, the common wild heath is by no means the least important; nor are we, on first consideration, aware for how large a proportion of our admiration of mountain scenery we are indebted to the rich purple hue which is thrown by this plant over the rugged sides of the hills, otherwise too cold and stony in their aspect to gratify the eye. With the idea of the heath we connect the path of the lonely traveller, or the silence of untrodden wilds; the haunt of the timid moor fowl, the hum of the wandering bee, or the gush of unseen water in the deep ravines of the mountains, working its way amongst the rocks, through moss, and fern, and matted weeds, until at length it sparkles up in the clear sun-shine, and then goes dancing, and leaping, yet ever murmuring, like a pleased but fretful child, on—on towards the bosom of the silent lake below.

But above all other vegetable productions, neither trees nor flowers excepted, the ivy is perhaps the most poetical. And why? not merely because its leaves are "never sere," nor because it hangs in fanciful festoons, glittering yet gloomy, playful yet sad; but because it does what so few things in nature will do—it clings to, and beautifies the ruin—it shrinks not from the fallen column—it covers with its close embrace the rugged face of desolation, and conceals beneath its rich and shining mantle the ravages made by the hand of time—the wreck which the tempest has wrought.

Besides this highly poetical idea, which forces itself upon every feeling mind, the ivy has other associations, deeply interesting in their character. It requires so many years to bring it to the perfection necessary for those masses of foliage, and dark recesses of mysterious gloom, which its most picturesque form presents, that we naturally connect with this plant the ideas of solemnity which are awakened by reflecting on the awful lapse of time. The ivy, too, is chiefly seen upon the walls of religious houses, either perfect or ruinous, where its heavy clusters of matted leaves, with their deep shadow, afford a shelter and a hiding place for the bat and the owl, and, in the ideas of the irrational or the too imaginative, for other less corporeal beings that flit about in the dusky hours of night. Thus, the ivy acquires a character of mystery and gloom, perhaps, even more poetical than that which strikes us when we see its glittering sprays glancing in the clear light of day, or waving in the wind around the gray turrets of the ruin, and suggesting that simile which has been so frequently the poet's theme, of light words and jocund smiles assumed by the broken-hearted to conceal the withering of the blighted soul.

It would be useless to proceed farther with this minute examination of objects, to each of which a volume of relative ideas might be appropriated. A few examples are sufficient to prove, that with this class of natural productions, the great majority of minds are the same in their associations. Would it might prove something better than a mockery of the loveliness of nature, thus to examine its component parts, and ask why each is charming! Far more delightful would be the task of expatiating upon the whole, of roaming at will upon the hills and through the woods, and embracing at one view, in one ecstatic thought, the unspeakable harmony which reigns through the creation. The pine, the oak, and the elm, may be magnificent in themselves—the willow, the heath, and the ivy, may each present a picture to the imagination; but what are these considered separately, compared with the ever-varying combination of form and colour, majesty and grace, presented by the forest, or the woodland, the sloping banks of the river, or the leafy dell, where the round and the massive figures are broken by the spiral stem or the feathery foliage that trembles in the passing gale—where the hues that are most vivid, or most delicate, stand forth in clear contrast from the depths of sombre shade—where every projecting rock and rugged cleft is fringed with a curtain of green tracery, and every glassy stream reflects again, in its stainless mirror, the variety and the magnificence of the surrounding groves? Yet what are words to tell of the perfection of nature, the glories that lie scattered even in our daily path? And what are we, that we should pursue the sordid avocations of life without pausing to admire?

In order that the harmony of sweet sounds may be distinctly perceived and accommodated to the taste, there must be a peculiar formation of the human ear; nor is it possible for the poetry of any object, even the most beautiful in nature, to be felt or understood without an answering chord in the human heart. There are many rational beings, worthy and estimable in their way, altogether insensible to the unseen or spiritual charm which lies in almost every subject of intellectual contemplation; who gaze upon the ivy-mantled ruin, and behold nothing more than gray walls with a partial covering of green, like the man so aptly described by Wordsworth, when he says—

"The primrose by the water's brim,
A yellow primrose was to him,
And it was nothing more."

But there are others, whether happier in this state of being it might not be easy to prove, but certainly more capable of intense and refined enjoyment, who, accustomed to live in a world of thought, and to derive their happiness from remote and impalpable essences of things, rather than from things themselves, cannot look on nature, nor behold any object with which poetical association holds the most distant connexion, but immediately a spark in the train of imagination is kindled, and consciousness, memory, and anticipation, heap fuel on the living fire, which glows through the expansive soul.

It is, still to speak figuratively, by the light of this fire, that they see what is imperceptible to other eyes. They can discover types and emblems in all created things; and having received in their own minds deep and indelible impressions of beauty and harmony, majesty and awe, can recur to those impressions through the channels which external things afford, and draw from thence a never-failing supply of the purest poetical enjoyment.

THE POETRY OF ANIMALS.

While flowers, and trees, and plants in general afford an immense fund of interest to the contemplative beholder, the animal kingdom, yet scarcely touched upon in these pages, is, perhaps, equally fertile in poetical associations. From the reflections of the melancholy Jacques upon the wounded deer, down to the pretty nursery fable of "The Babes in the Wood," the same natural desire to associate with our own the habits and feelings of the more sensitive and amiable of the inferior animals is observable, as well in the productions of the sublimest, as the simplest poet.

Burns' "Address to a Mouse," proves to us with how much genuine pathos a familiar and ordinary subject may be invested. No mind which had never bathed in the fountain of poetry itself—whose remotest attributes had not been imbued with this ethereal principle as with a living fire, could have ventured upon such a theme. In common hands, a moral drawn from a mouse, and clothed in the language of verse, would have been little better than a burlesque, or a baby's song at best; but in these beautiful and touching lines, so perfect is the adaptation of the language to the subject—so evident, without ostentation, the deep feeling of the bard himself, that the moral flows in with a natural simplicity which cannot fail to charm the most fastidious reader.

The lines in which Cowper describes himself as a "stricken deer," are also affecting in the extreme; but as my object is not to quote instances, but to examine why certain things are pre-eminently poetical, we will proceed to the considerations of a few individual subjects; first premising, that animals obtain the character of being so in a *greater* degree in proportion as we imagine them to possess such qualities as are most elevated or refined in ourselves, and in a *less* degree as we become familiarized with their bodily functions: because the majority of our ideas, in connexion with them, must then be of a gross material character, just as we may speak in poetry, of the "wild boar of the wilderness," while the tame hog of the sty is a thing wholly forbidden.

The elephant is allowed to be the most sagacious of the brute creation; but his sagacity is celebrated chiefly in anecdotes of trick and cunning, which qualities being the very reverse of what is elevated or noble in human nature, he possesses, in spite of his curious formation and majestic power, little claim to poetical interest.

The dog very properly stands next in the scale of intellect; and so far as faithful attachment is a rare and beautiful trait in the character both of man and brute, the dog may be said to be poetical; but we are too familiar with this animal to regard him with the reverence which his good qualities might seem to demand. We feed him on crusts and garbage; or we see him hungered until he becomes greedy, and neglected until he becomes servile, and spurned until he threatens a vengeance which he dares not execute.

The claims of the horse to the general admiration of mankind are too well understood to need our notice here, especially as they have already been examined in a former chapter. To the horse belong no associations with ideas of what is gross or mean. His most striking attribute is power; and the ardour with which he enters into the excitement of the chase, or the battle, gives him a character so nearly approaching to what is most admired in the human species, that the ancients delighted to represent this noble animal, not as he is, but with distended nostrils, indicating a courage almost more than animal, with eyes animated with mental as well as physical energy, and with the broad intellectual forehead of a man.

The ass is certainly less poetical than picturesque; but, still, it is poetical in its patient endurance of suffering, in its association with the wandering outcasts from society whose tents are in the wilderness, and whose "lodging is on the cold ground," in its humble appetites, and in its unrepining submission to the most abject degradation. Let us hope that the patience of the ass arises from its own insensibility, and that its sufferings, though frequent, are attended with little acuteness of sensation; but they are sufferings still, borne with a meekness that looks so much like the Christian virtue, resignation, that, in contemplating the hard condition of this degraded animal, the heart is softened with feelings of sorrow and compassion, and we long to rescue it from the yoke of the oppressor.

I have often thought there was something peculiarly affecting in the character of the young ass—something almost saddening to the soul, in its sudden starts of short-lived frolic. In its appearance there is a strange unnatural mixture of infant glee, with a mournful and almost venerable gravity. Its long melancholy ears are in perfect contrast with its innocent and happy face. It seems to have heard, what is seldom heard in extreme youth, the sad forebodings of its latter days; and when it crops the thistle, and sports among the briers, it appears to be with the vain hope of carrying the spirit of joy along with it, through the after vicissitudes of its hard and bitter lot.

The cow is poetical, not from any quality inherent, or even imagined to be inherent in itself, but from its invariable association with rich pastures and verdant meadows, and as an almost indispensable ornament to pictures of quiet rural scenery. Time was when the cow was poetical from her association with rosy maidens tripping over the dewy lawn, and village swains tuning the rustic reed; but since the high magnifier of modern investigation has been applied to pastoral subjects, milkmaids have been pronounced to be too homely for the poet's theme; village swains have been detected in fustian garments; and both, with their flocks, and their herds, and with pastoral poetry altogether, have been dismissed from the theatre of intellectual entertainment.

Nothing, however, that has yet been effected by the various changes to which taste is liable, has destroyed the poetical character of the deer. Our associations with the deer are far removed from every thing gross or familiar; we think of it only as a free denizen of the woods, swift in its movements, graceful in its elastic step, delicate in all its perceptions, and tremblingly alive to the dangers which threaten it on every hand. We imagine it retiring from the broad clear light of day, into the seclusion of the mountain glen; stooping in silence and solitude to drink of the pure waters in their bubbling and melodious flow; gazing on through the rocky defile, or in amongst the weedy hollows on the banks of the stream, with its clear calm eye, that looks too full of love and tenderness to be betrayed, yet ever watchful, from an instinctive sense of the multiplied calamities which assail the innocent and helpless; listening to the slightest sound of earth or air, the rustling of the spray that springs back from the foot of the fairy songster, or the fall of the leaf that flickers from bough to bough; and then—as the zephyr swells, and the gathering breeze comes like a voice through the leafy depths of the forest—bounding over the mossy turf, and away along the sides of the mountain—away to join the browsing herd, and give them intelligence of an approaching, but unseen foe. Or, when the chase is ended, and the wounded deer returns to pant away its parting breath in the same glen where it gambolled upon the dewy grass, a careless and sportive fawn, he comes back with weary foot and bleeding bosom, to slake his burning thirst in the same fountain where so often he has bathed his vigorous and elastic limbs. The woods are still peaceful, the birds sing on, regardless of his groans, the stream receives the life-blood from his wound, his brethren of the faithless herd again are browsing on the distant hills, and alone in his mortal agony he weeps and dies.

But of all the animal creation, birds have ever been the poet's favourite theme. In the beauty of their form and plumage, in their soaring flight, in their sensitiveness and timidity, and in the lightness and vividness of their movements, there is something to our conceptions so intimately connected with spirituality, that we can readily sympathize with the propensity of the imaginative, to imbody, in these gentle and ethereal beings, the souls of their departed friends; and of the superstitious, to regard them as winged messengers laden with the irrevocable decrees of an oracular fate.

It is a curious fact, that, in our ideal personifications of angelic forms, we do not perceive that they lose any thing of their intellectual or celestial character, by having appended to them the entire wings of a bird. Whether, from this association, we have learned to consider birds as less material than other animals, or whether, from the aerial flight of birds, the artist and the poet have learned to represent angelic beings as borne along the fields of air on feathery wings, it is certain that the capacity of flight loses none of its poetical sublimity and grace, by being connected in our notions with the only means of which we have any knowledge.

Birds, in their partiality for the haunts of man, offer a striking appeal to the sensitive and benevolent mind. Why should they cast themselves into the path of the destroyer, or expose their frail habitations to the grasp of his unsparing hand? Is it that they feel some "inly touch of love" for their imperious master, or that they seek from his power what his mercy too often denies? or would they ask, in the day of their distress, for the sparings of his plenty, and pay him back with the rich melody of their summer songs? Whatever may be the cause, they flock around him, as if the manly privilege of destruction had never been exercised upon their defenceless community. Yet, mark how well they know the nature of creation's lord. They tremble at his coming, they flutter in his grasp, they look askance upon him from the bough, they regard him with perpetual suspicion, and, above all, some of their species will forsake their beloved and carefully constructed habitations, if he has but profaned them with his touch. It can be no want of parental affection which drives them to this unnatural alternative, for how diligently have they toiled, with what exquisite ingenuity have they constructed their children's home, how faithfully have they watched, how patiently have they waited for the fulfilment of their hopes! Yet, in one fatal moment, the silken cord that strung together their secret joys is broken. Another spring may renew their labours and their loves, but they know it not. Their all was centred in that narrow point, and to them the hopes and the labours of a whole life are lost. The delicacy of perception which enables them to detect the slightest intrusion upon the sacred mysteries of their nest, gives them a character of acuteness and sensibility far beyond that of other animals; and it is a wonderful and mysterious instinct which makes them resign all they have loved and cherished, even when no change is perceptible to other eyes, and when it is certain that no injury has been sustained. It is a refinement upon feeling, which strikes the imagination with a strong resemblance to some of those mal-occurrences in human life, which divert the inner channel of the thoughts and affections, without the superficial observer being aware of any change—those lamentable encroachments upon the sacredness of domestic confidence, which, by a word—a look—a touch, may at once destroy the blessedness of that union, which is nothing better than a degrading bond after the spell of its secret charm is broken.

The nightingale, whose charmed lays have a two-fold glory in their native melody, and in the poet's song, claims unquestionably the first place in our consideration; though I own I am much disposed to think that this bird owes half its celebrity to the circumstance of its singing in the night, when the visionary, wrapped in the mantle of deep thought, wanders forth to gaze upon the stars, and to court the refreshment of silence and solitude. It is then that the voice of the nightingale thrills upon his ear, and he feels that a kindred spirit is awake, perhaps, like him, to sweet remembrances, to sorrows too deep for tears, and joys for which music alone can find a voice. He listens, and the ever-varying melody rises and falls upon the wandering wind—he pines for some spiritual communion with this unseen being—he longs to ask why sleep is banished from a breast so tuned to harmony—joy, and joy alone, it cannot be, which inspires that solitary lay; no, there are tones of tenderness too much like grief, and is not grief the bond of fellowship by which impassioned souls are held together? Thus, the nightingale pours upon the heart of the poet, strains which thrill with those sensations that have given pathos to his muse, and he pays her back by celebrating her midnight minstrelsy in song.

The skylark is, of all the feathered tribe, most invariably associated with ideas of rapturous, pure, and elevated enjoyment; such as we ourselves had glimpses of in early life, when the animal excitement of childhood, mingling with the first bright dawnings of reason, lifted us high into the regions of thought, and taught us to spurn at the harsh discipline of real life. From flights such as these we have so often fallen prone upon the earth, that they have ceased to tempt our full-fledged powers, and even if the brilliancy of thought remained to lure us on, the animal stimulus would be wanting, and we should be conscious of our utter inability on the first attempt to soar again. But the memory of this ecstatic feeling still remains, and when we think of the aspirations of purified and happy spirits, we compare them to the upward flight of the lark, or to the boundings of that innocent joy which we ourselves have felt, but feel no more. And then there is the glad voice of the lark, that spring of perpetual freshness, pouring forth its untiring and inexhaustible melody.

"Like an unbodied joy whose race is just begun."

Who ever listened to this voice on a clear spring morning, when nature was first rising from her wintry bed, when the furze was in bloom, and the lambs at play, and the primrose and the violet scented the delicious south wind that came with the glad tidings of renovated life—who ever listened to the song of the lark on such a morning, while the dew was upon the grass, and the sun was smiling through a cloudless sky, without feeling that the spirit of joy was still alive within, around, and above him, and that those wild and happy strains, floating in softened melody upon the scented air, were the outpourings of a gratitude too rapturous for words?

Nor is it the vocal power of birds which gives us the highest idea of their intellectual capacity. Their periodical visitations of particular regions of the globe, and the punctuality with which they go forth on their mysterious passage at particular seasons of the year, form, perhaps, the most wonderful propensity in their nature. It is true that instinct is the spring of their actions, and it is possible that they are themselves unconscious of any motive or reason for the important change which instinct induces them to make; but in speaking of the poetry of birds,

I wish to be understood to refer to the *ideas* which their habits naturally excite, not to the facts which they elicit. We know that birds are by no means distinguished, above other animals by their intellectual capacity, but so wonderful, so far beyond our comprehension, is the instinct exhibited in their transient lives, that instead of having always in mind the providential scheme which provides for the wants and wishes even of the meanest insect, we are apt to indulge our imaginations by attaching to the winged wanderers of the air, vague yet poetical ideas of their own mental endowments, and half believe them to be actuated by a delicacy of sense and feeling, in many cases superior to our own. Whether this belief, with which the minds of children are so strongly imbued, and which lingers about us long after we have become acquainted with its fallacy, be any bar to the progress of philosophical knowledge, I am not prepared to say; but certainly it is the very essence of poetical feeling; and for one visionary who would scruple to kill a bird for dissection because it had been the companion of his woodland walks, there will remain to be a thousand practical men who would care little what strains had issued from that throat, if they could but ascertain how the throat itself was constructed. It is precisely the same principle which inspires us with the sublimest ideas of the majesty of the universe, by imbodying in the stars, the mountains, the ocean, or the pealing thunder, some unseen, but powerful intelligence, that offers for our enjoyment a never-ending companionship in the woods and wilds, through an ideal personification of every thing sweet and fair. It is this principle which makes us hail the periodical return of certain birds, as if they had been thinking of us, and of our fields and gardens, in that far distant land, of which they tell no tidings; and, taking into consideration the changes of the seasons, had consulted upon the best means of escaping the dangers of the threatening storm: as if they had spread their feeble wings to bear them over the wide waste of inhospitable waters from the energy of their own hearts, and had come back to us from their own unchangeable and fervent love.

If it be poetry to gaze upon the mighty ocean with that strange, deep wonder with which we regard the manifestations of a mysterious, but concentrated and individual power—to feel that *he* stretches his unfathomable expanse from pole to pole—that *he* ruffles his foaming mane and rushes bellowing upon the circling shore—or that *he* lies slumbering in his silent glory, beneath the blaze of our meridian sun, and through the still midnight of the island gardens that gem the South Pacific; it is not less in unison with poetic feeling, nor less productive of ecstatic thought, to personify the trees, and the flowers, and the rippling streams, and to welcome with gratitude the fairy forms and glad voices that come to tell us of returning spring.

Who that has tasted the delights of poetry, would be deprived of this power of the imagination to people the air and animate the whole creation? Let the critic smile—let the tradesman count his pence, and reckon up how little imagination has ever added to his store—let the modern philosopher examine the leaf, and the flower, and the bird's wing, and pronounce them equally material and devoid of mind—let the good man say that poetry is a vain pursuit, and that these things are not worthy of our regard; I maintain that these notions, visionary as they are, tend to innocent enjoyment, and that innocent enjoyment is not a vain pursuit, because it may, and ought to inspire us with love and gratitude towards Him who has not only given us a glorious creation to enjoy, but faculties to enjoy it with, and imagination to make the most of it.

With the swallow we associate the ever-cheering idea of returning summer. We watch for its coming, and rejoice to hear the merry twittering voice, that seems to tell of a life of innocent and careless glee—an existence unruffled by a storm. As the summer advances, and we seek shelter from the noon-day heat in the deep shade of the leafy boughs that wave around the margin of the glassy stream, it is here that the swallow is not unfrequently our sole companion; and ever as we call to remembrance its swift yet graceful flight, we picture it darting from the pendent branches of the willow, stooping to cool its arrowy wing upon the surface of the glancing waters, and then away, swifter than thought, into mid air, to sport one moment with aerial beings. Again it sweeps in silence past our feet, over the spiral reeds, around, above us, gliding through the shadows, and flickering through the sunshine; but never resting, and yet never weary; for the spirit than animates its bounding bosom, and stretches forth its giddy wing, is one that knows no sleep until light has vanished from the world, no sadness until the sweets of summer are exhausted. And then arises that vague mysterious longing for a milder sphere—that irrepressible energy to do and dare what to mere reason would appear impracticable; and forth it launches with its faithful companions, true to the appointed time, upon the boundless ocean of infinitude, trusting to it knows not what, yet trusting still.

With the cuckoo, our associations are in some respects the same as with the swallow, except that we are in the habit of regarding it simply as a voice; and what a voice! How calm, and clear, and rich! How full of all that can be told of the endless profusion of summer's charms!—of the hawthorn, in its scented bloom, of the blossoms of the apple, and the silvery waving of the fresh green corn, of the cowslip in the meadow, and the wild rose by the woodland path; and last, but not least in its poetical beauty, of the springing up of the meek-eyed daisy, to welcome the foot of the traveller, upon the soft and grassy turf.

Above all other birds, the dove is most intimately and familiarly associated in our minds with ideas of the quiet seclusion of rural life, and the enjoyment of peace and love. This simple bird, by no means remarkable for its sagacity, so soft in its colouring, and graceful in its form, that we cannot behold it without being conscious of its perfect loveliness, is in some instances endowed with an extraordinary instinct, which adds greatly to its poetical interest. That species called the carrier pigeon, has often been celebrated for the faithfulness with which it pursues its mysterious way, but never more beautifully than in the following lines by Moore.

"The bird let loose in eastern skies,
When hastening fondly home,
Ne'er stoops to earth her wing, or flies
Where idler wanderers roam;
But high she shoots through air and light,
Above all low delay,
Where nothing earthly bounds her flight,
Or shadow dims her way.

So grant me, God, from every stain
Of sinful passion free,
Aloft through virtue's purer air,
To steer my flight to thee!

No sin to cloud, no lure to stay,
My soul, as home she springs,
Thy sunshine on her joyful way,
Thy freedom on her wings."

But neither the wonderful instinct of this undeviating messenger, nor even the classical association of the two white doves with the queen of love and beauty, are more powerful in awakening poetical ideas than the simple cooing of our own wood pigeon, heard sometimes in the silent solemnity of summer's noon, when there is no other sound but the hum of the wandering bee, as he comes laden and rejoicing home, when the sun is alone in the heavens, and the cattle are sleeping in the shade, and not a single breath of air is whispering through the boughs, and the deep dark shadows of the elm and the sycamore lie motionless upon the earth—or, in the cool evening, when the shadows, less distinct, are lengthened out upon the lawn, and the golden west is tinging here and there the bright green foliage with a brighter hue, when the shepherd is numbering his flock, and the labourer is returning to his rest, it is then that the soft sweet cooing of the dove, bursting forth, as it were, from the pure fount of love and joy within its breast, sounds like the lullaby of nature, and diffuses over the mind that holy calm which belongs to our best and happiest feelings.

From the timid moor cock, the "whirring partridge," and the shy water fowl that scarcely dares to plume its beauteous wing in the moonlight of our autumnal evening, when the floods are high, and the wind rushes whispering through the long sere grass, down to the russet wren that looks so gravely conscious of the proprieties of life, there is scarcely one class of the feathered tribe to which imagination does not readily and naturally assign an intellectual, or rather a moral character, associating it with feelings and capabilities, of which the little flutterer is (perhaps happily for itself) unconscious.

The peacock is a striking illustration of this fact. The beauty of his plumage is in all probability lost upon him, yet because it consists of that rich and gaudy colouring, which is consistent with our notions of what vanity delights in, and because the lengthened garniture of his tail requires that for convenience and repose he should often place himself in an elevated situation, he has obtained a character which there is little in his real nature to justify, and as an emblem of pride, is placed by the side of Juno in her regal dignity. This tendency of the mind to throw over sensible objects a colouring of its own, is also proved by the character which mankind have bestowed upon the robin redbreast, in reality a jealous, quarrelsome, and unamiable bird; yet such is the unobtrusive and meek beauty of its little form, the touching pathos of its "still small voice," and the appeals it seems ever to be making to the kindness and protection of man, that the poet perpetually speaks of the robin with tenderness and love, and even the rude ravager of the woods spares a breast so lovely, and so full of simple melody.

Birds as well as other animals, owe much of their poetical interest to the fabulous part of their history; thus, the pelican is said to feed her young with the life-blood flowing from her own bosom, and this unnatural act of maternal affection is quoted by the poet as a favourite simile for self-devotion under various forms. Of the swan it is said and sung, that in dying she breathes forth a strain of plaintive song; but even without this poetical fable, the swan is associated with so much that is graceful and lovely, that we cannot think of this majestic queen of the water, sailing forth like a snow-white gallery on the silver tide, without losing ourselves in a romantic dream of lakes and rivers, and that sylvan scenery which the swan is known to frequent.

We have yet given our attention only to those birds whose nature and habits are productive of pleasing associations. There are others no less poetical, whose home is in the desert or the mountain, whose life is in the storm or on the field of carnage; and it is to these especially that fabulous history has given importance and celebrity.

For its mysterious and gloomy character the owl is particularly distinguished; and such is the grave aspect of its countenance, so nearly resembling the human face in the traits which are considered as indicative of sagacity and earnest thought, that the ancients dignified this bird by making it the emblem of wisdom, though there seems to be little in its real nature to merit such exaltation. From the extreme timidity of the owl, and its habitual concealment from the light of day, it is difficult to become familiar with its character. We see it sailing forth on expanded wings in the gray twilight of the evening, when other birds have retired to their nightly rest; or we behold it in the distance a misty speck, half light, half shadow, just visible in the same proportion, and with the same obscurity of outline and colour, as in our infancy we fancied that spiritual beings from another world made themselves perceptible in this. Besides which, the voice of the owl, as it comes shrieking on the midnight blast, and its mysterious breathings, half sighs, half whispers, heard amongst the ivy wreaths of the ruin, all tend to give to this bird a character of sadness, solemnity and awe.

The raven, strikingly sagacious and venerable in its appearance, is still believed by the superstitious to be a bird of ill omen; and much as we may be disposed to despise such prognostications as the flight, or the cry of different birds, there is something in the habits, but especially in the voice of the raven, which gives it a strange and almost fearful character. It seems to hold no communion with the joyous spirits, to have no association with the happy scenes of earth; but leads a lengthened and unsocial life amongst the gloomy shades of the venerable forest, in the deep recesses of the pathless mountain, or on the rocky summit of the beetling crag that overlooks the ocean's blue abyss; and when it goes forth, with its sable pinions spread like the wings of a dark angel upon the wind, its hoarse and hollow croak echoes from rock to rock, as if telling, in those dreary and appalling tones, of the fleshy feast to which it is hastening, of the death-pangs of the mountain deer, of the cry of the perishing kid, and of the bones of the shipwrecked seaman whitening in the surge.

To the eagle mankind have agreed in assigning a sort of regal character, from the majesty of his bearing, and the proud pre-eminence he maintains amongst the feathered tribe; from the sublimity of his chosen home, far above the haunts of man and meaner animals, from the self-seclusion in which he holds himself apart from the general association of living and familiar things, and from the beauty and splendour of his sagacious eye, which shrinks not from the dazzling glare of the sun itself. Innumerable are the fables founded upon the peculiar habits of this bird, all tending to exalt him in the scale of moral and intellectual importance; but to the distinction conferred upon him by the ancients when they raised him to a companionship with Jove, is mainly to be attributed the poetical interest with which his character is universally invested.

There are many birds whose peculiar haunts and habits render them no less useful to the painter than the poet, by adding to the pictorial effect of his landscape. In the sheet of crystal water which skirts the nobleman's domain, and widens in front of his castellated halls, we see the stately swan; on the shady margin of the quiet stream, imbosomed in a copes-wood forest, the shy water hen; the jackdaw on the old gray steeple of the village church; and a company of rooks winging their social way, wherever the scenery is of a peaceful, cultivated, or rural character. By these means our inimitable Turner delights to give his pictures their highly poetical character. The heron is one of his favorite birds, and when it stands motionless and solitary upon a broken fragment of dark rock, looking down into the clear deep water, with that imperturbable aspect of never-ending melancholy which marks it out as a fit accompaniment of wild and secluded scenery, we feel almost as if the genius of the place were personified before us, and silent, and lonely, and unfrequented as these wilds may be, that there is at least one spirit which finds companionship in their solitude.

But above all other birds, the seagull, as it diversifies the otherwise monotonous aspect of the ocean, is an essential accompaniment to every representation of a sea view. Had the colour of this bird been red or yellow, or almost any other than what it is, it would have broken the harmony of the picture; but its breast is of the form of the ocean waves, and the misty hue of its darker plumage is like the blending of the vapoury clouds with the cold blue of the deep sea below. Not only in its colouring, but in the wild gracefulness of its movements, in its shrill cry, in its swift and circling flight, and in the reckless freedom with which it sails above the drear abyss, its dark shadow reflected in the hollow of the concave waters, and its white plumage flashing like a gleam of light, or like the ocean spray, from rock to rock, it assimilates so entirely with the whole character of the scene, that we look upon it as a living atom separated from the troubled and chaotic elements, a personification of the spirit of the storm, a combination of its foam and its darkness, its light and its depth, its swiftness and its profound solemnity.

Inferior to birds in their pictorial beauty, though scarcely less conducive to poetical interest, are the various tribes of insects that people the earth and animate the air; but before turning our attention to these, it may be well to think for a moment in what manner the poet's imagination is affected by fishes and reptiles. Of the poetry of fishes little can be said. Two kinds only occur to me as being familiar in the language of poetry, and conducive to its figurative charm—the flying fish and the dolphin. The former, in its transient and feeble flight, has been made the subject of some beautiful lines by Moore; and because of the perpetual dangers which await it from innumerable enemies, both in sea and air, it is often adopted as a simile for the helpless and persecuted children of earth; while the dolphin, from the beauty of its form, and the gorgeous colours which are said to be produced by its last agonies, is celebrated in the poet's lay as an emblem of the glory which shines most conspicuously in the hour of death.

> "————parting day
> Dies like the dolphin, whom each pang imbues
> With a new colour, as it gasps away:
> The last still loveliest, till,—'tis gone—and all is gray!"
>
> Byron.

In fearful pre-eminence amongst those animals commonly considered repulsive and degraded, is the serpent, whose history is unavoidably associated with the introduction of sin and sorrow into the world. Whether from this association, or from an instinctive horror of its "venomous tooth," it is certain that the serpent is more generally dreaded, and more loathed, even by those who do not fear it, than any other living thing; and yet how beautiful is its sagacious eye, how rich and splendid its colouring, how delicate the tracery of net-work thrown all over its glossy scales, how graceful and easy its meandering movements, as it winds itself in amongst the rustling grass, how much like one of the fairest objects in nature, a clear blue river wandering through a distant valley! Yet all these claims to beauty, which the serpent unquestionably possesses, entitle it the more to the contempt and abhorrence of mankind, by obtaining for it the character of insinuating guile, which the allurements it is recorded to have practised upon our first mother seem fully to confirm.

The toad, save for the "precious jewel in his head," can scarcely be called poetical, though not unfrequenty found in verse as a striking similitude for the extreme of ugliness, as well as for a despicable proneness to grovel in what is earthly and most abhorrent to our finer feelings, from its frequenting low, damp, unwholesome places, the banks of stagnant pools, or the nettles and lone grass that wave over the gloomy and untrodden ground where the dead lie sleeping in their silent rest.

The snail has certainly no strong claims to poetical merit; yet we often find it serving the purpose of simile and illustration, from its tardy movements, and the faculty it has of carrying about its home, into which it shrinks on the first touch of the enemy. And even the lowly worm has some title to the poet's regard, because of its utter degradation, and the circumstance of its being, of all living things, most liable to injury, at the same time that it is one of the least capable of resistance or revenge.

Passing slightly over the multitudinous family of insects, we leave the beetle to his evening flight—the grasshopper, whose merry chirp enlivens the wayside traveller—the bee, perhaps the most poetical of any, from his opposite qualities of collecting honey and diffusing poison—the locust, whose plagues are often commemorated—the hornet, to whose stings Milton describes Samson as comparing the accumulated agony of his own restless thoughts—the glow-worm, whose feeble light is like a fairy star, beaming upward from a world upon which all other stars look down—and the canker-worm, whose fatal ravages destroy the bloom of youth, and render void the prodigality of summer—passing over all these and many more, in which we recognise the familiar companions of the poet, we turn our attention to the butterfly and the moth, as being most associated with refined and agreeable ideas.

The butterfly is like a spiritual attendant upon the poet's path, whether he dreams of it as an emblem of the soul, fluttering around the fair form of Psyche, or beholds it in no less beautiful reality, sporting from flower to flower, and teaching him the highest intellectual lesson—to gather sweets from all.

We are apt in our childhood to delight in the legendary tales of fairy people inhabiting the groves, the gardens, or the fields, and regard with an interest almost superstitious, that mysterious circle of dark green verdure that remains from year to year marking the enchanted spot, where once they were believed to hold their midnight revels. Butterflies, in their exquisite colouring, their airy movements, and ephemeral lives, exhibit to the imaginative beholder no slight resemblance to these ideal beings, as they glide through the scented atmosphere of the parterre, nestle in the velvet leaves of the rose, or touch without soiling the snowy bosom of the lily.

The butterfly is also strikingly emblematical of that delicacy which shrinks from communion with all that is rude or base. Touch but its gorgeous wings, and their beauty falls away—immure the woodland wanderer in captivity, and it pines and dies—let the breath of the storm pass over it, and in an instant it perishes.

The moth is less splendidly beautiful than the butterfly. It has a graver character, and seeks neither the sunshine nor the flowers of summer; yet it is liable to be destroyed by the same degree of violence. Supported by the same slight thread of life, and scarcely perceptible amongst the evening shadows, except as an animated speck of moving mist, it yet possesses one striking characteristic, of which the poet fails not to avail himself—a tendency to seek the light, even when that light must prove fatal to its own existence. How many poetical ideas has this simple tendency excited! But enough on this fertile theme. The reader will doubtless be better pleased to examine the subject farther for himself, than to have additional instances of the poetry of animals placed before his view.

It is sufficient to add, in continuation of this subject, that without allowing ourselves time and opportunity to study the nature and habits of animals, we can never really *feel* that they constitute an important part of the world which we inhabit. We may read of them in books, and even be able to class them according to their names and the genera to which they belong, but they will not enter into our hearts as members of the brotherhood of nature, claiming kindred with ourselves, and entitled to our tenderness and love. Those who have known this fellowship in early life will never lose the remembrance of it to their latest day, but will continue to derive from it refreshment and joy, even as they tread the weary paths that lead through the dark passage of a sordid and troubled existence. The difference between those who study nature for themselves, and those who only read of it in books, is much the same as between those who travel, and those who make themselves acquainted with the situation of different countries upon a map. The mind of the traveller is stored with associations of a moral and intellectual character, which no map can suggest; and he who occasionally resigns his soul to the genuine influence of nature as it is seen and felt in the external world, will lay up a rich store of deep and precious thought, to be referred to for amusement and consolation through the whole of his after life.

Had Pope, our immortal poet, not cultivated this intimate and familiar acquaintance with the nature and habits of animals, he would never have thought them of sufficient importance to be made instrumental in conveying the following severe, yet just reproof to man.

"Has God, thou fool! work'd solely for thy good
Thy joy, thy pastime, thy attire, thy food!
Who for thy table feeds the wanton fawn,
For him as kindly spreads the flow'ry lawn.
Is it for thee the lark ascends and sings?
Joy tunes his voice, joy elevates his wings.
Is it for thee the linnet pours his throat?
Loves of his own, and raptures, swell the note.
The bounding steed you pompously bestride,
Shares with his lord the pleasure and the pride.
Is thine alone the seed that strews the plain?
The birds of heaven shall vindicate their grain.
Thine the full harvest of the golden year?
Part pays, and justly, the deserving steer."

THE POETRY OF EVENING.

Ascending in the scale of poetical interest, the seasons might not improperly occupy the next place in our regard, had they not already been especially the theme of one of our ablest poets. To describe the feelings which the seasons in their constant revolutions, are calculated to excite, would therefore only be to recapitulate the language and insult the memory of Thomson. There is one circumstance, however, connected with this subject which demands a moment's attention here. It is the preference for certain seasons of the year evinced by different persons, according to the tone or temperament of their own minds. There are many tests by which human character may be tried. In answering the simple question, "which is your favourite season?" we often betray more than we are aware of at the time, of the nature of our own feelings and character. It is no stretch of imagination to believe, certainly no misstatement of fact to say, that the young and the innocent (or the good, who resemble both) almost invariably make choice of spring as their favourite season of the year; while the naturally morbid and melancholy, or those who have made themselves so by the misuse of their best faculties, as invariably choose autumn. Why so few make choice of summer is not easy to say, unless the oppressive sense of heat is too powerful in its influence upon the body to allow the mind to receive any deeply pleasurable sensations, or because during the summer there is such a constant springing up of beauty, such an unceasing supply of vigour in the animal and vegetable world, that our ideas of spring are carried on until the commencement of autumn. There are a still smaller number of individuals who venture to say they love the dark days of winter, because, in order to find our greatest enjoyment in this season, we must possess a fund of almost uninterrupted domestic happiness, and few there are who can boast of this inestimable blessing; few indeed who, when thrown entirely upon the resources which their own hearts, their own homes, or their own families afford, do not sometimes wish to escape, if only to enjoy the refreshment of green fields, free air, and sunny skies.

The good and the happy, the young and the innocent, whose hearts are full of hope, find peculiar gratification in the rich promise of spring, in the growth and perfection of plants, the rejoicing of the animal creation, and the renovated beauty of universal nature. There is within themselves a kind of sympathy, by which they become a part of the harmonious whole, a grateful trust which accords with this promise, a springing up and growth of joyful expectation which keeps pace with the general progress of the natural world, and echoes back a soul-felt response to the voice which tells of happiness.

How different in all, except their power over the feelings, are the sympathies which are called forth by the contemplation of autumn! The beauty or rather the bloom of nature, is then passing away, and the gorgeous and splendid hues which not unfrequently adorn the landscape remind us too forcibly of that mournful hectic which is known to be a fatal precursor of decay. Every thing fades around us like our own hopes; summer with her sprightliness has left us, like the friends of our youth; while winter, cold winter, comes apace; alas! too like the chilling prospect that lies before us in the path of life. Thus, imagination multiplies our gloomy associations, and renders autumn the season best beloved by the morbid and cheerless, for very sympathy with its tendency to fade.

He who knew, perhaps better than any other man, the depth and the intensity of the mind's worst malady, tells us that—

> "The glance of melancholy is a fearful gift;"

and fearful indeed, is that insatiable appropriation to her own gloomy purposes with which melancholy endows her victims. Fearful would it be to read and sinful to write, how melancholy can distort the fairest picture, extract bitterness from all things sweet and lovely, darkness from light, and anguish—unmitigable anguish—from what was benificently intended to beautify and to bless.

Each day, also, has its associations, so nearly resembling those of the seasons, that it will not be necessary to examine in their separate characters the natural divisions of morning, noon, evening, and night. But evening, as being universally allowed to be highly poetical, may justly claim a large share of our attention.

> "Now came still evening on, and twilight gray
> Had in her sober livery all things clad."

These words occur immediately to every poetical mind on the first consideration of this solemn and lovely hour. Indeed, they occur so familiarly, that, if it were possible they could lose their charm, it would already have been destroyed by frequency of repetition. But these two lines contain within themselves a volume of poetic feeling, that will live imperishable and unimpaired, so long as the human mind shall retain its highest and purest conceptions of the nature of real poetry. The very words have a resemblance to the general lull of nature gently sinking into the silence of night—"Now came still evening on;" "twilight gray" presents us with more than a picture—with a feeling—a distinct perception of thin shadows, and white mists gradually blending together; and the last line completely imbodies in a few simple words, our ideas of the all-pervading influence of evening, with its universally tranquillizing, solemn and mysterious power.

The mystery of twilight is not the least charm it possesses to an imaginative and poetic mind. From the earliest records of intelligent beings, we learn that mystery has ever been inconceivably powerful in its influence upon the human mind. All false religions have been built upon this foundation, and even the true has its mysteries, for which we reverence it the more. Those subjects which excite the deepest veneration and awe, strike us with an indefinite sense of something which we do not—which we cannot, understand; and the throne of the monarch, by being veiled from vulgar eyes, is thus invested with a mystery to which it is greatly indebted for its support. Were all mankind clearly convinced of the inestimable value of true virtue, were they all noble, generous, and devoted, and were all sovereigns immaculate, they might then go forth amongst their people, defended only by their own dignity, supported only by the affection and esteem of their subjects. But since we have learned in these degenerate times that kings are but men, and since there are base natures abroad, ever ready to lay hold of and expose the slightest proof of fallibility in their superiors, it is highly necessary to the maintenance of regal majesty, that the sovereign should be raised above the cognizance of vulgar penetration; that properly initiated members should constitute the court, within whose penetralia the ignorant and common herd are not permitted to intrude; and that in order to give the mandate which issues from the throne, the awful solemnity of an oracle, its irrevocable veto should be uttered unseen.

It next becomes our business to inquire how mystery possesses this power to fascinate the strongest mind, and to lead captive the most tumultuous passions.

Along with mystery, there is invariably some degree of excitement; and excitement, if we may judge by the general conduct and pursuits of mankind, is, when not extended so as to create a feeling of pain, a universally delightful sensation. In speaking of a love of excitement, those who look gloomily upon human nature, are apt to describe it as a defect; but would it not be more philosophical, as well as more consistent with a grateful disposition, to regard this principle as having been implanted in our nature to stimulate us to exertion, and to render the various occupations of life a succession of pleasing duties, rather than of irksome toils?

That excitement is uniformly the accompaniment of mystery, is owing to this cause; mystery is not the subject of any one particular train of ideas, nor can it exclusively occupy the reasoning powers, for want of something tangible to lay hold of; but while the senses or feelings are strongly affected by that which is new, or strange, or fearful, or the magnificent, it opens a field in which all the faculties of the mind, set at liberty from physical restraint, may rush forth to expatiate or combat, without any one gaining the ascendency. Sometimes fear for a moment takes the lead, but the want of sufficient proof or fact to establish any definite cause of alarm, encourages hope; love peoples the unfathomable void with creatures of its own formation; or hate, revenge, and malice wreak their fury upon they know not what; while imagination, the sovereign queen of mystery, reigns supreme and undisturbed over her own aerial realm. Thus does mystery afford illimitable scope for the perpetual activity and play of all the thoughts or passions of which we are capable. By allowing liberty of operation to all, the violence of each is neutralized, and hence the power of mystery over the mind of man.

It may be argued, that mystery has often been the means of exciting the most violent passions, such as fear or superstition. Mystery has unquestionably been made by artful men the means of exciting the curiosity, and arresting the attention of their deluded followers; and thus rendering them more willing and servile recipients of false views, or base desires. But in order that either fear or superstition should be excited to any violent degree, it must have been necessary to dissolve the veil of mystery, and reveal distinctly some palpable object of dread, or subject of mistaken worship.

But to return from this digression to the more pleasing consideration of that delightful hour of day, which brings to every creature the most powerful and indissoluble associations with what it loves best.

"Home to the weary, to the hungry cheer,
To the young bird its mother's brooding wings."

Before the mystery of evening, if not in a higher degree, we are charmed with its repose. The stillness that gradually steals over the creation extends to our own hearts. Passion is lulled, and if we are not, we long to be at rest.

"I will return at the close of day," says the wanderer as he goes forth; and in the evening we begin to listen for his welcome, though weary step. "It is but another day of toil," says the labourer as he brushes away the morning dew, "In the evening I shall rest again;" and already his children are watching at the cottage door, and his wife is preparing his evening meal. All day the rebellious child has resisted the chastisements of love; but in the evening his soul is subdued, and he weeps upon his mother's bosom. We can appease the yearnings of the heart, and drive away reflection—nay, we can live without sympathy, until evening steals around our path, and tells us with a voice which makes itself be heard, that we are alone. In the freshness of morning, and through all the stirring occupations of busy noon, man can forget his Maker; but in the solemn evening hour he feels that he is standing in the presence of his God. In the day-time we move on with the noisy multitude, in their quest of sordid gain, or we wear without weariness or complaint the gilded chains which bind down the soul, or we struggle against the tide of time and circumstance, battling with straws, and spending our strength in fruitless warfare; but in the evening we long to find a path where the flowers are not trampled down by many feet, to burst the degrading bonds of custom, and to think and feel more like immortal beings; we see the small importance of those contested points about which so many parties are at war, and we become willing to glide on with the stream, without fretting ourselves about every weed or feather on its surface; esteeming peace of mind and goodwill towards men far before the defence of any particular set of opinions, or even the establishment of our own.

Evening is the time for remembrance; for the powers of the mind having been all day in exercise, still retain their activity, and being no longer engaged in necessary or worldly pursuits, branch out into innumerable associations, from things present and visible, to those which are unseen and remote, and which but for such associations might have been forgotten. The evening melody of the birds, stealing gently upon the humid air, and heard more distinctly than their noon-day song, calls up the image of some friend with whom we have listened to that sound; nor can we pursue our wonted evening walk without being reminded by the very path, the trees, the flowers, and even the atmosphere, of that familiar interchange of thought and feeling, never enjoyed in such perfection as at the close of day. But, above all other ideas connected with this hour, we love the *repose* of evening. Every living creature is then sinking to rest, darkness is stealing around us like a misty curtain, a dreamy languor subdues our harsher feelings, and makes way for the flow of all that is tender, affectionate, or refined. It is scarcely possible to muse upon this subject without thinking of the return of the wanderer, the completion of labour, the folding of the weary wing, the closing of innocent eyes in peaceful slumber, the vesper hymn, and the prayer or thanksgiving with which every day should be closed.

How is it, that when there is so much even in external nature to remind ungrateful man of his duty, he should be backward in offering that tribute which is due to the Author of all his blessings? Is it so hard a thing to be thankful for the bountiful sun, when we see what a train of glory goes along with his departing light? For the gentle and refreshing dews which come with timely nourishment to the dry and drooping plants? For those very plants, and their unspeakable utility and beauty? For all that the eye beholds of loveliness or magnificence, or that the ear distinguishes of harmony? But above all, for that unwearied sense of enjoyment with which it is possible for man to walk through the creation, rendering thanks to his Creator at every step.

Far be it from the writer of these pages to advocate the vain philosophy of past ages—the vague notion long since discarded from the rational world, that the contemplation of the grandeur, beauty, or even perfection of the universe, is sufficient of itself to lead the heart to God. I speak of such contemplation as being the natural and suitable exercise of an immortal mind, and of the glories of creation as corroborating evidence that a gracious will has designed the mystery of our being, and that a powerful hand continues to uphold the world which we inhabit. I speak of the soothing calm of evening, not with the puerile notion that mere sentimental musing is conducive to the vitality of the true spirit of Christianity—that spirit which is compelled to engage in active warfare with the world, and sometimes to maintain its stand amidst all that is repulsive to the poetic mind; but I speak of the evening hour as a season of repose and wholesome refreshment to this spirit, and of all other enjoyments derived from the admiration of nature as lawful, natural, and highly conducive to the feeling of thankfulness which unfailingly pervades the soul of the true Christian.

THE POETRY OF THE MOON.

To write a chapter on the moon, appears, at first sight, a task no less presumptuous in itself, than inevitably fruitless in its consequences—fruitless as regards that kind of interest which on behalf of the queen of night has been called forth and sanctified by the highest powers of genius, as well as abused and profaned by the lowest. To apostrophize the moon, even in the most ecstatic lays, would, in the present day be little less absurd than to attempt

> "To gild refined gold, to paint the lily,
> To throw a perfume o'er the violet,
> To smoothe the ice, or add another hue
> Unto the rainbow, or with lantern light
> To seek the beauteous eye of heaven to garnish."

Yet in order to prove that the moon is of all natural and sensible objects, pre-eminently poetical, no other facts need be adduced than these; that all the effusions of disordered fancy which have been offered at her shrine, since first the world began, have not deprived the queen of night of one iota of her regal dignity; not all the abortive efforts of deceptive art, (and not a few have presented a mockery of her inimitable beauty,) have, in the slightest degree impaired the charm of her loveliness; not all the allusions of sickly sentiment, or vulgar affectation, have sullied her purity; nor have all the scenes of degradation, fraud, or cruelty, which her mysterious light has illuminated, been able, even in these clear-sighted and practical times, to render less solemn and imposing, that soul-pervading influence, with which the moon is still capable of inspiring those who have not entirely subdued or sacrificed the tender, generous, or sublime emotions of their nature.

In power, and majesty, and glory, the sun unquestionably claims our regard before all other objects of creation. But the sun is less poetical than the moon, because his attributes are less exclusively connected with our mental perceptions. By combining the idea of heat with that of light, our associations become more sensitive and corporeal, and consequently less refined. The light of the sun is also too clear, and too generally pervading in its nature, to be so poetical as that of the moon. It leaves too little for the imagination. All is revealed to the eye; and myriads of different objects being thus made distinctly visible, the attention wants that focus of concentration which gives intensity and vividness to all our impressions.

"But the stars," some may ask, "are they not sufficiently distant and magnificent for sublimity—mild enough for purity—beautiful enough for love?" Yes; but they are too distant—too pure—too cold for human love. They come not near our troubled world, they smile not upon us like the moon. We feel that they are beautiful. We behold and admire. No wonder that the early dwellers upon earth should have been tempted to behold and worship. But one thing is wanting, that charm, whether real or ideal, which connects or seems to connect, our mental sufferings, wants, and wishes, with some high and unattainable source of intelligence—the charm of sympathy. Thousands of purified and elevated minds have expatiated upon the stars as the most sublime of all created objects, and so unquestionably they are;* but sublimity is not all that constitutes

* Every one disposed to doubt this truth, may find full conviction by reading in Montgomery's Lectures on Poetry, a few pages devoted to this subject; perhaps the most poetical effusion that ever flowed from an eloquent pen, inspired by a refined imagination, a highly gifted mind, and a devout spirit.

the essence of poetic feeling. The spirit of poetry dwells not always in the high and distant heavens, but loves to vary its existence by the enjoyment of tender and homefelt delights. Thus, we are not satisfied, even in our hightest intellectual pursuits, unless we find something to appropriate, and call our own; and thus while we admire the stars as splendid portions of the heavens, we both admire and love the moon, because, still retaining her heavenly character, she approaches nearer to our earth. We cannot look upon the stars without being struck with a sense of their distance, their unattainable height, the immeasurable extent of space that lies between the celestial fields which they traverse with a perpetual harmony of motion, and the low world of petty cares where we lie grovelling. But the moon—the placid moon, is just high enough for sublimity, just near enough for love. So benign, and bland, and softly beautiful is her ever-beaming countenance, that when personifying, as we always do, the moon, she seems to us rather as purified than as having been always pure. We feel as if some fellowship with human frailty and suffering had brought her near us, and almost wonder whether her seasons of mysterious darkness are accompanied with that character of high and unimpeachable dignity which attends her seasons of light. Her very beams, when they steal in upon our meditations, seem fraught with tenderness, with charity, and love: so that we naturally associate them in our own minds, not so much with supernatural perfection, as with that which has been refined and sublimated by a moral process. We call to remembrance the darkest imputation ever cast upon the moon, in those dark times when to be a goddess was by no means to be free from every moral stain; and then, in fanciful return for all her sweet, and cheering, and familiar light, we sometimes offer a sigh of pity to the vestal Dian, that she should have paid so dearly for having loved but once, and that with so pure a flame, that it disturbed not the dreams of a slumbering shepherd boy.

To prove that the moon is of all visible objects the most poetical, there needs no other evidence than the *number* of poetic lays in which she has been celebrated. The merit of these lays is proof of a totally different nature, and has nothing to do with the case in point; the inspiration being in the moon herself—the virtue of that inspiration in the souls of her votaries. Here however we find additional, and perhaps stronger proof of the same fact; for not only have poets of every age, and every country, found in the queen of night a never-tiring theme; but she has unquestionably the honour of having called forth some of the most memorable, and most brilliant effusions of poetic genius. To quote illustrative passages on this subject would be to fill volumes, and to make selections would be almost impossible, amongst instances so numerous and so fraught with interest; but there is one scene in the Merchant of Venice which deserves particular notice, for the natural and simple manner in which the poet has given us the most perfect idea of an exquisite moonlight night, apparently without effort, and almost without description. It is where the two lovers, escaped from danger and suspicion, first find time and opportunity for the quiet enjoyment which is best appreciated after imminent risk. In this picture (for it is nothing less) we behold most strikingly the master hand by which the scene is drawn. Here is no babbling 'about silver rays,' 'soft influence,' 'smiling light;' the passage commences merely with—'The moon shines bright;' and then so perfect is the enjoyment of the lovers, both in each other and in all that surrounds them, that they immediately strike off comparisons between that particular night, and others that have been vividly impressed upon their imaginations, not by observation, but by passages from (perhaps their favourite) authors, where the moon has been called in to aid the representation of some of the most striking scenes. Had the happiness of Lorenzo and Jessica been less absorbing, or had the night been less beautiful, they might have told us how, and upon what objects the moon was then shining. But with them all was complete. They had no comments to make upon the lovely night, which we are left to suppose too exquisite for description; and after amusing themselves and each other with simple, but most beautiful allusions to classic history, they very naturally fall into that playful humour, which belongs to perfect happiness, and descending from their poetic flights, turn upon each other the sportive badinage, which is more familiar to those who are but "earthly happy." They are then interrupted by the entrahce of a messenger; but still the mind of the poet having been filled to overflowing with his own idea, or rather his own intense feeling of this ecstatic night, he goes on after the first exuberance of fancy has been expended in mere association, to give us some description of the scene; and then follows that passage so highly imaginative and poetical, yet withal so simple, that it seems but to embody in words, the faint dreams that have floated through our own minds a thousand times without finding utterance:

"How sweet the moonlight sleeps upon this bank!
Here will we sit, and let the sounds of music
Creep in our ears; soft stillness, and the night,
Become the touches of sweet harmony.
Sit, Jessica. Look how the floor of Heaven
Is thick inlaid with patines of bright gold;
There's not the smallest orb, which thou behold'st,
But in his motion like an angel sings,
Still quiiing to the young-ey'd cherubims.
Such harmony is in immortal souls;
But, whilst this muddy vesture of decay
Doth grossly close it in, we cannot hear it."

In contemplating the different attributes of the moon, first, and most striking, is that distinctness of light and shade which characterise her influence over external nature. Here are no lesser lights, no minor shadows to constitute a medium between the two extremes. The whole earth is under the dominion of two ruling powers; and every material object presents on one side a surface distinctly visible, while the other is lost in impenetrable darkness. Not a wreath of ivy, a projecting cornice, or a broken turret, but the moon invests it with a beauty of her own, more attractive to the eye, and more potent in its influence upon the imagination, from the depth of mysterious shadow by which it is contrasted. Beautiful as her light unquestionably is, when it falls upon the verdure of the sloping bank, where every flower, and leaf and tendril have their shining surface contrasted with their shadow, we should scarcely pause to offer our tribute of admiration, by telling how often the poet's lay has recorded events which took place "on such a night," but that in glancing from this scene of silvery brightness, we behold the deep gloom of the surrounding woods, the narrow defile, or the hollow cave, within whose confines the queen of night, with all her power, and all her splendour, is unable to penetrate.

Another striking attribute of the moon, and one which seems more especially to bring her within the sphere of human sympathy, is her alternate darkness and illumination; which last is familiarly spoken of as a periodical visitation; for so powerful are the senses of the imagination, that it is with some difficulty we realize the truth, that when the moon is invisible to our eyes, she is in reality as present with us as when her soft light salutes us in our nightly wanderings. Thus we hear perpetually of the constancy, as well as the inconstancy of the moon; just as a similitude with either quality may suit the poet's need. Of her constancy, because, lost as she is to our outward perceptions, we are able to calculate with undeviating certainty the hour of her return; of her inconstancy, because how profound soever are the devotions offered at her shrine, that shrine is no sooner invested with the full splendour of her celestial brightness, than the ineffable light begins to wane, and finally disappears.

From the long established custom of appealing to the moon in our descriptions of mental suffering, we might almost be led to pronounce that melancholy was one of her chief characteristics, were not this poetical propensity easily accounted for, by the enjoyments of the generality of mankind being of such a nature as to confine their attention to social, stirring, mundane subjects of interest or excitement; and thus to leave little time, and less inclination, for making observations upon the moon: while under the influence of melancholy, which has in all minds the same tendency to silence, solitude, and contemplation, the eye is naturally directed to scenes of repose and serenity, and more than all, to the solemn aspect of the heavens. It is here that we look for peace, and we all can remember, when through the long watches of the sleepless night, the moon was our only companion, the only friend who was near us under the pressure of our calamity, or who appeared to sympathize in our distress.

Surely the sweet influence of the queen of night is in its own nature more cheering than melancholy. How many glad occasions of social and festive entertainment are regulated by the moon. "We will visit our friends when the moon is at the full"—"We will return by the light of the moon"—"We wait for the moon before we set sail," is the familiar language of every day; and how much more must the mariner on the mighty deep rejoice in her welcome visitations, and hail her nightly radiance as she rises over the unfathomable abyss. Shines not the moon through the grated lattice of the prison, from whence all other gentle comforters are excluded, smiling upon the criminal in his feverish sleep, and reminding him when he starts into waking consciousness, that while his brother man, perhaps weak, fallible, and faulty as himself, had he been similarly circumstanced, is able to pursue, impeach, and condemn, according to the strict authority of laws, which take no cognizance of want of knowledge, of early bias, and more than all, of peculiar and incalculable temptation; there is still mercy in the everlasting heavens—an eye that looks down upon his earthly sufferings, beholding through a clear, and steady, and impartial light, all that is hidden from the scrutiny of man; and that an humble, solemn, and heartfelt appeal, even from out his dungeon, beneath his chains, or upon the fatal scaffold, may yet be made to that higher tribunal, whose judgments are as unparalled in mercy, as unimpeachable in justice.

Is not the moon, amidst all the chances and changes that occur to us in this sublunary scene, still, still the same? We recall the sweet and social evenings, when the moon looked in upon our childish play, through the trellice-work of vine and jessamine that grew around our ancestral dwelling. How looks that dwelling now? The vine and the jessamine are rooted from the earth, the walls are broken down, and scarcely is one stone left upon another. Where are the companions of those happy hours? Some have paid the debt of nature, and are gone we ask not where; some are so altered in their loves and friendships, that we know them not, or perhaps, they know not us; and others are scattered abroad throughout the busy world, chasing their different objects of ambition or desire, in which we hold no share: even our own hearts, though they feel the same to us in their capability of suffering, having learned to beat another tune, to burn with different fires, to be vivified with a new life, or subject to a fatality which we were far from apprehending then. Yet the moon—the lovely moon, is still the same, shining on with the same ineffable effulgence—teaching us that constancy is not an empty name, though we and ours have failed to find the reality—that there is purity and peace beneath the heavens, though we are still wandering in fruitless quest of both—that there is an inexhautible fountain of loveliness and delight, though we have wasted ours.

And is not the moon most kind, most charitable, that she reveals no deformities, brings to light no defects, but ever shines on—

"Leaving that beautiful, that still was so,
And making that which was not."

Oh! it is wearisome in our daily existence to see the critic's eye for ever peering through a narrow focus of concentrated and partial light, to find out the specks upon the face of the sun, the soil of the lily, the footprints of the butterfly upon the velvet petals of the rose; listening with his ear sharpened to an acuteness that renders it sensible only of discord, to detect the misapplication of tone and emphasis in the eloquence that shakes the world, the wrong cadence in the voice that tells of anguish, the false note in the harmony of the spheres. Yet this is what men call wisdom—a wisdom which if it fails to subdue the ignorance and prejudice of mankind, at least destroys the capacity for appreciating the beauty and perfection of the creation, and the desire to bow with mute reverence and awe before its Creator. It is this wisdom which intrudes its unwelcome presence upon our daily walk, rendering that walk most wearisome, and the society we meet there, infinitely worse than solitude. But the night returns—the calm and silent night, and the sweet moon rising over the eastern hills, goes forth upon her pathway through the heavens. Perchance an envious cloud advances, and her form is obscured by misty vapours; but they pass away, and her smile looks sweeter than before. Upon the rugged precipice, the dark impenetrable forest, the restless waves of the ocean, "her soft and solemn light" is falling, beautifying whatever it shines upon, marking out as with a silver pencil the majestic outline of the crag or promontory, but leaving the deep and frightful cavern at its base still unrevealed; tinging with radiant lustre the light boughs that wave and dance as if with very gladness in her welcome beams, the sprays of glittering ivy, or the lofty turrets of the ancient tower, while passing in her peaceful progress over every scene of gloom and terror, she seems to cast the dark places of the earth into yet deeper shade; or, turning the foam of the angry billows into crests of sparkling light, the troubled track of the heaving bark into a silvery pathway, and the sails that flutter in the adverse gale, into the white pinions of some angelic messenger, she kindly offers to the imaginative beholder, a picture of sublimity for that of danger—of trust for anxious fear—of hope for murmuring and despair.

Is not the moon also a faithful treasurer of sweet and pleasant memories? We might forget (in this world there is much to make us forget) what we learned before our minds were tainted by the envious struggle for pre-eminence, and the necessity of sordid gain, or soured by the disappointments inevitably attending both. The worldly man, the sharp keen bustler of the city, sees little to call back his thoughts to the days of unsophisticated innocence, and still less to recommend to his now mature judgment, what he would call nothing better than his boyish blindness, to his own best interests. But the bodily frame in time wears out, the city feast becomes unpalatable to the sickly appetite, and civic honours are unable to support the head they crown. Sleepless nights succeed to wearisome days. Perhaps his attendant enjoys that repose, which he is unable to purchase with all his wealth. To sum up the amount of his gold, no longer relieves the aching void of his heart. There is a gnawing want still pressing upon him, even at this late hour of the day, which all his possessions are unequal to supply; and he begins at last to question, whether they may not have cost him more than their real value. Lost in a world of vague and unsatisfying thoughts, the moon steals in upon his meditations. It is not with him as with more feeling minds, that memory rushes back with one tremendous bound, but with his wonted caution and reserve, he begins to retrace the pilgrimage of past years, the silent moonbeams lighting him unconsciously on his way, and leading him by the chain of association back to his paternal home. He enters again the once familiar habitation. He takes possession of the chair appropriated to the darling boy, and along with it the many pure and lively feelings, which the world had chased away. He listens to his father's gentle admonitions, and feels the affectionate pressure of his hand, upon his then unruffled brow. He hears his mother's voice as she sings their evening hymn, and "Oh!" the man of wealth exclaims, "that I might be again that innocent and happy boy!"

If he who embarks his whole heart in the sordid avocations of life, is necessarily driven on to resign the noblest aspirations, and tenderest affections of his youth, the votaress of fashion becomes if possible more heartless, and more hardened in her servile and despicable career: it is possible from this cause that in order to act to the life the artificial character she has assumed, it is necessary that she should sometimes wear the semblance of feeling, just in that proportion, and according to that peculiar mode, which may best suit the selfish purpose of the moment; and this empty mockery of the best and loveliest attributes of human nature—of its affections, sympathies, and high capabilities, has a more debasing and injurious effect upon the mind, than the total forgetfulness even of their outward character. But the woman of fashion cannot always keep her thoughts directed to the same brilliant point. There will be moments when she suspects the potency of the idol to whom her only devotions have been offered. With her also the exhaustion of the bodily frame, will produce a pining after that which has been sacrificed at the altar of the world—a longing to lie down and rest, beneath the sheltering wings of the angel of peace. Perchance she has stolen unnoticed from the busy throng, to breathe for one moment with greater freedom at the open casement. She still hears the tread of the noisy dance—the music—the glad voices—and she feels what no heart is capable of feeling without a pang, that her presence is not necessary to the enjoyment of her reputed friends, and that when her head is laid within the grave they will still dance on, without being conscious that one familiar step is wanting in their merriment. Her soul is oppressed. She looks out beneath the high blue silent heavens, and the moon is there to welcome her as with a sister's smile. It is to the moon alone that all human beings can appeal with an inward sense of sympathy; and to the moon at last she ventures to utter that complaint, which no ear has ever heard. "It was not thus!" the melancholy strain begins, but tears—true, unaffected tears are rising, and she looks down upon the clustering jessamine, whose delicate stars gleam out in the moonbeams, and send forth their odorous perfumes upon the gales of night. It was not thus that she, that splendid mourner, weary with the weight of her own diamonds, and sick of the selfishness of her own chosen friends, looked up to the face of the pale moon, in those hours when the moon looks fairest—those happy hours when even she, the false one, was beloved. Her memory, the only faculty which she has not been able to pervert, returns to the bright season of sincerity and youth. Again she is walking by the side of one whom worlds could not have tempted to violate her confidence, or wound her love—one who was deserted for a worthless rival, in his turn to be cast off for another, and then a third, and so on, until the world at last became the only candidate for her affections, the only ruler of her heart. "It was not thus!" she exclaims, "that I was wont to look upon the moon. Oh! give me back the loves, the friendships of my early days. Restore the capability of trusting, even though I should still be deceived! Awaken in my soul the faculty of hope, though I should be disappointed still! Rekindle my affections, that I may feel the possibility of loving, though I should never be beloved again! Let me hear once more the voice of kindness, though it should be strange to mine ear! Let me listen to the language of truth, though it should condemn the whole of my past life!"

The mariner at midnight on the deep sea, looks forth when other eyes are sleeping, towards the bright opening in the eastern clouds, where the pale lustre of the rising moon gives welcome promise of her blessed visitation. Soon her full round orb appears in all its splendour, and the dark vapours float away, or, gliding gently past her beaming face, receive the soft reflection of her smile, before they pass into the undistinguishable chaos of night. High into the azure heavens she now ascends, while the lonely helmsman chants to the heedless gale the songs of his native land. He gazes upon the wide expanse of heaving water, and ever as his eye dwells upon that silvery track of light that seems to lure him away to another world, recollections which the bustle of the day keeps down, and thoughts dear as the miser's hoarded treasure, rise within his breast, fresh and spontaneous; and he thinks how the same moon shone upon the woodbine bower where he first wooed the village maid, who blushed in her innocent joy, and inwardly exulted in the short-lived happiness of being a sailor's bride. Has he not seen that bower again? Yes, and the woodbine was still lovely, but his bride had lost her maiden bloom, and the cares of a lonely and almost widowed wife had made her prematurely old. Again he has returned to that well-known spot—that haven of his dearest hopes and the babe that should have welcomed him with the kind name of father, was sleeping beneath a little grassy mound in the churchyard, while he had been far away in its hour of agony, and its last cry had been unheard by him. Once more he has returned to his deserted home. The mother too was gone to her place of rest, and two humble graves side by side were all the memorial that remained of his domestic happiness. What then? Does he wish that his marriage day had never dawned? would he extinguish the memory of the past? No, though amidst the stir of the busy day, or amongst his jovial comrades he thinks little of his wife and child, yet in the solitude of the night watches when the moon is above his head, and no sound is to be heard but the ripple of the water against the vessel's side, he blesses that mild and gentle remembrancer, that she visits him in his loneliness, to tell him those tales of tenderness to which his ear has become strange, and to open in his bold and hardy bosom those sweet fountains of human love which transform the character of the rude sailor into that of the avenger of the injured, the father of the orphan, and the protector of the helpless.

Thus ever sweet and pleasant to the watchful eyes of the wayfaring man, is the moon as she rises from her throne of clouds. He turns to gaze upon that welcome face, and thinks how many well-known and familiar looks are directed to the same object. Perchance he has been a wanderer through many lands, a voyager over the deep seas, a pilgrim of the world; yet ever on his wayward course, the same mild moon has been like a faithful and untiring friend, speaking to him amongst a strange people in the native language of his heart, and telling through the lonely night, sweet tidings of his wished-for home. Whether amid snow covered hills, through the frozen wilderness, along the skirts of the pine forest, far, far away, she guides the solitary Laplander? or, in more sultry climes looks down through the foliage of the waving palm tree, and glances over the bright surface of the welcome waters, where the Indian laves his burning feet: whether high above the tower, the minaret, or stately dome, she looks down, a silent and unmoved spectator, upon the thickly-peopled city, the perpetual stir, the hurry and the rush of busy life; or far away in the silence and solitude of some lone isle of the ocean, touching with her sparkling radiance the leaves and blossoms of that nameless and uncultured garden, and the rippling waves that rise and fall, and lull themselves to rest upon that unknown shore: whether through the richly curtained window of the palace, her modest light steals gently in, and gliding over the marble floor, or along the tapestried walls, rest in its silence and purity upon the crimson canopy of kings; or where the cottage of the herdsman stands upon the lone moor, silvers the mossy turf beside his door, covering the grey thatch of the mouldering roof with her garment of beauty, and looking in with her quiet and approving smile upon his homely mea., blessing the cup of which he drinks, and lighting the parents' way, as they seek the couch of their slumbering cherubs to ask a blessing for the coming day, to return thanks for the past, and then to enjoy the refreshment of peaceful and untroubled sleep; over the waste unpeopled desert, the rich and fertile fields which surround the habitations of men, the tempest-troubled ocean, or the hive of human industry, it is the same moon that meets the traveller's anxious gaze, and ever on his lonely and distant course he feels it to be the same whose rays are interwoven with the thread of his early existence.

Yes, it is the same moon whose silver crescent was hung in the blue heavens when the first night shadowed the infant world with its mighty and mysterious wing. It is the same moon that rocks the restless tides from shore to shore, with a monotony of motion that marks out the different epochs in the life of man, and over-rules his most momentous actions with a power which he is unable either to baffle or subdue. It is the same moon for the mystic celebration of whose metamorphoses, the king of Israel erected an edifice, the most splendid that human ingenuity could invent, or human labour construct. It is the same moon for the visible completion of whose perfect radiance, the Spartans, while yet their souls were fired with the noblest ambition, sacrificed their share of glory in the memorable field of Marathon. It is the same moon which inspires the most ecstatic dreams of the enthusiast, giving to his earth-born visions, a refinement and sublimity, which belong only to that imaginative realm, over which the queen of night presides. It is the same moon upon which the eyes of countless myriads are nightly gazing, but which never yet inspired one unholy thought, awakened one mean or sordid feeling, or called forth one passion inimical to the maintenance of "peace on earth and goodwill towards men." It is the same moon which personifies in her refulgent orb that bright link of spiritual connection between this troubled life, and one that is without anxiety, and without tears; hanging her single lamp of ineffable radiance above our nightly slumbers, like a beacon of hope to lure us to a better land—returning again, and again to this earthly sphere, to warn us of the danger of delay, to cherish our heavenward aspirations, and to teach us that there is a love, (Oh! how unlike the love of man!) as constant and untiring in its faithfulness, as slow to avenge disobedience and neglect.

THE POETRY OF RURAL LIFE.

Before entirely quitting the fascinating employment of tracing out the poetical associations of particular objects in nature, it is necessary to add a few remarks upon the effect produced upon the mind by rural scenery in general.

The great difficulty in the task I have undertaken, a difficulty which presents itself most strikingly at this stage of the work, is to avoid the folly of being too sentimental, or rather to escape the charge of wishing to lead the mind away from what is substantially useful, to that which is merely visionary. If the major part of society in the present day consisted of love-stricken poets and languishing girls, mine would indeed be a scheme unnecessary and ill devised; but as the tendency of our present system of education, our conversation, habits, and modes of thinking, is towards the direct opposite of sentimentality, we may fairly presume, that in the opinion of all candid and competent judges, this work will be considered harmless, to say the least of it; and that the writer will have due credit given for an earnest endeavor to assist in rescuing the spirit of poesy from the oppression of vulgar tyranny, and in guarding the temple of the muses from the profanations of avarice and discord.

The character of the cultivated portion of the present race of mankind is too practical, too bustling, too commercial, I might almost say, too *material*, to admit of the least apprehension that ideas should be brought to stand in the place of facts, that learning should be superseded by sensibility, or that vague notions about the essences of things should be preferred to a just and circumstantial knowledge of the actual substances of those things themselves.

It is unnecessary to state, that happiness, in one shape or another, is the great end we have in view, in all our pursuits and avocations; whether that happiness consists in amassing or expending money; in our personal and sensual gratifications, or in the aggrandisement of others; in maintaining the station to which, by birth or education, we have become attached, or in raising ourselves to a higher scale of society; in obtaining and securing to ourselves the refinements and luxuries of life, or in cultivating the mental powers; in looking far and deep, both into the visible and the intellectual world, for those principles of consistency, beauty, and harmony, which owe their development to an almighty hand; and in recognising the work of that hand in every thing around and within us, from the simplest object of sense, to the most sublime and majestic source of contemplation.

The question is not, under which of these forms mankind is most addicted to look for happiness, but under which of these forms the happiness there in found, is likely to be most conducive to the cultivation and refinement of that part of his nature which is committed to him as a sacred trust, and will have to be rendered up, either elevated or debased, for eternity. I know that poetry is not religion; and that a man may dwell in a region of poetical ideas, yet far from his God: but we learn from the Holy Scriptures, whose whole language is that of poetry, as well as by the slightest experimental knowledge of the subject, that poetry may be intimately associated with religion, and that, so far from weakening its practical influence, it may be woven in with our familiar duties, so as to beautify what would otherwise be repulsive, to sweeten what is bitter, and to elevate what we have been accustomed to regard as mean or degraded.

It is not thus with sordid or artificial life. Poetry neither can, nor will dwell there. The atmosphere is too dense, and those who inhale it acquire a taste for its impurities, upon the same principle as that on which the victim of habits more gross and vicious learns to love the odour of the deleterious bowl, because it is associated with the gratification of his brutal appetites.

I am far from wishing that all men were

poets; or that the practical and necessary rules of education, should give place to the lawless vagaries of fancy, or the impulse of feelings uncontrolled: but I do wish that these rules and the attention they require, did not occupy the whole season of youth, without leaving time then to *feel* that they are essential. I do wish that men and women too, would sometimes pause in their hurry after mere verbal knowledge, to think for themselves; and turn away occasionally from the pile of fresh books which every day sees placed before them, to study that which never was, and never can be written—the wide field of nature; not only as it lies spread before their actual view, but as it expands in their own minds, teaching them by the gradual unfolding of the eternal principles of truth, that we have faculties of the heart, as well as of the head, and that we must hereafter render an account of a moral as well as of an intellectual nature.

How far my impressions in favor of a country life, may arise from early habit and association, I am not prepared to say; and I must be candid enough to grant, that the state of society in remote and isolated districts, does not present an aspect at all calculated to support the idea that our moral faculties are improved in proportion to the means we enjoy of cultivating an acquaintance with external nature; but the fact that this opportunity alone is insufficient to produce the effect, by no means proves, that in conjunction with other advantages it is not powerfully conducive to the end desired. In the country, man may be as brutish, as stultified, and as incapable of every gentle or sublime emotion, as in the city he may be gross, selfish and insensible to the happiness and misery of others: but it is no more the fault of nature when the eye has not been opened to behold her beauties, than it is the fault of the musician when his auditors are without the sense of hearing. I speak of the enjoyment which nature is capable of affording, not of that which it necessarily forces upon man, whether he looks for it or not; nor does the fact, that remote dwellers in the country have amongst themselves a very low standard of intellectual merit, prove anything against my argument; since I believe it may be asserted with confidence, that no poet of eminence in his art, and but few intellectual characters remarkable for the best use of the highest endowments, ever lived, who had not at some time or other of their lives, studied nature for themselves, imbibed strong impressions from their own observation of the external world, and from these impressions drawn conclusions of the utmost importance to society at large.

He whose mind is once deeply imbued with poetic feeling, may afterwards enter into the ordinary concerns of life, and even engage in the active commerce of the world, without losing his elevated character. It is only when substituted for common sense, that poetic feeling can be absurd or contemptible. Blended with our domestic occupations, its office is to soften, harmonize, and refine; and carried along with us through the more conspicuous duties of social and public life, it is well calculated to remind us, that there is a higher ambition than that of accumulating wealth, and that we have capabilities for intellectual happiness, which may be freely and fully exercised without interference with our worldly interests.

It is not then by merely dwelling in the country, that men become poetical; nor by working their way by fair and honourable means, to pecuniary independence, that they necessarily sacrifice the best part of their nature: though it must be confessed, that the ordinary routine of city life, as it is generally conducted, has a tendency to extinguish, rather than excite poetic genius. The principal reason why it does this, is obvious to the candid observer. The mind as well as the body is always in need of food, and this necessity it naturally prefers to supply, with the least possible expense of pain or labour. If facts of great number and variety are continually set before us, little attention will be paid to principles; because facts can be received with no exertion, while principles must be investigated and examined, to be in any degree understood. In towns, the news of the day is eagerly inquired after, and public journals, travellers, and frequent meetings, furnish for the general demand a constant supply of facts; while in the country even facts have often to be sought for with considerable labour and industry, and can only be enjoyed, with long intervals between every fresh accession of intelligence. Thus a real energetic mind, learns to connect an immense number of ideas, with the few facts which do transpire in the country; but a mind of quiet and lethargic character, sinks into nothingness, and one of still lower grade, active only for loose or malicious purposes, fills up the void in social communion, with inferences falsely drawn, uncharitable inuendos ingeniously thrown out, and conclusions too frequently both injurious and unjust.

I have said that a great deal may be made of the few facts which do transpire in the country. "Impossible!" exclaims the precocious youth, learned alone in civic lore. "You only hear the news once a week, and as to your facts, what are they? The return of the swallow, seedtime, and harvest, a shower of rain, or a thunder storm; and what is all this to the community at large?" I answer, it is a great deal to those individuals who choose to reflect. It is true we are sometimes a week later than you, in learning what have been the movements of a certain foreign army, that a cabinet minister has been dismissed, and that an elopement has taken place in high life. There are even facts similar to these, which occur without ever reaching us at all, which is a proof that they are of as little importance to us, as the building of our rooks, the scattering of our grain, or the reaping of our corn to you. You snatch up the Morning Post, and read of this interesting elopement; we learn with as much interest that the kite has seized our favourite dove. You read that a once popular statesman has been overthrown, by the strength of opposing party; we hear that a former servant of our own, has been dismissed from his place. You read of the dismemberment of Poland; we are startled with the intelligence, a few hours earlier, that the fox has been making dreadful ravages amongst our poultry. What follows? Our conclusions are at least as philosophical as yours, and if you take time to reflect, it is most probable they will both amount to this—that the weak must be the victims of the strong, all the world over; that propensities to rapine, cruelty, and wrong, are permitted to deface the glory of the earth, for reasons which neither you nor we can understand; and that man, when he boasts too proudly of his superiority in the creation, forgets that in the most malignant and injurious attribute of the brute he is at least his equal.

And then our returning swallows, our seedtime, and harvest, our rains and thunder storms, of which you think so little; why they supply us with inexhaustible food for deep anxiety, earnest calculation, ardent hope, and trembling fear; and sometimes with gratitude as warm as if the success which crowned our labours, was visibly and palpably bestowed immediately by the hand of the Giver of all good. We hail the birds of spring, as the blessed messengers of hope —the seed is scattered in faith—the harvest is reaped in joy—the rains descend, and we give thanks for the opening of those fountains, whose source, and whose seal is above —the thunders roll, and we bow before the terrors of the Almighty.

Man *may*, unquestionably, enjoy the same sensations in the city. Surrounded by the work of human hands, he *may* look up and bless the power which bestowed such faculties and means upon his creatures; but it is a fact which few will pretend to deny, that the more the mind is interested and occupied with artificial things, the more it is carried away from the truth that is in nature; and the greater the number of objects which intervene between us and the great First Cause of all, the less fixed and reverential are our views of heaven. We know by reasoning that God is no more present in the rolling thunder than in the social meeting, or the secret thought; but our impressions are often stronger and deeper than our reasoning: and when we stand alone in the silent night, and look up to the starry heavens; when we watch the play of the lightning, or listen to the roaring blast; when we gaze upon the wide expanse of heaving ocean, or on the peaceful bosom of the lake, slumbering in its mountain cradle at the feet of its majestic guardians, whose brows are o'er the sky, mantled with clouds, or crowned with golden glory; when we watch the silvery fall of summer's evening dew, the sunset in the west, or the moon's uprising over the eastern hills, we naturally look upon these interesting phenomena as immediately influenced by an omnipotent hand, and advancing one step farther, penetrate within the veil, and find ourselves alone with God.

With regard to the mere amusements of the country, it is very natural for townspeople—such as are accustomed to games of skill and hazard—to dress-parties, plays, and concerts, to ask in what they can possibly consist. Let us in the first place observe a group of children at play beneath the flowery hawthorn, their cheeks suffused with the rosy hue of health, and their bright eyes sparkling with that inward joy which naturally animates the infant mind. Nobody can tell what they are playing at—they do not know themselves. They have no names or set rules by which their gambols are restrained; but when they start off from their sequestered retreat, bounding over the grass like young fawns, you see at once that it is the fresh air, the glowing health, and above all, the glorious liberty of the country which constitutes their enjoyment. Then they have an intimate and familiar acquaintance with every thing around them, with the woods and the winding paths, the song of the different birds, and the course of the streams that come down from the hills. Upon all or most of these the seasons have considerable influence, and the welcome appearance of spring, the withering of autumn, the heat of summer, and the winter's snow, have trains of association in the youthful mind, which supply them with a perpetual source of amusement, blended with instruction. Added to which, they not unfrequently have the care of domestic animals, and feel almost as much interest in their fate as in that of their fellow-creatures. They soon learn that their kindness allures, and that their rebukes repel. This makes them observant of the happiness and the misery of the creatures committed to their charge, and lays the foundation of social and benevolent feelings, which continue with them through the rest of their lives. As the mind acquires strength and begins to investigate, what a field of inquiry then lies before them—the fall of the rains—the density of the atmosphere—the gathering of clouds—the fertility of the earth—the principles of vegetation and vitality—the production of flowers and fruits—the source of streams—the planetary system—chemical agency—and the study of electricity, that mighty and mysterious power, which operates through earth and air in a manner yet but partially understood, though producing some of the most wonderful and sublime phenomena in nature.

Are these amusements of a kind to be neglected or contemned by a rational and intellectual being? Are they not rather such as we ought to seek every possible means of rendering familiar and attractive to the youthful mind? And surely there can be no means more likely than to retire sometimes within the bosom of nature, where the development of Almighty power is obvious above, around, and beneath us.

But above almost all other peculiarities belonging to a country life, I would place that homefeeling which has the power through the whole course of our lives to bring back the wandering affections, and centre them in one point of space—one point of importance, to a very limited portion of the community, but a portion consisting of our nearest and dearest connexions. In towns there can be comparatively little of this feeling. A man steps out of his door immediately upon common ground. The house he lives in is precisely like his neighbour's, one of a number which he returns to without attachment, and leaves without regret. But in the country, not only the grass we tread on, the paths, the trees, the birds that sing above our heads, and the flowers that bloom beneath our feet, but the very atmosphere around us, seem to be our own. There is a feeling of possession in our fields, our gardens, and our home, which nothing but a cruel separation can destroy; and when absent, far away upon the deep sea, travelling in foreign lands, or driven from that home for ever, we pine to trace again the familiar walks, and wonder whether the woods and the green lawn are looking the same as when they received our last farewell. In the haunts of busy life, the music of our native streams comes murmuring again upon our ear; we pause beneath the cage of the prisoned bird, because its voice is the same as that which cheered our infancy; and we love the flowers of a distant country when they resemble those which bloomed in our own.

There are other wanderers besides those who stray through foreign realms—wanderers from the ways of God. Perchance we have spurned the restrictions of parental authority, and cast away the early visitations of a holier love; but the homefeeling which neither change of place nor character can banish from our bosoms, renews the memory of our social ties, and draws us back to the deserted hearth. Along with that memory, associated with the soothing of affection which we have lived to want, and the wisdom of sage counsel which experience has proved true, the tide of conviction rushes in upon the burdened heart, and the prodigal rousing himself from the stupor of despair, exclaims, "I will arise and go to my father!"

It is difficult for those whose hearts and homes are in the city, fully to appreciate the enjoyment arising from rural scenery; but there are others whose homes are there, yet whose hearts are not wholly absorbed in city news, and scenes, and customs. These have probably, at some time or other of their lives, known what it was, not merely to make an excursion to Richmond, Hampstead, or Windsor, but to go far away into the country, amongst the hills, and the valleys, where the rattling of wheels, or the crack of the coachman's whip, was never heard. What, let me ask, were their sensations, as they rose higher and higher up the side of the mountain, at every step taking in a wider view of the landscape, until it lay beneath them like a garden, in which the ancient woods were fairy groves, and the rivers threads of silver, now seen, now lost, but never heard, even in their floods and falls, at that far height. What are the feelings of the traveller, when standing on the topmast ridge, a mere speck in that stupendous solitude, while the fresh breezes of an unknown atmosphere sweep past him, and he muses upon the past, and feels the impressive truth, that not only the firm rock on which he stands, but the surrounding hills, with their beetling brows, and rugged pinnacles, and hollow caves, are the same as on that great day when the waters of the deluge disappeared from the face of the earth—that the art of man is impotent against the imperishable fabric upon which he rests—that the ploughshare never has been there—nor track of wandering beast, nor nest of soaring bird, nor hum of laden bee—nothing but the winds, the rolling clouds, the lightning and thunder, those tremendous agents of eternal Power, before whom the boasted sovereign of creation lies trembling in the dust.

What are his feelings when he reflects that such as this new and mighty world appears to him, such it will remain when he and his, with their ambitious hopes and envied honours, are buried and forgotten! These are sensations peculiar to the situation, which words are inadequate to describe. Too deep for utterance, too powerful for language, they teach a wisdom more profound than is to be acquired in all the schools of man's devise. I would ask again, how the wanderer on the mountain's summit has looked back to the narrow sphere of social life which he has been wont to call the world? Its laws, conventional but arbitrary, by which his past conduct has been influenced, what are they here? Scarcely more important than those which regulate the movements of a community of insects, confined within the limits of a little mound of earth. Where now is the tremendous and potent voice of public opinion, resounding in authoritative tones from house to house, from heart to heart? Upon the mountain's brow, beneath the blue arch of heaven, it is silent, lost, and forgotten. Where are the toils, the anxieties, the heartaches, which consume the vitality of our existence, in the lower region of our sordid and selfish avocations? Already they have assumed a different character; and, despising the nothingness—the worse than nothingness of their ultimate end, he resolves to give them to the winds, and henceforth to live for some more exalted and noble purpose.

There is no danger that man should feel himself too little, or his Maker too great. If there were, he would do well to confine himself to a sphere, in which nothing is so obvious as the operation of man's ingenuity and power. But since we are all too much engaged in the strife, and the bustle, and the eagerness which is necessary to insure an average of material comforts; since individuality of character is too much sacrificed to the arbitrary rules of polished life; since by associating exclusively with man in an artificial state of being, the generous too frequently become selfish, the gentle hardened, and the noble debased: it is good to shake off occasionally the unnatural bondage by which the aspiring spirit is kept down, to go forth into the woods and the wilds, and to feel, though but for a day or an hour, that man was born for something better than to be the slave of his own bodily wants. Each time that we experience this real independence of mind, we ascend one step higher in the scale of moral existence; and if circumstance or dire necessity should prevent the frequent recurrence of such feelings, we may at least secure a solid and lasting good, by learning in this way to appreciate the mental elevation of others.

I am not, even on this subject, so blind an enthusiast, as to attempt to support my argument in favour of rural life on the ground of the greater appearance of vice in the town than in the country; because I am one of those who believe that the vacancy of mind, the gross bodily existence, the moral apathy, which too frequently prevail amongst persons who lead an isolated life, are quite as much at variance with the Divine law, as vices which are more obvious, and which consequently fall under the cognizance of human statutes. If amongst congregated multitudes we are shocked to find so much of riotous indulgence, treachery, outrage, and crime of every description, we are, on the other hand, cheered with the earnest zeal, the perseverance, the disinterestedness, which are brought into exercise to counteract these evils. While in the country, where men sit still and wonder alike at both extremes, the average of moral good is certainly not higher, because vice being less obvious, the fear of its fatal consequences does not stimulate to those meritorious exertions which proceed from true Christian love. The country may be abused as well as the town; and since the inhabitants of both, for the most part, fall into their stations from circumstances rather than inclination, or if from inclination, settle themselves at a time of life when they are incapable of judging of the privileges peculiar to either, it is not to be supposed that they will always make the best use of the advantages around them; and those which abound in great number and variety in the country, certainly add weight to the moral culpability of such individuals as live stupidly beneath the open sky, in the midst of fields, and woods, and gardens, without exhibiting more mental energy than is displayed by their own flocks and herds.

After remarking with regret upon the inertness and apathy of disposition too obvious in the country, we must in common justice observe, that where there does exist sufficient mental energy for the display of peculiar traits of character, such traits have a degree of strength and originality seldom found amongst the inhabitants of the city, where social institutions have a tendency to bring individuals together upon common terms, and thus to render them more like each other; and where the frequent contact of beings similarly circumstanced rubs off their eccentricities, and wears them down to the level of ordinary men.

The friendships and acquaintances of the country are formed upon a system essentially different from that which holds society together in more compact and congregated masses. The ordinary style of visiting in towns does little towards making people acquainted with each other. Commonplace remarks upon general topics—remarks which derive no distinctive character from the lips which utter them, fill up the weary hours of each succeeding visit; while the same education, and the same style of living, are observable in every different *set*, of which each individual is but a part—separate but not distinct. But in the country, where people meet more casually, and with less of common purpose and feeling, where they often spend a considerable time together under the same roof, thrown entirely upon their own resources, and unacquainted with any general or prevailing topic of conversation, they necessarily become more intimately acquainted with each other's natural character, with their individual bias of disposition, and peculiar trains of thought.

Dwelling apart from the tide of public opinion, they know nothing of its influence or power, and having established their own opinions, formed for themselves from their personal observation, their sentiments and remarks are characterised by their originality, and their affections by their depth. They are in fact, though less polished, less artificial, and less learned in mere facts than their brethren and sisters of the city, infinitely more poetical, because their expressions convey more meaning, their sentiments are more genuine, and their feelings more fresh from the heart.

In speaking of the intimate knowledge of individual character which rural life affords abundant opportunities of obtaining, we must not omit to mention the sum of happiness derived from this knowledge when it extends amongst our domestics, labourers, and dependent poor. The master of a family in the country resembles a little feudal lord, and if he makes a generous use of his authority, may be served as faithfully, and obeyed as implicitly through love, as any old English baron ever was through fear. The agricultural labourer becomes attached to the soil which he cultivates. He feels as if he had a property in the fields of his master, and this feeling extends not only to the produce of his toil, but, through many links of natural connection, to the interest of his master and the general good of his family; while on the other hand, his own wants and afflictions, and those of his wife and children, are made known through the kind visitations of charity, and soothed and relieved, with a familiarity and unison of feeling which goes almost as far as almsgiving towards alleviating the distresses of the poor. There can be no distrust between families that have dwelt together upon the same soil, in the mutual relation of master and servant, from generation to generation. Both parties are intimately acquainted with the characters they have to deal with, and each esteeming the other's worth, can look upon their little peculiarities with kindness, and even with affection; while the mutual confidence, good will, and clear understanding which subsist between them, constitute a sure foundation for substantial and lasting comfort.

These advantages, peculiar to rural life, may appear almost too homely and commonplace to be admitted under the character of poetical; but in their relation to the social affections, and to the principles of happiness —that happiness which is rational, intellectual, and moral, they are in themselves highly poetical, and must often be recurred to with tenderness and interest; at the same time that they supply the bard with subjects of pathos and pictures of delight.

Perhaps it may better please the fanciful reader to turn to themes of a more imaginary and unsubstantial nature, of which we find an endless variety in the associations afforded by rural habits, pursuits, and scenes. We have observed in the former part of this work, that scarcely a beast, a bird, a tree, a flower, or any other visible object exists, without an ideal as well as a real character; but we have not yet entered upon that region of poetic thought which is peopled with the imaginary beings of heathen superstition, and which to the mind that is deeply impressed with the beautiful imagery of classic lore, is perpetually associated with rural scenery. No sooner are the gates of fancy opened for the admission of these ethereal beings, than we behold them gliding in upon our favorite haunts, now floating upon the sea of air, dancing in the sunbeams, or reposing upon beds of violets; and then rushing forth upon the destructive elements, riding on the crested waves, or directing the bolts of death.

Wandering in our fields and gardens, Flora, with her ever-blooming cheek and coronet of unfading flowers, becomes our sweet companion, while with her ambrosial pencil, dipped in the hues of heaven, she tints the velvet leaves of the rose, scatters perfume over the snowy bosom of the lily, or turns in playful tenderness to meet the smiles of her wayward and wandering lover, the sportive and uncertain Zephyrus. We penetrate into the depth of the forest, and the vestal Huntress flits across our path with her attendant nymphs. While seated under the cool shadow of the leafy trees, or stooping over the margin of the crystal stream, the Dryads bind their flowing hair. The harvest smiles before us with the glad promise of the waning year, and joyfully the yellow grain is gathered in; but we see the deity of rural plenty, with her unextinguishable torch and crown of golden ears, wandering from field to field, heart-stricken, and alone; too mortal in her sufferings—too desolate in her divinity. We hail the purple morning, Aurora rises in her rosy car, driving her snowy steeds over the cloud-capped mountains, separating the hills from their misty canopy, and scattering flowers and dew over her fresh untrodden pathway through the verdant valleys. We turn to the glorious sun as he rises from his couch of golden waves, and ask the inspiration of Apollo for the verse or for the lyre. We sail upon the ruffled sea, where the Nereides, sporting with the dolphins, lave their shining hair; or where Neptune, striking his trident on the foaming waters, bids the deep be still. We hear the bellowing of the stormy blast, and call on Æolus to spare us; or we listen to the thunder as it rolls above our heads, echoing from shore to shore, and tremble lest the forked lightning should burst forth from the sovereign hand of Jove.

Fanciful as these associations are, (almost too fanciful to afford us any real enjoyment,) they unquestionably supply the poet with images of beauty not to be found in real life; and they have also an important claim upon our consideration, from the place they occupy both in ancient and modern literature; as well as from the effect which this system of imperfect and dangerous theology produced, in promoting the refinements of art, and softening the habits and feelings of a barbarous people.

It is pleasant to turn from such visionary sources of gratification to those which are more tangible and true—to the smypathy which every feeling mind believes it possible to experience in nature. There is no state of feeling to which we may not find something in the elements, or in the natural world, so nearly corresponding, as to give us the idea of companionship in our joys and sorrows. True, it would be more congenial to our wishes, could we find this companionship amongst our fellow-creatures; but who has not asked for it in vain? and turning to the woods, and the winds, and the blue skies, has not believed for a moment there was more sympathy in them than in the heart of man.

There is scarcely any human being so selfish as to wish to feed upon joy alone; and what a privilege it is, separated from those who could rejoice with us, that we can share our happiness with nature! The soaring lark, the bounding deer, and the sportive lamb, animated with a joy like ours, become our brethren and our sisters; while the same light buoyant spirit that fills our bosoms, smiles upon us from the shining heavens, glows beneath us in the fruitful earth, or whispers around us in the fresh glad gales of spring. But, under the pressure of grief, this sympathy is most perceptible and most availing, because sorrow has a greater tendency than joy to excite the imagination, and thus it multiplies its own associations by identifying itself with every thing that wears the slightest shadow of gloom.

I will not say that the world in general is more productive of images of sadness than of pleasure; but from the misuse of our own faculties, and the consequent tendency of our own minds, we are more apt to look for such amongst the objects around us; and thus in our daily observation, passing over what is lovely, and genial, and benign, we fix our minds upon the desolating floods, the anticipated storm, the early blight, the cankered blossom, the faded leaf, the broken bough, or the premature decay of autumn fruit. This, however, is no fault of nature's, but our own; nor does it prove anything against the argument, that, whether happy or miserable, we may find a responding voice in nature, to echo back our gladness, and to answer to our sighs; that every feeling of which we are capable, in its purest and least vitiated state, may meet with similitude, and companionship, and association in the natural world; and above all, that he who desires to rise out of the low cares of artificial life, whose soul aspires above the gross elements of mere bodily existence, and whose highest ambition is to render up that soul, purified rather than polluted, may find in nature a congenial, faithful, and untiring friend.

I cannot better conclude these remarks, than by quoting a passage from the writings of one, who possessed the enviable art of combining science with sublimity, and philosophy with poetic feeling.

"Nature," says Sir Humphry Davy, "never deceives us; the rocks, the mountains, the streams, always speak the same language; a shower of snow may hide the verdant woods in spring, a thunder storm may render the blue limpid streams foul and turbulent; but these effects are rare and transient—in a few hours, or at least days, all the sources of beauty are renovated. And nature affords no continued trains of misfortunes and miseries, such as depend upon the constitution of humanity, no hopes for ever blighted in the bud, no beings full of life, beauty, and promise, taken from us in the prime of youth. Her fruits are all balmy, bright, and sweet; she affords none of those blighted ones so common in the life of man, and so like the fabled apples of the Dead Sea, fresh and beautiful to the sight, but when tasted, full of bitterness and ashes."

THE POETRY OF PAINTING.

In turning our attention to the poetry of painting, we enter upon a subject which forms the first connecting link between the physical and the intellectual world. So far as painting is a faithful representation of external nature, it belongs to the sphere of the senses; but as it holds intimate connection with some of the noblest efforts and affections of the human mind, it is scarcely inferior to the art of poetry itself, in the value it derives from the diffusion of poetic feeling, through the countless varieties of style and character, in which it is exhibited to mankind.

The poetry of painting is perhaps more felt, and less understood, than that of any other subject to which we can apply our thoughts; nor is it easy to define what is the nature of the charm by which we are fascinated on beholding a picture in perfect accordance with our taste, especially as this taste varies so much in different individuals, and even in the same becomes more select in its gratifications, in proportion as it is more cultivated and refined.

That the poetry of painting is not mainly dependent upon the choice of subjects is clear, from the most simple and familiar scenes being rendered poetically beautiful by the pencil of an able artist; yet there are lines of demarcation beyond which even genius dare not venture, and which cannot be transgressed without the most glaring violation of good taste. It is where the associations are such as are not only vulgar in themselves, but totally destitute of any claim upon the feelings or affections of the mind. Nor is it in the representation of scenes the most gross and degraded (though such do little credit to the taste of the painter); yet in them the violent passions which agitate our nature are frequently most powerfully and strikingly exhibited. Look, for example, upon a representation of the lowest stage of intoxication, and surely the pencil of the painter can pourtray no subject more loathsome and repulsive; yet even here the associations are not necessarily such as are altogether debarred from connection with refined intellectual speculations. In contemplating such a picture, we think immediately of the high capabilities of man, and of the dangerous profanation and abuse of his natural powers, of the spotless infancy of the being before us, the love that watched over his youth, the hopes that were centered in his manhood, and that now lie grovelling beneath him in his fall. This class of subjects then is not entirely beyond the limits of the field of poetry, though it certainly requires some stretch of fancy to prove them to be within it; yet there is another class so decidedly and irrevocably excluded, that it may not be uninteresting to mark the difference between them, and of these a single instance will be sufficient.

I remember seeing in an exhibition of paintings at Manchester, a picture of a huge red brick cotton-mill, so well executed, and so appropriately placed, as to look very handsome in its way; and no doubt that way was all-sufficient to the owner, who had a train of sweet and pleasant local associations with this picture, enjoyed snugly to himself, which if they were not poetical, had most probably a weightier charm, and one which he would not have exchanged for the lyre of Apollo. The surface of the picture was almost entirely covered with the brick building, and by its side was the all important engine-house, with tall spiral chimney pointing to the sky, but alas! with no heavenward purpose. It was the picture of a manufactory, and nothing more—most probably the owner wanted nothing more. There was not, as there might have been, a broken foreground, denoting the rugged course of one of those polluted streams which murmur on (for what can still the voice of nature?) with the same melody as in its native woods, before the click of rattling machinery broke in upon the harmony of man's existence. There was no pale girl, with darkened brow and dejected form, returning to her most unnatural labours, a living and daily sacrifice to the triumphs of national prosperity; there was not even that deep and turbid stream, that dense and perpetually rising fountain of thick smoke, bursting, as if with indignation, from the gross confines of its narrow birthplace, first darting upwards in one compact and sable pillar, as if from the crater of a volcano, and then folding and unfolding its dark volume, until, assuming a more ethereal character, it floats away upon the gale, and ambitious of a higher union, mingles at last with the vapours that sail along the purer regions of the sky—no, there was nothing in this picture but a cotton-mill; and the wealthy owner, with a praiseworthy feeling of gratitude and respect for the origin of his prosperity and distinction in the world, had done his best to immortalize the object that was not only the most important, but the dearest to him on earth. Yet notwithstanding this was, in the opinion of at least one individual, a picture of great merit, it was unquestionably of that class to which no single poetical idea could by any possibility be attached. It is true that such a building as was here represented, need not be without its intellectual associations. It might give rise to some of the most profound speculations relative to trade, commerce, and the wealth of nations; all that I maintain is, that this picture could not in any way call forth the passions or affections of our nature, or awaken those emotions of the soul which constitute the very essence of poetry.

In order to render the poetry of painting a subject more tractable in an unskilful and inexperienced hand, it will be necessary to consider it under its three different characters—portrait, landscape, and historical painting. Of these three, portrait painting is decidedly the least calculated for the display of poetical feeling, not only because it is generally practised under the arbitrary will of those who possess neither taste nor understanding in the fine arts, but because there are so few subjects really worthy in themselves, and these few are too frequently beyond the reach of the artist; while the rubicund and wealthy citizen, having grown sleek upon turtle soup, after retiring with his rosy consort to their Belle Vue, or Prospect Cottage, in the suburbs of the town, deems it a suitable and gratifying appropriation of some portion of his hard-earned wealth, to employ one of the first artists of the day in making duplicates of forms, which a full-sized canvas is scarcely wide enough to contain, and faces, in which the expression of cent. per cent., and the distinctions of white and brown sauce, are the only visible characteristics.

While the painter is at work, sacrificing all that is noble in his art to the sad necessity for sordid gain, the gentleman insists upon a blue coat and buff waist-coat, but above all, upon a gold headed cane, which necessarily mars the picture with a bright yellow spot full in the centre. This however is a trifle by comparison, for the buttons help to carry off the glare of the gold, and the artist revenges himself by making the hand approximate to the same colour. It is in attempting to delineate the august person of the lady, that his skill and his taste are put to the severest test. With consternation in his countenance, he eyes the subject before him, and in the first agony of despair, queries within himself whether he cannot really afford to lose the offered reward. He ventures to remonstrate with great delicacy on some particular portions of the dress. But the lady is inexorable. It is a dress for which she has paid the highest price, and *must* look well. Money rules the day, and the painter, covering his palette with double portions of red and yellow, commences with his task. Upon the head of the fair sitter is a pink turban, interwoven with a massive gold chain, surmounting a profusion of flaxen ringlets, in the midst of which twinkle out two small blue eyes, faintly shaded by thin eyelashes of the palest yellow, while cheeks that might vie with the deepest peony, and a figure upon which is stretched, almost without a fold, a brilliant orange dress of costly silk, make up the rest of the picture.

It is upon the same principle, and with similar restrictions, that portrait painting is generally practised in the present day. But let the painter rule his subject, and the case will be widely different. He who is worthy of his art sees at once what are its capabilities. His imagination immediately places the object before him in some appropriate situation. He assigns to it a character of which it may be wholly unconscious—one to which it was by nature peculiarly adapted, though circumstances may have consigned it to a totally different destiny.

Perhaps there is no class of pictures in which the painter's want of taste is more frequently displayed, than in the portraits of children. We see them standing like wooden images, holding in one hand an orange never meant to be eaten, or flowers which it is evident they have not gathered; their hair smoothly combed, their frocks unruffled, and their blue morocco slippers unsullied by the dust of the earth. In short they are always dressed in their best to be painted, and the mother is often as solicitous about the pink sash, as about the likeness. The subject is unquestionably one of great difficulty, because the beauty of childhood consisting chiefly in the light easy movement of the playful limbs, it is almost impossible to make a child perfectly natural when at rest, and not sleeping; and it is here that the skill of the able artist is exercised in carrying on our thoughts to what the child will the next moment be doing. If he does not place in its hand a bunch of flowers, he throws into his picture a vivid atmosphere, in which we are sure that flowers are growing; and by slightly ruffling the fair hair, letting loose the folds of the dress, quickening the expression of the eye, and giving a playfulness to the almost open lips, an idea of life and motion is conveyed, and we are deluded into the belief that the very next moment the child will start off in pursuit of the butterfly, and that he will bring home with him a handful of flowers gathered from the gorgeous carpet of nature, or a wounded bird found in his woodland rambles, to place on the maternal bosom, which has so fondly cherished him, that he believes it to have benevolence enough for all the wants and sufferings in the world.

It is possible that the same artist may be called in to paint the portrait of a poor gentleman, who having nothing else to bequeath to his children, is prevailed upon to leave them a likeness of the form they have been accustomed to venerate. The painter finds him in a mean and humble dwelling, dressed in a manner that too plainly shows his long acquaintance with urgent wants and narrow means. Yet in the noble outline of the face, the fair and finely moulded forehead, when for a moment its wrinkles are smoothed down, but above all, in the symmetry of the mouth, and the graceful motion of the lips, he reads the sad history of that gradual fall from high station and noble fortune, which has never through the whole of a long life been able to degrade the soul; and in painting the portrait of this poor gentleman, he makes a picture worthy of a place amongst the aristocracy of the land.

Or he may be required to exercise his art in painting the likeness of one of the celebrated belles of the day. It is possible that the arbitrary laws of fashion may have concealed the beauty of a form that is perfectly Grecian in its contour. The painter casts down the stately and unnatural fabric from the head, and leaving a few dishevelled ringlets to wander over the snowey temples, binds up the rest of the hair so gracefully behind, as just to leave visible the noble pillar of the neck, which proudly supports the whole. It is also possible that the rigid rules of polished society, or early discipline, or sad experience, may have rendered cold, constrained, or artificial in its expression, a countenance that was originally capable of exhibiting the deepest passions, and the finest sensibilities of our nature. The artist whose eye is quickened to an almost supernatural acuteness of perception, sees all this; and in painting the portrait of one who is by compulsion a mere fine lady, he invests it with the beauty and the pathos of a heroine.

Nor is it in the skillful management of expression alone that the poetry of this art consists. Though this is unquestionably the most important, there are minor points, which cannot be neglected without so glaring a violation of good taste that the eye is offended; and as we have often had occasion to remark, no sooner are the senses unpleasantly affected, than the powers of the mind are arrested in their agreeable exercise, and the poetic illusion is totally destroyed. In the choice of costume, it is highly essential to the poetical charm of the portrait, that every thing wearing the character of constraint or conceit should be avoided. All those striking peculiarities which belong only to a class of beings whose feelings and avocations are entirely separate from the sphere of high mental refinement, or intellectual power, will be rejected by an artist of good taste. The coarse habit of the monk may be made subservient to the poetical interest of a portrait, because it is associated in our minds with ideas of reflection, study, and strict mental discipline; even that of a peasant is admissible, because his hardy frame may be animated by the bold independence and rude energy of a mountaineer; but he who would paint a butcher or a harlequin in their characteristic costume, must forfeit every pretension to the poetry of his art.

The local partiality of the Dutch painters has rendered this error strikingly conspicuous in some of their historical pieces. Whatever may be the merits of this school of artists, the national prejudice which retained the familiar costume, habits, and customs of their own peculiar people, even when representing the higher scenes and circumstances of life, proves them to have been but little qualified for the most noble and interesting branch of their art.

Besides the choice of costume, and of far higher importance, is the proper adjustment of colours, and other mechanical branches of the art of painting, which cannot properly be discussed in a chapter on poetry, but which are of unspeakable importance in producing that delightful combination of form and colour by which the eye is so entirely gratified as to repose in perfect enjoyment and to leave the imagination to wander as it will.

Entering upon the subject of landscape painting, it becomes much less difficult to specify in what the poetry of the art consists. There are certain fundamental principles from whence our ideas of the beauty of nature are derived, which the slightest sketch is capable of illustrating, but which cannot be neglected without offence even to the most indifferent beholder. Of these principles, light and shade are the most important and conspicuous. Thus two objects, one to receive the rays of light, and another to receive the shadow of the first, are sufficient to constitute a picture. Let one of these be the massive stem of an old tree, grey with time, and shattered with the storms of ages, wearing round its hoary brow a wild wreath of clustering ivy, and stretching forth one verdant branch, still clothed with dense foliage as in former years. Let the other be the weedy banks of a silent river, in whose clear depths the shadow of this ancient tree is reflected, and we have at once a scene of sufficient interest and beauty to rivet the eye and fascinate the imagination. Still much must depend, even in a scene so simple as this, not only upon the skilful conduct of the pencil, but upon the poetical feeling of the artist. Perhaps the subject may be better understood by illustrating it with a case in point.

It was, a few years ago, my good fortune to receive instruction from a gentleman,* who, whatever may be his other pretensions, must be unanimously acknowledged to be one of the most *poetical* artists of the present day; a fact which is sufficiently proved by the fearless and independent manner in which he can snatch up the most barren subject, and invest it with a mysterious beauty of his own creating. The piece which this artist first gave me to copy, was a pencil sketch of a rude entrance by a little wooden bridge, over a narrow stream, to what might be a copse-wood, or indeed a wood of any kind; for the whole picture contained nothing more than three or four trees, a few planks of time-worn timber, and the reedy banks of this stream or pool. My task was performed with diligence, and with no little self-approbation, for my friends pronounced it to be admirable; and I saw myself that

* Mr. Cotman, now professor of drawing at King's College, London.

the foliage of the oak was edged round with the most accurate precision, the rooks in the distance were eked out with the same economy of number, and the bulrushes that stood in the water were all manifestly tipped at the ends. While my heart bounded with internal triumph, I drew forth the interesting deposit from the portfolio in which I had conveyed it into the presence of my master, and impatiently watched the expression of his eye as he glanced over it. After looking at it for some time with less and less of what was agreeable in his countenance, he at last gave utterance to a low growl of disapprobation, and finally pronounced it to be bad in two ways—bad as a copy, and bad as a drawing. Although I was at that moment very much inclined to execrate the art so often called divine, I have since learned to look with feelings of interest almost like affection upon that simple drawing, to which my master, with a few strokes from his own able and accomplished penc[illegible] gave a character at once touching, beautiful, and poetic What was practically the work of this pencil, it would be foreign to my purpose (even were I able) to define. It is sufficient to say, that through the illusion of the eye, the mind was forcibly presented with the ideas of space and atmosphere. My drawing represented nothing but an even surface, covered with a minutely extended texture, woven according to the pattern, of oak leaves, reeds, water, or whatever the uninitiated pencil might vainly attempt to imitate. In the same picture, after it had received a few touches from an able hand, the most unpractised eye might behold a distinct representation of a quiet day in autumn. The rooks, which had been stationary and silent, were now winging their way towards that woodland scene, cawing at intervals with the musical and melancholy cadence, which at that particular time of the year, and especially at that particular distance, turns their harsh tones to melody. The passage of the wooden bridge had now become quite practicable, and after looking down into the bosom of the unruffled water, you might enter upon that unfrequented path, and hear the rustling of the withered grass beneath your feet; while high overhead were the majestic branches of old and stately trees, extended by the imagination beyond what was perceptible to the eye, farther and farther, into the silent depth of the forest.

From what I then saw of the metamorphosis wrought upon this picture, and what I have since learned by observation and experience, I am inclined to think that the poetry of landscape painting is dependent, in a great degree, upon the idea of *atmosphere* being clearly conveyed to the mind. That scene, however laboriously or delicately executed, which, from its want of general harmony, conveys no such idea to the mind, deserves not the name of a picture; but that which draws forth the emotions of the soul by a correspondence with impressions made upon it by the sun, the sky, the seasons, or the hour of the day, may be highly and intensely poetical, though simple and unpretending in itself. This idea must be strongly impressed upon the memory and the imagination of the painter before he begins his task. As in the natural world the colour and character of every visible object is affected by the air which is invisible, so in all representations of external nature there must be that perfect harmony pervading the whole scene, which is in keeping with any particular state of the atmosphere, of which the artist may wish to convey an impression to others; and thus, through the medium of form and colour operating upon the eye, the mind receives distinctly and forcibly the idea of that which possesses neither form nor colour in itself, and which no eye is capable of beholding.

I never saw the want of atmosphere more striking than in a picture full of peacocks. It was intended to illustrate the fable of the presumptuous jackdaw adorned in borrowed plumes; but the jackdaw was only to be found upon examination, for there were three peacocks nearly as large as life crowded into a moderate sized painting, and two of them having their tails expanded, the canvass was literally covered with feathers. These feathers, it is true, were beautifully executed, and had the piece been called a picture of peacock s feathers, it might have been admired; but there was a total absence of some of the most essential parts of a *scene*, and the eye turned away with weariness or disgust, while the mind remained uninformed as to the meaning of the painter, unimpressed with a single idea.

In describing this picture, my mind very naturally reverts to one in the same exhibition, almost immediately opposed to it in situation, but still more so in character. It was, if I recollect right, by one of the *Nasmiths*, and represented a sunset upon a level beach. The sky was still glowing with all the gorgeous tints of evening, but the sun was not visible, and there was neither cliff nor wave, nor headland to reflect his light. All was a complete flat, gilded with his sidelong beams, and the sea and the shore were alike unruffled. But the artist, acquainted with the principles of mind as well as matter, had not sent forth this mere flat to brave the consequent contempt of mankind. He had wisely given to his picture a focus of interest, without which it must have been a complete blank. We have before observed, that whatever is beautiful or sublime, does not create intense sensations of pleasure, without some link of human fellowship, either real or imaginary; so the painter of this picture had placed in the middle distance, or rather in the foreground of his piece, two human beings, whose tall shadows fell behind them on the ground. They might be fishermen consulting about the tides, or travellers resting by the way, or poets gazing on the golden sky; their dress and appearance revealed nothing, nor was it of consequence that they should. They were human, and that was enough. Imagination could supply the rest, and people that glowing scene with all the images, familiar or fantastic, that wait upon the sun's decline.

It was the perfect harmony of this picture which made the charm so irresistible—the illusion so complete; and whenever the delight or the beauty of landscape painting is considered, harmony must be acknowledged to be the basis upon which both are founded. It is true that the external aspect of nature presents perpetual contrast, both in form and colour; but this very contrast is in harmony with the whole: for our ideas of beauty are chiefly derived from the principles which pervade the external world, and amongst these we may reckon it not the least important that there can be no brilliant light, without deep shadow.

In speaking of the pleasure derived from painting, I have found in necessary to make frequent use of the word *illusion*, a word which might unquestionably be applied to many other sources of human gratification. But in reference to the illusion to which we willingly and necessarily submit ourselves, in order to find greater pleasure in the productions of the pencil, it may not be ill-timed to offer a few remarks in this place.

Those who have never studied the art of painting, intellectually, are not aware how much we are indebted for the pleasure we receive from it, to a natural process which takes place in the mind of the beholder. The painter who has no brighter materials than red and yellow clay to work with, can so dispose them as to represent the splendour and brilliance of a summer sunset, upon which we gaze till our eyes are almost dazzled with the refulgence of those burning beams. In the centre of his piece he places the glowing orb of day, smiling his brightest before he sinks to rest upon his couch of crimson clouds; on either side are trees whose foliage is bathed in the same golden hues, and if skilfully managed, they will form a vista terminating in excess of light; while the whole is enlivened by a group of panting cattle, some of them holding down their heads as if in the very prostration of patient endurance, while their tails are curled about in every possible variety of posture, to show with what assiduity they are lashing off the myriads of insects, whose busy and unceasing hum is almost loud enough to be heard. On first asking why the little spot of yellow paint which represents the sun looks so much more brilliant in the picture than on the palette, we are told it is the adjustment of the different grades of light which thus increases the brightness of the centre. But let the same colours be placed without any regard to form in the same order on the palette, and we behold nothing but a heap of paint, upon which we might gaze till doomsday without being dazzled. It is because we know that that particular appearance of the sun, the sky the earth, the trees, and the cattle, is in reality the invariable accompaniment of intense heat, so, on perceiving the same appearance in a picture, we persuade ourselves that it is so there. If in the same scene, and with precisely the same colours, the artist should represent the violence of a gale of wind; or if instead of the cattle, but in the same situation, and still with the same colours, he should place a leafless tree, a cottage with its roof covered with snow, and a miserable, half-starved man, vainly endeavouring to fold a blanket round his shivering limbs, there is no eye that would feel the same difficulty, in gazing on the picture, no mind, either of man or woman, that would be able, while contemplating such a scene, to undergo the process of (what is now commonly called) *realizing* the ideas of light and heat.

In the selection of animals, or individual objects thrown in from choice to diversify a picture, the landscape painter finds wide scope for the display of his poetic feeling. The introduction of fat cattle is an error into which none could fall who was not either a novice in his art, or an agriculturalist irrevocably wedded to the best system of rearing live stock. And why? Because our associations with fat cattle, whatever satisfaction they may yield in the kitchen or larder, are decidedly too gross and vulgar in their nature to afford any gratification in a poem or a picture. Far be it from the writer of this chapter to depreciate the value of fat cattle, or any other agricultural produce; but everything has an appropriate place, and there is but one kind of picture in which fat cattle would be in theirs. I will leave the reader to judge how far that kind is worthy of the graphic art. Let the subject be a red brick farm house, with a barn extending on one side, and a square plot of garden ground on the other, circular corn stacks, and a red-tiled pigeon house in front, with fields in the distance, smoothed down by constant culture, and intersected with neatly clipped hedgerows running at right angles all over them; then fat cattle would unquestionably be well placed in the foreground, and the picture, merely as such, would possess the beauty of harmony in all its parts, though it might be impossible to call it poetical.

After condemning an extreme case, the mind, by a natural effort, rushes towards its opposite in search of that gratification which it has failed to find, and the idea which now presents itself, is that of a wild and varied landscape, with distant mountains, rugged precipices, deep groves, green slopes, foaming cataracts, and wandering rills. Upon the verdant banks of one of these, beneath the shade of a "wide spreading beech," the artist places, immediately in the foreground, no less a personage than Apollo himself, while the Muses dance before him to the music of his lyre, and winged loves, and agile graces, skip from rock to rock, or float upon the ambient air. Does the picture please? No; because, in the first instance, it is not true to nature,* and wherever the conceit of man's imagination breaks in upon the harmony and pathos which belong to nature alone, the poetical charm must in some measure be destroyed; and, secondly, because in the picture of a landscape, the ideal of rural scenery should be distinct and predominant, which it is impossible it should be where characters so important as Apollo and the Muses are introduced. But let us still retain the landscape, and see whether something better may not be made of it. The artist who enters into the real spirit of poetry, will place upon the broken crags of the mountain a few shaggy goats, and perhaps a solitary stag, a wanderer from the herd, will be stooping over the side of the stream to lave its thirst in the cool waters of the forest. The foreground he will enliven with the rich colouring of innumerable wild plants, woven into a gorgeous carpet, which here and there gives place to a sharp projecting rock, or yields to the wild vagaries of a small silvery torrent, that sparkles up from a gray stone fountain, and after filling a rude trough, shoots forth in bubbling eddies, and then loses itself amongst the thick leaves and brushwood overhanging the little narrow bed, which with the strife of ages it has worked out for its own repose. Beside this fountain, a woman is standing, not an angel, or a goddess, but a simple peasant woman, whose dress, coarse but gorgeous in its colouring, corresponds with the rich and varied tints of the foreground. She has

* "My notion of nature comprehends not only the forms which nature produces, but also the nature and internal fabric and organizations, as I may call it, of the human mind and imagination."—*Sir Joshua Reynolds.*

just filled her pitcher from the pure stream, and is resting it for a moment on the side of the stone trough, before she treads back her lonely way to the herdsman's cottage, whose low thatched roof may be seen half hid by the sheltering trees. Here is at once a picture, which, by awakening our sympathies, calling to mind a thousand delightful recollections, and giving birth to the most agreeable associations, rivets our attention, delights our fancy, and demonstrates more clearly than would a volume of definitions, what it is that constitutes the poetry of painting; and in this manner, the most pleasing landscapes may be composed out of materials extremely simple, and sometimes even barren in themselves.

Perhaps no one was ever more intimately acquainted with the poetry of this branch of the art, than Salvator Rosa. In all his delineations of the savage dignity of nature, may be found a perfect correspondence between the subjects which he chose, and his manner of treating them. "Everything is of a piece, his rocks, trees, sky, even to his handling, have the same rude and wild character which animates his figures."

As the art of poetry may be classed under several different heads, so that of painting has, to the poetical observer, many distinctions of character not laid down in the technical phraseology of the schools. Leaving the more celebrated productions of the studio, to which there might doubtless be found corresponding specimens in the sister art, I will turn to a case in point, which to my mind is both striking and familiar. It is the resemblance of character between Bewick's woodcuts, and the poems of Robert Burns. It is true, the artist in this instance has confined himself to a mode of conveying his ideas so simple and unpretending, that the comparison hardly holds good between the productions of the pencil and the pen. All that I maintain is the similarity of talent, of tone of mind, and moral feeling, displayed in their separate works. We find in both the same adherence to nature, without ornament or affectation, and we discover the same pathos in those slight touches of which genius alone is capable, with the same freaks of fancy, lawless and unrestrained, describing as if in very wantonness, scenes the most grotesque, ludicrous, or familiar; and then soaring away amongst the wild, the melancholy, and sometimes the sublime, yet retaining throughout the same moral impress, either dignified or abused.

I was once so circumstanced as to become intimately acquainted with the private studies of an artist, whose talent bore so striking a resemblance to ballad writing, that I feel confident had circumstances in early life directed his choice to the pen instead of the pencil, he would have used it with equal facility, and probably with as much lasting fame. The subjects which came under my notice were extremely small, and seldom contained more than a little patch of mountain scenery, with two or three goats or wild sheep; yet such was the *character* of these fairy pictures, that while the eye dwelt upon them, the illusion was so perfect as almost to beguile the fancy with the belief, that the bleat of those wandering sheep, the scent of the purple heather, and the hum of the wild bee, were really present to the senses. You might gaze, and gaze upon those simple scenes until you felt the cool elasticity of the mountain breeze, and the influence of the clear blue sky, stretching pure and high and distant over the wide moor; while you wandered on, amongst the rustling furze and yellow broom, startling the timid moor-fowl, and rousing the slumbering lark to spread again its folded wing, and soaring into upper air, to sing another hymn of praise and thanksgiving to the Author of this perfect and wonderful creation, of which we feel ourselves in such moments to be no inconsiderable or unworthy part. What is there to remind us that we are unworthy? We feel not the stirrings of mean or sordid passion. We are away from the habitations of man. Away from the envy and strife, the tumult and contention, which mar the peace of his hereditary and social home. Away amongst the hills—away in the boundless and immeasurable realm of nature, where it is impossible not to feel the love of a benign and superintending Providence—not to behold the work of an omnipotent Creator—not to acknowledge the dominion of a pure and holy God. If we are not worthy of his countenance and protection when we feel and acknowledge all this, when we bow in simplicity and humble reverence before the all-pervading spirit that animates and sustains the world; when—when are the creatures of his formation to lift up the prayer of gratitude, and return thanks for the blessing of existence?

But to return to our subject. After all that has been said of the importance of copying from nature, a few remarks may be necessary in reference to this expression, which is capable of being very differently understood. To copy nature is not merely to make the sky above, and the earth beneath, or even, entering into minutia, to make the clouds grey, and the grass green. The artist may copy nature with the accuracy and precision of a Chinese,* and yet never paint a picture that will excite even momentary admiration. It is quite as necessary that he should be able to perceive with the eye, as to execute with the hand. He must learn to distinguish, to separate, and to combine; but above all, he must be able to form a whole, not out of the different parts presented at one particular moment to his eye, but, as nature is perpetually changing, and as no two yards of the earth's surface are precisely alike, he must compose a whole out of the various aspects of the natural and visible world, which he has at different times of his life observed, and of which his memory retains a distinct impression; and this proves again, that painting as well as poetry requires time and opportunity for receiving such indelible impressions, without which the works of the most talented artist would never exceed in merit the representations in a school-boy's sketch book.

Sir Joshua Reynolds remarks, in his admirable lectures, that Rubens makes amends for the local peculiarities of the Dutch school, by varying his landscape representations of individual places, confined and uninteresting in themselves, by the introduction of a rainbow, a storm, or some particular accidental effect of light; while Claude Lorrain, who well knew that taking nature as he found it, seldom produced beauty, composed his pictures from draughts which he had previously made from various beautiful views and prospects. It is a vulgar remark, often made upon pictures thus composed, that they are not true to nature, nor are they like a map, true to any given section of the earth's surface; *but they are true to that conception of perfect beauty with which nature animates the soul of the poet*, and which it is one of his greatest pleasures to see diffused over the external world. It is not by representing nature in detail, but in *character*, that the highest gratification is produced; and he must unquestionably be the best, as well as the most poetical painter, who conveys by his works an idea of the general character of the external world; in short, who paints not only for the eye, but for the mind. It is not the eye alone that is enlivened by the brilliance of a sunny morning, nor is it the eye alone that reposes where the sombre shades of evening fall upon our path. There must be so much of character in all representations of particular times and seasons, as to convey to the mind a corresponding idea of the general state of the sky, the air, the vegetable and the animal kingdom, by which such seasons are invariably accompanied. Thus the landscape painter, by cultivating a familiar acquaintance with the minute varieties, and the distinct characteristics of the visible world; but above all, by studying profoundly those phenomena by which all that we know of the mysteries of beauty, power, and sublimity are revealed, will be able out of such materials to compose a whole, whose highest recommendation it will be, that it addresses itself forcibly to the imagination of the beholder, and calls up a train of associations with feelings and ideas the most exquisite and poetical.

On the poetry of historical painting, volumes might be written—but as much, perhaps too much, has already been said on painting in general, I will merely add a few remarks on this particular branch of the art. It is obvious, on first turning our attention to this subject, that the grand requisite for a poetical painter, is a mind so cultivated and informed, and at the same time so warmed by enthusiasm, as to enable the artist to enter fully and deeply into the subject before him. As an instance of this we need only contrast the touching pathos, the wild grace,

* This remark does not refer to the figures upon china, but to the more elaborate paintings of the Chinese, where a delineation of every leaf on a tree is frequently attempted.

and beauty given by Gainsborough to all his cottage children, with some of our more modern and ephemeral productions, where a young lady with the airs and graces of a fashionable boarding school, or where at least a *lay* figure is dressed in rags and called a beggar girl. The little motherless looking children in Gainsborough's pictures offer a silent appeal to our best and tenderest feelings, and it is evident he must have powerfully *realized* in his own mind all that belongs to orphan-destitution, as well as to the simple habits and feelings of rustic life.

Next to this qualification for a poetical painter, is a capacity for combining a whole from particular and suitable parts, and the art of keeping all such parts in their proper degree of relation and subordination. If for instance a painter, in representing the death of a father of a family, should so far forget the dignity of his subject, as to make a favourite dog advance to the centre of the piece and lick his master's face, the unity of the whole would be destroyed; and instead of the feelings being affected by sympathy with the grief there represented, the general and very natural exclamation would be—"What can the dog be doing?" But let the afflicted family, next to their dying parent, be most conspicuous in the scene. Let the focus (if I may use the expression) of distress diverge amongst the domestics or less interested members of the household, and then in the distance the same dog might very properly be introduced, looking through the half open door with surprise and perplexity upon the unwonted scene, and standing with one foot lifted up as if doubting whether it were a place and time for him to venture in. The same kind of subordination with respect to light and colour is of immense importance in the formation of a scene. That picture which is broken up with a variety of spots of light and shade, can neither be agreeable to the eye, nor convey to the mind sensations of concentrated or powerful interest. But as the rules for the regulation of light and shade, as well as of form and colouring, belong more exclusively to the studio, I shall merely repeat in reference to this subject, that none of these rules can in any single instance be so violated as to offend the eye, or strike the fancy with an impression foreign to the purpose of the painter, without the charm of the whole being sacrificed. With the practical parts of his profession, the painter must make himself acquainted, upon the same principle that the poet learns the grammatical use of language, and studies the rules of composition; nor would a glaring breach of propriety of style be less pardonable in one instance, than a gross departure from the established rules of art in the other.

I am induced to make these remarks because we are perpetually nearing of the inspiration, rather than the cultivation of genius; and that the merit of a painting, rather than the misfortune of the painter, consists in his being self-taught. The only excuse that can be made for so glaring a misuse of language, is that it may serve the purpose of exciting in the vulgar mind higher notions of the influence of intellectual power. The constant labour and concentrated application which marked the lives of the most eminent painters, prove that immediate inspiration had little to do with the work of their hands. Indeed I know not what inspiration is, with regard to the fine arts; unless it be the first moving spring of action—the desire—the thirst for excellence obtained at any cost, which operates upon the talent and the will, prompting the one to seek and the other to submit to, all the laborious, irksome, and difficult means which are necessary for the attainment of excellence.

The painter knows well what it has cost him to compose one entire figure out of the various parts, which intense study has taught him are essential to any particular whole. He knows, but there is no need that he should tell the world, how many thousand sketches he has made of each individual limb, by how many heart-breaking failures the wreath of fame has been torn from his brow, what days and nights he has spent in the adjustment of the cloak of a favorite hero, how the head of his saint has been designed from sketches made in Italy, the feet of his martyr brought from Paris, and the hand of his goddess copied from that of his own lady-love at home, who had laid aside her stitching, and doffed her thimble, after many fruitless entreaties, consenting for five minutes only, and with the liberty of scolding all the time, to sit for the likeness of her hand. • And this is what the vulgar call inspiration! They speak too of expression in a portrait, just as if it were a sort of magical atmosphere thrown around the figure, and capable of converting form and colour of any description into a likeness. They do not take the trouble to observe that the eyebrows in the original are arched, and that the painter has made them straight; they are ignorant that the nostrils when depressed at one corner denote melancholy, when elevated vivacity and wit; that the artist can immediately produce a total change in the character of the mouth, by a slight alteration in the closing line; and that it is by a long course of study, experience, and unremitting labour, that he makes himself intimately acquainted, not only with the natural formation of the human countenance, but also with those muscular affections which accompany certain emotions of the mind; that by these means he is enabled not only to perceive, but to imitate the characteristic lines and features, and thus to produce what is called expression.

On dismissing the idea of inspiration from the art of painting, and acknowledging the necessity of study and experience, we see that a poetical painter, though elevated to the highest distinctions of genius, can only have attained that eminence by a process not improperly called education; though it may or may not have been conducted in strict conformity with academical rules. This process may be divided into three stages. First, he feels the moving spring of action—the ardent desire which prompts the young artist to look abroad into the works of the creation, to search out with penetrating and comprehensive vision, the eternal principles of things, and to discover and acknowledge wherever it is to be found, the imperishable essence of beauty. Thousands of human beings are alive to this state of feeling, who from want of suitable advantages, from different bias, in short, from necessity, are hindered from advancing farther in the walks of art; and therefore thousands are sensible of the poetical influence of painting, who have never touched a pencil, or only touched one to their own shame and disappointment. But let the young artist, stimulated with this burning desire—this unquenchable thirst for physical and moral excellence, submit himself to the strictest discipline of the schools, will his energy be impaired, his genius extinguished, or his enthusiasm subdued? No. No more than the poet in selecting suitable words as the vehicle to convey his ideas to mankind, will lose the Promethean fire which gives life and splendour to his verse: and just with the same facility can the painter strike off a perfect picture without adherence to established rules, as the minstrel can pour his harmonious thoughts in a language unknown to him before.

From the stern practice of the schools, the artist in time emerges, though only to extend the sphere of his education, and widen the field of those studies which the longest life of man is insufficient to complete. This brings us to the third and last stage, when the artist, still animated with the same enthusiasm, launches forth into the world. Having become thoroughly initiated into the use of the proper means, he is now able to apply both the ardour of his soul, and the labour of his hand, to the production of those splendid works which his mind is not less able to conceive, for having been made acquainted with their internal construction, their peculiar distinctions, and limitations. Fully qualified to enter the realm of poetry, he identifies himself with the author, and regarding his hero in his moral and intellectual character, invests him with a nobility of mien and stature, which, if it is not true to his physical formation, is true to nature; because his nature was noble, and the character which the historian is able to describe with the intervention of time, and the change of scene and circumstance, he must impress upon the canvass, as it were with one stroke, and concentrate into the space of a single moment, the accumulated influence, and power, and majesty, of a long life of glorious actions. Animated by the spirit-stirring influence of poetic feeling, he can now take captive the fallen monarch, in chains which his own hand flings around him; he can allure the sylvan deity into bowers of his own constructing; personify the impassioned minstrel with a harmony of colouring, like music to the eye; and tinge an angel's wings with the golden hues of heaven.

The greatest merit of painting is, that like poetry, it addresses itself to those principles of intellectual enjoyment, without which its greatest beauties would neither be appreciated or seen—principles implanted in the human mind, and often neither felt nor acknowledged, until called forth by the works of art. The pleasure we derive from painting, is commonly and superficially considered to be only as it is an *imitative* art. Why then do not coloured figures in wax, rank higher in the estimation of the world, than the more laborious and cumbrous productions of the sculptor? And why do not miniature landscapes, with the real elevation of hills, trees, and houses, made of cork or clay, and coloured to the hues of nature, please more than the level surface, on which form and distance are denoted merely by a particular management of colour, so as to represent light and shade? The fact is, that in such performances, however ingeniously managed, nothing is left for the imagination. We see the thing as it really is, pronounce it to be very pretty, and think no more about it; while those in which the effect alone is obvious, and the means enveloped in their proper obscurity, strike the beholder with feelings of wonder and admiration; while through the medium of the senses, he receives just so much information, as is necessary to set the imagination afloat upon an immeasurable ocean of thought. Let hands profane colour to the very life an Apollo or a Venus, and we should see nothing more than a fine man, and a pretty woman; but in contemplating them as they are, we behold the eternal principles of imperishable beauty, handed down to us from distant ages, conceived by one nation, appropriated by another, and acknowledged by all with the profoundest admiration.

Painting and sculpture, next to poetry, constitute the grand medium by which the sublimest ideas, and the most exquisite sensations are conveyed to the human mind. It is true the phenomena of nature are more essentially sublime, as well as beautiful; but nature speaks to us in a voice which we do not always hear, and cannot always understand. It is when nature is interpreted by the power of human genius, that we hear most forcibly, and if we do not understand, we *feel* the eternal truths which have their archetype in nature, and their corresponding impress in the soul of man.

THE POETRY OF SOUND.

Amongst the organs of perception by which ideas of sensible things are conveyed to the mind, it is only necessary here to notice those which are most important and obvious—the eye, and the ear. Painting forms the medium of connexion between the eye and the mind: language supplies the mind with ideas, through the medium of the ear. Our attention has hitherto been occupied by visible objects alone, and having conducted them to the mind through one avenue, it is necessary that we take up the subject of sound, in order that we may make a progressive approach by another.

Sound is perhaps of all subjects the most intimately connected with poetic feeling, not only because it comprehends within its widely extended sphere, the influence of music, so powerful over the passions and affections of our nature; but because there is in poetry itself, a cadence—a perceptible harmony, which delights the ear while the eye remains unaffected. The ear is also more subject than the eye to the influence of association, just in proportion as the impressions it receives are more isolated or distinct. The eye perceives a great number of objects at once, or in such rapid succession that they tend to destroy the identity of each, and so long as it remains unclosed, continues to behold, and to perceive, without a moment's intermission; but the ear, besides being compelled to receive sounds, merely as they are offered to it, without, like the eye, possessing the powers of searching, selecting, and investigating for itself, has its intervals of silence, which render the impressions that have been made more durable, and those which are to follow more acute. Wherever there is any visible object, the eye, and the mind through the eye, may receive pleasure, because light itself is beautiful, and the glancing sunbeams even on the walls of a prison, afford to the unfortunate dwellers within, associations which connect those beams with the glorious orb of day, the skies, the air, and a multitude of agreeable ideas which naturally present themselves; but the ear is much less frequently gratified than the eye, especially in towns where it is denied the negative enjoyment of silence. Compare the frequency of light and sunshine appearing even on the prison wall, with the occurrence of any sweet, or soothing sound within those gloomy precincts. Compare the beautiful specimens of art, the appearance of order, regularity, and magnificence to be seen in the city, with the perpetual tumult and din, by which the ear is distressed and annoyed. Compare the endless variety of charms presented to the eye by external nature, with the frequent silence which prevails in the country, and we shall perceive at once, that the ear is an organ less active, and less occupied than the eye; and thus we may account for its impressions being so intense, as well as so peculiarly fraught with associations the most powerful and affecting to the mind.

Why certain sounds should be agreeable or disagreeable to the ear may be best understood by examining the principles of music; which for more reasons than one, it would be unwise to introduce into the present work. The established fact that the ear is gratified by harmony, and pained by discord, is quite sufficient for my present purpose; but why, under certain circumstances, we are delighted with sounds which are in themselves, and separate from association, the most intolerable discord, may very properly form a subject of serious consideration here.

Perhaps one of the most striking, as well as most familiar instances of this kind, is the cawing of the rook. When this bird is taken captive and brought into your room, nothing can well be more offensive to the ear, more harsh, or discordant, than its voice; and yet the same voice heard in certain situations in the open air is proverbially musical—heard as a number of these social and sagacious inhabitants of the woods are winging their slow and solemn flight, while their shadows flit over the richly cultivated landscape, and approaching the abodes of man, they wheel round and round in graceful circles, returning homeward with the same speed, the same desire, and the same end in view, the language of the whole community reminding the listener of the voices of wearied but contented travellers, well pleased to return from their journey; while they congratulate each other upon the peace, the comfort, and the security which awaits them in their ancestral dwellings.

Though the language of the rook is extremely limited, and to those who know little of rural scenes or rural pleasures, extremely monotonous, it is capable of varying that language by a cadence of expression both familiar and interesting to the privileged class of beings who draw upon the inexhaustible resources of nature for their amusement and delight. In the spring, when the rooks first begin to be busy with their nests, their language, like their feelings and occupations, is cheerful, bustling, and tumultuous. Within the rookery it is perfect discord; but heard in the distance, it conveys to the mind innumerable pleasing associations with that delightful season of the year, and the universal alacrity and joy with which the animal creation resume their preparations for a new and happy life. But it is in the autumn, when the bustle of the spring and summer has subsided, that the language of the rook is most poetical. There is then a melancholy cadence in its voice, heard slowly and at intervals, which is in perfect unison with the general aspect of nature; nor is it difficult to suppose that this sagacious bird, perched upon the topmost bough of some venerable tree, is making observations upon the external world, and sympathising in the universal tendency to decay, exhibited in the scattered fruit, the faded foliage, and the withered grass.

Of the same description of sound is the bleating of the lamb, which in itself is as entirely devoid of sweetness and melody, as the cawing of the rook; yet the voice of the lamb has been so long and so intimately connected in idea with the season of spring, with green fields and sunny slopes, with scented hawthorn, yellow cowslips, rich meadows, and wandering rills; as well as with plenty, and innocence, and peace; that our best poets have deemed it no violation of the laws to which genius is amenable, to mingle the bleating of the lamb with the sweetest harmony of nature.

One more instance of the same kind will suffice—the croak of the raven, which exceeds the other two in the harshness and dissonance with which it strikes upon the ear; and yet how perfectly harmonious is the croak of the raven when it echoes amongst the rocky heights of the mountain, or rising from the rugged cliffs of the shore, mingles with the hollow and tumultuous roar of the ever restless ocean.

The voices of the innumerable singing birds, which people our gardens, fields, and groves, filling the air with one perpetual melody, are well known to every listening ear and feeling mind, both in their natural music, and in their poetical associations. From the sweet, plaintive notes of the robin, to the rich, full warble of the thrush and blackbird, they are in themselves, and separate from all relative ideas, most delightful to the ear, under almost all imaginable circumstances except one; and that is, when heard through the bars of the solitary prison to which the wild minstrels of nature are too often inhumanly condemned. The two most melancholy sounds in the world, are the song of the caged bird, and the voice of the street minstrel. It makes the heart that has been accustomed to the wild, joyous minstrelsy of nature, sicken to hear either. Suspended in his narrow cage, and excluded by an outer prison from all participation in the fresh and genial air, or hung without these walls in the heat and din and suffocation of the crowded city, perhaps the little prisoner feels a gleam of sunshine fall upon his plumed wing, and in an instant the fire of nature is kindled in his bosom. He may know nothing of the flowery fields, let us hope he possesses not the faculty of remembering what once he was; but in his bounding breast instinct supplies the place of memory and imagination, and he pines for he knows not what. Animated with the energy of a wild free life, he flutters his light wings with a quick and fairy motion, almost spiritual in its grace, and oh! how touching in the perpetual fruitlessness of its efforts to "flee away and be at rest." Still the life of its little soul is unsubdued, and it warbles out its longest, loudest notes, even there, as if in defiance of the power of man, or to prove that there is a power in nature, a power of expansion and vitality, beyond the reach of his controlling, contracting, and contaminating hand.

There is a scene exhibited every day throughout the summer months, in the outskirts of London, which it is possible to contemplate until the mind is filled with misanthropy, and we learn to loathe and shun our own species. In fields sufficiently remote from the city to admit of their being the resort of birds, men are accustomed to station themselves with a trap and snare, in order to obtain a supply of singing birds for the London markets. The trap is a large net, so contrived that it can be drawn up in a moment; the snare is a little chirping bird, tied fast to the end of a pliant stick, which rebounds with the flutter of its wings, and thus the bird alternately rising and sinking has something the appearance of dancing at will upon the light and buoyant spray. The man, the monarch of creation, all the while crouches on the ground to watch his prey, and when one little sufferer has by its fruitless struggles so well mimicked the movements of a joyous flight, as to allure its fellow victims into the snare, the fatal knot is drawn, the man chooses out from the number the sweetest songsters, and after depositing them separately in an immense number of little cages, brought with him for the purpose, they are conveyed to the market, purchased, and made miserable during the rest of their lives, for the delectation of London ears, and the benefit of society in general.

I know not whether it was the effect of my own fancy, or that such was really the fact, but the men whom I have seen employed in this business, looked to me uncommonly large, that is, personally large. There was so strange a contrast between their magnitude and that of the little fragile beings they were contending with upon such unequal terms; between the frantic fluttering of the decoy bird and the joyous flight of the free ones; between this system of deception, artifice and cruelty, and the open and manly performance of that Christian duty which teaches us to deal mercifully even with the meanest of God's creatures, that I have always considered this scene as amongst the most melancholy of those incident to a congregated mass of human beings in an imperfect state of moral cultivation.

But to return from this digression to the immense number and variety of sounds made conducive to the embellishment of poetry amongst which that of the wind is perhaps the most productive of poetical associations. Strike out this master chord from the harp of nature, and the music of the spheres would be harmony no more. Upon the bosom of the waveless sea; in the wide desert, where the sterile sand reposes unruffled; or in more domestic and familiar scenes, when the sky is concealed behind a dense mass of motionless cloud, when the flowers no longer tremble on their slender stems, and even the aspen leaves are still, a voice is wanting to remind us of the prevalence and potency of one mighty element; and we feel as if the great spirit of nature were either sleeping or dead. The least perceptible movement in the air, the slightest sound of the passing breeze as it whispers through the leafy boughs of the forest, fills up the dreary void; an all-pervading intelligence again lives around us, and the imaginative mind holds ideal intercourse with invisible beings, whose home is in the wilderness, and whose mystical companionship is the symbolical language in which nature is ever speaking to her children. According to the temper and construction of that mind, the voice of the wind brings tidings either joyful or melancholy. It may whisper in those low sweet tones which are sacred to the communication of happiness, or it may answer to the sadness of the soul in long plaintive notes that resemble a continued, unbroken, and universal sigh. It may tell of the gardens of the East, of the perfumes of Arabia that float upon its buoyant wings, of the cooling flow of sparkling waterfalls, of the "delicate breathing" of summer flowers; or of the bleak mountain, the howling wilderness, the deep echo of the gloomy cave, the rustling of the withered grass, and the waving of the boughs of the cypress. Precisely as the mind is affected it interprets the language of the wind, and receives its portion of joy or sorrow from the associations which that familiar sound conveys. This, however, can only be the case under ordinary circumstances. There are situations in which the howling of the wind so closely resembles the low monotonous wail of inexhaustible sorrow, that the pleasure it is known to afford to some individuals of particular taste and feeling, can only be accounted for by supposing that it forcibly reminds them, by contrast, of their own uninterrupted enjoyment. In the same manner, those who love to listen to the nightly tempest are wont to stir the fire and pity the sailors, and then turning inward to their own contracted circle of delight, congratulate themselves that it is broken in upon by no storms, invaded by no distress, and subject to no apprehensions of impending calamity.

Amongst the varieties of sound rendered familiar to us by their frequent and natural occurrence, the voice of the storm is the most potent in its influence. Whether it comes bounding and booming over the surface of the raging sea, or roaring through the stately forest, it is alike grand and terrific—alike full of association with images of majesty and awe, and ideas of partial or universal destruction by a mighty but unseen power. The speed with which it travels seems scarcely to admit of any distinction in the feelings which it awakens, but swift as the wind may be in its irresistible progress, it is not more so than thought, to which even a sudden explosion of matter affords time for the combination of a number of familiar ideas, by a process unknown to the mind in which it takes place. The raging of the tempest, to those who have never heard it with feelings alive to the poetry of nature, would be described as one continuous and monotonous sound; but to those who have, it is marked by a variety of distinctions, which accounts for the variety of sensations it occasions. To begin first with the hollow roar marking the interval when it seems to be retreating as if to gather strength, then the mighty gathering and the irresistible progress with which it rushes as swift as lightning through immeasurable space, leaving just time for the most appaling apprehensions, as it comes louder, and louder, and at last bursts upon us in one overwhelming tumult, mingling every imaginable combination of terrific sound, from the crash of falling matter, to the shrieks of w ld despair. And it is this combination of impressions, each bringing along with it a train of associations, which constitutes what is called the excitement of the scene—an excitement either distressing or invigorating, fearful or exquisitely delightful, according to the peculiar temper or capability of the mind of the listener.

There are three important attributes belonging to the wind, which combine to invest it with a character of intelligence. Motion, which gives the appearance of life to the external world; sound, which operates upon the mind through the medium of another sense, and resembles the universal voice of creation; and (if I may be allowed the expression) omnipresence, an attribute so potent in its influence upon our feelings, that from the searching, penetrating, and pervading power of the wind, we are accustomed to assign to it a character which differs little from actual personality. From ancient times down to the present moment, the wind is spoken of as a swift and faithful messenger. We say—"tell it not to the winds," lest they should carry the report to the utmost parts of the earth, and communicate the tidings to its inmost recesses; "Give thy sorrow to the winds," that they may bear it away on their elastic wings, and disperse it too widely for any single particle to remain perceptible, through the regions of illimitable space; and the great master magician who could wield at will all the passions of human nature, and all the influences of the elements, has thus powerfully represented the instrumentality of the winds in calling forth the self-upbraidings of a guilty conscience:

O, it is monstrous ! monstrous
Methought, the billows spoke, and told me of it;
The winds did sing it to me ; and the thunder,
That deep and dreadful organ-pipe, pronounc'd
The name of Prosper !—

Next to the sound of wind, that of water is perhaps the most poetical; whether it falls clear, and sharp, and tinkling drop by drop into the hollow basin of rock, or wanders through the woodland with a warbling and mellow voice, or glides in the sheeted water-fall down the sides of the mountain, with a soft and silvery sound, or rushes over its pent-up channel, in all the wild tumult of an impetuous torrent—whether rising and falling upon the distant shore, with a solemn and monotonous motion, or bellowing forth the mandates of the imperious ocean, it threatens to overwhelm and destroy, by sweeping every atom of moving or perishable matter, into the unsearchable abyss of its unfathomable waters; it is the same musical voice that salutes our ear, whilst wandering over the mountains, reposing in the valley, or meditating upon the wave beaten shore.

As the representation of water in a landscape, is said in the language of painters, to give repose to the picture by harmonizing with the colours of the sky, so the soothing and melodious sound of water, harmonizing with the winds. softens down the wild cry of different animals, and the sharp shrill minstrelsy of the woods, blending into one delightful symphony, the universal voice of nature. If anything can be added, to render this symphony more perfect—if the refinements of art may so mingle with the symplicity of nature, as to enhance our enjoyment of both, it is when sweet music is heard upon the water; for music is the great master key which unlocks the feelings and passions of mankind, bringing to light more hidden things than ever were called forth or revealed by the direct language of words. When plaintive, it addresses itself to sensibilities that have long been dormant, or never were awakened before, softening the flinty heart, and suffusing with the warm tribute of genuine tenderness, eyes that had forgotten to weep; when light and joyous, it touches as with electric power, the springs of animal motion and elasticity, and in an instant the dark brow becomes enlivened, the old resume their youth, the weary step is quickened, and the shadows of life are trampled down in the light and playful dance; when wild, and free, and national in its associations, it strikes the soul of the patriot, and the chains of the oppressor are burst asunder; while, planting himself on his native hills, with a step as firm as the beetling rock, a heart as invincible as the storm, and a front as undaunted as the mountain's brow, he defies the might of the invading foe, and nerves himself to defend his liberties or die; or when slow, and solemn, and majestic in its strains, it falls upon the spirit like the mantle of deep thought, soothing down the idle flutter of evanescent joy, the fruitless stirrings of ambition, the selfish and sordid cares that desolate the mind, and diffuses a holy calm, which if not religion itself, brings with it one of religion's best and sweetest attributes—the sanctity of peace.

The evil purposes to which music is capable of being applied, might afford a fertile subject for the pen of the moralist; its power over the human mind, is all that is attempted to be established here. Operated upon by this power, how many thousands of human beings have been led on to do, and to dare, what they would never have dreamed of attempting, but for the influence of this potent spell—potent in its immediate effects upon the feelings and affections, but, Oh! how much more potent in the recollections it awakens!

Music is the grand vehicle of memory, the key which unlocks the hoarded treasure of the soul. Words may define, and place before our mental perceptions, as in a map, all that has been; but music, suspending the active energies of the mind, addresses itself directly to the soul, in a voice that makes itself be heard, amongst the tumult and excitement of present things—the voice of the irrevocable past.

We listen, as to a curious specimen of art, to the national music of some distant country, about which we interest ourselves no farther than as it occupies a place upon the globe. We listen, we criticise, we remark upon the peculiarity of the air, and then turn away; but there may be one in the crowd of auditors—a heart-stricken exile from that very country—a wanderer without a home—driven about from one inhospitable shore to another, and stupified with the very extremity of his sufferings—he hears that well-known strain, and in an instant plunges into the very centre of his early attachments, and the warm comforts of his ancestral home. He sees again the stately woods that bounded his hereditary domain, and hears the rush of the torrent that guarded and defined its limits. He stands again upon his father's hearth, and feels himself a free-born man, proud to maintain and strong to defend his liberties and rights. The music ceases; a shadow like the sable pall of death falls upon the ideal picture, and again he stands upon a foreign land, an alien, desolate, and alone.

We have all known some blessed season of our lives, before the wheels of time had grown heavy with an accumulation of harassing cares, when the morning was bright upon our path, and the evening fell around us calm and serene as the repose of our own souls; when the friends we loved, loved us, and the smiles that betrayed our happiness were answered by smiles that told of gladness in return; when the fields and the woods, the mountains and the sky, were parts and pillars of that great temple, where we met to worship all that was sublime, eternal, and holy; when the moon was the centre of love and beauty, and the sun of life and light; when the rivers and wandering streams were a perpetual refreshment and delight, and the ocean was a flood of glory; when the dews, and the flowers, and the stars of night, blended their sweet influences together, and the song of the birds, the murmuring of the waterfall, and the whispering of the gentle gales, rose in a perpetual anthem of gratitude and joy; and when music, heard as it was heard then, told in its sweetest tones of all that we treasured of the past, all that we enjoyed of the present, and all that we hoped of the future. We have gone forth since then upon the pilgrimage of life, and the morning may have risen without brightness upon our path, and the evening may have come without repose; we may have missed the warm welcome of the eyes we loved, and the smile that was wont to answer to our own; we may have stood alone in the temple of nature without reverence, and without worship; we may have looked up to the queen of night without beholding her beauty, and to the sun without blessing his light; we may have wandered where the rippling flow of the crystal stream brought no gladness, and turned away from the ocean as from a desert plain; to us the dews may have fallen, the flowers may have bloomed, and the stars of night may have shone unheeded; and the grateful and harmonious voice of nature may have sounded without expression, wearisome and void. But let the music of our early days be heard again, and the floodgates of memory are opened; creation resumes the vividness of its colouring; the melody of sound is restored; and the soul, expanding her folded wings, soars once again up to her natural element of long forgotten happiness.

We have said that the song of the caged bird, and that of the street minstrel, are both sad; and yet how many millions pass on their daily walk, hearing, without regarding either. It is because music addresses itself to the most exquisite sensations of which we are capable, that its vulgar profanation is so peculiarly distressing; it is because of its own purity, and refinement, and adaptation to delicate feelings, and high sentiments, that we grieve over its prostitution to low purposes; it is because it is properly the language of ecstacy or woe, that we cannot bear to hear it sold for filthy pence, grudgingly doled out, or still more grudgingly denied. We hear, at intervals, amidst all the dust and tumult of the city, the tinkling sound of distant music, with the accompaniment of a voice that might once have been sweet. We listen to a lively strain that should have echoed through stately halls, amongst marble pillars, and wreaths of flowers. The voice of the minstrel is strained beyond its natural pitch, but no ear will listen; it is modulated, but no heart is charmed. The discord of city sounds, the rattle of wheels, and the busy tread of many feet, carry away the sound, and the sweetness is lost. A plaintive lay comes next, but it is alike unavailable in moving the multitude; and the wretched minstrels wander on, a living exemplification of the impotence of music performed without appropriate feeling, persisted in without fitting accompaniments of time and place, and poured upon ungrateful and inattentive ears.

The cultivation of music as a science, clearly marks the progress of national civilization. In almost all countries on the face of the earth, however simple or barbarous the state of their inhabitants, humble attempts to produce something like music have been detected, which proves beyond a doubt that there is a natural faculty or feeling in the human mind that pines for this peculiar enjoyment. As the eye is gratified with the blending of different colours, so is the ear regaled with the harmony of different sounds. The general aspect of the external world, and the wonderful construction of the organ of sight, show how admirably they are adapted to each other; yet much is left to the ingenuity of man, that he may exercise his faculties in carrying on the same principle of intellectual enjoyment derived from nature, and diffusing it through the region of art. As relates to the eye, this is most effectually accomplished by painting; as relates to the ear, by music. They each constitute links of the same degree of relative connection between the organs of sense and the operations of the mind. Painting is generally considered more intellectual than music, because it remains extant and tangible to criticism; while music is more instantaneous, and more evanescent in its effect upon the feelings; but they have both worked their way as an accompaniment in the progress of civilization and general refinement; they have both occupied the lives of many able men, requiring the exercise of much patience, and much intellect, to bring them to their present state of perfection; and they both afford pleasure, upon principles which form an important part of our nature, and are inseparable from it.

It is true there are human beings so strangely constituted that deficient in no other faculty, they yet declare themselves incapable of being charmed by music; but rather than consign them at once to the well-known anathema against "the man that has not music in his soul," I have sometimes fancied that these individuals were influenced by prejudice, or early bias, against music in some particular character; that they might probably each have their favourite song bird, and that if they could once be convinced that the music to which they professed themselves insensible, was only a different arrangement of the same notes they were accustomed to listen to with delight from a bird, they would no longer turn away with indifference from the music of the harp or the viol. There is one kind of music, which, above all others, I would make the test of their capability—the music of the voices of children. If they remain unmoved by that, the case would be fully proved against them, and there would appear no reason why sentence should not be immediately pronounced by declaring them

"Fit for treason's stratagems and spoils."

There is no sound that salutes us in our daily and familiar walk, more affecting than the voice of infancy in its happiest moods. It reminds us, with its fairy tones of silvery music, at once of what we are, and what we might have been; of all that we have lost in losing our innocence, of the flowers that still linger upon the path of life, of the sweetness that may yet be extracted from affection and simplicity, from tenderness and truth; and of the cherub choir that sing around the eternal throne.

The poetry of village sounds, when heard by the evening wanderer, scarcely needs description here. The clap of the distant gate, the bark of the faithful watch-dog, the bleat of the folded sheep, the faintly distinguished shout of some victorious winner in the village game, the cry of the child under the evening discipline, and the hum of many voices, telling of the toils of the past, or of the coming day, are all poetical when they come floating upon the dewy air; though each in itself is discordant, and such as we should shun a nearer acquaintance with. Yet such is their intimate and powerful association with the calm of evening's hour, the close of labor, and the refreshment of repose, that heard in the distance they are mellowed into music, and thus become symbolical of happiness and peace.

As if to multiply our sources of enjoyment, and allure the mind onward from sensible to spiritual things, echo seems to have assumed her mysterious place in the great plan of creation. As shadow in the visible world is more productive of poetical associations than objects which possess the qualities of substance, light, and colour, so is echo in the region of sound. It speaks to us in a language so faithful, yet so airy and spiritual in its tones, that we willingly adopt the fanciful conception of the poet, as the most natural and satisfactory manner of accounting for the existence of a being so sensitive and ethereal, as to be perpetually speaking in the language of the woods and waterfalls, yet never seen, even for a moment, in the depth of the cool forest, listening to the melody of the winds, or stooping over the side of the crystal fountain to catch the silvery fall of its liquid music. How could a being of intelligence be made so faithful, but by love; or so timid, but by suffering? And from these two common circumstances of love and sorrow, the poet has drawn materials for that beautiful and fantastic story, of echo sighing herself away, until her whole existence became embodied in a sound—a sound of such exquisite but mysterious sweetness, wandering like a swift intelligence from hill to hill, from cave to mountain crag, from waterfall to woodland, that he must be destitute indeed of all pretentions to poetic feeling, who can listen to the voice of echo without connecting it in idea with the language of unseen spirits.

As in the material world every visible object has its shadow, and every sound its echo, so in accordance with the great harmonious system of creation, no single idea is presented to the mind without its immediate affinity and connection with others; nor are we capable of any sensation, either painful or pleasurable, that does not owe half its weight and power to sympathy.

Such is the vital character of the principle of poetry, that touch but the simplest flower which blooms in our fields or our meadows, and the life-giving spell widens on every side, including in its charmed circle the dews, and the winds, light, form, and loveliness, the changes of the seasons, and an endless variety of associations, each having its own circle, widening also, and extending for ever without bound or limitation. Strike but a chord of music, and the sound is echoed and re-echoed, bearing the mind along with it, far, far away, into the regions of illimitable space; examine but one atom extracted from the unfathomable abyss of past time, apply it to the torch of poetry, and a flame is kindled which lights up the past, the present, and the future, as with the golden radiance of an eternal and unextinguishable fire.

To speak of the poetry of one particular thing, is consequently like expatiating upon the sweetness of a single note of music. It is the combination and variety of these notes that charm the ear; just as it is the spirit of poetry pervading the natural world, extracting sweetness, and diffusing beauty, with the rapidity of thought, the power of intelligence, and the energy of truth, which constitutes the poetry of life.

THE POETRY OF LANGUAGE.

Language, as the medium of communication, has the same relation to the ear and the mind, as painting has to the mind and the eye. The poetry of language, like that of painting, consists in producing upon the organs of sense such impressions as are most intimately connected with refined and intellectual ideas; and it is to language that we appeal for the most forcible and obvious proofs that all our poetic feelings owe their existence to association.

The great principle therefore to be kept in view by the juvenile poet is the scale (or the *tone*, as the popular phrase now is) of his associations; and this is of importance not only as regards his subjects, but his words: for let the theme of his muse be the highest which the human mind is capable of conceiving, and the general style of his versification tender, graceful, or sublime, the occasional occurrence of an ill-chosen word may so arrest the interest of the reader, by the sudden intervention of a different and inferior set of associations as entirely to destroy the charm of the whole.

Without noticing words individually, we are scarcely aware how much of their sense is derived from the relative ideas which custom has attached to them. Take for example the word chariot, and supply its place in any poetical passage with a one-horse chaise, or even a coach and six; and the hero who had been followed by the acclamations of a wondering people, immediately descends to the level of a common man, even while he travels more commodiously.

Dean Swift has a treatise on the "art of sinking in poetry," to which curious additions might be made by striking out any appropriate expression from a fine passage, and, without materially altering the sense, supplying its place with some vulgar, familiar, or otherwise ill-chosen word. For example,—

"Come forth, sweet spirit, from thy cloudy cave."
Come *out*, &c.

"But hark! through the fast flashing lightning of war,
"What steed of the desert flies frantic afar."
What steed of the desert *now gallops* afar.

"We shall hold in the air a communion divine."
We shall hold in the air *conversation* divine.

"Around my ivy'd porch shall spring
"Each fragrant flower that drinks the dew."
Each fragrant flower that *sups* the dew.

"To Bristol's fount I bore with trembling care
"Her faded form: she bow'd to taste the wave,
"And died."
She *stoop'd to sip* the wave.

"We thought as we hollowed his narrow bed,
"And smooth'd down his lonely pillow,
"That the foe and the stranger would tread o'er his head,
"And we far away on the billow."
"We thought as we hollowed his *little* bed,
"And *dug out* his lonely pillow,
"That the foe and the stranger would *walk* o'er his head, &c.

"Be strong as the ocean that stems
"A thousand wild waves on the shore."
Nine hundred wild waves on the shore.

"This life is all chequered with pleasures and woes."
This life is all *dappled*, &c.

There can scarcely be a more beautiful and appropriate arrangement of words, than in the following stanza from Childe Harold.

"The sails were fill'd, and fair the light winds blew,
"As glad to waft him from his native home;
"And fast the white rocks faded from his view,
"And soon were lost in circumambient foam:
"And then, it may be of his wish to roam
"Repented he, but in his bosom slept
"The silent thought, nor from his lips did come
"One word of wail, whilst others sate and wept,
"And to the reckless gales unmanly moaning kept."

Without committing a crime so heinous as that of entirely spoiling this verse, it is easy to alter it so as to bring it down to the level of ordinary composition; and thus we may illustrate the essential difference between poetry and mere versification.

The sails were *trimm'd* and fair the light winds blew,
As glad to *force* him from his native home,
And fast the white rocks *vanish'd* from his view,
And soon were lost *amid the circling* foam:

And then, *perchance, of his fond wish* to roam
Repented he, but in his bosom slept
The *wish*, nor from his *silent* lips did come
One *mournful word*, whilst others sat and wept,
And to *the heedless breeze their fruitless* moaning kept.

It is impossible not to be struck with the harmony of the original words as they are placed in this stanza. The very sound is graceful, as well as musical; like the motion of the winds and waves, blended with the majestic movement of a gallant ship. "The sails were filled" conveys no association with the work of man; but substitute the word *trimmed*, and you see the busy sailors at once. The word "waft" follows in perfect unison with the whole of the preceding line, and maintains the invisible agency of the "light winds;" while the word "glad" before it, gives an idea of their power as an unseen intelligence. "Fading" is also a happy expression, to denote the gradual obscurity and disappearing of the "white rocks;" but the "circumambient foam" is perhaps the most poetical expression of the whole, and such as could scarcely have proceeded from a low or ordinary mind. It is unnecessary however to prolong this minute examination of particular words. It may be more amusing to the reader to see how a poet, and that of no mean order, can undesignedly murder his own offspring.

To Liberty, by Shelley.

"From a single cloud the lightning flashes,
"Whilst a thousand isles are illumin'd around,
"Earthquake is *trampling* one city to ashes,
* * * * * * *
"But keener thy gaze than the lightning's glare,
"And swifter thy step than the earthquake's tramp;
"Thou deafenest the rage of the ocean; thy STARE
"Makes blind the volcanoes;————"

The images called up before the mind, by this personification of earthquake in the act of "trampling," and liberty "staring," are sufficiently absurd to destroy the sublimity of the poem.

To ————.

"Music, when soft voices die,
"Vibrates in the memory—
"Odours, when sweet violets *sicken*,
"Live within the sense they quicken."

A Dirge.

* * * * * * *
"Ere the sun through heaven once more has rolled,
"The *rats* in her heart
"Will have made their nest.
"And the *worms* be alive in her golden hair."

Song for Tasso.

* * * * * * *
"And if I think, my thoughts come fast,
"I mix the present with the past,
"And each seems *uglier* than the last."

Ode to Naples.

"Naples! thou heart of men, which ever pantest
"Naked, beneath the *lidless* eye of heaven!"

The same fault, as it applies to imagery rather than to single words, is still more frequently found in poetry, because the ear assists the judgment in its choice of words, but imagery is left entirely to the imagination. The same poet, rich as he is in passages of beauty, must still supply us with examples.

A Fragment.

"Thou art the *wine* whose *drunkenness* is all
"We can desire, O Love!"

A Vision of the Sea.

"'Tis the terror of tempest. The *rags* of the sail
"Are flickering in ribbons within the fierce gale;
"From the stark night of vapours the dim rain is driven,
"And when lightning is loosed, like a deluge from heaven,
"*She sees the black trunks of the water-spout spin*,
"And bend as if heaven was raining in."

The Fugitives.

"In the court of the fortress
"Beside the pale portress,
"Like a blood-hound well beaten,
"The bridegroom stands, eaten
"By shame:"

The Sunset.

"For but to see her were to read the tale
"Woven by some subtlest bard, to make hard hearts
"Dissolve away in wisdom-working grief;—
"*Her eyelashes were worn away with tears.*"

The Boat on the Serchio.

"Our boat is asleep on the Serchio's stream,
"Its sails are folded like thoughts in a dream,
"The elm sways idly, hither and thither;
"Dominic, the boatman, has brought the mast,
"And the oar and the sails; but 'tis sleeping fast,
"*Like a beast unconscious of its tether.*"

A vulgar proverb tells us that "seeing is believing;" and it is quite necessary to see, in order to believe, that the same poet who wrote that exquisite line,

"Its sails are folded like thoughts in a dream."

should go on to tell us in the language of poetry, that

Dominic, the boatman, has brought the mast,"

and that the boat itself

"Is sleeping fast,
"Like a beast unconscious of its tether."

The same poet has addressed himself to night, in language seldom surpassed for sublimity and grace; but even here he calls up one image which spoils the whole.

"Wrap thy form in a mantle grey,
"Star inwrought!
"Bind with thine hair the eyes of day,
"*Kiss her until she be wearied out.*
"Then wander o'er city, and sea, and land,
"Touching all with thine opiate wand—
"Come, long sought!"

LINES ON HEARING THE NEWS OF THE DEATH OF NAPOLEON.

* * * *

"And livest thou still, mother earth?
"*Thou wert warming thy fingers old*
"O'er the embers covered and cold
"Of that most fiery spirit, when it fled——."

It is an ungracious task to busy one's fingers in turning over the pages of our best writers, for the purpose of finding out their faults, or rather detecting instances of their forgetfulness; yet if any thing of this kind can assist the young poet in his pursuit of excellence, it ought not to be withheld; especially as it can in no way affect the decided merits of those who have so few flaws in their title to our admiration.

"What behold I now? (says Young,)
"A wilderness of wonders burning round;
"Where larger suns inhabit higher spheres;
"Perhaps the *villas* of descending Gods.
"Nor halt I here; my toil is but begun;
"'Tis but the threshold of the Deity."

The idea of "descending gods" requiring "villas," or half-way houses to halt at, is wholly unworthy of the dignity of the author of "Night Thoughts."

It is remarkable that Milton, whose choice of subjects would have rendered an inferior poet peculiarly liable to such errors, has a few, and but a very few, instances of the same kind.

"And now went forth the moon,
"Such as in highest heaven, arrayed with gold
"Empyreal; from before her vanished night,
"*Shot through* with orient beams."

Through the whole of the works of this master mind, the passage which describes the combat between Satan and the Archangel, is perhaps the most in danger of falling into burlesque, and even this has great sublimity and power: but the subject itself —a fleshly combat in the air, is one which necessarily requires such descriptions and allusions as we find it difficult to reconcile with our notions of ethereal or sublime. For instance, when

"From each hand with speed retired,
"Where erst was thickest fight, the angelic throng,
"And left large *field, unsafe within the wind*
"*Of such commotion.*"

And again, when the sword of Michael "shares all the right side of his antagonist" and

"A stream of nectareous humour issuing flowed
"Sanguine, such as celestial spirits may bleed."

This, and the minute description of the process by which the wound is healed, have little connexion with our ideas of the essential attributes of gods. Nor is there much dignity in the allusion made by Adam to his own situation after the fall, compared with that of Eve.

————"On me the curse *aslope*
"Glanced on the ground; with labour I must earn
"My bread."

But above all, in describing the building of the tower of Babel, our immortal poet seems wholly to have forgotten the necessary difference between the inhabitants of Earth, and those of Heaven.

"Forthwith a hideous gabble rises loud
"Among the builders; each to other calls
"Not understood; till hoarse, and all in rage,
"As mocked they storm; *great laughter was in heaven*
"*And looking down, to see the hubbub strange,*
"*And hear the din.*"—

It is into such incongruities as these, that young poets and enthusiasts, whether young or old, are most apt to fall: young poets, because they are not so well acquainted with the world, and with the tastes and feelings of mankind in general, as to know what particular associations are most uniformly attached to certain words; and enthusiasts, because their own thoughts are too vivid, and the tide of their own feelings too violent and impetuous, to admit of interruption from a single word, or even a whole sentence; and forgetting the fact that their books will be read with cool discrimination rather than with enthusiasm like their own, they dash forth in loose and anomalous expressions, which destroy the harmony, and weaken the force of their language.

The introduction of unpoetical images may however be pardoned on the score of inadvertency, but it is possible for such images to be introduced in a manner which almost insults the feelings of the reader, by the doggrel or burlesque style which obtains favour with a certain class of readers, chiefly such as are incapable of appreciating what is beautiful or sublime. One specimen of this kind will be sufficient. It occurs in a volume of American poetry.

"There's music in the dash of waves
"When the swift bark cleaves the foam;
"There's music heard upon her deck,
"The mariner's song of home.
"When moon and star-beams smiling meet
"At midnight on the sea—
"*And there is music once a week*
"*In Scudder's balcony.*"

* * * * *

"The moonlight music of the waves
"In storms is heard no more,
"When the living lightning mocks the wreck
"At midnight on the shore;
"And the mariner's song of home has ceased;
"His course is on the sea—
"*And there is music when it rains*
"*In Scudder's balcony.*"

What could induce the poet to spoil his otherwise pretty verses in this manner, it is difficult to imagine; but as this is by no means a solitary instance of the kind, we are led to suppose that the minds in which such incongruities originate, must be influenced by the popular notion of imitating Lord Byron, in the wild vagaries which even his genius could scarcely render endurable. What his genius might have failed to reconcile to the taste of the public, was however sufficiently effected, by the proofs we find throughout his writings, of the agony of a distorted mind, of that worst and deepest of all maladies, which hides its internal convulsions under the mask of humour, and throws around, in lurid flashes of wit and drollery, the burning ebullitions of a frenzied brain. There is a depth of experience, and bitterness of feeling, in the playful starts of familiar commonplace with which he forcibly arrests the tide of his own tenderness, or 'turns to burlesque" his own elevated sentiments, which sets all imitation at defiance; and might, if properly felt and fully understood, serve as a warning to those who aspire to be poets in the style of Byron, that to imitate his eccentricities without the power of his genius and the pathos of his soul, is as obviously at variance with good taste, natural feeling, and common sense, as to attempt to interest by aping the frolic of the madman, without the deep-seated and burning passions that have overthrown his reason.

Another prevailing fault in poetry, as intimately connected with association as the foregoing, is the introduction of words or passages, in which the ideas connected with them are too numerous, or too remote from common feeling and common observation, for the attention to travel with the same rapidity as the eye. Under such circumstances the mind must either pause and examine for itself, or pass over the expression as an absolute blank; in either of which cases, the chain of interest and intelligence is broken, and the reader is either wearied, or uninformed as to the meaning of the writer.

The same poet who has afforded us so many instances of his own faults, will serve our purpose again.

————————"the whirl and the splash
"As of some hideous engine, whose brazen teeth smash
"The thin winds and soft waves into thunder; the screams
"And hissings crawl fast o'er the smooth ocean streams,
"Each sound like a centipede."

Descriptions such as this, are beyond the power of the most vivid imagination to convert into an ideal *scene:* all is confusion, because the mind no sooner forms one picture, than other objects, differently coloured, are forced upon it, and consequently the whole is indefinite and obscure.

Again, in the Song of a Spirit—

"And as a veil in which I walk through heaven,
"I have wrought mountains, seas, and waves, and clouds
"And lastly, light, *whose interfusion dawns*
"*In the dark space of interstellar air.*"

Milton is by no means free from this fault. Witness his frequent crowding together of appellations, which even the most learned readers must pause before they can properly apply, as well as passages like the following, with which his works abound.

————————"There let him victor sway,
"As battle hath adjudged, from this new world
"Retiring, by his own doom alienated;
"And henceforth monarchy with thee divide
"Of all things parted *by the empyreal bounds*,
"*His quadrature, from thy orbicular world;*
"Or try thee, now more dangerous to his throne."

But of all our poets, Young is perhaps the most liberal in bestowing upon his readers examples of this kind. His ideas are absolutely ponderous. His associations crowd upon us in such stupendous masses, that we are often burdened and fatigued, instead of being refreshed and delighted with his otherwise sublime, and always imaginative style.

The poetry of language consists, therefore, not only of words which are musical, harmonious, and agreeable in themselves, but of *appropriate* words, so arranged as that their relative ideas shall flow into the mind, without more exertion of its own, than results from a gentle and natural stimulus. That quality in poetry which is most essentially conducive to this effect, is simplicity; and perhaps, from the humble ideas we attach to the word, simplicity is too much despised by those who are unacquainted with its real power and value. Yet is there nothing more obvious, upon reflection, than the simplicity of the language of some of our best poets. We feel that it is only from not having been the first to think of it, that we have not used precisely the same language ourselves. It contains nothing apparently beyond our own reach and compass. The words which terminate the lines seem to have fallen naturally and without design into their proper places; and the metre flows in like the consequence of an impulse, rather than an effort. Simplicity in poetry, when the subject is well chosen and skilfully managed, like order in architecture, where the materials and workmanship are good, establishes a complete whole, which never fails to please, not only the scientific observer, but even those who are least acquainted with the principles from which their gratification arises.

Our business thus far has been to point out what is not poetical in language; and so far as it serves to establish the fact, that the poetry of language, as well as that of feeling, arises from association, the task can scarcely be altogether uninteresting: but that which now lies before us is one of a much more grateful character.

We are told by Blair, that it is an essential part of the harmony (and consequently of the *poetry*) of language, that a particular resemblance should be maintained between the object described, and the sounds employed in describing it; and of this we give practical illustrations in our common conversation, when we speak of the *whistling* of winds, the *buzz* and *hum* of insects, the *hiss* of serpents, the *crash* of falling timber, and many other instances, where the word has been plainly framed upon the sound it represents.

Pope also tells us, in his Poetical Essay on Criticism,

"'Tis not enough no harshness gives offence;
"The sound must seem an echo to the sense.
"Soft is the strain when Zephyr gently blows,
"And the smooth stream in smoother numbers flows;
"But when loud surges lash the sounding shore,
"The hoarse rough verse should like the torrent roar."

And faithful to his own maxims, he thus describes the felling of trees in a forest:

"Loud sounds the air, redoubling stroke on strokes,
"On all sides round the forest hurls her oaks
"Headlong. Deep echoing groan the thickets brown,
"Then rustling, crackling, crashing, thunder down."

The words *alone, gone, no more*, are peculiarly adapted by their sound to the lengthened and melancholy cadence with which they are generally uttered; and *quick, lively, frolic, fun*, are equally expressive of what they describe. Of the same character are the following examples:—*whirring* of the partridge—*booming* of the bittern, &c.

"Scarce
"The bittern knows his time, with bill ingulft
"To shake the sounding marsh."

THE HORSE DRINKING IN SUMMER.

"He takes the river at redoubled draughts,
"And with wide nostrils, snorting, skims the wave.'

STORM IN SUMMER.

"The tempest growls————
————"Rolls its awful burden on the wind.
* * * * * * *

"Follows the loosen'd aggravated roar,
"Enlarging, deepening, mingling; peal on peal
"Crush'd horrible, convulsing heaven and earth.
"Down comes a deluge of sonorous hail,
"Or prone descending rain."

ON WINTER.

"At last the rous'd-up river pours along,
"Resistless, roaring, dreadful, down it comes" &c.
"Tumbling thro' rocks abrupt," &c.

"I hear the far-off curfew sound
"Over some wide water'd shore,
"Swinging slow with sullen roar."
"The reeling clouds
"Stagger with dizzy poise."—THOMSON.

"Have you not made an universal shout,
"That Tyber trembled underneath his banks,
"To hear the replication of your sounds,
"Made in his concave shores?"—SHAKESPEARE.

But above all our poets, he who sung in darkness most deeply felt and studied the harmony of his versification. Shut out from the visible world, his very soul seemed wrapped in music, and confined to that one medium of intelligence, through it he received as well as imparted, the most exquisite delight. Witness his own expression,—

——————— "to
"Feed on thoughts, that voluntary move
"Harmonious numbers."

"The multitude of angels, with a shout
"Loud as from numbers without number."

"The harp
"Had work and rested not, the solemn pipe,
"And dulcimer, all organs of sweet stop,
"All sounds on fret by string or golden wire,
"Temper'd soft tunings," &c.

The contrast between the two following passages, displays to great advantage the poet's art.

"On a sudden, open fly,
"With impetuous recoil, and jarring sound,
"Th' infernal doors; and on their hinges grate
"Harsh thunder."

"Heaven opened wide
"Her ever-during gates, harmonious sound,
"On golden hinges turning."

And again,—

"When the merry bells ring round,
"And the jocund rebecks sound,
"To many a youth, and many a maid
"Dancing in the chequer'd shade."

"Fountains, and ye that warble as ye flow
"Melodious murmurs, warbling, tune his praise."

"Now gentle gales,
"Fanning their odoriferous wings, dispense
"Native perfumes, and whisper whence they stole
"Those balmy spoils."

"Tripping ebb, that stole
"With soft foot toward the deep," &c

"Sabrina fair,
"Listen where thou art sitting
"Under the glassy, cool, translucent wave."

"At last a soft and solemn breathing sound
"Rose like a steam of rich distilled perfumes,
"And stole upon the air, that even silence
"Was took ere she was ware, and wished she might
"Deny her nature, and be never more
"Still to be so displaced."

"How sweetly did they float upon the wings
"Of silence, through the empty vaulted night,
"At every fall smoothing the raven down
"Of darkness till it smiled."

"Midnight shout and revelry,
"Tipsy dance and jollity."

"The sun to me is dark
"And silent as the moon,
"When she deserts the night,
"Hid in her vacant interlunar cave."—MILTON.

The measure of the following two lines is remarkably descriptive of the tardy leave-taking of our first parents, when they passed for the last time through the gates of Paradise.

"They hand in hand, with wandering steps and slow,
"Through Eden took their solitary way."

How bright and crystalline is the following description:

"How from the sapphire fount, the crisped brook,
"Rolling on orient pearl, and sands of gold,
"With mazy error, under pendent shades."

The following specimens, from different authors, are all illustrative of the harmony of numbers.

"How beautiful is night!
"A dewy freshness fills the silent air;
"No mist obscures, nor cloud, nor speck, nor stain
"Breaks the serene of heaven:
"In full orb'd glory yonder moon divine
"Rolls through the dark blue depths.
"Beneath her steady ray
"The desert circle spreads,
"Like a round ocean girded with the sky.
"How beautiful is night!"—SOUTHEY.

"From peak to peak the rattling crags among,
"Leaps the live thunder!"

"And first one universal shriek there rush'd,
"Louder than the loud ocean, like a crash
"Of echoing thunder; and then all was hush'd,
"Save the wild wind, and the remorseless dash
"Of billows: but at intervals there gush'd,
"Accompanied with a convulsive splash,
"A solitary shriek, the bubbling cry
"Of some strong swimmer in his agony."—BYRON

"And dashing soft from rocks around,
'Bubbling runnels join'd the sound."—COLLINS.

'That orbed maiden with white fire laden
"Whom mortals call the moon,
"Glides glimmering o'er my fleece-like floor
"By the midnight breezes strewn."—SHELLEY.

"Sad, on the solitude of night, the sound,
"As in the stream he plung'd, was heard around:

"Then all was still,—the wave was rough no more,
"The river swept as sweetly as before,
"The willows wav'd, the moonbeams shone serene,
"And peace returning brooded o'er the scene."
H. K. WHITE.

Gray is scarcely inferior to Milton in his musical versification; indeed so much less important are the subjects of his muse, and consequently so much more easily woven in with soft and musical words, that as regards mere versification he stands unrivalled in the literature of our country.

"Now the rich stream of music winds along,
"*Deep, majestic, smooth, and strong.*"

"Woods that wave o'er Delphi's steep,
"Isles, that crown th' Egean deep,
"Fields that cool Ilissus laves."

"Bright-eyed fancy, hov'ring o'er,
"Scatters from her pictured urn
"*Thoughts that breathe, and words that burn.*"

"Fair laughs the morn, and soft the zephyr blows,
"While proudly riding o'er the azure realm
"In gallant trim the gilded vessel goes;
"*Youth on the prow, and pleasure at the helm;*
"Regardless of the sweeping whirlwind's sway,
"That, hush'd in grim repose, expects his evening prey."

"Bright rapture calls, and soaring, as she sings,
"Waves in the eye of heaven her many-colour'd wings."

"Now the storm begins to lour,
"(Haste, the loom of hell prepare,)
"*Iron sleet of arrowy shower*
"*Hurtles in the darkened air.*"

"Now my weary lips I close:
"Leave me, leave me to repose."

Nothing can be more expressive of weariness than the simple words which compose these two lines. We could scarcely find in our hearts to detain the enchantress who utters them more than once, even were she capable of realizing to our grasp the imaginary dominion of a world.

The elegy written in a country churchyard is altogether the most perfect specimen of poetical harmony which our language affords; but like some other good things it has been profaned by vulgar abuse, and many who have been compelled to learn these verses for a task at school, retain in after life a clear recollection of their sound, without any idea of their sense, or any perception of their beauty. Stil. this elegy contains many stanzas, and one in particular, to which the ear must be insensible indeed if it can listen without delight.

"*The breezy call of incense-breathing morn,*
"The swallow twitt'ring from the straw-built shed,
"The cock's shrill clarion, or the echoing horn,
"No more shall rouse them from their lowly bed."

Amongst our modern poets, there is not one who possesses a more exquisite sense of the appropriateness of sound and imagery, than Moore. His charmed numbers flow on like the free current of a melodious stream, whose associations are with the sunbeams and the shadows, the leafy boughs, the song of the forest birds, the dew upon the flowery bank, and all things sweet, and genial, and delightful, whose influence is around us in our happiest moments, and whose essence is the wealth that lies hoarded in the treasury of nature. In reading the poetry of Moore, our attention is never arrested by one particular word. His syllables are like notes of music, each composing parts of an harmonious whole; and the interest they excite, divided between the ear and the mind, is a continued tide of gratification, gently but copiously poured in upon the soul. There is scarcely a line of his that would not gratify us by its sound, even were we ignorant of its sense; but the perfect correspondence between both is what constitutes the soul-felt music of his lyre.

It would be as useless to select passages from what is altogether harmonious as to point out particular parts in a chain of beauty, whose every link is perfect; but from an almost affectionate remembrance of the delight with which they first struck upon my youthful ear, I am tempted to quote a few examples powerfully illustrative of the poetry of language.

"Oh! had we some bright little isle of our own,
"*In a blue summer ocean far off and alone.*"

"*Not the silvery lapse of the summer eve dew.*"

"I saw from the beach, when the morning was shining,
"A bark o'er the waters move gloriously on;
"I came when the sun o'er that beach was declining,
"The bark was still there, but the waters were gone."

"There's a bower of roses by Bendemeer's stream,
"And the nightingale sings round it all the day long;
"In the time of my childhood 'twas like a sweet dream,
"To sit in the roses and hear the bird's song."

What a picture of innocent enjoyment is here! A picture whose vividness and beauty are recalled in after life as light and colouring only—whose reality is gone with the innocence which gave it birth.

In the poet's farewell to his harp, the last two lines are exquisitely poetical:

"If the pulse of the patriot, soldier, or lover,
"Have throbb'd at our lay, 'tis thy glory alone;
I was but as the wind passing heedlessly over,
"*And all the wild sweetness I wak'd was thy own!*"

A few more passages, quoted at random and without comment, will sufficiently illustrate what is meant by embodying in appropriate words, ideas which are purely poetical.

"So fiercely beautiful, in form and eye,
"*Like war's wild planet in a summer sky.*"

——— "who with heart and eyes
"Could walk where liberty had been, nor see
"*The shining foot-prints of her Deity.*"

"But ill-according with the pomp and grace,
"*And silent lull of that voluptuous place!*"

——— "and gave
"His soul up to sweet thoughts, like wave on wave
"Succeeding in smooth seas, when storms are laid."

——— "still nearer on the breeze,
"*Come those delicious dream-like harmonies.*—"

"Awhile they dance before him, then divide,
"Breaking like rosy clouds at eventide
"Around the rich pavilion of the sun—"

"'Tis moonlight over Oman's sea;
"Her banks of pearl and palmy isles
"Bask in the night-beam beauteously,
"And her blue waters sleep in smiles."

"To watch the moonlight on the wings
"Of the white pelicans, that break
"*The azure calm of Mœris' lake.*"

——— "when the west
"*Opens her golden bowers of rest.*"

"Our rocks are rough, but smiling there,
"Th' acacia waves her yellow hair,
"Lonely and sweet, nor lov'd the less,
"For flowing in a wilderness.

"Our sands are rude, but down their slope,
"The silvery-footed antelope
"As gracefully and gaily springs,
"As o'er the marble courts of kings."

Nor is the prose of this *delicious* bard less musical than his verse. The very cadence of his sentences would charm us, independent of their meaning, were it possible to listen without understanding; but his choice of words is such, that their mere sound conveys no small portion of their sense.

"Seldom, indeed, had Athens witnessed such a scene. The ground that formed the original site of the garden had, from time to time, received continual additions; and the whole extent was laid out with that perfect taste, which knows how *to wed Nature with Art, without sacrificing her simplicity to the alliance.* Walks, leading through wildernesses of shade and fragrance—glades opening, as if to afford a play-ground for the sunshine—temples, rising on the very spots where imagination herself would have called them up; and fountains and lakes, in alternate motion and repose, either wantonly courting the verdure, or calmly sleeping in its embrace—such was the variety of feature that diversified these fair gardens; and, animated as they were on this occasion, by the living wit and loveliness of Athens, it afforded a scene such as my own youthful fancy, rich as it was then in images of luxury and beauty, could hardly have anticipated.

"For, shut out, as I was by my creed, from a future life, and having no hope beyond the narrow horizon of this, every minute of delight assumed a mournful preciousness in my eyes, *and pleasure, like the flower of the cemetery, grew but more luxuriant from the neighbourhood of death.*"

"Every where new pleasures, new interests awaited me; and though melancholy, as usual, stood always near, her shadow fell but half way over my vagrant path, and left the rest more welcomely brilliant from the contrast."

"Through a range of sepulchral grots underneath, the humbler denizens of the tomb are deposited,—looking out on each successive generation that visits them, with the same face and features they wore centuries ago. *Every plant and tree that is consecrated to death, from the asphodel flower to the mystic plantain, lends its sweetness or shadow to this place of tombs; and the only noise that disturbs its eternal calm, is the low humming sound of the priests at prayer, when a new inhabitant is added to the silent city.*"

"The activity of the morning hour was visible every where. Flights of doves and lapwings were fluttering among the leaves, and the white heron, which had been roosting all night in some date tree, now stood sunning its wings on the green bank, or floated, like living silver, over the flood. The flowers, too, both of land and water, looked freshly awakened;—*and, most of all, the superb lotus, which had risen with the sun from the wave, and was now holding up her chalice for a full draught of his light.*"

"To attempt to repeat, in her own touching words, the simple story which she now related to me, would be like endeavouring to note down some strain of unpremeditated music, with those fugitive graces, those felicities of the moment, which no art can restore, as they first met the ear."

"The only living thing I saw was a restless swallow, whose wings were of the hue of the grey sands over which he fluttered. "Why (thought I) may not the mind, like this bird, take the colour of the desert, *and sympathise in its austerity, its freedom, and its calm!*"

It would scarcely be possible to exchange any one word in the writings of Moore for another more fitting or appropriate, nor can the young poet be too often reminded that it is *appropriateness* rather than uniform elevation of diction which he has to keep in view. There are certain kinds of metre to which peculiar expressions are adapted—expressions which even if the subject were the same, would be extremely out of place elsewhere; and here again Moore is preeminent for the skill with which he maintains (if we may so call it) the *proportions* of his verse, by keeping the familiar and playful language with which he sports like a child with his rainbow-tinted bubbles, always in their proper degree of subordination; so that they never break in upon the pathos of a sentiment, or check the flow of elevated thought.

Lines on the burial of Sir John Moore afford a beautiful instance of what may be called *tact* in the choice and application of words. It is not the splendour of an excited imagination flashing upon us as we read these lines, which constitutes their fascination; but the entire appropriateness of the words, and the metre, to the scene described. Simple as these verses are throughout—simple almost as the language of a child, and therefore to be felt and understood by the meanest capacity, they yet convey ideas of silence, solemnity, and power, such as especially belong to the hour of night, the awful nature of death, and the indignant spirit of the unconquered warrior.

Beyond the mere appropriateness of words, poetical language affords a deeper interest, in those rapid combinations of thought and feeling which a few words may convey, by introducing in descriptions of present things allusions to those which are remote, and which from being easily and naturally presented to the mind of the reader, glide in like the shadow of a passing cloud upon the landscape, without obscuring our view, or interrupting our contemplation of the scene.

Crabbe, who is by no means remarkable for the harmony of his numbers, abounds in passages of this kind; and it is to them that we are mainly indebted for the interest, as well as the power of his poetry. The first instance which occurs to me, is in the introduction to the sad story of the smugglers, and poachers—a story almost unrivalled for the natural and touching pathos with which it is described.

"One day is like the past, the year's sweet prime
"Like the sad fall,—for Rachel heeds not time;
"Nothing remains to agitate her breast,
"Spent is the tempest, and the sky at rest;
"But while it raged her peace its ruin met,
"And now the sun is on her prospects set;
"Leave her, and let us her distress explore,
"*She heeds it not—she has been left before.*"

Here is the story of the sufferer, told at once by a sudden transition from the description of her settled grief, to that which had been the bane of her past life—its melancholy cause. Yet the chain of association so far from being broken acquires tenfold interest from the transition of thought, and we hasten on to learn the particular history of this lonely being, who has experienced the most melancholy fate of woman—that of being "left."

Again, towards the conclusion of the same story, when Rachel finds the dead body of her lover, and, as if incapable of comprehending any further grief, takes no note of the intelligence that her husband is dead also.

——————"But see, the woman creeps
"Like a lost thing, that wanders as she sleeps.
"See here her husband's body—but she knows
"That other dead! and that her action shews.
"Rachel! why look you at your mortal foe?
"*She does not hear us—whither will she go?*"

Here we have three distinct ideas, not necessarily connected with each other, presented to us in quick succession, without any interruption to the interest excited by each individually. First, we see the dead body of the husband, and then "that other dead," with the total abstraction of the mourner, who in her silent grief sees only one, and this proves the strength of her affection, which life might have subdued, but which death reveals in all its overwhelming power; then follows the simple query, "whither will she go?" presenting us at once with a view of her future life, and its utter desolation.

Moore has many passages of the same description:—

"Here too he traces the kind visitings
"Of woman's love, in those fair, living things
"Of land and wave, whose fate,—in bondage thrown
"*For their weak loveliness—is like her own!*"

The reader may, without any flaw in the chain of association, pause here to give one sigh to the fate of woman, and then go on with the poet while he proceeds to describe other fair things, amongst which the stranger was wandering.

There is somewhere in the writings of Wordsworth a highly poetical passage, equally illustrative of the subject in question.

It is where he describes a mourner whose grief has all the bitterness of self-condemnation:—

"It was the season sweet of budding leaves,
"Of days advancing towards their utmost length,
"And small birds singing to their happy mates.
"Wild is the music of the autumnal wind
"Amongst the faded woods; but these blythe notes
"Strike the deserted to the heart;—*I speak*
"*Of what I know, and what we feel within.*"

When he leaves the subject which he has so beautifully described, to attest by his own experience, and by his knowledge of human nature, the truth of what he has asserted, our thoughts are not diverted from the original theme, but our feelings are riveted more closely to it by the force of this attestation, which meets with an immediate response from every human bosom.

In Gray's description of Milton, where he says:—

"The living throne, the sapphire blaze,
"Where angels tremble while they gaze,
"*He saw, but, blasted with excess of light,*
"*Clos'd his eyes in endless night.*"

The transition is immediate from what the poet saw, to what he suffered; yet the associations are highly poetical, and so clear as in no way to interfere with each other.

It is related of the Emperor Nero, when in the last mental agonies of his wretched life, he sought from others the death he shuddered to inflict upon himself, that finding none who heeded his appeal, he pathetically exclaimed, "What! have I neither a friend nor an enemy?" Although no man could possibly be thinking less of poetry than the fallen monarch at that moment, yet such is the language which an able poet would have used, to express the three separate ideas of the helplessness of Nero's situation, his pitiful appeal to the kindness of his people, and his internal consciousness that if he had not a friend, he had at least done enough to deserve the stroke of an enemy in his last hour.

Personification is another figure of speech by which poetica. associations are powerfully conveyed. It seems to be peculiarly in accordance with the infant mind—infant either in experience or in civilization, to identify every thing possessed of substance, motion, form, or power, with an intelligence of its own; hence the strong disposition shown by children to revenge themselves upon whatever has given them pain, and to battle, however vainly, with all that obstructs the gratification of their wishes; and hence those bursts of figurative language with which semi-barbarous people are accustomed to express what they deeply feel. As if to accommodate themselves to the natural tastes and feelings of mankind, originating in the principles of our nature, all good poets have made frequent use of this style, and always, when it is well managed, with great effect. How beautiful is the following passage from Barry Cornwall, where he speaks of the wind murmuring through the pine trees on mount Pelion:—

"And Pelion shook his piny locks, and talked
"Mournfully to the fields of Thessaly."

Shakespeare abounds in examples of this kind, in no one instance more touching or powerful than in the lament of Constance, after the French king tells her she is as fond of grief as of her child:—

"Grief fills the room up of my absent child,
"Lies in his bed, walks up and down with me;
"Puts on his pretty looks, repeats his words,
"Remembers me of all his gracious parts,
"Stuffs out his vacant garments with his form;
"Then have I reason to be fond of grief."

The following example from Cowper is remarkable for its elegance and beauty. Alluding to the lemon and the orange trees—

"The golden boast of Portugal and Western India,"

he says, they

"Peep through the polished foliage at the storm,
"And seem to smile at what they need not fear."

The next figure of speech noticed by Blair is metaphor, of immense importance to the poet, because, if for one moment he loses the chain of association, an image wholly out of place is introduced, the charm of his metaphor is destroyed, and his verse becomes contemptible. From Lord Bolingbroke, whose writings abound in beauties of this kind, Blair has selected one example of perfect metaphor. The writer is describing the behaviour of Charles the First to his parliament. "In a word," says he, "about a month after their meeting, he dissolved them; and, as soon as he had dissolved them, he repented; but he repented too late of his rashness. Well might he repent, *for the vessel was now full, and this last drop made the waters of bitterness overflow.*"

The works of Ossian abound with beautiful and correct metaphors; such as that on a hero: "In peace, thou art the gate of spring; in war, the mountain storm." Or this on woman: "She was covered with the light of beauty; but her heart was the house of pride."

Young, in speaking of old age, says,

"It should
"Walk thoughtful on the silent solemn shore
"Of that vast ocean it must sail so soon."

In the following lines Prior gives us an example of allegory, which may be regarded as continued metaphor.

"Did I but purpose to embark with thee
"On the smooth surface of a summer's sea,
"While gentle zephyrs blow with prosperous gales,
"And fortune's favour fills the swelling sails,
"But would forsake the ship, and make the shore,
"When the winds whistle and the tempests roar?"

Beyond these figures of speech, there yet remain hyperbole, apostrophe, comparison, and a variety of others, which the young poet would do well to study, and which are scientifically described in books expressly devoted to the purpose; I shall therefore pass on to the colloquial language of the Irish—the simple, unsophisticated, genuine, Irish, which has always appeared to me particularly imaginative, powerful and pathetic; but unfortunately for the writer, it is only heard in moments of excitement, of which the feelings alone keep a record, and this record being one of impressions rather than words, it is difficult to recall the precise expressions which, striking the chords of sympathy, produce a momentary echo to the music of the soul.

Mrs C. Hall, in an Irish story, illustrative of the strong and metaphorical language of the Irish peasantry, makes this observation proceed from the mouth of a poor man, who had listened to the recital of the misfortunes of one who was brave, just and virtuous.

"The gardener pierces the vine even to bleeding, and suffers the bramble to grow its own way."

But it is to the author of Traits and Stories of the Irish Peasantry, that we are chiefly indebted for our knowledge of what is peculiarly national and characteristic in his native language. He gives us a spirited and amusing chapter upon Irish swearing, by no means confined to those malevolent wishes which it would be a painful task to transcribe, but which, as they issue from the impassioned lips of the Irishman, have something of that sentimental nature (though far deeper in its character) triumphantly displayed by Acres before his friend. "May the grass grow before your door," conveys a striking picture of desolation and ruin. "May you melt off the earth like the snow off the ditch," is another figure of the same description.

If positive good had the power to neutralize evil, we might comfort ourselves in reading such expressions as these, with what the author goes on to tell us, that the Irish have a superstitious dread of the curse of the pilgrim, mendicant, or idiot, and of the widow and the orphan. And so high is his idea of the duty he owes to these, that his heart is ever open to their complaint, and his hand ready to assist them. Thus it is not uncommon for them to say of a man whose affairs do not prosper, "He has had some poor body's curse;" and a woman who unexpectedly receives a guest, welcome in no way except that she was a stranger and a wanderer without a home, is described as exclaiming, "The blessing o' goodness upon you, dacent woman."

The frequent recurrence of the word *heart* in its unlimited capacity, gives a warmth and fervency to their expressions of tenderness or sorrow. "The beloved fair boy of my heart." "Father! son of my heart! thou art dead from me!" "Heavy and black was his heart." "The world's goodness is in your heart." "Light of my eyes, and of my heart;" but above all, "*Cushla machree*—the pulse of my heart," is most expressive of that deep-toned affection which the heart alone can understand.

What can exceed the following words for refined yet genuine and fervent sympathy, such as those who have been intimately acquainted with suffering alone can feel; and hence it is that the Irish derive their pathos, for what strain of human misery can be touched, to which their own experience has not an echo?

"Hunger and sickness and sorrow may come upon you when you'll be far from your own, and from them that love you." Or, "He's far from his own the crather—the pretty young boy."

"*Mavourneen dheelish*—my sweet darling," is expressive of great tenderness.

"My father, the heavens be his bed!" when uttered with fervency has both solemnity and pathos.

In their good wishes the Irish are most ingenious. "May every hair of your honour's head become a mould candle to light you into glory." "May you live a hundred years and a day longer," which last words seem to be added from a sudden impulse, to throw another weight into the scale, or to heap another blessing into the measure already overflowing.

There is also a great deal of imagination in the manner in which they account for what they do not, or will not understand rationally: always referring directly to the principles of good or evil. Thus a hard and unjust steward who wore his ears stuffed with wool, was said to have adopted this custom that he might not hear the cries of the widow and the orphan.

In reply to instructions that were to prove his constancy, a peasant exclaims, "*Manim asthee hir*, my soul is within you." A mother thus regrets her son's approaching marriage, "You're going to break the ring about your father's hearth and mine." A broken-hearted mother exclaims, "My soul to glory, but my child's murthered!"

In a note by Crofton Croker, in his Fairy Legends, he remarks, "The Irish, like the Tuscans, as observed by Mr. Rose in his interesting Letters from the North of Italy, are extremely picturesque in their language. Thus they constantly use the word *dark* as synonymous with *blind;* and a blind beggar will implore you to 'Look down with pity on a poor dark man.'"

It may be observed here that the Irish, like the Scotch, by a very beautiful and tender euphemism, call *idiots*, *innocents*. A lady of rank in Ireland, the lady Bountiful of her neighbourhood, was one day asking a man about a poor orphan: "Ah! my lady," said he, "the poor creature is sadly afflicted with *innocence!*" And another peculiarity in the phraseology of the Irish, is their fondness for using what Mr. Burke would term "*sublime adjectives*," instead of the common English adverbs—very, extremely, &c. Thus an Irishman will say, "Its a cruel cold morning;" or "There's a power of ivy growing on the old church."

There is a peculiarity of constitution both mental and bodily, observable in the Irish people, for which it is difficult to account. One of their most amiable characteristics is the absence of satire, perhaps it would be more correct to say *contemptuous satire;* for the Irish are quick to see the ridiculous, but they can see without despising it. Unacquainted with that qualifying medium between what amuses them, and what excites their passions—that medium which an Englishman fills up with every variety and degree of contempt, they pass immediately from laughter to indignation; and thus amongst the least civilized classes of the Irish, the social meeting too often terminates in the deadly fray. Madame de Stael in speaking of the Italians, makes the same observation with regard to the absence of contemptuous satire from their national character; and it is to this amiable trait, in connection with great natural enthusiasm, that we may reasonably attribute the poetical constitution of both people. It is impossible to imagine that those combined ebullitions of music and verse, for which Italy has been celebrated, and which have unquestionably given a poetical tone to the character of her people;—that those bursts of impassioned feeling finding at the same time a language and a voice, should ever have flourished under the auspices of John Bull; or that he should have sat by, aud witnessed with delight those exhibitions of irrelevant tropes, and metaphors, and splendid perorations, and flashes of wit, and peals of passionate eloquence, for which Irish oratory has been distinguished. No; there is nothing more destructive to enthusiasm and poetry, indeed to genius in its most unlimited sense, than contempt. It is true, the calm judgment of the censor is often necessary to restrain the exuberance of undisciplined fancy, but he who *prides* himself upon being able to *put down* with a sneer, whatever is unnecessary in feeling, and extraneous in taste and imagination, ought to feel bound to supply, with something equally conducive to happiness, the void which this practice must necessarily occasion in the highest range of intellectual gratification.

If other evidence were necessary, beyond what is afforded by the nature of the human mind, to prove that poetry may not only be mingled with, but highly enhance all that we enjoy and admire, we have this evidence in the Bible, abounding as it does in every variety of poetical language which it has entered into the mind of man to conceive. A slight examination of the different meanings attached to words of common and familiar signification, will sufficiently illustrate the high tone of imaginative interest flowing through the whole.

The words I have selected are, hand, wing, foot, head, mind, heart, and soul, of which hand is perhaps the most unlimited in its application.

HAND.

His *hand* will be against every man, and every man's *hand* against him.—And the children of Israel went out with an high *hand.*—The day of their calamity is at *hand.* —The Lord made all that he did to prosper in his *hand.* The *hand* of the Lord is sore upon us.—For he put his life in his *hand*, and slew the Philistine.—As soon as the kingdom was confirmed in his *hand.*—I will set his *hand* also in the sea, and his right *hand* in the rivers.—In the shadow of his *hand* hath he hid me.—Would we had died by the *hand* of the Lord.—The *hand* of the Lord is gone out against me.—The *hand* of the Lord was strong upon me.—If thou wilt take the left *hand*, then I will go to the right; or if thou depart to the right *hand*, then I will go to the left.—Let not thy left *hand* know what thy right *hand* doeth.—I will remember the years of the right *hand* of the Most High.—A wise man hears at his right *hand.* —Let my right *hand* forget her cunning.—Is there not a lie in my *right* hand.—If thy *right* hand offend thee, cut it off.—They gave to me and Barnabas the right *hand* of fellowship.

Here we find the word *hand* is not only used for the instrument of performing, maintaining, and possessing, but that it supplies the place of power, in all its different modifications of will, action, and suffering.

WING.

As one gathereth eggs that are left, have I gathered all the earth; and there was none that moved the *wing.*—Ye have seen what I have done unto the Egyptians, and how I bore you on eagles' *wings*, and brought you unto myself.—A full reward be given thee of the Lord God of Israel, under whose *wings* thou art come to trust. And he rode upon a cherub, and did fly: yea, he did fly upon the *wings* of the wind.—Oh that I had *wings* like a dove! for then would I fly away and be at rest.—Hide me under the shadow of thy *wings.*—If I take the *wings* of the morning, and dwell in the uttermost parts of the sea.—Riches make themselves *wings.*—Wo to the land shadowing with *wings!*—The wind hath bound her up in her *wings.*—The sun of righteousness shall arise with healing in his *wings.*

The word *wing* is here used not only as the instrument of conveying aloft, or away; but as the means of sheltering and protecting; from the two different associations which we have with the flight of a bird, and the brooding of its young.

FOOT.

He will keep the *feet* of his saints, and the wicked shall be silent in darkness.—He maketh my *feet* like hinds' feet.—He that is ready to slip with his *feet*, is as a lamp despised in the thought of him that is at ease.—I was eyes to the blind, and *feet* was I to the lame.—He shall subdue the people under us, and the nations under our *feet.*—Suffer not our *feet* to be moved.—My *feet* were almost gone.—Lift up thy *feet* unto the perpetual desolations.—Her *feet* go down to death.—How beautiful upon the mountains are the *feet* of him that bringeth good tidings.—Thou hast put all things in subjection under his *feet.*—No man lifted up his *foot* in all the land.—The flood breaketh out from the inhabitant; even the waters forgotten of the *foot;* they are dried up, they are gone away from men.

We see by these passages that *foot* is used in a very unlimited sense, as a foundation and a stay, as well as a means of establishing, confirming, moving, overcoming, and destroying.

HEAD.

Yet within three days shall Pharaoh lift up thine *head*, and shall restore thee unto thy place.—Thou hast kept me to be the *head* of the heathen.—Thy blood shall be upon thine own *head.*—Though his excellency mount up into the heavens, and his *head* reach the clouds.—Mine iniquities are gone over mine *head.*—Blessings are upon the *head* of the just.—Thou shalt heap coals of fire upon his *head.*—Mine *head* is filled with dew.—Thou hast built thy high places at every *head* of the way.—Thy dream and the visions of thy *head* upon thy bed.—For this cause ought the woman to have power on her *head*, because of the angels.

We find *head* used here as it is in our ordinary language, not only as the chief portion of any whole, and the centre from whence our ideas flow; but as a figure it is most frequently made to stand for the highest part of man's nature—that which is most capable of being exalted or depressed—most calculated for receiving honour, as well as suffering degradation.

MIND.

And they put him in ward, that the *mind* of the Lord might be shown them.—Bring it again to *mind*, O ye transgressors.—Thou wilt keep him in perfect peace whose *mind* is stayed on thee.—Sitting clothed, and in his right *mind*.—The carnal *mind* is enmity against God. —Let every man be fully persuaded in his own *mind*.—Even their *mind* and conscience is defiled.—Be all of one *mind*.—It was in my *mind* to build an house.—To do good or bad of mine own *mind*.—I know the forwardness of your *mind*.—Gird up the loins of your *mind*.—Comfort the feeble-*minded*.—A double *minded* man is unstable in all his ways.

Here we see that in the language of scripture, precisely the same license is used as in that of our poets. The word *mind* represents an ideal centre from whence volitions flow, and relates almost exclusively to the understanding, the memory, and will.

HEART.

And God saw that every imagination of the thoughts of man's *heart* was only evil continually.—And Jacob's *heart* fainted, for he believed them not.—Pharaoh's *heart* was hardened.—Lay up these my words in your *heart*.—My brethren that went up with me made the *heart* of the people melt.—For the divisions of Reuben there were great searchings of *heart*.—And it was so, that when he had turned his back to go from Samuel, God gave him another *heart*.—David's *heart* smote him.—His *heart* died within him.—And God gave Solomon wisdom and understanding exceeding much, and largeness of *heart*, even as the sand that is on the sea shore.—His wives turned away his *heart*.—I caused the widow's *heart* to sing for joy.—A broken and contrite *heart*, O God, thou wilt not despise.—By sorrow of *heart* is the spirit broken. —I am pained at my very *heart*.—I weep for thee with bitterness of *heart*.—Out of the *heart* proceed evil thoughts.—Where your treasure is, there will your *heart* be also.—Did not our *heart* burn within us, while he talked by the way.—Love the Lord thy God with all thy *heart*.

The difference between *heart* and *mind* is here apparent. *Heart* comprehends the understanding and the affections, but has nothing to do with either memory or will, except as the affections may be considered as the moving cause of impressions upon the memory, and operations upon the will; while *mind* confined to the sphere of the intellects has nothing to do with the affections.

SOUL.

And man became a living *soul*.—Set your *soul* to seek the Lord.—The law of the Lord is perfect, converting the *soul*.—He satisfieth the longing *soul*, and filleth the hungry *soul* with goodness.—Fear not them which kill the body, but are not able to kill the *soul*: but rather fear him which is able to destroy both *soul* and body in hell.—He hath poured out his *soul* unto death.—My *soul* is weary of my life.—Unto thee, O Lord, do I lift up my *soul*.—We were willing to have imparted unto you, not the gospel of God only, but also our own *souls*, because ye were dear unto us.—In patience possess ye your *souls*. —He that winneth *souls* is wise.—Thou fool, this night shall thy *soul* be required of thee.—Take heed to thyself, and keep thy *soul* diligently, lest thou forget the things which thine eyes have seen.—Why art thou cast down, O my *soul*, and why art thou disquieted within me?—As the hart panteth after the water brooks, so panteth my *soul* after thee, O God!—My *soul* shall be joyful in the Lord.—Save me, O God, for the waters are come in unto my *soul*.—Unless the Lord had been my help, my *soul* had almost dwelt in silence.—My *soul* fainteth for thy salvation.—My *soul* is even as a weaned child.—I shall go softly all my years in the bitterness of my *soul*. —The Lord is my portion, saith my *soul*.—My *soul* doth magnify the Lord.

We now find that every attribute both of the *mind* and the *heart* are comprehended in the meaning of the word *soul*. Not only is the soul capable of willing, acting, and suffering, but also of loving; and when we pursue the idea of love through all its gradations, down to simple preference, we shall have traversed a region comprising every impulse by which our nature is capable of being influenced. But in addition to the most extensive signification of *mind* and *heart*, *soul* obtains a character more dignified and profound, from being associated with the principle of life—with man's moral responsibility—and with eternity.

In examining these few words we are struck with the idea, of how much they would lose in beauty and interest by being confined to their literal and absolute signification; and just in the same proportion would our intellectual attainments and pursuits be robbed of their ornament and charm, by being separated from the poetry of life.

THE POETRY OF LOVE.

On entering upon the poetry of the human mind, the passions naturally present themselves as a proper subject of interesting discussion; because as poetry belongs not so much to the sphere of intellect, as to that of feeling, we must look to the passions, as to the living principle, which gives intensity to perception, and vividness to thought. All mankind who are gifted with common sense, are capable of writing verses, but all cannot feel, and still less can all write poetically. In order to do this it is necessary to feel deeply. By the exercise of intellectual power we may learn what are the component parts of a flower, but this alone will never make us sensible of its beauty. The same power may collect and disseminate the truths most important to the well being of society, but it cannot enforce their reception. In short, though it may instruct, improve, invigorate, and supply the mind with a perpetual fund of information, intellectual power alone can never make a poet, nor excite that love of poetry—that ardent desire in the soul for what it feeds on, which gives to the poetic mind a refinement, an energy, and a sense of happiness unknown to that which subsists merely upon knowledge. Hence we may fairly conclude, that the man who is wholly dispassionate himself, and who has neither observed, nor studied the nature of passion in others, can never be a poet; any more than the artist who has never felt the exhilaration of joy, nor witnessed its effects, can represent in painting or marble a personification of delight.

To examine the passions individually would be a work of time and patience, or rather of impatience. We will therefore dismiss those which are malevolent or injurious to the peace of society; for though rage, envy, malice, jealousy, and above all the master passion of revenge, may supply the poet with images of majesty, and horror, which give to the productions of his genius a character of depth and power; yet as those to which we are about to turn our attention are so much more congenial to the peaceful spirit of the muse, we will devote our time solely to the consideration of the poetry of love, and grief.

First then we begin with love; a subject hourly trampled in the dust, and yet hourly rising from its degredation with fresh life, and fresh vigour, to claim, in spite of the perpetual profanation of vulgar familiarity, the best and warmest tribute of the poet's lay. By love I do not mean that moderate but high-toned attachment which may be classed under the general head of affection —of this hereafter. For the present I am daring enough to speak in plain prose, and even in this enlightened day, of the love of May-day queens, and village swains; of the love of Damon and Delias; of the love which speaks in the common-place of sighs and blushes, as well as of that which never told its tale; of the love which Milton thought worthy of being described in its purest, holiest character; and of the love which lives and glows in the pages of every poet from Milton down to Byron, Burns, and Moore.

That all who have touched the poet's magic pen, have at one time or other of their lives made love their theme, and that they have bestowed upon this theme their highest powers, is proof sufficient to establish the fact that love is of all the passions the most poetical; a fact in no way contradicted or affected by the vulgar profanation to which this theme more than any other has been subjected. All human beings are not capable of ambition, of envy, of hate, or indeed of any other passion; but all are capable of love, in a greater or less degree, and according to certain modifications; it follows therefore as a necessary consequence, that love should form a favourite and familiar theme, with multitudes who know nothing of its refinements, and high capabilities.

The universal tendency of love to exalt its object, is a fact which at once gives it importance, dignity, and refinement. Importance because of its prevalence amongst mankind; dignity, because whatever raises the tone of moral feeling, and disposes towards kindly thoughts of our fellow-creatures, must be conducive to the good of society; and refinement because it enters into the secrets of social intercourse, and delights in nothing so much as communicating the happiness it derives from all that is most admirable in art and nature. If that is a contemptible or insignificant passion under whose influence more has been dared, and done, and suffered, than under any other; then is the human mind itself contemptible, and the name of insignificance may very properly be applied to all those impulses of human nature which have given rise to the revolutions of past ages, and the most conspicuous events which mark the history of the world.

It seems to me that love originates in a mixture of admiration and pity. Without some feeling of admiration, no sentient being could first begin to love; and without some touch of pity, love would be deficient in its character of tenderness, and that irresistible desire to serve the object, which impels to the most extraordinary acts of disinterestedness and devotion. I grant that after love has once taken possession of the heart, it becomes a sort of instinct, and can then maintain an existence too miserable, and degraded, for a name, long after admiration and even pity have become extinct. But in the first instance there must be some quality we admire to attract our attention and win our favour, and there must be some deficiency in the happiness of this object, which we think we can supply, or we should never dream of attaching ourselves to it. It may be asked since love sometimes fixes itself upon an inferior object, degraded below the possession of dignity or virtue, where then can be the admiration? I answer, that in such cases the mind that loves must be degraded too, and consequently it is subject to call evil good, and may thus discover qualities admirable to its perverted vision, which a more discriminating eye would turn from with disgust. Again, it is still more reasonable to ask when love is fixed upon an object apparently the centre of happiness, to which prosperity in every shape is ministering, where then can be the pity? We all know that the appearance of happiness is deceitful, and we all suspect that even under the most flattering aspect, there is a mingled yarn in the web of life, which renders the experience of others, like our own, a mixture of joy and sorrow; but if a being can be found in whose happiness is no broken link, no chord unstrung, who has no false friend, no flattering enemy, no threatening of infirmity, no flaw in worldly comfort and security; I would answer the question by asking, is human happiness of so firm and durable a nature that once established, it remains unshaken? No; the summit of earthly felicity is one of such perilous attainment, that the nearer we see any one approaching it, the more we long to protect them from the danger to come—to stretch out our arms, and if we cannot prevent, at least to break their fall. We feel towards such an one, that the day will come when they may want a real friend, a firm support, a true comforter, and we hasten the bond that unites our fate with theirs, that we may be ready in the days of "trial and wo."

If admiration did not form a competent part of our love, we should not feel so ardent a desire as is generally evinced, to obtain for the object beloved, the admiration of others. We long for others to behold them with our eyes, that they may participate in our feelings and do what we consider justice to the idols of our imagination; and though this can seldom be the case to the extent of our wishes, we know that to listen to the well-merited praises of those we love, is (at least to women) the most intense enjoyment this world can afford. To purchase this gratification what anxiety we endure, what study we bestow, what ardent desire we experience, that they may commit no errors cognizable to the world's eye; but steering an open, honourable, upright course, may defy the scrutiny of envious eyes, and claim as their due from society at large, that tribute of admiration which we are ever ready to bestow. But the unspeakable anguish with which we behold any departure from this honourable course of conduct, is perhaps the strongest proof, how intimately our sense of all that is admirable in the human character is interwoven with our affections. I do not pretend to say, that we are all so influenced by right feeling, or so well assured of the precise line of demarcation between good and evil, as to lament over the errors of those we love, exactly in proportion to their moral culpability. Far from it. But let that which all hearts can feel—let the stigma of the world's disgrace fall upon them—let it at the same time be voluntarily incurred, and richly merited, and ye who tell us of the loss of friends or fortune, of poverty, or sickness or death, match the agony of this conviction if you can. No; it has neither companion nor similitude. In the wide range of human calamity there is not one that bears any proportion to this.

It may be said of pity also, that there are cases in which we are scarcely aware of its forming any part of our love; but is not our love at such times languid, spiritless, and inert? No sooner does sickness or misfortune assail the object of our regard, than it assumes a new life, and all that was dear before, becomes doubly valuable beneath the pressure of affliction, or on the brink of the grave. How often has pity brought to light a love whose existence we were unconscious of before; and those whom we should once have deemed it impossible to regard with tenderness, have become, under the shadow of misfortune, the objects of our most devoted affection.

The power which love possesses of enhancing our enjoyments, is of itself sufficient to entitle this sentiment to a high place amongst those that are most influential in their operations upon the human mind. I appeal to the young, or rather to the old who have not forgotten their youth, whether love has not at some period of their existence, given a life and vividness to the aspect of creation, a music to sound, and an intensity to all their capabilities of simple and natural delight, which, while the enchantment lasted, seemed to raise the pleasures of earth above this sublunary sphere, though in remembrance it claims nothing but a passing smile, or perhaps a faint sigh of regret, that we have lost so much of what constitued the life of our early existence. We smile because we have lived to awake from our delusion—to know that the sunshine which then appeared to us a flood of radiance pouring its golden streams over hill and grove, and diffusing the principle of happiness through all the secret mysteries of nature, was but the ordinary light of day, liable to be obscured by mists, and hid from us by the intervention of dense snd gloomy clouds. We smile because the brook that murmured at our feet with such continuous and unbroken melody, to our young imaginations pure, and clear, and vivid, like the secret springs of unsophisticated feeling, since then has wearied us with the constant monotony of its sound, seeming to tell of little else than pebbles and clear water. We smile, because the song of at least half the birds whose voices were then all music, has degenerated into a mere chirp; but most of all we smile, because that bright being whose brow was garnished with a glory—at whose feet we would have laid the accumulated treasures of the whole world had we possessed them—the idol whom irreligiously we had placed upon the high altar of the soul, has stepped down from that exalted pedestal, and passing forth into the world endowed only with the customary functions of humanity, has mixed in the common avocations of life, and become

"An eating, drinking, bargain-making man."

Or if after such a retrospection, perchance we sigh, it is not so much with any positive regret, as with a vague sense of some indefinite loss—a mere illusion—a false colouring—a deceitful tone—an evanescent charm which owed its existence to the infatuation of the mind, and yet we sigh; because not the longest period of man's natural life, not the rapid and entire success of all our schemes, not the riches of prosperity poured into our lap, around our feet, and even beyond the circle of our hopes, can restore what is lost to us, when we are driven to the conviction that we can love no more. It was an idle phantasy, we tell ourselves in after life, and we join in the ridicule that reprobates this foolish passion; but would we not give all that time and tears have purchased for us, to sit again in the bright sunshine, to look round upon the fields and the woods, to listen to the singing of the birds, and without the excitement of art, or the aid of borrowed attributes, to feel each individual moment sufficient in its fulness of felicity to lull the memory of the past, and soothe down the anxieties of the future, concentrating into one point of present time, all that we spend after years in search of, and realizing without purchase, and without sacrifice, in one single isolated particle of blissful experience, the happiness for which countless myriads are pining in vain.

It is a strong proof of the poetical character of love, that all the contempt, and all the ridicule it meets with in the world, are unable to deprive it of the legitimate place which it holds in the popular works of our best authors. Caleb Williams is the only novel that occurs to me, in which the interest of the story is in no way connected with love. The author has supplied this deficiency, by conducting the reader through his pages with an intensity of anxiety, scarcely equalled elsewhere; but well as this story is penned, we arrive in the end at the unsatisfactory conviction, that we have been reading an uncongenial, hard, bad book, the whole tenor of which is in direct opposition to the good providence of God. It may be remarked, in connexion with the same fact, that Sir Walter Scott after he had spell-bound the public by the easy natural flow of his first poems, tried his skill upon the battle of Waterloo, and produced one which it is difficult to read, though the same master hand is there. He has since atoned for this want of fealty to the tender passion, by the most delicate and judicious distribution of it through the whole of his novels, where we find always enough, and (what is saying a great deal for the writer) never too much. At the same time however that love forms an essential part in our popular works of fiction, it seems to be inconsistent with the genius of the English nation, to make it the entire, or even the leading subject of any particular work. Richardson approaches the nearest to this extreme, but his novels are more remarkable in this day, for presenting minute descriptions of human character, of the social habits and customs of the times in which he lived, than as dissertations upon love. Miss Porter, kind as she is in mating all her characters, and marching them off the stage in couples, gives us battles innumerable, with lively exhibitions of valour, patriotism, and various other passions, good and evil, among which her love scenes form a very small, and certainly a very inferior part. And Miss Edgeworth, "the great enchantress," who manages love with more tact, and often with exquisite pathos, introduces it always with due subserviency to that substantial, sound moral, which to the honour of her sex and the benefit of her fellow-creatures, she makes the chief object of her clear, well regulated, and comprehensive mind.

We have no work in our language which bears any resemblance to the sorrows of Werter or to Corinne, each admirable in their way, and far above the praise of an ordinary pen. No Englishman could possibly have written either. He could not have resigned himself so entirely to any subject of a tender and evanescent nature, as to have studied it metaphysically. The spirit of sarcasm is so predominant in the English constitution, that he would have laughed at his work before it was half completed, and the other half would have remained unfinished, for fear of bringing upon himself the contempt of his friends, and the sneers of his enemies. The loves of Black-eyed Susan, Will Watch, and Roderick Random, are more pleasing to John Bull; because such is his extreme sensitiveness on the score of ridicule, that as soon as the fatal smile appears, love, such as it is in these and similar productions, can be dismissed altogether as a joke, and no more need be said or done about it. But to be convicted of sentimentality—to be detected in the act of exhibiting or infusing, pathos, would be a dilemma as unprecedented, as insupportable to that powerful subborn genius, the grand aim of whose life is never to commit himself; and that man is unquestionably committed—committed beyond the power of redemption, who writes a book about love. Still even to critics—to John Bull, who on the score of non-commitment, constitutes himself the chief of critics, love must be allowed to have the power of developing human character beyond what is possessed by any other passion, sentiment, or feeling.

There is a class of beings so numerous that they form a very important, and in many respects a very useful part of society, who can listen to the most enchanting music, with ears, and thoughts, and memory alive only to the sound of individual notes, imprinting them separately upon the tablet of their minds, in order that they may be carried home, pricked down upon paper, and played upon their own pianos; or who on beholding the finest specimens of ancient painting, or sculpture, immediately—before they have had time to take in the whole view. snatch out the ready sketch-book, and with that energy which men exhibit in associating themselves and their own powers with all that they admire, apply the busy pencil to the outline, in order that they may exhibit to their wondering friends a pattern of the colouring of the ancients, of a Roman sandal, or a Grecian nose. Even by this class of beings, the most impervious to the tender passion, love must be acknowledged to be a *fine study*, because it draws forth the capabilities of the human mind, and brings forward its leading features into a strong light.

The first effect which love produces upon the imagination is that of exalting or ennobling its object, and upon the principle of adaptation, it consequently extends a similar influence over the mind where it exists. Under favorable circumstances, and before it reaches the crisis of its fate, it has a natural tendency to smooth down the asperities of the temper, to soften the manners, and to diffuse a general feeling of cheerfulness and good will even beyond the sphere of its immediate object. But under circumstances of an opposite description, love is remarkable for exhibiting in its train all the evil and frailty which belong to our nature. We are seldom betrayed by any other passion to throw aside entirely that veil, beyond which pride conceals her hidden store of private faults and follies. But love is stronger than pride; and it is besides so absorbing in its nature, that we are apt to forget while devoting ourselves to one object, the figure we are exhibiting to the eyes of the world, the secrets we are disclosing, and the open revelation we are making of our "heart of hearts."

"Love," says a popular and powerful writer, "is a very noble and exalting sentiment in its first germ and principle. We never loved without arraying the object in all the glories of moral as well as physical perfection, and deriving a kind of dignity to ourselves from our capacity of admiring a creature so excellent and dignified; but this lavish and magnificent prodigality of the imagination often leaves the heart a bankrupt. Love in its iron age of disappointment becomes very degraded—it submits to be satisfied with merely external indulgences—a look—a touch of the hand, though occurring by accident—a kind word, though uttered almost unconsciously, suffices for its humble existence. In its first state, it is like man before the fall, inhaling the odours of paradise, and enjoying the communion of the Deity; in the latter, it is like the same being toiling amid the briar and the thistle, barely to maintain a squalid existence, without enjoyment, utility, or loveliness."

Shakespeare has done little towards giving dignity to this passion, though he seems to have been intimately acquainted with its influence upon the human mind. The reason is obvious. Love is a familiar feeling, associating itself with mankind in their daily walk, and entering into the ordinary and domestic scenes of life; it therefore speaks in a language simple and familiar, scarcely admitting of poetical ornament, except in memory or imagination; and as the drama compels all persons to speak for themselves, almost exclusively from the impulse of the moment, they can only speak of love in the colloquial language of the day, which language changing with the tastes and fashions of the world, that of Shakespeare's dramatic characters, when they speak of love is not only offensive to modern ears, but degrading to the sentiment itself—a sentiment which always maintains the most elevated character where the proprieties of life are most scrupulously observed, and the standard of moral feeling is the highest. Yet Shakespeare has left a striking proof that he could reverence this feeling, in the following beautifu. stanza.

"Let me not to the marriage of true minds,
  Admit impediments. Love is not ove
That alters when it alteration finds,
  Or bends with the remover to remove.
Oh! no! it is an ever fixed mark,
  That looks on tempest and is never shaken:
It is the star of every wandering bark,
  Whose worth's unknown although its height be taken.
Love 's not Time's fool, though rosy lips and cheeks
  Within his bending sickle's compass come;
Love alters not with his brief hours and weeks,
  But bears it out even to the edge of doom."

It would be wholly at variance with nature, were the poet to make his characters speak in tropes and metaphors, with classical allusions, and rounded periods, of the passion whose powerful influence was then upon them. No man ever yet could speak or write poetically, for any length of time, of the love he was then experiencing. Thus it is only by occasional touches of feeling that burst upon us in all their genuine intensity, that the depth of the sentiment is discovered. Our language may be forcible and affecting, but it is impossible that it should be elaborate when we are feeling acutely; and there is a certain identity with self; an exclusiveness, giving something like sacredness to the sensations which belong to love, that renders an open, full, unsparing exposure of it repulsive, even in the pages of the poet. It is this sacredness, which, above all other things constitutes the poetry of love. Those who live under its influence possess, so long as that influence lasts, a secret treasure, and often betray by their inadvertent expressions, and by a speaking smile, that they believe themselves to be enjoying an inward source of satisfaction, which their companions know not of. Imagination invests with a peculiar importance and a mysterious charm, all the minutiæ of life, as it is connected with one individual being, and the mind broods over its own private and particular hoard of joy, with a constant watchfulness and jealousy lest the world, that fell spoiler, should break in and pollute, even if it had no inclination or ability to steal.

Under the influence of love, we are suspicious even of ourselves. We shrink from making it the common topic of conversation. It is a feeling which admits of no participation. We would not, if we could, make converts, any farther than our admiration extends; and as there is no sympathy to be obtained by communication, no one at all acquainted with the world, or with the principles of human nature, would ever tell their love, were it not for the power which this passion possesses to overthrow the rational faculties, to blind perception, and to silence experience, holding the wise man captive in the leading strings of second childhood, and drawing him on from one folly to another, until at last he awakes from his dream, and feels, like the unfortunate bellows-mender, that he is wearing an ass's head. No sooner is the spell dissolved, than he turns upon his fellow-creatures the weapons of ridicule, dipped in the venom of his wounded pride; he laughs the more in order that he may appear to make light of his recent bonds, and thus revenges himself for his own mortification.

Those who are wise enough to profit by the experience of others, learn to keep silence on this theme, but it pervades their thoughts and feelings not the less. It is present with them in the morning when they awake, and in the evening when they seek repose. It is cradled in the bosom of the scented rose, and rocked upon the crested waves of the sea. It speaks to them in the lulling wind, and gushes forth in the fountain of the desert. It is clothed in the golden majesty of the noonday sun, and shrouded in the silver radiance of the moon. It is the soul of their world, the life of their sweet and chosen thoughts, the centre of their existence, which gathers in all their wandering hopes and desires. Here they fix them to one point, and make that the altar upon which all the faculties of the soul pour out their perpetual incense.

Burns, who has written of love more frequently, yet with more simplicity of sweetness than any other of our poets, strikingly illustrates the potency of this sentiment in associating itself with our accustomed amusements and avocations. There was no object in nature which he did not find it possible to compare or contrast with the reigning queen of his affections; but the memory of one, above all others, he has immortalized in strains as touching and poetical, as ever flowed from a faithful recollection, a warm imagination, and a too fond heart.

The lines beginning

"Thou lingering star with less'ning ray,"

are, or ought to be, too familiar to every reader of taste and sensibility to need repetition here, as well as those to Highland Mary, equally expressive of ardent and poetical feeling, a feeling which all the rough usages of the world were unable to deprive of its tenderness, and which all the allurements of vice and folly were unable to divest of its purity. In glancing over the pages of this genuine bard of nature, we are every moment struck with the particular pathos with which he speaks of love. Read as an instance the following lines, so unlike anything that we meet with in the productions of the present day.

"Had we never lov'd sae blindly,
Had we never lov'd sae kindly,
Never met or never parted,
We had ne'er been broken-hearted.

"Fare thee weel, thou first and fairest!
Fare the weel, thou best and dearest!
Thine be ilka joy and treasure,
Peace, enjoyment, love, and pleasure!

"Ae fond kiss, and then we sever;
Ae fareweel, alas for ever!
Deep in heart-wrung tears I'll pledge thee,
Warring sighs and groans I'll wage thee."

Or,—

"Not the bee upon the blossom,
In the pride o' sunny noon;
Not the little sporting fairy,
All beneath the summer moon!

Not the poet, in the moment
Fancy lightens on his e'e,
Kens the pleasure, feels the rapture,
That thy presence gies to me."

Or again,—

"Altho' thou maun never be mine,
Altho' even hope is denied;
'Tis sweeter for thee despairing,
Than aught in the world beside."

And where in the records of feeling can we find a more affectionate description of love and poverty contending against each other, than in the following song; the first and last stanza of which I shall quote for the benefit of those who are too wise to think of love, who are too happy to have ever been compelled to take poverty into their calculations, and who are consequently unacquainted with the fact that both together struggling for mastery over the wishes and the will, create a warfare as fearful and desolating as any which the human heart is capable of enduring.

"O Poortith cauld, and restless love,
Ye wreck my peace between ye;
Yet Poortith a' I could forgive
An 'twere na for my Jeanie.
O why should fate sic pleasure have,
Life's dearest band untwining?
O why sae sweet a flower as love,
Depend on fortune's shining?

* * * *

"How blest the humble cotter's fate!
He woos his simple dearie;
The silly bogles, wealth and state,
Can never make them eerie.
O why should fate sic pleasure have,
Life's dearest bands untwining?
Or why sae sweet a flower as love,
Depend on fortune's shining?"

Moore has done much, perhaps more than any other man was capable of doing, to render this hackneyed theme agreeable to modern tastes, by arraying the idol whose divinity the public had begun to question, in every kind of drapery, graceful and gorgeous, and placing it in every possible variety of light and shadow. Yet throughout the many elegant lines which he has devoted to this subject, there are none which occur to my recollection more poetically simple and touching than these.

"A boat sent forth to sail alone
At midnight on the moonless sea,
A harp whose master chord is gone,
A wounded bird that has but one
Unbroken wing to soar upon,
Are like what I am without thee."

In the pages of Shelley we find more freshness, and sometimes more pathos. There is a vividness in his thoughts, and in the character of his mind, which we may well believe to have proved too keen and restless for the mortal frame in which his delicate, sensitive, and ethereal spirit was inclosed—too refined for the common purposes of life, too brilliant for reason, and too dazzling for religion, and too exquisite for repose. The following lines have great poetical beauty.

"Ah! fleeter far than fleetest storm or steed,
Or the death they bear,
The heart which tender thought clothes like a dove
With the wings of care;
In the battle, in the darkness, in the need,
Shall mine cling to thee,
Nor claim one smile for all the comfort, love,
It may bring to thee."

And the following fragment, addressed to love itself, with the exception of the first line, which is in extremely bad taste, is perhaps without its equal in poetry of this description.

"Thou art the wine whose drunkenness is all
We can desire, O Love! and happy souls,
Ere from thy vine the leaves of autumn fall,

"Catch thee and feed from their o'erflowing bowls
Thousands who thirst for thy ambrosial dew;—
Thou art the radiance which where ocean rolls

"Investest it; and when the heavens are blue
Thou fillest them; and when the earth is fair
The shadows of thy moving wings imbue

"Its deserts, and its mountains, till they wear
Beauty like some bright robe;—thou ever soarest
Among the towers of men, and as soft air

"In spring, which moves the unawakened forest,
Clothing with leaves its branches bare and bleak,
Thou floatest among men; and aye implorest

"That which from thee they should implore:—the weak
Alone kneel to thee, offering up the hearts
The strong have broken—yet where shall any seek

"A garment whom thou clothest not?"

From love, as a passion, it is truly delightful to turn to the consideration of love in its more social and domestic character; and here again we find the same poet offering to his wife the noblest tribute of affection, in language as tender as it is elevated and pure.

"So now, my summer task is ended, Mary,
And I return to thee, mine own heart's home;
As to his queen some victor knight of faery,
Earning bright spoils for his enchanted dome;
Nor thou disdain that ere my fame become
A star among the stars of mortal might,
If it indeed may change its natal gloom,
Its doubtful promise, thus I would unite
With thy beloved name, thou child of love and light.

'The toil which stole from thee so many an hour
Is ended, and the fruit is at thy feet!
No longer where the woods to frame a bower
With interlaced branches mix and meet,
Or where with sound like many voices sweet
Waterfalls leap among wild islands green
Which formed for my lone boat a lone retreat
Of moss-grown trees and weeds, shall I be seen;
But beside thee, where still my heart has ever been."

It is worthy of remark, that these lines form the introduction to a work in which the poet concentrated all the powers of his genius. The merits of this work have nothing to do with the fact, that it was the richest offering he had to lay upon the shrine of affection, and that that offering was dedicated to his wife.

The late amiable Bishop of Calcutta, a less exceptionable poet, and a less eccentric genius, has left us a beautiful and affecting tribute to affection, under the same pure and sacred form; and the woman who could inspire these lines ought to have been satisfied for the rest of her life, never to receive the incense of less hallowed praise.

"If thou wert by my side, my love!
How fast would evening fail
In green Bengala's palmy grove,
Listening the nightingale!

"If thou, my love! wert by my side,
My babies at my knee,
How gaily would our pinnace glide
O'er Gunga's mimic sea!

"I miss thee at the dawning ray
When on our deck reclined,
In careless ease my limbs I lay,
And woo the cooler wind.

"I miss thee when by Gunga's stream
My twilight steps I guide,
But most beneath the moon's pale beam
I miss thee from my side.

"I spread my books, my pencil try,
The lingering noon to cheer,
But miss thy kind approving eye,
Thy meek attentive ear.

"But when of morn and eve, the star
Beholds me on my knee,
I feel, though thou art distant far,
Thy prayers ascend for me.

Then on! then on! where duty leads,
My course be onward still,
O'er broad Hindostan's sultry meads,
O'er bleak Almorah's hill.

"That course, nor Delhi's kingly gates,
Nor wild Malvah detain,
For sweet the bliss us both awaits
On yonder western main!

Thy towers, Bombay, gleam bright, they say,
Across the dark blue sea,
But ne'er were hearts so light and gay,
As then shall meet in thee!"

If the language of a pure and dignified attachment, proved by long trial, refined by suffering, clothed in humility, and wholly divested of weakness or selfishness, was ever wrung out by the power of affliction from the inmost recesses of an elevated and virtuous mind, it is in the words of Mrs. Hutchinson, where she speaks of the love of her lamented husband.

"There is only this to be recorded, that never was there a passion more ardent and lesse idolatrous; he loved her better than his life, with inexpressible tendernesse and kindnesse, had a most high obliging esteeme of her, yet still considered honour, religion, and duty above her, nor ever suffered the intrusion of such a dotage as should blind him from marking her imperfections: these he looked upon with an indulgent eie, which did not abate his love and esteeme of her, while it augmented his care to blot out all those spotts which might make her appeare lesse worthy of that respect he payed her; and thus indeed he soon made her more equall to him than he found her; for she was a very faithful mirror, reflecting truly, though but dimly, his own glories upon him, so long as he was present; but she that was nothing before his inspection gave her a faire figure, when he was removed, was only filled with a darke mist, and never could again take in any delightful object, nor return any shining representation. The greatest excellencie she had was the power of apprehending, and the virtue of loving his: soe as his shadow she waited on him every where, till he was taken into that region of light, which admitts of none, and then she vanished into nothing. 'Twas not her face that he loved, her honour and her virtue were his mistresses, and these (like Pigmalion's) images of his own making, for he polished and gave form to what he found with all the roughnesse of the quarrie about it; but meeting with a compliante subject for his own wise government, he found as much satisfaction as he gave, and never had occasion to number his marriage among his infelicities."

This beautiful illustration of love combines all that is essential to the most ardent, as well as the most ennobling sentiment, and wants nothing but metre to entitle it to a high place in the scale of poetical merit.

There remains one important observation to be made on the subject of love, that it marks the progress of national civilization, and the improvement or the deterioration of public morals. Love, above all other passions, is capable of producing the greatest happiness, or the greatest misery; of being the most refined, or the most degraded. It may be associated with the highest virtue, or made the companion of the lowest vice. Where a nation or a community is the most licentious, love is the least respected. Where deference is paid to moral laws, and religious duties, love is regarded as the bond of domestic union, the charm which diffuses a secret, but holy influence over our domestic enjoyments. In patriarchal times, when men were dispersed over the face of the earth in separate families or tribes, love dwelt among them like a patient handmaid, ministering to their private comfort, but wholly uninfluential in directing their important movements. In the days of chivalry, when men, following the standard of false glory, maintained their possessions by force of arms, sacrificed ease, honesty, or life, to the laws of honour, and the adventures of knight-errantry, love was worshipped as a goddess, whose inspiration endowed her votaries with superhuman power, and whose protection was a shield of adamant. And thus through the different changes of national character and customs, love adopts itself to all, luxuriating in the indulgence of artificial life, or sharing the drudgery of corporeal toil.

Even in individuals, it is not going too far to say, that low notions of the nature and attributes of love, bespeak a vitiated mind, and show, like the "trail of the serpent," in the garden of Eden, that the principle of evil has been there. There is in its elevated nature, a character of constancy, truth, and dignity, which constitutes the essence of its being, and no pure eye can behold it robbed of these, without sorrow and indignation.

It is this faculty of adaptation to all circumstances and states of being, which renders love so entirely subservient to the purposes of the poet; because it takes the tone of the times, as well as that of individual character, and participating in good or evil, calls forth these opposing principles in all their power.

Besides the love here spoken of, poetry abounds in descriptions of that which assumes the sober garb of friendship, and which is perhaps of all others the most substantial support to the human mind, through the difficulties and temptations necessarily encountered in the journey of life. A friend well chosen is the greatest treasure we can possess. We have in such a friend the addition of another mind, whose strength supplies our weakness, and whose virtues render us ambitious of the same. We see frequent instances that men alone in the world—unknown, and unvalued, will commit errors, we might say vices, from which the well-timed warning of a friend would have restrained them, and stain their character with follies, for which, if a friend had blushed, they too would have been ashamed. All the endearing associations which enhance our pleasures, or console us under affliction, are centred in the name of friend. When the stroke of adversity falls upon us, the sympathy of a true friend takes away half its heaviness. When the world misunderstands our meaning, and attributes bad motives to what are only ill-judged actions, we think (with what satisfaction those who have experienced the feeling alone can tell) that there is one who knows us better. When good fortune comes unexpectedly upon us, in a tide too sudden and too full for enjoyment, we hasten to our friend who shares the overplus and leaves us happy. When doubtfully we tread the dangerous path of life, misdirected by our passions, and bewildered by our fears, we look for the hand of friendship to point out the safe footing, from whence we shall bless our guide. When wounded, slighted, and cast back into the distance, by those whose fickle favor we had sought to win, we exclaim in the midst of our disappointments, "There is one who loves me still!" And when wearied with the warfare of the world, and "sick of its harsh sounds, and sights," we return to the communion of friendship, as we rest after a laborious journey, in a safe sweet garden of refreshment and peace. There is unquestionably much to be done in the way of cultivating this garden, and maintaining our right to possess it; but it repays us for the price, and when we have exercised forbearance, and interchanged kind offices, and spoken, and borne to hear, the truth, and been faithful, and gentle, and sincere, we find a recompense in our own bosoms, as well as in the affections of our friend.

There are yet other modifications of [illegible]e such as that which constitutes the ch[illegible] of domestic union—the love of brothers and sisters; and lastly, and most to be revered as the foundation of family concord and social happiness, we might almost say of moral feeling, the love which subsists between parents and children, uniting on one hand the tenderest impressions we have received with the first lessons we have learned; on the other, the warmest affection, with the weightiest responsibility. The weakness and the waywardness of a child watched over by parental love, directed by parental care, and reclaimed by parental authority, are so frequently alluded to in the Scriptures, when describing the condition of man in reference to his Maker, and in themselves harmonize so entirely with that relation, that we use the name of "*Heavenly Father*," not only in obedience to scriptural authority, but because we comprehend in these holy words, the highest object of our love, our gratitude, and our veneration.

We cannot better conclude this chapter than with the following appropriate lines by Southey.

'They sin who tell us love can die.
With life all other passions fly,
All others are but vanity.
In heaven ambition cannot dwell,
Nor avarice in the depths of hell.
Earthly these passions, as of earth,
They perish where they have their birth.
But love is indestructible;
Its holy flame for ever burneth,
From heaven it came, to heaven returneth;
Too oft on earth a troubled guest,
At times deceived, at times oppressed,
It here is tried and purified,
And hath in heaven its perfect rest;
It soweth here with toil and care,
But the harvest time of love is there.
Oh! when a mother meets on high
The babes she lost in infancy,
Hath she not then, for pains and fears,
The day of wo, the anxious night,
From all her sorrows, all her tears,
An over-payment of delight!"

THE POETRY OF GRIEF.

The poetry of grief is exhibited under so great a variety of forms, all capable of so wide a difference in character and degree, that it will be necessary to speak of the sentiment of grief, first, under that mild and softened aspect which assumes the name of sadness or melancholy, and then as a gloomy passion, absorbing every faculty of the soul.

Of all the distinctive characters assumed by grief, from simple sadness to wild despair, melancholy is the most poetical, because while it operates as a stimulant to the imagination, its influence is so gentle as to leave all the other intellectual powers at full liberty to exercise their particular functions. Burton speaks of melancholy as engendering strange conceits—as quickening the perceptions, and expanding the faculties of the mind; and Lord Byron, scarcely less intimate than this quaint old writer with the different mental maladies to which our nature is liable, describes the "glance of melancholy" as "a fearful gift."

"What is it but the telescope of truth
Which strips the distance of its phantasies,
And brings life near in utter nåkedness,
Making the cold reality too real?"

When melancholy takes possession of the soul, we lose as it were the perspective of our mental vision. We forget the relative proportions of things, and mistaking the small for the great, or the distant for the near, magnify their importance, examine their particular parts, and fill our imaginations with their nature and essence. This is in fact "making the cold reality too real;" for though there is much of truth in the vivid perceptions ef melancholy, it is truth misplaced; truth with which the wise man has little to do, but which ministers powerfully to the wretchedness of the "mind diseased."

Being in our nature as liable to pain as we are susceptible of pleasure; and by the neglect of our privileges, and abuse of our faculties, subjected to the experience of even greater suffering than enjoyment; it necessarily follows, that those views of the condition of man which are tinctured with the sombre hues of melancholy, should be regarded as the most natural as well as the most interesting. There is little poetry in mirth, or even in perfect happiness, except as it is contrasted with misery; and thus all attempts to describe the perfection of heavenly beatitude fail to interest our feelings. The joys of heaven are, according to the writers who have ventured upon these descriptions, chiefly made up of luxuries which in this world money alone can purchase, and money is connected in our ideas with toil and strife, with envy, and jealousy, and never-ending vexation; or they consist of fountains always pure, flowers that never fade, and skies which no cloud has ever obscured—things which we find it difficult to conceive: or of perpetual praises sung by an innumerable host of saints—an employment which we are not yet able to separate from ideas of monotony and weariness. Far more touching and more descriptive of that state to which the experienced soul learns to aspire as to its greatest bliss, are those descriptions and allusions abounding in the Holy Scriptures, and particularly in the Book of Revelations, where a great multitude which no man could number, are seen standing around the throne arrayed in white robes, and with palms in their hands: and when the question is asked, who are these, and whence came they? it is answered, "these are they which came out of great tribulation—they shall hunger no more, neither thirst any more; neither shall the sun light on them, nor any heat. For the Lamb which is in the midst of the throne shall feed them, and shall lead them unto living fountains of waters: and God shall wipe away all tears from their eyes." Here the allusion to the sufferings and wants of our moral nature is continued throughout, forming that natural and necessary contrast with perfect happiness, which is the very essence of poetry. Such expressions as these come home to the heart that has known tribulation, and therefore can conceive the blessedness of eternal repose—which has known the anguish of mortal sorrow, and therefore can appreciate the healing of the heavenly Comforter.

Everything that deeply interests our feelings has some connexion with our own condition, or some accordance with our own tastes. All who experience a healthy state of mind have a keen relish for happiness; but all are not so free from envy or selfishness as fully to enjoy the happiness of others; and that which falls to our own share is so absorbing in its nature, that we feel little inclination to pour it forth in poetical descriptions, at least while its influence lasts; and when it is over, it can only be alluded to with a certain degree of sadness and regret. It has been justly observed, that it requires a more amiable temper of mind to laugh with those who laugh, than to weep with those who weep; and experience must have taught all who have made the experiment that it is less difficult to excite interest by detailing our sorrows, than our joys. Our friends weep *with* us, but *for* themselves; and perhaps at the bottom of their hearts are not grieved to find that they do not suffer alone. But when we fly to them, full of our own individual hopes and joys, they often unconsciously throw some damp upon our ecstatic emotions, or coldly turn away, deeming us selfish, and inconsiderate to have wholly forgotten their situation in the enjoyment of our own.

Lord Byron, the most melancholy of all our poets found a home in every heart. The love-lorn maiden fed upon his pages, well pleased to read expressions which described a passion hopeless and irremediable as her own; the disappointed and the dissolute discovered there the language of a sympathy, which they sought in vain of the giddy world around them; but above all, the misanthrope curled his contemptous lip, and gloried in having found a high and titled bard who scorned mankind as he did. It would be difficult to point out the productions of any light and joyous poet, which have been equally popular and equally penetrating to the soul of the reader. Some there are which have been great favourites with the public; but such for the most part have been recommended by the force of their satire, and the poignancy of their jests, rather than for the pure stream of rational happiness flowing through their strains.

It is scarcely necessary to repeat, that poetry, in order to meet with a welcome in the world, must address itself to the feelings of mankind as they are, not as they should be. It may be, and unquestionably has been, the means of raising in the soul a high tone of moral feeling, of purifying what is gross, and subduing what is harsh; but this can only be effected by establishing a chain of connexion between our low wants and wishes, and that which is high, and pure, and holy. Happiness therefore—happiness without alloy, can never be a suitable theme for the muse until we enter upon a state of existence where it shall more frequently be our experience. But melancholy, towards which all our feelings have some tendency, either immediate or remote, will add a charm to the language of poetry so long as it is understood and felt by all. Descriptions of life without its cares and sorrows, would appear to us little less wearisome and unnatural than landscapes without shadow; but those which are varied by the sombre colouring borrowed by experience from the hand of grief, exhibit the principles of harmony, and the essential characteristics of truth.

It has been wisely ordered by the Author of our being, that we should be stimulated to action by certain wishes and wants arising within ourselves. Had man, constituted as he now is, been placed in a situation of perfect enjoyment, it must necessarily have been one of supineness and sloth, in which his mental powers would have experienced no exercise, and consequently no improvement. Thus when we look with regret upon the daily wants of mankind, and feel disposed to regard them as a defect in his nature, or an error in his morals, we do not reflect that they are parts of a powerful machine, so constructed and designed as to awaken and stimulate man's highest capabilities, yet so liable to derangement, misapplication, and abuse, as to be frequently converted by his ignorance, or want of care, into the engine of his own destruction. It was the want of some medium of communication which first led to the use of certain sounds as signs of our ideas, and it was the same want which produced such an arangement of these sounds as to constitute a copious language; it was the want of some sweet influence to soothe the asperities of pain, and labour, and fatigue, which prompted the cultivation of music; it was the want of some visible and substantial personification of their own ideas of beauty and grandeur, which operated upon the genius of the first artists, and produced those massive but sublime attempts at sculpture which arose among the Egyptians, and were afterwards improved upon by the more refined inhabitants of ancient Greece; and it was the want of a higher tone of language, suited to the most elevated conceptions of the human mind, which first diffused the refreshing stream of poetry over the world, gave the charm of melody to the hymns of Israel's minstrel king, inspired the father of ancient verse with those heroic strains which still delight the world, found a language and a voice for the impassioned soul of Sappho, fired the genius of Euripides, and which still continues, though often unknown and unacknowledged, to tune to harmony the poet's secret thoughts, operating upon the springs of sympathy and love, like the airs that touch unseen the chords of the Æolian harp.

But above all, it is under the influence of sorrow that this want is felt. Joy is sufficient of itself; the soul receives it, and is satisfied. But sorrow is burdensome, and the soul would gladly throw it off; and because it cannot give what no one is willing to receive, would cast it upon the winds, or diffuse it through creation's space. The mind that is under the influence of melancholy, knows no rest. It is wearied with an incessant craving for something beyond itself. It seeks for sympathy, but never finds enough. It is dissatisfied with present things, and because the beings around it are too gross or too familiar to offer that refined communion for which it ever pines, it pours forth in poetic strains the transcript of its own sorrows, trusting that the world contains other sufferers at least half as wretched as itself, who will read, with a pity too distant to offend, descriptions of a fate more lamentable than their own.

There needs no greater proof that melancholy is poetical, than the effect it produces upon the imagination, converting everything into its own bitter food. Under the influence of melancholy, the voice of friendship often sounds reproachful and always unfeeling when it speaks the truth; the looks of gladness worn by others, are proofs of their want of consideration for ourselves; acts of kindness are instances of pity, and pity, under such circumstances, always appears accompanied with contempt. Love is ap to attack those who are victims of melancholy, but it is always in some forbidden shape; and religion, which is, or ought to be, the sovereign balm for all mental maladies, appears to them like a sacred inclosure drawn around a chosen few, from which they are eternally shut out. If they read the Bible, they turn to the lamentations of Jeremiah, Ecclesiastes, or the Book of Job; and seated on a cushion of ease, in the full enjoyment of health, and wealth, and luxury of every kind, they believe themselves to be as severely tried, as miserable, and perhaps as patient, as the heroic sufferer. If they go forth into the fields, the flowers either look wan and sickly, or mock them with their gorgeous hues; the tree spread around a gloomy shade; the streams murmur, as everything on earth has a right to do; the birds and the insects that flutter in the sunshine, are poor deluded victims of mortality, sporting away their short-lived joy; the clouds which vary the aspect of the landscape, and the calm blue heavens, are emblematical of the "palpable obscure" in which their own fate is involved; and if the sun shines forth in his glory, it is to remind them that no sun will ever more rise to disperse the darkness of their souls. Instead of indulging in those wide and liberal views which embrace the perfection and beauty of the universe, they fix their attention upon objects single and minute, choosing out such as may most easily be connected with gloomy associations. In the gorgeous hues of the autumnal foliage, the eye of melancholy can distinguish nothing but the faded leaves just separated from the bough, and flickering downwards on the reckless wind, with those dizzy and convulsive movements which are wont to precede an irrevocable fall; from amongst the cheerful songsters of the grove, it singles out the bird with wounded wing; it perceives the rifled nest, and knows by the scattered plumage that the spoiler has been there; throughout the flowery wilderness of the fields, or the gorgeous bloom of the cultivated garden, it sees only the blighted blossom, the broken stem, or the fatal ravages of the canker-worm; in the heavens, it beholds only the setting sun, the waning moon, or the feeble star that glitters in a world of gloom; in the animal kingdom, it selects those species which prey upon each other, and turns from the sportive gambols of the lamb, to the kite that hovers over the feathery brood, or the tiger and the cat that torture ere they devour their victims; in the city, it is sensible only of poverty, disease, and accumulated crime; and in the social circle, it sees only the lip of scorn, the pale cheek, or the averted eye. Over the calendar of births, marriages, and deaths, the melancholy hold themselves peculiarly privileged to mourn, because, in the first instance, another sentient and responsible being is added to the dark catalogue of those who come into the world to sin and suffer; in the second, an additional proof is about to be exhibited before the world of the fallacy of human hopes, and the disappointment which inevitably attends our pursuit of earthly happiness; and the third is an awful evidence of that fatal doom to which we are all hastening. In short, there is nothing natural or familiar, sweet or soothing, good or great, which does not set the gloomy and morbid imagination afloat upon "a sea of troubles:" and it is this exuberance of fancy, this illimitable range of thought, this fertility of the mind in producing objects of mournful associations, which constitutes the poetry of melancholy.

"I have of late," says Hamlet, "(but wherefore I know not,) lost all my mirth, forgone all custom of exercises: and, indeed, it goes so heavily with my disposition, that this goodly frame, the earth, seems to me a sterile promontory; this most excellent canopy, the air, look you, this brave o'erhanging firmament, this majestical roof, fretted with golden fire, why, it appears no other thing to me, than a foul and pestilent congregation of vapours. What a piece of work is man! How noble in reason! how infinite in faculties! in form, and moving, how express, and admirable! in action, how like an angel! in apprehension, how like a god! The beauty of the world, the paragon of animals! and yet to me, what is this quintessence of dust? Man delights not me—nor woman neither."

We now come to the consideration of grief as a passion, under which character there is one peculiarity to be remarked, tending powerfully to invest it with the poetical charm it unquestionably possesses—it is the peculiar force and vividness of some of our perceptions while the mind is under the immediate influence of grief. It is true we cannot reason, nor calculate, nor detect the weakness of sophistry, because the mind in this state is incapable of action. The only faculty awakened in it, is that of receiving impressions; a power considerably heightened and increased by the total suspension of its active operations. But it is to trifles alone that this power is applied—to things of no importance, and such as hold no relative connexion with the cause of grief. Thus the criminal at the bar, though wholly incapacitated for taking into consideration the nature of the laws by which he is tried, looks round upon the judge, the witnesses, and the whole court; and with an acuteness and vividness of perception which seem actually to be the means of forcing every unwelcome object upon his sight, he beholds the breathless and expectant multitude around him, from amongst whom he is able to distinguish, and single out particular faces, which, if he is happy enough to escape the dreaded doom, will remain impressed upon his memory till his latest day. The messenger who brings us evil tidings, is, for any thought or interest that we bestow upon him individually, a mere intelligence, a voice, a breath of air; and yet we find afterwards that we have involuntary noted down in characters never to be obliterated, his countenance, his dress, his manner, and the tones in which his errand was delivered. We watch by the bedside of the dying, our very souls absorbed by the near prospect of that fearful dissolution which is about to deprive us of a child, a parent, a friend or a brother, unconscious that our thoughts have wandered for one moment from what was most important or impressive in that awful scene; yet in after life, even when the heavy wheels of time have rolled over us, laden with other accidents and other griefs, we are able to recall, with a distinctness almost incredible to those who have never known it, the particular aspect of that sick chamber—the folded curtains—the pillow without rest—the wild delirious wanderings—the countenance of the nurse—the voice of the physician—and all the other minutiæ of that mournful scene.

It is with the tide of feeling as with a swollen river. The violent and overwhelming force of the torrent bears along with it innumerable fragments from the desolated shore. While the stream rushes on, swollen and tumultuous, these fragments are scarcely distinguishable amongst the whirlpools, and rapids, and roaring falls; but when it subsides and again glides calmly within its natural boundaries, they rise to the surface and afford clear and palpable evidence of the tremendous strength and violence of the overwhelming flood.

Lord Byron has described with his wonted power and pathos this capability of the mind, when under the influence of grief, in that most affecting (I might almost say most beautiful) of his poems "The Dream." In the melancholy scene so forcibly exhibiting the deep but silent anguish of plighting the hand without the heart, how naturally do the thoughts of the gloomy being he has chosen to represent, rush back to the season of his first—his only love, and settle upon the last agonizing moment of separation, which life has now no power to equal by any future suffering. A minor poet, or a less experienced reasoner, would have centred all the recollections of the heart-stricken bridegroom in the person of the lady herself; but Lord Byron, who could at his own pleasure make use of expressions as delicate as poetical—as poetical as true, colouring the whole scene with those ethereal tints which belong to the hightest genius, merely alludes to the sacred object of such deep, and fervent, and forbiding thoughts as a "*destiny*;" while he gives us the minor parts of the picture, clear, and distinct as they would be in the memory of one who could feel and suffer like himself.

——————"He could see
Not that which was, but that which should have been
But the remembered chambers and the place,
The day, the hour, the sunshine, and the shade,—
All things pertaining to that place and hour,
And her who was his destiny, came back
And thrust themselves between him and the light.
What business had they there at such an hour?"

We might add to what has already been said of grief, the pleasure which it is supposed to afford in recollection; a subject much sung and celebrated by the poets, bu one to which I confess myself too ignorant, or too obtuse to be able to do justice. Still we all know there are those who can linger over the grave recently closed over their heart's treasure, who love to revisit scenes of former suffering, and dwell in lengthened detail upon the sorrows they have endured; and I am inclined to believe that such are the individuals best qualified to describe the poetry of grief; rather than those who shrink from all retrospection of their own experience, and hurry on through life to find in the future what has failed them in the past.

We turn from this subject to the consideration of grief under that peculiar character which appears to claim more than its due share of interest, and which by the world is called *first grief.*

The first grief generally arises from disappointment in love, death of parents, change of fortune, or neglect of friends; all sufficient causes of sorrow, yet by no means so powerful or durable in their effects, as the accumulated cares, crosses, and afflictions, which beset us in after life. This grief is comparatively without association, and therefore, though touching and pathetic in the extreme, because it falls upon the young, and often upon the beautiful, cannot in the experience of the mourner be comparable to those in which are combined the accumulated sufferings that arise from memory, and anticipation—the recollection of happiness that never can return—the fear of future evil yet more intolerable than the present.

The first grief is unquestionably a fertile subject for the poet, because it supplies all the interest arising from strong contrast; as a sudden blight falling upon the luxurious vegetation of a productive soil, affords more matter for affecting and melancholy description, than the leafless desert stretched out in its perpetual sterility beneath a burning sun.

The first grief comes to the young heart like the rough wind to the blossom—like the early frost to the full blown flower—like the gathering vapours to the smiling sun—like the dark cloud to the silver moon—like the storm to the summer sea—like the sudden influence of all those fatal accidents which deface the lovely and verdant aspect of nature; not like that dull monotony of constant care which experience proves to be far more intolerable, but which the poet rejects for its very weariness. The tears which dim the eye of youthful beauty are wholesome, natural, and refreshing, compared with those which wear away the waning sight. When youthful beauty weeps, what heart so callous as not to be touched with pity? What benevolence so limited as not to extend to the fair sufferer the consolation of love, and the comfort of protection? There is something in our very nature which makes us yearn with peculiar tenderness over those who mourn for their first grief. They have never troubled us with their complaints before. We have been wont to see them light and joyous, bounding forth upon their mortal race; but now their speed is checked, the wished for goal has vanished from their sight, the stimulus is withdrawn, and unable either to pause, or to retrace their rapid way, they begin to feel that the long dull path before them must be trod by many a weary step. We have learned this truth ourselves, we know that all who live must learn it, and yet to spare those who are untutored in life's harsh discipline, though but for another year—a day—an hour of innocent enjoyment, we would almost be willing to bear a fresh stroke of the axe to which we have already become accustomed—the loss of another branch—the blight of another bough.

It is this tenderness, felt and acknowledged by all, which gives the charm of ideal loveliness to the tears of the young mourner, which heightens the interests of those afflictions that are but a faint type of what life has yet in store, and which in fact constitutes the poetry of the first grief.

Another and perhaps the most legitimate cause of grief is death; a calamity common to all, but not felt the less for being alike incident to the young, and the old; the good, and the evil; the rich, and the poor; the noble and the abject. Under all other afflictions we may school ourselves into the belief that some hope of remedy or alleviation yet remains; but our reflections upon this fatal catastrophe are uniformly stamped with that word of awful and irrevocable import—*never.** Never more shall we listen to the voice whose familiar tones were like the

* Madame de Stael has remarked upon the words *no more*, that both in sound and sense they are more descriptive of melancholy meaning than any other in our language. If not before these, at least second in the scale, I would place the single word *alone*, and next to this *never*. I have heard of a poor maniac, who spent her life in singing or chanting this word three times repeated "*never—never—never*," in a mournful cadence composed of six different notes of music; and it might afford matter of interesting speculation to the poet, to ask what was the nature of her grief, that could *never* die—of her loss that could *never* be restored?

memory of sweet music heard in childhood —never shall the beaming eye whose language was better understood than words, light up the secrets of our souls again—never shall the parental hand be laid upon our own with the earnestness of experience, and the warmth of love—never shall the innocent prattle of those cherub lips now sealed in death awaken us from our morning slumbers—never shall the counsel of that long tried friend guide us again through the mazy paths of life. We might have lived and perhaps we have, without their actual presence; seas might have rolled between us; and wide countries separated their home and ours: but to believe in their existence was enough—to think that they looked upon the same world with ourselves —that the same sun rose to them and to us —that we gazed upon the same moon—and that the same wind which breathed its spiritual intelligence into our ears, might in its wild and lawless wanderings, have sighed around their distant dwelling. But above all, that the time might come when we should yet meet to recognize the same features, though changed by time—the same voice though altered in its language—and the same love, though long estranged, yet never totally extinguished. We must now satisfy ourselves that this can *never* be; and why? not from any cause which the power and ingenuity of man can remedy, or the casuality of after events avert; but simply because the vital principle which never can be revived, is extinct, the functions of humanity are destroyed, and the friend of our bosom is no more.

It is true that religion points to the ethereal essence existing in a happier sphere, directs the attention of the mourner to the undying soul, and urges on his hope to an eternal union; but we have earthly feelings too frequently usurping the place where religion ought to reign; and love that is "strong as death," turns away from the Heavenly Comforter, and will not be consoled. Love holds a faithful record of the past, from which half the interest, and half the endearment must now be struck out, rendering the future barren, waste, and void. Love keeps an inventory of its secret treasures, where it notes down things of which the higher faculties of the soul take no cognizance—the smiles—the tones of mutual happiness—the glowing cheek—the sunny hair—the gentle hand—the well known step—and all that fills up and makes perfect the evidence of long cherished affection; exchanged for what? For the motionless and marble stillness of death, and the cold, unnatural gloom of that deep sepulchre which conceals what even love itself has become willing to resign—for the sad return to the desolate home—the silent chamber—the absent voice—the window without its light—the familiar name unspoken—the relics unclaimed—the harp untouched—the task unfinished—the blank at the table unfilled up—the garden walks untrodden—the flowers untended—the favourite books closed up as with a seal—in short, the total rending away of that sweet chord, without which, the once harmonious strains of social intercourse are musical no more.

The effect produced upon the mind by the contemplation of death, is of a character peculiarly refined and gentle. We necessarily forgive the dead, even though they may have been our enemies: and if our friends we remember their virtues alone. They have lost the power to offend again, and therefore their faults are forgotten. It is true, there are associations with the bodily part of death which scarcely come under the denomination of refined, but from these our nature shrinks; even the common nurse performs her last sad office in silence, and delicacy shrouds in everlasting oblivion the mortal remains of the deceased. It is the task of the poet to record their noble actions —their benevolence—their patient suffering —their magnanimity—their self-denial; and while he performs this sacred duty, his bosom burns with enthusiasm to imitate the virtues he extols.

The loss of fortune is another cause of grief, not less severely felt for being of common occurrence. Those who have never tasted the real bitterness of poverty, tell us in the language of philosophy, that the loss of fortune is a very insufficient cause for the grief of a wise man; that our nature is not degraded when our bodies are clad in homely garments; and that the friends whose esteem is worthy of our regard, will follow us as willingly to the clay cottage, as to the "courts of kings." This might be all very true, did reason alone govern the world; but we have another law—the law of feeling, more potent in its influence upon the affairs of mankind; and in this law the poet is often much better instructed than the philosopher. The poet knows that to attempt to remove the pressure of the calamities of life, by reasoning, however plausibly, upon their transient or trifling nature, is not, in effect, to speak the language of common sense; because it does not adapt itself to the feelings of those to whom it is addressed, so as to render it available or even intelligible. As well might we tell the victim of raging fever, that it is absurd to thirst again, because he has but lately moistened his lips, as endeavour to persuade him who suffers from the loss of worldly wealth, to be comforted, because it is vain to grieve. The poet's sphere being one of feeling, he has within himself so quick and clear an apprehension of all the sources of human pain or pleasure that he sees and understands at once why the change of fortune, the deprivation of accustomed privileges and enjoyments, and the gradual sinking to a lower rank in social life, should occasion the deepest sorrow and regret. Were reason the sole regulator of our passions and propensities, we should never grieve; because we are taught by the experience of every day, that good may arise out of what we have blindly called evil; and because we are assured upon the highest evidence, that our worldly affairs even when darkest and most perplexed, are under the government of a gracious and unerring Providence: but the experience of every day teaches us also, that these important truths have not their proper weight in human calculations. Who, for instance, can meet with equanimity the clamorous attacks of suspicious creditors, whose claims he knows he is unable to supply? Who can bear the mute appeals of those who have been dependent upon his bounty and protection, when he has no longer the power to offer either—the looks estranged of former friends; for friendship in the world is not what it is fabled to be in books, but will sometimes deviate from the rule of Scripture, by showing respect unto the persons of men—the reproaches, covert and open, which always fall upon those whose success has not been equal to their endeavours; as if the affairs of this life were so regulated, that to succeed in obtaining money were the highest proof of merit—the gradual declension (owing to the taking away of props on every side when most needed) into a lower grade of society, where intellectual refinement is little valued, and difficult to be maintained—the signs of envious triumph exhibited by those who in our better days would have been our enemies if they had dared. Who can endure all these, and an endless variety of other causes of suffering incident to fallen fortune, and yet so fortify his soul by sage reasoning that it shall feel no anguish? No; the poet knows what is in nature and in man; and therefore he finds a fruitful theme of never-failing interest in the fountain of his own feelings, which, through the medium of poetic language, is so conducted, as to mix, and blend, and harmonize with those of others.

A well known cause of grief, and one familiar to every poetic mind, is loneliness. In one sense it may be said that the poet is never alone; but let us ask how it is that he learns to make

—"him friends of mountains; with the stars,
And the quick spirits of the universe
To hold his dialogues ——?"

Perhaps there never was a poet who had not first sought to find in his own species that real sympathy, for which he becomes afterwards satisfied to substitute the ideal. It is impossible but that the elevated and finely constituted mind should often find itself alone, and if morbid and too sensitive, as such minds generally are, it must be always so in the common haunts of human kind. The poet who can be satisfied with nothing less than entire communion and sympathy of soul, is alone in the crowded city, where, amidst the rush of thousands of busy feet not one is found to pause because he is near—alone in the garden's flowery paths, where there is no eye to look for beauty and delight in the same objects with his—alone beneath the starry canopy of heaven, where none will join his midnight rambles---alone at the altar, where his peculiar faith is liable to be contemned---alone in the season of grief---alone in the hour of joy---alone in all those ecstatic emotions which give the power of life and action to the highest faculties of our nature, raising it above the common level of ordinary existence—alone in those moments of weakness and dependence, when the soul is hungering after that intellectual sustenance which never yet was found in the selfish or sordid avocations of life, pining for the consolations of a higher sympathy than the world affords, and ready to lean upon the veriest reed for its support. To feel all this without the power either of communicating or receiving what is most intimately connected with the soul, is true loneliness; and therefore the poet, escaping from the contact of uncongenial minds, flies to his own peculiar home in the bosom of nature, where, if the intercourse he meets with be ideal, it is sufficient to satisfy a mind etherealized like his; especially as it differs from that of the world, in being such as will neither mock nor mar the harmony of his own breast. But this intercourse is not in reality ideal. The Author of our being has so constructed the world, animate and inanimate, that there are laws of sympathy and association unmarked by the obtuse perceptions of sensual beings, which connect the different, and to us apparently incongruous parts of the universe, so as to form an entire and perfect whole.

We read of a solitary prisoner immured within the bare walls of a dungeon, who tamed a spider, and even loved it; because the principle of love was strong within him, and he had no other object for his affections. Love is but one of the many stimulants that urge us on to seek through the world for objects on which these affections can be lavished, and situations in which they may be indulged; and if deprived of the power of gratifying our tastes and wishes by change of scene or circumstance, imagination will do her utmost to transform what is repulsive in itself, into an object of tenderness, interest or admiration: for such are the bounds which connect our intellectual nature with the material world, that the mind must lay hold of something to grapple with, appropriate, or destroy. It cannot exist alone and separate from association.

As it is the nature of all grievances to awaken suggestions of their own remedy, so the poet, after deeply experiencing the grief arising from loneliness, learns to satisfy his soul in its pining after a spiritual communion with all that is pure, and lovely, and sublime, by an ideal converse with nature. Having found the objects of his search but seldom, or where they existed, but faintly revealed amongst the children of men, he returns with fresh ardour, and renewed desire to the solitude of the sequestered valley, the heights of the trackless mountain, or the echoing shores of the ever restless sea; not because he actually believes, what his muse sometimes fantastically describes, that "myriads of happy spirits walk the air unseen," delivering their earthly errand to his privileged and attentive ear; but because there exists in his bosom an insatiable love of what is sweet,and calm, and soothing, which he finds in the freshness and repose of nature—an intense enjoyment of what is elevated, and majestic, which crowns his labour in climbing to the mountain's brow—a deep sense of power, and grandeur, and magnificence, which leads him to the ocean's brink, to pour his soul forth in its native element—the true sublime.

The last character under which we shall attempt to describe the poetical nature of grief, is that of pity—a sentiment so admirably adapted to the relief of the wants and sufferings of humanity, that we regard it as one of our greatest blessings; because we owe to pity half the kind offices of life, never feeling the pain it awakens in ourselves, without feeling also some laudable impulse, and seldom witnessing the signs of it in others, without hailing them as omens of good. Indeed so powerful is the influence of pity, that it is the first refuge of innocence—the last of guilt; and when artifice would win from feeling what it wants merit to obtain from discretion, it never fails to appeal to pity with an exaggerated history of suffering and distress.

But for the gentle visitations of pity, the couch of suffering would be desolate indeed. Pain, and want, and weakness would be left to water the earth with tears, and reap in solitude the harvest of despair. The prisoner in his silent cell, would listen in vain for the step of his last earthly friend; and the reprobate beneath the world's dread stigma, involving in wretchedness and ruin, would find no faithful hand to lift the pall of public disgrace, and reclaim the lost one from a living death. But more than all, without pity, we should want the bright opening in the heavens through which the radiance of returning peace shines forth upon the tears of penitence—we should want the ark of shelter when the waters of the deluge were gathering around us—we should want the cloud by day, and the pilliar of fire by night to guide our wanderings through the wilderness.

The grief arising from pity is the only disinterested grief we are capable of; and therefore it carries a balm along with it, which imparts something of enjoyment to the excitement it creates; but for its acuteness of sensation, we have the warrant of the deep workings of more violent passions, which pity has not unfrequently the power to overcome. History affords no stronger proof of this, than when Coriolanus yielded to the tears of his mother, and the matrons of Rome, what he had refused to the entreaties of his friends, and the claims of his country.

But if pity, connected with the power of alleviating misery, is mingled with enjoyment, pity without this power is one of the most agonizing of our griefs. To live amongst the oppressed without being able to break their bonds—amongst the poor without the means of giving—to walk by the side of the feeble without a hand to help—to hear the cries of the innocent without a voice to speak of peace, are trials to the heart, and to the will, unparalleled in the register of grief. And it is this acuteness of sensation, connected with the unbounded influence of pity, and the circumstance of its being woven in with the chain of kindness, and love, and charity, by which human suffering is connected with human virtue, that constitutes the poetry of grief in its character of pity—a character so sacred, that we trace it not only through the links of human fellowship, binding together the dependent children of earth; but also through God's government, up to the source of all our mercies, where, separate from its mortal mixture of pain, pity performs its holy offices of mercy and forgiveness.

THE POETRY OF WOMAN.

After what has already been said of love and grief, we feel that to treat at large upon the poetry of woman, must be in some measure to recapitulate what forms the substance of the two preceding chapters; because, from the peculiar nature and tendency of woman's character, love and grief may be said to constitute the chief elements of her existence. That she is preserved from the overwhelming influence of grief, so frequently recurring, by the reaction of her own buoyant and vivacious spirit, by the fertility of her imagination in multiplying means of happiness, and by her facility in adapting herself to place and time, and laying hold of every support which surrounding circumstances afford, she has solely to thank the Author of her life, who has so regulated the balance of human joys and sorrows, that none are necessarily entirely and irremediably wretched. On glancing superficially at the general aspect of society, all women, and all men who see and speak impartially, would pronounce the weaker sex to be doomed to more than an equal share of suffering; but happily for woman, her internal resources are such as to raise her at least to a level with man in the scale of happiness. Bodily weakness and liability to illness is one of the most obvious reasons why woman is looked upon as an object of compassion. Scarcely a day passes in which she has not some ache or pain that would drive a man melancholy, and yet how quietly she rests her throbbing temples; how cheerfully she converses with every one around her, thus beguiling her thoughts from her own sufferings; how patiently she resigns herself to the old accustomed chair, as if chained to the very hearth-stone; while the birds are warbling forth their welcome to returning spring, and she knows that the opening flowers are scenting the fresh gales that play around the garden where she may not tread, and that the sunny skies are lighting up the landscape with a beauty which she may not look upon—it is possible, which she never may behold again. Yet what is all this to woman? Her happiness is not in physical enjoyment, but in love and faith. Give her but the voice of kindness—the pure sweet natural music of the feminine soul, to soothe her daily anguish—to cheer her nightly vigil, and she will ask no more: tell her of the green hills, the verdant woods, and the silver streams, of the songs of the birds, and the frolic of the lambs, of nature's radiant beauty glowing beneath a cloudless sky, and of the universal gladness diffused through the animal creation—tell her all this, in which she has, personally, no participation, and she will be satisfied, nay, blest.

In the natural delicacy of woman's constitution, however, we see only one of the slightest of the causes of suffering peculiar to her character and station in society; because her feelings are so entirely relative and dependent, that they can never be wholly, or even half absorbed by that which is confined to her own experience, without reference to that of others. There are unquestionably many exceptions to this rule, but the rule is the same notwithstanding; and I desire to be understood to speak not of women individually, but of the essential characteristics of woman as a genius. Amongst these characteristics, I am almost proud to name her personal disinterestedness, shown by the unhesitating promptness with which she devotes herself to watchfulness, labour, and suffering of almost every kind, for, or in lieu of others. In seasons of helplessness, misery, or degradation, who but woman comes forward to support, to console, and to reclaim? From the wearisome disquietudes of puling infancy, to the impatience and decrepitude of old age, it is woman alone that bears with all the trials and vexations which the infirmities of our nature draw down upon those around us. Through the monotony of ceaseless misery, it is woman alone that will listen to the daily murmurings of fruitless anxiety, and offer again the cup of consolation after it has been petulantly dashed at her feet. It is woman who withdraws not her sweet companionship from that society whose intercourse is in sighs and tears. What is it to her that the brilliance of wit is now extinguished, the favourite anecdotes untold, and silent all the flattering enconiums that flow from love and gratitude. It is enough for her that the lips now sealed by grief, the eye now dim with tears, and the heart now tortured with agony, are dear—dearer in their unutterable wo, than the choicest pleasures of the world, did they centre in herself alone. No; woman will not leave the idol of her worship because the multitude have turned away to bow before another shrine, because the wreaths have faded away from the altar, or because the symbols of religion are no more. She hears the popular outcry that her vows are offered to a false deity, but she will not believe, because her faith makes it true. A higher object of devotion is pointed out to her, but she clings to that which her imagination has invested, and still invests, with all the attributes of a celestial being; until at last it falls before her, a hopeless and irrecoverable ruin, and then, after vainly struggling to hide its degradation, she goes forth into the wilderness alone.

For the poetry of her character, woman is chiefly indebted to her capability of feeling, extended beyond the possibility of calculation, by her naturally vivid imagination; yet she unquestionably possesses other mental faculties, by no means inconsiderable in the scale of moral and intelligent beings. Those who, depriving woman of her rightful title to intellectual capacity, would consign her wholly to the sphere of passion and affection; and those who, on the opposite side, are perpetually raving about her equality with man, and lamenting over the inferior station in society which she is doomed to fill, are equally prejudiced in their view of the subject, superficial in their reasoning upon it, and absurd in their conclusions. In her intellectual *capacity*, I am inclined to believe that woman is equal to man, but in her intellectual *power* she is greatly his inferior; because, from the succession of unavoidable circumstances which occur to interrupt the train of her thoughts, it is seldom that she is able to concentrate the forces of her mind, and to continue their operations upon one given point, so as to work out any of those splendid results, which ensue from the more fixed and determinate designs of man. To woman, belong all the minor duties of life, she is therefore incapable of commanding her own time, or even her own thoughts; in her sphere of action, the trifling events of the moment, involving the principles of good and evil, which instantly strike upon her lively and acute perceptions, become of the utmost importance; and each of these duties, with its train of relative considerations, bearing directly upon the delicate fabric of her mind, so organized as to render it liable to the extremes of pain or pleasure, arising out of every occurrence, she is consequently unable so to regulate her feelings, as to leave the course of her intellectual pursuits uninterrupted.

Suppose for instance, a woman is studying Euclid when she hears the cry of her child; in an instant she plunges into the centre of her domestic cares, and Euclid is forgotten. Suppose another, (for such things have been,) deeply engaged in the dry routine of classic lore, when suddenly the fair student sees something in the eye of her tutor, or hears something in his voice, which puts to flight the Roman legions, and dismisses the Carthaginian queen to weep away her wrongs unpitied and alone. Suppose a woman admitted within the laboratory of a chymist, and listening with the mute attention of a devotee to his learned dissertations upon his favourite science, when, behold, her watchful eye is fixed upon the care-worn brow and haggard cheek of the philosopher, and she longs to lead him away from his deleterious drugs and essences, into the green fields, or home to the quiet comforts of her own fire-side, where she would rather cherish his old age with warm clothing and generous diet, than ponder upon the scientific truths he has been labouring to instil into her mind. Suppose another studying the course of the stars, when by one of those involuntary impulses by which thoughts are let into the mind we know not how, the form of her departed friend rushes back upon her memory, and suddenly, beneath that heavenly host, whose sublimity her rapt soul had been almost adoring, she stands alone, a weak and trembling woman; and asks no more of the glistening stars, than some faint revelation of her earthly destiny—some glimmering of hope that she may yet be permitted to shelter herself beneath the canopy of domestic and social love. Suppose a woman mentally absorbed in the eventful history of past times, pondering upon the rise and fall of nations, the principles of government, and the march of civilization over the peopled globe; when suddenly there is placed in her hand a letter—one of those mute messengers which sometimes change in a moment, the whole colouring of a woman's life, not only clothing in shade or sunshine the immediate aspect of nature and surrounding things, but the illimitable expanse of her imaginary future. A letter to a woman is not a mere casual thing, to be read like a newspaper. Its arrival is an event of expectancy, of hope, and fear; and often seems to arrest in a moment the natural current of her blood, sending it by a sudden revulsion, to circle in a backward course through all her palpitating veins. In the instance we have supposed, the letter may convey the sad intelligence of the sickness of a friend or relative, who requires the immediate attention of a faithful and devoted nurse. The book is closed. The quiet hours of reading, and study, are exchanged for the wearisome day, the watchful night, the soothing of fretfulness, and the ministration of comfort and kind offices; while the heroes of ancient Greece are forgotten, and the Cæsars and the Ptolemies are indiscriminately consigned to an ignominious tomb.

It is owing to circumstances such as these, daily and even hourly occurring, that women are disqualified for great literary attainments; and every impartial judge will freely acknowledge that it is not her want of capacity to understand the fundamental truths of science and philosophy; but her utter inability from circumstance and situation, diligently to pursue the investigation of such truths, and when clearly ascertained, to store up and apply them to the highest intellectual purposes, which constitutes the difference between the mental faculties of woman and those of a nobler sex.

Nor let the pedant call this a defect in woman's nature; that alone can be a defect by which anything is hindered from answering the purpose for which it was designed.

Man is appointed to hold the reins of government, to make laws, to support systems, to penetrate with patient labour and undeviating perseverance into the mysteries of science and to work out the great fundamental principles of truth. For such purposes he would be ill qualified, were he liable to be diverted from his object by the quickness of his perception of external things, by the ungovernable impulse of his own feelings, or by the claims of others upon his regard or sensibility; but woman's sphere being one of feeling rather than of intellect, all her peculiar characteristics are such as essentially qualify her for that station in society which she is designed to fill, and which she never voluntarily quits without a sacrifice of good taste—I might almost say, of good principle. Weak indeed is the reasoning of those who would render her dissatisfied with this allotment, by persuading her that the station, which it ought to be her pride to ornament, is one too insignificant or degraded for the full exercise of her mental powers. Can that be an unimportant vocation to which peculiarly belong the means of happiness and misery? Can that be a degraded sphere which not only admits of, but requires the full developement of moral feeling? Is it a task too trifling for an intellectual woman, to watch, and guard, and stimulate the growth of reason in the infant mind? Is it a sacrifice too small to practice the art of adaptation to all the different characters met with in ordinary life, so as to influence, and give a right direction to their tastes and pursuits? Is it a duty too easy, faithfully and constantly to hold up an example of self-government, disinterestedness, and zeal for that which constitutes our highest good—to be nothing, or anything that is not evil, as the necessities of others may require—to wait with patience—to endure with fortitude—to attract by gentleness—to soothe by sympathy judiciously applied—to be quick in understanding, prompt in action, and, what is perhaps more difficult than all, pliable yet firm in will—lastly, through a life of perplexity, trial, and temptation, to maintain the calm dignity of a pure and elevated character, earthly in nothing but its suffering and weakness; refined almost to sublimity in the seraphic ardour of its love, its faith, and its devotion.

The same causes which operate against the intellectual attainments of woman, unfit her for arbitrary rule. Queen Elizabeth, one of the most distinguished of female sovereigns, was womanly in nothing but her vanity and artifice. She was ready at any time to sacrifice her lover to her love of power; and those affairs, said to be of the heart, which rendered her despicable in old age, were nothing better than flirtations founded upon personal adulation, selfishness, and caprice. But deficient in the nobler characteristics of generous feeling, in enthusiasm, and devotedness, she was the better qualified to maintain her regal dignity, and to pursue those deep-laid schemes of policy and ambition which raised her to a level with the greatest potentates of Europe; while her ill-starred rival, Mary of Scotland, a "very, very woman!" who, with the richest endowments of head and heart, might, as a wife, have proved a blessing to any man who had the good feeling to appreciate her worth, raised to the throne, became the bane of her empire; and as a queen, was eventually the most unfortunate that ever let in misrule and rebellion upon her state, or brought down disgrace and destruction upon herself.

It is only in her proper and natural sphere, that woman is poetical. Self-supported, as a sovereign or a sage, she wants all her loveliest attributes. That which stands alone, firmly, and without support, can never supply the mind with so many interesting and poetical associations, as that which has a relative existence and is linked in with the chain of creation by the sympathies or necessities of its own nature. A single barren hill, in the midst of a desert, without sunshine, without shade, without verdure, or any perceptible variety in its surface, would afford little to interest the feelings of the poet. It might serve as a landmark to the bewildered traveller; but without the light of the sun, or the shadow of intervening clouds upon its summit, without the garment of verdure, or the varieties of beetling rock, and precipice, and deep ravine around its sloping sides; and above all, without its "mighty shadow in a weary land," it could not be an object upon which the eye would linger with delight, or the excursive faculty of imagination find food and exercise. The ıghtest bird that plumes its wing upon the leafy bough, or, "tuning its native wood notes wild," soars up to the clear expanse of heaven's ethereal blue; the frailest plant twining its parasitical arms around the supporting stem, lavishing its prodigal sweets upon the morning air, or scattering its faded leaves upon the gales of the wilderness; the faintest cloud that sails before the face of the moon, basking for a moment in her vestal smile, wearing her silver livery, and then wreathing her forehead in fantastic folds of mist and vapour before it floats away, formless, and void, into the dark abyss of unfathomable night, are objects in themseives, in their attributes, relations, and associations, infinitely more poetical than the single mountain: and it is precisely upon the same principle, that woman with her boundless sympathies, her weakness, her frailty, her quick perceptions, her inexhaustible energies, in all that constitutes the very essence of her character, is more poetical than man.

Yet notwithstanding all this, in the art of writing poetry, women prove themselves decidedly inferior to the other sex; for the same causes which retard their progress in the more laborious walks of science, are equally forcible here. Beyond a very limited extent woman is incapable of concentrated, fixed, and persevering attention. We have many instances that she can, as it were out of the momentary fulness of her own heart, "discourse most eloquent music," but she is unequal to any of those lasting productions of poetic genius, which continue from age to age to delight the world. I am unwilling however even in this instance to attribute to her mental inferiority, what appears to me as more probably owing to the uncontrolled influence of her imagination, the faculty most essential to the poet, which women possess in so great a degree, that its very exuberance of growth prevents the ripening of those rich fruits of which its profusion of early blossom gives deceitful promise. The imagination of woman may be compared to a quick growing plant, which shoots out so many slender twigs and tendrils, that the main stem is weakened, and the whole plant unable to raise itself from the earth, continues to bud and blossom, and send forth innumerable shoots which altogether form a beautiful group of flowers and verdure, but nothing more; while the imagination of man resembles a stately tree, whose firm and continuous stem, exactly proportioned to the support and nourishment of the numerous branches in their subordinate place completes the majesty, the utility, and the beauty of the whole. The imagination of woman is sufficiently vivid and excursive to take in the widest range of poetical sublimity, but unfortunately it meets with so many interruptions in that range, and deviates so often from its proper object to waste itself upon others of minor importance, that it seldom attains any laudable end, or accomplishes any lasting purpose.

It is impossible for those who have merely *studied* the nature of woman's mind, to comprehend the rapidity of her thoughts, and the versatility of her feelings. Touch but one sensitive chord, and her imagination takes flight upon the wings of the butterfly over the garden of earth, up into mid air, beyond the lark, that sweetest intelligencer of sublunary joy, higher, still higher, through illimitable space, ascending to the regions of peace and glory, and passing through the everlasting gates into the communion of saints, and blessed spirits, whose feet "sandalled with immortality," trace the green margin of the river of eternal life.

Would that the imagination of woman had always this upward tendency, but, alas! it is not satisfied even with the fruition of happiness; it cannot rest even in the bosom of repose; it is not sufficiently refreshed, even by that stream whose waters make glad the celestial city. The light of some loved countenance perchance is wanting there, and the spirit, late soaring on delighted wing, now plunges downward amongst the grosser elements of earth, while lured on by the irresistible power of sympathy, it chooses rather to follow the erring or the lost through all the mazy windings of sin and sorrow, than to rise companionless to glory.

With such an imagination, startled, excited, and diverted from its object, not only by every sight or sound in earth or air, but by every impulse of the affections and the will, it is impossible that woman in her intellectual attainments should ever equal man, nor is it necessary for her usefulness, her happiness, or the perfection of her character, that she should. As she is circumstanced in the world, it is one of her greatest charms, that she is willing to trust rather than anxious to investigate. While she does this she will be feminine, and while she is feminine she must be poetical.

The power of adaptation is another quality, which, next to imagination, is strikingly conspicuous in woman, and without which she would lose half her loveliness, and half her value. There is no possible event in human life which she is unable, not only to understand, but to understand feelingly; and no imaginable character, except the gross or the vile, with which she cannot immediately identify herself.

It is considered a mere duty, too common for observation, and too necessary for praise, when a woman forgets her own sorrows to smile with the gay, or lays aside her own secret joys to weep with the sad. But let lordly man make the experiment for one half hour, and he will then be better acquainted with this system of self-sacrifice, which woman in every station of society, from the palace to the cottage, maintains through the whole of her life, with little commendation, and with no reward, except that which is attached to every effort of disinterested virtue. It is thought much of, and blazoned forth to the world, when the victim at the stake betrays no sign of pain; but does it evince less fortitude for the victim of corroding care to give no outward evidence of the anguish of a writhing soul? —to go forth arrayed in smiles, when burning ashes are upon the heart?—to meet, as a woman can meet, with a never-failing welcome the very cause of all her suffering? —and to woo back with the sweetness of her unchangeable love, him who knows neither constancy nor truth?

It is unquestionably the exercise of this faculty of adaptation, which attaches to woman's character the stigma of artifice. She has no power to command, therefore to attain her purpose she can only win; and in order to win, she must in some measure adapt herself to the feelings of those who hold the object of her wishes in their keeping. But for one instance in which this is done to serve a selfish purpose, we might count a thousand where it is done for pure sympathy and love, and tens of thousands where she submits to the disappointment of her dearest hopes, without attempting, even in this humble manner, to obtain what she desires.

Women can not only adapt themselves to the habits and peculiarities of others, but they can actually *feel* with them—enter into their very being and penetrate the deep recesses of their souls. Thus they are no less interesting in themselves, than really interested in what they hear and see. In society they have the character of being diligent talkers, but are they not good listeners also? And where they do not actually listen, they can pretend to do so, which answers the purpose of the speaker just as well. A truly agreeable woman knows how to give a quick and delicate turn to conversation, so as to avoid an unpleasant dilemma or produce a pleasing effect; she knows how, and to whom, to address her good things, and never wastes them upon the wrong person; she discovers the secret bias of the character, and bends the same way, or opposes so gently, that resistance becomes an agreeable amusement; she reads the eye, and discourses eloquently in the language of the heart; and she allows herself caprice enough to ruffle the monotony of life, but not sufficient to create tumult or confusion. Without diving so deep as to be lost, she glides over the surface of things and makes herself acquainted with their nature, and their importance in the aggregate of life. She can enter into the different elements of human nature, and assuming every variety of form of which it is capable, can endure every change of time, and place, and circumstance, and, what is most wonderful, retain her own identity in each. Al this she can do with little of the "borrowed aid of ornament." The charm is within herself, and like the great enchantress of the Nile, she imparts it to everything around her.

For want of the power which is in nature,

our writers of romance are compelled to make all their heroines beautiful—to place them upon thrones, or beds of violets—to spangle them over with pearls, and blanche them to the whiteness of snow—to wreath them with roses, and scatter flowers beneath their feet—to endow them with all languages, and all gifts of music and eloquence, pouring forth the wisdom of the sage from the lips of the cherub. But it is not so in common life; there is a witchery in nature which it is impossible for art to attain, and a truly charming woman clad in russet weeds, may darn her husband's stockings and be charming still.

Yet after all, it is not by the examination of any particular talent, faculty, or endowment, that we become acquainted with the true poetry of woman's character; for such is her liability to be affected by every change of circumstance, and such her capacity for receiving pain and pleasure, that we must always speak of her in reference to her state of feeling, rather than her capability of mind. Her thoughts for the most part, are combinations of indistinct ideas, which flow together in a tide too rapid, too impetuous, and too generally directed by her affections, to admit of the strict government of right reason. She beholds not only the present and the palpable, but the contrast, and the similitude of everything around her. The past and the future are spread before her like pictures, whose colouring varies with the tone and temper of her own mind. In one moment, the vivid glow of happiness is diffused over the scene, and in the next, the sombre shadow of despair. Exulting in the acquisition of some unexpected joy, what a glad free spirit is that of woman, soaring without bound or limitation, far beyond the reach of fear, and spurning at the apprehension of future pain—under the pressure of affliction, how sad, how low, how utterly cast down! Bursting forth upon the wings of hope, the soul of woman knows no impediment. Impossibility is no barrier to its course. It sees that which is without form, hears voices in the depth of silence, and lays hold of things which have no tangible existence.

All this may be called absurd, and so it would be, if the allusions of the mind were not permitted to lift us occasionally above the grossness and heaviness of life. Without this mysterious power to create food for its own felicity, the mind of woman would sink beneath its burdens, and instead of a bright, vivacious being, ever the first to welcome sunshine—the last to yield to gloom, woman would be alike wearisome as a companion, feeble as a helpmate, and impotent as a comforter. All this would be absurd too, if the sphere of woman were the same as that of man; but as a woman I am well convinced that those peculiarities for which she is too frequently ridiculed and despised, arise either from the excess or the abuse of natural qualities, which under proper discipline, might have been made conducive to her own, and other's happiness.

The want of stability, consistency and depth, is perceptible only in woman's intellectual pursuits. In all that belongs to her affections, and her social duties, she is faithful, sincere, and firm. It is true, she is called fickle, but as has been remarked by an amiable and talented writer, "her inconsistency is of the head rather than of the heart."* Believing what she hopes, she takes her friends upon trust, and loving rashly, must necessarily be often deceived; but it does not follow that if the object of her affection could retain the character with which her own fancy invested it, she would not still love with the same constancy, and "love for ever."

From the varied and fluctuating nature of woman's feelings, as well as from their power, their expansion, and their depth, it is impossible to say individually what she is, or what she might be, because the ordinary routine of life, particularly of polished life admits of little development of the passions and affections. It is only in cases of trial that she proves herself, and therefore all writers who have drawn from nature, in attempting to delineate the character of woman, have done it by a few impressive strokes, rather than by general description.

Amongst numerous instances of this kind abounding in the works of Shakspeare, I shall point out one which bears most strik-

* Mrs. Sandford, author of "Woman in her Social and Domestic Character."

ingly the impress of a master hand. It is the last speech of Desdemona in the horrible scene of her murder. Æmilia, her attendant, hears her dying voice, and, beginning to suspect there has been foul play, exclaims,

"O, who hath done
This deed?"

"Nobody; I myself; farewell:
Commend me to my kind lord; O, farewell!"

is answered by the wretched victim. Who can read these lines without acknowledging the writer's profound and intimate acquaintance with the heart of woman? First, Desdemona answers "*Nobody*," from the impulse of a sudden desire to clear her husband from suspicion; but immediately recollecting that this will not be sufficient, she adds, "*I myself;*" and then to complete the whole—to give the climax to her faithfulness and devotion, she continues, "*Commend me to my kind lord*"—to that very lord whose hand was just unloosed from its fatal hold, and who stood beside her neither penitent nor triumphant, but literally stupified with the magnitude and the horror of the deed which yet he had not the power to behold as a crime.

Another instance of a gentler and more pleasing character, occurs in Wallenstein, as translated by Coleridge, where the princess, after the death of Max, claims the tenderest office of friendship from her faithful companion.

THEKLA.

"Now gentle Newbrun, show me the affection
Which thou has ever promised; prove thyself
My own true friend and fellow-pilgrim.
This night we must away.

NEWBRUN.

"Away! and whither?

THEKLA.

"Whither! *There is but one place in the world.*
Thither where he lies buried!"

In these few words we see the magnitude of woman's love, and the absorbing nature of her grief. Herself and the whole universe sink into nothing in comparison with that single point of space. She is surprised that her friend should ask "whither," and almost reproaches her for not remembering that there is now "*but one place in the world.*"

Lord Byron has in many instances proved both his talent and his taste, by giving us the true poetry of woman's character in a few touching words. I shall select one remarkable for its simplicity and pathos. It occurs in Cain, after the perpetration of the first murder, where the fratricide has received the malediction of one parent, and been driven out by the other. Adah, whose character is beautifully and justly drawn throughout, remains with him after the others have departed, and addresses him in these words:—

ADAH.

"Cain! thou hast heard we must go forth. I am ready,
So shall our children be. I will bear Enoch,
And thou his sister. Ere the sun declines
Let us depart, nor walk the wilderness
Under the cloud of night,—Nay, speak to me,
To me—thine own.

CAIN.

"Leave me!

ADAH.

"*Why all have left thee.*

CAIN.

"And wherefore lingerest thou? Dost thou not fear
To dwell with one who hath done this?

ADAH.

"I fear
Nothing except to leave thee, much as I
Shrink from the deed which leaves thee brotherless.
I must not speak of this, *it is between thee*
And the great God."

There can be no stronger bond to a firm and faithful woman, than that "*all have left*" the object of her love. Adah feels this, and offers no other reason. Besides which she utters no reproach; enough has already been said, and like a pure spirit descending upon earth for purposes of love and mercy, she stoops with her husband beneath his degradation, and though confessedly shrinking from the fatal deed, meekly and reverentially places it solely between him "and the great God."

In order to define with greater precision what it is that constitutes the poetry of woman's character, we must enter yet more closely into her individual feelings, and for this purpose it is necessary to trace her experience through the different stages of existence, in which we behold her as a girl, a maiden, a wife, a mother, and an old woman.

It is difficult to say which is least important in the scale of human beings—a little girl or an old woman; but certainly the former inspires us with a kind of tenderness, which is rarely, too rarely, bestowed upon the latter. So long as the sphere of her childish enjoyments is unassailed by affliction, especially by that heaviest of all domestic calamities, the loss of a kind and judicious mother, the existence of a young girl is happy as it is innocent. With her, day after day dances on in the perpetual sunshine of domestic love, and night only comes to remind her of the shelter of the maternal wing. Directed by the impulse of her feelings towards those duties which are to be her portion in after life, she tends her flowers, cherishes her pet lamb, or nurses the wounded bird; and true to the dictates of nature, devotes her feeble strength, her earnest thoughts, and her ardent wishes to the happiness of others. If from the mal-administration of domestic discipline she should become selfish, her sole gratification continues to be derived from surrounding things, and she never seeks it in the centre of her own bosom, but remains dependent still. It may be, that she is sometimes unreasonable in requiring more than she bestows, but the perfect abandonment with which she throws herself upon the good will and generosity of others, ought at least to claim their protection, if it fails to ensure their esteem.

But let us suppose any of the dark visitations of sin and sorrow to fall upon the domestic scene. It is then that the rosy girl is called in from her play, to watch and wait, to bear the harsh rebuke, to know the innocent wish denied, to sympathize with the untold grief, to cultivate a premature acquaintance with the outward signs of inward wo, and to feel what it is to have the cherub wings of childhood burdened with the cares of age. Perhaps the maternal voice is hushed, and the hand that used to smooth her nightly pillow cold in the grave. Who then is left to pity the little mourner, as silently, and unobserved, she passes on through life, seeking for what the whole world is too poor to bestow—a second mother?

Time passes, and the impulse of affection mingles with the dawn of reason. Her intellects are limited to the regular routine of education, while her passions are left free: and thus her feelings become matured, while her talents remain in the bondage of infancy. If the page of history is held up before her, she sees it not as it is, but in the vivid colouring of her own imagination. She will not learn the truth, because it accords not with her aspiring hopes, and ardent wishes, which have already taken precedence of her knowledge. She cannot listen to the lore of past ages, because she is busy combating present disappointments, and just beginning to feel that her efforts are in vain; for the voice of experience, louder that that of instruction, rises above the light carolling of joy, and will be heard. Her buoyant spirit repelled, as easily as it is attracted, mounts in exultation, or sinks in despair, and occupies with its alternations of pain and pleasure, those hours which ought to be devoted to the cultivation of the intellectual powers. Thrown by her natural dependence upon the esteem and affection of those around her, woman learns to regard the smile of approbation as the charmed spell by which the gates of happiness are opened; and to look for the frown of contempt as the signal of her darkest doom. Trembling between these two extremes, there can be no wonder that she should study every means to attain the one, and avoid the other: and this is what the world calls vanity; while it is in fact an ardent, and in some measure a laudable desire to do, and to be, that which is most agreeable to others, purely because it is gratifying, not to herself but to them; and an involuntary shrinking from all which can repel, disgust, or in any way offend, because to be the source of dissatisfaction, to give pain, or to excite uneasiness, is most abhorrent to the natural delicacy and generosity of her own mind.

It is on the verge of womanhood that we see the female character in its greatest variety and beauty; while the rich colouring of fresh-born fancy, the warm gush of genuine feeling, and the high aspirations of ambitious youth, are yet unsubdued by the tyranny of custom, or forced back into the bursting heart by the cold hand of experience. Woman, fresh as it were from the garden of Eden, while the loveliness of her first creation is still lingering around her, blended with the melancholy symbols of her fall, in her character and attributes, her beauty, her tenderness, and her liability to danger and suffering, is all that the poet can desire to inspire his happiest lays.

It is in this stage of her existence, while love, her most insidious enemy, folding his rosy wings, lies shrouded at the bottom of her heart, ready to rush forth on his impetuous flight towards the highest point of happiness, or the lowest depth of wo, that woman lays hold of friendship as her greatest solace and support. Her mind is agitated with a world of indefinite thoughts and feelings which she is unable to communicate, because she does not understand them. While they are confined within her own bosom, she feels like one burdened with an immense and incalculable load, and therefore, she seeks the society of those, whose sympathy, arising from a similarity of feeling, supplies the want of a common medium of communication. Ardently desiring to find in her friend all those qualities which she most admires, and prone by nature to believe whatever she desires, she pauses not to enquire whether the choice she makes is not rather the result of her own necessities, than a tribute justly paid to virtue; and thus the two friends similarly circumstanced, and mutually in need of each other, trust most implicitly to the strength and durability of their attachment: and happy is it for those to whom experience does not teach the emptiness of what the world calls friendship. I do not say the *worthlessness*, because that cannot be worthless, which supplies us with enjoyment for the present, and wisdom for the future.

Nor let the world be quarrelled with because its friendships do not always last. Formed out of the warm feelings of youth—feelings which it would be impossible to carry on with us through life, it is but reasonable that we should lose our friendships as we journey onwards, or that retaining them, their character and mode of exhibition should be wholly changed; because we cease in some measure to feel the want of them, and therefore they can no longer repay us for the expenditure of time, and thought, and affection, which in their original ardour they required. We have other objects in pursuit, different aims, and hopes, and wishes. We have become more concentrated in our feelings, and therefore have less disposition to give out the love that once flowed in a tide too rapid and impetuous to be restrained. But let us pause, and ask, have we found anything to compare in the genuine and heartfelt happiness it affords, with the social hours of unguarded confidence—the truth—the tears—the affections which belonged to the friendships of our early youth?

I am far from from asserting that we may not have friends—true and zealous friends—friends who would protect our reputation as their own, through every stage of life; but they are for the most part such, as having lost their enthusiasm, are become keenly observant of our faults, and strict to correct them, rather than tender and faithful confiders in our virtue: such as, wearied with our peculiarities, vainly endeavour to make us submit to the common rule, and finding their endeavours ineffectual, grown niggardly in their charitable allowance for our deviations; not such as looked kindly on our foibles, because they made a part of us, and felt if we were better, that they could not love us more: such as freely enter into our views and feelings, when in full accordance with their own established notions of what is praiseworthy and prudent; not such as are the last to step forward and tell us we have been in error, purely because they would be the last to give us pain. Such friends as these we should do wisely to keep along with us even to the end of life—they are in fact the only *true* friends, because they are true to our best interests: but, oh! they are not like the friends who loved us in our early youth!

To return to woman in her girlish days. How beautifully has our own fair poetess, whose lays, mournful as they are musical, remind us of the fabled melody of the dying swan, described the particular yearning of the heart with which the experienced observer regards the tender years of woman.

"Her lot is on you—silent tears to weep,
And patient smiles to wear through suffering's hour
And sumless riches, from affection's deep,
To pour on broken reeds—a wasted shower!
And to make idols, and to find them clay,
And to bewail that worship—therefore pray!

"Her lot is on you!—to be found untir'd,
Watching the stars out by the bed of pain,
With a pale cheek, and yet a brow inspir'd
With a true heart of hope, though hope be vain!
Meekly to bear with wrong, to cheer decay,
And, Oh! to love through all things—therefore pray!"

Trace her experience to the next stage of her existence, and woman is more poetical still; because so long as her youth and beauty inspire admiration—so long as there is any thing to be gained by her favour, she is subjected to the deceitful flatteries of man, whom she is naturally desirous to please, not only as her superior, guide, and friend, but as he holds the reins of government, and can therefore deprive her of all or most of her pleasures. As a girl, she was deceived only by her own heart, she is now deceived by the general aspect of society. Way is made for her to walk forth as a queen, and when suppliants bow before her, no wonder that they should assume the dignity of one, and learn to love the sceptre placed for a moment of mockery in her feeble hand. Trusting and sincere herself, she dreams not of falsehood, and when told that she is beautiful, she looks in the mirror and believes it true. Finding that beauty is the only sure title to the admiration of that sex, which it is her wish and her interest to please, she values her personal charms as her richest dower; and if she smiles not from the fullness of a glad heart, but because smiles are lovely, frowns to produce effect, or sighs to excite a momentary interest, it is because she has learned in her intercourse with society that she must be *personally* lovely to be beloved, and *personally* interesting to avoid contempt.

When we think of the falsehood practised towards women, at that season of life when their minds are most capable of receiving impressions, and when their intellectual powers, just arriving at maturity, are most liable to serious and important bias, we can only wonder that there should be any substantial virtue found amongst them. But as there is a time to sleep, and a time to awake, so there comes to almost all women, a time when their eyes are opened to the truth—when their beauty charms not, and their step is heard without a welcome—when they tune the harp without an audience, and speak unanswered—when they smile without imparting happiness, and frown without exciting alarm—when others step forward to receive the adulation once offered to them, while they are thrust down from their imaginary thrones, by the very hands which supported them in their ascent. Compelled to descend, though sometimes gradually, from the state of ideal exaltation to which she has been raised, woman—weak woman, catches at every slender hold that may break her fall. To the last voice that speaks flatteringly, she listens with an avidity which subjects her to the ridicule of the world; while to the last kind hand that is held out to her, she clings with a despairing energy, an ardent gratitude, which permit her not to perceive its unworthiness. Hence follow the absurdities for which she is more blamed than pitied, and the rash sacrifice of herself, for which she meets with little mercy from the world. But the censor of woman should be a woman herself, to know what it is to have lived in that vortex of falsehood, flattery, and dissipation, which surrounds a young and beautiful female; and then to pass away into the sullen calm of neglect—to have basked in the warm and genial atmosphere of real or pretended affection; and then to "bide the pelting of the pitiless storm," with which envy never fails to assail her whose capability of loving has outlived her charms—to have listened to the voice of adulation, breathing her praises like a perpetual concert all around her; and then to hear nothing but the cold dull language of truth, exaggerated into harshness, or sharpened into reproof—to have lived a charmed life, under the fascination of man's love, in the very centre of all that constitutes ideal happiness, ministered to on every hand, and feeding, like the butterfly, upon the flowers of life, without a wish ungratified, a thought untold, or a tear unpitied; and then upon the world's bleak desert to stand alone! I repeat, that the censor of woman should be a woman herself—a woman who has been admired, and then neglected.

We have here spoken only of women whose personal charms recommend them to general admiration, because it is of these alone that the poet delights to sing; yet such is the influence of personal admiration in checking the growth of moral and intellectual beauty, and engendering selfishness and vanity, that we are inclined to believe the deep pathos of the feminine heart is to be found in the greatest perfection concealed behind the countenance that has seldom attracted the public gaze. It is in such hearts, whose best offerings are rarely estimated according to their real value, that disinterested affection, in all its natural warmth, lives and burns for the benefit of the suffering or the beloved; that enthusiasm and zeal, tempered down by humility, are ever ready for the performance of the arduous duties of life; and that ambition, if it exists at all, is directed to the attainment and diffusion of more lasting happiness than mere beauty can afford.

In the capacity of a wife we next observe the character of woman, and it is here, if ever, that she learns the truth—learns what is in her own heart, and what are her duties to herself and others. Not that she learns all this through the gentle instrumentality of affection, but by the moral process of experience, which if less congenial to her taste, is more forcible in its convictions, and more lasting in its effects. In assuming this new title, woman is generally removed to a new, and often to a distant sphere, where she has to take her stand in society upon common ground. None within the circle to which she is at once admitted, know precisely what she *has been*, and therefore every eye is open to see what she *is*. All the little caprices, and peculiarities, nurtured up with her bodily growth in the bosom of her own family, not only forgiven there, but indulged from the fond consideration that "it was always her way," or, "that she was always thus," now stand forth for the full discussion, and impartial inspection of the many, who, seeing no just reason why such should have been her way, and no plausible pretext for her being always thus, soon contrive means to convince her, if not by personal information, by the unanimous opinion of society, that the more entirely she lays aside such peculiarities of character, the more she will be respected and valued. Nor is this all. She has perhaps a stronger corrective within her own household. Her husband begins to see with the eyes of the world. His vision no longer dazzled by her beauty, or his judgment cheated by her caresses, he involuntarily, and often without sufficient delicacy, points out faults which he neither saw, nor believed her capable of possessing before. "Why did I marry?" is the question which every woman, not previously disciplined, asks of herself under such circumstances, "why did I marry, if not to be loved and cherished as I was in my father's house?" Such are her words, for she has not yet learned to understand her own heart; but she means in fact, "why did I marry, if not to be flattered and admired as in the days of courtship, when the competition for my favour excited unremitting assiduity in all who sought to win it, and who, because they knew my vanity and weakness, sought to win it by these means alone?" The answer is an obvious one—because it is not good for us to go deluded to our graves, and therefore merciful means have been designed, as various as appropriate to compel us to open our reluctant eyes upon the truth; and woman as a wife, does open her eyes at last, from the dream in which her senses have been lulled, while with the tide of conviction, as it rushes in upon her newly-awakened mind, come serious thoughts, and earnest calculations, and deeper anxieties; with higher hopes, and nobler aims, and better regulated affections to counterbalance them.

As a mother we next behold woman in her holiest character—as the nurse of innocence—as the cherisher of the first principles of mind—as the guardian of an immortal being who will write upon the records of eternity how faithfully she has fulfilled her trust. And let it be observed that, in assuming this new and important office, she does not necessarily lose any of the charms which have beautified her character before. She can still be tender, lovely, delicate, refined, and cheerful, as when a girl; devoted to the happiness of those around her, affectionate, judicious, dignified, and intellectual as when a wife only; while this new love, deep as the very wells of life, mingles with the current of her thoughts and feelings, giving warmth and intensity to all, without impairing the force or the purity of any. Yet while her attributes remain the same, her being is absorbed in the existence of her child. Now more than ever she forgets herself, deeming nothing impossible which has reference to her own devotedness, and its good—computing neither time, nor space, nor capability in the single consideration of its happiness—regarding neither labour, watching, nor weariness, as worthy of a thought in comparison with its lightest slumber, or its minutest pain.

If the love of a mother be considered as an instinct which pervades all animated nature, it is not the less beautiful when exhibited in the human character, for being diffused throughout creation; because it proves that the Author of our being, knew that the distinctive attributes of humanity would be insufficient to support the mother through her anxieties, vexations and cares. He knew that reason would be making distinctions between the worthy and the unworthy, and prematurely consigning the supposed reprobate to ruin; that fancy would make selections, and dote upon one while it neglected another; that caprice would destroy the bond of domestic union; and that intellectual pursuits would often take precedence of domestic duties. And therefore he poured into woman's heart the same instinct which impels the timid bird to risk the last extremity of danger for her helpless young. Nor let any one think contemptuously of this peculiar capability of loving, because under the extinct it is shared with the brute. It is not a sufficient recommendation to our respect that it comes immediately from the hand of our Creator—that we have no power to control or subdue it—that it is "Strong as death"—and lastly, that it imbues the mind of the mother with equal tenderness for her infirm, or wayward, or unlovely child, as for him who gives early promise of personal as well as mental beauty? But for this wonderful provision in human nature, what would become of the cripple, the diseased, the petulant or the perverse? Who would be found to fulfil the hard duties of serving the ungrateful, ministering to the dissatisfied, and watching over the hopeless? No. There is no instance in which the providential care of our heavenly Father is more beautifully exhibited than in that of a mother's love. Winding its silken cords alike around every natural object, whether worthy or unworthy, it creates a bond which unkindness cannot break. It pursues the wanderer without weariness, and supports the feeble without fainting. Neither appalled by danger, nor hindered by difficulty, it can labour without reward, and persevere without hope. "Many waters cannot quench" it; and when the glory has vanished from the brow of the beloved one, when summer friends have turned away, and guilt, and misery, and disgrace have usurped their place, it steals into the soul of the outcast like the sunbeams within the cell of the prisoner, lighting the darker dungeon of the polluted heart, bringing along with it fond recollections of past happiness, and wooing back to fresh participation in the light and the gladness that still remain for the broken and contrite spirit.

If the situation of a wife brings woman to a right understanding of her own character, that of a mother leads to a strict knowledge of her own principles. Scarcely is any one so depraved as to teach her child what she conscientiously believes to be wrong. And yet teach it she must, for its "clear pure eyes" are fixed upon hers to learn their meaning, and its infant accents are inquiring out the first principles of good and evil. How, with such a picture before her, would any woman dare to teach what she did not implicitly, as well as rationally, and from mature examination believe to be true. In a few days—hours—nay, moments, that child may be a cherub in the courts of Heaven. What if a stain should have been upon its wings, and that stain the impress of a mother's hand! or if its earthly life should be prolonged, it is the foundation of the important future that the mother lays. Other governors in after years may take upon themselves the tuition of her child, and lead him through the paths of academic lore, but the early bias—the bent of the moral character—the first principles of spiritual life, will be hers, and hers the lasting glory or the lasting shame.

There is no scene throughout the whole range of our observation, more strikingly illustrative of intellectual, moral, and even physical beauty than that presented by a domestic circle, where a mother holds her proper place, as the source of tenderness, the centre of affection, the bond of social union, the founder of each salutary plan, the umpire in all contention, and the general fountain of cheerfulness, hope, and consolation. It is to clear up the unjust suspicion that such a mother steps forward; to ward off the unmerited blow; to defend the wounded spirit from the injury to which it would sullenly submit; to encourage the hopeless, when thrown back in the competition of talent; to point out to those who have been defeated, other aims in which they may yet succeed; to stand between the timid and the danger they dread; and, on behalf of each, and all, to make their peace with offended authority, promising, hoping, and believing, that they will never willingly commit the same fault again.

Even amongst her boys, those wayward libertines of nature's commonwealth, the mother may, if she acts judiciously, be both valuable and dear; for wild and impetuous as they are when they first burst forth from the restraints of childhood, and rush on regardless of every impediment and wholesome check, as if to attain in the shortest space of time, the greatest possible distance from dependence and puerility, they are apt to meet with crosses and disappointments which plunge them suddenly back into the weakness they have been struggling to overcome, or rather to conceal; and it is then that a mother's love supplies the balm which their wounded feelings want, and provided they can mingle respect with their affection they are not ashamed to acknowldege their dependence upon it still.

It may here be observed how much depends upon the word *respect*. When the boy respects his mother, she is associated with his highest aspirations, and therefore he has pride as well as pleasure in her love. But he will not respect her merely because she has nursed him when an infant. No. He must find as he gains experience, a perfect accordance between the principles of virtue and the instruction he first heard from his mother's lips, as well as the rules by which her own conduct is regulated. It is this respect mingled with natural affection, that constitutes the strongest and most durable bond which is woven in with the life-strings of the heart; that draws back the wanderer to his home; and is the last, the very last, which the reprobate casts off.

In turning from the contemplation of a mother in the midst of her family, to that of a mere old woman, we make a melancholy descent from important usefulness to neglected imbecility. Perhaps we have been dwelling too much upon what ought to be, but the bare mention of an *old woman* brings us down at once to what is. To inquire why it should be thus, belongs more to the writer on morals than on poetry; yet so it is —that woman who has been cherished in her infancy and flattered in her youth, who has been exalted to the most honourable station which her sex can fill, and who has spent the meridian of her life in toils and anxieties for the good of others, becomes in old age, a mere proverb, and a by-word—a warning to the young and the gay of what they must expect—a similitude for all that is feeble and contemptible—an evidence of the destructive power of time—a living emblem of decay.

It is true the mother is a mother still, and greatly is it to be feared, that where she sinks into a state of total neglect, it is from the absence of all feeling of respect in the minds of her children; nor are there wanting instances to prove this fact—instances in which the want of youthful beauty has been more than supplied by the loveliness of a mind at peace with all the world, and with its God; where the weakness of old age has been dignified by the services of a well-spent life: and where the wants and wishes of second childhood have been soothed by affection, whose vital principle is gratitude, and whose foundation is esteem. But we speak of the world, and the things of the world as we find them, and we find old women so frequently neglected and despised, that it becomes a duty, as well as a pleasure, to show, that though bereft of every other charm, they may still be poetical—poetical in their recollections, beyond what human nature can be in any other state or stage of its existence.

It is an unkind propensity that many writers have, to make old women poetical through the instrumentality of their passions, exaggerating them into witches and monsters of the most repulsive description, and that not so much "to point a moral," as "to adorn a tale;" but in such instances the writer is indebted to their recollections for all the interest which his unnatural exhibitions excite—to flashes of former tenderness shooting through the gloom of despair—to bright and glowing associations following in the wake of madness—and to once familiar images of love and beauty, re-animated by a strange paradox, at the touch of the wand of death, and bending in all their early loveliness over the brink of the grave.

Infinite indeed beyond the possibility of calculation, must be the recollections and associations of her, whose long life, from its earliest to its latest period, has been a life of feeling—whose experience has been that of impressions, rather than events—and whose sun goes down amidst the varied and innumerable tints which these impressions have given to its atmosphere. Endued with an inexhaustible power of multiplying relative ideas, how melancholy must be the situation of her who was once beloved and cherished, now despised and forsaken—who in her turn loved and cherished others, and is now neglected. If she be a mother—one of those fond mothers who expect that mere indulgence is to win the lasting regard of their children, what sad thoughts must crowd upon her at every fresh instance of unkindness, and every additional proof that she has fallen away from what she was, both in her own and others' estimation. Over the brow that now frowns upon her, she perhaps has watched with unutterable tenderness through the long night when every eye but hers' was sleeping. The lips that now speak to her coldly, or answer her with silence when she speaks, she has bathed with the welcome draught when they were parched and burning with contagious fever. The scorn with which her humble pretensions are looked down upon, arises in the hearts of those for whose higher intellectual attainments she has made every sacrifice, and exerted every faculty. And what if she be unlearned in the literature of modern times, she understands deeply and feelingly the springs of affection, and tenderness and sorrow. She knows from what source flow the bitterest tears, and

> "How sharper than a serpent's tooth it is
> To have a thankless child."

She sees the young glad creatures of another generation sporting around her, and her thoughts go back to the playmates of her childhood—some reduced to the lowest state of helplessness or suffering—some dead and some forgotten. She hears the reluctant answer when she asks a kindness of one of the merry group, and she thinks of the time when kindness was more freely granted her, though far less needed than now. She starts at the loud laugh, but cannot understand the jest, and no one explains it to her listening ear. She loses the thread of earnest conversation, and no one restores the clue. She sits within the social circle, but forms no link in the chain of social union. Her thoughts and feelings cannot harmonize with those of her juvenile companions, and she feels in all its bitterness, that least tolerable portion of human experience—what it is to be desolate in the midst of society—surrounded by kindred and friends, and yet alone.

In looking at the situation of woman merely as regards this life, we are struck with the system of unfair dealing by which her pliable, weak and dependent nature is subjected to an infinite variety of suffering, and we are ready to exclaim, that of all earthly creatures she is the most pitiable. And so unquestionably she is, when unenlightened by those higher views which lead her hopes away from the disappointments of the present world, to the anticipated fruition promised to the faithful in the world to come. But the whole life of woman, when studied with reference to eternity, presents a view of the great plan of moral discipline mercifully designed to assist her right conduct through the trials and temptations which surround her path. In childhood she is necessarily instructed in what belongs to social and domestic duty, and here she learns the difficult but important task of submitting, and of making her own gratification give place to that of others. In youth she is plunged into a sphere of greater temptations, and of more intense enjoyments, where her experience, embracing the widest extremes of pain and pleasure, teaches her all the different means to be made use of in avoiding or palliating the one, and promoting the other. As a wife and a mother she has an opportunity of acting upon the knowledge thus acquired, and if her practice does honour to her theory, it is here that she obtains an importance, and derives a satisfaction, which might be dangerous even to a disciplined mind, did not age steal on and diffuse his sombre colouring over the pleasant pictures to which her affections had given too warm a glow, and which her happiness had persuaded her to be satisfied with contemplating. But this cold, blank medium intervening between life and eternity —between beauty and ashes—between love and death, comes to warn her that all she has been desiring, is but as the scattering of the harvest to be reaped in heaven; that all she has been trusting in, is but typical of that which endures for ever; and that all she has been enjoying, is but a foretaste of eternal felicity.

Let then the aged woman be no longer an object of contempt. She is helpless as a child; but as a child she may be learning the last awful lesson from her Heavenly Father. Her feeble step is trembling on the brink of the grave; but her hopes may be firmly planted on the better shore which lies beyond. Her eye is dim with suffering and tears; but her spiritual vision may be contemplating the gradual unfolding of the gates of eternal rest. Beauty has faded from her form; but angels in the world of light may be weaving a wreath of glory for her brow. Her lip is silent; but it may be only waiting to pour forth celestial strains of gratitude and praise. Lowly, and fallen, and sad, she sits amongst the living; but exalted, purified, and happy, she may arise from the dead. Then turn if thou wilt from the aged woman in her loneliness, but remember she is not forsaken of her God!

THE POETRY OF THE BIBLE.

In tracing the connexion of poetry with subjects most frequently and naturally presented to our contemplation, we observe how it may be associated with our pursuits, so as to give interest to what is familiar, to refine what is material, and to heighten what is sublime. We now open the Bible, and find that poetry as a principle of intellectual enjoyment derived from association, is also diffused through every page of the sacred volume, and so diffused, that the simplest child, as well as the profoundest sage, may *feel* its presence. This in fact, is the great merit of poetry, (a merit which in no other volume but the Bible, can be found in perfection,) that it addresses itself so immediately to the principles of feeling inherent in our nature, as to be intelligible to those who have made but little progress in the paths of learning, at the same time that it presents a source of the highest gratification to the scholar and the philosopher. Let us refer as an example, to the first chapter of Genesis:

> In the beginning, God created the heaven and the earth.
>
> And the earth was without form and void; and darkness was upon the face of the deep. And the Spirit of God moved upon the face of the waters.
>
> And God said, Let there be light; and there was light.

A child but just grown familiar with the words contained in these verses, not only understands their meaning here, but feels something of their sublimity—something of the power and the majesty of the God who could create this wonderful world, whose Spirit moved upon the face of the waters, and who said, *Let there be light: and there was light!* While learned men of all ages have agreed, that no possible combination of words, could express more clearly and powerfully than these, the potency of the first operations of almighty power of which mankind have any record.

We have more than once observed that poetry must have some reference, either uniformly or partially, to our own circumstances, situation, or experience, as well as to the more remote and varied conceptions of the imagination; and in the Scriptures, we find this fact fully illustrated. Witness the frequent recurrence of these simple words—*and God said.* We are not told that the mandates of almighty power issued forth from the heavens, but simply, *that God said:* a mode of speech familiar to the least cultivated understanding, yet in no danger of losing its sublimity as used here, because immediately after, follow those manifestations of universal subordination, which give us the most forcible idea of the omnipotence of Divine will.

Again, after the transgression of our first parents, when

——— they heard the voice of the Lord God walking in the garden in the cool of the day: and Adam and his wife hid themselves from the presence of the Lord God amongst the trees of the garden.

And the Lord God called unto Adam, and said unto him, Where art thou?

And he said, I heard thy voice in the garden, and I was afraid, because I was naked; and I hid myself.

What description of shame and abasement can be more true to human nature than this? But the character of Cain affords the earliest, the most consistent, and perhaps, the most powerful exemplifications of affections and desires perverted from their original purity and singleness of purpose. Cain, the second man who breathed upon the newly-created earth, felt all the stirrings of envy and jealousy, precisely as we feel them at this day, and he

——— talked with Abel his brother: and it came to pass, when they were in the field, that Cain rose up against Abel his brother, and slew him.

And the Lord said unto Cain, Where is Abel thy brother? and he said, I know not: am I my brother's keeper?

And he said, What hast thou done? the voice of thy brother's blood crieth unto me from the ground.

And now art thou cursed from the earth, which hath opened her mouth to receive thy brother's blood from thy hand;

When thou tillest the ground, it shall not henceforth yield unto thee her strength; a fugitive and a vagabond shalt thou be in the earth.

And Cain said unto the Lord, My punishment is greater than I can bear.

Behold, thou hast driven me out this day from the face of the earth: and from thy face shall I be hid; and I shall be a fugitive and a vagabond in the earth; and it shall come to pass, that every one that findeth me shall slay me.

And the Lord said unto him, Therefore whosoever slayeth Cain, vengeance shall be taken on him sevenfold. And the Lord set a mark upon Cain, lest any finding him should kill him.

And Cain went out from the presence of the Lord.—

Am I my brother's keeper? is a question with which we are too apt to answer the reproaches of conscience, when we have violated the most important trust or neglected the duties which ought to be the dearest in life. And what sufferer under the first infliction of chastisement, consequent upon his own transgressions, has not given utterance to the expressive language—*my punishment is greater than I can bear?* Thus far this striking passage contains what is familiar and natural to every human being, but beyond this, yet at the same time connected with it, it has great power and even sublimity, in no instance more so, than where it is said, that *Cain went out from the presence of the Lord.*

The peculiarly emphatic manner in which the Lord promises to bless Abraham, saying—

I will bless them that bless thee, and curse him that curseth thee: and in thee shall all the families of the earth be blessed.

As well as afterwards when—

——— the Lord came unto Abram in a vision, saying, Fear not, Abram: I am thy shield, and thy exceeding great reward—

is comprehensive and full of meaning beyond what more elaborate language could possibly convey. And also after the separation from Lot, where the Lord said unto Abraham,

Lift up now thine eyes, and look from the place where thou art, northward, and southward, and eastward and westward:

For all the land which thou seest, to thee will I give it, and to thy seed for ever.

And I will make thy seed as the dust of the earth: so that if a man can number the dust of the earth, then shall thy seed also be numbered.

Arise, walk through the land in the length of it, and in the breadth of it; for I will give it unto thee.

Then Abram removed his tent, and came and dwelt in the plain of Mamre, which is in Hebron, and built there an altar to the Lord.

Here the act of stretching the sight to the *northward, and southward, and eastward, and westward,* and *walking through the land in the length of it, and in the breadth of it,* presents to the mind ideas of space and distance, at once simple and sublime; and when we read that whenever the faithful patriarch found rest in his wanderings, *he built there an altar to the Lord*, our thoughts are led on by a natural transition to our own experience, to ask what record we have left, or could leave in the past, to prove that the same divine presence was with us in our journey through life.

The story of Hagar is one of great poetical interest. We pursue the destitute mother and her helpless child into the solitude of the wilderness, and behold a picture which has become proverbial for the utter desolation which it represents. Compelled by a stern necessity, with the ultimate good of which she was wholly unacquainted, the mother goes forth as she believes, unfriended and alone, to trust herself and the treasure of her affections to the mercy of the elements, and the shelter of the pathless wilds, unconscious that her peculiar situation is made the especial care of the Father of the fatherless, and the Protector of the forlorn.

> And the water was spent in the bottle, and she cast the child under one of the shrubs.
>
> And she went, and sat her down over against him a good way off, as it were a bow-shot; for she said, Let me not see the death of the child. And she sat over against him, and lift up her voice and wept.
>
> And God heard the voice of the lad; and the angel of God called to Hagar out of heaven, and said unto her, What aileth thee, Hagar? Fear not; for God hath heard the voice of the lad where he is.
>
> Arise, lift up the lad, and hold him in thine hand; for I will make him a great nation.

And in the following chapter, where Abraham, faithful, even to the resigning his dearest treasure, goes forth with his son, prepared to render him up if the Lord should require it at his hand;

> And Isaac spake unto Abraham his father and said, My father? and he said, Here am I, my son: and he said, Behold the fire and the wood: but where is the lamb for a burnt offering?
>
> And Abraham said, My son, God will provide himself a burnt offering: so they went both of them together.

How strong must have been the faith of the patriarch at that moment; or if not, how agonizing his feelings as a father! But if there were any of the natural struggles of humanity between his faith and his love, they are sealed to us, by the simple and beautiful conclusion,—*so they went both of them together.*

Yet it is not merely in particular instances, such as may be singled out for examples, that we see and feel the poetry even of the historical parts of the Bible. The separate accounts of the creation and the deluge, handed down to us in language the most intelligible and unadorned, present to the imagination pictures of sublimity so awful and impressive, that it seems not improbable we may in some measure have derived our ideas of sublimity and power, from impressions made by our first reading of the Bible. Beside which, we find descriptions of the desert, and the wilderness, the wells of water, and the goodly pastures, of the intercourse of angels with the children of men, and of the visitations of the Supreme Intelligence, if not personally, in the different manifestations of his power and his love—as a voice, and an impulse—all conveyed to us in language as simple as if a shepherd spoke of his flocks upon the mountain—as sublime as if an angel wrote the record of the world.

Nor is the poetry of the Bible by any means confined to those passages in which the power of the Almighty is exhibited as operating upon the infant world. The same influence extending over the passions and affections of human nature, is described with the most touching pathos, and the most impressive truth. That moving and controlling influence, so frequently spoken of as *the word of the Lord* coming with irresistible power upon the instruments of his will, is nowhere set before us in a stronger light, than in the character of Balaam, when he declared that if Balak would give him his house full of silver and gold, he could not go beyond the word of the Lord his God to do less or more. Not even when he stood upon the high place amidst the seven altars with the burning sacrifice, and all the princes of Moab around him, and knew that the express object of his calling was to curse the people whom the most high had blessed; yet here, before the multitudes assembled to hear the confirmation of their hopes, he was compelled to acknowledge how those hopes were defeated, saying,

> —— Balak, the king of Moab, hath brought me from Aram, out of the mountains of the east, saying, Come, curse me Jacob, and come, defy me Israel.
>
> How shall I curse, whom God hath not cursed? or how shall I defy, whom the Lord hath not defied?
>
> For from the top of the rocks I see him, and from the

hills I behold him: lo, the people shall dwell alone, and shall not be reckoned among the nations.

Who can count the dust of Jacob, and the number of the fourth part of Israel? Let me die the death of the righteous, and let my last end be like his!

And Balak said unto Balaam, What hast thou done unto me? I took thee to curse mine enemies, and, behold, thou hast blessed them altogether.

And he answered and said, Must I not take heed to speak that which the Lord hath put into my mouth?

Although Balaam knew that by obeying the word of the Lord he was sacrificing the favour of his master, who had promised to promote him to honour, yet again, when brought to the top of another mountain with the vain hope of escaping from the power of Omnipotence—when seven altars were again built, and seven bullocks and seven rams sacrificed, the people of Moab were again told, that the Lord

—— hath not beheld iniquity in Jacob, neither hath he seen perverseness in Israel: the Lord his God is with him, and the shout of a king is among them.

Disappointed and defeated, Balak now very naturally exclaims, *Neither curse them at all, nor bless them at all.* Yet still willing to try for the third and last time, the power of man against his Maker, he leads Balaam to the top of Mount Peor, where the same ceremonial gives the sanction of truth, and the majesty of power, to the words of the prophet; and here it is that he pours forth for the last time, a blessing, still richer and more unlimited than before, beginning with the beautiful and poetic language,

How goodly are thy tents, O Jacob, and thy tabernacles, O Israel!

As the valleys are they spread forth, as gardens by the river's side, as the trees of lign aloes which the Lord hath planted, and as cedar trees beside the waters.

To those who are best acquainted with the poetry of the human heart, the sad history of Jephthah and his daughter affords particular interest, told as it is in language never yet exceeded for simplicity and genuine beauty, by any of the numerous writers who have given us, both in prose and verse, imaginary details of this melancholy story.

And Jephthah vowed a vow unto the Lord, and said, if thou shalt without fail deliver the children of Ammon into mine hands,

Then it shall be, that whatsoever cometh forth of the doors of my house to meet me, when I return in peace from the children of Ammon, shall surely be the Lord's, and I will offer it up for a burnt-offering.

So Jephthah passed over unto the children of Ammon to fight against them; and the Lord delivered them into his hands.

And he smote them from Aroer, even till thou come to Minnith, even twenty cities, and unto the plain of the vineyards, with a very great slaughter. Thus the children of Ammon were subdued before the children of Israel.

And Jephthah came to Mizpeh unto his house, and behold his daughter came out to meet him with timbrels and with dances: and she was his only child; beside her he had neither son nor daughter.

And it came to pass, when he saw her, that he rent his clothes, and said, Alas, my daughter! Thou hast brought me very low, and thou art one of them that trouble me: for I have opened my mouth unto the Lord, and I cannot go back.

And she said unto him, My father, if thou hast opened thy mouth unto the Lord, do to me according to that which hath proceeded out of thy mouth; forasmuch as the Lord hath taken vengeance for thee of thine enemies, even of the children of Ammon.

The character of Samson displays in a powerful manner that combination of strength and weakness, which too frequently produces the most fatal and irrevocable ruin. It is a character well worthy of our greatest poet, yet one, to the interest of which, his genius could add nothing, and (what is saying much) could expatiate upon without taking anything away. We first behold Samson as the man before whom the Philistines trembled, after rending the lion, and scattering thousands with a single arm, stooping to the dalliance of a false and worthless woman—three times deceived—wantonly and wickedly deceived, yet trusting her at last with the secret of his strength. Next, betrayed into the hands of his enemies, we find him,

"Eyeless in Gaza, at the mill with slaves."

And lastly, as if this punishment were not sufficient, he is led forth and placed between the pillars in the public hall of entertainment, to make sport at the festival of his enemies, rejoicing in his weakness and his bonds; where the indignation of his unconquerable soul finally nerves him for that tremendous act of retributive vengeance, by which the death of Samson is commemorated.

The story of Ruth is familiar in its touching pathos, to every feeling heart; as well as intrinsically beautiful to every poetic mind. What for instance can exceed the description of the separation of the sisters, when their mother entreats them to leave her.

And they lifted up their voice and wept again: and Orpah kissed her mother-in-law; but Ruth clave unto her.

And she said, Behold, thy sister-in-law is gone back unto her people, and unto her gods: return thou after thy sister-in-law.

And Ruth said, Entreat me not to leave thee, or to return from following after thee: for whither thou goest, I will go; and where thou lodgest, I will lodge: thy people shall be my people, and thy God my God:

Where thou diest, will I die, and there will I be buried: the Lord do so to me, and more also, if aught but death part thee and me.

In speaking of poetry as it relates to the passions, and to the minor impulses, and finer sensibilities of human nature, as well as to the scenes and circumstances most calculated for their developement, we have no hesitation in pointing out the life and character of Saul, as one, abounding perhaps more than any other in the Scriptures, with poetical interest. The book of Job is one of poetry itself, yet the character of the sublime sufferer does not afford the variety exhibited in that of Saul. Prostrate in the dust of the earth, and still holding communion with the Deity, we behold him as an isolated being, struck out from the common lot, and set apart for a particular dispensation, whose severity was sufficient to fill a more human heart with bitterness. But the experience of Saul is that of a more ordinary man, with whom we can fully sympathize, as we go along with him through those great national and social changes, by which men of common mould are often placed before the world in a point of view so striking and important, as to entitle them to the name of great. We recognize in the king of Israel the same motives and feelings by which men in all ages have been influenced; yet while we speak of him as a less extraordinary character than Job, it is only so far as the features of his character are more intelligible and familiar to our observation and experience; for every thing recorded of him in his eventful history, bespeaks a mind imbued at the same time with power and sensibility, and a soul capable of the extremes both of good and evil.

We behold him first a simple youth—a choice *young man, and a goodly,* so unconscious of the high honour which awaited him, that when Samuel emphatically asks, "Is not the desire of the people on thee, and on thy father's house?" he answers with perfect humility and simplicity of heart,

Am not I a Benjamite, of the smallest of the tribes of Israel? and my family the least of all the families of the tribe of Benjamin? wherefore then speakest thou so to me?

Yet,

—— it was so, that when he had turned his back to go from Samuel, God gave him another heart.

We have no reason to suppose an ambitious heart, but rather a heart enlarged with a conception of the favour of the Almighty, and filled with the spirit of prophecy, and with all heavenward aspirations; so that, under a sense of the responsibility of sending forth as a king, an edict among his people, he built an altar unto the Lord, and asked counsel of God before he went down after the Philistines. Thus far we find him obedient as a man, and faithful as a sovereign; for his heart was yet uncorrupted by the temptations which surround a throne: but the power of leading and governing others, soon produced its natural and frequent consequence—a disposition to be guided by his own inclination, and to resist all higher authority. Thus, when commanded to go and smite the Amalekites, and utterly to slay both men and women, infant and suckling, ox and sheep, camel and ass, he spared Agag and the best of the sheep, and of the oxen, and of the fatlings, and of the lambs, and all that was good, and would not utterly destroy them; thereby transgressing the great paramount law, no less necessary for the right government of an infant mind, than for an infant world—the law of obedience.

Then came the word of the Lord unto Samuel, saying,

It repenteth me that I have set up Saul to be king: for he is turned back from following me, and hath not performed my commandments. And it grieved Samuel; and he cried unto the Lord all night.

And when Samuel rose up early to meet Saul in the morning, it was told Samuel, saying, Saul came up to Carmel, and, behold, he set him up a place, and is gone about, and passed on, and gone down to Gilgal.

And Samuel came to Saul: and Saul said unto him, Blessed be thou of the Lord: I have performed the commandment of the Lord.

And Samuel said, What meaneth then this bleating of

the sheep in mine ears, and the lowing of the oxen which I hear?

And Saul said, They have brought them from the Amalekites: for the people spared the best of the sheep and of the oxen, to sacrifice unto the Lord thy God; and the rest we have utterly destroyed.

Then Samuel said unto Saul, Stay, and I will tell thee what the Lord hath said to me this night. And he said unto him, Say on.

And Samuel said, When thou wast little in thine own sight, wast thou not made the head of the tribes of Israel, and the Lord anointed thee king over Israel?

And the Lord sent thee on a journey, and said, Go and utterly destroy the sinners of the Amalekites, and fight against them until they be consumed.

Wherefore then didst thou not obey the voice of the Lord, but didst fly upon the spoil, and didst evil in the sight of the Lord?

After this reproof from Samuel, Saul again endeavours to justify himself by proving that the reservation he had made was solely for the purpose of sacrificing to the Lord, when the prophet emphatically asks,

Hath the Lord as great delight in burnt offerings and sacrifices, as in obeying the voice of the Lord? Behold, to obey is better than sacrifice, and to hearken than the fat of rams.

To Samuel, who seems hitherto to have stood in the capacity of an intercessor between him and the Divine Majesty, Saul now humbles himself, and entreats that he will pardon his sin, and turn again with him, that he may worship the Lord. And when still rejected, he humbles himself yet more, and prays (Oh! how naturally!) that at least the prophet will honor him before the people, that the world may not witness his degradation. And now Samuel yields, but we are told soon after that he came no more to see Saul until the day of his death; nevertheless he mourned for him, and the Lord repented that he had made Saul king over Israel.

And the Spirit of the Lord departed from Saul, and an evil spirit from the Lord troubled him.

How descriptive is this passage of this gradual falling away from Divine favour, which sometimes darkens and weighs down the soul, filling it with gloomy thoughts, and sad forebodings, long before the melancholy change is perceptible in the outward character. And how strikingly does it illustrate the hidden, and to us mysterious workings of the great plan of Providence, that the future king of Israel, already secretly appointed by Divine commission, should be the minstrel chosen to come and charm away, with the melody of his harp, the evil spirit from the mind of his predecessor in authority; and that Saul should arise relieved and refreshed by the music of the instrument of his future torment. For it is not long before envy enters into his heart, adding its envenomed stings to the anguish he is already enduring. He hears the song of the dancing women as they meet him with tabrets and with joy, answering one another, and saying, that Saul hath slain his thousands, and David his tens of thousands, and he asks, *What can David have more but the kingdom?* Yet after this he promises him his daughter in marriage, but quickly repenting him of the purposed honour, bestows her upon another. Again, hoping she may be a snare to him, he offers him his second daughter; and then we are told that he *saw and knew that the Lord was with David, and that his daughter loved him. And Saul was yet the more afraid of David; and he became his enemy continually:* yet once more at the earnest intercession of Jonathan, Saul consents to receive David again into his presence.

And Jonathan called David, and Jonathan shewed him all those things. And Jonathan brought David to Saul, and he was in his presence as in times past.

And there was war again: and David went out and fought with the Philistines, and slew them with a great slaughter; and they fled from him.

And the evil spirit from the Lord was upon Saul, as he sat in his house with his javelin in his hand: and David played with his hand.

And Saul sought to smite David even to the wall with the javelin; but he slipped away out of Saul's presence, and he smote the javelin into the wall: and David fled, and escaped that night.

The struggle was now passed The early tendency of the soul of the king to seek, and to do good, was finally subdued, and he went forth to pursue the chosen of the Lord, as an open and avowed enemy; yet, envouring to justify himself by proving that David had first risen up against him, he appeals to his servants, and fully conscious that his cause would not stand the test of impartial examination, he appeals to their interest, and to their compassion, rather than to their judgment.

Hear now, ye Benjamites; will the son of Jesse give every one of you fields and vineyards, and make you all captains of thousands, and captains of hundreds;

That all of you have conspired against me, and there

is none that sheweth me that my son hath made a league with the son of Jesse, and there is none of you that is sorry for me, or sheweth unto me that my son hath stirred up my servant against me, to lie in wait, as at this day?

Filled with rancour and jealousy, heightened by the rising fame and influence of David, Saul pursues him to the wilderness of Engedi, where we meet with a remarkable instance of forbearance on the part of a persecuted man. With the skirt of the king's robe in his hand, David shows him that he had advanced so near his person as to have been able with the same facility to destroy his life, but that he spared him from reverence for the Lord's anointed. When, struck at once with a sense of his own recent danger, with the honourable dealing of one whom he believed to be an enemy, with the sight of the man he had once loved—loved in the days when his heart was not as now, seared with the worst of passions; and perhaps touched more than all with the tones of the voice which in those happier days had been his music, Saul exclaims, *Is this thy voice, my son David?* and then *he lifted up his voice and wept.* After this burst of tenderness, his heart is opened to express the full sense he had of David's superiority, and the strong feeling ever present to his mind, that he should one day be compelled to resign the reins of government into his hands.

And he said to David, Thou art more righteous than I: for thou hast rewarded me good, whereas I have rewarded thee evil.

And now, behold, I know well that thou shalt surely be king, and that the kingdom of Israel shall be established in thine hand.

A second instance of a similar kind occurs, in which Saul appears to be struck, though less forcibly, with the generosity of David, whom he still addresses as his son, and of whom he again prophesies, that he "shall do great things, and shall still prevail." But these transient ebullitions of former feeling pass away before the gathering influence of David, and Saul humbles himself to seek consolation under his falling fortunes from the last miserable and barren resource of the utterly destitute in soul. Samuel is dead, and though the king had, from the impulse of his better judgment, put away all who had familiar spirits, and wizards, out of the land, he stoops to disguise himself, and to go at midnight to cast his forlorn hopes upon the enchantments of the witch of Endor

And he said to the woman, I pray thee, divine unto me by a familiar spirit, and bring up him, whom I shall name unto thee.

And the woman said unto him, Behold, thou knowest what Saul hath done, how he hath cut off those that have familiar spirits, and the wizards, out of the land: wherefore then layest thou a snare for my life, to cause me to die?

And Saul sware to her by the Lord, saying, As the Lord liveth, there shall no punishment happen to thee for this thing.

Then said the woman, Whom shall I bring up unto thee? And he said, Bring me up Samuel.

And when the woman saw Samuel, she cried with a loud voice; and the woman spake to Saul, saying, Why hast thou deceived me? for thou art Saul.

And the king said unto her, Be not afraid: for what sawest thou? And the woman said unto Saul, I saw gods ascending out of the earth

And he said unto her, What form is he of? And she said, An old man cometh up; and he is covered with a mantle. And Saul perceived that it was Samuel, and he stooped with his face to the ground, and bowed himself.

And Samuel said to Saul, Why hast thou disquieted me, to bring me up? And Saul answered, I am sore distressed; for the Philistines make war against me, and God is departed from me, and answereth me no more, neither by prophets, nor by dreams: therefore I have called thee, that thou mayst make known unto me what I shall do.

Then said Samuel, Wherefore then dost thou ask of me, seeing the Lord is departed from thee, and is become thine enemy?

And the Lord hath done to him as he spake by me: for the Lord hath rent the kingdom out of thine hand, and given it to thy neighbour, even to David:

Because thou obeyedst not the voice of the Lord, nor executedst his fierce wrath upon Amalek, therefore hath the Lord done this thing unto thee this day.

Moreover the Lord will also deliver Israel with thee into the hand of the Philistines: and to-morrow shalt thou and thy sons be with me: the Lord also shall deliver the host of Israel into the hand of the Philistines.

Then Saul fell straightway all along on the earth, and was sore afraid, because of the words of Samuel: and there was no strength in him; for he had eaten no bread all the day, nor all the night.

How affecting is this picture of the abject state of a fallen king—fallen not so much from earthly honour, as from the countenance and protection of the King of kings. Even Saul, the envious persecutor of his unoffending successor, becomes an object of compassion, when he answers to the question of Samuel, "Why hast thou disquieted me?" "*Because I am sore distressed.*" And when it is said that "he stooped with his face to the ground," and finally "fell straightway all along upon the earth," there can scarcely be a stronger description of total abandonment of soul under a deep sense of the overwhelming might of Omnipotence; as well as of a melancholy presage of the entire uprooting of all that he had trusted and gloried in. Yet scarcely trusted in, for he had greatly feared the thing which was about to come upon him, and which the awful voice of the prophet risen from the dead had solemnly confirmed.

The doom of the king of Israel was now sealed. And when the Philistines arose and fought against Israel, and "followed hard after Saul and his sons, and the Philistines slew Jonathan, and Abinadab, and Melchi-shua, Saul's sons;"

And the battle went sore against Saul, and the archers hit him; and he was sore wounded of the archers;

Then said Saul unto his armour-bearer, Draw thy sword, and thrust me through therewith; lest these uncircumcised come and thrust me through, and abuse me. But his armour-bearer would not; for he was sore afraid. Therefore Saul took a sword, and fell upon it.

Through the whole of this history, we trace the same strong and natural developement of feeling, which all our most talented authors aspire to in their descriptions, and upon which they chiefly depend for the poetical interest of what they describe. But while in the character of Saul are forcibly portrayed the fatal workings of the passions of envy, jealousy, and remorse, accompanied with many of those delicate shades, which denote the latest yearnings after good, and the earliest tendency to evil, the character of David is scarcely less poetical in its strength, and beauty, and consistency, varied by a few instances of natural weakness, producing their own atonement in the humiliation, the abasement, the agony of mind, and the final welcome back to Divine love, by which they are succeeded.

The attachment between David and Jonathan is perhaps the most beautiful and perfect instance of true friendship which we have on record. As a shepherd, and a prince, their first covenant is made.

Then Jonathan and David made a covenant, because he loved him as his own soul.

And Jonathan stripped off the robe that was upon him, and gave it to David, and his garments, even to his sword, and to his bow, and to his girdle.

And we see the same covenant binding them together through all the changes of their after life; for Jonathan, who loved the simple minstrel boy that charmed away the evil spirit from his father, knew not the envy of Saul when that minstrel became a man of war, and multitudes were gathered beneath his banner. And David, persecuted as he was by the father of his friend, never once betrayed towards him or his, the bitterness of an injured spirit, but followed him even to his death, with the reverence due to the Lord's anointed. It is then that he pours forth, both for Saul and Jonathan, that beautiful and affecting lamentation, which no language can exceed in poetry and pathos.

The beauty of Israel is slain upon thy high places: how are the mighty fallen!

Tell it not in Gath, publish it not in the streets of Askelon; lest the daughters of the Philistines rejoice, lest the daughters of the uncircumcised triumph.

Ye mountains of Gilboa, let there be no dew, neither let there be rain, upon you, nor fields of offerings: for there the shield of the mighty is vilely cast away, the shield of Saul, as though he had not been anointed with oil.

From the blood of the slain, from the fat of the mighty, the bow of Jonathan turned not back, and the sword of Saul returned not empty.

Saul and Jonathan were lovely and pleasant in their lives, and in death they were not divided: they were swifter than eagles, they were stronger than lions.

Ye daughters of Israel, weep over Saul, who clothed you in scarlet, with other delights, who put on ornaments of gold upon your apparel.

How are the mighty fallen in the midst of the battle! O Jonathan, thou wast slain in thine high places.

I am distressed for thee, my brother Jonathan: very pleasant hast thou been unto me: thy love to me was wonderful, passing the love of woman.

How are the mighty fallen, and the weapons of war perished!

There is an instance of maternal affection recorded in the 21st chapter of the same book, which in speaking of the strength of human passions ought not to be passed over without notice. It is where David was commanded to destroy the remnant of the house of Saul, and seven sons of the late king were delivered up into his hand, but he spared Mephibosheth, the son of Jonathan, because of the Lord's oath that was between David and Jonathan.

But the king took the two sons of Rizpah, the daughter of Aiah, whom she bare unto Saul, Armoni and Mephibosheth; and the five sons of Michal, the daughter of Saul, whom she brought up for Adriel, the son of Barzillai, the Meholathite;

And he delivered them into the hands of the Gibeonites, and they hanged them in the hill before the Lord: and they fell all seven together, and were put to death in the days of harvest, in the first days, in the beginning of barley harvest.

And Rizpah, the daughter of Aiah, took sackcloth, and spread it for her upon the rock, from the beginning of harvest, until water dropped upon them out of heaven, and suffered neither the birds of the air to rest on them by day, nor the beasts of the field by night.

Of all the instances, imaginary or real, handed down to us by fable or history, we have not one of a more intense and devoted love than this. A solitary woman seated upon a rock, watching the wasting bodies of her two dead sons, day after day—night after night—with no shelter but the open canopy of heaven—no repose but the sackcloth spread upon the rock, an emblem of her own abasement—no hope but to see the last—the very last of all she loved—no consolation but her constancy—no support but the magnitude of her own incommunicable grief. It was the beginning of harvest, and the feet of a busy multitude might come and go beneath that solitary rock—the shout of gladness—the acclamation of the joyous reapers might be heard from the valleys below; but there she sat in her loneliness upon the dismal watch tower of death, faithful to her silent and sacred trust, *suffering neither the birds of the air to rest on them by day, nor the beasts of the field by night.*

The whole life of the prophet Elijah, especially his last appearance upon earth, is remarkable for an interest whose *least* recommendation is that of being highly poetical; for deeply as this subject has occupied the heart of the writer, it must be confessed that in pursuing it through the Holy Scriptures, and tracing its connexion with the revelation of those sacred truths upon which depend our hopes of eternity, the consideration of poetry loses much of its importance by comparison, and the task of the writer becomes like that of one who culls with adventurous hand, the flowers that grow around the fountain of life. This view of the subject would of itself be sufficient to prevent any near approach to the doctrinal parts of the Scriptures, whose strictly spiritual import, though still couched in language both figurative and poetical in the extreme, places them above the reach of ordinary discussion, in a sphere more exclusively appropriated to considerations of infinitely greater importance.

Some further progress may however be justifiable in the course we hope we have hitherto pursued without profaning what is pure, or violating what is sacred; and we consequently pause at that passage in the book of Kings, in which the prophet Elijah is described as escaping from his enemies into the solitude of the wilderness, where, casting himself upon the ground, he exclaims, "It is enough; now, O Lord, take away my life, for I am not better than my fathers."

Such were the human feelings contending for the empire of his mind, that he was almost weary of the service of his Divine Master, accompanied as it was with disappointment, hatred, and persecution. How simple, and yet how admirably adapted to his peculiar state, are the means here adopted to bring him again to a sense of the superintending care and love of his heavenly Father.

And as he lay and slept under a juniper tree, behold, then an angel touched him, and said unto him, Arise and eat.

And he looked, and behold, there was a cake baken on the coals, and a cruse of water at his head. And he did eat and drink, and laid him down again.

And the angel of the Lord came again a second time, and touched him, and said, Arise and eat; because the journey is too great for thee.

And he arose, and did eat and drink, and went in the strength of that meat forty days and forty nights unto Horeb the mount of God.

And he came thither unto a cave, and lodged there, and behold, the word of the Lord came unto him, What dost thou here, Elijah?

And he said, I have been very jealous for the Lord God of hosts: for the children of Israel have forsaken thy covenant, thrown down thine altars, and slain thy prophets with the sword; and I, even I only, am left; and they seek my life, to take it away.

And he said, Go forth, and stand upon the mount before the Lord. And, behold, the Lord passed by, and a great and strong wind rent the mountains, and brake in pieces the rocks before the Lord; but the Lord was not in the wind: and after the wind an earthquake; but the Lord was not in the earthquake.

And after the earthquake a fire; but the Lord was not in the fire: and after the fire a still small voice.

And it was so, when Elijah heard it, that he wrapped his face in his mantle, and went out, and stood in the entering in of the cave. And, behold, there came a voice unto him, and said, What dost thou here, Elijah?

Where, through the wide range of modern literature can we find a passage to be compared with this, for the conciseness and simplicity with which ideas the most sublime and elevated are conveyed into the mind? The prophet had been looking, (perhaps impatiently) for some striking exhibition of Almighty power amongst the children of men, forgetful of the secret springs of action, and action itself being alike under the control of Omnipotence; when his faith and his confidence are reanimated by witnessing one of those tremendous and awful convulsions of the elements, by which forests are uprooted, and rocks overthrown, accompanied with the internal conviction that the immediate presence of the Lord was not there. Again, an earthquake shakes the world; but the Lord is not in the earthquake; after the earthquake a fire, but the Lord is not in the fire. No; though such are the open manifestations of his power, by which he makes the nations tremble, yet the prophet was convinced that the war of the elements might exist, and the destruction of the earth ensue, without that sensible presence of the Almighty, for the want of which his soul was fainting. At last, after the fire, there came a *still small voice*, and Elijah felt that the Lord was near, that he was not forsaken, and that, independent of the outward symbols of illimitable power, the Creator of the world is able to carry on his operations in the mind of man, by the desire of the heart, the silent thought, or the secret impulse directed towards the accomplishment of his inscrutable designs.

A great proportion of the Holy Scriptures is not only poetical, but real poetry. Under this head the song of Moses, and the children of Israel, is the first instance that occurs. In this song, the passage of the children of Israel through the Red Sea, the overthrow of Pharaoh's host, and the wonderful dealing of the Lord with his chosen people, are commemorated in language highly figurative and sublime.

The Lord is my strength and song, and he is become my salvation: he is my God, and I will prepare him an habitation; my father's God, and I will exalt him.

Thy right hand, O Lord, is become glorious in power: thy right hand, O Lord, hath dashed in pieces the enemy.

And in the greatness of thy excellency hast thou overthrown them that rose up against thee: thou sentest forth thy wrath, which consumed them as stubble.

And with the blast of thy nostrils the waters were gathered together, the floods stood upright as an heap, and the depths were congealed in the heart of the sea.

Who is like unto thee, O Lord, among the gods? who is like thee, glorious in holiness, fearful in praises, doing wonders?

Thou stretchedst out thy right hand, the earth swallowed them.

Thou in thy mercy hast led forth the people which thou hast redeemed: thou hast guided them in thy strength unto thy holy habitation.

Thou shalt bring them in, and plant them in the mountain of thine inheritance, in the place, O Lord, which thou hast made for thee to dwell in, in the sanctuary, O Lord, which thy hands have established.

The Lord shall reign for ever and ever.

When Moses pours forth before the people his last public testimony to the mercy, the might, and the vengeance of the Almighty, it is in the same powerful strain of poetical fervour.

Give ear, O ye heavens, and I will speak; and hear, O earth, the words of my mouth.

Do ye thus requite the Lord, O foolish people and unwise? Is not he thy father that hath brought thee? Hath he not made thee, and established thee?

Remember the days of old, consider the years of many generations: ask thy father, and he will shew thee, thy elders, and they will tell thee.

When the Most High divided to the nations their inheritance, when he separated the sons of Adam, he set the bounds of the people according to the number of the children of Israel.

For the Lord's portion is his people; Jacob is the lot of his inheritance.

He found him in a desert land, and in the waste howling wilderness; he led him about, he instructed him, he kept him as the apple of his eye.

As an eagle stirreth up her nest, fluttereth over her young, spreadeth abroad her wings, taketh them, beareth them on her wings:

So the Lord alone did lead him, and there was no strange God with him.

To me belongeth vengeance, and recompense; their foot shall slide in due time: for the day of their calamity is at hand, and the things that shall come upon them make haste.

For the Lord shall judge his people, and repent himself for his servants, when he seeth that their power is gone, and there is none shut up, or left.

And he shall say, Where are their gods, their rock in whom they trusted?

And again, the last blessing of Moses is delivered in language full of poetry.

And he said, The Lord came from Sinai, and rose up from Seir unto them; he shined forth from mount Paran, and he came with ten thousands of saints: from his right hand went a fiery law unto them.

And of Joseph he said, Blessed of the Lord be his land, for the precious things of heaven, for the dew, and for the deep that coucheth beneath,

And for the precious fruits brought forth by the sun, and for the precious things put forth by the moon,

And for the chief things of the ancient mountains, and for the precious things of the lasting hills.

There is none like unto the God of Jeshurun, who rideth upon the heaven in thy help, and in his excellency on the sky.

The eternal God is thy refuge, and underneath are the everlasting arms, and he shall thrust out the enemy from before thee; and shall say, Destroy them.

Israel then shall dwell in safety alone: the fountain of Jacob shall be upon a land of corn and wine, also his heavens shall drop down dew.

Happy art thou, O Israel: who is like unto thee, O people saved by the Lord, the shield of thy help, and who is the sword of thy excellency! and thine enemies shall be found liars unto thee; and thou shalt tread upon their high places.

These two examples are, however, inferior to the song of Deborah and Barak, for the high tone of metaphorical ornament, characterizing the whole of that incomparable specimen of poetical imagery, which immediately strikes us with the idea of its having been the archetype of some of the finest passages in Ossian, as well as the original from which many of our own notions of the beauty and melody of language are derived.

Praise ye the Lord for the avenging of Israel, when the people willingly offered themselves.

Hear, O ye kings; give ear, O ye princes; I, even I, will sing unto the Lord; I will sing praise to the Lord God of Israel.

Lord, when thou wentest out of Seir, when thou marchedst out of the field of Edom, the earth trembled, and the heavens dropped, the clouds also dropped water.

The mountains melted from before the Lord, even that Sinai from before the Lord God of Israel.

And the princes of Issachar were with Deborah; even Issachar, and also Barak: he was sent on foot into the valley. For the divisions of Reuben there were great thoughts of heart.

Why abodest thou among the sheepfolds, to hear the bleatings of the flocks? For the divisions of Reuben there were great searchings of heart.

Gilead abode beyond Jordan: and why did Dan remain in ships? Asher continued on the sea-shore, and abode in his breaches.

Zebulun and Naphtali were a people that jeoparded their lives unto the death in the high places of the field.

The kings came and fought; then fought the kings of Canaan in Taanach by the waters of Megiddo: they took no gain of money.

They fought from heaven; the stars in their courses fought against Sisera.

The river of Kishon swept them away, that ancient river, the river Kishon. O my soul, thou hast trodden down strength.

Curse ye Meroz, (said the angel of the Lord,) curse ye bitterly the inhabitants thereof; because they came not to the help of the Lord, to the help of the Lord against the mighty.

Blessed above women shall Jael the wife of Heber the Kenite be; blessed shall she be above women in the tent.

She put her hand to the nail, and her right hand to the workman's hammer: and with the hammer she smote Sisera; she smote off his head, when she had pierced and stricken through his temples.

At her feet he bowed, he fell, he lay down: at her feet he bowed, he fell; where he bowed, there he fell down dead.

The mother of Sisera looked out at a window, and cried through the lattice, Why is his chariot so long in coming? why tarry the wheels of his chariots?

Her wise ladies answered her, yea, she returned answer to herself:

Have they not sped? have they not divided the prey; to every man a damsel or two? to Sisera a prey of divers colours, a prey of divers colours of needle-work, of divers colours of needle-work on both sides, meet for the necks of them that take the spoil?

So let all thine enemies perish, O Lord: but let them that love him be as the sun when he goeth forth in his might.

Were it possible to take away the poetry from these passages, and leave their sense entire, we should then see how much they owe in intellectual beauty, to that peculiar style of language, which adorns the whole of the Scriptures. It would, however, be a vain attempt to remove one, and leave the other untouched; because their sense as well as their poetry consists in allusion, and association. We are not merely told of that, which it is the direct object of the inspired minstrels to describe, but our thoughts are extended beyond to an infinity of relative ideas, which neither crowd upon nor neutralize each other, but all flow naturally and easily into the same stream of enjoyment, mingling with and accelerating its uniform and uninterrupted course.

We now conclude this minute examination of the Scriptures, not only because it is unnecessary for our purpose to pursue it further, but because we should soon arrive at those portions of the sacred record, which consist entirely of poetry, the most genuine and sublime. We have already seen enough to convince us that the same principle which is associated with our highest intellectual enjoyments, is diffused—copiously diffused throughout the written revelation of eternal truth, a revelation whose wonderful adaptation to every variety of human nature, feeling, and condition, carries along with it the clearest evidence of its divine authority. Coeval with the infancy of time, it still remains, and widens in the circle of its intelligence. Simple as the language of a child, it charms the most fastidious taste. Mournful as the voice of grief, it reaches to the highest pitch of exultation. Intelligible to the unlearned peasant, it supplies the critic and the sage with food for earnest thought. Silent and secret as the reproofs of conscience, it echoes beneath the vaulted dome of the cathedral and shakes the trembling multitude. The last companion of the dying and the destitute, it seals the bridal vow, and crowns the majesty of kings. Closed in the heedless grasp of the luxurious and the slothful, it unfolds its awful record over the yawning grave. Sweet, and gentle, and consoling to the pure in heart, it thunders and threatens against the unawakened mind. Bright and joyous as the morning star to the benighted traveller, it rolls like the waters of the deluge over the path of him who wilfully mistakes his way. And, finally, adapting itself to every shade of human character, and to every grade of moral feeling, it instructs the ignorant, woos the gentle, consoles the afflicted, encourages the desponding, rouses the negligent, threatens the rebellious, strikes home to the reprobate, and condemns the guilty.

It may be observed, that all this might have been effected without the instrumentality of the principle of poetry; and so unquestionably it might, had the Creator of the human heart seen meet to adapt it to different means of instruction; but as that heart is constituted, the delicate touches of feeling to be found in every part of the Holy Scriptures accord peculiarly with its sensibilities; the graceful ornaments which adorn the language of the Bible correspond to the impressions it has received, the ideas which have consequently been formed of the principles of taste and beauty; and by no other medium that we are capable of conceiving, could the human heart have been more forcibly assured of the truths to which belong eternal life.

Had the Bible been without its poetical character, we should have wanted the voice of an angel to recommend it to the acceptance of mankind. Prone as we are to neglect this banquet upon which the most exalted mind may freely and fully feast, we should then have regarded it with tenfold disdain. But such is the unlimited goodness of him who knew from the beginning what was in the heart of man, that not only the wide creation is so designed as to accord with our views of what is magnificent and beautiful, and thus to remind us of his glory · but even the record of his immediate dealing with his rational and responsible creatures, is so filled with the true melody of language, as to harmonize with all our most tender, refined, and elevated thoughts. With our established ideas of beauty, and grace, and pathos, and sublimity, either concentrated in the minutest point, or extended to the widest range, we can derive from the Scriptures a fund of gratification not to be found in any other memorial of past or present time. From the worm that grovels in the dust beneath our feet, to the track of the leviathan in the foaming deep—from the moth that corrupts the secret treasure, to the eagle that soars above his eyry in the clouds—from the wild ass of the desert, to the lamb within the shepherd's fold—from the consuming locust, to the cattle upon a thousand hills—from the rose of Sharon to the cedar of Lebanon—from the crystal stream gushing forth out of the flinty rock, to the wide waters of the deluge—from the barren waste to the fruitful vineyard, and the land flowing with milk and honey—from the lonely path of the wanderer, to the gathering of a mighty multitude—from the tear that falls in secret, to the din of battle, and the shout of a triumphant host—from the solitary in the wilderness, to the satrap on his throne—from the mourner clad in sackcloth, to the prince in purple robes—from the gnawings of the worm that dieth not, to the seraphic visions of the blest—from the still small voice, to the thunders of Omnipotence—from the depths of hell, to the regions of eternal glory, there is no degree of beauty or deformity, no tendency to good or evil, no shade of darkness or gleam of light, which does not come within the cognizance of the Holy Scriptures; and therefore there is no impression or conception of the mind that may not find a corresponding picture, no thirst for excellence that may not meet with its full supply, and no condition of humanity necessarily excluded from the unlimited scope of adaptation and of sympathy comprehended in the language and the spirit of the Bible.

How gracious then—how wonderful, and harmonious, is that majestic plan by which one ethereal principle, like an electric chain of light and life, extends through the very elements of our existence, giving music to language, elevation to thought, vitality to feeling, and intensity, and power, and beauty, and happiness, to the exercise of every faculty of the human soul!

THE POETRY OF RELIGION.

Nor are the Holy Scriptures the utmost bound of the sphere through which poetry extends. With that religion which is the essence of the Bible, it may also be associated. The power of human intellect has never yet worked out from the principles of thought and feeling, a subject more sublime than that of an omnipotent Being presiding over a universe of his own creating. There have been adventurous spirits who have dared to sing the wonders of a world without a God, but as a proof how much they felt the want of this higher range of poetical interest, they have referred the creation and government of the external world to an ideal spirit of nature—a mysterious intelligence, single or multiplied, smiling in the sunshine, and frowning in the storm, with the mock majesty of omnipotence.

Again, the propensities of our nature—the low grovelling hopes and fears that agitate the human heart, when centred solely in what is material, without connection with, or reference to eternal mind, as subjects for the genius of the poet, are robbed of half their interest, and all their refinement; but when the feelings which form the sum of our experience are regarded as the impress of the hand of our Creator, when the motives which lead us on to action are considered as deriving their stimulus and strength from almighty power, and when the great chain of circumstances and events which influence our lives are linked in with the designs of a superintending Providence, they assume a character at once poetical and sacred, a colouring which blends the light of heaven with the shades of earth, and an importance which raises them from what is ordinary and familiar, to what is astonishing and sublime.

The most serious objection ever advanced against poetry, is that of its not *necessarily* constituting any part of our religion, and being in no way *essential* to our spiritual progress. Upon precisely the same principles it might be argued, that beauty does not necessarily form any part of utility, and that happiness is not essential to the moral constitution of man. The same answer will apply in both cases; and it is one which ought to be sufficient for creatures of limited perceptions like ourselves. It has seemed meet to the Author of our existence so to construct our mental and bodily functions, that we shall derive pleasure from the principle of beauty diffused throughout the external world, and that we shall be lured on by a perpetual thirst for enjoyment to that which is our only true and lasting happiness; as well as so to constitute our perceptions and feelings that poetry shall be one of our chief sources of intellectual gratification, at the same time that it is intimately blended with the highest objects of our desire; so that in the pursuit of ultimate and eternal good, we have no need to resign the society of this unwearying friend, whose companionship is a constant refreshment and delight.

I would humbly refer both these subjects to the unlimited goodness of a gracious God. If the beauty and magnificence of the visible creation is not essential to practical utility, let us look upon it as a free gift, liberally offered for the promotion of our happiness; and if poetry does not appear to our finite views to be in reality a part of religion, let us consider how they are associated, and gratefully acknowledge their connexion, rather than presumptuously attempt to separate what the principles of our nature teach us to unite.

We will first speak of the poetry of religion as it is exhibited to the world, in some of the various modes of worship which mark the civil and religious history of man.

Under the terrific rule of tyranny and superstition, religion has ever been the first to suffer and the last to yield; and whether we contemplate the martyr at the stake, singing his triumphant hymns amongst the circling flames; or pursue the silent devotee to the secret recesses of the mountain, or the wilderness, where the bond of Christian brotherhood is strengthened and confirmed by the horrors of an impending fate which threatens to leave that bond alone unbroken, of all that have sweetened and supported life, we see and feel, that the might of mortal suffering, gives even to the most humble victims of cruelty and oppression, a dignity which entitles them to the highest place in the scale of poetical interest.*

So far as poetry is connected with the exercise of fortitude, resignation, and ardent zeal, it is exhibited by the martyr in its holiest character. Suffering even to death, and such a death! yet suffering triumphantly, that the glory of God may shine with additional brightness before the eyes of men, and that unbelievers may behold the majesty and the power of the faith for which he dies. Nor has it been always the man of iron mould, of unshaken nerve, and inflexible resolve, who has died triumphant at the stake. Creatures of delicate and gentle form have been led forth from the hall and the bower, and they too have raised the cry of exultation that they were deemed worthy to set the seal of suffering to the cause they loved. Eyes that have never dwelt save on the fairest page of human life have gleamed out from amidst the lurid flames, and looked up in calmness and in confidence to the mercy that lies hid beyond the skies; hands whose gentle office had been the constant ministration of tenderness and charity, have been clasped in fervent prayer, until they mingled with the ashes of the sinking pile; brows around which the cherub locks of youth were woven, have borne the fatal ordeal, and betrayed no sign of shrinking from the fiery blast; and voices whose sweet tones were once the natural minstrelsy of happiness and love, have been heard above the crackling embers, and the shouts of brutal acclamation, hymning to heaven the pure melodious strains of a seraphic joy. Fresh from the fount of domestic peace, young, innocent bosoms have been torn to bleed and writhe in the centre of the torturing fire, and trembling with the last throbs of mortal agony, have borne their unflinching testimony to the fervour of their faith. The cry of an agonized parent bursting from the surrounding throng, may have reached the sufferer in the flames, the eye that was once the beacon of his hopes may have glanced upon him through the dense and thickening smoke, and thoughts dear as the memory of early love, may have rushed upon his soul even there, bathing it in the tenderness of childhood, and melting down his high resolve, which, but for that sustaining and unquenchable zeal, would yet have sent him forth a worthless wreck upon the troubled ocean of life after the promised haven had been in sight, the pilot near, and the anchor of eternal hope ready to be cast for ever into the foundation which no storms can shake. Yet even here his faith remains immoveable, and he shakes off the lingering weakness of humanity, his joyful spirit already anticipating the unbounded fruition of its promised felicity.

Let us contemplate the awful scene one moment longer. The excitement has subsided; the cry of the merciless spectators is heard no more; the smoking pile becomes one universal ruin; and the living form so lately quivering with the intensity of quickened and agonized sensation, is mingled with the silent dust. Are there not footsteps lingering near that fatal spot? Are there not looks too wild for tears, still fixed upon the white ashes with which the idle breezes are at play? Are there not hearts whose inmost depths are filled with bitterness, and thoughts of vengeance, and dreams of impious daring, and fierce, bold scrutiny of the ways of Providence, and presumptuous questioning if these are the tender mercies of the Most High? Yes; such has ever been the effect of persecution upon the human mind, and never is the infidel so firmly fortified against conviction, as when he contemplates the wrongs and the wretch-

* In justice to herself, the writer must here observe, in speaking of the poetry of religion, how forcibly she is struck with what some would call the *puerility* of the task she has undertaken; because this subject necessarily brings under serious observation the all important truths for which we ought to be willing either to live or die as duty may require; and before which all intellectual considerations, even that of poetry itself, vanish into comparative nothingness. She would however hope that her task may be pursued without irreverence, and that she may point out the poetry of religion with a distinct feeling of its weightier and more essential attributes, in the same way that a beholder may expatiate upon the architecture of a cathedral, without reference to the purpose for which the building was originally designed and to which it is still appropriated.

edness which man, infuriated with a blind and superstitious zeal inflicts upon his brother.

We turn from this scene of horrors to the aspect presented by religion under a milder form of persecution, or rather under one whose influence is more remote, and we follow a little company of faithful worshippers to their tabernacle in the mountains, where their canopy is the starry sky, and their altar the rude rocks of the wilderness. Upon the summit of a beetling precipice, a sentinel keeps watch, and while he looks to the sombre woods, the hollow caves, or the dim and distant heights, if haply he may discern the movements of an insiduous enemy, hymns of praise and adoration are heard from the congregation in the valley, as, echoing from crag to crag, the deep full anthem of devotion rises on the evening breeze. Then the devout and heartfelt prayer is offered up, that the true Shepherd will vouchsafe to look down upon and visit the scattered remnant of his flock, that his voice may yet call them into safe pastures, and that he will pour out the waters of eternal life, for the support of the feeble, the refreshment of the weary, and the consolation of the "sore distressed."

It is in such scenes and circumstances, that the followers of a persecuted faith become indeed brethren in the fellowship of Christ. Suffering in a common cause, apprehending the same danger, and led on by one purpose, the vital bond of the society extends and lives through all its members. Discord enters not into their communion, for the world is against them, and they can stand under its cruelty and oppression by no other compact than that of Christian love; jealousy pours not its rankling venom into their hearts, for they are hoping to attain a felicity in which all are blest; ambition sows not the seeds of selfishness amongst them, for their reward is one that admits of no monopoly—of which all may partake, without diminishing the portion of any: and after this pure and simple worship, how sacred, how fervent is the farewell of the brethren on separating for their distant home. Some have to trace the dubious sands of the sea-beaten shore, some the lonely sheep-track on the mountains, and some the hollow bed of the wintry torrent, whose thundering waters have worked out for themselves a rugged pathway down the hills; but all are accompanied by the same deep sense of outward danger, and internal peace—all have the same bright stars to light them on their silent way, and the same spiritual help to support their weary steps. They know not but the homes they are seeking may have become a heap of ruins; but they have learned to look for an everlasting habitation where the spoiler may not come. They know not but the sword of persecution may have severed the chain of their domestic happiness; but they feel that every link of that chain can be reunited in a world of peace. They know not but the shadow of destruction may have fallen upon all that beautified and cheered their earthly path; but they are pilgrims to a better land, and they have only to press onward in the simplicity of humble Christians, and the gates of the celestial city will soon be won.

Religion, stigmatized with the world's contempt, and hunted from the earth by the powerful emissaries of public authority, is ever the religion of the heart and the affections. Were it otherwise it could not stand its ground; but dignity and disgrace, temporal enjoyment and temporal suffering, even life and death, become as nothing in comparison with that righteous cause which men feel themselves called upon faithfully to uphold before a disbelieving people, for the glory of God and the benefit of their fellow creatures. If it be a test of the love which a man bears for his brother, that he will lay down his life for him, the test of suffering must also apply to his religion; and pure and devoted must be the love of him, who holds himself at all times in a state of readiness to lay down the last and dearest sacrifice upon the altar of his faith. Yes; that must be love indeed, which overweighs all earthly and natural affections, which separates the mother from her weeping child, the husband from his wife of yesterday, the friends who had been wont to take sweet counsel together, and last, but not least, which tears away the fond endearing thoughts of promised happiness from the heart around which they cling when it beats with the fervour of youthful hope, and rejoices in the anticipated sunshine of bright days to come, in which the lovely and the loved may dwell together in peace and safety even upon earth. It is not a light or common love that can thus sever the strongest ties of human life, and fortify the soul not only to endure all that our nature shrinks from, but to resign all that our nature teaches us to hold dear.

From the worship of the heart, we turn to that of the sanctuary—from religion robbed of its external attributes, restrained, and persecuted, and driven inward to the centre of volition, and sealed up in the fountains of spiritual life ; to that which powerful nations combine to support, before which suppliant monarchs bow, and which, supreme above the regal sceptre, sends forth its awful and imperious mandates through distant regions of the peopled world.

We enter the magnificent and stately edifice consecrated to the worship of a God no longer partially acknowledged, or reverenced at the risk of life, and we mark the pomp and the ceremonial designed to recommend that worship to the general acceptance of mankind. Through the richly variegated windows, bright beams of golden splendor are glancing on the marble floor, and lighting up the monumental tablets of departed worth. Deeds of heroic virtue, long since forgotten but for that faithful record, are dimly shadowed out upon the tombs, and the sculptured forms that bend in silent beauty over the unbroken slumbers of the dead, point with an awful warning to the inevitable doom of man. Above, around, and beneath us, are the storied pages on which human labour has inscribed the memorial of its power—the barriers raised by art against the encroachments of time—the landmarks graven upon stone, which denote the intellectual progress of past ages. We gaze upon the tessellated aisle, intersected with alternate light and shadow, where the stately columns, terminating in the solemn arch, rise like tall palm trees in the desert plain, whose graceful branches meet in stately grandeur above the head of the wayfaring traveller, while he pauses to bless their welcome shade, and thinks how lovely are the green spots of verdure in the wilderness—the fertile islands that beautify a waste and troubled sea. We listen, and the measured tread of sober feet is the only sound that disturbs the silence of that sacred place—we, listen, till the beating of our own hearts becomes audible, and we almost fear that a "stir—a breath" should break the slumbers of the dead—we listen, and suddenly the tremendous peal of the deep-toned organ bursts upon our ear, and sweet young voices, like a symphony of pure spirits, join the heavenly anthem as it rises in a louder strain of harmony, and echoes though every arch of the resounding pile. The anthem ceases, and the sound of prayer ascends from a thousand hearts, as variously formed as the lips from whence that prayer proceeds, yet all uniting in the worship of one God—all reverentially acknowledging his right to reign and rule with undisputed sway.

Perhaps it is the hour of evening worship, and instead of the bright sunbeams glancing through the many-tinted windows, and penetrating into the distant recesses of the cathedral pile, artificial lights of inferior lustre gleam out here and there, like stars in the midnight sky, making the intervening darkness more palpable and profound. It is the hour when "every soft and solemn influence" is poured most profusely upon the prostrate soul, when the sordid and mercenary cares of the day are over, and religion, like an angel of peace, descends upon the troubled spirit that knows no other resting place than her sanctuary—no other shelter than her brooding wing. It is the hour when all our warmest, purest, and holiest affections gush forth like rills of sweetness and refreshment, watering the verdure of the path of life, and producing fresh loveliness, and renewed delight. It is the hour when prayer is the natural language of the devoted soul, and here the humble penitent is kneeling to implore the pardon promised to the broken and contrite heart—there the parent devoutly asks a blessing upon his family, and his household, upon the wife of his bosom, and the children of his love—here the poor mendicant bares his pale brow before the eye of heaven, and stands without a blush in that presence to which wealth is no passport, and from which poverty affords no plea for rejection—there the rich arbitrer of magisterial law, humbly bends his knee, and acknowledges, that without the sanction of divine authority the judgment of man must be vain, and his sentence void—here the miserable outcast from society, glides unnoticed along the silent aisle, and bending beneath the shadow of a marble column, bathes her hollow cheek with tears whose sincerity is unquestioned here—there the gaily habited, admired, and cherished idol of the same society folds her white hands upon her bosom, and feels the deep aching void which religion alone is sufficient to supply—here the rosy lips of cherub infancy lisp the words of prayer, more felt than comprehended amidst the awful grandeur of that solemn scene; and there the wrinkled brow of age is illuminated with the overpowing brightness of anticipated joy, while feeble accents, broken by the tremors of infirmity and pain, tell of the gladness of renovated life.

It is this variety of sight and sound, mingled together into one scene, and united in the same holy purpose, which constitutes a harmony so true to the principles of human nature, as well as to the character and attributes of the Divine Being, and the relation between him and his lowly and erring creatures, that we cannot contemplate such worship without aspiring to partake in its reality—we cannot feel its reality without being raised higher in the scale of spiritual enjoyment.

If, retiring from this scene, we follow the penitent to his secret cell, we behold him lacerating his bleeding limbs, and torturing out what he believes to be the demon of his natural heart; or we watch him through the tedious hours of solitary musing, when the sun is shining upon the walls of his convent, upon the green flowery valley where it stands, and upon the glancing waters of a river whose pure fresh streams glide on with a perpetual melody, through woods, and groves, the verdant beauty of whose mazy labyrinths look like the chosen walks of wandering angels. While the bright sun is shining upon a scene, the pale monk sits brooding over the transgressions of his youth, and counting a never-varying circle of dull beads; or, stooping his cold forehead to the stony floor, he closes every avenue of rational enjoyment, and believing this immolation of his nature is the sacrifice his God requires, pledges himself to the same abstinence, the same penance, and the same abasement through all the long years of his after-life.

It is not, most assuredly, to the *nature* of such worship, that we would accord the meed of poetical merit; but to the earnestness, the sincerity, the total dedication of heart, which its votaries display, and which might sometimes bring a blush of shame upon the less devoted followers of a more enlightened faith.

Nor is the simplicity of a less ostentatious form of worship inferior in its accordance with the true spirit of poetry. There is not much to fix the gaze of the beholder in the quiet congregation of a village church, or in the little band of lowly suppliants who bend the knee within the walls of the conventicle, and listen to the impassioned eloquence, bursting in extemporaneous fervour, from the lips of the humble labourer in the vineyard, whose reward is not the gift of sordid gain, but the soul-sustaining consciousness of walking in the ways of truth, and yielding the tribute of obedience where simply to obey is to enjoy. There is not much to interest the *mere* spectator in such a scene; but there is much to cheer the spirit of the philanthropist in the contemplation of the earnest zeal, the strict integrity, and the devotional fervour which inspires this staunch adherence to what conscience points out as a better way than that established by former ages, supported by national authority, and persevered in by thousands from a blind partiality for old customs and familiar forms.

Far be it from the writer of these pages, to draw invidious comparisons between one creed and another, or to join the public voice which makes destruction rather than edification the object of its tumultuous outcry. Whatever is the subject of popular belief, or the common ground on which mankind concentrate their energies and hopes, it argues the proper exercise of moral feeling, when those who dissent from such belief have the courage and integrity to avow that dissent in the face of a disapproving world—

when those who depart from such ground, do so in Christian love, and charity, and with full purpose of heart.

It is when entertaining these views of moral rectitude, that we behold with peculiar interest a congregation of schismatical worshippers, and even if we cannot join in the peculiar form of their devotional duties, we can at least rejoice that there are independent minds, ready to shake off the bondage of established opinion, and freely and fully to acknowledge whatever they conscientiously believe to be the truth, making the testimony of their own faith supreme above the authorities of this world, and preferring the service of God before the gracious countenance of men.

There are cases too, when this system of worship comes home to the affections of the people unprovided for by the established religion of the land. There are obscure and isolated beings, dwelling in remote or thinly peopled districts, by whom the sound of the Sabbath bell is seldom heard, and to whom the welcome visitation of a Christian minister would scarcely be known, but for the pilgrim preacher, who penetrates, not only into the solitary cottage of the herdsman on the mountain, but into the lowest haunts of savage life, where, instead of the simplicity of pastoral innocence, he finds the brutality of rustic vice. Nor must we judge of the announcement of a village prayer meeting, or the appearance of an itinerant preacher, by what we ourselves should feel, if compelled to listen to his wild eloquence, stirring up the unsophisticated mind to enthusiasm, if not to pure devotion. We must picture the poor and destitute old man, infirm and helpless, racked with pain, and trembling on the brink of the grave, weary of life, yet dreading the darkness and the uncertainty of death, his anguish never soothed by the voice of kindness, nor his heart enlightened by the words of comfort or instruction. We must picture him day after day, and night after night, the sleepless, restless victim of lassitude and disease, without a thought beyond the narrow bounds of his miserable hovel, or a feeling separate from the pangs that torture his emaciated frame. To such an one, perhaps the wandering minister imparts the sanguine hope that animates his own soul, when suddenly the couch of suffering is converted into one of triumph. He who cannot read, can *feel* the words of life; and joyfully he clasps his trembling hands in full assurance of an immortality from whose inexhaustible happiness, the poor, the despised, and the needy are not shut out.

Or we turn to the cottage of the lonely widow who has lost the sole prop of her declining years, whose children are distant or dead, who sit from morn till night in the silence of her desolate home, pursuing the same monotonous range of limited and painful thought—looking alternately from her narrow lattice upon the wide bare surface of the distant hills, or back again to the white ashes that lie upon her silent hearth. It is to such a being (and there are many whose existence is a little more enlivened by mental or spiritual excitement) that the social prayer meeting becomes an object of intense and incalculable enjoyment, the communion of fellow Christians a living and lasting consolation, and the record of divine truth the source of vital interest and delight.

There are in the darkest and most degraded walks of life, coarse, blind votaries of mere animal gratification, outcasts from the pale of intellectual as well as moral fellowship, gross bodily creatures, who sink the character of man beneath the level of the brute—men whose haunts are the polluted habitations of guilt and shame, whose feelings are seared with the brand of public infamy, and whose souls are blasted with the contagion of lawless thoughts and despicable purposes, and passions uncontrolled. By such men the paths that lead to the house of prayer are more despised than the gates of hell, and rather than seek the pardon of an offended God, they impotently defy his power. But at the same time that they are boasting of their recklessness, and making an open parade of the impious prostitution of their souls, the worm that dieth not has begun its irresistible operation upon their hearts, and the darkness and horror which surrounded them in their solitary hours assume a tenfold gloom. They hear of religion, and they hate the name; but with their hate is mingled a secret trust in its efficacy to remove the intolerable burden under which they groan. They scorn to join the congregation of openly professing worshippers, though but to hear the nature of religion explained; but without implicating themselves, they can go forth into the open fields to listen to, and mock the less authorized enthusiast, pouring his unpremeditated eloquence upon the wondering ears of thousands, who would not have listened to his voice elsewhere. And such are the means by which the hardened sinner is not unfrequently awakened from his gross and brutal sleep, the outcasts from the society drawn back within the wholesome limitations of a decent life, and the reprobate reclaimed from the dangerous error of his ways.

Nor let the more enlightened Christian despise such humble means, whose chief merit is their unbounded extent, added to their adaptation to extreme cases, and whose efficacy, proved by the observation of every day, is a sufficient warrant for their lawfulness. With the too frequent abuse of these means, poetry holds no connection; but it is their least recommendation to say, that poetry is intimately associated with their power to awaken the dormant energies of the mind, to penetrate the heart, and mingle with the affections, and to let in the glorious light of immortality upon the benighted soul.

Of all the public ordinances of our religion, that which appoints one day in seven for a season of rest, is perhaps the most productive of poetical association, and as such has ever been a favourite theme with the imaginative bard. In a world such as we inhabit, and with a bodily and mental conformation like ours, it is natural that rest should become (especially in advanced age) the object of our continual desire, and that regarding it superficially, as it appears to us in the midst of the cares and perplexities of ordinary life, we should learn to speak of it as our chief good; although it is probable that in a purer sphere, and endowed with renovated powers of action and perception, we should find that constant activity was more productive of enjoyment. Even here, the word rest is one of comparative signification, for those who have an opportunity of making the experiment become more weary of continued repose than of continued exertion. Still the pining of the heart is ever after some portion of natural and necessary rest, and the Sabbath, where it is regarded with right feelings, affords a beautiful and perfect exemplification of the provision made by our Heavenly Father, to meet the wants and the wishes of humanity.

Those pitiable beings whose mental existence is supported by a perpetual succession of excitements, are wholly incapable of conceiving what the Sabbath is to the mechanic, the labourer, or even to the man of business, whose heart is with his family, while his head and hands are occupied in the daily traffic of mercantile affairs. To such a man the Sabbath is indeed a day of refreshment, as well as rest—a day in which he can listen to the prattle of his almost unknown children, and look into their opening minds, and cultivate a short—alas, too short acquaintance with the sources of domestic happiness—it is a day on which he can enter into the free unreserved companionship of his own fireside, and, feeling that he has a possession in the esteem and the approbation of those around him, in the moral rights of man, in the institutions of religion, and in the heritage of an immortal creature, he aspires to a higher and more intellectual state of being than that absorbed in the continual pursuit of wealth. If then he loves the Sabbath, it is not merely because it relieves him from the necessity of laborious exertion, but because it makes him a wiser and a better man.

The mechanic has the same reason, and the same right to welcome this day. Indeed it seems to be the peculiar privilege of those who spend their intervening hours in toil and trouble, to appreciate the enjoyment of the Sabbath, so far as it affords them an interval of cessation from irksome cares. Rightly to enjoy, and fully to appreciate the value of the Sabbath, requires the association of a higher range of thought and feeling, such as religion alone can supply.

If in the busy town, and for those who tread the beaten paths of life, there is much to interest the heart in the recurrence of the Sabbath—in the chiming of innumerable bells at stated intervals of public worship, in the gathering of vast multitudes assembled for one common purpose, and that the holiest of which our mortal nature is capable, and in the general aspect of sobriety, order, and profound respect which pervades the thickly-peopled city, how much more is to be felt where man exists in a state of greater simplicity, in the rude home of the peasant, or in those little groups of humble dwellings gemming the fertile plain, in the midst of which the tall village spire rises and points to heaven. It is not here as in the city, that the loud peal of many bells announces the hour of prayer, but the single bell tolling at intervals, is converted into music by the fresh pure morning air, and the many simple and delightful associations connected with that well-known sound. Perhaps a beloved and revered minister is there to welcome his people once again within the fold of Christian communion; families separated by the occupations of the week, now meet to offer up their fervent prayers together; the the village pauper stands upon the same foundation as the village lord, and looks upward with the same calm countenance to meet the light of heaven; the comely-habited maiden closes the wicket of her father's garden, and hastens at the universal call; while the feeble steps of infancy and age, blending their weakness and their humble confidence together, are heard slowly advancing along the solemn aisle. No sooner is the simple service ended, than a cordial recognition takes place between the pastor and his congregation, and often between those who meet too seldom—the rich and the poor—the exalted and the lowly: and kind questions are asked of the suffering or the absent, followed by visits of Christian love, and words of consolation, to those who are debarred the privilege of meeting their brethren and their friends within the consecrated walls of the church.

It is on these days, that through the stillness of the summer air, we often hear the mournful cadence of distant and harmonious voices, singing at intervals their low sweet requiem over the bier of a departed friend, as they bear him to his last long home beneath the outstretched arms of the sheltering elms, that skirt the precincts of the dead, and cast their sombre shadows athwart the beams of the declining sun. Perhaps it is a venerable parent who has been quietly translated to his place of rest, and the tears of the surrounding mourners fall into the grave without bitterness, and almost without regret; for the poor have happier thoughts of the last call announcing the termination of mortal suffering, than those whose progress through this world is less interrupted with hardship, toil, and pain.

But it is quite as possible that the lifeless form for which that bier is spread, should have been the rustic beauty of the fair and the festival, the pride of the village the belle who bore away the palm of admiration from her less lovely sisters who now stand weeping by her side, without one touch of envy, or one wish, except to call her back to trace again the flowery meadows, to sing her songs of native melody, and to meet them with her ever-beaming smile of youth and joy. But it may not be. And she who was so fondly cherished, so tenderly beloved, so flattered and admired, is consigned to the cold prison of the tomb, and left to the unbroken silence of her solitary sleep.

With the Sabbath evening in the village, are connected a thousand agreeable associations, which those who are not alive to the true poetry of life, are unable to enjoy. Nor is it the least portion of the satisfaction afforded by this day, to see the cattle that have borne their share in the labour of the week, without participating in its reward, browsing in the cool pastures, or resting their toil worn limbs upon the sunny slopes of the verdant hills. The shady lanes around the village afford shelter and refreshment to many a persecuted animal that knows no other day of rest; and as we pass along, we see groups of rosy children wandering hand in hand in quest of wild flowers, or the purple fruit of the bramble, which seems to be the only unalienable property of childhood; or we meet with families going half-way home with a beloved son or daughter, whose portion of servitude is now cast in some distant hamlet, from whence the occasional return is an event of long promise, and widely participated joy. Around the open door of the peasant are other groups of more infantine beauty, and as the father stands beside them, with the Bible in his hand, the fond mother looks alternately at him and them, as if the whole wealth of her existence were centered in these her household treasures; while retiring into some quiet nook of the cottage or the garden, the little patient pupil of Sabbath discipline carefully cons his lesson for the coming week. Farther on within a neatly trimmed enclosure, where the red daisy, and the dark green box, mark out the boundary lines surrounding the rose tree, the sweet briar, and the climbing honeysuckle, stands the quiet habitation of an ancient dame, who diligently spells out the meaning of the sacred page, in uninterrupted loneliness and peace. In the distance we hear the sound of many voices joining in hymns of prayer and praise—the old and the young—the feeble and the firm, raised together in one delightful symphony of gratitude and love: and if scattered here and there, we find little companies of the idle, the thoughtless, or the gay, they are still those whose outward decency—whose fresh bright looks of health and happiness, evince a respect for the Sabbath, and a participation in its universal calm.

It is after the contemplation of scenes like these, that we return to our homes, more happy in the thought, that the young have their serious moments, the widely separated their time of meeting, the ignorant their seasons of instruction, the old their consolation, and the weary their day of rest.

It is not however to the public offices of religion, that its poetical interest is confined. If we look into the private walks of life, we behold this powerful principle working the most important revolutions in the moral character of man—if into the midst of families, we find it severing or uniting the firmest links of natural connexion—giving solemnity to the sad parting—over the glad meeting after long separation diffusing a holy joy—imparting reverence to the attributes of age—purity and happiness to the cheerful smiles of childhood—and presiding with its sanctifying influence over all the different offices of duty, and charity, and love—or if we look into the human heart, it is here that religion is seen controlling the fiery passions of youth, subduing the stubborn will, softening down the asperities of nature, and mingling with the springs of earthly feeling the pure, inexhaustible waters of eternal life.

How would the fond mother endure with fortitude the sad farewell, that separates the son of her hopes from the genial atmosphere of domestic peace, if she did not in her heart consign him to the more judicious care of his heavenly Father? or how would she send him forth alone to trace his distant and dubious pathway through the wilderness of life, but for her faith in the guiding hand which she implores to direct him through its manifold temptations, to lead him safely through its dangers, and bring him back to her yearning bosom unspotted from the world. It is the internal support derived from religion that nerves her for the trial, and reconciles her to the after hours of watchfulness and care, when she may look in vain for tidings from the wanderer, and calculate with fruitless anticipation upon the hour of his return.

It is the same feeling of religion not unfrequently excited to enthusiasm, that tears away the youthful devotee from all the joys of nature, and the endearments of domestic love; clothing her fair forehead in the mournful vestments of monastic gloom, and shadowing the young cheek from which the last rose has faded, with the sable pall of a premature and living death.

It is religion too that steals upon the soul of the contemplative student, and lures him him away from the haunts of convivial mirth, from the excitement of the flowing bowl, and from the ambition of the sordid or the gay, to devote the highest powers and energies of his mind to the edification of his fellow creatures, and the spring time of his existence to the service of his God.

It is this support which keeps alive the hope of the heart-stricken wife, as she pursues her reprobate husband through the dark windings of his sinful course, wooing him back with her unfailing gentleness to the comforts of his home, watching over him in his unguarded moments, with the balm of Christian consolation ever ready for his hour of need, and supplicating with incessant prayers, that a stronger arm than hers may be stretched out to arrest the progress of his erring steps.

Without this active and living principle, operating upon the various dispositions of mankind, we should never witness those instances of self denial in the cause of virtue, which afford the strongest evidence of the all-sustaining efficacy of religion. How, for instance, would the compassionate maiden find strength to reject her worthless lover, because the stain of guilt was upon his brow, and because his spirit refused to bow down and worship at the altar of her God, if the claims of duty were not paramount to those of affection? And yet such things have been; and warm, young hearts, whose cords of happiness were rent asunder by the fierce and fiery trial, have chosen for themselves a solitary lot, separate and distinct from the sphere of their long cherished enjoyments, and have dwelt in peace and resignation under the guiding influence of the one divine light, by which all others, from whence they had ever derived hope or gladness were extinguished.

Yes; and the man of strong affections, whose downward tendency in the career of worldly occupation, had reduced a tender wife and helpless children to the last extreme of poverty and wretchedness, has been visited with powerful temptation in his hour of weakness, when his perceptions of right and wrong were so confused with bodily and mental suffering, that the limitations of moral good seemed to be yielding to the encroachments of physical evil, when the wants of his starving family were bursting forth in audible and heart-rending appeals for which he had no answer, when the shadows of despair fell around him, and squalid misery encircled his cold hearth. And he too has stood his ground, strong in the confidence that real good, or lasting happiness, never yet was purchased by the sacrifice of virtuous rectitude.

But if we measure the strength of the principle by the weakness of the agent it inspires, we would point out, above all other instances of its operative power, that in which a child looks boldly in the face of authority, and daring the retributive judgment which must inevitably follow, openly and freely tells the truth. Sometimes a single falsehood, or a mere evasion would save the little culprit from the pain of public ignominy, from the fury of a tyrant master, and from the punishment that, even in anticipation, checks the warm current of his youthful blood, and sends a shivering thrill through every nerve and fibre of his trembling frame. But he has been instructed by parents whose word he cannot doubt, to believe that there is a good and gracious God looking down upon the children of earth, caring for their sufferings, listening to their prayers, teaching them his holy law, and encouraging them to regard the performance of it above all the enjoyments afforded by the world; and knowing that a strict adherence to the truth is one of the essential points of that law, the penitent child, even with the tears of anguish on his cheek, pronounces the decisive word of truth which seals his sentence upon earth—the word which rejoicing angels bear to the courts of heaven, as the richest tribute humanity can lay before the throne of its Creator.

These are but single instances, chosen out from a mass of evidence, clearly proving that religion in its influence upon the affections, in its intimate connexion with those important scenes and circumstances of life, from which we derive the greatest pain or pleasure, in short, in its supreme dominion over the human heart, is, above all other subjects, that which possesses the highest claim to the regard of the poet; not only as being most productive of intellectual gratification, but most worthy of him who aspires to the right exercise of the loftiest attributes of mind.

A superficial view of religion may lead to the popular and vulgar notion, that its practical duties are incompatible with true refinement of feeling, and elevation of thought; but is not that the most genuine refinement which penetrates into the distant relations of things, and cements, by mental association, the visible and material—the familiar or the gross, with powerful impressions of moral excellence, and beauty, and happiness? Is not that the most elevated range of thought which combines the practical and temporal affairs of men, with the eternal principles upon which the world is established and governed?

We know of nothing that can so fully and so beautifully adorn the ordinary path of life, as religion; because it imparts a spiritual essence to all our customary actions and pursuits, in which the slightest portion of good and evil is involved. We can imagine nothing to exceed in tenderness the merciful dealing of our heavenly Father with his erring and rebellious creatures; and as there is nothing to equal the perfection of the Divine character, so there is no sublimity comparable to that of his nature. Nor is this all. We have said that poetry must come home to our own bosoms in order to be truly felt, and religion teaches us that we have a portion in everlasting life—an inheritance in eternity—that the hopes and the fears which stimulate our actions, the powers and the energies with which we are endowed, are not merely given us for the brief purposes of temporal existence—to play their little part upon this sublunary stage—to animate frail creatures that must perish in the tomb, but as links woven in with the great chain of being to be unfolded in a sphere without limitations, in a "world without end."

We would not depreciate the freeness, and the fulness of the benefits of religion, by saying that the poet has a participation in their delights, beyond that enjoyed by others; because we reverently believe the nature of religion to be such as to adapt it to every understanding, render it available in every condition of humanity, and sustaining, and consolatory to every heart. But we have no hesitation in pronouncing it impossible for the poet to reach the same intellectual height, without the aid of religion, as when he soars on angels' wings up to the gates of heaven—to touch the strings of human feeling so powerfully, as when his hand is bathed in the pure fountains of eternal truth.

How for instance would he expatiate upon beauty or excellence, if they had no archetypes in heaven? How would he describe the calamities which tear up the root of domestic peace, and agonize the tortured bosom, if neither prayer nor appeal were wrung out by such wretchedness, and directed to a spriritual power by whom the calamity might be averted? How would he solemnize the vow, or seal the blessing, or ratify the curse, without the sanction of divine authority? or how might his soul aspire to the sublime, without expanding its wings in the regions of eternity?

No; there is nothing which the poet need reject in the religion of the Bible, or the religion of the heart; but rather let him seek its benignant and inspiring influence, as a light to his genius, a stimulus to his imagination, a guide to his taste, a fire to his ardour, an impetus to his power, and a world thrown open to his enjoyment.

IMPRESSION.

Hitherto we have bestowed our attention upon what essentially belongs to poetry, as a medium for receiving and imparting the highest intellectual enjoyment. We now come to the qualifications for composing poetry—the fundamental characteristics of the poet. All persons of cultivated understanding, endowed with an ordinary share of sensibility, are more or less capable of *feeling* what is poetical; but that all, even amongst those who attempt it, are not equal to *writing* poetry, is owing to their deficiency in some or all of the following qualifications:—capacity of receiving deep impressions — imagination — power — and taste. These qualifications we shall now consider separately, beginning with the first, which for want of a better term, I have called impression.

We have already seen how poetry derives its existence from the association of ideas, as well as how such associations must arise out of impressions, and it follows as a natural consequence, that if this be necessary to enable a man to feel poetry, it is still more so to qualify him for writing it. Impressions are, in fact, the secret fund from whence the poet derives his most brilliant thoughts—the material with which he works, the colouring in which he dips his pencil when he paints—the inexhaustible fountain to which he applies for the simplicity of nature, and the force of truth.

We have before observed, that it is impossible to trace a great proportion of our associations to their original source, because we cannot recall the impressions made upon our mind in infancy; but we know that in that early stage of life. when we were most alive to sensation, all the impressions which we did receive, must have been connected with pain or pleasure, and that hence arise preference and antipathy, hope and fear, love and hatred. We have the authority of Dr. Johnson, as well as that of our own observation for asserting, that children are not naturally grateful, and from the history of man in a barbarous state, we learn that he is not naturally honest. The reason is, that both the infant and the savage have received pleasure from self-indulgence, but not from the exercise of any moral duty; and therefore it is evident that greater maturity of mind is necessary for the formation of those ideas which arise out of impressions made by the social intercourse of mankind. Yet in a very early state of existence we are capable of deriving more simple ideas from impressions whose strength and durability constitute the riches of the poet.

Perhaps the first of this description is, the idea of power, naturally arising in the mind of a child, from the bodily force by which its most violent attempts at resistance are easily overcome. But in order to be deeply impressed with this idea, it is necessary that we should have witnessed some manifestation of power beyond the reach of man's utmost capabilities, and this we behold in the tremendous violence of the winds, the rage of the ocean, the cataract, or the volcano.

The idea of number multiplied to infinity comes next, and this it is reasonable to suppose may originate in the contemplation of the stars. We may not be able to recall to our remembrance the time when our own minds were first awakened to a conception of the splendour of the heavens; but we have an opportunity of observing in others the rapt and astonished gaze with which they first regard the stars in reference to their number, and how the opening mind expands as one after another of these nightly suns rises, and dawns upon it—first seen in separate points of light—then in groups—then multitudes—then fields spangled all over with shining glory—then wider fields—and so on, until at last the idea of number loses all limitation, and the child conceives for the first time, that of infinity.

From the contemplation of a widely extended view, we have unquestionably derived our notion of space. Why this idea, arising out of an incalculable number of objects, in themselves ordinary and familiar, should obtain the character of sublime, it is not easy to determine, unless it be that the same expansion of mind is as necessary to receive these two impressions, as to contemplate the nature of unlimited power, which is universally accompanied with sensations of awe, and sometimes of terror.

Duration is generally the last which the mind receives of these impressions, and when extended to eternity, it is the most important. This idea does not arise like that of infinity, from objects of calculation, nor like power, from any connexion with impulse or sensation; but steals quietly upon the mind from deep and earnest meditation, sometimes upon objects which have existed from time immemorial, sometimes upon those which will exist for ages yet to come. We gaze upon the ivied walls of the ruined edifice, whose very structure bears evidence of the different manners, customs and occupations of those who once surrounded the now deserted hearth. We walk into the spacious banqueting-room whose walls once echoed to the songs of festivity or triumph, and there the bat holds nightly converse with the owl. We listen to the rush of the evening breeze amongst the deep dark foliage of the firmly-rooted trees, which have arisen out of seeds scattered by the wandering winds amongst the desolation of fallen magnificence. Even then the pile must have been a ruin, and we see by the broken pillar whose base is buried in the earth, what an accumulation of matter time must have strewn around it, to raise the level of the surrounding earth, from its foundation to its centre. We look through the wide yawning aperture that seems to have been a richly-ornamented window, and there, where the gallant knight once laid his conquering sword at the feet of smiling beauty, where the minstrel tuned his lyre, and sung the praise of heroes now forgotten, where the snow white hand of the courtly dame was wont to rest as she looked forth upon the sloping lawn, marking the long shadows of the stately trees, of which neither root nor branch remain; now the rude nettle rears his head, the loose bramble waves in the wind that whistles through the broken arch, birds of dark omen, inhabitants of desolation, pass to and fro on dusky wing, and the loathsome toad, and poisonous adder creep in amongst the shattered fragments of sculptured stone and mouldering marble, to find themselves a hiding place and a home. As we contemplate all this, the mind is naturally carried back to the time when these emblems of decay had their beginning. We think that there were ruins then; that ages still more remote had theirs; and thus as we travel through the dim obscurity of pre-existent time, our retrospective view at length fades and is lost in the sublime idea of uncreated power.

Or we look onward from the present time —on—on, to a mysterions futurity, when we and ours shall be forgotten. We cannot build up without reflecting that there is also a time to pull down, and in laying the foundation of an edifice, or in witnessing its erection, it is natural to ask, "Where shall I be when of these stones not one remains upon another?" We plant the sapling oak, and watch it year by year, slowly extending in its circumference and its height, and we think of the time when children now unborn shall play beneath its shade, when we shall have been gathered to the only place of earthly rest, and when the very soil in which that tree is planted, shall have become the property of those who never heard our names. It is by extending such reflections as these ad infinitum, that imagination passes from small to great, from infancy to age, and from time to eternity; and thus we form all the idea that we are capable of conceiving of that which has no beginning, and can never end.

There is one other mental conception—the idea of a God, intimately connected with those here specified, which mankind have endeavoured by every means, natural and artificial, reasonable and absurd, pleasing and terrible, to introduce into the mind, before the mind is prepared for receiving it; and hence follow the unworthy notions, the irreverent language, and the low attributes, by which the majesty of the Divine Being is too frequently insulted.

If we might so speak without presumption, we should say, that God, jealous of his own honour, had chosen in this instance, sometimes to baffle the ingenuity of man, by first throwing open to the human mind, the contemplation of his attributes, and then by his own appointed means, inscrutable to our perceptions, concentrating them all in one sublime and ineffable thought, which flashes through the brain like a quickening fire, and bursts upon the soul with the light of life.

I would still be understood to speak poetically. I know that there are modes of reasoning by which men of sound understanding must almost necessarily arrive at a belief in the existence of a God. But rational evidence, and the evidence of sensation, are two different things. We often assent to facts of which we do not *feel* the truth. And it is this *feeling* as it gives vitality to belief, that I would call the *impression* from which we derive the most lasting and distinct idea of a God. Yet at the same time that I speak of such impressions as evidence, which the Divine Being vouchsafes to give us of his own existence, I speak of them only as corroborating evidence following that of reason, and of no sort of value where they directly contradict it. Separate from the mental process by which the idea is first conceived, this evidence refers rather to the state of the mind as a recipient; and such impressions as are here spoken of poetically, may therefore, exist independent of rational conviction. Without such conviction, however, they are liable to lead to the most egregious and fatal errors, but with it they establish truth, and render it indelible.

It is of much less importance to the poet, than to the philosopher, whether impressions of this abstract nature, arise out of the immediate operation of divine power, or from a combination of conclusions previously drawn, which the mind is often able to make use of without being aware of their existing in any rational or definite form, and which we can never fully understand, unless the study of the human mind should be reduced to a practical science. The poet may often use expressions which accord with the former notion, just as he would describe the hand of Omnipotence covering the mountains with eternal snow, but let us hope that he is wise enough seriously to entertain the latter; and if sometimes he makes a sudden transition from effects to causes, without regarding the intermediate space, let us do him the justice to believe that it is from the very sublimity of his own genius, which stoops not to take cognizance of means, but rather in searching out the principles of sensation, thought, and action, plunges at once into the fountain of life, and refers immediately to the great first Cause.

Thus the full and entire conviction of the being of a God, may come upon us precisely as God pleases, and force itself upon our hearts in the way which he sees meet to appoint. Galen is said to have received this impression from unexpectedly meeting in his solitary walks with a human skeleton; and just as easily may the infidel be reclaimed from his ignorance by any other means adapted to the peculiar tone and temper of his own mind—by the chanting of a hymn, or the peal of rolling thunder—by the prayer of an innocent child, or the destruction of a powerful nation—by the gathering of the plenteous harvest or the desolation of the burning desert—by the faded beauty of a falling leaf, or the splendour of the starry heavens—by the secret anguish of the broken spirit, or by accumulated honours and unmerited enjoyment—by the blessings of the poor, or the denunciations of the powerful—by the visitations of divine love, or by the terrors of eternal judgment—in short, by the natural sensations of pain or pleasure, arising from any of the causes immediate or remote, by which the attributes of Deity may be forced upon the perceptions of the soul, and concentrated in the idea of one indivisible, and omnipotent Being.

Subsequent to the idea of a God, arise distinct perceptions of moral duty—of what we owe to him as the creator and preserver of the world, as well as the founder of the laws by which our lives ought to be regulated. We have before observed that, immediate self-gratification is the earliest motive upon which we act, but we now become sensible that this motive must give place to others of a more remote and abstract nature. With the first impressions of pain and pleasure, we learned to separate evil from good. We now learn that there is a deeper evil to which pleasure is frequently the prelude, and a higher good which can sometimes only be attained by passing through a medium of pain.

Our first strong impressions of a moral nature are of beauty and excellence. We should call beauty merely physical, did it not comprehend what belongs to fitness and harmony, as well as to colour and form. In all that is exquisite in art we are struck with the idea of beauty in connexion with others; as, with all that is magnificent in nature we combine with the same idea, those of motion or sound, form or colour, light or shade, splendour or majesty, utility or power; but we are perhaps never more impressed with *mere* beauty than when contemplating a flower—gorgeous in its colour as the resplendent heavens—pure in its whiteness as the winter's snow. The eye that can gaze without admiration upon a flower, deserves to be prematurely dim; for what is there on earth more intensely beautiful! and yet how frail! so that scarcely does the breath of praise pass over it, than its delicate petals begin to droop, and its stem that once stood proudly in the field or the garden, bends beneath the fading glory which it bears. Yet the same flower, supported by the hand of nature, and sheltered beneath her maternal wing, burst forth in the wilderness, where we are too delicate to tread, opened its gentle eye full underneath the sunbeams from which we turn away, rested on the thorns which startle us at every step, poured forth its odours upon the blast from which we shrink, drank in the dews which chill our coarser natures, endured the darkness of the solitary night from which we fly with terror, and derived its nourishment from the common earth, which we spurn, until we learn to value the latest friend whose arms are open to receive us.

Excellence, like beauty, is of kinds so various, and degrees so numerous, that it is only by a combination of impressions that we arrive at the idea of excellence in its abstract nature; but when once formed, it constitutes the point of reference, and the climax of all that we admire and love; and therefore it is of the utmost importance to the poet, that his standard of excellence should not only be acknowledged as such by the enlightened portion of mankind, but that it should be as high as the human mind can reach, and at the same time so deeply graven upon his own heart, that neither ambition, hope, nor fear, nor any other passion or affection to which he is liable, can obliterate the impression, or supplant it by another.

All our ideas of intellectual as well as moral good are of a complex nature, arising not so much out of impressions made by things themselves, as by their relations, associations, and general fitness or unfitness one to another; hence it follows that the mind must be naturally qualified for receiving decided impressions of simple ideas, so as afterwards to make use of them, in drawing clear deductions, by comparing them one with another, and combining them together. How, for instance, would the poet describe the general influence of evening twilight, if he had never really felt its tranquillizing power as it extends over the external world, and reaches even to the heart? or how would he be able to convey a clear idea of the virtue of gratitude, if he had never known the expansion of generous feeling, the ardent hope of imparting happiness, and the disappointment of finding that happiness unappropriated, or received with contempt?

That there are men of common perceptions, who "travel from Dan to Beersheba," saying that all is barren, and that there are men of more than ordinary talent, who, deficient neither in imagination, power, nor taste, are yet unable to write poetry, is evidently owing to their want of capability for receiving lively impressions; for wherever such impressions exist, with sufficient imagination to arrange and combine them so as to create fresh images, with power to embody them in forcible words, and taste to render those words appropriate and pure, either poetry itself, or highly poetical prose, must be the natural language of such a mind.

We should say that opportunity for receiving agreeable impressions, as well as capacity for receiving them deeply, was essential to the poet, were it possible that any human being, even of moderately cultivated understanding, commanding the use of language, and acquainted with the principles of taste, should have been so entirely excluded from all contemplation of what is admirable, both in the external world and in human nature, as to have conceived no just idea either of physical or moral beauty. It is however of immense importance to the poet that he should have formed an early and intimate acquaintance with subjects regarded as poetical by the unanimous opinion of mankind—that he should have gazed upon the sunset until his very soul was rapt in the blaze of its golden glory—that he should have lived in the quiet smile of the placid moon, and looked up to the stars of night, until he forgot his own identity, and became like a world of light amongst the shining host—that he should have watched the silvery flow of murmuring water, until his anxious thoughts of present things were lulled to rest, and the tide of memory rolled on, pure, and clear, and harmonious, as the woodland stream—that he should have listened to the glad voices of the birds of spring, until his own was mingled with the universal melody of nature, and strains of gratitude and joy burst forth from his overflowing heart—that he should have seen the woods in their summer vesture of varied green, and felt how beautiful is the garment of nature—that he should have found the nest of the timid bird, and observed how tender its maternal love, and how wonderful is the instinct with which the frailest creatures are endowed—that he should have stood by the wave-beaten shore when a galley with full sails swept along the foaming tide, and impressed upon the tablet of his heart a perfect picture of majesty and grace—that he should have witnessed the tear of agony exchanged for the smile of hope, and acknowledged—feelingly acknowledged, how blessed are the tender offices of mercy—that he should have heard the cry of the oppressed, and seen the breaking of their chains, with the inmost chords of his heart's best feelings thrilling at the shout of liberty—that he should have trembled beneath the desolating storm, and hailed the opening in the tempestuous clouds from which the mild radiance of returning peace looked down—that he should have bent over the slumbering infant, until his imagination wandered from the innocence of earth to the purity of heaven—that he should have contemplated female beauty in its loveliest, holiest form, and then by a slight transition, passed in amongst the angelic choir, and tuned his harp to celebrate its praise, where beauty is the least of the attributes of excellence—in fine, that he should have bathed in the fount of nature, and tasted of the springs of feeling at their different sources, choosing out the sweetest, the purest, and the most invigorating, for the delight of mankind, and the perpetual refreshment of his own soul.

As in society it is impossible to know whether any particular language has been learned until we hear it spoken, so it would be difficult to single out individual instances of the existence or the absense of deep impressions; because a mind may be fully endowed with this first principle of poetry, and yet without the proper medium for making it perceptible to others, we may consequently never be aware of the presence of such a capability even where it does exist. It will, however, eminently qualify the possessor for feeling and admiring poetry, and thus it is but fair to suppose, that there are many individuals undistinguished in the multitude, who possess this faculty in the same degree as the most celebrated poet, but who for want of some or all of the three remaining requisites, have never been able to bring their faculty to light. Where, amongst the four requisites for writing poetry, this alone is wanting, however highly cultivated the mind of the writer may be, and however mature his judgment, this single deficiency will have the effect of rendering his poetry monotonous and unimpressive, even where it is, critically speaking, free from faults; because it is impossible that he should be able to convey to others clear or forcible deas of what he has never felt clearly or forcibly himself. Dr. Johnson was a poet of this description; and on the other hand, instead of pointing out instances, we have no hesitation in asserting that every man who has written impressively, ingeniously, powerfully, and with good taste, has been possessed, in an eminent degree, of the faculty of receiving and remembering impressions.

IMAGINATION.

Imagination is the next quaufication essential in the poetic art. As a faculty, imagination is called creative, because it forms new images out of materials with which impression has stored the mind, and multiplies such images to an endless variety by abstracting from them some of their qualities, and adding others of a different nature; but that imagination does not actually create original and simple ideas, is clear, from the fact that no man by the utmost stretch of his rational faculties, by intense thought, or by indefatigable study, can imagine a new sense, a new passion, or a new creature. Imagination, therefore, holds the same relation to impression, as the finished picture does to the separate colours with which the artist works. Judiciously blended, these colours produce all the different forms and tints observable in the visible world; and by arranging and combining ideas previously impressed upon the mind, and shaping out such combinations into distinct characters, imagination produces all the splendid imagery by which the poet delights and astonishes mankind. When he describes an object new to his readers, it is seldom new to himself, or if new as a whole, it is familiar in its separate parts. If for instance he sings the praises of maternal love, he refers to the memory of his own mother, and the strong impression left upon his mind, by her solicitude and watchful care—if the song of the nightingale, he recalls the long summer nights, ere forgetfulness had become a blessing, when to listen was more happy than to sleep—if the northern wind, he hears again the hollow roar amongst the leafless boughs, that was wont to draw in the domestic circle around his father's hearth—if the woodland music of the winding stream, he knows its liquid voice by the rivulet in which he bathed his infant feet—if the tender offices of friendship, he has enjoyed them too feelingly to forget their influence upon the soul—or if the anguish of the broken heart, who has not the transcript of sorrow written even on the earliest page of life?

These are instances in which the poet draws immediately from experience, and where his task is only to transmit to others the impression made upon his own mind; but there are other cases where the idea conveyed is derived from a combination of impressions, and this is more exclusively the work of imagination.

The poet who has never seen a lion may use the image of one in his verses, with almost as much precision as the poet who has; because he knows that its attributes are courage, ferocity, and power, and he has been impressed with ideas of these attributes in other objects. He knows that its roar is loud, and deep, and terrific, and he has distinct impressions of the meaning of these words also. Its colour, form, and general habits, he becomes acquainted with by the same means; and thus he makes bold to use the name and the character of the lion to ornament his verse. In the same manner he describes the sandy desert, and with yet greater precision; because he has only to add to the sands of the sea shore, with which he is perfectly familiar, the two qualities of extent and burning heat, and he sees before him at once the wide and sterile wastes of Arabian solitude. Or if the human countenance be the subject of his muse, and he endeavours to invent one that shall be new to himself as well as to his readers, it is by borrowing different features from faces which have left their impress on his mind: and upon the same principle he proceeds through all that mental process, which is called creating images, and which gives to the works of the highly imaginative, the character of originality; because from the wide scope and variety of their impressions, they are able to select such diversified materials, that when combined, we only see them as a whole, without being aware of any previous acquaintance with their particular parts.

Where distinct impressions, power, and taste are present in full force, and imagination alone, out of the four requisites, is wanting, we speak of the poet as one who borrows from the thoughts of others, or one whose images are too ordinary and common place to interest the reader; because, either limited by the nature of his own mind to a narrow range of ideas, or indolent in the search of materials necessary for his work, he has laid hold of such as fell most readily within his grasp, and these being few and familiar, and unskilfully arranged, we recognise at once the gross elements of the compound, and see from whence they have been obtained.

Deficiency of imagination is the reason why some, who would otherwise have been our best poets, are *mannerists*. It is true they may be so from partiality, almost amounting to affection, for some peculiar character or style of writing; but that they are blindly addicted to this fault, is much more frequently owing to their want of capability to conceive any other mode of conveying their ideas.

Lord Byron was unquestionably a writer of the former class. From the variety of his style, the splendour of his imagery, and the brilliant thoughts that burst upon us as we read his charmed lines, it is impossible to believe that his imagination was incapable of any scope, of any height, or any depth, to which it might be directed by inclination; but in the characters he portrayed he may justly be called a mannerist, because he evidently preferred the uniformly dark and melancholy; and chose out from the varied impressions of his own life, that sombre hue, so deeply harmonizing with majesty and gloom, which he spread over every object in nature, like the lowering thunder clouds above the landscape; varying at times the wide waste of brooding darkness, with short-lived but brilliant flashes of sensibility, and wit, and lively feeling, like the lurid streaks that shoot athwart the tempestuous sky, lighting up the world for one brief moment with ineffable brightness, and then leaving it to deeper—more impenetrable night.

As instances of mannerism arising from the actual want of imagination, we might bring forward a long list of minor poets, as well as inferior writers of every description, without however descending so low as to those who have not consistency of mind sufficient for maintaining any particular system of thought, or style of composition. Yet of imagination, as well as impression, we are unable to say decidedly that it does not exist, because, like impression, it only becomes perceptible to us through the medium of words; and as all individuals are not able to use this medium with force and perspicuity, we necessarily lose many of the brilliant conceptions of those around us. We may however assert as an indisputable fact, that poetry of the highest order was never yet produced without the powerful exercise of the faculty of imagination.

As a wonderful instance of the force and efficacy of imagination, as well as of impression, power, and taste, we might single out Milton, were it not that power is more essentially the characteristic of his works. He has equals in the other requisites of a poet, while in power he stands unrivalled.

But, supreme in the region of imagination is our inimitable Shakespeare; and that he is inimitable is perhaps the greatest proof of the perfection of his imaginative powers. The heroes of Byron have been multiplied through so many copies that we have grown weary of the original; but who can imitate the characters of Shakespeare? And yet how perfectly human is every individual of the multitude which he has placed before us—so human as to be liked and disliked, according to the peculiar cast of mind in the persons who pronounce upon them; just in the same manner as characters in ordinary life attract or repel those with whom they come in contact. Every one forms the same opinion of the Corsair, because he has a few distinctive qualities, by which he is known and copied; while no two individuals agree upon the character of Hamlet—a character of all others perhaps least capable of imitation. Yet let us ask, is Hamlet less natural than Conrad? Quite the reverse. If ever the poet's mind conceived a perfectly original man, it is Hamlet, in whose mysterious nature is displayed the most astonishing effort of imagination; and yet so true is the dark picture to the principles of human nature, that we perceive at once the representation of a creature formed after the similitude of ourselves.

The fact is, that though as a whole it stands alone, even in the world of fiction, in all its varied parts it consists of the ordinary and familiar features of humanity; and in thinking of this wayward and capricious being, whose accumulated wrongs and miseries have almost stupified his energies, whose melancholy, natural or induced, has converted the "brave, o'erhanging firmament" into "a pestilent congregation of vapours," we feel with him in all his weakness, as with a man; and for him with all his faults, as for a brother. In memory too, how distinct is Hamlet from all the creations of inferior minds! He seems to occupy a place in history, rather than in fiction; and in searching out the principles of human feeling, we refer to him as to one whose existence was real, rather than ideal. This may be said of all Shakespeare's characters, and so powerful is the evidence of truth impressed upon them, that where he chooses to depart from circumstantial fact, our credence clings to him in preference to less imaginative historians.

Perhaps the most remarkable fact in connection with the genius of this wonderful writer, is the immense *variety* of his characters. In almost all other fictitious writings, we recognize the same hero, appearing in different forms—sometimes seated on an eastern throne, and sometimes presiding over the rude ceremonial of an Indian wigwam; while the same heroine figures in the "sable stole" of a priestess, or in the borrowed ornaments of a bandit's bride. But the people of Shakespeare amongst whom we seem to live, are in no way beholden to situation or costume, for appearing to be what they really are. They have an actual identity—an individuality that would be distinctly perceptible in any other circumstances, or under any other disguise.

One of the favorite painters of our day, or rather of yesterday, has but three heads, which serve all his purposes—an old man with white hair and flowing beard, a Grecian female, and a semi-roman hero; and in the same way many of our writers make use of three or more distinctions of character—a hero and a heroine—a secondary hero to thwart their loves—a secondary heroine to assist either one party or the other—perhaps to play at cross purposes with her mistress or her friend: and a fool or buffoon, (who varies least of all,) to rush upon the stage when more important personages are likely to be reduced to a dilemma. But in Shakespeare even the fools are as motley as the garb they wear; and the women, who with other writers vary only from the tender to the heroic, are of all ages, and of all distinctions of character and feeling; while amongst the immense number of men whom he introduces to our acquaintance, there is no single instance of greater resemblance than we find in real life. Perhaps the nearest approach to similarity is in the blundering absurdities of justices of the peace, or country magistrates, a class of people with whom ("if ancient tales say true") it is probable the poet may have been brought into no very pleasing kind of contact, and hence arises the vein of satire which flows through every description of their conduct and conversation.

Beyond this, there is another striking proof of the wonderful extent of Shakespeare's imaginative powers. Throughout the whole of his plays we never recognize the man himself. In the works of almost every other writer, the author appears before us, and we become in some measure acquainted with his peculiar tone of mind and individual cast of character; but Shakespeare is equally at home with the gloomy or the gay, the licentious or the devout, the sublime or the familiar, the terrific or the lovely. We never detect him identifying himself either with the characters, or the sentiments of others; and though we wonder, and speculate upon the mind that could thus play with all the feelings of humanity, Shakespeare himself remains invisible and unknown, like a master magician regulating the machinery which at the same time conceals his own person, and astonishes the world.

The Tempest is generally considered the most imaginative of Shakespeare's plays, and certainly it contains little, in scenery, or circumstance, that can be associated with ordinary life. In the character of Prospero, we are forcibly struck with the originality of the conception; because it combines what is not to be found elsewhere—the art of a necromancer with the dignity of a man of honour and integrity; and when he lays down his magic wand, "unites the spell," and doffs the mantle of enchantment, he stands before us, not debased and powerless, but full of the native majesty of a nobleman and a prince. To his daughter, the pure and spiritual Miranda, one of our most talented, yet most feminine writers,* has so lately done, perhaps more than justice, that nothing can be added to her own exquisitely poetical description of the island nymph, who has "sprung up into beauty beneath the eye of her father, the princely magician; her companions the rocks and woods, the many-shaped, many-tinted clouds and the silent stars; her playmates the ocean billows that stoop their foamy crests, and run rippling to kiss her feet."

Of Ariel, the "delicate Ariel," that most ethereal essence that ever assumed the form of beauty in the glowing visions of imagination, what can we say? so entirely and purely spiritual is this aerial being, that we know not whether to speak of *him* as calling up "spirits from the vasty deep," rolling the thunder clouds along the stormy heavens, whelming the helpless mariners in the foaming surge, and dashing their "goodly bark" upon the echoing rocks; or if *her*, gentle, willing, and obedient, hastening on ready service at a moment's bidding, and asking for the love, as well as the approbation, of the island lord. We know of nothing within the range of ordinary thought from which the character of Ariel can be borrowed, and certainly it is the nearest in approach to a perfectly original conception, of any which in our literature adorns the page of fiction.

Of Caliban, too monstrous for a man—too fiendish for a beast, it may also be said that he is entirely the creature of imagination; and indeed throughout the whole of this astonishing drama, the mind of the author seems to have taken the widest possible range of which human genius is capable. The very existence of these beings upon a solitary island, isolated and shut out from human fellowship, involves, in difficulties as strange as insurmountable to ordinary powers, the usual course of thought and action, and renders it infinitely more reconcilable to

* Mrs. Jameson.

our prejudices, that Prospero, in such a situation,

——" with the stars,
And the quick spirits of the universe"

should hold "his dialogues."

How beautiful, amidst all the complicated machinery of her father's magic, is the delicate simplicity of Miranda! She wonders not at the prodigies around her, because her trust and her love are centered in her father, and she believes him to have power to dissolve as well as to enforce the spell; yet why he should exercise this power for any other than humane and gracious purposes, she is at a loss to conceive, and therefore she ventures to call his attention to the wreck of a "brave vessel" which she has first seen dashed amongst the rocks, and then she adds—

"Had I been any God of power, I would
Have sunk the sea within the earth, or e'er
It should the good ship so have swallow'd, and
The freighting souls within her."

Finding the natural disposition to wonder and inquire, just dawning in her mind, Prospero thinks it time to explain the mystery of their situation, and then follows that touching and beautiful description of their former life, their wrongs, and sufferings, which, occasionally interrupted by the jealousy of the narrator, lest the attention of his child should wander, and by her simple ejaculations of wonder and concern, is unparalleled alike for its imaginative charm, and for its accordance with the principles of nature. For instance, when Miranda is questioned by her father whether she can remember a time before she came into that cell, and whether she can recall such by any other house, or person, or image, she answers—

"MIRANDA.

"'Tis far off;
And rather like a dream than an assurance
That my remembrance warrants: Had I not
Four or five women once, that tended me?

PROSPERO.

Thou hadst, and more, Miranda. But how is it
That this lives in thy mind? What seest thou else
In the dark backward and abysm of time?
If thou remember'st aught ere thou cam'st here;
How thou cam'st here thou may'st.

MIRANDA.

But that I do not.

PROSPERO.

Twelve years since, Miranda, twelve years since,
Thy father was the duke of Milan, and
A prince of power.

MIRANDA

Sir, are not you my father?"

Again, when Prospero describes the horrors of their situation afloat upon the sea, how natural and feminine is her reply, and his, how full of tender and yet noble feeling!

"PROSPERO.

* * * * *

"In few, they hurried us on board a bark,
Bore us some leagues to sea; where they prepar'd
A rotten carcass of a boat not rigg'd,
Nor tackle, sail, nor mast; the very rats
Instinctively had quit it. There they hoist us
To cry to the sea that roar'd to us; to sigh
To the winds, whose pity, sighing back again,
Did us but loving wrong.

MIRANDA.

Alack! what trouble
Was I then to you!

PROSPERO.

O! a cherubim
Thou wast, that did preserve me! Thou didst smile,
Infused with a fortitude from heaven,
When I have deck'd the sea with drops full salt."

Ariel's description of the tempest raised by the command of Prospero, is such as none but the liveliest imagination could have inspired.

"ARIEL.

"All hail, great master! grave sir, hail! I come
To answer thy best pleasure; be't to fly,
To swim, to dive into the fire, to ride
On the curl'd clouds; to thy strong bidding task
Ariel, and all his quality.

PROSPERO.

Hast thou, spirit,
Performed to point the tempest that I bade thee?

ARIEL.

To every article.
I boarded the king's ship: now on the beak,
Now on the waste, the deck, in every cabin,
I flam'd amazement. Sometimes I'd divide
And burn in many places: on the top-mast,
The yards, and bolt-sprit, would I flame distinctly,
Then meet, and join: Jove's lightnings, the precursors
O' the dreadful thunder clap, more momentary
And sight outrunning were not. The fire and cracks
Of sulphurous roaring, the most mighty Neptune
Seem'd to besiege, and make his bold waves tremble,
Yea, his dread trident shake."

After all this, the imperative magician requires yet farther service, when Ariel, in language true to a nature more human than his own, meekly reminds his master of the promised freedom for which his spirit is ever pining.

"ARIEL.

"I pray thee:
Remember, I have done thee worthy service,
Told thee no lies, made no mistakings, serv'd
Without or grudge or grumblings: thou didst promise
To bate me a full year.

PROSPERO.

Dost thou forget
From what a torment I did free thee?

ARIEL.

No.

PROSPERO.

Thou dost; and think'st it much to tread the ooze
Of the salt deep;
To run upon the sharp wind of the north;
To do me business in the veins of the earth,
When it is bak'd with frost."

There is certainly too much of harshness and contempt to suit our feelings, in the language which Prospero addresses to his "tricksy spirit." But yet sometimes, when Ariel asks of the diligent execution of his master's mission, "Was't not well done?" and receives a gracious answer full of approbation; when the magician turns away from coarser natures to welcome with smiles his invincible messenger in the air; and especially when at last he dismisses him, with

"My Ariel,
This is thy charge; then to the elements
Be free, and fare thou well!"

Thus breaking his bondage with the gentleness of affection; we have only to extend our thoughts a little farther beyond the sphere of common life, and we feel that a spirit, gentle, and pure, and elastic, like that of Ariel, would be more than soothed by a single word or look of kindness—more than rewarded with all it could desire, centred in the glorious blessing of liberty.

Even the monster Caliban has also an imagination amongst all his brutalities, or how could he thus describe the influence of the magic spell, by which his being was surrounded?

"Be not afear'd, the isle is full of noises,
Sounds, and sweet airs, that give delight, and hurt not.
Sometimes a thousand twanging instruments
Will hum about mine ears; and sometimes voices,
That if I then had wak'd after long sleep,
Will make me sleep again: and then, in dreaming,
The clouds methought, would open and show riches,
Ready to drop upon me; that when I waked,
I cried to dream again."

The following passage, well known to every reader, can never become too familiar, or lose its poetic and highly imaginative charm by repetition:

———" these our actors,
As I foretold you, were all spirits, and
Are melted into air, into thin air:
And, like the baseless fabric of this vision,
The cloud-capt towers, the gorgeous palaces,
The solemn temples, the great globe itself,
Yea, all which it inherit, shall dissolve;
And, like this unsubstantial pageant faded,
Leave not a rack behind. We are such stuff
As dreams are made on, and our little life
Is rounded with a sleep."—

How beautiful, and still imaginative is the scene, in which the heart of the magician begins to melt for the sufferings of those he has been afflicting with retributive justice!

"Say, my spirit,
How fares the king and his followers?

ARIEL.

Confined together
In the same fashion as you gave in charge;
Just as you left them; all prisoners, sir,
In the lime grove which weatherfends your cell;
They cannot budge, till your release. The king,
His brother, and yours, abide all three distracted;
And the remainder mourning over them,
Brim-full of sorrow and dismay; but, chiefly,
Him that you term'd the good old lord, Gonzalo,
His tears run down his beard, like winter drops
From eaves of reeds: your charm so strongly works 'em,
That if you now beheld them, your affections
Would become tender.

PROSPERO.

Dost thou think so, spirit?

ARIEL.

Mine would, sir, were I human.

PROSPERO.

And mine shall.
Hast thou, which art but air, a touch, a feeling
Of their afflictions? and shall not myself,
One of their kind, that relish all as sharply,
Passion'd as they, be kindlier mov'd than thou art?
Though with their high wrongs I am struck to the quick,
Yet with my nobler reason, 'gainst my fury
Do I take part: the rarer action is
In virtue than in vengeance: they being penitent,
The sole drift of my purpose doth extend
Not a frown further. Go, release them, Ariel!
My charms I'll break, their senses I'll restore,
And they shall be themselves.

ARIEL.

I'l fetch them, sir.

PROSPERO.

Ye elves, of hills, brooks, standing lakes, and groves;
And ye, that on the sands with printless foot
Do chase the ebbing Neptune, and do fly him,

When he comes back; you demy-puppets, that
By moon-shine do the green sour ringlets make,
Whereof the ewe not bites; and you, whose pastime
Is it to make midnight mushrooms; that rejoice
To hear the solemn curfew: by whose aid
(Weak masters though ye be,) I have bedimm'd
The noontide sun, call'd forth the mutinous winds,
And 'twixt the green sea and the azur'd vault
Set roaring war: to the dread rattling thunder
Have I given fire, and rifled Jove's stout oak
With his own bolt; the strong-bas'd promontory
Have I made shake: and by the spurs pluck'd up
The pine and cedar: graves at my command,
Have wak'd their sleepers; op'd, and let them forth,
By my so potent art. But this rough magic
I here abjure: and when I have requir'd
Some heavenly music, (which even now I do,)
To work mine end upon their senses, that
This airy charm is for, I'll break my staff,
Bury it certain fathoms in the earth,
And, deeper than did ever plummet sound,
I'll drown my book."

It is easy to bring proofs of the existence of imagination—more easy from the pen of Shakespeare than from that of any other writer; but what language shall describe its power! what hand shall reach to the utmost boundary of space and time—from the source of light to the centre of darkness—from the heights of heaven, to the depths of hell, to draw forth the attributes of imagination, and embody them in a visible sign? Countless as the varieties of human character are those of the nature and office of this active principle; and whatever is the tendency of the mind—to happiness or misery—to good or evil, imagination, faithful to the impulse of the feelings, ranges through creation, collecting sweets or bitters—delicious food, or deadly poison.

This faculty, more than any other, bespeaks the progress, or the declension of the immortal soul. Like the dove of peace, it soars with the spirit in its upward flight—like the ominous raven it goes before it in its downward fall. To those who seek for beauty and happiness, imagination lifts the veil of nature, and discloses all her charms, unfolds the rosebud to the morning sun, wakens the lark to sing his matins to the purple dawn, or folds back the mantle of misty clouds, and calls upon the day-beam to arise; while those who close their eyes upon the loveliness that smiles around them, it darkens with a tenfold gloom, sharpening the thorns that lie beneath their feet, stunning the ear with the harsh tumult of discordant sounds, rousing the bellowing deep with storm and tempest, pouring the waters of bitternes upon the pleasant paths of earth, and calling upon the troubled elements to bring their tribute of despair.

What then is imagination to the good or to the evil? An angel whose protecting wings are stretched out above the pathway to the gates of heaven—a demon whose ghastly image beckons from precipice to gulf—down, down into the fathomless abyss of endless night: a gentle visitant, who brings a tribute of sweet flowers—a fearful harbinger of storms and darkness: a voice of melody that sings before us as we journey on—a cry that tells of horrors yet to come: a wreath of beauty shadowing our upward gaze—a crown of thorns encircling a bleeding brow: a wilderness of verdure spread beneath our wandering steps—an adder in that verdure lurking to destroy: a comforter whose smile diffuses light—an enemy whose envenomed arrow rankles in the heart: a joyful messenger going forth upon an embassy of love—a hideous monster howling at the gates of hell.

True to the impulse of nature, imagination rushes forth with certain aim, and never brings home sweets to the malevolent, or poison to the pure heart; but penetrating into paths unknown, gathers riches for the supply of confidence and hope, or collecting its evidence from "trifles light as air," sharpens the pangs of envy and mistrust.

There are who treat imagination as a light to be extinguished—a power to be overcome—a demon to be exorcised. But ask the child who sits with sullen brow beneath unnatural discipline, whether imagination is not pointing to flowery paths, and stimulating his unbroken will to seek them in despite of stripes and tears. Ask the self-isolated misanthrope, when lonely and unloved he broods over the dark future and the joyless past, whether imagination does not call up images of social comfort, of friendly intercourse, and "homefelt delight," which his sad solitude can never know. Ask the pale monk whose daily penance drags him to an early grave, whether imagination steals not with the moonbeams into his silent cell, whispering of another heaven than that of which he reads—a heaven even upon earth, to which a broken vow a church in arms, a name struck out from the community of saints, are in comparison as nothing Ask the criminal at the gallow's foot, when chains, and judges, and penitence and priests, have done their utmost to fortify his soul for its last mortal struggle, whether imagination does not paint the picture of his cottage in the wood, with her whose prayers he has neglected, fondly watching for his return, and whether the voices of his children come not on the wandering gale, as they lift their innocent hands to heaven, and bless their father in their evening hymns.

Yes; and the stern moralist, who would strike out imagination from the soul of man, must first extinguish the principle of life. What then remains? That those who have the conduct of the infant mind, should seek to stamp it with a living impress of tne loveliness of virtue, and the deformity of vice; and that the passions and affections should be so disciplined, that imagination, the busy faculty which must, and will exist, and act, either for happiness or misery, for good or evil, may bring home to the hungry soul food fit for the nourishment of an immortal being, and dispense from out the fulness of a grateful heart, the richest tribute man can offer at the throne of God.

POWER.

Power, in connexion with the art of writing poetry, admits of two distinctions—as it relates to language and to mind. The former, however, is always dependent upon and subservient to the latter; but the power of mind may exist where there is little or no facility in the use of appropriate words. Were it possible that powerful language could proceed from an imbecile mind, the effect would be, that of heaping together ponderous words, and incongruous images, so as to extend and magnify confusion, without rendering any single thought impressive.

That the force of our ideas must depend in great measure upon the strength of our impressions, is as clear, as that the vividness of a picture must depend upon the colours in which it is painted; but in addition to impression, there is a tide of feeling which flows through the mind of man, in different degrees of velocity and depth, awakening his imagination, stimulating his energies, and supporting him under every intellectual effort. This tide of natural feeling obtains the character of enthusiasm, or power, according to the concomitants with which it operates. If connected with great sensibility, and liveliness of imagination, without clear perceptions, sound judgment, or habits of deep reasoning, it is with strict propriety called enthusiasm; and as such works wonders amongst mankind. Indeed we are indebted to enthusiasm for a great proportion of what is new in theory, and experimental in practice; as well as for most of the astonishing instances of valour, enterprize, and zeal with which the page of history is enlivened and adorned. But enthusiasm, while it partakes of the nature of power in its first impulse, is essentially different in its operation. Enthusiasm in action aims at one point of ardent desire, and regards neither time, nor space, nor difficulty, nor absurdity, in attaining it; while true mental power, in strict alliance with the highest faculties of the mind, is the impetus which forces them into action, so as to accomplish its purpose by the concentrated strength of human intellect directed to an attainable object.

When this principle is diffused through the medium of language, it imparts a portion of its own nature, commanding conviction, stimulating ardour, and rousing determined action; or, bursting upon the poetic soul like sunshine through the clouds of morning, it opens the book of nature, and reveals a new world of light and loveliness, and glory. It creates not only conviction and approval, but actual sensation; and thrills through the awakened feelings, like those tremendous manifestations of physical force, which by the combined agency of different elements produce the most wonderful, and sometimes the most calamitous results.

Were it possible that in any human mind, its faculties could have a complete and evident existence and yet lie dormant, we should say of such a mind that power alone was wanting; but since there must be some power to stimulate the slightest voluntary act, we must speak of this faculty as being always present, and existing in a greater or a less degree. Persons deficient in this faculty and no other, are always content to imitate; and as a proof that they possess the other requisites for successful exertion, they sometimes imitate with great ability and exactness, while they shrink from the very thought of attempting any thing without a model, from an internal consciousness of inability. That many venture to strike out into new paths without attaining any thing like excellence, is owing to the want of some other mental quality; and that some continue to pursue such paths to their own shame, and the annoyance of their fellow creatures, arises from their enthusiasm, not from their power. Yet while many wander on in this eccentric course, without ever being aware of their inability to succeed, we believe that no man ever yet voluntarily commenced a deliberate undertaking, without some internal evidence of power, where it really did exist. A sudden effort is no test, because time is not allowed for the mind to examine its own resources; but the man who has this evidence, will work out his determined way, though all the world should pronounce him incompetent, and exclaim at his absurdity.

It may be asked, if this evidence always accompanies the possession of power, how is it that certain individuals have not been aware of its existence until circumstances have called forth their energies? I answer, it is the test alone which brings this confidence to light; but even these individuals, for any thing which history tells us to the contrary, may have had in their private walk precisely the same sensations on commencing any trifling undertaking, as afterwards accompanied their more public and splendid career. We are not told with what energy or skill Cincinnatus cultivated his farm, but we have no proof that he did not feel the same consciousness of power in conducting his agricultural pursuits, as in regulating the affairs of the commonwealth of Rome. Still it would be absurd to maintain that power always exists in the same mind in an equal degree. There are physical as well as other causes why this should not be the case. There must to every individual, liable to human weakness and infirmity, be seasons when merely to think definitely requires an effort—when *desire fails*, and *the grasshopper becomes a burden;* but when the poet speaks of the bliss-ful moment of inspiration, we suppose it to be that in which all his highest faculties are in agreeable exercise, at the same time that the operations of mental power are unimpeded.

Amongst our poets, those who display the greatest power of mind, are Milton, Pope, and Young. Had Young possessed the requisite of taste, he would perhaps have rivalled even Milton in power; but such is his choice of images and words, that by the frequent and sudden introduction of heterogeneous and inferior ideas, he nullifies what would otherwise be sublime, and by breaking the chain of association, strikes out, as it were, the key-stone of the arch. Nor is this all. The ponderous magnitude of his images, heaped together without room for adjustment in the mind, resembles rather the accumulation of loose masses of uncemented granite, than the majestic mountain, of which each separate portion helps to constitute a mighty whole. Still we must acknowledge of this immortal poet, that his path was in the heavens, and that his soul was suited to the celestial sphere in which it seemed to live and expand as in its native element. We can feel no doubt that his own conceptions were magnificent as the stars amongst which his spirit wandered, and had his mode of conveying these conceptions to the minds of others been equal to their own original sublimity, he would have stood pre-eminent amongst our poets in the region of power.

In order to prove that the poetry of Young is too massive and complex in its imagery to be within the compass of natural and ordinary association, it is unnecessary to quote many instances. Those who are most familiar with his writings—even his greatest admirers, must acknowledge, that in one line of his works, they often meet with matter, which if diffused and poetically enlarged upon, would fill pages, better calculated to please, as well as to instruct.

"How poor, how rich, how abject, how august,
How complicate, how wonderful is man!
How passing wonder He who made him such!
Who centr'd in our make such strange extremes!
From different natures, marvellously mix'd,
Connexion exquisite of different worlds!
Distinguish'd link in being's endless chain!
Midway from nothing to the Deity!"

Thus far the mind may keep pace with the writer, and, especially by the last two lines, must be impressed with ideas at once clear, imaginative, and sublime. Those which immediately follow are less happy.

"A beam ethereal, sullied, and absorb'd!
Though sullied and dishonour'd, still divine!
Dim miniature of greatness absolute!
An heir of glory! a frail child of dust!
Helpless immortal! insect infinite!
A worm! a god! I tremble at myself,
And in myself am lost."——

One instance more, and we turn to passages of a different character.

"Lorenzo, blush at terror for a death
Which gives thee to repose in festive bowers,
Where nectars sparkle, angels minister,
And more than angels share, and raise, and crown,
And eternize, the birth, bloom, bursts of bliss."

It is really a relief to pass on from this laborious collection of disjointed ideas, to instances of more perfect sublimity, which also abound in the works of the same poet. What can exceed in power and beauty his first address to Night?

"Night, sable goddess! from her ebon throne,
In rayless majesty now stretches forth
Her leaden sceptre o'er a slumb'ring world.
Silence how dread! and darkness how profound!
Nor eye nor list'ning ear an object finds;
Creation sleeps. 'Tis as the general pulse
Of life stood still, and nature made a pause,
An awful pause! prophetic of her end."

Again, his appeal to the Divine Inspirer of his solemn thoughts, is full of majesty and power.

"Man's Author, End, Restorer, Law, and Judge!
Thine, all; day thine, and thine this gloomy night,
With all her wealth, and all her radiant worlds.
What night eternal, but a frown from thee?
What heaven's meridian glory, but thy smile?
And shall not praise be thine, not human praise,
While heaven's high host in hallelujahs live!
O may I breathe no longer than I breathe
My soul in praise to Him who gave my soul,
And all her infinite of prospect fair,
Cut through the shades of hell, great Love, by thee,
O most adorable! most unadorn'd!
Where shall that praise begin which ne'er should end!
Where'er I turn, what claim on all applause!
How is night's sable mantle labou ed o'er,
How richly wrought with attribu es divine!
What wisdom shines! what love! This midnight pomp
This gorgeous arch, with golden words inlaid!
Built with divine ambition! nought to thee:
For others this profusion. Thou, apart,
Above, beyond, O tell me, mighty Mind!
Where art thou? shall I dive into the deep?
Call to the sun, or ask the roaring winds,
For their Creator? shall I question loud
The thunder, if in that the Almighty dwells?
Or holds He furious storms in straiten'd reins,
And bids fierce whirlwinds wheel his rapid car?

"The nameless He, whose nod is nature's birth;
And nature's shield, the shadow of his hand;
Her dissolution, his suspended smile!
The great First—last! pavilion'd high he sits
In darkness, from excessive splendour, borne,
By gods unseen, unless through lustre lost.
His glory, to created glory bright
As that to central horrors: he looks down
On all that soars, and spans immensity."

Young's description of truth is also strongly characterized by power.

"See from her tombs as from an humble shrine,
Truth, radiant goddess, sallies on my soul,
And puts delusion's dusky train to flight;
Dispels the mist our sultry passions raise
From objects low, terrestrial, and obscene,
And shows the real estimate of things,
Which no man, unafflicted, ever saw,
Pulls off the veil from virtue's rising charms;
Detects temptation in a thousand lies.
Truth bids me look on men as autumn leaves,
And all they bleed for as the summer's dust
Driven by the whirlwind: lighted by her beams,
I widen my horizon, gain new powers,
See things invisible, feel things remote,
Am present with futurities; think nought
To man so foreign as the joys possess'd;
Nought so much his, as those beyond the grave."

After all, it is not so much in extended passages, as in distinct thoughts, and single expressions, that we feel and acknowledge the power of this dignified and majestic writer. "Silence and darkness! solemn sisters!" is a striking illustration of how great an extent of sublimity may be embodied in a few simple and well chosen words; and it is unquestionably to beauties of this description that Young is indebted for his high rank amongst our poets.

The same faculty of mind is exhibited under a different character in the writings of Pope. Power as an impulse is less apparent here, but in its mode of operation it is more uniform and efficient. Pope is less an enthusiast than Young, and therefore he pays more regard to means; whilst the agency by which these means are brought to bear upon their object seems to be slumbering in silent pomp. The genius of Young gives us the idea of continued, extraordinary, and sometimes ineffectual effort—even in the dead of night counting the stars, grappling with darkness, and grasping at infinity; while we imagine that of Pope seated on a throne of majesty, collecting, combining, and controlling the elements of mind, by authority, rather than by direct force. The power of Young resembles that of a volcano, an earthquake, or a storm of thunder—that of Pope is like the flow of a broad and potent river—too copious to be interrupted in its course—too deep to be impetuous. And as it would be impossible to form any idea of the general agency of such a river by observing any particular portion of its surface, so it would be unjust to the character of Pope, to attempt to convey an adequate idea of his power as a poet, by any particular selection from his writings. One instance, almost too well known to need repetition, will serve our purpose.

"All are but parts of one stupendous whole,
Whose body Nature is, and God the soul;
That, chang'd through all, and yet in all the same,
Great in the earth, as in the ethereal frame,
Warms in the sun, refreshes in the breeze,
Glows in the stars, and blossoms in the trees,
Lives through all life, extends through all extent,
Spreads undivided, operates unspent,
Breathes in our soul, informs our mortal part,
As full, as perfect, in a hair as heart;
As full, as perfect, in vile man that mourns,
As the rapt seraph that adores and burns;
To him no high, no low, no great, no small;
He fills, he bounds, connects, and equals all."

As a proof that the exercise of power is not dependent upon the magnitude or sublimity of the subject described, we will add another passage from the same writer—a singular paradox—an example of power exhibited in the description of a spider's web!

"The spider's touch, how exquisitely fine!
Feels at each thread, and lives along the line."

Here we have distinct ideas of the most delicate sensibility, the most acute perception, and the wonderful expansion and duration of the principle of life, in connection with the frailest, and one of the least perceptible objects in nature, without in any way interfering with our distinct ideas of that object; an evidence of mental power, well worthy of the genius that unbound the lyre of Homer, and awakened fresh music from his immortal strains.

But it is in contemplating the nature of Milton's genius, in its connection with power, that we behold at once the full force of a stupendous impulse, associated with the greatest possible facility in the use of the best means of action. The difference to be observed in the character of power, as exhibited in the poetry of Pope and Milton, is, that the former affects us rather as the written transcript of well concocted thoughts; while the latter, bursting forth from the natural, and immediate, and constantly operating force of an enlightened and vigorous mind, opens for itself—for us—for the whole world and for ages yet to come, the gates of a paradise of thought, pours in an overwhelming flood of light, and diffuses through a region of unexplored sublimity, the loveliness of nature and the harmony of truth.

In reading the poetry of Milton, we have perpetual evidence of his inspiration—of the fulness of the fountain of poetic feeing, whose copious streams are rich in majesty, and beauty, and spiritual life; and we are satisfied that the fountain could never have been sealed save by a hand divine. One tributary and mighty spring was closed, but the waters only became more pure and harmonious, and derived from their divine original a more seraphic sweetness—a grandeur more sublime. We feel that Milton could not but have written as he did. He was less capable of subduing the impulse of his soul, than of finding a language suited to its highest aspirations: and it is this uncontrollable impulse operating in conjunction with the noblest faculties of human nature, which constitutes his power.

We cannot better illustrate the power of Milton's muse, than by selecting from his works, passages descriptive of the two opposite principles of good and evil. On the character of Satan the poet has bestowed so much of the native energy of his genius, that we scarcely feel as we ought to, that it is the nature of evil to degrade and debase.

"Forthwith upright he rears from off the pool
His mighty stature; on each hand the flames,
Driven backward, slope their pointing spires, and, roll'd,

In billows, leave in the midst a horrid vale.
Then with expanded wings he steers his flight
Aloft, incumbent on the dusky air,
That felt unusual weight; till on dry land
He lights, if it were land that ever burned
With solid, as the lake with liquid fire;
And such appeared in hue, as when the force
Of subterranean wind transports a hill
Torn from Pelorus, or the shattered side
Of thundering Ætna, whose combustible
And fueled entrails thence conceiving fire,
Sublimed with mineral fury, and the winds,
And leave a singed bottom all involved
With stench and smoke: such resting found the sole
Of unblessed feet."

——————" he, above the rest
In shape and gesture proudly eminent,
Stood like a tower; his form had yet not lost
All her original brightness, nor appeared
Less than archangel ruined, and the excess
Of glory obscured: as when the sun new risen
Looks through the horizontal misty air
Shorn of his beams; or from behind the moon,
In dim eclipse, disastrous twilight sheds
On half the nations, and with fear of change
Perplexes monarchs."

"He spake: and to confirm his words, outflew
Millions of flaming swords, drawn from the thighs
Of mighty cherubim; the sudden blaze
Far round illumined hell: highly they raged
Against the Highest, and fierce with grasped arms
Clashed on their sounding shields the din of war,
Hurling defiance toward the vault of heaven."

——————" The other shape,
If shape it might be called, that shape had none
Distinguishable in member, joint, or limb;
Or substance might be called that shadow seemed,
For each seemed either; black it stood as night,
Fierce as ten furies, terrible as hell,
And shook a dreadful dart; what seemed his head,
The likeness of a kingly crown had on.
Satan was now at hand, and from his seat
The monster moving, onward came as fast
With horrid strides: hell trembled as he strode.
The undaunted fiend what this might be admired;
Admired, not feared; God and his Son except,
Created thing nought valued he, nor shunned;
And with disdainful look thus first began."

——————" I fled, and cried out, Death!
Hell trembled at the hideous name, and sighed
From all her caves, and back resounded, Death!"

——————" Horror and doubt distract
His troubled thoughts, and from the bottom stir
The hell within him; for within him hell
He brings, and round about him, nor from hell
One step, no more than from himself, can fly
By change of place; now conscience wakes despair,
That slumbered; wakes the bitter memory
Of what he was, what is, and what must be
Worse; of worse deeds worse sufferings must ensue.
Sometimes towards Eden, which now in his view
Lay pleasant, his grieved look he fixed sad;
Sometimes towards heaven, and the full blazing sun.
Which now sat high in his meridian tower.
Me miserable, which way shall I fly
Infinite wrath, and infinite despair?
Which way I fly is hell; myself am hell;
And, in the lowest deep, a lower deep
Still threatening to devour me opens wide
To which the hell I suffer seems a heaven.
Oh! then, at last relent: is there no place
Left for repentance, none for pardon left?
None left but my submission; and that word
Disdain forbids me, and my dread of shame
Among the spirits beneath, whom I seduced
With other promises and other vaunts
Than to submit, boasting I could subdue
The Omnipotent! Ah me! they little know
How dearly I abide that boast so vain,
Under what torments inwardly I groan,
While they adore me on the throne of hell,
With diadem and sceptre high advanced,
The lower still I fall, only supreme
In misery: such joy ambition finds."

We now change the subject, and see how the same genius can ascend from the lowest depths of hell, to the highest regions of purity and bliss, tuning his harp to strains that harmonize with both.

"No sooner had the Almighty ceased, but all
The multitude of angels, with a shout
Loud as from numbers without number, sweet
As from blessed voices, uttering joy, Heaven rung
With jubilee, and loud hosannas filled
The eternal regions."

"Immortal amaranth, a flower which once
In Paradise, fast by the tree of life,
Began to bloom: but soon for man's offence
To heaven removed, where first it grew, there grows,
And flowers aloft, shading the fount of life,
And where the river of bliss through midst of heaven
Rolls o'er Elysian flowers her amber stream:
With those that never fade, the spirits elect,
Bind their resplendent locks, inwreathed with beams;
Now in loose garlands thick thrown off, the bright
Pavement, that like a sea of jasper stone,
Impearled with celestial roses smiled.
Then crowned again, their golden harps they took,
Harps ever tuned, that glittering by their side
Like quivers hung, and with preamble sweet
Of charming symphony they introduce
Their sacred song, and waken raptures high;
No voice exempt, no voice but well could join
Melodious part, such concord is in heaven."

"So spake the cherub; and his grave rebuke,
Severe in youthful beauty, added grace
Invincible: abashed the devil stood,
And felt how awful goodness is, and saw
Virtue in her shape how lovely: saw, and pined
His loss."

"Hail, holy light, offspring of heaven first born,
Or of the Eternal co-eternal beam!
May I express thee unblamed? Since God is light,
And never but in unapproached light
Dwelt from eternity; dwelt then in thee,
Bright effluence of bright essence increate.
Or hear'st thou rather pure ethereal stream,
Whose fountain who shall tell? Before the sun
Before the heavens thou wert, and at the voice
Of God, as with a mantle didst invest
The rising world of waters dark and deep,
Won from the void and formless infinite."

"And chiefly thou, O Spirit, that dost prefer
Before all temples he upright heart and pure,
Instruct me, for thou know'st; thou from the first
Wast present, and with mighty wings outspread
Dove-like sat'st brooding on the vast abyss,
And mad'st it pregnant; what in me is dark,
Illumine; what is low, raise and support;
That to the height of this great argument,
I may assert eternal Providence,
And justify the ways of God to men."

"Henceforth I learn, that to obey is best,
And love with fear the only God; to walk
As in his presence; ever to observe
His providence; and on him sole depend,
Merciful over all his works, with good
Still overcoming evil, and by small
Accomplished great things, by things deemed weak
Subverting worldly strong, and worldly wise
By simply meek; that suffering for truth's sake
Is fortitude to highest victory,
And to the faithful, death the gate of life;
Taught this by his example, whom I now
Acknowledge my Redeemer ever blessed."

If power be the faculty which presents us most clearly and forcibly with ideas that lie beyond the scope of ordinary thought, there is then a power in beauty, as well as in sublimity—a power in the language of the affections to awaken their echo in the human heart, and in pure and holy aspirations, to call us back to all the good we have forsaken, and to lead us forward to all that yet may be attained.

That beautiful and majestic hymn in which Milton describes our first parents, as calling upon the creation—upon every bright and glorious creature—to join in the solemn praises of their universal Creator, comprehends all that we can imagine, both of the harmony of verse, and the force of mental power. Widely as we may have wandered from the purity and the innocence of the first inhabitants of paradise, this morning hymn seems to burst upon us like the dawn of a brighter day, when gratitude and love shall again become the natural language of the re-illumined soul. We see around us even now the same attributes of divinity—the sun, the "eye of this great world," the moon that "meets the orient sun," and the "fixed stars"—we feel "the winds that from four quarters blow"—we hear the warbling flow of the fountains—

"The birds,
That singing up to Heaven's gate ascend"—

we behold the world of animate and moving life—creatures that "in waters glide," or "stately tread the earth," or "lowly creep," and we acknowledge them to be the work and the care of an Almighty hand; but where is the fresh impulse of undeviating will to worship that Almighty Father? will it return with the contemplation of his attributes, and stimulate us to a more faithful service, or inspire a holier love?

We are not among those who would limit the means appointed by Omnipotence for winning back the wanderer from the fold, and we have no hesitation in saying, that it is impossible studiously to examine, and seriously to consider the well directed aim of Milton's genius, without feeling a fresh conviction that such should be the high and glorious purpose of all human intellect—to dignify the immortal nature of man—to throw open as far as human powers permit, the great plan of Divine benevolence, and to teach the important lesson, that where we cannot wholly understand, we may humbly admire, and where we cannot penetrate, we should trust.

In connexion with mental power, there remains some distinction to be made in its mode of operation. There is a power of intellect, and a power of feeling. The writings of Pope bear the most striking evidence of the former, those of Byron will serve as an example of the latter. Pope addresses himself to man's reason, and wields conviction like a thunderbolt. Byron appeals to the soul through its strong sympathies and passions, and spreads over it the shadow of the mighty wings of a dark angel. But the genius of Milton combining the powers of both, and pausing in its flight from heaven to hell, treads the verdant paths of Eden with the footsteps of humanity, reposes in the bowers of earthly bliss, and pours the lamentation of a broken and a contrite spirit over the first sad exile of the progenitors of sin and death.

We cannot complete our tribute to the power of Milton's mind, without referring to his prose, as well as to his poetical compositions; and here we find that strong internal evidence of his calling and capability to work out what mankind in future ages should wonder at and approve; accompanied with a deeply reverential feeling, that even with such capabilities, he was but an humble instrument whose highest office was to assist and promote the purposes of the Most High. And when he levels the powerful aim of his majestic mind against the abuse, and the oppression of a suffering church, it is with the full conviction that such is the solemn duty laid upon his soul.

"For surely (he acknowledges) to every good and peaceable man, it must in nature needs be a hateful thing to be the displeaser and molester of thousands; much better would it like him doubtless to be the messenger of gladness and contentment, which is his chief intended business to all mankind, but that they resist and oppose their own true happiness. But when God commands to take the trumpet, and blow a dolorous or jarring blast, it lies not in man's will what he shall say, or what he shall conceal."

Milton then describes, in language scarcely less remarkable for its power than for its poetical fervour, the self-upbraidings he should ever have felt in after life, had he neglected this high and holy call to rescue the church from degradation.

"Timorous and ungrateful, the church of God is now again at the foot of her insulting enemies, and thou bewailest; what matters it for thee, or thy bewailing? when time was, thou couldst not find a syllable of all that thou hast read, or studied, to utter in her behalf. Yet ease and leisure was given thee for thy retired thoughts, out of the sweat of other men. Thou hast the diligence, the parts, the language of a man, if a vain subject were to be adorned or beautified; but when the cause of God and his church was to be pleaded, for which purpose that tongue was given thee which thou hast; God listened if he could hear thy voice among his zealous servants, but thou wert dumb as a beast; from henceforward be that which thine own brutish silence hath made thee. Or else I should have heard in the other ear; slothful and ever to be set light by, the church hath now overcome her late distresses after the unwearied labours of many of her true servants that stood up in her defence; thou also wouldst take upon thee to share amongst them of their joy: but wherefore thou? where canst thou show any word or deed of thine which might have hastened her peace? whatever thou dost now talk, or write, or look, is the alms of other men's active prudence and zeal. Dare not now to say or do any thing better than thy former sloth and infamy; or if thou darest, thou dost impudently to make a thrifty purchase of boldness to thyself, out of the painful merits of other men; what before was thy sin, is now thy duty, to be abject and worthless. These, and such like lessons as these, would have been my matins daily, and my evening song. But now by this little diligence, mark what a privilege I have gained with good men and saints, to claim my right of lamenting the tribulations of the church, if she should suffer, when others, that have ventured nothing for her sake, have not the honour to be admitted mourners. But if she lift up her drooping head and prosper among those that have something more than wished her welfare, I have my charter and freehold of rejoicing to me and my heirs."

The manner in which Milton speaks of the first stirrings of his youthful genius—the first impulse of inspiration, is worthy of the effect it has produced, and still continues to produce upon mankind.

"I began thus far to assent both to them and to divers of my friends at home, and not less to an inward prompting which now grew daily upon me, that by labour and intense study, (which I take to be my portion in this life,) joined with the strong propensity of nature, I might perhaps leave something so written to after times, as they should not willingly let it die."

The poet then describes the high and mighty compass of the work which he contemplated, speaking uniformly of the great endowment of extraordinary intellect as a gift to be exclusively devoted to the honour and instruction of his country, and the glory of his God.

———"To celebrate in glorious and lofty hymns the throne and equipage of God's almightiness, and what he works, and what he suffers to be wrought with high providence in his church; to sing victorious agonies of martyrs and saints; the deeds and triumphs of just and pious nations, doing valiantly through faith against the enemies of Christ; to deplore the general relapses of kingdoms from justice and God's true worship. Lastly, whatsoever in religion is holy and sublime, in virtue amiable or grave, whatsoever hath passion or admiration in all the changes of that which is called fortune from without, or the wily subtleties or refluxes of man's thoughts from within; all these things with a solid and treatable smoothness to point out and describe. Teaching over the whole book of sanctity and virtue through all the instances of example, with such delight to those especially of soft and delicious temper, who will not so much as look upon truth herself, unless they see her elegantly dressed; that whereas the paths of honesty and good life appear now rugged and difficult, though they be indeed easy and pleasant, they will then appear to all men easy and pleasant, though they were rugged and difficult indeed.

———"A work not to be raised from the heat of youth, or the vapours of wine; like that which flows at waste from the pen of some vulgar amourist, or the trencher fury of a rhyming parasite; nor to be obtained by the invocation of dame Memory and her siren daughters, but by devout prayer to that eternal Spirit, who can enrich with all utterance and knowledge; and sends out his seraphim, with the hallowed fire of his altar, to touch and purify the lips of whom he pleases."

This is indeed quoting at great length, but the temptation is great also, to support with the highest authority what has been asserted, that true mental power is always accompanied with the consciousness of its existence, and that the noblest exercise of this power is to promote the intellectual happiness, as well as the moral good of the human family, and to "justify the ways of God to man."

We know not that our language contains

any thing comparable in poetic fervour, and sublimity, and power, to the solemn appeal to the Divine Being with which Milton closes his second book on the Reformation. After summing up a list of evils present and to come, he adds—

———"I do now feel myself inwrapped on the sudden into those mazes and labarynths of hideous and dreadful thoughts, that which way to get out, or which way to end, I know not, unless I turn mine eyes, and with your help lift up my hands to that eternal and propitious throne, where nothing is readier than grace and refuge to the distresses of mortal suppliants. And it were a shame to leave these serious thoughts less piously than the heathen were wont to conclude their graver discourses.

"Thou therefore that sittest in light and glory unapproachable, Parent of angels and men! next thee I implore, omnipotent King, Redeemer of that lost remnant whose nature thou didst assume, ineffable and everlasting love! and thou, the third subsistence of divine infinitude, illumining Spirit, the joy and solace of created things! one Tripersonal godhead! look upon this thy poor and almost spent and expiring church, leave her not thus a prey to these importunate wolves, that wait and think long till they devour thy tender flock; these wild boars that have broke into thy vineyard, and left the print of their polluting hoofs on the souls of thy servants. O let them not bring about their damned designs, that stand now at the entrance of the bottomless pit, expecting the watchword to open and let out those dreadful locusts and scorpions, to reinvolve us in that pitchy cloud of infernal darkness, where we shall never more see the sun of thy truth again, never hope for the cheerful dawn, never more hear the bird of morning sing. Be moved with pity at the afflicted state of this our shaken monarchy, that now lies labouring under her throes, and struggling against the grudges of more dreadful calamities.

"O thou, that, after the impetuous rage of five bloody inundations, and the succeeding sword of intestine war, soaking the land in her own gore, didst pity the sad and ceaseless revolution of our swift and thick coming sorrows; when we were quite breathless, out of thy free grace didst motion peace, and terms of covenant with us; and have first well nigh freed us from antichristian thraldom, didst build up this Britannic empire to a glorious and enviable height, with all her daughter islands about her; stay us in this felicity, let not the obstinacy of our half obedience and will-worship bring forth that viper of sedition, that for fourscore years hath been breeding to eat through the entrails of our peace; but let her cast her abortive spawn without the danger of this travailing and throbbing kingdom: that we may still remember in our solemn thanksgivings, how for us, the Northern Ocean even to the frozen Thule was scattered with the proud shipwrecks of the Spanish Armada, and the very maw of hell ransacked, and made to give up her concealed destruction, ere she could vent it in that horrible and damned blast.

Milton then goes on with somewhat too much of the rancour of a zealot to stigmatize and condemn the enemies of the church, but still his language is so perfectly illustrative of what we have attempted to describe as mental power, that we conclude only with the end of the chapter. Of those whom he has been denouncing, he says,

"Let them take counsel together, and let it come to nought; let them decree, and do thou cancel it; let them gather themselves, and be scattered; let them embattle themselves, and be broken; let them embattle and be broken, for thou art with us.

"Then, amidst the hymns and hallelujahs of saints, some one may perhaps be heard offering at high strains in new and lofty measures, to sing and celebrate thy divine mercies and marvellous judgments in this land throughout all ages; whereby this great and warlike nation, instructed and inured to the fervent and continual practice of truth and righteousness, and casting far from her the rags of her old vices, may press on hard to that high and happy emulation to be found the soberest, wisest, and most Christian people at that day, when thou, the eternal and shortly expected King, shalt open the clouds to judge the several kingdoms of the world, and distributing national honours and rewards to religious and just commonwealths, shall put an end to all earthly tyrannies, proclaiming thy universal and mild monarchy through heaven and earth; where they undoubtedly, that by their labours, counsels and prayers, have been earnest for the common good of religion and their country, shall receive above the inferior orders of the blessed, the legal addition of principalities, legions, and thrones into their glorious titles, and in supereminence of beatific vision, progressing the dateless and irrevoluble circle of eternity, shall clasp inseparable hands with joy and bliss, in overmeasure for ever.

"But they contrary, that by the impairing and diminution of the true faith, the distresses and servitude of their country, aspire to high dignity, rule, and promotion here, after a shameful end in this life, shall be thrown down eternally into the darkest and deepest gulf of hell, where under the despiteful control, the trample and spurn of all the other damned, that in the anguish of their torture, shall have no other ease than to exercise a raving and bestial tyranny over them as their slaves and negroes, they shall remain in that plight for ever, the basest, lowermost, the most dejected, most underfoot, and down trodden vassals of perdition."

TASTE.

Taste, the last mentioned of the four requisites for writing poetry, is by no means the least important, because its sphere of operation belongs so much to the medium through which poetical ideas are conveyed, that even where impression, imagination, and power exist, we may lose by the absence of taste, all the sensible effect of their presence, as well as all the pleasure naturally arising from their combined influence.

We speak of taste as belonging chiefly to the medium of the poet's ideas, because in the choice and arrangement of his subjects, he uses a higher faculty (or rather a higher and more profound exercise of the same,)—the faculty of judgment; in its nature so nearly allied to taste, that we are inclined to describe taste as a superficial application of judgment. Both are faculties whose office it is to take note of the fitness of things generally, the one by casual observation of them, the other by mature consideration of their nature. Taste applies chiefly to those qualities which immediately strike our attention without much exercise of thought, such as beauty and harmony; while judgment admits within its compass the weightier considerations of present utility, and ultimate good.

If, for example, we say of a lady that she dresses with taste; we mean with due regard to beauty of form, harmony of colours, and general suitableness to her appearance—if with judgment, we mean with regard to her pecuniary means, her character, and station in life; but the operation of the mind in the exercise of taste, and judgment is the same, differing only in the subjects to which it is applied. In both cases we draw conclusions from the general nature of the subjects considered, those of which taste takes cognizance, being superficial and evident to the senses, its conclusions are prompt, and immediate; and thus it erroneously obtains the character of an intuitive power, directing the choice at once to what is most suitable, or best. In the tasteful arrangement of a group of flowers, we are apt to suppose it is an instinctive impulse by which they are so placed before us, as to display their beauties to the greatest advantage, and produce the most agreeable effect; but it is in fact upon conclusions previously drawn from the principles of pleasure, that the mind operates in contrasting the colours so as to make one heighten the brilliancy of another, and combining the whole group so as to render not only colour, but form, and character conducive to the beauty of the whole.

If taste and judgment differ only in being exercised upon different subjects, it may be asked, why then are not the individuals best skilled in the arrangement of flowers, able legislators, and profound logicians? It is because there are many minds possessed of the faculty of judgment yet wholly incapable of taking into consideration the nature, relation, and application of the laws which regulate public action, and private thought; but if such individuals could be made to understand these laws, there is no reason why they should not judge as correctly of their effect as of that of a group of flowers. In order to compose a tasteful bouquet it is only necessary that we should have clear perceptions of form and colour; in order to invent laws for the government of nations, or systematize the thoughts and "imaginations of man's heart," we must have distinct ideas of physical force, and moral good, of action, and motive, of power, and integrity.

It is a familiar, but not the less important and comprehensive fact, that every thing has a proper place; and the faculty which enables us to ascertain by instantaneous perception what is, or is not the proper place of any object, is taste—that by which we ascertain the same fact by conviction is judgment. We admire, and derive pleasure from the operation of the former; we reverence, and derive benefit from that of the latter. Our looks, words, movements, and trifling pursuits come under the cognizance of taste; nor let its superficial character lessen the value of this universal test of beauty and harmony, which are the two grand sources of our enjoyment. It is not the profound nature of the cases in which it acts, but their frequent recurrence in the ordinary walks of life, as well as their immense variety and number, which renders the influence of taste so important to our happiness. If from the causes upon which it operates, we are liable to receive pain or pleasure every moment of our lives, the cultivation of this faculty must indeed be of no inconsiderable weight in the aggregate of human affairs; yet how to cultivate it so as ultimately to produce the greatest good, is a delicate and difficult question. Refined to the most acute perception of all the degrees which lie between the remote extremes of beauty and deformity—of pleasure and pain, taste is any thing but a blessing; unless where there is judgment to go deeper into the essential qualities of things, and to discover a moral good beneath a physical evil; because the outward aspect of our world, even with all its loveliness, and the external character of our circumstances, even with all our enjoyments, are such as often to present pictures repulsive and abhorrent to perceptions more delicate than deep. But the cultivation of taste when confined as it ought to be to its proper place, and limited to its proper degree, is eminently conducive to our happiness, and eventually to our good. Taste should even rule itself, and set bounds to its own existence, for its laws are as much violated when we are too sublime for useful service, and too delicate for duty, as when we descend to the use of vulgar epithets, and ape the absurdities of our inferiors.

As a proof of the immediate application of taste, we seldom wholly approve of the language and customs of past ages. That the same astonishing productions of art which adorned the most enlightened eras of Grecian history, should remain to be models of excellence at the present day, is because of their relation to the senses, whose power in assisting the judgment is limited to a *degree* of cultivation; but language and social customs having more immediate relation to the intellectual and moral constitution of man are continually fluctuating, or progressing, without any perceptible limitation to their capability of improvement. We cannot look back to the literature of the past century, and pay our just tribute to its superiority in force of expression, without at the same time being struck with words and phrases, which to say the least of them, arrest our attention, and often impede, by the difference of their associations, our perception of their sense and application. Indeed so wide is this difference, that many minds endowed with fine taste and sensibility, are now incapable of appreciating the beauties of Shakespeare; though we own there is some cause to suspect of such minds, that they are deficient both in imagination and power, or they would unquestionably be lifted above what appear to us now the absurdities of this extraordinary writer, by the unrivalled splendour of his mighty genius. Insensible to the brilliance of a great luminary, which reveals a world of glory, these fastidious critics take the light of their tiny perceptions into partial spots of shade, and extracting from thence the rank nettle or the wandering weed, cry out that by their own delicacy they have made this laudable discovery. Better would it beseem an elevated soul to pass on, and leave such blemishes unnoticed; or to prove its just and noble admiration of true genius, rather than its capability of discovering petty faults.

Where the poet is gifted with judgment, and not with taste, he is compelled to ponder at every verse; and while he weighs the merit of his subject, compares his ideas, and new models his expressions, the warmth of his poetic fervour is expended, and that which ought to appear to us as if it flowed from a natural and irrepressible impulse, becomes painful and laborious, both to himself, and to his readers. But he who is gifted with a high degree of taste, calls in the aid of this important faculty, the lively exercise of whose immediate power directs him to the choice of expressions in which to clothe his ideas, striking out what is defective, and selecting what is appropriate, with the rapidity of an instantaneous impulse. One kind of metre admits of a pompous array of words, another of expressions volatile and gay—one of abrupt and broken, another of smooth and flowing sentences. One subject requires a correspondence of solemn or melancholy sound, another of the rapid movements which belong to lively joy. One scene calls forth the glowing ornament of eastern magnificence, another, the cold majesty of the frozen north. For the description of one passion the poet must adorn his muse with the attributes of love and beauty, for another he must place in her hand the lighted brand of fury and destruction. All this is the work of taste, and when no law, either intellectual or moral has been violated; when the customs and regulations of society have been consulted, and no feeling or prejudice offended; when propriety, and order, and harmony, have ruled the poet's theme, and verse; and when supreme regard has been paid to beauty, both in its physical and intellectual character, we may confidently pronounce the writer to have possesed a more than common share of taste.

On this subject we may go yet farther. We may say of the faculty of taste, that it makes the nearest approach to what we are in the habit of calling inspiration; because it is the direct rule of propriety in action:

and were the perceptions of man so quick and clear as to carry the same principle along with him through all the transactions of his life, he would always act rightly. But, beyond the surface of things, man is unable to judge at sight. Reflection requires time and effort, often more of both than he is willing to bestow, and even when he is willing, the right period of action is lost before he has decided upon the right means.

By contemplating the character and operation of taste, we arrive at a dim and distant perception of one of the attributes of the Divine nature; and even this imperfect view reveals a world of wonder in which imagination is bewildered, and understanding lost. We know the rapidity of thought with which we decide in a moment, even during an instantaneous movement, which is the most graceful, the most effective, or the best mode of acting; and it may not perhaps be derogating from the supreme majesty to suppose that the same effort of omnipotent mind, created out of Chaos a universe of worlds, not only designing their form and regulating their movements, in the centre of infinity; but also designing and regulating their internal constitution, down to the slightest impulse of an infant's will, the meanest weed that lurks within the forest glade, or the minutest insect that skims along the surface of the summer lake. The power of judging when limited to a narrow sphere of operation constitutes the superiority of man above the brutes; the power of judging universally, instantaneously and infallibly, belongs to God alone.

We have said, and we repeat it with reverence, that the faculty of taste in the single consideration of its mode of operating, bears an humble relation to what we conceive of infallibility; because its decisions are so prompt as to apply to immediate action, and so extended as to comprehend all relative circumstances; or else it does not exist: for let a sound be harsh, where it should be soft; or soft, where it should be harsh; let a movement be quick, or slow, as circumstances do not warrant; let a shadow, or a gleam of light break in upon the sphere of beauty; let a word be found misplaced, or a thought ill-timed; in short, let any single thread in general concord be broken, and taste is sacrificed: consequently, as our mental and material world is constituted, the dominon of taste must extend over a very limited and narrow sphere.

The difference of taste to be found amongst mankind, and the want of a universal standard of reference, have excited almost as many arguments in the sphere of poetry and the arts, as the difference of creeds in the religious world. This subject seems to be most satisfactorily decided, by attaching to the majority the same importance in taste as in politics. The exercise of taste being to find the medium between all objectionable extremes—the centre of eccentricity—it follows of necessity, that whatever is admired by the greatest number, must possess the greatest share of intrinsic excellence. But here, as in other cases, it is highly important to make a distinction between mere numbers, and numbers qualified to judge; for how should that judgment be a test of merit, to which merit is neither apparent nor intelligible? The gallery audience in a theatre may be well qualified to pronounce upon the height, the breadth, the complexion, or the agility of a favourite actor; but who would appeal to them to know whether he had exhibited to the life the workings of deep-seated feeling, or entered into the mental mysteries of an intellectual character? When, therefore, we speak of the majority of opinions being the strongest proof of the presence of good taste, we would confine those opinions, not merely to a few learned men, the established critics and censors of the day, but to the whole of the enlightened public, who constitute a community too numerous for long continued prejudice, and too intelligent for egregious error.

Why then, it may be asked, does a false taste sometimes prevail, even amongst this community, as in the case of Byron,* whose poetry so powerfully affected men's minds, as to leave behind it a disrelish for all other? A false taste may exist amongst the few, from partial impressions, and local preju-

* The inequalities of Byron's style, naturally lead the writer to speak of his poetry in a manner that may at times appear paradoxical: this remark of course can only apply to the extremes, unworthy of so great a mind, to which his eccentric genius sometimes descended.

dices; but a false taste can only exist amongst the many, from the universality of the same impressions false to the principles of nature, and the same prejudices opposed to the principles of good sense; a phenomenon which it is not often our misfortune to behold; and I should account for the extraordinary bias given to the public taste by the works of Byron, as arising from the power of his genius rather than the peculiarity of his style; and the generality of readers not giving themselves trouble to make the distinction, they are still thirsting for the same style, in the vain hope of finding it connected with the same genius. Happy would it be for mankind, for public taste, and public morals, if the same mind, purified from all alloy, could return again to earth, to prove to the world that the same power may be directed to higher purposes without losing its influence, and the same beauty, and the same harmony, be touched by a hand more true to the principles of eternal happiness.

In looking for instances of the display of taste in poetry, it is necessary to confine our observation to the present times; for as we have before remarked, that which was in strict accordance with good taste a century ago, is not so now; because the different customs and manners of mankind have introduced different associations; and expressions which formely conveyed none but elevated and refined ideas, are now connected with those of a totally different nature. We are inclined to think that the works of Milton would have afforded the finest example of taste, as well as power, in the age in which he lived, because in cases where the senses have dominion—the accordance of sense with sound, for instance—he is inimitable. But the language of Milton is sometimes too quaint for modern ears, and in his pages we occasionally meet with single words that startle us with associations foreign to what is now considered as poetical.

We cannot quote a more perfect example of taste in modern language, than the writings of our poet Campbell, in which, especially his Pleasures of Hope, it would be difficult to find an ill-chosen word, or an idea not in strict accordance with the principles of harmony and grace. The presence of taste being, however imperceptible, except by the absence of faults, it is difficult to bring forward instances in particular passages of the influence of this powerful but still indefinable charm. The following lines, familiar to every reader, or rather every admirer of poetry, are remarkable for their adaptation of language, and harmony of sound.

"Primeval Hope, the Aönian muses say,
When man and nature mourn'd their first decay;
When every form of death, and every wo,
Shot from malignant stars to earth below;
When Murder bared her arm, and rampant War
Yoked the red dragons of her iron car;
When Peace and Mercy, banish'd from the plain,
Sprung on the viewless winds to Heaven again;
All, all forsook the friendless guilty mind,
But Hope, the charmer, linger'd still behind."

And in the description of the fate of the "hardy Byron," how perfectly does the sound of each line correspond with its sense, flowing on like a continued stream of melody, without interruption from any word or idea not purely poetical.

"And such thy strength-inspiring aid that bore
The hardy Byron to his native shore—
In horrid climes, where Chiloe's tempests sweep
Tumultuous murmurs o'er the troubled deep,
'Twas his to mourn misfortune's rudest shock,
Scourg'd by the winds, and cradled on the rock,
To wake each joyless morn, and search again
The famish'd haunts of solitary men;
Whose race, unyielding as their native storm,
Know not a trace of nature but the form;
Yet, at thy call, the hardy tar pursued,
Pale, but intrepid, sad, but unsubdued,
Pierced the deep woods, and hailing from afar,
The moon's pale planet, and the northern star:
Paused at each dreary cry, unheard before,
Hyænas in the wild, and mermaids on the shore;
Till, led by thee o'er many a cliff sublime,
He found a warmer world, a milder clime,
A home to rest, a shelter to defend,
Peace and repose, a Briton and a friend!"

The idea conveyed in the following lines, is well worthy of a poetic mind. Others seem to have felt the same, but none have done more ample justice to the feeling, than the elegant bard from whom we quote.

"Who that would ask a heart to dullness wed,
The waveless calm, the slumber of the dead?
No; the wild bliss of nature needs alloy,
And fear and sorrow fan the fire of joy!
And say, without our hopes, without our fears,
Without the home that plighted love endears,
Without the smile from partial beauty won,
Oh! what were man?—a world without a sun."

And when the poet exclaims,

"Cease, every joy, to glimmer on my mind,
But leave—Oh! leave the light of Hope behind
What though my winged hours of bliss have been
Like angel visits, few and far between,"—

we feel that to such a mind, hope would come as a blessed messenger, whose tidings would be of things sublime, and pure, and elevated above the low wants and wishes of a material existence.

We know of but one word in the whole of this beautiful poem which is at variance with good taste, and we quote the line, not from the pleasure of pointing out a single fault in the midst of a thousand merits, but for the purpose of showing how forcibly an error in taste strikes upon the attention and the feelings of the reader.

"The living *lumber* of his kindred earth."

We are ready to imagine from this line, that the author has scarcely been aware of the high degree of beauty and refinement which pervades his work. "Lumber," in the poetical writings of Pope, might have occurred without any breach of taste, because his concise and forcible style is more characterised by power, than elegance; and lumber might, therefore, have been in keeping with the general tone of his expressions. But here, where all is music to the ear, and harmony to the mind, this uncouth word is decidedly out of place; and while longing to exchange it for another, we can only wonder that there should be but one small blemish in so many fair and beautiful pages of genuine poetry, adorned throughout with the most tender, refined, and elevated thoughts.

Gertrude of Wyoming is another poem strikingly illustrative of the influence of taste. In the death-song of the Indian chief, we observe how skilfully the poet has blended the indignant spirit of an injured man, with the strong affections, wild metaphors, and wilder visions, of that interesting and dignified people.

"And I could weep;—th' Oneyda chief
His descant wildly thus began;
But that I may not stain with grief
The death-song of my father's son!
Or bow this head in wo;
For by my wrongs, and by my wrath!
To-morrow Areouski's breath,
(That fires yon heaven with storms and death,)
Shall light us to the foe:
And we shall share, my Christian boy!
The foeman's blood, the avenger's joy.
* * * * * *
But hark, the trump—to-morrow thou
In glory's fires shall dry thy tears:
Even from the land of shadows now
My father's awful ghost appears,
Amidst the clouds that round us roll
He bids my soul for battle thirst—
He bids me dry the last—the first—
The only tears that ever burst
From Outalissi's soul;
Because I may not stain with grief
The death-song of an Indian chief."

Campbell's "lines on leaving a scene in Bavaria," full of the deep pathos of poetic feeling, afford one of the most splendid instances of the power of that faculty, which can strike with the rapidity of thought the chords of true harmony, and waken the genuine music of the soul—the echo of its deep, but secret passions. We cannot read these lines without feeling that there is a language for the wounded spirit—a voice amidst the solitudes of that

"Unknown, unploughed, untrodden shore,"

whose melancholy cadence is in unison with the feelings which we may not, dare not, utter; and we inwardly bless the mournful minstrel for the wild sweet melody of his most harmonious lyre. Were we to attempt to quote passages from these lines, the temptation would extend to the whole of this inimitable poem, we can only recommend it to the reader as one of the finest specimens of poetic taste, as well as poetic feeling, which our language affords.

After all that has been said on the subject, we feel that taste is something to be felt, rather than defined, yet of such unparalleled importance to the poet, that wanting this requisite, he may sing for ever, and yet sing in vain. As well might the musician expect to charm his audience, by playing what he assures them is the finest music, on a broken or defective instrument, as the poet hope to please without making himself thoroughly acquainted with the principles of taste—perhaps we should rather say, with what is, or is not in accordance with its rules, for as a principle, taste has not yet arrived at a definite state of existence; and if the young poet should read "The pleasures of Hope" with reference to this subject, and not feel in his very soul the presence and the power of taste, he might bid adieu to the worship of the muses, and devote his genius to objects less elevated and sublime.

CONCLUSION.

We have now examined the four requisites for writing poetry, to none of which it would be wise to assign a station of pre-eminence, because they are equally necessary to the success of the poet's art—impression to furnish lasting ideas, imagination to create images from such ideas, power to strike them out with emphasis and truth, and taste to recommend such as are worthy of approbation, and to dismiss such as are not. We have also been daring enough to maintain that poetry, as a principle, pervades all nature, and if the fact be acknowledged that poetry is neither written with that ardour, nor read with that delight, which characterised an earlier era in our history, it becomes an important and interesting inquiry, *What is the cause*?

That imagination should be exhausted, is a moral impossibility; because the creation of a thousand images in no way disqualifies for the creation of a thousand more; any one quality extracted from a former image, and added to the whole or a part of another, being sufficient for the creation of one, that shall appear to the world entirely original or new. That power should be expended, is no less an absurdity in thought; because that being the vital principle by which thoughts are generated, man can only cease to think when he ceases to feel, and only cease to feel when he ceases to exist. And that taste should have lost its influence over the human mind, is equally at variance with common sense; because with increased facility in collecting and comparing evidence for the establishment of true excellence, taste must unavoidably become more definite in its nature, and more determinate in its operations. Beyond this, we may ask, is there any thing in the customs, occupations, or mode of education peculiar to the present day, which hinders the exercise of imagination? We should rather say, that its sphere of action is widened to an incalculable extent. Is there any thing that weakens the mind, or destroys its native power? No. The habits of the present race of men are distinguished by indefatigable industry, and general application, and regulated by those laws of strict and unremitting discipline, which are universally acknowledged to strengthen the understanding, and invigorate the mental faculties. Is there any thing to warp the public taste, and establish a false standard of merit? Never since the world began, were mankind more penetrating, and at the same time more extensive in their observations, more universally free from the shackles of tyranny and superstition, as well as from all uniformly prevailing prejudice, than now. It is clear then, that the deficiency in our poetical enjoyments arises from a want of the due proportion of clear and deep impressions. We have not stored up the necessary materials for imagination, power, and taste to work with, and therefore the machinery of the mind, so far as relates to poetry, remains inactive. We possess not the key to its secret harmonies, and therefore the language of poetry is unintelligible to our ears.

The silence of our ablest poets, and the want of any leading or distinguished poem to fill up the present vacuum in our literature, sufficiently prove the fact to which we allude. The last popular work of this kind that issued from our press, was "The Course of Time;" but its popularity rather resembled an instantaneous flash, than a steady and lasting light. It forced its way in the flush of the moment to every respectable library in the kingdom—was read with wonder—closed with satisfaction—and, what is very remarkable, affords no quotations. Since this time we have had none to awaken a general interest. We see many noticed by the reviewers—kindly and encouragingly noticed, and we doubt not their title to such approbation; but we do not deny ourselves one ordinary indulgence that we may buy them, or when they are bought, look upon them as a solid mass of substantial happiness set apart for our private and insatiable enjoyment. We do not reverence the authors of our felicity, as if they were beings of a gifted order, endowed with a superhuman capacity of penetrating into the souls of men. We do not listen when they tell us of our own secret passions, as if we heard the music of an inspired minstrel, nor when they sing of the revolutions of time, as if a potent and oracular voice dealt out the destiny of mankind. Either we have grown indifferent, and heedless, and almost deaf to the language of poetry, or the spirit of the art has ceased to operate in producing those harmonious numbers that were wont to charm the world.

Yet when the facilities for acquiring knowledge are multiplying every day, when it has become almost as difficult to remain unlearned, as to learn, when the infant mind is trained up to the continual application of its faculties in all the different branches of art and science, when the memory is stored with a fund of information which at one time would have been deemed incredible, when not only the ordinary and beaten track of learning is thrown open to the multitude, but flowery and meandering paths are devised to entice, and woo, and charm into the bowers of academic lore, is it possible there can be any defect or disadvantage in the general system upon which youth is trained?

If it be the ultimate aim of mankind to ascertain of what materials the world is made, and out of these materials to construct new facilities for bodily enjoyment, that we may eat more luxuriously, move more rapidly, repose more softly, clothe more sumptuously, and in short, live more exempt from mental, as well as bodily exertion, I should answer, that the present system of education, and the general tone of thought and conversation, was the best that could possibly be devised. But in looking at the means, we are too apt to disregard the end. In devoting our endeavours to the attainment of knowledge, to forget the attainment of wisdom; and take credit to ourselves for having spent an active life, when it has been wholly unproductive of any increase in the means of happiness, except what mere activity affords.

We know that nature is no less capable of producing poetical ideas, than it was when gifted men were inspired by the cool shade, the glowing sunshine, or the radiance of the moon. We have attempted to prove, that the same beauty, and the same connexion with refined and elevated thought may still be found in the external world, and that the soul of man is still animated by the same passions and affections, as when genius kindled the fire of poetry, and, lighting up the charms and the wonders of creation, stimulated the enthusiasm of him who deems himself "creation's heir." It follows then as a necessary consequence, that the *connexion between man and nature*, is not the same; that he holds no longer the spiritual converse with all things sweet and lovely, solemn and sublime, in the external world, that was wont to fill his soul with admiration and love, and to instruct his heart in the feeling of the presence of an invisible intelligence, connected with his own being by the indissoluble bond of sympathy, real or imaginary. Man now studies nature as a map, rather than a picture—with reference to locality, rather than beauty. He sees the whole, but he studies only the separate parts, and to his systematic mind, the vegetable, animal, and mineral kingdoms, are distinct subjects of consideration, scarcely to be thought of in the same day. He looks around him with microscopic eye, and if his attention fixes upon the rich and varied foliage of the ancient forest, it is to single out particular specimens of trees and plants, and to class them according to Linnæus; while from the musical inhabitants of these woods, he selects his victims, and applies the same minute examination to the organs from whence the sweetest melody of nature flows. The idle butterfly, fluttering above his woodland path, or resting upon the unsullied petals of the delicate wild rose, has neither charm nor beauty in his eye, unless he counts the spots upon its wing. The mountain rises in the distance, and he hastens to examine the strata of which it is composed. The vapours roll beneath him, and he ponders upon the means of their production. The stars are shining above in all the majesty of cloudless night, and he counts the number, and calculates the distance of the worlds of light.

All these we freely grant are right and fitting occupations for a rational and intellectual being; but when pursuits of this kind, instead of the end to which they lead, are made the *sole business of man's life*, the natural consequence must be, to render him familiar indeed with nature, but familiar on such terms that he is in danger of forfeiting his reverence for the creator, and losing sight of the connexion between the material and the moral world.

We are not so blindly wedded to the vagaries of imagination as to speak of this thirst for definite knowledge, as an evil. Far from it. But when the unenlightened, or the imbecile mind becomes infected with this fever of acquisition; when the juvenile philosopher is merely talking about what he ought to feel; when the puny artist no sooner beholds a tree, than he thinks it necessary to sketch it; when the student of nature tears in pieces every bird and insect that falls within his grasp; when books without number are eagerly inquired for, looked into, laid aside, and never understood; when the finished and fully-educated young lady displays her knowledge of the phraseology of foreign languages, and her ignorance of the spirit of her own; when the youthful metaphysician discourses eloquently upon the nature and laws of mind and matter, and hears with total vacuity of understanding that there is a *moral* law; we cannot help feeling that something is wanting of the ultimate end of education, and that the mind may be stored with knowledge, and yet be too ignorant of the right means of applying that knowledge to render its possessor wise.

The man of comprehensive mind, capable of appreciating all things according to their real value, will cultivate this knowledge of material things for the sake of the truths which it establishes, and the consequences to which it leads; and will no more content himself with this examination of external nature, than the sculptor will rest satisfied with having discovered the block of marble, out of which his figure is to be formed.

If the question might be asked without implying an ignorant and stupid want of reverence for knowledge in general, we should propose for the consideration of those who regret the absence of poetry from the world of letters, whether the defect so obvious in the literature of the present day, may not arise, in the first place from the competition, and the consequent labour that is now actually necessary to secure the means of subsistence; and in the second, from the public mind being too fully occupied with the acquisition of *mere* knowledge, to allow time for receiving deep impressions, without which it is impossible either to write, or to feel poetically. If, for instance, in the cases already specified, the attention be wholly occupied in ascertaining the precise form of a leaf, where will be the impression of the majestic beauty of the forest? if in dissecting the organs of sense, what general idea can be formed of the melody of sound? if in examining the wing of the butterfly, what observation can be made upon its airy and fantastic flight? if in discovering the component parts of a cloud, how should the graceful involutions of the cloud be seen? if in chiseling out minute fragments from the side of the mountain, how should a deep sense of its grandeur pervade the soul? or if in merely counting the stars as separate spots of light, where will be the lasting impress of their glory?

The modern observer having had little time, and less inclination for the relative ideas which the contemplation of such objects affords to the poetic mind, they pass away from his thoughts as soon as his practical purpose has been fulfilled, and never afterwards are recalled as links in the chain of association connecting the material with the ideal world. When the wild winds of autumn sweep the many tinted leaves from the forest; like the ruder blasts of a less physical calamity, despoiling the fair pictures of spiritual beauty; the summer garniture of green and golden foliage lives no longer in remembrance. The woodland songster breathes no more; and the living voice that answered the universal language of nature from the fields, the groves, and the silvery waterfalls, is forgotten. The butterfly that lately fluttered round him like a winged flower escaped from Flora's coronet, a spotted specimen of a particular tribe—classed according to its name, lies before him faded, and lifeless, and dismantled of its beauty—the memory of its aerial rambles extinguished with its transient and joyous life. The cloud has passed, and all its graceful and fantastic wreaths of mingled mist and light, floating upon the pure ocean of celestial blue, like a spirit half earthly half divine, wandering on its upward journey to the realms of bliss, have vanished with the sunbeams that gave a short-lived glory to its ephemeral existence. The lofty and majestic mountain no longer rises on the view; and his towering summit pointing to the sky, the deep ravines that cross and intersect his rugged sides like the foot prints of the retiring deluge—the light upon his golden brow, and the dark shadows that lie beneath like the frown of a mighty monarch whose will is life or death—all these have passed away from thought and memory, and a tiny particle of stone—a grain of granite remains in the hand of the modern philosopher, as his sole memorial of a mountain. Or when he grasps the telescope, and strains his eye to count the stars; before his labours cease, a dim line of light begins to mark out the eastern horizon, and one after another the stars retire before the brighter radiance of ascending day, like guardian angels who have watched the wanderer through his dark, and dubious, and earthly way, relinquishing their faithful trust before the unfo ding gates of Heaven. But the mere man of science retires into his closet, and pricks out the constellations in separate spots, better satisfied to have ascertained the perceptible number of stars in any given section of the hemisphere, than to have felt their light, their glory, and their magnificence, reigning and ruling over the midnight world.

We repeat, that no mind can be poetical whose exercise is confined to mere physical observation, and whose sphere of action excludes all those modes of receiving and retaining impressions which are either immediately or remotely connected with the feelings, the passions, and the affections.

The nature of our being admits of two important distinctions—physical and moral. And it is the great merit of poetry, that it constitutes an indissoluble bond of union between the two. We could not have been sensible of the different nature of good and evil, but for our capacity of receiving pleasure and pain. It is thus we learn to love whatever is conducive to our happiness—to hate or avoid whatever is productive of pain; and it is this love, or this hatred, extending though an illimitable number of degrees and modifications, which constitutes the very essence of poetry and which, were poetry struck out from the world would disappear along with it, and leave us nothing but a mere corporeal existence, unconnected with the attributes of an imperishable and eternal life.

It may be a subject of something more than curiosity, to ask what the world would be without poetry. In the first place we must strike out beauty from the visible creation, and love from the soul of man. We must annihilate all that has been devised for ornament or delight, without a bodily and material use. We should no longer need a centre of light and glory to illuminate the world, but the same principle of light uniformly diffused, without reflection, and without shadow, would supply the practical purposes of man. The moon might hide her radiance, and the stars might vanish, or remain only as spots of black upon a dusky sky, to guide the nightly traveller, and lead the adventurous bark across the sea. Half the feathered songsters of the woods might plume their wings for an eternal flight, and the rest might cease from their vocal music, and let the woods be still. Rivers and running streams might glide on without a ripple or a murmur—reflecting no sunshine—adding nothing to the harmony of nature; and the ocean might lie beneath a heaven without clouds or colour, stretched out in the waveless repose of never-ending sleep. The trees might rear their massive trunks without their leafy mantle of varied green, the flowers might bow their heads and die; and the wild weeds of the wilderness that weave themselves into a carpet of rich and varied beauty, might perish from the earth and leave its surface barren and unclothed. Of animal life, the beasts of burden, and the fleshly victims of man's appetite, would alone remain; while in man himself, we must extinguish his affections, and render void his capacity to admire; and having moulded the creation to a uniform correspondence with his earthly and coporeal nature, we must leave him to the exercise of his faculties—first, to see, without beholding beauty—to hear, without distinguishing harmony from discord, or to distinguish without preference—to esteem the effluvium of the stagnant pool as delicate an odour as the perfume of the rose—to taste without regard to flavour—and to feel with equal indifference the downy pillow, or the rude couch where the hardy peasant seeks repose. Then in the higher regions of his mental faculties, to observe, without any sense of sublimity—to calculate without arriving at an idea of infinity—to measure, without reference to illimitable space—to resist, without forming a conception of absolute power—to build without reflecting upon duration—to pull down, without looking forward to annihilation. And in the vacant sphere of passion and affection, to receive benefits, and remain insensible to favour—to stand on the brink of destruction, without terror—to await the result of experiment, without hope—to meet without pleasure—to part without grief—and to live on with the same uniformity of existence, without emotion—not idle, for that would imply a sense of the pain of labour, and the pleasure of repose ; but perpetually active, yet active without desire. Such would be the world, and such the condition of man, were all that appertains to the nature of poetry extinct.

Were it possible to concentrate the dark features of this gloomy picture into a small compass, it would be in the simple idea of the exclusion of beauty from nature, or of the perception of beauty from the soul of man. Beauty is not necessary to our bodily existence. Nature would afford the same corporeal support, did we look upon her varied character with a total absence of all sense of admiration. Why then is this ineffable charm diffused through all creation, its essence so mingled with man's nature, that where he finds food for admiration, he finds intellectual enjoyment; and where he finds it not, he thirsts for it as for a fountain of excellence, until he works his way through difficulty and dangers to participate, even in the smallest measure, of its inexhaustible supply of pure and natural refreshment.

That this insatiable desire for beauty forms a part of the constitution of man, is sufficiently proved by his still following the same principle in art, after he ceased to recognise it in nature. As the facilities for bodily enjoyment are multiplied, improved, and refined, man becomes luxurious and artificial in his habits. He withdraws from all familiar acquaintance with natural things, and surrounds himself with all that is curious in human invention, and exquisite in the work of human hands. But still the principles of beauty, derived from external nature, pursue the slave of art, and he studies how to imitate the variety, the splendour, and the magnificence, which the meanest peasant may enjoy in greater perfection, without invention, and without price.

Perception of beauty is one of the most decided characteristics, by which man is distinguished from the brute. We discover no symptoms of admiration in animals of a lower grade than ourselves. The peacock excites no deference from the splendour of his plumage, nor the swan from her snow white feathers, and the verdant fields in their summer bloom, attract no more, than as their flowery sweets allure the insect tribe, who in their turn are followed by their foes. To man alone belongs the prerogative of appreciating beauty because admiration is graciously designed as the means of leading him on to moral excellence.

There are philosophers who argue against the existence of positive enjoyment. I am ignorant, and I feel no anxiety to learn what they can say to prove that admiration,—true admiration, untainted by the remotest touch of envy, is not positive enjoyment—that, when the soul expands with a conception of excellence, unseen, unknown, unfelt before—of excellence, not merely as it relates to fitness for physical purposes ; but of that which combines the principles of intellectual beauty, with the attributes of our moral nature—excellence which leads us into a new world of thought to expatiate in fields of glory, and to drink of the waters of immortality, it knows no positive enjoyment. For never was the enlightened mind excited to the highest sense of admiration, without feeling an extension of being beyond the narrow limits of mortal life; and this expansion naturally conducts us into a sphere of illimitable felicity. Hence arise the different heavens which mankind have constructed for themselves out of the materials of earthly enjoyment, and hence our internal evidence of the belief, that the true heaven promised to the faithful, will comprehend all that we pine for of happiness, all that we admire of beauty, and more than all that we can conceive of excellence.

This intense perception of beauty—this tribute of the heart to excellence—this admiration of physical and thence of moral good, which dignifies the mind with the noblest aims, is so nearly allied to poetic feeling, that we question whether one could exist without the other; and if the diminution of poetic fervour be symptomatic of a decreased capacity of admiration, we have to look, not only to the depreciated character of our literature, but of our taste, and our morals. Nor is this view of the subject too widely extended to be supported by reason, since the first step to improvement is to *admire* what is better—the nearest approach to perfection, to *admire* all things worthy, in their true proportion—and to *admire* that most which is supremely good.

Is it then a thing of small importance that we should cease to admire? that we should lose, not only the most brilliant portion of our literature, but the happiest moments of our existence? We have observed what a void would be left in the natural world by the extinction of poetic feeling, we have now to consider what a void would be left in the world of letters by the absence of poetry as an art. We must not only seal up the fountain from whence flows the melody that has softened down the asperities of our own passions; but turning to the page of history, and tracing back the connexion of civilization with poetry, we must strike out from the world the influence of the mighty genius of Homer, in refining the manners of a barbarous people, in transmitting to posterity a faithful record of their national and social character, and in kindling in other minds the sparks of embryo genius, from that ancient period down to the present time. And if the influence of this single poet be insufficient to establish the general importance of poetry, we have that of other poets, inferior perhaps in their individual power, but deriving importance from their number, and the greater facility with which their influence has been diffused.

It may be answered, that we have still the works of these poets to refer to for amusement and instruction. And are we to rest in this low and languid satisfaction, which extends to nothing but our poetry? We have the same conveniences of life which belonged to our forefathers; are we satisfied with them? The same use of machinery; are we satisfied with that? We have the same knowledge of the surface of the globe—we can count the same number of stars—and class the same kinds of animals and plants; and are we satisfied? We have the same knowledge of chemistry, electricity, hydrostatics, optics, and gravitation; and yet we are not satisfied. No:—the principle of improvement—the desire of progress, extends through every manual occupation, through every branch of science, and through every variety of art, and leaves the region of poetry a void, for future ages to wonder at, and despise. It is our ambition to impress upon the page of history the advance that has been made in every other field of intellectual operation; but we are satisfied that history should record a time when the genius of the English nation cast off the wreath of poesy, and trampled her brightest glories in the dust—when the harp of these once melodious isles was silent—and when the march of Britain's mind was unaccompanied by the music of her affections.

Next in importance to the impressions derived immediately from nature, are those derived from books, which if less obvious to the senses, and consequently less distinct, instruct the mind with greater facility and precision; and we behold another cause of the absence of deep impressions, in the excessive reading which characterises the present times. It is not certainly the most gracious mode of pointing out the evil, for those who multiply books to complain of their being read; but by *excessive* reading we desire to be understood to refer to that voracious appetite for books which exceeds the power of digestion.

Time was when a well-written book had an identity in the hearts of its readers—a place in memory, and almost in affection—its choice passages referred to for illustration on every momentous occasion, and its pointed aphorisms quoted as indisputable evidence of truth. Through the sentiments cf the author, we became acquainted with his personal character, and took him with us into solitude as a companion who would never weary; and into society as the supporter of our arguments, and the prompter of our most brilliant thoughts.

Such were the times when Goldsmith, Addison, and Johnson, accompanied us in the circle of daily communion with our fellow creatures, and we looked around us, and discovered the same principles of thought and action which their minds had suggested, operating through all the links of human fellowship, through all the changes of worldly vicissitude, and through all the varieties of station and circumstance in which man—the same being, is to be found. Such were the times, when by every mountain side, or "wimpling burn," we found the versatile spirit of Burns, animated by the fresh invigorating breeze of morning; or, leaning in musing attitude over the arch of the rustic bridge, and listening to the melodious flow of the rippling stream as it worked its way through rocks and reeds, scorning to linger in its woodland course, even beneath the fascination of a poet's gaze—we saw his keen eye mark the flight of the "whirring partridge," and then look wistfully upon its fall, as if he rued the deed; orhe has turned upon us with the lively sallies of his playful wit, half pathos, half satire, but ever the genuine language of a noble heart, and a poetic soul. Such were the times, when we shaped out our own ideas, and traced them to their origin, according to the principles of Locke, whose very soul was mingled with the atmosphere of our private studies, watching over the eccentric flights of imagination, and calling back the mind to its proper exercise upon sensible or definite things. Such were the times, when every flower, and every tree, was associated with the fairer flowers and loftier trees of Milton's Paradise; when our conceptions of peace, and purity, and happiness, were immediately derived from his descriptions of the short-lived innocence of our first parents; and when our visions of celestial and infernal beings were arrayed in the glory of his own genius, or shadowed out by the mighty power of his majestic mind.

It is not thus in the present day. Books are now spoken of as certain quantities of printed paper; and authors, a class of men too numerous to be distinguished, mix with the multitude, creating less emotion by their bodily presence, than the bare idea of an author created formerly. This general diffusion of knowledge—this removal of the barriers by which literature has hitherto been restricted to an enlightened few, is unquestionably a national, and public good; but it calls for a greater effort of intellectual power to render the influence of mind as potent as it is extensive. Unless this effort is made, the effect of the present system will be, to generalize the principle of intelligence so as to neutralize the two extremes, which have separated the highly-gifted from the wholly-unenlightened; and while the lower class of minds are better taught, and better cultivated, the average of talent will be the same, because we shall want the light of those brilliant geniuses that rose like suns amid a world of stars.

It is necessary, therefore, not that we should read fewer books, but that we should read them more studiously; and as knowledge is advancing with rapid strides, that we should endeavor to keep pace with it, by a more definite application of solid thought to the subjects laid before us in such number and variety. It is the *mode* of reading, not the number of books read, that forms the sum of the evil here alluded to; and we appeal to any one conversant with the society of the present day, whether it is not wearisome to the ear, to listen to the catalogue of *names* of books, and *names* of authors, which form the substance of general conversation, (except where politics take precedence of literature, and the names of public men are substituted for the nature of public measures,) instead of the facts those books record, the arguments they maintain, the truth they establish, or the genius which adorns their pages; and still less do we hear of the manner in which they develope the nature and principles of the mind of the writer.

When we behold the piles of heterogeneous literature, which not only fill the libraries of the learned, but load the tables of the man of business—not books which have descended from his forefathers, and will remain an heir-loom in his family for ages yet to come, to be read some twenty years hence when he shall have retired to the quiet of the suburbs, and the comfort of a gouty chair; but books beyond count, voluminous and large, poured in as the circulating medium of a literary society, to be read in five days, and then forwarded under the penalty of a fine, to the next happy member of the club; when we know too that the gentleman comes home from his office at six in the evening, and returns to it at nine the next day, his intervals of leisure including the necessary occupations of dining and sleeping; and when we know that his wife (a reader also) has seven children, a sick governess, and two idle servants, and that half her days are spent in imparting or receiving the felicity of morning calls; when we add to this the subscription of the same individuals to three or four libraries for the benefit of their children, as well as of themselves, and the necessity of glancing through all the books that fall into the hands of their boys and girls; but above all, when we turn over the pile of books, look at their titles, and see—A treatise on the characteristics of mind—A key to paper currency—The lives of all the heroes—General observations on the visible creation—System of banking detailed—Antediluvian remains—Interior of the earth explained—London, and its inhabitants—Refutation of the Mahomedan creed—The world at one view—with voyages. and travels to every section of the earth's surface;—when we consider all this, we can only wonder at the prodigious compass of the minds of those who imagine it possible for them to read, mark, and properly digest the contents of these books within the stated period allowed for their perusal; and still more we wonder at hearing it fearlessly asserted that they have been read.

It is not necessary to ask, what definite impressions we receive from this style of reading, which is indeed a mockery of that vital participation in the elements of another, and a more enlightened mind, whose influence is to raise that of the reader almost to a level with the author, leaving behind it when the book is closed, a freshness, a vigour and a capacity of production, like that which follows the retiring waters of a rich and fertilizing stream.

When the best mode of remedying an evil is beyond our reach, we naturally and wisely adopt the next best. Thus, instead of allowing our ideas to be diluted, diffused, and rendered indefinite by this overwhelming tide of literature, if we cannot gain more time for reading, nor quicken our understandings by a fresh impetus, we should do well to read *some* books attentively, thoughtfully, and feelingly: and what if we do go into society wholly ignorant even of the names of others, we may perform the useful part of listeners, and shall no more sacrifice our claim to intellectual merit by such ignorance, than we shall forfeit our title to the admiration awarded to personal embellishment, by not *wearing* a specimen of every gem.

Every stage of civilization, as well as every condition of civilized society, is marked by some strong characteristics which indicate the prevailing and national tone of manners and morals, as well as what are the chief objects of intellectual pursuit. By conversation we obtain the most immediate, and by literature the most profound knowledge of what these characteristics are, and what they denote. We should say in familiar language, that *utility* was the order of the present day; and such unquestionably should be the aim of every well directed mind; but there is a physical, and moral utility connected with the two distinctions of our nature, and it is a subject of no small importance to inquire, which of these distinct portions of our being is most productive of happiness, and consequently most worthy of cultivation.

The utility to which we now generally appeal in computing the value of our own endeavours, or those of the rest of mankind, is chiefly confined to physical advantages, and operates by material agency. The utility which ought to be the ultimate aim of every enlightened being, comprehends all that ennobles and exalts the mind. In the facilities now invented for the acquisition of knowledge of every kind; in the increased cultivation and dissemination of letters; in the assistance afforded to individual research, by public institutions and societies of every description for the concentration and diffusion of talent, we see the *means* by which the nature and condition of man is to be improved; but if we limit our views to these *means*, and rest satisfied with the occupation, and activity necessarily accompanying the attainment of knowledge, we shall never behold the desirable *end*—the attainment of *wisdom*—which we understand to mean, the application of knowledge so as to produce the greatest sum of moral good.

That knowledge is not happiness, we are taught by the experience of our own hearts, by the observation of every day, and by the undying record of the king of Israel, who knew and felt, perhaps more deeply than any other man, the harassing and destructive conflict of high intellectual powers at war with ungoverned passions, and an ill-regulated will.

The cultivation of the intellectual faculties can only lead us to a knowledge of the nature of things generally. It cannot inspire us with an ardent desire to appropriate some, and to avoid others. Unless as some philosophers maintain, we only need to know what is best, and our preference for it will follow, as a necessary consequence. It may be a weak, and certainly it is a womanly mode of reasoning, to argue that we must be taught, not only to know, but to *love* what is best, because desire arises entirely out of a moral, as knowledge arises out of an intellectual process. It arises in fact out of our early impressions of pleasure and pain, and is so distinct from a knowledge of the quality of the thing desired, as not unfrequently to be at variance with our judgment, and to lead us in pursuit of what we know to be unproductive of ultimate good. Hence arise all the *wilful* errors committed by mankind, errors so evident and so numerous, that we can only envy the philosopher who looked upon the conduct of his fellow creatures, and upon his own heart, yet saw and felt no desire except for what he believed to be morally excellent.

We are told that the errors which are committed arise from mistaken views of the nature of good and evil, and that these views are acted upon, because the good we perceive is present and obvious, while that with which it ought to be compared is remote. But when a man whose sole subsistence depends upon the produce of his garden, preferring ease and indolence to activity and labour, suffers that garden to run to waste, it is not because he is ignorant of the consequences that must ensue, but because he has learned to love the gratification of corporeal inclination more than any other thing, and therefore he determines to obtain it at any risk. The fact is, that in such cases, our mental calculations are generally more numerous, and more correct, than we are willing to acknowledge to the world, and while we act from the immediate impulse of desire, we disown all conviction that we could have acted better, in order to lessen our culpability in the eyes of others.

The first stirrings of desire arise out of sensation, long before we are capable of estimating good and evil. We feel the impressions of pleasure and pain, consequently we desire to repeat the one, and to avoid the other; and as we are long in understanding the pleasure remotely derived from virtue, so it is long before we see the necessity of cultivating our moral nature in such a manner as to enable us willingly to sacrifice the lesser good for the greater, and to love most what is intrinsically best. In the mean time the mind is gaining new impressions of a less and less corporeal nature, and as they are invariably accompanied with some degree of pleasure or pain, the desire naturally belonging to the sensation of pleasure gains additional strength, and fresh impulse, until it gradually assumes the warmth and vitality of affection, which prompts us to seek certain things in preference to others, perhaps more worthy of our regard, and sometimes to obtain them at any cost, and at the risk of any consequence.

As it is of infinitely more importance what we are, than what we know; and as our moral conduct is more influenced by what we love, than by what we understand, because we naturally pursue that which we love best, rather than that which we know to be so; so in order that our desires, and consequently our affections, may be properly directed, it is necessary that all our impressions connected with the nature of good and evil should be distinct and durable, and founded upon truth: and the science which leads to the proper selection and arrangement of early impressions—the origin of desire—the direction of the affections, and consequently the formation of the moral character, is that which we would earnestly recommend to the attention of the busy public, as conducive to the highest and most lasting utility.

It is with this view of the subject of utility, that the writer of these pages has dwelt so long upon the nature and importance of poetry, and laboured (it may be fruitlessly to others, but certainly not without enjoyment to herself,) to enforce the desirableness of cultivating poetry as an art, and of cherishing poetic feeling as a source of intellectual enjoyment.

Upon the principle of our desires arising out of our impressions of pleasure and pain, there is an importance—a wisdom in poetry, beyond what a superficial observation would lead us to suppose. It is because poetry addresses itself immediately to our feelings, and appeals to the evidence of our individual impressions to attest its truth, that it becomes a powerful engine of instruction, enforcing while it inculcates, and stimulating while it teaches. If while we learn an important truth, we have the testimony of our feelings to confirm it, how much stronger is the impression? The orator whose object is to rouse the public mind to indignation and violence, and active force against a tyrant, or a usurper, does not merely argue upon the natural rights of man, and the principles of law and justice; but he calls the attention of the people to their ruined homes, to their desolate hearths, and draws pictures of the hunger, and want, and squalid misery with which they are too feelingly acquainted.

We have a striking instance of the difference between addressing the judgment, and addressing the feelings, in the two orations on the death of Julius Cæsar, delivered by Brutus and Mark Antony. Brutus, whose noble mind disdains all artifice, appeals at once to the "wisdom" of the people, and justifies the fatal deed he has just committed, by dwelling upon one single stain in Cæsar's character—his ambition. But who in that motley crowd regarded Cæsar's ambition, unless it touched himself? The soul of Brutus was capable of apprehending in the ambition of one man, an enemy to the many—a destroyer of the rights and the liberties of the Roman people; but it was an evil too remote for the multitude to be impressed with, and though they offered a prompt, and at the moment a sincere acknowledgement, that what Brutus had said was just and true, we see how soon they could turn, and listen, and grow furious, under the influence of that master-piece of eloquence, by which Mark Antony gradually led their attention away from Cæsar's ambition, and the remote idea they might have formed of its consequences, to the bloody spectacle of his bleeding body, the gaping wounds still testifying that it was the hand of a friend—a loved and trusted friend, that had shed the proudest blood in Rome.

> "But yesterday the word of Cæsar might
> Have stood against the world; now lies he there,
> And none so poor to do him reverence."

Lest the people should not be sufficiently excited by this spectacle—by what they could all immediately understand—the direct infliction of cruelty, the artful orator makes another appeal to their feelings, which immediately strikes home. He tells them of Cæsar's will, from which they were individually and personally to derive benefit, and then the fire he had so studiously endeavoured to kindle burst forth, and weeping for Cæsar as for a public benefactor—a patriot—a god, they direct the fury of their indignation against the conspirators, and threaten the direst vengeance upon the head of Brutus.

This appeal is in strict accordance with the spirit of poetry, which convinces not so much by the evidence of what we know, as what we feel. It required time for the Romans to reflect upon the nature of ambition, and even then they could not bring home its remote consequences to the conviction of their bosoms; but they were instantaneously impressed with horror on beholding the lacerated body of Cæsar, they all felt that the friends in whom he had trusted should have been the very last to do the bloody deed, and they felt also that the man, who while he lived had formed those generous plans for their benefit which his will attested, ought in his death to be lamented and avenged.

If sufficient had not already been said to establish the fact, that the influence of poetry arises from its connexion with our feelings, we might refer to the history of all nations, in whose early stages of civilization, poetry has held a prominent part. And why? Because in describing what is beautiful, or refined, or conducive to happiness, it has been supported by principles inherent in the human mind—principles upon which are founded our impressions of pleasure and pain. Knowledge in its prosaic form, as it is usually conveyed into the mind, can only instruct; but poetry charms while it instructs. Knowledge requires the evidence of facts, and the aid of reflection, and reasoning to establish its truth. Poetry teaches by a different process. Telling of others what we experience in ourselves, it engages in the cause of truth, all that we fear of evil, and all that we desire of good; and sometimes in the fabulous history of imaginary beings, imparts the profoundest knowledge of the principles of thought and action.

It remains only to add a few remarks on the subject of happiness, as connected with our condition in the present world. There are rigid disciplinarians who regard enjoyment as a dangerous appendage to that condition—who, shrinking from the idea of enjoyment as an end in itself worthy of attainment, look upon it rather as a snare to lure us into hidden mischief. If enjoyment is of no importance to our being, (we might say to our *well being*,) why then is beauty diffused throughout creation, or why is the principle of happiness derived from beauty implanted in the soul of man? What, in short, is the value of anything without enjoyment, either immediate or remote? For, when we speak of ennobling or exalting the human mind, it is but in other words to speak of increasing its capability of enjoying that which is supremely excellent. Our natural desire of enjoyment, is the principle upon which we teach all moral truths. We speak of particular things as conducive to the happiness of ourselves or others, and even the infant mind is convinced that they are desirable from its own vivid impressions of the sensations of pleasure. When we teach a moral lesson of practical difficulty and pain, it is still in the same way, by comparing present suffering with the greater and more lasting happiness that will ensue; and when one individual is to benefit by the suffering of another, we point out the internal satisfaction attending all benevolent actions, and the general happiness of a life of duty.

Without enjoyment, we should be without desire, and without desire, we should be without action—we should also be without love—without every good and virtuous impulse, and above all, we should be without gratitude; for those who endeavour to teach the duty of gratitude, while they withhold the means of innocent enjoyment, are guilty of an insult to common sense, and a presumptuous violence of the benign plan of Providence.

How different is the dealing of the Creator with his creatures! How much has he spread before them of beauty and sublimity! How prodigally has he blessed their existence with sweetness and harmony, for which we can imagine no other purpose than that of promoting the happiness of his dependent children, and of leading them by their experience of temporal enjoyment, to desire that which is eternal. For how should we form a conception of happiness, having had no impression of pleasure; or how should we desire it, having had no foretaste of enjoyment?

It follows then, that there is utility in being innocently happy—utility of the most extensive compass, and the highest character, which poetry is of all our intellectual pursuits most capable of promoting. Let us then no longer reject this heaven-born messenger of a more refined and spiritual existence; but let us call with united voice upon our silent minstrels, and bid them tune once more the melodious harps to which in early life our souls have thrilled; let us enter again into the field of nature, not only with eyes to examine, but with hearts to feel; let us woo back imagination to come and bear us up on her elastic wings, above the gross elements of mere corporeal life—not to separate us by the idle vapours of distempered fancy from the duties of rational and immortal beings but to sweeten those duties with a more ethereal essence, and to dignify them with a character more sublime. Above all, let us accept the additional source of enjoyment which poetry affords, not with the excitement of a transient indulgence, as an idle toy for pleasant pastime in our vacant hours, but with gratitude and humble reverence towards the Giver of every good and perfect gift, as a rich and gracious blessing, whose high purpose is to promote the intellectual happiness of man, and the glory of his Creator.

THE END.

PICTURES

OF

PRIVATE LIFE.

BY MRS. ELLIS

AUTHOR OF "WIVES OF ENGLAND," ETC.

"Would you judge of the lawfulness or unlawfulness of pleasure, take this rule: whatever weakens your reason, impairs the tenderness of your conscience, obscures your sense of God, or takes off the relish of spiritual things;—in short, whatever increases the strength and authority of your oody over your mind, that thing is sin to you, however innocent it may be in itself."

AUTHOR'S EDITION

COMPLETE IN ONE VOLUME.

New-York;

EDWARD WALKER 114 FULTON-STREET.

AN APOLOGY FOR FICTION.

To write a book which is intended, and calculated, solely for the readers of fiction, and prefix to it an apology addressed to the non-readers of fiction, appears somewhat paradoxical; yet as a member of a religious society, whose sentiments are openly and professedly at variance with works of this description, I would not willingly oppose the peculiarities of many whom I regard with gratitude, esteem, and admiration, without offering in my own vindication some remarks upon the nature of fiction in general.

Fiction may, or may not be, subservient to the purposes of moral instruction. The following are some of the abuses to which it is most liable:—the delineation of unnatural characters, by the combination of such qualities as never did, and never could exist in one human being; and the placing such creatures of imagination in scenes and circumstances where the common sympathies of our nature find no place; and where the mind of the reader, in order to follow them with interest, must be elevated to the highest pitch of absurdity, and the feelings strained beyond their proper and healthy tone; and when I add to this, the shameless prostitution of talent, with which some writers have confounded the nature of good and evil, making vice interesting, and virtue insipid, by investing one with the fantastic drapery of romance, and stripping the other of all that can please the eye or charm the senses, by describing the most astonishing instances of integrity, generosity, and self-denial, as arising solely from an amiable heart, without the assistance of religion, or the control of good principle, I am willing to allow that fiction has often been, and is well calculated to be, a most powerful engine of demoralization.

On the other hand, when a writer keeps steadily in view the development of moral truth, when his characters are all of our "mixed essence," drawn from the scenes of every-day life, animated with our feelings, weak with our frailties, led into our difficulties, surrounded by our temptations, and altogether involved in a succession of the same causes and effects which influence our lives, his productions may be called fictitious, but they cannot be false. To me they appear at least as lawful as those of the painter, and for this reason I have ventured to call my stories, Pictures of Private Life.

Suppose, for instance, an artist wished to exhibit to the public a personification of old age. Perhaps he would paint an old woman in her cottage. But this would not be all. In order to present the idea more complete, he must place before our eyes the interior of her habitation, her ancient furniture, the old fashioned chair on which she is resting, her crutch at her side, her knitting, or her spinning wheel, her kettle and her cat. Now though such an old woman, with her furniture, such a chair, spinning wheel, crutch, kettle, and cat, never did exist, yet the picture may be true; because the idea of old age could not well be conveyed without the representation of the scene being thus filled up;

and in proportion as the subject is more complex, the collateral circumstances will be more studied, and frequently more numerous.

In the same way the fictitious writer labours, and for the same end; with this advantage, that the supposed lapse of time, affords him an opportunity of tracing causes to their effects. If, for instance, his subject be virtue, that virtue must be tried; and therefore he brings in a variety of circumstances all subservient to one purpose. Virtue must be contrasted with vice; and therefore other characters are introduced, and made to speak, and act, in a manner the most opposed to the words and actions of virtue. Virtue when allied to clay, must not be complete, and without flaw, because that would be unnatural, and convey an idea of a superhuman being; virtue must therefore sometimes fall away from its high purpose, in order that it may learn humility, and look more earnestly for the guiding hand of Providence; and, lastly, virtue must have its reward. In this manner the writer is involved in a great variety of imagery, and may sometimes have the management of characters, which, if separately and independently considered, would not be worth his while to delineate.

Various means may be employed to produce the same end. As individuals we must all labour according to our calling. Some preach virtue, some only practise it, some make a picture of it, and some a poem, and some (perhaps the lowest in the scale of moral teachers) adorn it with the garb of fiction, that it may ensure a welcome, where it would not otherwise obtain an entrance.

To meet with an attentive and willing listener is no less difficult than to find an able teacher. Fiction may be compared to a key, which opens many minds that would be closed against a sermon. Nor is it without authority in the writings of sincere and zealous christians. The wide range of allegory affords innumerable subjects for instruction and delight, and many a weary wanderer through the valley of the shadow of death, has been cheered by the remembrance of Bunyan's pilgrim. But the Scriptures themselves afford the highest evidence that this style of writing may be made serviceable, as a means of reproof and conviction. Let us confine our attention to one example. Where can we find anything comparable to the affecting story of the ewe lamb? Had the prophet Nathan addressed the king of Israel at once as a violator of the laws of virtue, honour, and generosity, he would probably have found him so effectually defended by the pride of human nature, as well as by the dignity of his office, that he would have failed to reach his heart; but by the simple story of the ewe lamb, he touched at once upon that chord of feeling, which seemed ever ready to vibrate with sweetest melody, in the soul of the Royal Psalmist; and then followed that emphatic application "thou art the man!"

It is in this manner, by the contemplation of ideal characters that we are sometimes led on towards conviction; our feelings become softened in sympathy with theirs, we unconsciously pronounce our own condemnation, and conscience makes the application.

Although willing to allow that fictitious writing is the most humble means of moral instruction, I am still earnest in endeavouring to maintain its utility, especially on the ground that it finds its way to the dense multitude who close their eyes upon the introduction of purer light.

Happy, happy is it for those whose hearts are open to receive "Christ as their

Schoolmaster," who have learned to desire the "sincere milk of the word." In their select and privileged communities, the bible spreads before them a wide field of never ending wonder and delight, and religion is a hallowed word, uniting all their sympathies into one bond of peace and love.

Let us look into the next stage of advancement towards moral excellence, and here we see religion obscured by the mists of party prejudice, still worshipped, but frequently disguised, and misunderstood. A little lower and religion holds a disputed sway, contending with the spirit of the world, for a small portion of the heart. Lower still, and her power and her excellence are called in question; but before we arrive at that class by which her image is dethroned, and her institutions violated, let us regard that immense mass of beings whose perceptions are so imperfect, whose minds so unenlightened, and whose feelings so absorbed by the trifling affairs of a busy world, that they can hardly be said to have learned to think. It is from amongst these that I have ventured to lift up my voice; it is for these that I have thought, and felt, and written. In vain might instruction be laid before them in a weightier form. Their pursuit is pleasure, their food excitement. And since books of fiction are a kind which thousands will continue to write, and tens of thousands to read, I have endeavoured to do my little part towards blending with amusement some of those serious reflections, which in the often shifting scenes of a restless life, have occupied my own mind; not without earnest longings, that I myself were amongst those who are already prepared to receive truth without fiction, light without clouds, good without alloy.

CONTENTS.

PICTURES OF PRIVATE LIFE.

THE HALL AND THE COTTAGE.

"A weary lot is thine, fair maid,
A weary lot is thine;
To pluck the thorn thy brow to braid,
And press the rue for wine!"
ROKEBY.

CHAPTER I.

"MY mother was a lady," said Anna Clare, a beautiful girl of eighteen, to her meek and quiet looking friend, Mary Newton, who sat at the door of her father's cottage, busily employed in preparing her little brothers and sisters for the coming sabbath. "My mother was a lady, and though she had the misfortune to marry into a lower sphere, she never forgot her own superiority."

"Perhaps it would have been better for her if she had," replied Mary.

"So far from forgetting it," continued her friend, "she strove continually to impress upon my mind, the importance of imbibing, and retaining, her own notions of that distinction of birth and education which she valued so highly; and, above all things, warned me against forming any low connexion in marriage."

"But did she make you understand exactly whereabouts in society to place yourself? for that must clearly be made out, before you can know whether you look above or below you; and in my opinion it is one of the worst evils arising from alliances such as your mother's, and one which those who enter into them must have bitterly to lament, that their offspring occupy a doubtful and unsettled station; for if possessed of any ambition, they will be perpetually struggling to establish their claim to the rank of one parent, and looking down with contempt upon the other; and here Anna, allow me to speak a little of my mind respecting yourself, for I have often thought it would be better for you, if you would recollect that you are not entirely your mother's child, but that you bear the name, and live under the protection of a plain and homely man, who has always been to you a kind and indulgent father. But I fear my advice is not agreeable to you."

"Excuse me," replied Anna, endeavouring to look polite, because she really felt angry; "excuse me, Mary, if I say it is not quite agreeable; not because I cannot bear to hear the truth, but because you have not the kind of tact which is requisite to render advice pleasing.

"And excuse me, Anna, if I say that I do not believe any tact can render advice pleasing to those who do not mean to follow it.

After this, there was a long pause between the two friends, during which, Anna tried to forget what had passed, while Mary struggled to subdue her personal feelings, so that she might speak calmly and seriously, what she was determined her friend should hear.

"Anna," said she, "we have been long friends—friends in infancy—friends at school. Shall we not continue friends, now that we are about to enter upon the cares of women, and may need each others help? But mind me, Anna, friend is a serious word, and ought not to be lightly used. By being friends, I do not mean that we are merely to walk out together, and read together, and hear each other's love stories. No, I mean that we are to stand by each other through life, through evil report, and good report—to watch over each other for good, and to speak boldly and openly, yet kindly and tenderly, all that we think of each other. This is my notion of a friend; and if you think I am so meek and low, that I dare not be all this to you, you are very much mistaken, for I never will be humble friend to any one, no, not to you, Anna, dearly as I love you."

Anna, who had advanced nearer to Mary while she was speaking, now, with tears in her eyes, besought her forgiveness; and they parted for that night, with more true love than they had felt for months before.

Mary went in with the stockings she had darned, and commenced the operation of washing her little brothers and sisters before they went to bed, while Anna sauntered home by moonlight, musing as she went; then trimmed a new bonnet for exhibition the next day, and tried a new tune on her guitar before she retired to bed, where her dreams were scarcely more visionary than those which usually occupied her waking hours.

Neither of these young persons was of the class properly called poor. Their fathers were both small farmers, a description of people once numerous in Great Britain, now very much decreased by the loss of those who have fallen into abject want, and those who are scrambling up the dangerous ladder of luxurious extravagance.

The house in which Mary lived ought not, in the present day, to be called a cottage, because it could neither be etched, nor sketched into any thing, that would not be altogether disgraceful to the pages of a lady's album. It was a small, square-looking house, built of red brick, with a green door at the termination of a gravel walk to which you passed through a little gate, green also, and flanked on either side by green paling On entering the door, you saw on the right hand a common sitting room, with a brick floor, and on the other, a neatly garnished parlour, used only on Sundays, with a carpet and a sofa, and a chimney piece ornamented with a pair of beautiful hand-screens, "wrought by no other hand, I ween," than that of Anna Clare.

If the habitation of the Newtons was incapable of being metamorphosed into a picture, Mary herself was equally incapable of being transformed into a heroine. Neither her size, her figure, nor her face, was calculated to distinguish her from the many.

Her dress was neither picturesque nor fashionable, and her hair, neither raven, nor flaxen, golden, nor auburn, but just such as no poet or painter could make any use of, was braided over a forehead, neither high, nor marble pale. In short she was just the sort of person of which we fancy the multitude is composed, when we look out upon a crowd of people. While Anna's was a face, which the eye would discover and single out from amongst a thousand, and set the imagination to work to ponder upon whence it could have come, and whither it might be going. From her mother she had learned to place an undue value upon the symbols of wealth; but it seemed as though she had inherited, by nature, all that could adorn and give outward excellence to the highest station. Slender, delicate, and graceful in her figure, she had exactly the kind of taste, which enabled her to set that figure off to advantage; while her raven hair, because she knew not how to dress it fashionably, was always dressed becomingly. Her complexion was clear and glowing, and her dark eyes had that peculiar light of joy, and innocence, which is seldom seen in those that have looked long upon the world.

These simple charms, however trifling in description, may yet be accounted dangerous gifts; and such they have often proved to the poor inhabitant of the cottage. But there is a gift of far more fatal consequence to the peace of woman's mind, when that mind has not been disciplined by a rational education. "A quest for hidden knowledge," with a deep sense of the sublime and beautiful, which those who have never looked on nature's face with the eye of a poet, or a painter, can in no way comprehend. And this was Anna's portion too. How mournfully misplaced! For, beneath her father's humble roof, where she ought to have been, and, no doubt, under other circumstances, would have been, a kind and dutiful daughter, she was now dreaming away her existence in a world of visions, of which the every-day duties of common life formed no part.

Anna had early imbibed a taste for the accomplishments which adorn the higher stations in society. Music and drawing had been taught her by her mother; and being naturally of an aspiring mind, she had prevailed upon her father to allow her the advantage of instruction in oil painting, in the hope of rendering her genius more profitable. This was an important step in the *ladder* of distinction, in consequence of which all the well disposed young women in the neighbourhood agreed to call her a genius, while all the young men toasted her as a beauty; the women wishing internally that she had less of the one quality, the men that she had less of the other. But Anna valued both. Her beauty was delightful to her as a painter, no less than as a woman; and her genius was the magical key, which opened to her mental vision the wide field of taste, and sentiment, and feeling; a field so dangerous to enter upon, that those who have ventured within its charmed precincts, have too often returned to the beaten track of life with weary, and unwilling steps, wishing in vain to call back the happy thoughts of simplicity and youth, which made the paternal home a haven of rest, and life itself an enjoyment.

Anna's new bonnet had not been trimmed in vain; for on the following morning, while the sun shone upon a cloudless sabbath in July, the inhabitants of the little village of L——, were astonished by a blaze of beauty and fashion, at their parish church.

Mary had no time to make observations on the new comers, for with her constant and fruitless attempts to restrain the wonder and admiration of her little flock, and her earnest and zealous endeavours to keep her own attention fixed upon the service, she found enough to do; but Anna, not being quite so fully engaged, had leisure to set down in her memory the whole family of the Langleys, just come to spend the summer months at their country seat.

First, the old gentleman, Sir Thomas, with his white hair and sleek countenance, and his one idea perpetually recurring to the moor game, about to be shot by his hopeful son.—Lady Langley, with her towering crest of plumes and ribbons; come down into the country to be great.—Miss Langley, looking soft, delicate, and languid, but alas! not very young; come down into the country to brace up a feeble constitution for the ensuing winter, and to lay up a store of good works, to be held in memorial in her favour, by establishing Sunday schools, and soup societies.—Miss Julia Langley, a beauty of five winters, returning from an unsuccessful campaign; come down into the country to sketch waterfalls, and babble of Corinne.—And the heir apparent, young and handsome, for what earthly purpose could he be come?

Anna had time for all these reflections and enquiries, and a thousand more, by no means omitting the conclusion that Frederick Langley was the most brilliant and moving spectacle she had ever before witnessed in the form of man.

One look, and only one, she had ventured to fix full upon his countenance, when immediately his glass was raised, and Anna felt, that for a long time she was the object of his fixed and steady attention; but for all that, she did not completely turn away, nor take any effectual measures to relieve herself from the embarrassment of her situation, though anger and shame heightened the crimson that spread itself all over her beautiful face.

Before the service was over, Mary had forgotten that any strangers were at church, and Anna had forgotten every thing beside. Mary returned home with serious thoughts, to perform the duties in her domestic circle; and Anna went that afternoon with less than her wonted alacrity, to take her part as teacher in a Sunday school, some years ago established by the good clergyman of the parish, and so steadily supported, as to need little patronage from Miss Langley.

Miss Langley, however, could not withhold the blessing of her countenance. Miss Julia could find no better amusement for the Sunday afternoon; and Frederick thought there might be a chance of his meeting again with the fair vision of the morning.

The door of the school-room opened—Anna looked up, and from that moment, she thought as little of the alphabet, the catechism, and even of the bible itself, as any of her little pupils.

"Come here to me," said Miss Langley in a tone of authority, to one of the older girls, who was just taxing her attention to answer in her turn, the question of the teacher. "Come here to me, and tell me, if you can, what took place at the building of the Tower of Babel?"

"Confusion of tongues," thought the teacher, "and I wish it may not be come to us."

"What a charming study!" exclaimed Julia, singling out a little curly-pated urchin, who laughed and blushed, and wondered what she meant.

"Take that, you little ——" said Fredeick, throwing a sixpence on the floor, "and buy yourself a stick, instead of breakiug mine." Then, turning to Anna, "A charming amusement," continued he, seating himself upon the bench beside her, "I wish I might be a pupil." But the method he had chosen for commencing an acquaintance was not suited to the taste of his companion. It savoured too much of the Hall and the Cottage. To be singled out as a village beauty, and addressed with the familiarity of town-bred insolence, was not the distinction at which she aimed; and rallying her wandering thoughts, she assumed an air of dignity, and endeavoured to resume her task.

The young gentleman finding he had mistaken the subject of his attentions, and his sisters being equally disappointed in theirs, the party withdrew, leaving the young people in wonder at their gauze and laces, the old at their folly and assurance.

CHAPTER II.

"I TOLD you," said Frederick Langley to his sister, the next morning, "I to.d you we should all be miserably disappointed in coming to this abominable old Hall, for you see we have neither field sports in the day, peasants dancing on the green in the evening, nor ghosts ranging through the corridor at night. How, in the name of ennui, do you mean to exist?"

"Heaven only knows how Pa, and Ma, and Susan will exist," replied Julia; "but for my part, I am going out to sketch, when the dew is off the grass; and then you know, Lord B—— comes down to shoot in August, and your horses come on Saturday, and I am sure you will let me ride Phillis again."

"Lord B—— is a great bore," replied her brother; "and it always rains on the moors, and my horses don't come till Monday, and you shall not ride Phillis, because you always spoil her paces. But come, the dew is off the grass, and I have so much that is amiable in my temper just now, that I can afford to go out with you to sketch, and cut your pencils into the bargain, provided only, you will go my way."

The fact was, the young gentleman had determined, if possible, to see Anna Clare again. Had his first advances been received with the simper of a rustic coquette, it is probable that all interest about her would have ceased then, and there; but the look of wounded pride, and delicate reserve, with which she withdrew from his familiarity, combined with her beauty, to make a more lasting impression on his mind.

"This is the cottage," said he, leading his sister up to the door of William Clare, for he had made out the night before, not only Anna's residence, but much of her character, and the nature of her occupation.

"But where are you leading me?" asked Julia. "I know nothing of these people, what can you possibly be going to do in this sweet cottage?"

"Leave that to me," said her brother, leading her away from the beautiful scene on which she would gladly have staid to gaze; for the cottage of William Clare had long been the envy of the surrounding neighborhood. Though precisely on the same footing as the Newtons, with regard to property and rank in life, his house and garden had acquired, during the reign of Mrs. Clare, an air of taste and gentility, which his daughter was equally desirous to support. Perhaps the chief difference in the two habitations was, that the windows of one had been made to open out upon a green lawn; while those of the other terminated a little more than half the length in a broad seat, on which Mary used to sit and read to her father, when the children were asleep and all was quiet within and without. Each had their parlour of high and low degree, but the Clares trod always on a carpet, and Anna had her paintings, her guitar, her album, and her books, placed with studied negligence about the room, so as to give it a totally different character from even the best parlour of the Newtons.

Anna was at this moment practising an air which had lately caught her fancy, and accompanying it with a low and simple voice, which, though altogether untutored in scientific rules, was sufficiently attractive from its natural sweetness, to arrest the attention of the curious intruders; who, having advanced to the open window, stood in delighted astonishment gazing upon the lovely songstress; while Anna, startled by a rustling amongst the leaves around the window, looked up with no less astonishment than she had excited.

Had there even been time to recur to the affront of the preceding day, it would all have been atoned for, by the kind and polite manner in which Frederick apologised for the intrusion.

He said they were strangers in search of the picturesque; who had come to solicit the assistance of Miss Clare, to point out the beauties of the surrounding scenery, hoping that her taste would enable them to select some subject for a sketch, not altogether beyond the compass of moderate powers.

"I am quite a learner," added Julia, "and if you can assist me, I shall be for ever indebted to you."

By this time Anna had ushered them into her little sitting room; and taking up a large portfolio with just confidence enough to show her extreme devotion to the art, spread before them her own beautiful and highly finished drawings, of such simple and rural scenes, as the country around afforded; at the same time apologising for their want of interest, by saying that she had never been far from her native country, or seen any of the great and magnificent features of nature. For a few moments the woman gave place to the artist, and she went on with enthusiasm, "I sometimes think, that if heaven has a blessing in store for me, it must be, that I shall gaze on the blue sky of Italy!" But the eyes of Frederick Langley, fixed upon her earnest countenance, brought back every latent spark of womanly feeling, and not even the rapturous expressions of his sister, as she turned over the drawings, could again wean her from the consciousness that she was a genius, and a beauty, in the act of entertaining high born and fashionable guests.

"And you paint too," exclaimed Julia, looking up at a picture in which the artist had given to the subject of one of the drawings the vivid colouring of a masterly hand, and a warm imagination.

"That painting is not mine," said Anna; "yet I do paint a little, though I have practised for so short a time, that I am ashamed to exhibit my productions; but if you will pardon my presumption, and do not mind the litter of my room, perhaps I shall be able to amuse you for a few minutes, by allowing you to laugh at my barbarous attempts;" and saying this, she led the way to a small room lighted from above, where all "appliances and means" which her humble circumstances afforded, were spread around.

Amongst the confusion of unfinished pictures, all denoting industry and talent, was a portrait of herself, which immediately caught the wandering eye of Frederick.

"Oh! that," said Anna, blushing, "I know not what to say for that, or how to apologise for having spent my time upon so worthless a subject; except that it is always recommended to young artists to practise upon themselves, and in this instance, at least, I may escape the charge of vanity, for in looking at that portrait I always find an antidote."

"If the picture offends your eye, I will take it home with me," said Frederick, laying violent hands upon the treasure; and a scene ensued of laughing, blushing, pleading, and palliating, which is not necessary to describe; while Julia, who, to say the worst of her, was only idle and superficial, neither envious nor spiteful, looked round with amazement at the perseverance of her new acquaintance, and began to speculate upon the amusement and benefit of cultivating her friendship, for a few weeks, during their stay in the country.

A sketching excursion was soon proposed, and Anna did the honours of the country with so much vivacity, and good nature, that Frederick and his sister returned home, delighted with their new-made friend.

"They have been with me all the morning," said Anna, as she passed the garden of James Newton on her way home, and saw Mary at the door.

"Who have been with you?"

"Miss Julia Langley and her brother—the sweetest girl you ever saw."

"What—her brother?"

"How provoking you are, Mary, I am sure you understand me."

Better perhaps, than you understand yourself, thought her friend.

"Well, Anna, I will try to understand, then, that Miss Julia Langley is the sweetest girl I ever saw—and her brother?"

"I am not quite so decided about him," said Anna, with some confusion; "but they are so fond of painting, of music, of poetry, and of every thing that is delightful."

"Then I am sure they must be fond of you," thought Mary, as her eye dwelt upon the countenance of her friend, who leaned over the garden gate with her bonnet thrown back from her naturally sweet face, now more than usually animated. The company, the excitement, and the exercise of the morning, had given to her complexion a more vivid glow; and while the light breeze played idly with the "tendrils of her raven hair," the whole picture presented to the eye of the beholder, a perfect personification of health, and innocence, and joy.

Mary gazed for a moment with delighted admiration, for in her heart there was no taint of selfishness, or envy; but a cloud suddenly gathered upon her brow, for she thought of the dangerous gifts which heaven had bestowed upon this poor motherless creature; and her heart yearned towards her, with the tenderness of a sister, that she might watch over her, and be the means of assisting her to turn all these brilliant endowments to a good account.

"Why do you look so grave," asked Anna, "now when I feel so happy?" for to her the trees were more rich in foliage, the fields more verdant, and the skies more heavenly blue, than she had ever seen them before. But Mary could not well explain herself. It was too soon to warn her of her danger, and to croak over those evils which we do but faintly apprehend, has seldom a good effect upon the young and ardent mind. They parted therefore without any further explanation, and it was many days before they met again.

These days passed away with Mary, leaving nothing behind but the satisfaction of having gone through her usual routine of homely duties; while to Anna they were fraught with circumstances of deep interest—high hopes, and brilliant dreams of coming pleasure; what they left behind she did not stay to inquire, for hers was not the heart to look back.

A tour was planned to the Highlands of Scotland; and Julia Langley, always delighted with new faces, and having formed a most romantic and ardent friendship for the beautiful young cottager, insisted that she should accompany them; and not all the indignation of her mother, nor the remonstrances of her sister, could change her purpose.

"You are not going yourselves," said this amiable patroness of genius, "and therefore it can be of no consequence to you."

"But Lord B——, Lady C——, and Miss Manning," said her sister—"they have never been accustomed to associate with low persons; you will make yourself the jest of the whole world by these absurd fancies."

"And disgrace your family," said her mother.

"The party is of my forming," continued the immoveable young lady. "Lord B— always does as I like; Lady C— agrees with her brother; and poor Miss Manning has not the spirit to complain; besides, have I not an undoubted right to take an artist in my train, if I think proper?"

And thus, with a great deal of dispute, and many uncharitable remarks upon the unconscious object of this discussion, which might not otherwise have been called forth, the affair was at last decided to Julia's satisfaction; for she was the youngest in the family, and though not very young, could still coax and wheedle, and insist with so much pertinacity, as not unfrequently to carry her point against them all.

It cannot be supposed that Anna's strength of mind was proof against this temptation. Pluming herself upon the professions of her amiable young friend, and encouraging the vain hope that her service as an artist would amply remunerate the party for any expense or trouble they might incur on her account, she joyfully fell in with the proposal, and with a light and bounding heart, ran over the fields to tell Mary Newton the good tidings.

She had gone through the whole plan, and was expatiating upon some of its branches, before the unusual gravity of Mary's countenance arrested her attention, and, with a somewhat altered manner, she observed,

"You are always so serious now, Mary, when I come to tell you any thing."

"And that, I suppose, is the reason why you come so seldom."

"Was I not here last Friday?—no, it was Monday—no, I cannot tell when it was."

"It was the Sunday evening before last."

"Surely not so long ago as that. Well, I have been too much engaged with sketching and other things, to know how the time passes away."

"You have been in a sort of dream, I think, Anna, from which I hope the time has come for you to rouse yourself."

"You mean with regard to the Langleys. It is no dream, Mary, for I love them all; except the old people, and that proud and sanctimonious daughter of theirs."

"Then excepting the young gentleman, which you are bound to do in common delicacy, there remains one of the ancient and honourable name of Langley, whom you love—Miss Julia."

"Yes, I do love her, and will love her, and will go into Scotland with her too, and return to you, Mary, the happiest creature in existence; my brain and my portfolio filled with images of lakes, and rivers, and mountain scenery."

"May I, as a friend, ask you one plain question?;"

"Yes, a thousand."

"Will you travel at your own expense?

Anna's face was covered with confusion, and she replied with difficulty,

"I cannot say exactly that I shall, but I hope to make some return."

"Anna, my friend, my own dear friend, you are deceiving yourself. What return can you possibly make to this high family for the honour which they intend to confer upon you? It is the part of an independent mind to refuse, not with insult, but with gratitude, all offers of unnecessary kindness for which there is no probability of making any adequate return; more especially to the great, because the chance of being able to do any service to them is so much smaller. Indeed, there is nothing but the closest, and most intimate friendship, that can justify the giving, and receiving obligations, without any calculation as to the relative situation of the parties. Here, and here only, I would give and receive, without a debtor and creditor account."

Anna said something about Miss Julia's friendship for herself, but Mary interrupted her with warmth—

"And have you, Anna Clare, lived to give the name of friendship to that which springs up between two young persons who have only strolled together for a few sunny hours by the side of woods and waterfalls? No, if you will turn away from the truth, you compel me forcibly, rudely, but I hope not unkindly, to place it before your eyes. Miss Julia Langley is a sweet tempered, flippant, light-hearted creature, at least so she appears to us; who is interested by your talents, and charmed by your beauty, but more especially delighted with your willingness to oblige and serve her; yet, in her wide world of fashion and of folly, you can act but a very trifling part, and will consequently be very lightly esteemed. For what have you to boast of, that she cannot find and possess, in far greater perfection, elsewhere, except, perhaps, your beanty? and when, I would ask, was beauty a bond of union betwixt two women? Here, in this remote village you are a wonder, and a genius. Your paintings delight and astonish us; but these people have been abroad, and have seen the works of great masters, and even their own money can procure them such as you would hardly dare to copy. Your music, though exactly such as I delight to listen to, and sweeter, far sweeter to me than the song of birds, or any thing that I can remember since my poor mother used to sing these children to sleep; what would it be to their ears, when compared even with the meanest performance of an Italian opera girl? Oh, Anna, if you wish to be loved, if you wish to be valued, you will stay with us!"

"I will return to you, dear Mary, and we shall only be absent a few weeks."

"And in those few weeks what may you not endure? you, who have never been accustomed to insult or neglect."

"If I did not expect to be treated in all respects as an equal," said Anna, her indignation rising, "the finest scenery in the world should not tempt me to go beyond my native village."

"Then deceive yourself no longer; for this never can be, it is not in the nature of things that it should be. I have not spoken to you much of late, but I have watched you with the anxiety of a sister, and, though no sister could love you better than I do, trust me, I am not blind to your follies. No, Anna, I have seen the change in your dress and manner. I have seen what you endeavoured to conceal from yourself. It was but last Sunday, after service, that I observed you stop to speak to old Eleanor in the church-yard, while all the time your eye was fixed upon the door at which you thought the Langleys would come out; and when you found they had gone the other way, you listened no more, and thought no more of old Eleanor or her rheumatism, but skipped over the stile, and flew round by the lane, where you were sure to see them; but finding yourself too far in advance, you stooped down to tie your sandal, though I am sure it did not need it; and then Lady Langley swept past you with such a look of scorn, as I would not have brought upon myself for the richest jewel in her possession.

"And now, Anna, may I ask you to believe, that the pain I have given by my plain speaking, has not been from envy, or for sport; but merely, that you might see your conduct in its true light; for these things are beneath you, and I know you despise them as much as I do; but the notice of these people has turned your head. Let me entreat you to feel above them, as you really are: above them in all that is really excellent, though far below them in all which they esteem so."

When Mary had finished speaking, her friend remained silent for a long time, and though they walked together through the fields to the cottage of William Clare, their conversation was on indifferent topics, for Mary wisely judged it would be safest to leave Anna to the influence of her own reflections.

CHAPTER III.

We may read, and think, and converse, about humble merit, and high-born insignificance, folly or depravity, until we actually believe we have attained to the true discernment of good and evil, and are ready, under all circumstances, to choose the one, and to refuse the other; yet so forcible are the impressions received through the medium of the senses, that we are often led to wonder at the fallacy of our own conclusions. There is something, for instance, so imposing in the first entrance of a well-bred person at your door; compared with that of the plain man of homely merit, who stumbles over your staircase, sets down his hat upon your drawings, and clenches your hand in a grasp of Herculean strength. There is a great deal, too, in the soft tones of the well-modulated voice, with which well-bred persons address you: their kind looks when they choose to wear them; the rustling of their costly silks; their perfumery and cambric handkerchiefs; but above all, the ivory fingers with which they touch and seem to hallow whatever is worthy of their attention. These, and a thousand other trifles, too insignificant to find a name, combine to form parts of that scenery, which dazzles and bewilders the mental vision of those who are just entering the theatre of life.

How well soever Anna Clare might have been fortified and supported before she went to rest, by the sage admonitions of her friend, her noble resolutions vanished on the following morning, like mist before the summer sun; for the carriage of Sir Thomas Langley rolled up to the door, and a troop of young ladies, and fine gentlemen, rushed in to alarm, as they were pleased to say, "the beautiful enchantress in her fairy bower."

Could the beautiful enchantress have known how little they had really thought of alarming, or pleasing, or doing any thing else, but kill time;—could she have known what weary, dissatisfied, and listless feelings they really brought with them to the fairy bower, she might have been better able to appreciate their many flattering expressions; which to them meant nothing, and cost nothing, but which were set down by Anna to refer to on some future day, when her vanity should tax her memory to contribute to its maintenance.

Alas, that such a day should ever come! That flowers which were culled in the summer of youth and happiness, and thrown by with a prodigal hand, should come to be singled out, one by one, in search of exhausted sweetness, to revive the drooping spirit that has laid up no more substantial treasure for its hour of need.

Surely there is nothing upon earth that demands our pity more than this. Not the foolish bird fluttering in the snares of the fowler; nor the flower that has burst into blushing beauty, on a morning of storms; nor the child that has stolen to the brink of the precipice to play, can be more melancholy objects of consideration, than an amiable and lovely woman, who is drawing from the fountains of vanity and love, her only sources of happiness and hope. And yet who speaks of her danger? Those who stand aloof in unassailed security, and have never known the insatiable thirst of pampered vanity, nor fallen into the snare of earthly love. Should the deluded creature awake to a sense of her own awful situation, who rushes to the rescue? She looks back upon her sister woman, and the strong arm of malevolence and envy is put forth to urge her to destruction; to accelerate her fall. She leans upon her brother man, and he, more treacherous, but not less cruel, while he covers her with the garment of praise, and pours upon her head the oil of joy, at the same time places on her brow the poisoned chaplet, crying, "Peace, peace, where there is no peace." Like the priests of old, who with merriment and dance, and song, led forth the unconscious victim wreathed with flowers, to bleed upon the altar of sacrifice.

Lady B—, Lady C—, and Miss Manning, were amongst those who rushed into Anna's parlour. They were of the party for the Highlands; all things were in readiness, and on Monday morning they were to set out.

When Monday, the eventful day, arrived, Anna took a hasty farewell of the Newtons: and now she stood at the gate leading up to her father's door, and the old man stood beside her, ever and anon, wiping from his eyes tears, that were not altogether shed for sorrow, for he was proud of the distinction which had been shewn his daughter; but it was a long journey, and the dear child had never been far from the paternal roof before. And Phebe, the old servant, was there too, busily employed in providing every thing for the comfort of her darling; weeping and wiping her eyes with her apron, without trying to conceal her tears.

Now, though it is a pleasant and easy thing for the writers of romance to make their heroines glide and skim over the earth, without any of the common appendages of matter, it cannot be denied of Anna Clare, (though grevious to relate,) that while standing at her father's gate, she was literally surrounded by those various and vulgar articles, classed under the undignified name of luggage; that, when the carriage of the wealthy baronet drove up, Phebe was in the very act of drawing from her housewife a piece of white tape to secure the fastening of a green plaid bag, and that when Lord B——'s footman touched his hat, and offered his services to see every thing adjusted, (though at the same time a whisper passed through the menial train, that they had had trouble enough with their own things, and that now their was no room left,) William Clare described in circumstantial detail, how there was a hair trunk with a wrapper, a bag, a shawl, and a cloth cloak, besides a basket of prog, which Phebe held in her firm grasp, determined to place it herself in the hand of her young mistress, while the cloak, she insisted, must go inside too, for the evenings were cold, and the dear child had nothing on.

Could any thing, to Anna's feelings, exceed the confusion of this moment, during which the serene party sat in smiling wonder at the scene?

Her father, forgetful of every thing but the departure of his child, had slipped on an old slouched hat, that was wont to hang in the remotest corner of the passage; and Phebe! surely she was possessed with the demon of provocation, for she kept the little basket until she could herself place it upon Anna's lap, and thrust in the old grey cloak, spreading it over the costly silk dress of Lady C——, which had never been brought into contact with so rude a material before.

In fact, that moment was fraught with a combination of annoyances, which no words can describe; but which some have felt so forcibly, as to acknowledge that the poor and mean pay dearly in this small coin, for aspiring to participate in the pleasures of the rich and great.

Mary watched them round the brow of the hill, and as soon as they had vanished from her sight, she covered her face with her hands, and burst into tears.

"What are you weeping for?" asked little Martha, looking up in her sister's face. You need not be in trouble about Anna Clare, for I never saw her look half so happy in my life."

"I hope she is happy," said Mary.

"Then why do you weep? Will she not come back?"

"She may come back, my love,—but not tc me," was Mary's inward response.

Perhaps there are no few words by which we more frequently deceive ourselves than these, "I will come back to you," or, "you will return to me." The birds of spring, the flowers of summer, and the rich tints of autumn, may all come back. The playmates of our infancy, and the friends of our early years, may all return. But will they return unchanged, or shall we be able to meet them with the same glow of feeling unalloyed. Many, who have looked with wonder and delight on the splendour of the setting sun, have turned away with sickness of soul from the glory of his rising beams. Many who have bid adieu to summer, have drank from the well-spring of her loveliness, rich draughts of happiness and love, have met her again, without recognizing her fair form; without one ecstatic bound upon her flowery carpet,—one moment of joyous exultation in the softness of her sunny breeze! And thus it must be for thus it has been ordained, by a wise and merciful father, to teach his erring children, that all the treasures by which they are surrounded, are only lent them for a brief space of limited enjoyment, and that here they have no continuing city.

CHAPTER IV.

Light, and bounding were the hearts, which Miss Julia Langley had gathered round her; herself the centre of the magic circle, if not the source from whence their pleasure flowed, there needed no addition to her enjoyment, except that Lord B—— should declare himself more clearly, and this desideratum, nothing could be more likely to produce, than the present arrangement of affairs.

They had not proceeded many stages, however, before the discovery of certain glances of admiration directed to a part of the carriage where she was not sitting, led her to ask herself, whether it would not have been quite as prudent to leave Anna Clare at home.

Lord B——thought otherwise, and judging from her situation in life, that she could not be very fastidious in the choice of an admirer, or the style of his address, annoyed her by the most pointed and familiar attentions; until, repeatedly repulsed by her coldness, he determined to punish her by neglect.

Lady C——, neither young nor enthusiastic, had not travelled many days, before she had to lament bitterly over the inconveniences of the journey; and Miss Manning deep in the lore of Scotch novels, was disappointed and disgusted, because every old woman was not a Meg Merilies, and every young one a Flora Mac Ivor. Books of poetry and romance where referred to on every occasion, and closed with the natural but mortifying conclusion, that the Scottish nation must be miserably degenerated.

Anna Clare was the only one of the whole party who was well grounded in the real history of the "land of the mountain and the stream."

She had been accustomed to read in peace and in private, and had stored up in a naturally good memory such facts, as now rendered her company a valuable acquisition, to those who were not previously disposed to make too high an estimate of her powers of pleasing.

Finding herself of real service to her friends, her confidence began to increase; and with her confidence, her happiness, her vivacity and even her beauty too; until Frederick Langley felt himself emboldened to declare, what his heart alone had hitherto borne witness to,—his extreme admiration of Anna Clare. But his was not flattery in the gross. It consisted in that silent course of respectful attention, so irresistible to a delicate mind; shown chiefly by a desire to be informed by her knowledge, decided by her judgment, and directe y her taste; and if there was more of te derness in his lock and manner towards her than was quite consistent with their relative situations, it was only just so much as to encourage her to ask of him in preference to any one beside, those little services, which constitute the chief bond both of friendship and of love.

How often do we find persons, entering into the most intimate, and the most serious connections in life, not so much from any similarity of mind or sympathy of feeling, as from the manner in which they have been thrown together, have become associated with, and indebted to each other. Is not this, then, another reason amongst the many, why the poor ought to shun rather than seek, all familiar association with the great; and why the great should cease to amuse themselves with those summer friendships with their poorer neighbours, which at best can only serve on one hand, to wile away the monotony of a few months' residence in the country; and on the other leave nothing behind but emptiness and disappointment? This, however, is but the bright side of the picture. Look again, and we see more conspicuously a long list of fatal consequences; amongst which are written in legible characters, the base flattery of the low, and the falsehood of the great; the envy of the poor, and too frequently their ruined innocence.

Before the expiration of one entire week, the spirits of the tourists had begun to flag; and even Anna felt it difficult at all times to support her vivacity, upon which depended the good will of the party.

Though born to an humble lot, she was not of a robust constitution, nor had ever been accustomed to any kind of hardship. Miss Julia had her woman, and Lady C—— was almost inseparable from hers; but no one attended upon Anna to see that her bed was aired, or to carry her dry shoes.

There are few things we are more ready to profess our determination to do than this, —to "take care of ourselves, when nobody cares for us; and yet, somehow or other, there are many harder duties which we perform with more pleasure, so much are we accustomed to estimate our own worth by the opinion of others.

Anna had no heart to look after these little comforts and conveniences, and therefore felt the want of them the more; and sometimes her thoughts would return to old Phebe, and then she wished she had taken leave of her more kindly. But her greatest mortification was to find, that the labours of her pencil, so far from remunerating her friend for her numerous and unlooked-for favours, could never by any alteration of place or plan, be made agreeable to the whole party. Sometimes they could not possibly wait for her, and the drawing must remain half done; while they wondered that she put away so many unfinished pieces: then they dared to say it was very good, but really they could not recognise the spot; for this very reason, because they had not staid to observe it.

Oh! it is a wearisome, heartless, and life-spending service, to live by the power of pleasing! The miner has his stated portion doled out to him, and digs in undisturbed security; and the galley-slave knows, while he toils at the oar, that the utmost stretch of his sinews, is all that his tyrant master can require; but the miserable child of genius, who feels that he must starve and shiver in the shade, or tax his talents, and sharpen his wit, and torture his sensibility, to purchase the genial smiles of patronage: may not his life be compared to the lingering death of the dolphin, whose dying agonies produce those beautiful varieties of colour, which astonish the delighted beholder?

Annoyed, perplexed, and disappointed, Anna Clare began to think a little more of Mary Newton than she had done at first; and but for the kindness of Frederick Langley would really have looked with fearful apprehension to the future.

It happened one day, while left alone to sketch what her gay companions were soon tired of looking at, that they wandered round the foot of the hill, and came again un-

risen; except to Lord B——, who, having acknowledged for a brief space its limited ascendancy, now determined, if possible, to extinguish its fading light.

Anna perceived, yet could not understand the change; but Frederick saw and understood it all.

"She shall never be made unhappy by your caprices," said he to his sister, one day after a warm discussion on the subject, while the unconscious object of it was left sketching on the bleak side of a hill, alone, and altogether unregarded by all in the party, except one. But there was one who never wholly deserted her, who would return to the spot where she was seated, with kindness and consideration, to watch the progress of her pencil, to approve, and often to correct: for his eye was as true to the beauties of nature, as his mind was quick to discern, and his heart warm to enjoy them.

Frederick Langley was not merely a man of pleasure; he possessed noble and generous feelings, the extent or existence of which he hardly knew; for he had as yet never felt himself called upon to take any active part in life, or to choose betwixt pleasure and duty.

Along with these good feelings, however, he inherited his mother's pride, and a high sense of family distinction; and then, with all were blended the taste and the delicacy of a highly cultivated mind, by which its good qualities were developed, and its bad ones concealed; while a handsome person, and manners unusually gentle and attractive, rendered him as dangerous a companion as could well be found, for the young enthusiast. And then, they were associated together in scenes, where the distinctions of polished life were necessarily forgotten—where man had seldom been, at least, where it was impossible to drag along with him the insignia of his greatness—where nature ruled supreme over her own realm, of lake, and stream and mountain. Every thing to be admired here they could admire together; every thing to be enjoyed, their hearts could rejoice in with unrestrained delight. Together they could climb the brow of th mountain to watch the glories of the rising sun, free alike to the prince and to the peasant. Together they might sail upon the glassy surface of the clear lake, that spreads its silver bosom as kindly to the fisherman's humble prow, as to the light galley, streaming with the pennons of rank and power.—Happy mortals! together they could pour forth their young hearts at the shrine of nature, and what future circumstance in life would be able to separate them after this?

Is nature, then, the goddess to whom we are directed to offer all our vows? Let us stay one moment to consider what nature is.

In speaking of nature, we are too apt to confine our ideas to the origin of all that is estimable in our hearts and affections; and to look for the principle of evil, to something quite without ourselves, as if the good and evil of our mixed essence, belonged not equally to her realm. Surely the history of man might teach us to mistrust our favorite idol; for was it not nature that strengthened the arm of the first murderer? and is it not nature in our own bosoms that responds to the voice of the tempter?

If, then, nature be the queen of the blue heavens, when they are cloudless, is she not equally so of the storm? If she slumbers in a bower of roses, does she not awake in deep caverns when earthquakes and volcanoes desolate the land? If she leads forth the young affections, and gives to generous feeling its ecstatic glow—to love, its syren smile—and to pity, its pearly tear—are not the passions also of her training?—the fiery passions, that rage and war, and make the heart a wilderness? Surely, then, there must be a holier compact, a covenant more sacred, than that which is made at the shrine of nature.

CHAPTER V.

Excitement is not the natural food of the human mind. It may for a while, give life to imagination, and quicken sensibility; but like other stimulants, it is destructive both to the health of the body, and to the soundness of the mind; and like other stimulants, it leaves behind an aching void.

Anna Clare lived, moved, and had her being, in this deceitful element. Her beauty was the glow of animated feeling, and her genius more resembled the vivid, and uncertain sparkling of electric fluid, than the steady light of a fixed star.

Disturbed with the suspicion now almost amounting to certainty, that the short-lived friendship of Miss Julia was exhausted, she suffered herself to dwell perpetually upon the kindness of her brother, as her only source of consolation; while inwardly harassed and perplexed, by thoughts which it was impossible to communicate, she rushed with redoubled ardour into new enjoyment, in the vain hope of extinguishing every painful recollection of the past, and quieting every apprehension for the future.

This state of feeling was not calculated to last long; and a new evil, hitherto unthought of, began to steal rapidly upon the rest. Days of hurry and fatigue, and nights of sleepless anxiety, had followed each other in such rapid succession, that in spite of all her efforts, first, to be well, and then to appear so, she found her health and strength were rapidly declining. A violent cold, the consequence of keeping on wet clothes, was probably the immediate cause; for now a total loss of appetite with frequent cold shiverings, and other fervish symptoms, gave alarming intimations of approaching illness. They were travelling through a wild and inhospitable looking country; and ah! how did Anna think of her own home, of all its slighted comforts, but most of all, of Mary Newton. The thoughts of returning while she had yet the power, was perpetually upon her mind. But then the means!—Once or twice it was upon her lips to ask Frederick Langly—No! she could ask any thing of him but money; and money of any one, rather than him. And yet, he was the only one of the whole party who had hitherto noticed her indisposition; which soon, however, became sufficiently obvious to all; and a consultation was held one night after she had retired to bed, upon the best manner of proceeding either with or without her.

"We can never exist in this horrid place until she pleases to recover," said Lord B——, "that's a dead certainty. Why you might expect better accommodation if you were travelling post to the ——. The hostess looks as if she were planning where to bury us; and that great Highland lass, her daughter, sharpening knives to cut our throats!"

Julia, perplexed beyond measure, at last thought of appealing to medical advice; and a lad half asleep was dragged out of the chimney corner, and mounted on a blind pony, to make what speed he could to the nearest doctor, who lived at the distance of seven miles.

In the mean time the party amused themselves with such fare as their quarters afforded, and all but Frederick forgot the cause of their anxiety. He was absent and thoughtful; and neither the witticisms of Lord B——, nor the raillery of the ladies, could induce him to assume a gaiety which it was impossible for him to feel, while fully aware of the awful and critical situation of Anna Clare. Not merely awful and critical as regarded her life, but there were other considerations that weighed heavily upon him, now that she seemed likely to be so lightly shaken off by his sister.

The doctor came and pronounced it impossible for Anna to be removed without endangering her life.

"Julia," said Frederick, as he led his sister into an outer room, "you will not think of leaving this poor creature alone?"

"No, certainly not alone, but what would you advise me to do?"

"If I was my kind hearted sister," said he, laying his hand upon hers, "I would stay with her myself."

"Who, I?—you know that I am the worst nurse in the world. Besides, it may turn out some shocking fever, most probably infectious; and then I might be dead and buried in this horrid country, before any one in England knew."

"I would not leave you, Julia," said her brother, still hoping he might prevail.

"No no," said she, resigning his hand, it is too much to ask of me; but I will speak to Nevil; perhaps she might be induced to stay, and yet I hardly know what I shall do without her."

Nevil was spoken to and resolutely re-refused, adding, that she must really be compelled to resign her situation, if such a thing were required of her.

"Then what on earth can I do?" exclaimed Julia, returning to her friends, who unanimously protested against remaining another day at such a place; and yet, when the comfort of the poor cottager was the subject of consideration, they looked round and protested it was a vastly comfortable sort of inn for that part of Scotland, and just the thing for those who wanted to be quiet; the landlady, a very decent sort of woman, and the Highland girl the best creature in the world; until, encouraged by these assurances, Julia at length determined upon doing what her better feelings refused to sanction,—leaving this young and helpless creature, alone, and ill, in a strange land. But she would speak to the doctor herself; she would engage a nurse, and do all things considerate and kind, and then surely Frederick could not blame her.

Frederick did blame her, however, and severely too, though silently; for he said to himself, "if my sister has really the heart to leave her, that heart is not worth appealing to."

Anna slept little that night; but in the morning the fever abated, and she fell into a dreamy sort of slumber, not deep enough to prevent her hearing occasionally the tread of bustling feet, and other signs of preparation which she could not understand. Whenever she looked up, too, there was an old woman seated at the foot of the bed, whose cold glassy eyes were fixed upon her face, but the weariness of exhausted nature overcome her curiosity, and she slept again.

Once (she hardly knew whether it was a dream or a reality) a gentle voice asked if she were awake; the old woman's finger was lifted up, and the reply was, "Then I won't disturb her, but see that you take care of her;" and soon after the carriage wheels rolled away from the door, and Anna slept quietly till near mid-day, when she awoke to the full possession of her senses, and the consciousness of her forlorn and deserted situation. She was left, alone, at a little village, in the north of Scotland, with neither strength nor money to take her home. Appalling as was this conviction, the poor invalid determined to rise, and endeavor to shake off her weakness; and in order to rid herself of the unwelcome attentions of her stranger nurse, she descended, with feeble and tottering steps, to the little parlour below, which the merry party had so lately deserted.

Every thing here was cold and dreary: the fire had not been lighted, and a north wind was blowing through the open window, that looked out upon the side of a bleak hill, round which wound the road, where the marks of the carriage wheels were still visible.

All was now so still, that Anna could distinctly hear the cry of a fretful child, and the chiding of an angry mother, from a house on the opposite side of the street, if street it might be called; the bleating of some wild sheep amongst the heath; and the rustling of the wind through the branches of some old firs that grew beside the window, and creaked, and moaned in the blast, as if complaining of their lonely and melancholy fate.

Anna's feelings, peculiarly alive at this time, to sights and sounds of wretchedness, gathered around her a host of images too painful for endurance, and she burst into tears exclaiming, in true bitterness of soul, "Mary, my friend, my only friend, surely there will need no lesson after this to teach me that I am poor, and blind, and miserable!"

The pressure of a gentle hand upon her arm called back her wandering thoughts;—called back the colour to her pale cheeks, and to her heart the warm glow of life and hope; for it was Frederic Langley who stood beside her.

"I thought you were all gone," said the poor girl, as soon as the hurry and confusion of her feelings allowed her to speak. "Why did you not leave me?"

"I answer in the words of your favourite poet, 'Why, all have left thee:' and though he has wisely and justly given this simple and touching expression to the lips of woman, yet, trust me, there are men, who can be faithful, and kind, when women are heartless and cruel."

"I do trust you," said Anna, with warmth. "I was just saying, I had but one friend in the world; but you have been more to me than a friend."

"Say a brother, if you please Anna, and then we shall be at ease with each other; but let us have a fire, and shut out this cold wind, and make our prison as comfortable as we can. You are not so very ill, I hope and trust, but that we shall be able to meet our party at Edinburgh in the course of a few days."

He then explained how he had taken his horse early in the morning, and ridden out under pretence of calling upon a college acquaintance who was then shooting in the Highlands, leaving a message for his sister, that if he found his friend at home, he should probably not join them again before they reached the city, which he hoped they would do by the end of the following week.

How vain are the struggles of the most determined will against the encroachment of disease!

Anna Clare would at this time have given worlds, had she possessed them, to shake off the weariness, the langour, and all other symptoms of approaching illness, that were rapidly stealing upon her. For a short time her spirits rallied, for the presence of Frederick was a great stimulus; but it needed both his support, and that of the nurse, to enable her to regain her little comfortless chamber, where she was doomed to spend many wearisome days of sickness and sorrow, varied only by intervals of stupor and delirium,—days that were counted by Frederick with the anxiety, if not exactly with the affection of a brother.

The fever at length abated; and Anna, feeble as a child, once more looked out upon the hills, and the purple heath, now bright in the sunshine of a cloudless autumn day.

The time was fast approaching for Julia and her party to be at Edinburgh on their way home. The time was fast approaching, and yet Anna was so weak, it would have been madness to attempt the journey. No expence or trouble would have been spared by Frederick which might enable him to attain his object, and place his poor friend again under the protection of his sister before they reached home; for, pleasant as it might be to linger amongst the hills, with this beautiful young creature, he felt that upon this crisis depended her good name with his family at least, if not with her own. Could they join their party in time, she might be helped forward by easy stages, and her own appearance would sufficiently justify the story of her illness; but if she remained alone with him, what story could he make sufficiently plausible to satisfy the enquiries of the uncharitable, and the scruples of the envious?

At this juncture a letter arrived from Julia. Frederick was alone, and eagerly tore open the seal. It had been detained upon the road, and now told the sad tidings, that the fair writer and her friends would leave Edinburgh on that very day, having waited for Frederick as long as their patience would allow.

"It is all over," said he, throwing the open letter upon the table. "It is all over, and we must make the best of it."

It was past midnight when he awoke from

his reverie. He was sitting with his feet upon the bars of a little grate that contained the expiring embers of a turf fire. "No, no,' said he, starting from his seat, and snatching up the candle, now burnt down into the socket. "Her protector I must be, but no more; and for this reason I will see her as little as possible." So saying he retired to rest, with that solid satisfaction of heart, which the applause of the world cannot give, nor the venom of its envious tongue destroy.

His time was now spent chiefly in shooting, and Anna being unable to amuse herself with her usual pursuits, felt hers hang heavily upon her hands.

CHAPTER VI.

It was on one of these long and lonely days, that a letter was brought to the invalid, sealed with the crest of the Langleys, and directed by a female hand. Her own trembled as she opened it, and read as follows.

"Miss Clare will probably be surprised that I should have taken the trouble to address a person in her situation; but regard to myself, and my family will no longer permit me to be silent. From my sister and her friends I have learned all the particulars of your strange conduct; and can only wonder that we have not been more sensible of the deep and wicked artifice by which you endeavoured to seduce the affections of our beloved brother;—too prone, alas! to fall into the snares of Satan. With regard to the future, my object in writing, is to request or rather to insist, that you will never make any other claim upon our family, of any kind whatsoever, resting assured, that such claims would be rejected with contempt, if not punished by the law.

"Wishing you may experience a sincere and heartfelt repentance for all your transgressions, I venture to subscribe myself,

"Your Christian Friend,
"SUSAN LANGLEY.

"P.S. My sister does not know of my writing. She is extremely sorry on your account, and can with difficulty be persuaded that you have been so very artful and depraved. Lord B.—alone has had the good sense to discover, and the sincerity to speak the truth.

"You will do well to burn this, and say nothing to my infatuated brother."

Poor Anna! she read the letter again, and again, turning it backwards and forwards, and looking alternately at the direction, and the contents, to assure herself of the reality. Her senses had been stupified by long illness; and it seemed almost impossible for her to comprehend the whole truth. No tears came to her relief. A single kind word would have brought them in torrents. One exclamation at last burst from her lips. "Oh! Mary, you warned me of insult and neglect, but you never warned me of any thing half so horrible as this!"

When Frederick Langley returned that night, the invalid was still sitting in the little parlour, her cheeks flushed with burning crimson, and her eye bright and wandering. Shocked by the wildness of her looks, and her unconnected and hurried answers to his simple questions, he asked the nurse if any thing particular had occurred during his absence; and she told him that a letter had arrived about noon, and that since then she had not been able to persuade the young lady to take the least thing, nor even to move from her chair.

Frederick returned, and seating himself beside Anna, took her feverish and burning hand, while, in a firm and determined manner, he began to question her about what had passed.

"Circumstances," said he, "over which we have no controul, have placed us in a strange and difficult situation. To be your protector has become my duty, as it would at any time have been my pleasure; but in order that I may serve you entirely, it is necessary, that with me you should have no reserve. I therefore call upon you as a friend, and one who is entitled to make such a demand, to tell me what has distressed you."

Anna made no reply; but the quivering of her pale lips gave sufficient evidence of her internal struggle. At last she drew forth the letter, and opening it with trembling fingers, placed it in Frederick's hand. Rage and indignation gathered on his brow, while his eye glanced rapidly over its contents. His mind had been prepared for such an attack, and he had no need to read it twice; but tearing the letter into a thousand pieces, he thrust them through the bars of the grate, and spoke not till every atom was consumed. "There," said he, "is an end to this specimen of my sister's hypocrisy and malice, and I wish we could say the same of all the mischief it has done. But do not mind it, my good girl; you have done nothing that is wrong in the sight of heaven. Your heart is as pure as the snows of these mountains; and they shall be compelled to acknowledge it."

With the consciousness of her own innocence, Anna tried to comfort herself, and in some measure she was comforted; but how to return was the question that perplexed them both. It was strange, that in this critical juncture, the principle of evil, ever ready to furnish ways and means, did not suggest to Frederick, that now, when Anna's reputation had received so severe a blow, it would be requiring comparatively but a small sacrifice, to ask her to remain with him, or to consent to seek with him, some more genial climate, where her health and happiness might be restored. To say that he did not think of it, would be much to venture upon any of his sex, in a similar situation; but Frederick Langley was an honourable man, and spurned the idea of taking an unfair advantage, especially of a woman. Besides, he did not yet know the strong impression made upon his own affections; nor how often, after his return to college, the fair image of Anna Clare would present itself; first, animated, brilliant, and gay, as he had seen her at her father's house; then, feeble, helpless, but still beautiful, as she now sat before him, writing at intervals, as she could bear the fatigue of writing to her friend, Mary Newton. And wonder not, gentle reader, that the short and incoherent letter which follows, should have cost the poor writer the greatest possible fatigue, both of body and mind; so humbling are the consequences of illness;—so incomprehensible the construction of the human frame.

"Dear Mary,

"When I last wrote to you, I was happy. Happy in the contemplation of all that could delight me,—the clear skies, the mountains, and the streams; and now, if I write of mountains, it will be of the mountains of grief that are upon my heart; if of streams, it will be the streams that flow from my eyes. I have fallen into great trouble since my illness. I am still very weak, and my hand trembles so, that you will not believe this to be my writing; but indeed Mary, it is the writing of your own friend—your friend, who is now humbled in the dust. Yet do not mistake me, I am guiltless in the sight of heaven; and only wish I could feel my innocence to be a greater consolation. Frederick Langley has been to me—but I will tell you when we meet, how kind, how delicate, how generous his whole conduct has been: and you, I know, will believe it; for whatever my faults may have been, I never was guilty of deceiving you. In the mean time, I entreat you to think kindly of me, and to try to make my father and yours think so too; for indeed Mary it was illness, and not inclination, that kept me here. Pray for me, dear Mary, for I am weak, both in body and mind; and these cruel Langleys will trample me into the grave."

Before Anna's letter reached its destination, rumour had been busy in her native village. That the tourists had returned without her, and that Frederick too was left behind, became the subject of general remark. Some said they had gone round by Gretna Green; and some that they had gone off to Italy. All wondered, and many took to themselves credit, for having predicted the consequences; though still ignorant what these consequences were.

Whether it was the insinuations thrown out against his daughter, which at this time particularly affected William Clare, was difficult to know; for he was a man of few words: but all remarked that he was altered; and when Mary spoke of it to her father, he shook his head and looked grave, and said some mysterious words about his affairs; which led her to suspect that all was not going well with his worldly concerns. Indeed, he had never been a money-making man. Quiet and unpretending in his own habits, he had indulged his daughter in every gratification which his humble means could afford. And now, when that daughter became the "theme of gossips' story,"—when the whispers of those who delight to carry evil tidings, told of her folly and hinted at her disgrace; it fell with inexpressible poignancy upon the anxious heart of the doating parent. Mary tried to comfort him; but, though she fully convinced him of the falsehood of the reports, and that his darling child would return to him as innocent as ever, with additional claims upon their love, from her illness and suffering; still the many tongued monster would make itself heard, and he could not be comforted.

Those who have never heard a name beloved, coupled with sin and shame, and trembled lest it might be justly too, have never tasted the true bitterness of the cup of misery.

All other draughts may be sweetened; but this is beyond the power of flattery, for it does not reach the object—of hope, for the blackness of desolation has already fallen upon our Goshen—and of religion, for the more we love God, and delight in the beauty of holiness, the more we linger after the stray sheep, and lament that the gates of paradise should be closed upon the lost one.

Mary went every day to the house of William Clare, to see that he fared comfortably, and that every thing was done to make his solitary evenings pass as pleasantly as circumstances would allow; for the days were now fast shortening, and the old man came in to his lonely fire, shivering with the sharp winds of autumn.

It was on one of these evenings when Mary had staid with him later than usual, for they had fallen into a long and earnest conversation about Anna, that a carriage drove up to the door, and Anna herself rushed into her father's arms. But, oh! how unlike the rosy girl, with whom they had so lately parted. When the first joy of welcome was over, she sunk into a chair, pale, and exhausted, and burst into tears. Mary wept too, and the father; but his were not tears of sorrow, for now he believed that Anna had come back the same innocent and guileless creature she had left them. True, she was sadly altered; but this was not the alteration he had feared. Yes, she was sadly changed; but then she had looked up to him again and again, with her clear bright eyes, in which there was no cloud, nor the least shadow of shame—and his heart was at rest.

Mary could not leave them; and they sat together that evening, the father, and the daughter, and the friend, united in fresh bonds. The old man spoke seldom. Mary busied herself with those little attentions which tell more of welcome than the kindest words, and that gentle and beautiful young creature looked alternately at her father and her friend, with smiles that betrayed how her poor heart had been yearning for their love.

To the good management of Frederick Langley, the invalid owed every thing. He had travelled with her in company with the old nurse, until they reached the last stage, and then, leaving them to pursue their journey with the confidence that they could meet with no further difficulty, he proceeded to

Cambridge, to recommence his studies, and to forget, if possible, the fair image of Anna Clare.

To the three friends who were re-united, (Mary hoped to separate no more,) the first days of returning confidence were days of nappiness; as the first taste of the cup of duty, is often sweet and pleasant to willing lips. It is the second, and the third, that contain the drops of bitterness. It is the after-trial that proves the spirit; for the heart is deceitful, and after many fair promises, will return to its idols, again and again like the rebellious children of Israel.

CHAPTER VII.

MARY could not always be with her friend; and now the season was fast approaching, when household comforts are most valued, and household troubles most deplored—the dark days, and the cold rains of November. The flowers and the plants, which had grown around the window of Anna's little parlour, weaving themselves into garlands of beauty, were all withered and beaten down. Pools of water stood upon the gravel walks, and when the door was opened the angry tempest rushed in, and Anna and her father were both feeble, and little able to contend with storms of any kind.

This chilly season is the time when the heart draws upon its little store of hoarded treasures; or it may be, when it broods over its secret griefs. It is the time when happy faces are lighted up at the cheerful fire; or when the solitary sits musing in tenfold loneliness; when the rich and the gay delight themselves with artificial pleasures; and when the poor are made to feel the reality of their poverty.

While the summer lasts, the bright and bountiful summer, that grudges not to spread her beauties in the path of the lowliest pilgrim, it is not difficult for those who are raised above abject want, to vie with their more opulent neighbours, provided only their residence be in the country; for there the skies form a canopy more splendid than the hand of the great father of painting itself could produce. In the ever varying tints of the foliage, they have tapestry of the richest and most brilliant hues; and what loom can furnish a carpet like the green turf beneath their feet?

But when winter comes, the stern aspect of poverty presents itself in undeniable gloom. Around one fire the whole family must gather in; young, and old; boisterous, and quiet; barbarous, and civilized, must sit down together; and then if there should happen to be one aspiring spirit amongst the number, which has soared upon the wings of fancy to a higher realm of thought and feeling—alas! what a fate is hers!

Anna Clare felt all the distinctions of riches and poverty, more powerfully than words can describe; and though she was spared the misery of contending with coarse and uncongenial minds, she found that one simple duty, of being cheerful, which she owed both to her father and herself, indescribably irksome.

There are those who shut themselves up in retirement, thinking that danger exists only in the pleasures of the world, and safety in their exclusion. But let them look well to the choice they have made, and ask, whether the evils of solitude may not be as offensive in the sight of their Creator as those of society. For themselves, they have an undoubted right, both to know, and to choose, what is best; but there are hearts that can bear witness to the sins of solitude; to the sins, and the sufferings too.

Hearts, that have been weighed down with the leaden stupor of melancholy, until every affection was swallowed up in self, every feeling lost in the ocean of misery, from whence no gentle dew is exhaled, as an offering of gratitude to heaven.

This winter would indeed have been a long and heavy season to Anna Clare, had she not been able to resume her favourite amusement; to which she returned with her wonted avidity, as soon as her strength would allow. The sketches she had made in Scotland, became more valuable to her every day, in proportion as she forgot the pain, and dwelt only on the pleasure with which they were connected; and from these she busied herself to compose a picture, which should exceed all her other performances in excellence of colouring, and execution. To her eye, it was like a vision of paradise; for there was the blue lake on which they had sailed; and, stretching far out into its quiet bosom, was the point of rock, tinged with the rays of the setting sun, where the happy party stood while she was sketching: the broken foreground, the rich purple heath, and the scattered fragments of stone, on which Frederick and herself were seated. Anna painted, improved, and gazed upon this picture, until it became a sort of idol to her; but it was not before her father talked of the price she would ask for it, that she was aware of her own idolatry; and scornfully as her proud spirit at first rejected the old man's sordid notion, after circumstances occurred, which tended very much to reconcile the idea.

It was evident to many, and now could no longer be concealed from Anna, that her father was failing, both in purse and person. She had no wish to encroach unnecessarily upon his limited means; but she felt, more painfully than ever, her own inability to assist him; she felt, also, the want of many comforts, both for herself and her father, which she had never thought of before; for she was still extremely delicate, and the winter's cold seemed more than her slender frame could bear.

"If I had but a warm cloak," she said to herself, one day, after a visit to Mary Newton; and then, the thought of her picture presented itself, to be rejected and returned to a thousand times, before she could really make up her mind to part with it.

The love of a mother to her offspring is known even to the brutes; and there are many other natural affections, common to all; but the love of a painter for his picture, is what few can imagine, because few have known it. And if he do sometimes value his performance at what the world considers an unreasonable rate, let it not be set down solely to an inordinate love of gain; for in his picture, he beholds the clear skies, the work of his own hands, all bright and glowing, as if no cloud had ever cast a shadow on his path; the trees, in their perpetual verdure, and the seas, the lakes, and rivers, that know no storms; but most of all, his eye delights to dwell upon the portrait of a friend; for when he looks on that, memory brings back the time when it was painted—the kind words that were spoken, and the feelings that were shared together. Time may change the original. Alas! we all know, that time can wrinkle the fair cheek, and dim the sparkling eye with tears; and oh! more than all, can estrange the heart, and turn away the current of the affections; but this mute and motionless image bids defiance, alike to the ebb and flow of human passions, and to the chilling touch of time.

After many a lingering .ook, not unfrequently blended with tears, Anna at last determined upon the sale of her painting; which accordingly was set in an elegant and costly frame, and sent to stand the test of vulgar criticism, in the window of an artist's repository, in the neighbouring town.

The picture, however, was not sold, though the frame was paid for; and Anna was obliged to fold herself, once more, in a cloak that was neither warm nor handsome.

CHAPTER VIII.

"There is nothing puzzles me so much to account for," said Anna to her friend, "as, how you should always be so happy."

"Can you tell me," replied Mary, "why that little robin bears so patiently the winter's cold; and sings so cheerfully when he feels the first gleam of sunshine? It is because he has never flown to warmer climates, but contented himself with such things as God has placed around him."

"But you surely do not mean to say, that in my situation, you could be happy?"

"In your situation, Anna? I would not, willingly, give way to envy of another's portion, or repining at my own; but sometimes, when I am weary, and the children have been troublesome, and I see you sitting so quietly in your elegant parlour, just following your own pursuits, without any one to tease or interrnpt you, it does seem to me that yours is a privileged lot. But, mind me, I would not change with you, if I had to take into the bargain all the idle fancies that possess your brain. Constant exertion, has been a great blessing to me; but far before this, and next to the immediate protection of Providence, I ought to reckon the instruction and example of a good mother. A mother, who taught me to be content with my humble portion, and to cultivate such habits and desires, as would make that portion happy. So, you see, there is no merit in my being contented, because this, as well as every other good thing I am capable of, was taught me by my mother."

Anna was silent for a long time, and when she resumed the conversation, it was with a slight apology for the freedom of the remark she was about to make; and then smiling, lest it should appear too serious, she went on.

"There is another thing, Mary, equally incomprehensible to me, and that is, how you can love that homely and quaint young man, Andrew Miller."

Mary coloured deeply, but not with shame; for her attachment to Andrew Miller had already been acknowledged before her father, and many of her friends; and so high was her estimation of the worth of his character, that she could not hear without indignation, the least slight, or insult connected with his name.

"I will tell you," said she with some warmth, "if you can listen to so plain a story, why it is that I love that homely and quaint young man. We have known each other from infancy. For a long time we went to the same school. I was dull at learning, and he was always ready to help me out. I was not, in my early years, so dutifu. a daughter as I ought to have been; and he used to tell me kindly, and seriously, what he thought of my conduct. I was often fretful, and ill tempered when he reproved me; and yet he never would forsake me, nor give up the hope that I should live to have a clearer view of my own true interest; and to all these I will now add, if you please, a true woman's reason,—I love Andrew Miller, because he loves me." "You are a good girl, Mary," said her friend. "I would laugh, if I dared, at your Damon and Delia sort of love; but it ill becomes the miserable to make a jest of the happy. Have you never a Philander for me?"

"You may laugh if you will, Anna, and make a jest of my love, though not of my lover; but there is no greater proof of the error in which you have been educated, than the contempt with which you would reject the pretensions of an admirer in your own sphere of life; and yet, to live in single and stately blessedness upon a very slender income, is a fate for which you are by no means prepared; and to be carried off by a hero of romance, is a privilege not often enjoyed by the damsels of the present day."

Anna knew of but one hero, with whom her own fate could in any way be connected even in idea; one who was never forgotten, but so seldom named, that the two friends seemed, as if by mutual consent to have ceased to make him a topic of conversation. It is true, the young enthusiast had returned with his fascinating qualities deeply engraven on her heart, and his praises ever ready to flow from her lips; but finding how extremely difficult it was to do him justice, without describing scenes that wore a sort of doubtful character betwixt love and friendship, which might reasonably be misunderstood by her friends, since they were not very clear, even to herself: she ceased, by degrees, to name either him or his merits; and Mary ceased also, contenting herself with the belief, that no correspondence was kept up between them, and trusting to the well known propensity of young gentlemen to forget young ladies, especially when absent; besides, they had both other things of deep interest to converse about. The health of William Clare was failing rapidly, and every one predicted that he would not live to see another spring; and dark sayings were heard about his worldly affairs, and harsh comments were made upon his useless daughter. Anna's health was also extremely delicate, and she would often talk to Mary of the cold Scottish blight, from which, she believed, she never should recover.

Under these clouds the poor artist and her father spent the month of December; and Christmas, the happy time of good cheer and hearty welcome, brought nothing for them but that long train of gloomy realities, with which this merry-making season is associated in the minds and memories of those who have had to drink of the bitter draught of poverty.

No rosy school-boy threw open the door of William Clare; no cheerful party gathered round his hearth; no games nor festivities echoed in his silent home;—but a sickly daughter leaned her head upon her hand, in musing attitude, her eyes fixed upon the glimmering of a scanty fire, which just gave light enough to show the vast accumulation of bills and papers piled up on the mantelpiece. The night was dark, a heavy fall of snow lay thick upon the ground, and a fierce wind howled around their dwelling, searching every crevice of the doors and windows. The old man was dozing in his arm chair, and Anna sat beside him, pale and motionless as a marble statue, when suddenly a loud knock was heard at the door, and they both started, one from sleeping, and the other from waking dreams.

It was a long time before the old servant could unbar the door, and Anna stood trembling and agitated, she knew not why. The foot of a man was heard stamping off the light snow, and she began to think he never would come in.

"Is your mistress at home?" said a kind and well known voice, so unlike all other voices,—so impossible to be mistaken!——

A few evenings after this, the members of a book society, established by Miss Langley, held their meeting at the house of Mr. Blanchard the surgeon, where two maiden ladies, of unspeakable age, amused themselves with the following conversation:—

"Dear Mis Langley, she has so little time for writing, and yet what a kind letter I have received from her this morning." And the lady spread forth a neatly folded sheet of the finest writing paper, in which a few wavy lines, extenting far and wide, told how much the amiable writer was interested in the improvement of the inhabitants of her dear village of L——, and how truly she was, &c. &c.

"There is one thing, however," continued the lady, "in which I confess I am in the dark. Miss Langley recommends the study of Belles Letters, and, between ourselves, I cannot recollect ever having heard of them before. Now you, who have so good a memory, may perhaps be able to help me out, for as I mean to order the book to night, you know it will be quite as well to say something of the style of the publication, its size, price, &c.

The lady appealed to drew her hand across her forehead, and then confessed she had read the book; but really, it was very odd, she could not call to mind whether it was an octavo or duodecimo. "Ah! here comes my nephew, charming boy! even he has imbibed this love of literature. How delightful to meet with such young and ardent minds engaged in the same laudable pursuit."

At this instant a rosy-faced, red-handed, blustering young man, dressed in a short coat, and slashing a riding-whip about his own legs, and sometimes the legs of his neighbours, walked, or rather waded into the room; and after staring at the young ladies, and stumbling over the toes of the old ones, at last turned to meet the welcome of his aunt, though with no very cordial greeting on his part.

"Which is pretty Miss Clare!" said he, before the lady had concluded her encomiums on his love of literature. "I came to see Miss Clare, and I'll take my oath there isn't a pretty face in the room. Jim Bowles tells me she's grown confounded plain, and hasn't any colour at all.

"Speaking of the Langley's" said the aunt, "what can have brought the young gentleman into the country again at this time of the year ?"

"Why, don't you know that his horses are kept at Langley Hall, and that Lord B——'s hounds will throw off on Preston Common on Thursday; and a glorious run we mean to have !" and then the young Nimrod set up his hunting yell in the very ear of her who had just begun to hope that he would at last "get understanding."

As soon as this noisy intruder had withdrawn himself, and the old ladies could again hear themselves talk, they went on, with lowered voices, to hope, but really they could not help fearing, that young Mr. Langley had come down with some particular view. "It was a sad affair, very sad, but such things must be expected from bringing people up so much above their situation."

They had long thought the girl was more like a play-woman than a respectable farmer's daughter. Respectable, indeed, he was not; for it was well known he could not meet his payments this Christmas, and that all would have to be sold up; and then they wondered how much the moreen window curtains would go for; and then, more interesting still, they branched off into the merits of some articles which they had lately purchased for themselves; comparing the price, and the quality of each, with many other items not noted in the records of the book-society of L——.

CHAPTER IX.

There are harsh natures that cannot enter into a situation, such as Anna Clare's, who would say that she was bold, imprudent, and sought what she deserved to find, her own destruction. But surely, they can never have known how plausible is the first appearance of earthly love, to those whose hearts are yet warm with the glow of youth, and unhackneyed in the ways of the world. So pure, so disinterested, so entirely divested of every thing either gross or mean, is the first growth of this dangerous passion, at least in the breast of woman.

Anna felt all this, without one suspicion of the candour and integrity of her lover; nor had he hitherto harboured a thought that was injurious to her. In him she saw only the kind friend and companion of her summer rambles, come back, to her, when friends are dearest—in the winter, when there are few external sources of enjoyment; and oh! more than all, in the winter of the soul!

To the gaze of vulgar admiration Anna had indeed lost much of her beauty with her bloom; but to Frederick she was more lovely than before. It is true, she was much paler; her look of rosy health was gone; yet the colour had not so entirely forsaken her cheeks, but that it was ready to come back with every varying emotion, brighter and purer, and more spiritual in its variations.

There were traces of deep thought too upon her clear forehead, but so gently marked, as to seem only as if the finger of sorrow had lightly touched, and then withdrawn itself, unwilling to mar the beauty of so fair a picture. Perhaps she was graver too; and it was evident from her whole deportment, that experience had been her sage companion—experience, whose counsels are, or ought to be, so salutary; whose rejected lessons are so appalling when they rise up in judgment against us. When Frederick first beheld her, she was like the creature of a poet's dream; but now a stranger might assign to her the station of a wife, a mother, or a friend. She was then more beautiful to gaze upon; now, more fitted to be loved; and he had come back with the idea, almost amounting to conviction, that it was impossible to live without her.

"*Respice finem,*" is a motto, that we should all do well to adopt, and never lose sight of through the dangerons pilgrimage of life; but, most of all, it behoves the woman who listens to a tale of love, to "look to the end."

Anna Clare had no such extended vision, nor ever asked herself of what intrinsic value the love of Edward Langley could be to her; but listened, as weak and foolish woman will listen, while the only man who had ever fascinated her young imagination, poured forth his soul in high sounding professions of never ending attachment. Mary Newton was now forgotten; the bleak winter vanished, the snow melted, and all but her aged father, seemed to wear the cheerfulness of spring.

Frederick had said all that the most ardent lover could say;—he would leave Cambridge in April, and then his travels would commence. She was to go with him to Italy, where her health would be restored, and her skill in painting perfected, under the first masters. Nor was it until some days after his departure that this thought occurred to her,—he had never mentioned one word about marriage, of the consent of his family, or any of those business-like concerns, which she was willing to believe did not often intrude upon an attachment, pure and romantic like theirs; and therefore she was satisfied, at least, she told her heart a thousand times that she was so; but still, whenever she determined upon telling Mary Newton all that had passed, there was something which put a stop to her words, and she never could bring herself to make a complete disclosure, even to this faithful friend.

We know, that when there exists between two intimate friends a resolution not to converse upon one particular subject, which is intensely interesting to one or both, a separation, or suspension of intimacy, is the natural consequence; and thus it was with them; for Anna felt that she was keeping back what ought to be told, and Mary was a little piqued that so slight a circumstance, as the visit of a young gentleman, should have destroyed their long cherished confidence: nor could any thing less than illness have brought her again to be so frequent a visiter at the house of William Clare, until some confession had been made. But the old man was failing fast, and she could not allow Anna to be left alone with him; and therefore she came often in the day, and sometimes staid through the night, and yet the two friends would frequently sit in silenee together, both feeling that they were not to each other what they ought to be.

At length, however, the death of William Clare, put an end to all reserve, for they had more serious things to do, and to think about, without consideration of their relative situations.

James Newton and Andrew Miller were his executors; and when they came to the winding up of his affairs, it was discovered that there would barely be sufficient for the discharge of his debts, without leaving any thing for the maintenance of his daughter.

When Anna was first told of this, she heard it in silence; but she never slept on the following night, and her feverish symptoms returned, with an accumulation of distressing feelings, which terminated in a severe attack of the same disorder from which she had suffered in Scotland.

Mary was her faithful and unremitting attendant, and soon had the satisfaction of seeing her restored; her mind too, was more at ease, and she could speak calmly of the past, and of the future; though not of Frederick Langley. About him there was still a mystery, which Mary could not fathom, especially when Anna, in speaking of the future, added a hope, that she should not long be burdensome to her friends.

"Anna, dear Anna," said her friend, "let me never hear that word from you again. I cannot make professions, nor say that you shall come to live with my father and me; though I am sure you would be welcome to every one of us; but we live so differently to what you have been accustomed to, that I know you would not be happy. I have, however, not been idle during your illness. I have determined and acted upon a plan, which I hope will make all things easy. I will marry Andrew Miller. I suppose you know that he has taken this farm; and then you can live with us. We have only been waiting because I thought the girls were too young to take charge of the family at home; but now, I dare say, they will do very well, with me so near them: and if you do not like to be altogether what is called dependent, they shall come to you every day, and you shall instruct them in those things, which either I did not know myself, or had no time to teach them.

Anna stretched out one thin and burning hand to meet that of her friend; while with the other, she strove to conceal the tears that were now fast falling from her eyes; but she could not speak, for thoughts rushed upon her, some too painful, and some too pleasing for utterance.

"I have told Andrew," resumed Mary, with her wonted simplicity; "and he, poor fellow, is pleased enough. I wish you could just tell me that it pleases you, for I cannot see why you should weep so, when Andrew, and I, and my father and the children, will all be made so happy. Perhaps you will consider of it;" and so saying, she left the room, and Anna, giving full vent to her feelings, sobbed aloud.

"She is too good to me," said the poor girl, a little recovering herself, "they are all too good; it is my rebellious heart, that will not let me be happy. Oh! Frederick Langley, what have I to do with you? what have I to do with any thing but sickness and poverty?—why cannot I sit down contentedly, to be what they called me, the 'village schoolmistress!'"

CHAPTER X.

The next circumstance of any importance, which took place at the village of L——, was the marriage of Mary Newton and Andrew Miller. A large concourse of friends and relatives assembled, and Anna put off her mourning, and figured for that day as a bridesmaid. The tables of James Newton groaned with plenty; good fare, and hearty welcomes, were bountifully dispensed; the children laughed and played tricks with every body, and the old people hobbled in to give the happy pair their blessing. There was not a repining spirit in the whole party, and even Anna looked pleased, and strove to smile at the coarse jests of the neighbours; for, blush not, gentle reader, such things will prevail in times of festivity, even among those who were formerly shepherds, and shepherdesses; Damons and Pastorellas.

Andrew Miller was a man of strong, useful understanding; cultivated, at least informed, but not refined; perhaps in his share of knowledge, as much above his wife, as she was superior to him in the delicacy and sensibility which belong to her sex.

Though constant in the performance of every duty, whether religious, or social; by no means forgetting such as belong to charity, and good neighbourhood; he scarcely knew how to extend his pity to those who suffer from imaginary evils, and strew thorns in their own path. Thus, his gentle helpmate was often obliged to screen her friend from his censure, and even in spite of her good management, he would sometimes, without the least idea of causing pain, give utterance to plain truths, which wounded Anna's pride, and Mary's feeling. There were besides, little points of vulgarity about him, continually striking upon the delicate nerves of the fair heroine; and one single weakness, by no means confined to Andrew Miller, was a constant source of irritation and annoyance,—he was extremely fond of hearing himself read, though by no means a good reader, at least, in Anna's estimation; for she thought of Frederick Langley, and the fine tones of his well modulated voice, when he read to her in that little village in the Highlands, and the moments flew so rapidly along.

Perhaps there are few things in which the cultivation, or refinement of the intellectual powers is more perceptible, than in the style of a person's reading; for how well soever these untaught readers may understand the meaning of the author, it seems impossible tc give his words the proper tone and emphasis, without a regular parrot-like training; and when they read from a book, precisely the same expressions which they make use of every day, they seem bound to torture their words into a totally different sound, merely because they are in print. The books too, which Andrew Miller made choice of, were more ancient than the grandmother from whose library they had descended; and then he would give long histories of that grandmother, who had been a great personage in her day, and figured as mayoress in the town of——; of the alderman, and what property the different branches of each family then possessed; with accounts of houses that were pulled down, chapels that were built, levels that were drained, navigations that were made, and commons that were enclosed in his father's time. And yet Andrew Miller was a good man, and ought not to have been despised; for the number of good men is not so great as to make them worthless. Yes, he was indeed a good man, for he endeavoured to keep the service of his Maker continually before his eyes: to make it the rule of his actions during the day, and the subject of his prayers at night. A strict supporter of the established religion of the land; he served his king with integrity and uprightness, and his God with fidelity and zeal.

If he made an idol of any thing, it was his wife; and well he might, for she was a good and kind one; and he was proud and happy in the possession of such a treasure. But her sickly, pining friend, he could not understand; nor why she was not as cheerful as himself and Mary; so he fixed upon the absence of religion as the cause, and perhaps he was not so far wrong, as in the means he adopted to remedy the evil, for he read the Bible to her till she was weary of hearing it; and good books in such numbers, that she forgot both their nature and their names: and all the while her wandering spirit would fly to happier climes, and clearer skies, leaving the dull realities of life behind.

The first coming of spring is peculiarly delightful to those whose minds are at peace; who feel the importance and the pleasure of entering upon another year of duty and enjoyment; and can look up to their Creator with thankfulness, that he has given them a taste to enjoy the one, and a reasonable hope of being able to perform the other.

The first pale snow drop that burst from its icy prison, Mary gathered, and presented to her friend; and the first motherless lamb that Andrew brought in, she would have given her too, thinking it might amuse and interest her; but Anna's heart was far away from the simple pleasures of the cottage, and she cared for none of these things.

When the first song of the lark was heard one bright sabbath morning, as they walked to church, Mary looked up to the skies, and inwardly blessed the God of nature, who had placed her in a world so beautiful and happy; while Anna bent her eyes upon the earth, and wished that little bird was singing over her grave; and yet, she had the firmest reliance upon the truth and fidelity of her lover; but for all that she was not happy. She believed, too, that he would come again, and find her, even in her obscurity; and yet she was not happy. All around her was contentment and peace; and yet she was not happy.

Ah! that we could always compel ourselves to institute a strict, impartial, and thorough investigation, into the causes of our unhappiness. That we would make an enquiry which admits of no tampering, why we are not, as the merciful Author of our being designed we should be, numbering our blessings, and counting the favours which his gracious hand bestows upon us? Would not such an enquiry generally produce the conviction, that we are not giving up the whole heart to him, who has an undoubted right to rule over it? That we are making no better than a conditional covenant, that, if he will grant us some particular request, we will then serve him; or, turning to idols of perishable clay, which in a single moment may be broken into fragments at our feet.

"What am I, O Lord, that thou shouldst thus be mindful of me? O make me more worthy to partake of thy mercies!" was the simple and earnest prayer of Mary, every night before she retired to rest; while Anna became a stranger to the duty of prayer altogether.

For the present she knew of no blessings, at least she felt none, for which to be thankful; and for the future, she had but one overpowering wish, and if that should be denied, she believed it so utterly impossible to be resigned, that she never even supplicated help from that Being to whom all things are possible; and thus being unable to say, with full sincerity of heart, "Even as thou willest, O my father," she forsook that Father in the morning of her days, and went on her way repining.

April came at last, to Anna's anxious wishes; and with it a letter announcing the intended return of Frederick Langley. He was to take up his residence at the Hall for a few weeks, until all arrangements were made for his journey—for *their* journey; for he never spoke of going abroad, or of the future, without associating Anna with his plans of pleasure; and yet, there was nothing said of marriage, but a hint was delicately dropped, that their meetings must be neither public nor frequent.

The thrill of delight with which Anna first read the letter, was soon turned to sickness of soul, for she could not show it to her friend; and she must carry on a system of deception with that friend to whom she owed so much.

Well may the anguish of a troubled conscience be compared to the gnawing of a worm, which dieth not. To bear about with us continually the consciousness that we are harbouring some sinful purpose, which we dare not reveal, lest the kind hearts that are beating for our happiness should stagnate with horror, or shrink away with disgust;—to fix our weary eyes upon any object, rather than the countenance of a well tried friend, who is watching us with looks of tenderness and trust;—to seek, yet dread the darkness when we lie down at night, and to awake in the morning with a trembling sense of exposure, in the bountiful and glorious light of another day. Surely, of all the hard portions which the human heart has perversely selected for itself, there can be nothing to exceed this in piognancy of suffering.

The day arrived, on the evening of which Anna was to meet her lover, and she could not help thinking, that Mary's eye followed her with uncommon scrutiny; and when she stole out in the twilight hour, she felt like a guilty thief who is about to wrong his trusting master.

Is there any beauty in a beloved countenance that can clear away the darkness of a troubled spirit? Or is there any music in words of love that can charm away the reproaches of the still small voice?

Anna felt there was none; and returned that night to her solitary chamber, with heaviness of heart; but yet there was a spell upon her, which she could not, would not break, and all night long she wearied herself with dwelling upon and comparing such pictures of the future, as love, romance, and contempt of humble life, combined to present. On one side, there was her poverty, her dependence, her weak health, and inability to struggle with the rough accidents of life; her loneliness, for she felt alone, with those who could not enter into her heart of hearts; and the loathing with which she looked round upon the common herd, with whom she must necessarily associate, with all except Mary, and Mary was—married. On the other side was a bright vision of golden uncertainties, too dazzling to be looked upon with steady eyes. All that the poet dreams of when his soul is most elevated above the gross things of matter,—all that the painter pictures, when his spirit takes the wings of the morning, and soars into its native regions of light; and, above all, there was that secret voice, for ever pleading with the heart of woman, to lean upon the broken reed of earthly love, to glide upon its glassy surface, to repose in its bower of thorny roses.

CHAPTER XI.

It was a part of the system by which Frederick Langley quieted his own conscience, and imposed upon Anna's understanding, that he urged her to do nothing contrary to her own inclination. If she would commit herself to his protection, and forsake her country, and her friends, it was to be of her own choosing; he only promised her unchanging fidelity, a speedy rescue from poverty, dependence, obscurity and contempt; and a free and happy life, in a land rich with delightful associations, where her feeble constitution might be invigorated, her taste gratified, and her genius encouraged; and where an attachment pure and unchanging as theirs, might be indulged without fear of the censorious moralist, or the anathema of the rigidly righteous.

Anna listened till her senses were bewildered, and a dense mist seemed to obscure her perception of right and wrong.

"It is for souls like yours," continued he, "to spurn the laws that were only made for baser natures. Your beauty was not given to fade in the damp fogs of England; your heart to pine in the solitude of a country village. Your noble spirit shall bear you to a land where it may roam at will amongst all that is exquisite in art, and magnificent in nature." And thus the man went on; and the woman listened, like our first parent, to the voice of the tempter; until the one, clear, divine injunction, was forgotten in the contemplation of a picture of ideal happiness, which now took possession of her whole soul. Could this picture, and all the disobedience which its realization involved, have been described to her in the unvarnished language of vulgar truth, she would, most probably, have turned away with horror and disgust, at once declaring herself incapable of an act of such enormity. But it is the peculiar province of that power, which too frequently takes possession of the young and ardent mind, under the character of sentiment, romance, taste, feeling, or whatever fanciful designation its victims choose to bestow upon it, to invest, with a sanctity of its own creating, whatever is brought within its magic circle; subjecting every sentiment to the censorship of the poet; judging of every action by the criterion of "good taste." And thus, many whose talents have fitted them to be a light, and a wonder to the world, having spurned at the precepts of religion, as inventions to frighten fools: and having trampled on the laws of morality, as intended only to restrain the base and vulgar herd, have themselves passed away from this state of existence, without having fulfilled one rational purpose, or leaving anything behind but a blank or a ruin to tell where they have been. And it is in imitation of these eccentric stars, that minor lights give up their little ray of usefulness, and dance, and glimmer, and expire, like the ignis fatuus of the morass.

> "Who listens once will listen twice;
> Her heart, be sure, is not of ice,"

Has been said by one who well knew the weakness of the human heart; and in this manner Anna Clare proved that hers was not of adamant. Time flew on, and yet her decision was not made; the evil day was put off, and surely there could be no sin in thinking of it till that day should really come.

"Recollect," said Frederick, one evening when they were about to part, "that you have yet given me no promise, and that in three days, I shall be gone."

Anna stood for sometime in speechless and motionless silence; and then said softly but audibly. "Then in three days I must either go with you, or be left behind."

Were there no words she could bring in opposition to that fatal journey but this simple expression of total and solitary bereavement; "I must be left behind; a sound that touches so painfully upon the heart of woman. Anna felt all its force, and exclaiming with convulsive effort, "Then I will go;" she tore herself from her delighted lover, and hurried over the fields, and through the little gate, opening immediately beside the door, that was once her father's. She entered: it was the time of evening prayer. Andrew, his wife, and servants, were gathered together in the performance of this holy duty; and Anna knelt down beside them. But O! what a contrast to the quiet and peaceful inhabitants of that dwelling. Her hair fell around her in loose tresses, her cheek was flushed, and her eye wild and wandering. She uttered no response to the prayers—she joined not the hymn which that night arose to heaven.

Mary went with her friend to her own apartment, for she thought she must surely be ill, and might want something; so setting down the candle she said she would stay with her until she went to sleep.

"No, no," said Anna, "you are very kind, but I would rather be alone."

"Then I will come again;" and so saying, she left the room, and when she returned, it was with the quiet step of a mother who fears to wake her child. Finding Anna was not asleep, she stooped over her, and said she had just come to see that she was comfortable, and wanted nothing.

"There is one thing I want;" said Anna, for her heart was melted, and she stretched out her arms to meet the embrace of her friend. "I want you to pray for me. I am a weak and sinful creature; but I cannot tell you all now. No, Mary, you must leave me, for I am so very sinful, that even your presence is not welcome to me."

And thus they parted for the night.

In the morning Anna was not disposed to be more communicative, nor Mary to intrude upon her confidence; so they both went through the day with more than usual reserve. But Mary's suspicions were awakened, and having heard that Frederick Langley was in the neighbourhood, it was not difficult to surmise the rest. There was beside, a slight appearance of preparation in Anna's room, and Mary's fears were wrought up to the most agonizing apprehensions.

It was on the night before that fixed upon for the departure of the lovers, that, after a long season of communion with her own heart, Mary entered the chamber of her friend, determined not to leave it, until she had wrung from her a full confession.

Anna was still up, and busy with something which she hastily concealed. Her looks were confused, and her whole manner was constrained and embarrassed.

"Anna," said Mary, seating herself, and extinguishing her candle, "I have come to talk with you, for a little while. I know that my company is an intrusion, and I once thought, that if ever I should arrive at this conviction, I should leave you for ever. But I am not yet prepared to leave you, Anna, though you seem disposed to shake me off. So I have come to ask you a single question, and because I am in earnest, in serious and sad earnest, I will speak at once to the point; and now ask you, Anna Clare, if you are not in the secret of your heart, harbouring a design, upon which you cannot, before you go to rest this night, pray for the blessing of Almighty God?"

Anna bent her eyes upon the ground, and was silent for some time; but at length she roused herself.

"I will never be guilty of telling a deliberate falsehood to you or to any one; and since, by evasion, I should stand as much committed in your eyes as by a disclosure of the whole truth, I will tell you that to-morrow night, Frederick Langley will set off for Italy;—at eleven o'clock, his carriage will pass your gate, and,—I am to be his companion!"

A long silence followed, for Anna had nothing more to say, and Mary was not prepared for so sudden, so awful, a termination to all her love, and all her kindness. Thoughts of tenderness, mingled with the recollection of early years, rushed upon her, too powerfully for utterance; and she burst into tears.

"I know what you are thinking of," continued Anna, "you are thinking of my ingratitude to you. And, ah! Mary, when I am laid upon my death-bed, I shall think of it too."

"I believe I was," replied Mary, "but it was a selfish and unworthy thought." And then, taking the hand of her friend, she continued, "Let us turn our attention to weightier considerations. Let us think where that death-bed may be! But first, tell me truly, did my senses deceive me." And she quesoned Anna, in such plain and homely words, that the poor victim of self-deception, who had been cheating her understanding with the language of poetry, shrunk back, wounded and terrified, from Mary's strict and determined investigation of the truth; while all that she could venture in her own defence, was a few words about her lover's devoted and generous attachment.

"Oh! trust him not;" replied Mary, "the generosity of man wakes only while his passions sleep. And as for his love, think not of it. A few years will pass away, and he will laugh at the village girl who was the plaything of his youth; and she will be dying in that far country, where there is not a single friend to protect her."

"Mary, you do not know, it is impossible that you should know, the strength of a love like ours."

"Then, because you wander out by moonlight, and read verses, and sing love-songs together, you think you know better than we do, what belongs to true and faithful love. Listen to me, my poor infatuated friend. I cannot speak in polished language, but I will tell you a plain truth. The man who leads you from the path of duty, and calls upon your generosity for the sacrifice of your good name, is not your lover; he is your enemy. No, though he may follow, flatter, and serve you, I repeat what I have said, he is your deadliest enemy; but he who strives to correct your foibles, who points out your faults, who loves you most tenderly, when you are serving God, even though you should at the same time, be neglecting him; with this man, you may reasonably hope to live happily on earth,—with this man, you may hope to live more happily in heaven. I know that you look down with contempt, upon the affection which subsists between Andrew Miller and myself; but that humble man, whom you despise, would sooner part with his right hand, than he would make me a fit object for the finger of malice to point at, with scorn and derision."

"Then will you, Mary, never look upon me nor call me your friend again?"

"That is a question which I am hardly prepared to answer. I have striven to reason with you coolly, and without throwing into the scale the least particle of individual feeling, for we ought to look up to higher considerations; but since you have asked me, I will say that I do not believe there is any circumstance in life that can tear away my deep-rooted love for you, Anna, nor any situation in which I would forsake you. I like not professions; but I do feel that in the lowest pit of wretchedness and vice, I should be ready to seek you, and if it were possible, to save you. Nay, do not weep, Anna, you surely must have believed as much as this of me before, or else my conduct has sadly belied my feelings; but I will talk no more of myself; it is for you, that I feel this torturing anxiety; for you who have dwelt in the bosom of a kind family—who have been brought up in the nurture and admonition of the Lord—are you prepared to meet the common adversities of life, without a home in your sickness, a friend in your sorrow, or the consolations of religion in your remorse? Are you prepared to live on, from day to day, without asking the blessing of your Creator, at your lying down, and your uprising? Are you prepared to be hurried to the grave, by the hands of unpitying strangers, with no tear shed over you, no memorial, but in the wounded spirits of those who would gladly remember you no more? And this, Anna, is but an outline—but a faint sketch of the fate to which you are about to consign yourself. Fill it up, with all that you can imagine of wretchedness, and the picture will not be less true. I know too well that I have little to offer you on the other side; little, as regards the things of this world; but oh! let me intreat you to trust in Him, who can make a path for his people through the wilderness. We cannot tell when the precious manna will fall, nor discern which is the rock that will be smitten, nor say in what quarter the pillar of fire will first appear; but we know that his promises are sure, and that he will never leave, nor forsake his suffering people. Into his hands I commit you, beloved friend of my youth, farewell, and may his blessing be upon you."

On the following morning, a note was brought to Anna, which she read hastily, and then presented in silence to her friend. It ran as follows.

"Dear Anna,

"I have but a moment of time to tell you, that I still keep to my purpose of going to night; and as a proof how much I leave you to the liberty of your own choice, I propose the following plan. At eleven my carriage will be at the gate. You of course, will be at your window. If you are still generous enough to make me happy, you shall wave a white handkerchief, and I will fly to you; but should anything have occurred to alter your determination, and I see no sign, I will pass on, and the world will be to me a wilderness. "F. L."

"Thank God!" exclaimed Mary "you are not forsaken. Here is an easy escape for you. Strengthen yourself for the trial, and all will yet be well. This plan is admirable, for you will never meet again, and the temptation will be so much less." But Anna turned away from these congratulations to hide her tears; for Mary, in her uncontroulable exstacy, had hit upon the expression of all others least calculated to convey anything like pleasure to the mind of her friend. "You will never meet again."

Finding it almost impossible, for minds under the influence of such opposite feelings, to meet together through this critical day, in anything like confidence, Mary busied herself more than usual with her domestic affairs, and Anna spent nearly the whole time in the solitude of her own room. Once, or twice, Mary knocked at her door, but as Anna opened it without saying a word, she made some indifferent enquiries about ordinary concerns, and left her to the meditations of her own heart; wisely judging, that after having said all she could when the ear of friendship was open, to urge her with repeated arguments and entreaties, would only be defeating her own purpose, by strengthening the opposition of her friend.

It was a quiet day in April, but there were no showers nor any wind, and the sun shone out upon the opening flowers; the buds burst forth, and the bees were awakened from their long sleep; the birds were busy with their nests, singing as they built their summer homes; the fields were green, and the lambs, in merry troops, gambolled over the smooth lawn that lay beside the garden and orchard of Andrew Miller, who stood for a long time upon the threshold of his door, as if hesitating which he should most enjoy—the fair face of nature smiling in her loveliness without, or that which perpetually blessed his peaceful home within. You would have thought, to see that man, when he looked around him, that his cup of happiness was full, and yet, when he turned to enter, there was an expression upon his countenance that seemed to say, "I have yet more."

At the pleasant window of a chamber in that same house, a window that looked out upon the same lawn, and was lighted up by the same cheering sunshine, sat a melancholy creature, almost without life, and apparently without motion. That glorious sunshine fell upon her cheek, as upon a marble statue; that fair landscape smiled before her in vain; and those merry birds,—what was their ceaseless song to her who knew neither sound of joy, nor sight of loveliness; to whom the heavens were darkness, and the earth a desert?

The evening came, the gray, still evening; and the birds that had been busy all the day, folded their weary wings to rest. The curtain of night fell silently, and Anna was alone,—alone, in the presence of her God.

It is not difficult to cherish in our hearts an evil purpose, while engaged in the active scenes of life, and associated with beings, frail and erring as ourselves; for the bustle of business, and the dissipation of society, both tend to drown the whispers of the still, small voice. But in the solitude and silence of the night, when we are taught from our cradles to believe, and feel in our inmost souls, that an Almighty being is watching over us; that he who spangled the blue vault with an innumerable multitude of stars, and led forth the silver moon along her pathway in the heavens, and spread the silent and refreshing dews upon the earth, and hushed the winds at his bidding, is regarding with eyes of benignity and love, the creatures whom he has sent, for some wise purpose, to trace out their pilgrimage through a life of trials and temptations. Ah! it needs a heart of adamant, to look out upon a slumbering world, and up to the glorious heavens, and yet keep this evil purpose unchanged.

Anna Clare was more than commonly alive to the sweet influences of nature, and perhaps no other medium could have been found so effectual, to restore, to its proper tone, her wandering and distracted mind.

There was a sound of distant wheels.—No! it must have been the rustling leaves of the poplar, for this was not the hour;—again, it was no deception, she heard them afar off, and they came nearer and nearer, to the appointed place, and stopped. For a few moments all was silence, and then the carriage rolled on, and the sound died away upon the breeze. It was but for a few moments that her spirit had to struggle with temptation, but were they not ages in their intensity of suffering.

CHAPTER XII.

Let not those who make great sacrifices to duty, be led on by the hope of immediate reward. When a limb is severed from the human body, the first terrible stroke is not all that has to be borne; there are after seasons of pain and suffering, that must, inevitably, be endured: and when an idol of clay is broken in the dust, it requires time for humbling reflection, before its votaries can be convinced of the reality.

Mary had not entered the chamber of her friend, because she wished her to look for assistance to a higher power. She therefore retired into her own closet, and spent the dreaded time in prayer; but she too heard the carriage wheels, and knowing when they passed on, that her friend was no longer in danger, she rose up with the thankfulness of one who has experienced a merciful deliverance.

Those who would devote themselves to the service of their fellow-creatures, must be prepared for many an ungrateful return—for many a heart-rending repulse; to which, nothing but the consciousness of being about their Master's business, can reconcile the sensitive mind. Those who would save a sufferer from death, must often present an unwelcome draught to lips that loathe its bitterness; and those who would save a soul from sin, must bear with that rebellious soul in all its struggles to return; for it is not by one tremendous effort that the bonds of earthly passion can be broken. The work in which they are engaged, is a work of patience, not of triumph; and there must be long seasons of painful endurance, of watchfulness, and prayer, which nothing but a deep and devoted love to the heavenly Father, whose service they are engaged in, can possibly enable them to sustain.

When Mary entered the chamber of her friend, early on the following morning, she found her agitated, feverish, and restless.

"I am not resigned," were the first words that Anna spoke; "I wish I had gone."

"But you must be convinced, that the choice you made, was a right one."

"I can hardly say that it was my choice. I wished to go, and yet had no power to wave the handkerchief; there was something so still, so calm, all around me: and I thought of that beautiful hymn, which we learned when we were children, 'Though no man seeth thee, yet God seeth thee;' and it seemed to strengthen me for my trial."

"Then let us together offer up our thanks to Him, who stretches out his hand for the deliverance of his rebellious creatures, when they will not struggle for themselves."

"But I am not sufficiently thankful yet, Mary; perhaps the time may come when I shall bless you for what you have done."

"Oh! not me, Anna; you have nothing for which to bless me; you should only bless that Being, who gave me a heart to love, and a wish to save you."

"But I am not saved yet;—I commit no sin, because I have no temptation. I submit, because resistance is vain, but I do think, that if Frederick Langley would come back and speak one kind word to me, I would go with him at this instant."

Mary inwardly thanked God that such a trial was not likely to be repeated; and she bore with Anna's murmurings, day after day, without reproach, and even without repining; for she believed that brighter hours would come, and that her beloved friend would live to see more clearly, and to feel more calmly.

And here let us pause awhile, to enquire what is the cause, and the root of that suffering, which an inexperienced writer has attempted to describe, it may be, from her own want of mental power, with a feeble and useless pen. Is it not in the cultivation and encouragement of those feelings which are not calculated to afford either satisfaction to ourselves, or benefit to others;—in the planting in our own garden, those seeds which are only capable of ripening in a totally different soil?—in an inordinate desire after those pleasures which, however lawful in themselves, are and ought to be, unattainable to us; and a consequent looking down upon such as are set before us, with indifference or disgust? Oh! that we would teach ourselves—that some kind friend would teach us, rightly to value, and properly to use, that wisdom that is given to man, that he may profit withal;—that wisdom which compels us to believe that he who created us knows best for what situation we are most fitted, in a world where so many different degrees of moral and physical beauty are, no doubt for wise purposes, permitted to exist; and that when we are desiring what belongs not to our own sphere, and indulging in the vain thought, that in some other station we could be more virtuous, and more happy, we are in fact murmuring against the decrees of Providence and arraigning the wisdom of Almighty God.

What is the sum of misery brought upon the world by this dreadful delusion, no pen can describe. How many with wounded spirits and aching hearts, have looked back to the morning of life, when this important choice was made, betwixt contentedness with the things that are, and desire of those which might be! In thousands of instances it has been the root of that fatal malady, which is called a broken heart; and in the present, it well nigh cost the sufferer her life;—her wretched, earthly, perishable life, not that which is eternal: for in the quiet hours of a lingering illness, other thoughts arose that wore a different character. The strength of earthly passion was subdued, the clouds of earthly prejudice were swept away, before the clear dawn of undeniable truth; late, awfully late, when it first shines upon the steps that are descending to the grave,—when it first lights up the eye that is about to close for ever.

CHAPTER XIII.

When the jocund summer came, and spread her smiling flowers in the path of Andrew and Mary, Anna was not able to participate in their enjoyment. She was too feeble to take exercise, and the evening dews, to others so cool and refreshing, to her were chill, and damp, and cheerless. But she never allowed herself to complain; she never spoke of Italy, and the name of Frederick Langley never passed her lips; only, sometimes when she drew shivering to the fire, Mary could see that the tears were in her eyes, and then she knew that her spirit had flown away to distant lands.

It was but twelve short months since that proud family came into the neighbourhood. Since Anna was rich in the possession of youth, and health, and happiness; and now what a picture of melancholy did her faded form present;—of melancholy, but not of despair; for she never murmured, and sometimes her countenance would be lighted up by a smile, that showed how much she was striving against the tide of painful and contending emotions, which often seemed ready to rush in and overwhelm her reason. It was a faint and sickly smile, that told more than tears, what her heart had passed through. Like the first gleam of sunshine, on the landscape which the tempest had laid waste:—the first budding of the trees, when the whirlwind has torn their branches.

The autumn of this year was unusually mild and genial; and so gentle and imperceptible was the progress of Anna's disorder, that Mary saw no reason for alarming apprehension. It was, undoubtedly, a frail tenement to which her spirit held, but there were no symptoms of immediate danger. Much depended upon care and quiet; and here all circumstances were in her favour, for no one could have a better nurse than Mary, and no place could be more quiet than the village of L——, when the Langleys were not there to disturb it.

Day after day passed on with its little routine of domestic duties; rumour was silent, and scandal slept, for Anna Clare was ill, and poor, and those who had once envied, could now afford to pity her.

On one fine Sabbath morning in September, when Mary returned from church, she found that her friend had risen without any assistance, had dressed herself, and was seated in a high-backed arm chair, formerly occupied by her father.

"You should not have done this," said Mary; "you know it is too much for you."

"I believe now that it is too much for me, but I did not think so an hour ago. Perhaps it might be the effect of fever, but I felt capable of any thing; so much alive, that while the church bells were ringing, I fancied I could really go along with you; and now I have hardly strength to tell you how foolish I have been."

Mary begged she would take some refreshment and tell her at some other time; but it would not do, she was all animation and excitement, and could not be silent.

"Mary, I have been praying this morning that I may live till—till he returns from Italy. You will allow me to see him then, for there can be no harm in seeing him when I am so near the grave. I have thought of all that I will say, and indeed, Mary, it is not of earthly love, but of heavenly, that I shall talk to him then; and it may be, when he sees how I am changed, that he will listen to me. I will tell him of the hours we have both wasted, of the time that may yet be redeemed, and surely he will listen to me; and oh! Mary, if it be the will of heaven that I should at last be instrumental in his good, it will repay me for all that I have suffered."

Here their conversation was interrupted by the entrance of a neighbour, a young woman who was on friendly terms with both, and often came to sit with Anna, when Mary was engaged with more active occupations. The young woman took a seat, and they talked together about the affairs of the village, the Sunday School, the clergyman, and the sermon, to which they had that day listened. Mary all the while stealing anxious glances at the countenance of her friend, now more than usually animated, and beaming with a strange and radiant beauty, that was almost supernatural. On her cheek there was a glow so bright and vivid, in her eyes such clear and dazzling splendour, and upon her smooth forehead such calm and unearthly paleness, that it seemed as if, in compassion to her young spirit, the last awful struggle, the last terrible separation, had been done away, and its earthly companion had been permitted to pass into the regions of eternity, refined and pure as that spirit itself.

Mary gazed for some time, thinking little of the conversation, until suddenly attracted by the sound of a never-to-be-forgotten name.

"Speaking of the school," said the young woman, "reminds me of the Langleys. Have you heard the news? that old Sir Thomas is dead, and the young gentleman, now Sir Frederick, is coming down with his bride to take possession of his estates?"

A deadly paleness stole over the countenance of the poor invalid, and a cold shivering crept slowly over her whole frame.

Mary had time to conceal her friend from the observation of her visiter, by standing up, and arranging the pillows upon which she leaned; while her eye caught the shadow of a heavy cloud, which she pointed out, fearing it portended rain; in consequence of which the young woman took a hasty leave, and returned home.

With Anna all suffering was now suspended; and for a few moments life itself seemed to be extinct. When she again opened her eyes, she was stretched upon her own bed, and Mary was bending over her. It was some time before returning consciousness brought back the whole truth in its terrible reality: but it came at last, and, pressing the gentle hand which had been chafing her temples, earnestly and affectionately between both her own, she looked up into the face of her friend, and said, in a faint, but audible whisper, "So soon, Mary! I did not think it would have been so soon."

From this time she never spoke again of Frederick Langley, nor made the least allusion to any circumstance connected with him. She was quiet and peaceful, and resigned to die;—to die, but not to live.

It appears an easy and a pleasant thing, to the soul that is weary of the toils of mortality, to lay down the burden of the flesh, and soar away into a higher realm of purer and more ethereal existence; and thus no sooner is the future shrouded in darkness, than to die becomes the choice of the sentimentalist, in preference to a patient endurance of the ills of life.

Anna Clare had felt for a long time that she was gently and gradually passing away from the world, or rather the world was losing its importance, and even its place in her visions of futurity; and, therefore, she concluded that death must be at hand: yet, had she fondly pictured to herself one scene, before the last, and dwelt upon it with a childish intensity of interest; a scene, in which her lover should return, and beholding her altered form so wasted by sickness and sorrow, should listen to her parting prayers, and let her last admonitions sink deep into his heart. For this she had made frequent and earnest supplications, and for this she had felt willing to die; and perhaps, if the truth were fully known, she had appropriated to herself some little merit for the generosity of the sacrifice, and had been somewhat charmed by her own disinterestedness of feeling,—a disinterestedness that was sorely put to the test, when she found that he, on whom she had bestowed so much concern, had chosen for himself another companion through the pilgrimage of life; and that, if its rough passages were to be smoothed for him by a female hand, that hand must not be hers. Night and day, this humbling truth, with all its heartless and dreary accompaniments, was present to the mind, until death became no longer her choice, for to her it seemed impossible to live.

To go forth again into the wilderness, after having pined in the desert;—to set sail again upon the stormy ocean, with frail bark, and doubtful pilot, with trembling compass, and shattered mast;—to meet again the crosses, and disappointments, and vexations of life; with hopes that have been blighted in the bud, and desires that have failed, and patience that has not had its perfect work, requires more true fortitude, and resignation to the divine will, than to draw back from the brightest earthly prospects, and sink into an early grave: and yet so it was with the miserable invalid, that her disease made no progress, and she found herself, after the expiration of the winter months, not only alive, but evidently gaining strength; and painful duties, which in her weakness she had set aside as utterly impracticable, now came crowding upon her in terrible magnitude and hated reality. And then the indescribable gloom, and darkness of that little chamber, in which she first arose from her sick bed, and looked out again upon a world, which presented nothing to her perverted eye but an interminable waste of barrenness.

How little do we know ourselves! Anna Clare had imagined, that in the calmness with which she had welcomed the approach of death, there was mingled no inconsiderable share of willing submission to the will of a gracious and overruling Providence; but where was that submission now? Alas! it had only been conditional; for no sooner was the decree gone forth, that she must live, and not die, then her heart was torn with repining, and her cup of wretchedness was full.

There is nothing more selfish than melancholy; and lamentable is it to find, that the sentimental world have invested this absorbing malady with a kind of interest which makes it rather sought than shunned by vast multitudes of young ladies who, too indolent to exert themselves, hang their heads for weariness; grow sallow for want of exercise, and sigh for want of fresh air; who read novels for want of rational excitement; fall in love for want of something else to do; fancy themselves heroines because they are in fact, nothing; and drawl out to troops of confidential friends, long histories of imaginary troubles, because they know no real ones. The victims of this disease may be known by their perpetually babbling about pains and palpitations. Nerves occupy their attention when they wake, nightmare when they sleep, and self always. Their dearest friends may sicken and die, they are too languid to nurse them; a miserable population may be starving around, they are too delicate to feed them! afflictions, privations and crosses, may be sent amongst the circle in which they exist—they "have a silent sorrow," so deep-seated and overwhelming, that they can neither pity nor relieve them; and they would rather give a lecture on their own distresses, than listen to the rejoicing of a multitude. If they escape the temptation of a sinful world, to which their minds are peculiarly open, from having had raised up in them a false appetite, a craving for unwholsome food, it is but to drag on a neglected, weary, and loathed existence, and to arrive at the confines of the grave without having gathered one flower to sweeten it; and to look forward into eternity without having insured one rational ground of hope to glimmer in the gulf of darkness.

Such is the history of the last stage of the existence of many a melancholy young lady; who, while she was young, might very beautifully have hung her harp upon the willows, and the world at first might have sighed over its silent chords, and pitied the mute minstrel: but neither a silent harp, nor a mute minstrel, will long engage the sympathy of the world. We must either play for its pastime, or labour in its service. Its stirring communities extend not their patronage to any quiescent member, and if we will sit down by the way side, while our more energetic companions pass on, the inevitable consequence will be, that we shall be left behind, if not actually trampled under their feet.

CHAPTER XIV.

"Is there nothing," said Andrew Miller to his wife, one day, as they walked to the house of a neighbour; "is there nothing that can be done for this poor young woman? Do you really think, that if she could get out a little into the fresh air, it would not do her good?

Mary had so long dreaded this remark, that it was almost a relief to her when it was made; and yet she knew not what to say in behalf of her friend: for she believed in her heart that she was now capable of performing many active duties, yet she saw her every day, languid, listless, and weary of herself. It was a delicate and painful task to rouse her; as Mary was situated, peculiarly so; for it seemed almost like grudging her the indulgencies of sickness: but if she would not rouse herself, it must be done for her; for there was neither kindness or wisdom in permitting her to be so lost; and, therefore, one fine Sunday afternoon, when Anna had ventured down stairs to join the family, and had even been attracted to the door, by little Martha's exclamation about primroses and violets; Mary was glad to make use of a message from old Phebe, as an introduction to the lecture, which she intended should follow, if necessary.

"Old Phebe!" exclaimed Anna, as soon as she heard the name, "I had quite forgotten poor Phebe! Where does she live?"

"She lives in the thatched house at the end of the lane; and, I assure you, she has not forgotten you, for she often asks about you; and the last time I saw her, she desired me to tell you, as soon as you were able to walk out, that she had something to tell you which I suppose is a secret, for she wished you to go alone."

"What can it be?" said Anna, "I will certainly go to-morrow, or at any rate as soon as the weather is mild."

"We shall hardly have it milder than to day."

"Oh! but you know I have not walked for so long!"

"I would walk with you to the door. It is but a hundred yards, and the poor old woman would be so glad to see you. Besides, it may be something of consequence, for she looked very grave, and very earnest when she told me."

The tale of Mahomed and the mountain, probably did not occur to Anna at the time, or she might very reasonably have asked, why the old woman could not come to her; so after a great deal of bargaining with her curiosity, which refused to be satisfied with any thing short of payment in full, she muffled herself up, and leaning on the arm of her faithful friend, walked, to her own amazement, quite up to the cottage, without any extraordinary fatigue.

Phebe's little room had been swept and sanded. The door was set open to admit the scent of sweet-briar, and southern-wood; the kettle was humming on the fire; and she herself, with neatly pinned kerchief, and white apron, sat beside the open window, poring over the pages of her Bible; with which she was too fully occupied to observe that any one approached; but when she did look up and saw the face that was dearest to her on earth, she met that altered countenance with the welcome of a mother to her child; for she had rocked Anna Clare in her cradle, and sung her to sleep on her bosom, and knelt at the death-bed of both her parents.

"Poor thing!" said Phebe, when she had a little recovered herself, "you must have been very ill; I am sure you must; or you would have come to see me before: but more especially, you would have let me nurse you, for sometimes when trouble is nearest, kenn'd faces are dearest. That was a sad day to me, and a heavy heart I had, when I asked if I might go and be with you, and they told me, as if from yourself, that "Miss Clare would rather be alone." So I thought most likely, poor thing! she's out of her mind, and then I feared it would shortly be all over with you; though I can't say you look so bad as I expected."

At this time Anna was looking much better than she really felt; for Phebe's severe, though unintentional reproof, had called into her cheeks the burning blush of shame.

She had indeed been ill, but not for a long time so ill as to prevent her seeking the cottage of her old nurse; whose well-meant kindness she had rejected, purely from a desire to resign herself more entirely to the indulgence of her own secret and selfish sorrow.

"Aye," continued the old woman, "I knew you must be very bad, for you were never one to neglect a tried friend; but thank God, I have lived to see you out again, so we won't spend the time in talking over troubles. Sit down, and I will tell you how I am getting on, for I dare say you are anxious to know." Anna sat down, and though she could not force herself to express much anxiety, her talkative companion nevertheless went on.

"Well then, when all was sold up,—but I said I would not talk of troubles—the executors provided me with this cottage; and the next thing was to find something to do. For a long time I was, I must say, rather hardly put to it; but as soon as I heard of the family coming back to the Hall, I made bold to go and ask for the washing. And, though I did not think the lady very pleasant at first, my request was granted, no doubt, through the kindness of Sir Frederick; for he followed me out by the back gate, and asked about the family, I mean about you, and I told him you were dying of a bad illness, all owing to that cold you caught when you were away so long in the North; after which he asked me no more questions, but told me my request should be attended to, and went back into the house. The very next day who should I see coming in at my door, but Sir Frederick himself. He looked round at first, as if to be sure that no one was here; and then taking out his pocket book, unfolded several notes, and choose out a bill of fifty pounds. He then began, I thought rather awkwardly, to say that he feared Miss Clare might want many things in her illness, which the Millers could not afford; and therefore he had come to leave some money with me for her especial use, to be laid out without her knowledge,

I looked at the note, and I saw the fifty as plain as I see that book; nay I believe, I looked twice before I ventured to speak my whole mind; but I did at last; and told him, that Miss Clare would never thank any body for taking money privately for her; that she had friends in her own station of life, that would not see her want; and if they failed her, there was me; poor, and old, though I was; yet I thanked him he had put it in my power to work for her; and I knew that Miss Clare would at any time, rather have a sixpence of my earning than a hundred pounds of his. I then begged his pardon for my freedom, but I said I had lived long with your family, and I had never known any of you stoop to do a mean action; and I did think it would be mean for me to take money for those who had no right to it. Now tell me if I did wrong, for I had you in my heart all the time, and I tried to speak as you would have spoken; else, may be, I might have taken the money, for I knew you wanted it ill enough."

"Thank you, thank you," said Anna, "you did perfectly right." And the indignant flash of her eye sufficiently confirmed her words.

They then talked on other subjects, and Anna felt more cheerfu than she had done for many past months.

"You shall not go home and tell them that I would not give you a cup of tea;" said the old woman, and she rose up and bestirred herself, that her young mistress, as she always called her, might be refreshed in time to return before it was late. Anna could not refuse her hospitality, and it was wonderful with how much relish she partook of Phebe's tea, and cakes hot from her oven.

It was a clear and quiet afternoon in April; so still and cloudless, that all things seemed to acknowledge the influence of the sabbath, except the rooks, that were wheeling about over-head with as much noise as if the world depended on the building of their nest, and the rearing of their young.

"There is but one thing that troubles me," said Phebe, as they walked together down the lane, "and if I might make bold to ask you, I think it would be a comfort to me; just to come and read to me, sometimes, when you are quite well; but not before;

for I never was a scholar, though I can spell something out in the Bible, but the tracts that Mrs. Miller leaves me, I cannot puzzle them out at all. This good woman does sometimes read them to me, and says she would do it oftener, but she has no time; for it is wonderful how much she does in the village, besides attending to her family, and teaching her brothers and sisters their lessons."

"Teaching them their lessons!" exclaimed Anna, for a loud peal was now rung upon her conscience, and she seemed in one moment to awake to a full and perfect sense of her own negligence and ingratitude.

"Good night, Phebe," said she, when they parted at Andrew's door, "send for me whenever you are at liberty, and I will come and read to you."

With an unaltered manner, Anna that evening joined the family of her friend. She was, it is true, much distressed, when looking back upon her past life; and while they all knelt down in prayer together, her cheeks were bathed with tears of sincere and heartfelt penitence. But now it was an active sorrow that she felt; a sorrow that powerfully urged her to begin a new life, and redeem her lost time. In the morning, however, the difficulties attending upon the commencement of a different course, appeared much greater than they had done, with the stimulus of the evening to oppose them; and she lay awake a long time, pondering upon the possibility of performing the arduous duties which presented themselves.

Could she really go down to Mary, with a formal proposition to take upon herself the education of her brothers and sisters? It was almost impossible! For besides involving herself in a long series of disagreeable occupations, it would seem like an acknowledgement of her past culpability, and neglect; and she felt little disposition to bear the triumphant looks which she knew that Andrew would throw towards his wife, while he seemed to say, "So she has come to her senses at last."

"No, no," said she, covering up her head with the bed-clothes, "I cannot do it yet!" and then she thought of all the little Newtons one after another, their red faces, and coarse hair, their chilblains and worsted stockings, and corduroy trowsers; and she was quite sure it was impossible; so she took her breakfast once more in her own room; but the morning was fine, and she soon after arose, and opening her window, looked out into the garden, where Andrew was digging, and Mary standing beside him in earnest conversation.

"I should be very glad to do it," said the husband, as he stamped upon his spade; "but these times are so pinching, and really our expenses this year will be very considerable. Let me see: how much would a quarter's schooling be!"

"I would not ask you," said Mary, "if I had time to teach her, but you know I have as much as I can manage with our own young people."

"I wish that trouble was off your hands:" said he of the spade.

"That it might be," replied the wife, "if I would consent to let my father send them to school; but I always put him off, thinking it will be a nice thing for Anna when she recovers."

"In my opinion she never will recover," murmured the husband; and then they went to another part of the garden, leaving Anna to digest, with what appetite she might, the bitter food they had so unconsciously set before her.

After a struggle of a few moments, her decision was made, and she went down to her friend, who was already surrounded by her little flock, Mary's own words, "a nice thing for Anna," still ringing in her ears.

"I have come to help you, Mary," said the invalid.

"Thank you, thank you," replied her friend, "but you must take this chair by the fire," from which she arose, and placing before Anna the table, and the desk, left her for a while, on the plea of other engagements, kindly thinking that her first instalment into office would be more easily endured alone.

It is scarcely possible that any one should wish to know how the business of that morning was carried on. Those who have laboured in a school with a sad heart, and a weak body, know that it is an occupation which bids defiance to all the powers of description.

Many were the anxious glances turned towards Mary's stately clock that day, both by the scholars and their poor mistress. At last, in its own good time, it struck the welcome hour of twelve; and books were violently shut, and slates clattered, and bonnets with one string snatched up, and nailed shoes grated on the floor, and benches replaced, and all the noisy party took their leave; except little Martha, who, silently stealing towards Anna's chair, and looking up into her face with affectionate concern, said, "I am glad to see you better again, Miss Clare."

"Thank you, my love," said Anna, as she tried to lift the little girl upon her lap; but finding she had not yet sufficient strength, she bent down her face to Martha's rosy cheek, while her tears fell fast, and mingled with the glossy ringlets of the child.

In the afternoon the boisterous little party come again; but Mary insisted upon attending to them herself during half the day, until Anna was stronger and better able to bear the fatigue. She would very gladly give them up to her in the morning, for she had many other occupations which she could not well neglect; so soon, however, as Anna was able to bear with them all the day, she made no farther resistance, and it was astonishing how cheerful the young schoolmistress found herself when the clock struck five, and she felt that a very important, though somewhat irksome duty, had been faithfully performed.

The evenings were now growing long enough for a walk after tea, and Anna could not deny herself the luxury of walking alone, sometimes with a volume of Byron in her hand, and sometimes with the reins of imagination let loose, that fancy might roam at will over the pleasures of the past, and feast again from the forbidden tree; the inevitable consequence of which was, that she always returned from these walks with an additional cloud upon her brow, and a heavier load upon her heart.

"Are you going to walk this evening, Anna?" said her friend, one day as they were just finishing an early tea.

Anna replied that she was; and Mary then proposed that she should go with her to see a poor girl who had been dreadfully burnt, to which Anna, not being able to state her objections, reluctantly consented.

On their way, Mary told Anna the history of this poor creature, whose recent accident, indeed, formed the only incident of any interest, in her whole life; for she was a pauper from a distant parish, about the age of sixteen, who had come to exchange her services for her bread, in the family of a very small farmer in the village of L——. It was supposed, that having risen one morning early to light a fire, she had fallen asleep while blowing it; for when her shrieks had roused the family, she was found lying upon the hearth, but never was able to explain what was the real cause of the accident.

The mistress of the house, neither very kind, nor very prudent, could only shriek in concert with the girl; and the master added his bass, wondering why people need have such creatures in their houses; for she had always eaten more than she was worth; and when the doctor was sent for, he would not stir an inch towards the place before he had informed himself to what parish she belonged, and whether he was likely to obtain a full and speedy remuneration for his pains.*

"She is a great sufferer," continued Mary, "she has been laid upon her bed without the power to move, for ten weeks; and there is no prospect of her recovery. Yet no one cares whether she lives or dies, except for the trouble she is to them. She has so many frightful wounds, that she requires a great deal of support, and I do believe she is grudged by the parish every morsel that she

* A fact.

eats. And all day long, her master and mistress are quarrelling about her; the one declaring that she cannot do without some help to nurse her, and the other saying all kinds of cruel things in her hearing, about parish beggars hanging on their hands, and eating the bread out of their mouths."

By this time the two friends had reached the house. They knocked, and after waiting a long time, the door was opened by a slovenly woman, who let them in, with many complaints, that she was now never fit to be seen by any one. She then showed them into a little sleeping room, on the ground-floor, where, on a narrow bed without hangings, lay the poor orphan girl; her cheerful rosy face peeping over the bed-clothes that were none of the whitest. Her eyes were wild and bright with fever, her teeth white and prominent, while, with every appearance of hunger, she was gnawing a well-picked bone; not that she was really too scantily supplied, but the state of her body occasioned a continual craving for food.—On seeing Mary, she laid down the bone and smiled; for this was not her first visit, and she had never heard any one speak to her so kindly as Mary in her whole life.

Mary asked her a few questions, and then, determined that her friend should see for herself what real misery there was in the world, she folded down the bed clothes before she could be aware of her intention, and exposed, to her astonishment and horror, the whole of one shrivelled arm and shoulder.

"I dare say you think it looks very bad, ma'am," said the poor girl to Anna; "but dear me! I'm quite easy now. It's when they move me that I suffer most. Perhaps I don't bear it so well as I might; for they tell me I should not complain: it's they that ought to complain who have all the trouble; and a deal of trouble they have, I'm sure, though it's no fault of mine. It's ten weeks now, ma'am, since it happened; and if it was not for this good lady, I should feel the time long; but she comes every two or three days, and then it's something to think about between times, so that I get on very well, except for the dressings and the movings, as I said before."

"And you want for nothing?" asked Mary.

"Oh! no, nothing. I have every thing I can desire."

"And your mistress is kind to you?"

"She's kind in her way, ma'am; but that's very different from your way."

Mary then offered to read to her, requesting her to choose out of a number of tracts, or, if she preferred it, a chapter of the Bible. The girl chose the latter, and while Anna sat listening to Mary's gentle but untutored voice, she could not help wondering how it was that she felt so much happier that evening than when she walked out alone, or with only Byron for her companion.

"This you must allow to be a real misery," said Anna, when they left the house.

"I should indeed say it was a real misery," replied her friend, "if he who sends afflictions to try his creatures did not bountifully dispense his mercies too. I have seen this poor child often, yet have I never heard her complain. And if a countenance might be trusted, I should say that she was not only resigned, but cheerful. It is true, she is treated with what we should call cruelty, and neglect; but never having known the comfort of kindness, she does not feel the want of it. She knows that she must die; and yet I do believe this poor friendless creature is blessed upon her sick bed, with such glorious visions of a future life, as a king might wisely give his crown to purchase. Then ought not this, Anna, to be a lesson to us; and a warning to look well into ourselves, and see, when we complain and feel unhappy, whether the fault is not with our own hearts; and try, whether by some act of self-denial, the giving up of some idol, or the performance of some needful duty, accompanied always by earnest and humble prayer, we cannot remove the burden from our spirits, and look with cheerfulness and gratitude upon a world, where so much is designed and calculated to give us pleasure.

On the following day Anna recollected that she had never yet fulfilled her promise to Phebe, and, therefore, when the evening came, she took with her a tract which Mary had recommended, and went to sit an hour with her old friend, whom she found in the same room, still clean and comfortable, though she was herself busy ironing and preparing an extensive assortment of clean linen for the Hall.

Anna sat down, and though her eye sometimes caught the initials of Frederick Langley, and rested for a moment upon the elegant muslin dresses spread forth before the fire, she got through with the tract much to Phebe's admiration, and with some little interest even to herself; and when she rose up to go away, she had the satisfaction of feeling, that a kind duty had been performed to a poor and tried, and faithful servant who richly deserved it at her hands.

CHAPTER XV.

Anna Clare now began, for the first time since her illness, to think of returning to her pencil; for the mornings were bright and sunny; the family of Andrew Miller rose and breakfasted early, and her pupils never came before ten o'clock.

Her painting room, once to her the happiest spot on earth, had been scrupulously kept by Mary, unoccupied, and undisturbed; but it was a painful thing at first to enter that room, more especially to take up her pencil and her palette, and seat herself again before her easel. For when thus seated, there came back such busy crowding images; such "fragments of disjointed things," so fraught with melancholy interest, that it was almost impossible to proceed with any hope of success. Besides, what subject to choose, became a difficult question, for all were now alike to her—except those which she dared not venture to look upon; and then, who that was qualified, either to commend or to correct, would see her performance?

Oh! how we miss, in our accustomed pursuits, the eye whose watchful glance has been as a light around our feet! a light it may have been, which served only to dazzle and bewilder; but what resplendent luminary in after-life, will ever beam upon our path with a brightness like this!

Anna at last discovered amongst her drawings, a scene on one of the lakes of North America, which she fancied might be made into a painting; and this being safe ground to work upon, she set about it in a very diligent and laborious manner, although from long disuse, her right-hand seemed almost to have forgot its cunning.

With this work she was one day busily employed, about the hour of noon, when Mary announced, with some degree of embarrassment and confusion, a call from Lady Langley.

This lady was the daughter of an earl, whose interest had secured Sir Frederick a seat in Parliament; and for this reason, and this alone, some persons were daring enough to say that he had married her. The match, it is true, had been very speedily made up when they were both in Italy, and whatever the lady's merits might be, it was clear to any beholder that beauty had not been the attraction, on her part at least. She was, however, a kind, patronizing sort of woman, active, and busy about other people's affairs, having none of her own, and Sir Frederick being mostly in town. It was her pride, as well as her pleasure, to stand at the head of everything of importance transacted in the village of L—— and having heard much of the usefulness of Mrs. Miller, she had come to talk over with her the management of infant schools, and other charitable institutions, in the hope of finding this good woman a willing instrument in her hands, for the promotion of her many, and often changing plans, for ameliorating the condition of the poor. There was, besides, a lurking curiosity in her mind to see Mrs. Miller's friend, about whom she had heard some very contradictory reports. So soon, however, as this friend made her appearance, all that had been said to her disparagement vanished from the lady's recollection; for on the very first sight of Anna, she took to her amazingly, and determined to draw her out and to patronize her.

With her warmest feelings excited, she requested an introduction to Anna's painting room; and looking with every appearance of delight upon the American scene, in which the most ordinary combination of prussian blue and raw sienna, gave a very imperfect idea of the distant heavens, she turned to the fair artist, and asked if she did not feel happy in her sky.

"Oh! extremely happy," was Anna's inward response; but she had not ime to make a more audible reply, for the lady ran on with the greatest volubility, not contenting herself with generalizing about tone and colouring, but venturing fearlessly upon the sympathies and antipathies of colour; handling, foreshortening, and bringing out; until Anna, bewildered with astonishment, began to wonder whether her illustrious visiter really knew a great deal, or nothing at all, about the matter.

"Ha! you paint portraits, too!" exclaimed the lady, looking up to a likeness of William Clare, painted by his daughter. "Charming study!—What a dear old man!—quite patriarchal with his white locks! What would I not give for a portrait of Sir Frederick!" she continued, in a more emphatic and earnest tone; at the same time laying her white hand upon Anna's arm, who felt no inclination to withdraw her own, since it suffered nothing by the comparison.

"Is it possible? could I prevail with you?"

"I never paint gentlemen."

"Ah! you mean young gentlemen; you would not mind an old married man, like Sir Frederick?"

"I never go from home to paint any one."

"Indeed! that's very cruel; but perhaps, if Sir Frederick could be prevailed upon to come to you; and yet, I don't know, it is almost impossible now to catch him for two minutes."

"I believe I must decline the honour altogether."

"Why, what is the matter? Perhaps you think I should be jealous. The last thing on earth I should think of; for, between ourselves, Sir Frederick is now so much engaged with public affairs, that he cares no more for beauty than I do for business."

"Indeed!" said Anna, with well acted astonishment.

There was a looking-glass in that painting-room (ask not why!), placed in the best possible situation; and in this mirror, were at this time reflected the figures of the two ladies, in clear and striking contrast. The temptation was irresistible. One glance was all that Anna ventured; but that glance was sufficient to bring the glow of womanly triumph into her face, heightening the beauty which she would not at this moment have exchanged for a diadem; for Lady Langley was a little, hard-featured woman, with dull grey eyes, and a complexion with which all the colours of the rainbow, either singly or collectively, must eternally antipathise.

The different reflections which the telltale mirror had excited, followed each other much more rapidly than they could possibly be described; and all the while the eloquent lady went on.

"Did you ever see Sir Frederick? He is, I assure you, the best subject in the world for a picture. His hair is not so dark as yours. Why, bless me! (her eyes dilating to their utmost width) you are exactly like a picture I found soon after we married, hid behind a trunk. I did not observe it while you looked so pale, but now it's very odd, I never saw a greater likeness in my life. I remember asking Sir Frederick about that picture, and he told me some story about its being painted by an Italian artist."

"I should like to see it," said Anna, with well affected curiosity, as soon as she had recovered her self-possession.

"You shall, if I can find it; but that is hardly probable, for I believe it was put away in one of those large haunted rooms, at the top of the house, where no one dares to go alone. But I'll go myself, and send it to you. It certainly has more colour than you have now, and looks—I will not say younger, but happier. However, you shall see it yourself:" and so saying, the busy lady wished them a good morning, and hurried home.

"A good natured little woman," said Anna, as soon as she and Mary were left to themselves. "Sir Frederick had a fine taste for beauty."

"Hush, hush, Anna; take care what you say."

"Nay, I would not for the world say any thing against this good lady, who seems so graciously disposed towards her humble servant; but did you ever see any thing like her choice of colours—a bright lavender! Nay, do not look so grave, Mary, I will not say another word if I displease you; but do you know I have been solicited to paint a portrait of—Sir Frederick."

"Impossible!"

"Yes, I assure you it was so; and now, Mary, what do you say, shall I dress myself 'all in a green mantel,' as ladies do in story books,

> "And hie me to Sir Frederick's Hall,
> And to his lady's bower,
> And ask the menials great and small,
> Which is the fairer flower?"

"I think I can trust you."

"Trust me, Mary! you may indeed trust me. For all the wealth this lady possesses, and her rank, if she could bestow it upon me, I would not place myself in such a situation.

In the course of a few hours a parcel was brought to Anna, which she took into her painting room, and unfolded alone, with the door barred, her chair placed beside the fire, and her feet resting upon the fender.

It was indeed her own picture: too like herself: for it was much the worse for the time which had passed since it was painted.

"You have been ill treated too," said she, as she looked at the dusty edges, and the broken canvas, which never had been thought worthy of a frame. It was the same picture which had once been seized as a prize, and borne away in triumph, now rescued by the hand of idle curiosity, from the darkest lumber-room in the great mansion of him who had gazed upon it with eager admiration.

Anna looked at her poor slighted portrait for a long time, and then exclaimed, "Lady Langley, you have richly repaid me! When I saw you in the mirror I felt a moment's triumph; now yours is the triumph, and mine the humiliation. You are not conscious of what you have done; but I thank you from my heart;' and so saying, she laid the picture on the fire, and was quietly watching the smoke and flames curl over it in fantastic wreaths, when, suddenly recollecting that it might be enquired for, she folded it again in its cover, and never looked at it from that time; nor is there any reason to suppose that it was ever thought of again, within the proud walls of Langley Hall.

CHAPTER XVI.

When the first difficulty of returning to her wonted pursuits was over, Anna applied herself to them with as much diligence as ever; and in this manner the summer passed away cheerfully and contentedly, with all the household of Andrew Miller; but most of all, with Mary, for she saw that her friend was returning to her former, nay, to her better self; and this had long been the first wish of her faithful heart. Lady Langley called often, and really took a good deal of pains to cultivate an intimate acquaintance with "the lovely artist," as she called her; but Anna had the loud warning of experience still sounding in her ear, and in this instance there was little temptation to risk a second trial of her strength; for, added to her great repugnance to go to the Hall, or to meet Sir Frederick in any way, she felt so little interest in his lady, as sometimes to meet her civilities with coldness, almost bordering on contempt. And thus, in proportion as Anna endeavoured to turn away her eyes from the dazzling superfluities of polished life, she acquired the power of perceiving and admiring much that had before escaped her notice, in her own humble walk; and with this power came also a degree of charity and general benevolence, which made it by no means a difficult task to listen, with respectful attention, to Andrew's long stories; and perhaps Mary never was happier than when she saw her husband and her friend talking and smiling together on terms of cordial familiarity.

Music and painting were to Anna almost a necessary relaxation after the dust and the drudgery of the school-room; and often, when the clock had struck the welcome hour of twelve, she would take her guitar into the garden, and seat herself in an arbour which Andrew had made almost impervious to the weather, solely for her safety and accommodation. For years she had been in the habit of composing ballads of that humble description, which, to one chance of being thought rather pretty, risk twenty of being pronounced very poor; and now, unconscious of a listener, she amused herself with singing the following words:—

MARY LEE;

A BALLAD.

"I'd go to the world's end for thee,
Sweet Mary Lee!
I'd pluck the flowers of Araby,
And bring them home to thee!

I never loved before,
Sweet Mary Lee;
And I'll never love another
Though I break my heart for thee.

I listen to the nightingale,
Because she sings like thee;
Oh! I'd go to the world's end for thee,
Sweet Mary Lee!

Shew me the summer flower,
That has turned to the blast,
All her sweet scented leaves,
And kept them while it pass'd:
Shew me the lovely woman,
And gladly will I see,
One who has never lent her ear,
To man's perjury.

So shalt thou find a wiser
And fairer it may be;
But not a kinder maiden,
Than poor Mary Lee.

Her love it was not given,
Unsought by thee;
She hears thy voice of kindness yet,
Poor Mary Lee!

Look on her cheek so deadly pale,
And on her cloudy brow;
And ask of thy ungrateful heart,
Where is her beauty now?

Oh! it was soon to leave her
Who was so true to thee,
Who never would have served thee so,
Poor Mary Lee!

She never told to any,
What thy falsehood made her feel;
She bore her griefs in secret,
But her wounds they would not heal.

And now a lonely maiden
At evening you may see,
Wandering on the wild heath,
Poor Mary Lee!

Oh! pale is now her fair cheek,
And slender is her form,
She neither seeks the sunshine,
Nor shelters from the storm.

And hast thou quite forgotten
All she was to thee,
Hast thou not a kind thought
For Poor Mary Lee?

Thou'rt sitting in thy bright bower
With thy lovely bride;
Weaving summer garlands,
To bind her to thy side.

Weave them well, and gently,
Lest they rend away;
Oh! it is not flowers that can bind,
Nor love of yesterday.

Weave them well and fondly,
And fair let them be;
But will she ever love thee,
Like poor Mary Lee?

Anna had finished the last verse, and was just humming it over in a kind of reverie, when she was startled by the crackling of the garden fence, and two beautiful setters rushed past the entrance of the arbour; nor was this all—the shadow of a tall figure fell upon the walk—it was Sir Frederick himself! He had been out shooting; and while about Andrew Miller's fields, the sound of Anna's guitar had attracted him towards the spot where she was singing. The words he had heard before, and the air he well knew, and had often praised, when sweet sounds were not to him of such rare occurrence. He was naturally fond of music; and as Lady Langley neither played mechanically, nor, had any music in her soul, he felt the greater pleasure in hearing unexpectedly this well-remembered ditty. Indeed, for a moment he forgot every thing else; and when he leapt over the fence, it was from a sudden impulse of feeling, without any definite design, and in the same manner he addressed himself to the songstress with the familiarity of former days, saying, it was a long time since he had heard his old favorite ballad.

It is not to be supposed that Anna could, all at once, command herself sufficiently to reply; or that her countenance betrayed no outward sign of *inward* emotion; for there did at first rush into her cheeks such deep and burning crimson, as gave to her dark eyes the sparkling brilliancy of their former beauty; but she soon recovered herself, and rising up with respectful dignity, asked after the health of Lady Langley.

Sir Frederick said no more about the ballad; it was impossible to go on; both felt there was no common ground on which they could meet; every thing was too distant or too near.

Amongst the few advantages that women possess over the nobler sex, is an indescribable sort of tact, by which, in difficult circumstances, they can apply themselves with every appearance of indifference, to common pursuits, or common topics of conversation; and thus by an external show of cheerfulness, and sometimes levity of demeanour, they often veil from the eye of the superficial observer, hidden fountains of deep and impassioned feeling.

In this way Anna Clare was able to talk to her companion as they walked towards the house, of the beauty of his dogs, and the scarcity of game, of the weather, the harvest, and as many other things as she could possibly think of, before they reached the door. Here she stopped; and begging Sir Frederick would walk in, and partake of some refreshment, assured him that Mr. and Mrs. Miller were both at home, and would be most happy to offer him any thing their house afforded. But Sir Frederick declined taking advantage of their kindness, and gravely wishing her a good morning, whistled up his dogs, and walked away.

Anna rushed into the house, and finding Mary alone, threw her arms around her neck, and playfully kissing her forehead, "There," said she, "I have borne it well! For once in your life, Mary, give me one word of unqualified praise, for I have been walking in the garden with Sir Frederick Langley, and never did the sainted mother of a convent carry herself more distant, or more erect."

"Then I will say you are a good girl," replied her friend; "or rather, a wise and prudent woman."

"So wise and prudent Mary, that if you were not married, we would establish a community of holy sisters, and I would be the lady abbess."

The rigid moralist may probably be astonished that any credit should be due to Anna, for having resisted the temptation of flirting with a married man; but let us pause a moment, to consider what flirtation is.

Flirtation may be the idle frolic of an innocent girl; but it too frequently is a game deeply played by a designing and self-interested woman. It may be carried on at all ages, and by all classes of society, in all scenes, and circumstances of life: in the court, and the cottage; the crowded theatre, and the house of prayer: by the miss, and the matron; the flaunting belle, and the fanatical devotee, who casts up her clear eyes with the solemn asseveration that she knows no sin. Deformity does not preclude the possibility of its existence, nor beauty divest i of its hideous reality. Flirtation may raise or depress the snowy eye-lid, and distort the wrinkled cheek with smiles; add sweetness to the melody of song, and soften the harsh tones of discord; flutter in the ball-room in its own unblushing character, and steal under the mask of friendship upon the private peace of domestic life, like the serpent when it coils its vile and venomous folds within a bower of roses. And for what great purpose does flirtation thus work its way as a pest upon society? Its sole object is to appropriate to itself, that which it has no power of returning; too frequently robbing the faithful and devoted heart of the rich treasure of its best affections, and offering in repayment the distorted animation of a jaded countenance, the blushes of mimic modesty, the forced flashes of a faded eye, and the hollow smiles that simper on a weary lip.

Had Anna Clare been possessed with the demon of flirtation, she would have raised her eyes to those of Sir Frederick, with exactly the expression which she knew (and what woman with fine eyes does not know?) would have gone nearest to the source of long buried feeling. She would have sung that silly ballad again, perhaps with trembling and hesitation, but still she would have sung it, or have tried to sing it; and then towards the close of the performance, her eyes would have been cast down, and a tear might have stolen from beneath their long dark lashes, and her voice grown gradually more plaintive, until at last it died away in a kind of distant melody, leaving her quandam lover and herself in the most exquisite reverie imaginable; from which she would most probably, at last have started with a pretended effort at self-mastery; and then, as she rose to leave the arbour, and while Sir Frederick stooped for her guitar, she would have pointed to the blue ribbon, by which it was wont to be supported on her fair shoulder, saying, it was the same which he gave her when in Scotland, and that she cherished such memorials of past pleasure, as all that her existence had now to make it worth enduring: and then tears again, but not too many, lest her countenance should be disfigured. By this time they would have had the choice of two paths; the one leading directly to the house, and the other round by a melancholy walk, shaded with trees, and dark with evergreens. Without any appearance of design, she would have chosen this walk in preference to the other; first stooping down to gather a little sprig of forget-me-not, and placing it near her heart. The conversation might then have been led by delicate and ingenious management to former scenes, conveying the most touching allusions to sentiments and feelings, cherished in vain, and mourned over in secret bitterness of soul. And thus by the time they had reached the door of Andrew Miller, they might both have been at so high a pitch of excitement, that Anna might have forgotten her friend, her poverty, and her pupils, and Sir Frederick might have paid the same compliment to his lady. And after all this, Anna might have laid her hand upon her heart, as thousands have done on similar occasions, and said that she meant no harm.

She might, it is true, have done nothing, and said nothing, which, singly examined and considered, bore the stamp of evil; but what a farce, what a folly, is this self-exculpation; for by these secret movements from the side of virtue, of which no earthly judge can convict us, we place ourselves immediately on the side of vice; and to the early practice of this system of manœuvering, though apparently innocent, and too often pleasing in itself, how many have to look back with sorrow and regret from the gloomy close of a despised and friendless old age; it may be, from the miserable abode of folly, and wretchedness, and crime. The weight of culpability rests not upon any individual circumstance; it is the manner, it is the motive, it is the feeling by which every act and word is accompanied which constitutes the sin: and a deep and deadly sin it will be to many in the great day of account, when their secret thoughts are laid open.

Oh! that women would be faithful to themselves! It makes the heart bleed to think that these high-souled beings, who stand forth in the hour of severe and dreadful trial, armed with a magnanimity that knows no fear; with enthusiasm that has no sordid alloy; with patience that would support a martyr; with generosity that a patriot might be proud to borrow; and feeling that might shine as a wreath of beauty, over the temples of a dying saint;—it makes the heart bleed to think, that the noble virtues of woman's character should be veiled, and obscured, by the taint of weak vanity, and lost in the base love of flirtation; making herself the mockery of the multitude, instead of acting the simple and dignified part of the friend, the wife, or the mother; degrading her own nature, by flaunting in the public eye the semblance of affection, when its sweet soul is wanting;—polluting the altar of love by offering up the ashes of a wasted heart. Oh! woman, woman! thousands have been beguiled by this thy folly, but thou hast ever been the deepest sufferer?—Thine is a self-imposed and irrevocable exile from all, for which the heart of woman pines in secret; over which it broods in her best hours of tenderness and love. Talk not of domestic happiness—it can be thine no more. The plague-spot is upon thy bosom, and its health, and purity, and peace, are gone forever. Thou hast fluttered forth upon the giddy winds, like the leaf that wantons from the bough; the same uncertain blast may lay thee at the root of the parent stem, but it will only be to fade, and wither, and die. Oh! dream not of returning, when tired of idle wanderings; for thy return can only be that of the weary dove to her forsaken nest, cold, and cheerless, and desolate!

CHAPTER XVII.

For some weeks after this time, the attention of Lady Langley was too much occupied by an invalid brother, lately arrived from from Spain, where he had been wasting his time and his constitution, to allow her any leisure to think of the fair artist; who consequently, pursued her morning, and noon, and evening duties, without fear of interruption:—duties that became every day more easy, from the diligent and faithful manner in which they were performed:—

"Sweet are the uses of adversity."

And sweet is the return of the willing spirit after it has tasted the bitterness of disobedience. But Anna Clare was not yet to find her "perfect rest." Temptation was in store for her, against which she was to defend herself, without the aid and counsel of her friend.

Seated one day amongst her little flock, listening to the monotonous recitation of dry lessons, she was surprised by the following note from the hall:—

"Lady Langley begs the greatest favour upon earth of her, who alone has the power to grant it, Lord Carrisbrooke has returned, the shadow of his former self. The doctors have pronounced his case incurable,—he fails daily. In a few months, perhaps weeks, nothing will be left to me of my only brother, but——his likeness, if you consent to oblige me. I know the task will be difficult, for he is an invalid in every sense of the word. His disease is an affection of the heart, which makes him nervous and irritable in the extreme; so that, were I to engage an artist from town, it might be weeks before we could make sure of one sitting. You are on the spot, and I can send for you at the happy moment when he is most at ease. I will not insult your feelings by offering any thing of the nature of an equivalent for what no money can repay. What I ask of you, is an act of great and unmerited kindness. I think you know me well enough to believe, that I shall not be unreasonable or ungenerous; I therefore propose, in order to avoid all future difficulty on my part, and all unnecessary delicacy on yours, that you paint my brother's portrait on the same terms for which I should employ an artist from town; and believe me, that in so doing, you will confer an everlasting obligation on your friend,

"Lucy L——."

For a few moments Anna pondered upon the contents of this note; but it was a case, which to a generous mind, admitted of no hesitation, and she gave her full and free consent to wait upon her Ladyship, at any time she might appoint.

And then arose the dreadful mistrust of her own qualifications, with a horror of the nervous invalid, and the torturing anxiety which such an operation must inflict, both upon the performer and upon the patient, or rather the impatient. These however, are agonies which none but the portrait painter can imagine; for the heartless herd of lookers on, who can remark with indifference that they do not catch the likeness, after turning it into every possible direction; or who burst into peals of admiration at their own discernment, on discovering a resemblance to some face as unlike that of the sitter, as if, in attempting a greyhound, you had painted a toad, know not what whithering anguish is shooting through every bone and sinew of the poor artist, as he (or more unfortunately she) sits looking imploringly at the subject of her performance, to see whether patience has really doled out her last minute of mispent time.

They mean no harm—they know not what they do: but the emptying their coffers at the feet of the painter, would be a poor remuneration for the torture they inflict.

A few mornings after this, Anna received an early summons to appear at the Hall. With trembling knees, and throbbing heart, she entered the apartment, which had been carefully prepared by Lady Langley's orders; and then with what confidence she could command, busied herself in arranging the window-shutters, placing her easel, and making ready her own simple apparatus; while a well-stuffed invalid chair, covered with crimson damask, and a rich ottoman, standing near it, gave alarming indication of the state and dignity of its future occupant.

Having finished all her preparatory work, she was glancing from her brushes to her blank canvas, and wondering what kind of figure would fill the vacant chair, when Lady Langley hurried in, exclaiming with breathless delight, "He is coming, I declare, quite of his own accord, and in the best humour imaginable!"

Anna looked round, and saw the tall figure of a man, wrapped in a purple cloak, whose rich lining of crimson velvet was not able to impart the slightest glow of health or warmth to his countenance—a countenance that well might have puzzled Lavater, —calling forth his ecstatic smiles, and no less frequent tears.

Lord Carrisbrooke was much above the common height of ordinary men; and an unusually fine forehead, over which a profusion of raven hair, added to something of aristocratical dignity in his manner, made him look taller than he really was. His hair was slightly silvered about the temples, but so gently, that the white touches seemed only to be a part of the gloss by which its intense blackness was relieved. His eyebrows were dark and regular, and finely arched over eyes which had once been bright and beautiful; while a high and commanding nose, thin lips, and noble chin, formed the outline of the face which Anna had engaged to study, hour after hour, yet whose varying and doubtful expression seemed to set all study at defiance.

Lady Langley did her best to place her brother comfortably in his chair; and then, after bustling to and fro a few times from him to the artist, and back again from the artist to him, said something about her melons and her garden, and hurried out of the room.

With a countenance of despair, Anna watched the door as it closed after her ladyship; while Lord Carrisbrooke, as soon as he had ascertained that she was really gone, drew his cloak around him, let down his dark brows, and fixed upon his innocent companion such a look of terrific scrutiny as few women could have borne. Anna, however, suspecting it was only a trial of her self-possession, went on as well as she was able, when Lord Carrisbrooke addressed her in a hollow and constrained voice, assuring her that he was a member of the Holy Inquisition, sent over by the Spanish Government as a spy.

"I could more easily imagine your lordship one of the Knights Templars," replied Anna.

"Excellent And you shall be my Rebecca." And immediately his countenance changed to an expression infinitely more insupportable.

It was impossible to proceed. After many unsuccessful trials, Anna at last laid down her palette and her pencil, and, rising from her seat, addressed Lord Carrisbrooke with the greatest gravity and earnestness of manner.

"Since your lordship appears determined to frustrate, instead of facilitating, the performance of a task which I have undertaken as a painful duty,—a task which would not, under any circumstances, be agreeable to me, I must decline making any further attempt; and will therefore, with your lordship's permission, inform Lady Langley that the portrait is given up."

The inquisitor was completely at a loss what to make of all this; a blush, a giggle, or a simper, was what he had expected to produce. The blush, indeed, there was, and a more brilliant one he thought he had never seen; but there was no smile, nor the least approach to one; and when he saw the artist quietly preparing to take her leave, he wished her well seated again, without any compromise of his own dignity. This, however, was impossible, and he was obliged to beg her pardon for the past, and promise better for the future.

Anna was soon busily at work again; and Lord Carrisbrooke, in unbroken silence, pondered upon her strange expressions. Painful duty,—task,—anything but agreeable,—&c. "Many ladies," thought he, "would be proud to paint my likeness, and some would be happy; but this country damsel, I dare say, would rather paint her own Damon." At last he began to think aloud.

"And pray, may I ask what induces you to undertake what is avowedly so disagreeable to you?"

"Because I believe Lady Langley is unable to find any other person to do it for her; and because I am poor and want money."

Lord Carrisbrooke was puzzled again; and shocked at his own want of consideration, when he thought that he had been throwing difficulties in the way of one who was performing an unpleasant task for the sake of money, of which she appeared to be in great need; for nothing else, he imagined, could have wrung from her such a confession.

The dignity with which she at first acknowledged herself to be conferring an obligation upon Lady Langley, and then such an avowal of her station and circumstances as must at once place her in a sphere immeasurably beneath himself, was a complete mystery. But Anna had purposely done this; for she had made a strong determination, against which her pride was not able to prevail,—that she would undertake this portrait as an artist, not as a friend; and when she saw what manner of man Lord Carrisbrooke was, she felt equally determined that he should know that she was occupying a poor, and what he would consider a contemptible, situation in society. And in order to render this disclosure as little painful as possible, she made it at first, openly and boldly, and then, thought she, "there will be a barrier betwixt us which he will have no inclination to overstep, and I shall have no character to support but that of a poor artist, defending myself by a little dignity, if it should be necessary."

Lord Carrisbrooke, finding himself foiled in all his attempts to elicit anything like amusement from his companion, began to grow weary of his position; when a happy thought struck him, and he asked Anna if she were fond of music?

"Maurice, my fellow, has learned to play wonderfully well on the guitar since we were in Spain, and he has, besides, such a tolerable voice, that I often endure his music, when I can endure nothing else. If you can endure it too, he shall come and play to me, for I am growing miserably restless, and making the folds of my cloak very unclassical?"

Anna said, she should like it above all things; so Maurice was called in; and, seating himself a little behind his master, cleared his voice, and began—

"I SAW my lover mount on the war-horse in his pride,
I wish'd I was the soldier, who mounted by his side;
Light was the feather, waving from his crest,
Rich was the mantle he folded on his breast.
The summer comes again, to the bird and the bee,
But Alphonso Carnairo returns not to me!

Tell me ye wild winds, sweeping o'er the plain,
Fell he on the battle-field, with the noble slain?
Tell me thou pale moon, smiling from on high,
Where sleeps my lover, that near him I may die?
The summer comes again, to the bird and the bee,
But Alphonso Carnsiro returns not to me!

I look to the blue hills that part me from my home,
How could my young heart ever wish to roam!
Fair is the land of the olive and the vine,
But flowers may be smiling where bosoms may pine,
The summer comes again to the bird and the bee,
But Alphonso Carnairo returns not to me!"

"Enough of that ditty," interrupted Lord Carrisbrooke. "Let the poor lady seek her lover without our assistance, and think of something else."

Maurice screwed up the strings of his instrument, and began again.

"BRAID no more thy hair for me,
Fast my hours are flying;
Sunny dell, and flow'ry lea,
Spread their summer charms for thee;
Mary, I am dying!

Lay the jewell'd wreath aside;
Fast my hours are flying;
Health, and peace, and hope, and pride,
Dwell with thee, my lovely bride,
Mary, I am dying.

Soon thy lip shall smile again,
Fast my hours are flying;
Grieve not for thy lover's pain,
Sighs, and tears, alike are vain,
Mary, I am dying!

Lov'd and loveliest, fare thee well!
Fast my hours are flying;
Lonely thou wilt hear the knell,
Solemn sound of passing bell,
Mary, I am dying!"

Whilst Maurice sang this song, the features of his master relaxed into an expression of the deepest melancholy. The air was plaintive, and the words, though possessing little merit in themselves, were painfully touching to one, who felt himself so near the brink of the grave. Anna was struck with their aptness, and affected almost to tears, as she observed the change they had wrought; but still more so, when Lord Carrisbrooke, with that peculiar smile which is worn only by the wretched, said, in a playful and subdued voice, "Maurice, how dolorous you are: you'll sing me into my grave before I am ready for it."

Maurice looked up with anxiety and distress.

In their exchanging glances might be read, the trust of a long-tried and generous master; and the simple and devoted love of a faithful servant, whom nothing but death could separate from his lord; and to whom that long-dreaded separation would make the world a wilderness, through which he would thenceforth be a wanderer without a home.

Anna marked the expression, and saw, that, however harsh and rude Lord Carrisbrooke might be to her, he could be kind, and gentle, and familiar, even to a dependant, and an inferior.

Great obligations create strong attachments in generous minds. Lord Carrisbrooke was not prodigal of his affections, but Maurice had been to him in a foreign land, what no one else could be. He had nursed him through long illness, humoured his caprices, and borne with his irritable temper, when goaded almost to madness by the falsehood and ingratitude of others; and his master valued him accordingly.

Nearly a week passed away without any farther demand upon the services of the artist, and when Anna saw Lord Carrisbrooke again, there was a frightful alteration in his looks. His eye was hollow and sunken, his brow contracted with pain, and his whole countenance darkened, as with a cloud.

"I see you are horrified," said he, observing Anna's look of concern. "I have been wretchedly ill. They have bled, and blistered, and half killed me: but now I have escaped from their clutches for a while, and am, fair Angelica, very much at your service; for a Tancred, or anything else you like. So to business if you please, as the case admits of no delay. Let me see,—I may possibly hold out another month.—one sitting a week,—will that finish it?

Anna was indeed so horrified, that she had no remark to make, but went on as she was desired; while Lord Carrisbrooke remained impenetrably silent, and would have been motionless, but for the pain he was evidently enduring, which often compelled him to change his position.

"I fear your Lordship is in great suffering," said Anna, "I will paint no more today."

"No, no, I can bear it vastly well,—the worst is over for a while; I am only afraid of faintness. Give me that phial, and then, if you please, go on.

There is no time to be lost, and my lachrymose sister would cry herself into the grave, were I really to withdraw my presence from this blessed earth,

"And leave the world no copy."

Lord Carrisbrooke had scarcely done speaking, when an ashy paleness stole over his countenance, making it yet more ghastly; and in his breast there was a struggling, as if for the very breath of life. Anna flew to the bell.

"Don't ring," said he, with all the strength he could command. "Maurice is always so distressed, and Lucy had better not know; you are a stranger, and will not care. It will be over in a moment;——may I lean upon your arm?"

The arm that never refused its help to the needy, was willingly stretched out; and while he spoke the last words, the eyes of the haughty and stoical Lord Carrisbrooke were raised with the imploring helplessness of a child. It was but for a moment; and then the heavy lids were closed, and nothing but a slight working of the underjaw gave any signs of life; while Anna raised his dark hair, and bathed his pale temples, and performed all those little offices of kindness so familiar to the heart and hand of woman.

"Oh! say not woman's love is bought,"

by smiles, and flattery, and deceit. By deceit, it may be, but let him who would make sure of this prize, debase himself by the vilest of all treachery. Let him wear the mask of suffering, if he knows not the reality. Let sickness waste his frame, and sorrow set her seal upon his brow. Let poverty clench him in her iron grasp, and infamy track his footsteps; and want, and weakness, and misery, beset him in his daily path;—then, while his boon-companions fill his vacant chair with mirth, and "set the table in a roar," let him seek refuge in the tenderness, and the generosity of woman; and see whether she, who withstood his fascinations amidst the blaze of popular applause, the pride of beauty, and the pomp of power, will not be ready again, and again, to offer the cup of consolation to his ungrateful lips, while she drinks the dregs of bitterness herself.

Let the man who is merciless to the faults of his weak sister, look back to the days of his infancy, and ask whose watchful eye bent over him in his cradle, on whose bosom he wept away the first sorrows of existence; and who sung him with her gentle voice to rest? Who protected his weakness, and soothed his complainings, and turned his tears to joy? Who sat by his sick-bed and watched, but never wearied, through the night; forgetting her own existence, in the intensity of her anxiety for his? Who taught his young lips to utter the first accents of prayer? Who, when the ills of life pressed heavily, poured balm into his wounded spirit, and who at last will shed tears of sincerest sorrow upon his grave? Is it not a bright being of the sisterhood of those of old, who stole away in the darkness of the morning, to offer spices and precious ointments as a last tribute of affection to their beloved Master, after man had set his seal upon the door of the sepulchre, and left him alone to his eternal rest?

CHAPTER XVIII.

HAD Lord Carrisbrooke thought it worth his while to practise upon his young companion all the arts of fascination, of which he had once boasted himself the master, he would probably not have excited so deep a feeling of interest, as his weakness and suffering had called forth; and long did the intervening days appear to Anna before she was again summoned to her appointed task.

The next time the artist was seated at her easel, Lord Carrisbrooke felt himself so much better, as to be able to converse with ease and pleasure; and now to his wandering and delighted auditor, he poured forth the rich treasures of a mind, stored with almost every kind of information, selected with taste and judgment, from a life of constant amusement and variety; and did not hold himself above the trouble of being agreeable, even in obscurity, and to a simple country girl; for he saw that she had understanding enough to appreciate his own talents, and sensibility to feel gratified by his endeavour to please: to say nothing of the vanity of both, which formed the chain of connection between their spirits, blending all agreeable ideas and associations into one bond of sympathy.

"Are you going to a party, Anna," said Mary to her friend one day, as she watched her, altering a beautiful silk dress, to the fashion of the day.

"A party, Mary! how came you to think of such a thing? I am only making this frock more fit to paint in, for I am positively ashamed of going to the Hall the figure I have lately been."

There is a look of penetration in some eyes of dark grey, which is more insupportable to the object of their scrunity, than the flashing of more brilliant and sparkling orbs; and Mary fixed upon the face of her friend this searching expression; and Anna felt that she was looking at her, though their eyes did not meet.

It was in vain that she tried to change the current of her thoughts. She felt that she was blushing, and she felt also, that she was convicted in an act of eggregious folly. At last, when she could bear it no longer, she laid down her work, and exclaimed,

"Mary, you are too deep for me. You have discovered what I was trying to conceal from myself; that I have really been taking all this pains, to make myself look more pleasing and more ladylike, in the eyes of a man, who is shuddering on the brink of the grave. I thank you from my heart, Mary, for your well-timed and gentle warning. You see I am again beset with temptation. It is a hard lesson that I have to learn; for no sooner is one branch of vanity cut off, than it puts forth another; but if He will give me help, to whom alone belongs the glory of victory, I will be worthy of your friendship yet, Mary." And with this laudable resolution, Anna went to her own room, and after locking up her silk dress, cast a farewell glance at the mirror, before she went to her morning's occupation. It was only intended for one glance, but the wind had been busy with her raven hair; and sorry we are to say, that Anna looked again and again; for there were ringlets to arrange, and a pink handkerchief to adjust, so as to give a glow to her faded complexion.

Lord Carrisbrooke had again sunk into his usual state of brooding melancholy, probably from an increase of his bodily infirmities, bringing, as they not unfrequently do, an increased longing to retain a life, of which those who cling to it with the greatest pertinacity, often profess to be the most weary; and he might besides have his own private reasons for dreading his impending doom.

Anna saw at one glance that he was worse; and though she made no remark, yet she found many excuses for altering the folds of his cloak, that she might at the same time place his cushions more comfortably, offer him refreshments, or soothe him, with kind words; never so touching as when whispered near to the ear, in the sweet tones of womanly tenderness.

There was something in the situation of Lord Carrisbrooke deeply and painfully affecting to a sensitive mind; and it afforded him no small degree of gratification, to find that Anna was affected by it.

He had wandered through the world as a stranger, extracting from society every thing but what he most wanted;—the communion of a kindred soul—the pure and devoted affection of a guileless and unsophisticated heart. In vain he had tried to make any lasting impression upon the feelings of woman, as he had found her, in the magic circle of fashion, glittering in deceitful charms, and decked in false smiles; and often had he exclaimed, after returning to his own chamber, "My poor Maurice loves me better than any of them."

His sister, it is true, regarded him with what some would call passionate fondness; and he knew, that when the hour of parting should draw near, she would be overwhelmed with anguish, and drowned in tears; but he knew also, that her light step would skip over the church-yard before his grave was green.

And yet, what bond of union could possibly exist between the haughty Lord Carrisbrooke, and the humble Anna Clare? He, surrounded by luxury and wealth, yet suspended but for a few brief moments above the gloomy grave; and she, a simple country maiden, apparently pursuing her homely path with patient steps. Yes, there was a bond betwixt them. The bond of sympathy, felt and acknowledged by both. Sympathy of taste, and thought, and feeling; sympathy of high purpose, and noble sentiment; sympathy, which no difference of rank or station can subdue; sympathy in the inward yearnings of the spirit, which struggled in vain to support its own existence; clinging in its weakness to the veriest reeds of earth, and rejecting again and again, the offer of that hand which alone is mighty to save.

It was in the cheerful month of June, that the noble invalid and the young artist, sat together at an open window, during the quiet morning hours, before the Hall was disturbed by visiters, and while the dew was yet upon the grass. For now they often found both time and inclination to converse, and Lord Carrisbrooke cast his melancholy eyes around upon the clear landscape, the blue hills, the shining river, the green slopes, and the deep shadows of the trees; but neither the fair landscape, nor the scent of summer flowers, the hum of bees, nor the song of merry birds, brought gladness to his soul, for he was losing his firm step upon the joyous earth, and looking almost his last upon the smiling flowers, and listening to the jocund birds, that would soon be winging their happy flight above his grave.

"You will be here," said he, as if continuing the mournful train of his reflections, "You will be here when summer comes again, and—I,—" He paused and looked earnestly at Anna. Words were upon her lips which might have been applicable in such an hour, but she dared not utter them. How did her spirit yearn to answer, "And you will be in heaven!" All that woman can say, with eyes that shine through tears, was written in her countenance; but she made no audible reply, and her companion went on quoting the words of Antony,

"I am dying, Egypt, dying.'

"A fatal malady is preying upon my heart, yet I brave it out to the world, and none, but my faithful Maurice, knows that I endure any other than bodily suffering; even he knows not the cause, but to you I will confess, that when I think of launching forth upon the boundless ocean of eternity, I feel like a fearful child, about to enter upon a region of impenetrable darkness.

"In my ride the other day, I saw a poor woman sitting at the door of her cottage, reading her Bible; and oh! how I envied that humble creature, feasting upon what, to her, were the words of eternal truth."

"The same book," said Anna, "is open to all; and it is the perfection of that volume, that its sacred truths are equally applicable, its moral precepts equally serviceable, and its religious consolations equally available, to the high and the low, the rich and the poor the happy and the miserable."

Lord Carrisbrooke shook his head. "My mother forced me when a child to learn long lessons from the Bible, as a punishment when I did wrong; and I have never been able to read it since."

"If you would but try, my Lord," said Anna.

"Will you read it to me?" replied his Lordship. And then he smiled as dying men have no right to smile.

"I would do anything," said Anna, in her own guileless manner, "to make you less melancholy, less desponding; and I would suffer anything, were it possible for me to be instrumental in raising your thoughts to a participation in those hopes, which alone are able to support the soul in its hour of mortal trial."

"How is this?" said Lord Carrisbrooke, and while he spoke and looked earnestly at Anna, tears, burning tears, were in his eyes; and he stretched forth his thin and wasted hand, and grasped her arm with something of unearthly energy. "My course through this world has been short and eccentric; winning the wonder of the many, and the love of the few. Had I not dived beneath the shallow surface of profession, my sated vanity might have revelled in fruition; yet have I never known from my cradle until this hour one friend who cared about my soul."

"Your Lordship has been very unfortunate! Amongst the first of earthly blessings which heaven bestowed upon me, was a faithful friend; a friend whose counsel and kindness have been as a light upon my path."

"And will you be this friend to me?"

"Impossible, my lord!"

"Why impossible?"

"Because you are a man, noble, and wealthy, and accomplished; and I am a woman, young, and poor, and unprotected."

"And for these qualities I love you better; and surely for those, you cannot respect me the less!"

"My lord, that very weakness which excites your tenderness, and that dignity which awes me into respect, are incompatible with the fair and equalizing nature of friendship."

"Then call it love, if you will. It matters little what name is given to an intimacy like ours, to be dissolved in a few brief moments; but oh! do not leave me to myself. Come often; sit with me till you are weary; and, above all things, tell me how to make death less horrible. Ah! you are going again, going to gather roses, and sit within your sunny bower, and listen to the birds that warble overhead, and feel the breath of summer fan your blooming cheek, and think not of the weary hours that I am spending. Indeed why should you? I am nothing to you, I can be nothing, and have no right to trouble you with my fruitless complainings."

Anna held out one hand, while with the other she concealed her face; and wishing the miserable invalid a good morning, went her way to muse upon the various branches and bearings of the word "interesting;" a word so important in the vocabulary of the sentimentalist, that it appears to possess the talismanic property of discovering whatever is worthy of consideration either in nature or art.

"How interesting!" exclaims the enthusiast, and immediately her beau ideal is clothed in a mantle of imaginary beauty. Within may be an empty void, it matters not. Vanity or vice may lurk below, they are alike unheeded. Misery and disappointment may lie shrouded beneath, they are endured with the patience of a martyr. And why? Because the object is interesting, and consequently it becomes an idol.

Again—When anything earthly, or unearthly, has received the fatal condemnation of being pronounced uninteresting, how utterly hopeless and vain is every attempt to force it upon the attention of those, who have been accustomed to look only through the false medium of sickly sentiment. Unheeded, unnoticed, by them, uninteresting philosophy may labour in secret over the investigation of truth, uninteresting charity may go forth upon her errands of mercy, uninteresting resignation may watch beside the lowly bed of sickness, and offer up from unfeigned lips her last soul-felt prayer; and what to them is the incense of uninteresting piety, though it should burn upon the altar of the heart, consuming all that is gross and perishable, and purifying the immortal spirit for a new existence in the regions of eternal light.

CHAPTER XIX.

THE ambition of doing good, is often the last effort of expiring vanity in an amiable mind, and the resolution to do good is unquestionably laudable in the abstract; but with this excellent resolution there are not unfrequently certain accompaniments, such as these; I shall make myself valuable, I shall be more beloved, my name will be exalted among the people; and mournful it is to observe, that the mind of woman is peculiarly liable to fall away from its high purpose, into these snares and pitfalls, which are so placed along the christian's path, that there is no footing to be found upon the pilgrimage of life, without its own temptations, and besetments.

Possessed with these aspiring hopes, Anna Clare retired to her own chamber; and while she turned over various volumes, and referred to different texts of scripture, which she conceived might aid her purpose, there not unfrequently flitted across her mind the encouraging assurance, that "he who converteth a sinner from the error of his ways, shall save a soul from death, and hide a multitude of sins."

Having fixed at last upon the conversion of Count Struensee, Anna hastened early to the Hall on the following morning, with hope in her countenance, and triumph n her heart.

"You must read it to me," said Lord Carrisbrooke, "for there is something in your voice that charms away my evil genius."

So Anna opened her little volume, and sat down, and thought she had never been so well employed in her whole life; but, in spite of all her sanguine expectations, she could not help perceiving, that the thoughts of her noble auditor went not along with her, at least with her book, and that his eye never rested upon anything but her face, and when she closed the book as an experiment to try whether his attention was really fixed, he made no remark upon it but seizing the white hand by which it was held out to him, pressed it to his lips, with every expression of gratitude and admiration.

"It will not do," said Anna, as she walked home that morning: and when she met the calm countenance of her friend, she was more than ever convinced that she had been wrong; her pupils too were rejoicing in their prolonged holiday, and she herself was returning weary and dispirited, and not a little disposed to be dissatisfied with all around her.

"This picture takes you a long time to paint," said Mary: and Anna who was so conscious that it might have been completed in half the time, felt a reproof in the remark which it was not intended to convey. "I can finish it at one more sitting," was her consolation as she went to rest that night; and she did finish it, and was more than ever concinced on the following morning, that the work of reformation was at an end, at least that its triumphs were not for her; that Lord Carrisbrooke had been amusing himself, and gratifying his own vanity by the interest he had excited in her mind; and that in order to give this interest a deeper character, he had expressed all, and perhaps something more, than he really thought, and felt, at the prospect of the awful doom that was impending.

Oh! woman, in thy mysterious and often eventful life, thou hast many a hard lesson of humility to learn; and, perhaps, none can be more painfully instructive, than that which teaches thee, that in thy noble and generous desire to serve thy fellow creatures, thou has been aspiring too high. Learn, then, from the experience and the warning of others, learn while thy young heart is yet unscathed by disappointment, that thy sphere of merit is a lowly one; and above all things, go not forth upon the mighty ocean, in the presumptuous hope, that thou shall be able to pilot the stately vessel into port; let the heavy prow heave on upon the billows of destruction; thy feeble help cannot avail; thou canst only be drawn within the vortex, engulphed, and lost for ever. Thy little bark is made to float amongst the shoals and shallows of the shore, to warn the ignorant of danger, to gather up the wreck, to save the perishing, and to comfort the forlorn.

The last meeting between Lord Carrisbrooke and Anna was a painful one, through which nothing could have supported her, but the fruits of a sorrowful experience, and a heightened sense of duty.

"It is better, much better;" said she, as she walked home that morning; and yet tears were every instant starting in her eyes, and sometimes there seemed to be whispered in her ear, as if by a rebellious and unsubdued spirit, "I was but seeking to cheer the last moments of a dying man."

Unable to enter into the affairs of Mary's household, she retired to her own chamber; and here, upon reflection, she was confirmed in her belief that the path she had chosen was a wise and prudent one. The words, "touch not, handle not," were continually recurring to her mind. "These things are not for thee." Will he repent at thy bidding; who has lived to the mature age of manhood, in the habitual contempt of religion, and forgetfulness of his Creator? Will he be subdued by thy charming, whose heart is as the flinty rock! Or will thy reasoning convince him, who has exhausted the powers of an acute and penetrating mind, without having discovered the immutable excellence of eternal truth? "Touch not, handle not," but go thou into thy secret chamber, and when no eye seeth thee, offer up thy earnest prayers, that he who knoweth the path of the eagle in the heavens, will turn away the wanderer from the error of his ways: and, seek not thou to be the instrument. Look out upon the sufferings of thy fellow creatures; diligently watch the opportunity of fulfilling every duty; search the recesses of thy own soul, and see whether thy appointed task be not sufficient, without aspiring higher.

It was some weeks after this time, at the solemn close of a sabbath evening, that Anna Clare sat alone and silent at the window of her own chamber. The golden tints of the setting sun were fading away; the hum of the village was subsiding; the shepherd was folding in his sheep; the silvery dew was falling; and one pale planet shone out from the clear and distant heavens.

How strange that, upon such a scene, the principal of evil should dare intrude! Alas! for our heroine! she looked not forth with joy and thankfulness, but tears were stream ing from her eyes, and she was repining, that amidst so much peace and loveliness, her path must be alone; whether amongst flowers, or thorns. The beauty of the flowers and the anguish of the thorns, must be enjoyed, and endured alone.

Where now was her lately acquired submission, her patience, and resignation? Selfishness and vanity, had again been contending for the empire of her heart, and she was reaping the bitter fruit of their destructive warfare. For a short time her former self returned, to pine, and suffer; and when she thought of the mysterious and highly gifted character, in whose feelings she was just beginning to hold a share, when stern duty warned her to withdraw, it seemed to her, that she alone, of all mortal creatures, was singled out to resign whatever was most intimately connected with her heart of hearts.

At last, her murmuring thoughts found utterance in words.

"Every thing on earth has its little sphere of enjoyment, in which it can meet and participate with others. Coarse spirits have their social intercourse. Friend meets friend, around the humble hearth. In all the affairs of human life,—in commerce as well as religion, multitudes congregate together, and pursue in concert the great end of their existence. The very brutes—the flocks that feed upon yon sloping hill, enjoy the refreshing dews of night together. The birds have their companions in the woods, to whom they can utter a response. All the sweet flowers of night and day, have their appointed time for looking up in unison to heaven. The stars have their own bright family, shining through the blue expanse. Every intelligence in nature has its kindred essence; but I have nothing!"

Anna's complaining ceased, and she was looking out again, when the solemn sound of a passing-bell fell upon her ear—she shuddered and turned within. In the twilight she could just perceive that some one approached. It was Mary, who came with the tidings that Lord Carrisbrooke was dead. In an instant, Anna was restored to her better self. That sudden and awful sound, and the unexpected appearance of her, who had so often stood beside her as a guardian angel, bringing a silent reproof, where none was spoken; the stillness of the hour, and the recollections of the past, all mingling together, might have overpowered a spirit more hardened and perverse than Anna's.

"Mary," said she, laying her hand upon the arm of her friend, "there is one duty which we have never, since the days of our infancy, performed together, except in public. Let us kneel down in this quiet chamber, and enter into a fresh covenant with our Heavenly Father, that we will drink of the cup which he has poured out for us, even though it should be gall and bitterness. That we will walk in the path which he has pointed out, though it should pierce our feet with thorns; and that we will never turn away, nor be unfaithful to his service, though we know that it requires us to give up all and follow him," And then, from her eloquent lips, and overflowing heart, she poured forth her gratitude and praise to that Being who had thus far conducted her through the wilderness; who had borne with her spiritual idolatries, who had given her a friend as a faithful guide, and whom she now implored to look down from his habitation in the heavens, upon the weakest worm of his creation.

Bound by fresh ties of more than earthly union, the two friends had knelt together; together they rose, and the embrace with which they separated that night was warm and pure, as in the days of their first love.

Her feeble steps recalled from their slight wandering, her good resolutions confirmed after their short lapse, Anna Clare went onward in the path of duty; for she had learned to mistrust herself, and consequently to shun temptation. And having found how incompatible with true happiness is the gratification of vanity or ambition, she confined her hopes and wishes, and even her laudable desire to be of use, within the humble sphere in which her lot was cast.

On the reading of Lord Carrisbrooke's will, it was discovered that he had bequeathed the sum of one thousand pounds to the artist who painted his portrait: and with this sum added to the well earned reward of her daily labours, Anna contrived not only to maintain a respectable and genteel appearance, but often to comfort the distressed, and supply the wants of the needy.

Gentle reader, forgive the writer of this story, that she has no better fate in store for her heroine, even in the season of "the first grey hair," than that of a respected and respectable old maid; not a fretful, fuming thing, of false ringlets, and false smiles, but a woman of delicate and tender feeling, of calm dignity, and unbounded benevolence, who mourned no longer that earth afforded her no object, or rather no idol, on which she might lavish the warm feelings of an affectionate heart; for she had learned to pour forth into a thousand channels, "that charity which suffereth long and is kind."

Alas! to the rescue of Anna Clare, from the shades of vulgar oblivion, there came no belted knight, no steel-clad warrior; no prince in disguise discovered her to be the alien daughter of his house; nor did a superannuated nabob make her the heiress of an Indian fortune; but she continued to dwell in the home of her friend,

"Happy and giving happiness;"

and though highly gifted with those qualities, which might reasonably attract the attention of the wealthy and the noble, she never ventured beyond her own lowly sphere, but was content to remain, where she had not only the wish, but the power to bless. That enthusiasm which had given wayward wings to her inexperienced fancy, became tempered by religion, into energy and hope; energy, that shrank not from the humblest, as well as the most arduous duties; and hope that burned brighter and brighter, to the close of a useful and well spent life. Nor were the tastes and the enjoyments of her early years extinguished, but properly directed and restrained; for Anna Clare could still wander forth on dewy evenings, even when her cheek had lost its bloom; but her wanderings now more frequently terminated in errands of kindness to her humble friends, and though she could still look around her with delight on the charms of nature, the world was no longer a mere picture, admired only for the harmony of its colouring, and the grouping of its different objects; but for the harmony of its creation and government, and the mysterious and admirable adjustment of its different parts, beneath the wonder-working hand of the great Artificer. And she could still pause to look at the village spire, but it was not merely to observe how beautifully it arose from the masses of dark foliage, and pierced the azure sky; it was to meditate upon the privileges of living in a christian land, where the people of Christ may rest under the banner of his love, to hear his divine precepts, and to offer up their prayers together; and if there still were times when she was rapt in admiration at the splendour of the setting sun, it was with a hallowed feeling of thankfulness for that resplendent sign of daily assurance, that he who holds our being in his hands, departs not from his own wise and merciful design, in which the "heavens declare the glory of God, and the firmament showeth his handy work."

ELLEN ESKDALE.

Gone from her cheek, is the summer bloom,
And her breath has lost its faint perfume,
And the gloss has dropp'd from her golden hair,
And her cheek is pale but no longer fair.

And the spirit that sate on her soft blue eye,
Is struck with cold mortality;
And the smile that play'd on her lip has fled,
And every charm hath now left the dead.

Like slaves they obey'd her in height of power,
But left her all in her wintry hour;
And the crowds that swore for her love to die,
Shrunk from the tone of her last faint sigh,
And this is man's fidelity!

Barry Cornwall.

CHAPTER I.

Will my young friends forgive me, if, under the character of a fictitious story, I should in reality preach them a sermon; and that on the gravest of all possible subjects—on the subject of death?

We learn, from an immense number of the publications of the present day, how the righteous pass away from works to rewards; and, from the public papers, how the murderer and the malefactor expire on the scaffold; but there is an extent of intermediate space filled up by those of whose fate we know comparatively nothing; those who act, unheeded, their little part upon the stage of life, then die, and are forgotten.

It is from this class of beings that I have selected the individual who is to furnish to the attentive reader food for serious reflection during the perusal of a few dull pages, in order that we may lift the veil by which the moral secrets of the fashionable and well bred may be concealed from vulgar observation, and see for once how an amiable and very beautiful young lady may die.

There lived in a certain large city, a family of the name of Eskdale, consisting of a highly respectable gentleman, his lady, and three daughters. To describe them individually would be a waste of words and patience, they were so much like half the people one meets and visits with. One thing, however, ought to be remarked about this family, though by no means peculiar to them, that, while living in a populous city, where the loud death bell was often heard to toll, and where as often a solemn funeral was seen to pass along the streets; yet, for themselves, they never thought of death. It is true they had been made acquainted with some instances of fatality within their own sphere of observation; for once their white muslin dresses came home from the washerwoman's uncrimped, because, as she said, her youngest daughter then lay a corpse in the house; and their old footman Thomas Bell, died in the workhouse the day before the five shillings which they sent him reached his necessities. And, in high life, too, had they not known it? Had they not all worn fashionable mourning for their most revered monarch, King George the Third? And had they not lost a maiden aunt? And were not the fountains of their grief staid by a legacy of six thousand pounds? Yes,—they remembered all these things, and yet they looked upon death only as a frightful and far-off monster, who might never come to them; so they lighted up their drawing-room, and let down the rich damask curtains, and drew in the card-tables, and never thought of death. Perhaps one reason might be, they had never known sickness. It is true the mother sometimes presented, at the breakfast-table, a countenance pale and cloudy as a morning in November, but the evening party always found he adorned with ready smiles, and new made blushes:—smiles that betrayed no meaning, and blushes that told no tale but one.

Ellen Eskdale, the youngest of the three fair sisters, was at this time, making her first appearance in the fashionable world. She had grown prodigiously during her last year at school, and now, though a little in danger of becoming too stout, was as lovely a young creature, both in form and face, as you could well behold.

"A little in danger of growing too stout," has a very serious sound to a young lady, and yet it was much whispered among Ellen's friends, that in a few years she would be monstrous. The gentlemen thought otherwise, and swore it was all envy, for they could not see a fault in Ellen Eskdale, and perhaps she did not see many in herself; for she had ears to hear all that love and flattery could offer, and eyes to see, when gazing in the tall mirror, that love had hardly been too partial, or flattery too profuse. Though trained, and pushed, and bribed forward, in all the accomplishments of the age, Ellen's chief excellence was in music; and never did she look more beautiful than when her light and ivory fingers touched the harp; for then a rich mass of sunny hair fell over her cheek and forehead, often thrown back with girlish carelessness, when she forgot herself in any of her favourite airs. She had been well taught, and her parents had paid dearly for the loss of a fine girl, and the substitution of a fine lady; but yet she was not wholly refined from the dross of nature; for her wild and merry laugh was sometimes heard resounding through the rooms, to the dismay of her mother, and the astonishment of her guests; as the bird that has been taught to sing in measured notes, will sometimes return to his own sweet melody, telling of woods, and streams and mountains, and breathing forth the inward yearnings of that spirit, which it is impossible for art to subdue.

CHAPTER II

Could the bright eye, the blooming cheek, or the polished forehead—could all, or any of the attributes of beauty, support us in the hour of trial, or cheer us on the bed of sickness, they would then be worth cherishing, and mourning for; but there must be something else, my young friends, to render the pilgrimage of life a path of pleasantness and peace. Rich as you may be, the grave has closed over the possessor of greater wealth than yours. Fair as you may be, the worm has fed upon a cheek as lovely. Young as you may be, death has laid his icy hand upon those who have not numbered half your years. But, as this is not the style of preaching which I have the talent, or you the patience to pursue, we will, if you please, return again to the family of the Eskdales; not as they first beheld them, but after a summer had passed away; and the assemblies, the concerts, the plays, and the parties of another winter had commenced.

Ellen was still the centre of attraction, and still she was not wholly sophisticated, but would sometimes look, and speak, as if at the bottom of her heart there were left some latent feeling, that struggled to be free from the yoke of fashion—that rose in fruitless efforts to assert itself no longer the slave, but the minister of pleasure.

These ebullitions of feeling, however, came like angel visits; and when they did come, they were so faint, so ill-defined, and generally so mixed up with various and contending emotions, that no one knew from whence they flowed. whether from heaven, or earth; no—not even the fair possessor herself; only the ladies wondered at those times how so young a girl could venture to talk sentiment; still more how she could make it answer, when they had so long talked it in vain; and, at the same time, the gentlemen would begin to doubt whether they might not do worse than make serious proposals to Ellen Eskdale.

Miss Eskdale, the oldest sister, had been striving for the last five years, to attain that footing in society, which had been awarded to Ellen, apparently without any effort of her own. In loveliness, her own face would not stand the test of a comparison with her sister's; and in accomplishments she was far behind her; so taking to herself another standing, or rather, hanging her orb in another sphere, she determined that their rays should never intercept each other, and having failed to be a beauty, Miss Eskdale became a blue; and corresponded with (at least wrote to) great authors, and patronized poor ones, and held in her charmed possession the first manuscript copies of half the bright effusions that annually come forth, to delight or disappoint the expectant winter circle.

Of the second sister it could not well be said that she had ever been guilty of any aim at all, and, therefore, feeling no loss in her sister's gain, she would often kindly, and almost affectionately, fall in with her wild fancies, when Ellen's exuberance of spirits exacted from others a somewhat unreasonable submission to her own whims and follies; for Ellen was not merely a beauty, she possessed a ready invention, and versatility of talent, which, added to her natural good humour, and buoyancy of mind, gave an air of freshness and originality to whatever she said or did. Her path was not the beaten track of custom; she delighted in eccentricities, and charmed her mother's guests by a thousand schemes for their entertainment, which they had never heard of before; taking this precaution, in every thing she introduced, that her own should be a brilliant and striking part. In case of a failure, she never sat down with an air of despondency, but immediately took up some other plan to cover her defeat, so that the company were sure to go away well satisfied at last.

In this manner the gay evening parties came and went; and who was happier than Ellen Eskdale?

Of all the young gentlemen who flocked to her father's house, there was none more constant in his visits, more attractive in his person, or more pointed in attentions, than Harry Wentworth, a young man of enviable fortune, just whiling away the winter months, before commencing his travels on the Continent.

It was, for a long time, matter of doubt with the two elder sisters, which of the three could possibly be the object of attraction, but the whole secret had been revealed to Ellen during a long moonlight walk by the side of the river, late in the autumn, when a party of pleasure had been formed to visit the ruins of a castle, situated some miles up the stream. Ellen had always been afraid of water, and Wentworth was happy to be her escort on the shore. The dew was falling heavily, the grass was thick and long, and Ellen found a more dangerous enemy than she had feared; for she dated from this night the commencement of a quick and frequent cough, which was at times, exceedingly troublesome. But it was surprising how little she thought or cared about the cough; for, on this night, her lover had declared himself, and though she had insisted that nothing should be said on the subject, as she was quite too young to think seriously of such a thing, she had kindly promised that she would try to think of it; and there is every reason to believe that it did really occur to her thoughts almost as often as her lover himself could desire. There was such unspeakable satisfaction in knowing that the very man, whom her sisters were trying every art to fascinate, was secretly and surely devoted to her. He was so handsome too—so gay—so fearless—so playful in his disposition—and in every thing so much like herself—Oh! it was worth all the world to hear the whispers of Harry Wentworth, when he tried amongst the crowd, to catch her attention for a moment, while she would pass on with affected carelessness, not unfrequently returning to assure herself of the reality.

THE SPIRIT OF JOY.

Daughter of sor w, weeping and sad,
Cast the dark weeds from thy brow;
Come with the spirit of joy and be glad,
Come from the fountains of woe.

I'll bear thee away on a sunbeam so bright
I'll deck thee with flowers so gay,
I'll bathe thee in oceans of liquid ligh
And chase all thy tears away.

For I come from the mountain, the heath, and the dell,
I come with the hunter's wild horn,
I have bid the grim deserts of darkness farewell,
And I dance on the clouds of the morn

I live in the sunshine of summer's bright hours,
I sport on the butterfly's wing,
All mine are the treasures of April's glad showers,
And mine the rich odours of spring.

I spurn at the temple, the tower, and the dome,
I laugh at the labours of man;
Far, far, in the blue sunny sky is my home,
And my realm is the rainbow's wide span!

These words, with an exquisite accompaniment, Ellen had been singing to a crowded audience, with so much spirit and animation, that she seemed herself to personify the ideal being of whom she sung. Before her light fingers touched the harp, she had cleared her white forehead and sparkling eyes from the shadow of rich curls that veiled, without concealing, her beauty: and now the colour of her cheek was deepened by a blush of varying emotions, in which were mingled and combined some of the most powerful feelings that are wont to agitate the breast of woman; the shame of attracting every eye, the triumph of conscious power, and, mightest and most prevailing, the wild fervour of the enthusiast.

It was a habit some people said, a trick of Ellen's, as soon as her performance was ended, to divert the earnest attention of the company by some playful sally, quite irrelevant to the subject, or else to escape at once into obscurity; and, on this occasion, as on many former ones, she succeeded in finding a vacant seat beside Harry Wentworth, who seldom joined the herd of admirers, to worship the star of the multitude, but delighted to see that star direct its partial rays to him.

CHAPTER III.

"What is all this harangue about?" said she to her lover, after they had listened, for a few moments, to a little party of grave personages, gathered round Miss Eskdale.

"Your sister," replied he, "is edifying her friends on the subject of suicide; she is telling them the nature of different poisons, and what is the readiest mode of quitting the world."

"Oh! that does not concern me," said Ellen, "for I shall never be tired of living; shall you, Harry?"

"Not if you will promise to live with me."

"Now, tell me the truth for once," said she, looking up into his face,—"the truth, and nothing but the truth; for, mind you, I have a charm by which I know a falsehood, and you have told me a great many of late; tell me then, truly, whether you could live without me?"

Wentworth paused for a moment, and then coolly answered—"I think I could."

Ellen had been gazing on his face with the sweet confidence of a child, and, perhaps it was the steady look of her clear and cloudless eyes which, somehow or other, had impelled him, almost unconsciously, to speak what she had demanded, the whole truth; which he did at once, boldly, and thought no more about it; but, had he been a nice observer of woman's character, he would have seen that the ready smile of expectation had passed away from Ellen's lips,—

that the blush had faded from her cheek,—and that though she instantly took up a new print, and began to expatiate upon its beauties with rapturous enthusiasm, she bent down her head lower than was necessary, that her thick falling ringlets might conceal her altered countenance, while she wiped from her eye the first tear that Harry Wentworth had ever made her shed.

It might be that he did not know the degree of feeling of which Ellen was capable; or that, in his own heart there was no such deep and hidden fountain; for he never dreamed that he had given pain, and would almost rather have wept himself, than that eyes so beautiful should have been dimmed with tears. It was, however, but a light and passing cloud, and those eyes again beamed forth in all their wonted brightness; music and dancing drowned the evening in noise and confusion, and all was sunshine and glad summer beneath the roof of Mr. Eskdale, in spite of the wintry blasts that howled without.

"What can be the matter with Ellen Eskdale?" said a lady to her companion, one evening, as they returned home from the play?"

"Oh, in love, to be sure," was the reply; for her companion was a gentleman.

"She need not pine away for that," said the lady, "for Wentworth seems as much in love as she does. She must be ill; that cold of hers lasts so long. Did you not observe, the other day, at Mrs. Beverley's, how she leaned upon the harp, and how dreadfully worn-out she looked after the first dance?"

"As for the leaning upon the harp," replied he of the charitable sex, "it was to show off her figure; and young ladies always look languid, when they can, to excite interest."

"Well, continued the lady, these beauties never last. I wish poor Mrs. Eskdale may not lose her daughter yet."

It was true enough: Ellen was now often so weary that she could hardly walk up stairs, when the family retired to rest; and in the morning there was a cold glassy look about her eyes, that might well have startled the fears of a more anxious and experienced parent; and her mother did at last begin to think something must be the matter; for Ellen could not sing as she was wont; the highest tones of her voice were almost entirely gone, and she seldom got through a piece of music without a violent fit of coughing.

"Poor girl! she has quite outgrown her strength," said the mother; "she must have tonics." So Ellen tried tonics, and her cough was worse than ever; but it was not before she was obliged to give up dancing too, that the family had recourse to medical advice.

"A slight pulmonary affection," said the doctor; and he rubbed his hands, for he saw before him a good winter's work.

Some persons, on looking back, would have been alarmed to see how much had been given up during the last few weeks; but Ellen only laughed, and told Wentworth she was growing quite a saint; and that after Christimas, she would put on a plain cap, and go and sit with sister Cartwright, at her class-meetings.

All could have been borne; her bad nights, her cough, her weakness,—and all borne cheerfully, but now the ill-natured old doctor forbad her going out, except in the middle of the day, and when the weather was mildest. Her evenings must be spent at home, quietly, and without any excitement. If the family would stay with her, and Harry Wentworth, and two or three others would come, it might be endured; but sometimes she was left entirely alone: and, worst of all, had run through the last volume of the last novel before they returned. On Sunday, however, she had them all safely enough, and Wentworth too, and a merry evening they managed to pass together; for they had everybody to describe, and to mimic; and when Ellen had their follies second-hand, 't was almost as entertaining as if she had seen them herself. But even these amusements began to pall upon her; and sometimes, when they looked round for her ready laugh, she had turned away her face, and was quite unable to laugh at all.

Oh, the emptiness of folly, when mortal sickness falls upon the heart!

It was at the close of one of these sabbath evenings, when her sister and Wentworth had been unusually animated, that Ellen suddenly burst into tears, and left the room.

"What is the matter with that silly girl?" said Miss Eskdale; "she grows so fretful, there is no such thing as pleasing her."

"No," said her sister Mary, "you should not say so; Ellen was never fretful, but her spirits are so weak now, that the least thing overpowers her," and so saying, Mary followed her up stairs.

It was well that she did; for the poor girl having at last given full vent to her feelings, in a violent fit of hysterics, the rupture of a blood-vessel was the natural and fearful consequence.

From this time Ellen never spent the night alone: Marston, a middle-aged woman, who had been in the family for many years, had a bed placed beside her, and she was reduced to the necessity of being in all respects an invalid.

Still there seemed to be no immediate danger. It was a case which needed care and quiet. Marston was an excellent nurse, and the kindest creature in the world; so there was no need to sit much with Ellen, especially as the dear girl was not allowed to converse; and thus she was left hour after hour, to muse in solitude; for those who were nearest and dearest to her, knew not that love that will steal into the darkened chamber, and watch by the bed-side of a beloved object, not only enduring, but choosing that faithful vigil, before all the pleasures of the world—that soul-felt and expressive stillness, when affection, like the evening dew, sheds her silent influence on the drooping soul.

There was no immediate danger:—Ellen's excellent constitution rallied again, and she was able, once more, with the help of Marston, to pace slowly to and fro in her room, casting many a wistful glance at the dull window, that looked out upon a square of formal garden, where the shrubs were matted up, and here and there a wasted drift of dirty snow told of a chilly and humid atmosphere, with all its melancholy accompaniments. Ellen gazed, and gazed, till she was wearied out; and then she turned within, and opened her box of trinkets, which had pleased her so often; but now they failed in producing any other effect than a slight touch of pain—it might be a faint apprehension that what had been would never be again, which had well nigh brought the tears into her eyes; so she asked Marston for her music, but music, without either voice or instrument, is the dullest thing in the world, and this failed her too. What could she do? Swallow her sleeping draught two hours before the time, and beg of Marston to assist her into bed, for she was weary of herself and every thing beside.

In a few days, however, Ellen had so far recovered as to regain the wonted tone of her mind, and with this transient and delusive convalescence, came busy thoughts of that world in which she had been so bright a star—that ungrateful world, that never missed nor mourned her waning light.

As soon as her strength would permit, she amused herself with looking through her wardrobe. One by one, her rich dresses were unfolded; the dressmaker was called in, to alter them to her present shape, and ah! it was like a mockery of the grave, to see her tall thin figure, decked out in the vestments of fashion, and folly, and to hear her difficult and laborious breathings, and the short quick cough that perpetually interrupted her directions, as she told how the trimmings, the fullness, and the folds, were to be so placed, as to conceal the alteration in her wasted person.

Oh! it needs religion to wean us from the things of earth!

CHAPTER IV.

There is nothing like a return to the domestic scenes, and pursuits of a family, for giving spirits to an invalid; and Ellen, when released from the prison of her own room, really fancied she was gaining strength. With her returning spirits, the hopes of the family returned, and with their hopes, the longing to be again in the world, just to tell Lady B. that dear Ellen was recovering; and then the party at Sir Robert Long's, could they refuse that, now that Pa and Sir Robert had had a difference about their game; it would look as if the ladies of the family wished to keep it up—no, they must go, and not one of them only, but all. Marston would sit with Ellen; so they dressed themselves, and kissed her very kindly, and left her; and she sat for a long time listening to the sound of the carriages, as they rolled along the street, each conveying its rich freight to the door of the wealthy Baronet.

It so happened, on that day, that Wentworth had not been invited, and hearing that his mistress was again visible, and having nothing else to do, he went and knocked at that busy door, that was for ever turning on its hinges. Oh, how well did Ellen know his step, as he lightly skipped up the stairs! she tried to meet him at the door of the drawing room: but her breath failed her, and she could only look a welcome kinder than words.

When her lover first beheld her, he started back; for there is a disease which makes rapid inroads upon beauty, in the course of a few days, without the sufferer being aware of any change; but he soon recovered himself, and began to apologize for his long absence, by a thousand excuses, which Ellen often interrupted by her exclamations of pleasure, that he had come at last, and so opportunely.

"I began to think that you would never come again, it is so long since you have been here. Oh, I am so glad to see you, it is so dull shut up here alone, when they all leave me; but come, sit down, and be as happy as you can, and tell me all that you have seen and heard since we last met; but do not make me laugh, for I have a wretched feeling here," (laying her hand upon her breast,) "and laughing hurts me worse than anything;" so they sat down together, and fixed their eyes upon the fire, and were both silent for a long time.

"Did you ever see any one in a consumption?" was the first question which Ellen asked; and her lover started, for he had been thinking of the very same thing.

"No, I never did, and hope I never shall; your illness is not consumption, dear Ellen; it is not, it shall not be."

"Then what can be the meaning of all this fever; and why cannot I get rid of this horrid cough; I strive against it, indeed I do; and sometimes I think it is all fancy, I feel so well; but oh! Harry Wentworth, if it should be!" And she fixed her eyes upon him, with such an expression of wild and convulsive agony, that he almost shrank away.

Wentworth was not entirely a stranger to the thought of death, but he had only thought of dying as a man, or a soldier, in the cause of honour, or on the field of battle; the certain symptoms of a lingering and fatal malady had never before been present to his observation; and now, when he looked upon the being he had regarded as least mortal, and met the glaring of the hollow eye, and saw the falling away of the fair cheek, the wasting of the once rounded lips, and felt the earnest pressure of the thin and feverish hand, his spirits failed within him; for it was beyond what his imagination had ever pictured, what his fortitude was able to endure, and he felt that he had no consolation to offer in such an hour as this.

It is true he loved her—but how? Not as a fellow-pilgrim through a vale of tears, journeying on towards a better land:—not as a creature of high hopes and capabilities, whose talents are to be matured, and whose good feelings strengthened into principle. He loved her as man too often loves woman, for the sake of her bright eyes, her shining hair, and the symmetry of a graceful and elastic figure. He loved her as a fair and charmed creature, who was to be exclusively his own—to minister to his gratification, to soothe him when weary, and to supply fresh stimulus to his tastes, when sated with fruition. How then should he find consolation for such an hour as this! He could only fold to his bosom this frail and fading beauty—kiss off the falling tears—and tell her, that she would not, could not die.

Oh! it needs religion to reconcile us to the thought of death!

After this distressing interview, Wentworth had no disposition to come again; and, if he had, it would probably have been in vain, for the poor invalid was very soon confined to her own room, and strictly forbid to see any one, except her own family, who now were all sufficiently concerned at the sad change, and would probably have made any sacrifice of their wonted amusements to save her.

Mrs. Eskdale was by no means an unfeeling woman, though her fears had been late in taking alarm; but now she felt, in its full force, how much dearer to her was the life of her child, than all her wealth, her rich furniture, and her fashionable guests.

But what could she do? The ablest physicians were consulted, and there was no hope;—her child must die! Regardless of the wonted placidity of her countenance, she wandered from one stately room to another, by habit adjusting all the little ornaments which had been misplaced, without knowing what she did; and often both she and her daughter stole, on tiptoe, into the sick-room, asking the inexhaustible question, did Ellen want anything; but never staying long beside her, for the stillness was intolerable to them, and they knew not what to say,—Marston was an excellent nurse, and Ellen wanted nothing. Poor *child!* she wanted that best of friends, a friend who will kindly and candidly tell her the truth; for though she knew that she was daily giving up one thing after another, and gradually losing ground, such is the deceitful nature of this disease, that she did not feel at all certain it would terminate in death. Her physician was the only person who thought of revealing the awful truth, and a consultation was held on the subject, to consider whether it should be done, and how.

"It may be right," said one, "but I could not tell her for the world;" and another, and another, excused herself, until, at last, the lot fell upon the physician, a man who had neither wife nor child, nor knew any thing of the sensibilities of woman's heart; so he took up his cane, and went straight into the sick-room, and sat down by the bed-side.

"It has been thought right, ma'am," said he, and he cleared his voice; "it has been thought right, by your family, to depute me to be the bearer of unwelcome information;" and he paused again, for Ellen turned away her head. "I doubt not, ma'am, you understand my meaning;—all has been done that medical skill affords, but there are diseases which baffle the art of the physician; something, however, may yet be done to alleviate suffering; and allow me to assure you ma'am, that nothing shall be omitted on my part.

Ellen gave no sign of intelligence, either by word or motion. She had by this time buried her face in the pillow, so that, if he had said more, she would not have heard it; and the physician, with the satisfaction of having discharged his duty, rose, and gravely and quietly took his leave.

Indeed, every one in the house seemed to think they were doing their duty. Pills were compounded, physicians were fee'd, parties were given up, bells were muffled, and knockers wrapped in leather,—what more could they do? Nurses were hired, receipts were borrowed, and fruits of every description were purchased at any cost,—they could do nothing more! and still the poor girl lay stretched upon her uneasy bed, her face turned towards the pillow to hide the profuse perspiration that stood in pearly drops upon her forehead, and the still more copious flow of burning tears, which gave some evidence to the beholder of the uncontrollable agony within.

They could, indeed, do nothing more; for death had set his seal upon that beautiful form, and she was sinking into the fathomless depths of eternity—passing away, in the pride and the promise of her youth, from all its glory, and from all its exquisite enjoyments; while those who had cherished her infancy, and exulted in her ripened years; who knew that they were rearing an immortal fabric to stand for ever, a witness of their faithfulness or their neglect, looked upon their miserable child, and wrung their helpless hands, and mingled their melancholy wailings with hers; but no one pointed out a ray of hope, or spoke one word of comfort, or even thought of the blessed Saviour, who walked upon the troubled waters in the majesty of his benignant love. Trembling, fearful, hopeless, she was about to be pushed off from the frail bark of mortality; and where now were all the energies of that strong and buoyant heart? Hope, that burns brightest in the youthful bosom—hope, that too often deceives us in the intricate wilderness of life, but is ever ready to stand forth in undeniable reality on the brink of the grave—where was Ellen's hope? Weeping over the ruins of her own "fantastic realm," and faith, her sober sister, came not in that hour of need,—and why? because she had been sought only to give stability to idle professions, and vain promises, and giddy smiles, and had never been solicited to preside over her own peculiar province, the life, the duties, and the death-bed of the Christian.

The medicine, which was sent that afternoon, soothed the patient into a long slumber, from which she awoke considerably refreshed, and sat up, as usual, during part of the evening; indeed she felt so well as almost to question the doctor's infallibility, and could not help asking Marston if she thought there was really no hope.

"Oh! yes ma'am, a great deal of hope when the warm weather comes.

"Warm weather! how you talk woman! it is now the depth of winter, and the spring cannot come for months yet; but oh! I dare not think about the spring; and she fell into a long fit of childish weeping, partly the effect of the opiate she had taken. "Marston," said she, as soon as she regained some degree of self-command, "I wish you would tell Mr. Wentworth what the doctor thinks; but stay, give me paper, I will write;—no, I cannot guide the pen; do steal out, and ask to see him yourself, and tell him he must come once again. I will send for him when I am at the best, for I would not for the world distress him, poor fellow." So, one evening, when she felt able to bear it, he was sent for and came with Marston into the room where Ellen lay, stretched out upon a sofa, which had been placed beside the fire for her accommodation, when weary of her bed.

Poor girl! she had felt strong enough before her lover came, but now, when he walked silently up to her, and affectionately took her hand,—but most of all, when she heard again the well-remembered tones of his rich and manly voice, it seemed as if the ties that bound her to the world were drawn about her with fresh power, and in that moment, she tasted the full bitterness of death.

Wentworth asked a few kind questions, and that was all, for he had not a single word of comfort to offer, and there was a choaking in his throat, which almost forbade him to say anything.

Ellen all the while lay still and motionless; she did not raise her eyes, nor speak one word; yet the lids were not so closely shut, but that one big tear after another stole from beneath the long silken lashes, and wandered unheeded down her hollow cheek, where a single bright spot of burning crimson told its fearful tale.

It is impossible to say how long this painful silence might have lasted, had not the door opened, and Marston beckoned Wentworth out.

"You will be so good as to remember,

Sir," said she, "that I have strict orders not to admit any one, I should, therefore, thank you to leave us as soon as possible."

When Wentworth returned, he gently took up Ellen's long, thin hand, that lay stretched out as pure, and almost as lifeless as marble, and said, in a quiet voice, that he feared it was time for him to leave her. Then, and not till then, she raised her eyes, and looked full into his face.

There is an expression in the eye that is lighted up by the fever of consumption, which those who have not seen it never can imagine, and which those who have seen it never can forget. It was in vain that the poor sufferer struggled to speak. Her lips quivered, but she had no words to express the anguish of her soul. Wentworth stooped down, that his ear might catch the sound, if there were any, and with the hand that was disengaged, she raised from his brow the thick curls of raven hair, and then gently circling his neck with her slender arm, drew him still nearer, and pressed upon his forehead her farewell kiss; saying at the same time, in a low whisper, "It is the last!"

And this was all; and he, who had so loved her in this world, parted with her on the brink of another; left her at the gates of death, without one word about eternity to cheer her on her awful way.

Here let us draw a veil over the closing scene. He to whom time has no limits—to whom opportunity gives no advantage—to whom all things are possible, is, doubtless, able to carry on his own work of preparation in the soul, even when the sufferer dies and makes no sign.

It is the task of the writer to describe, as well as feeble powers are able to describe, the external evidence of that struggle, which must naturally attend the dissolution of the earthly tenement, to those who have not ensured a place in any higher habitation.

The heart alone knoweth its own bitterness, and the heart alone beareth witness, with anguish unutterable, to that which is in reality the sting of death—the victory of the grave.

CHAPTER V.

In a few days the public papers announced the death of Ellen, youngest daughter of Charles Eskdale, Esq., and all the ceremony of preparation for the deepest grief went on in the still busy family.

On the sixth day after this melancholy event, Wentworth found himself to his great surprise, still thinking of Ellen. It was true and faithful, and looked well not to forget her; but to bear about with him continually the remembrance of her loveliness, and his own loss, was a weakness of which he had not conceived himself capable; so he filled another bumper of champaign, and determined to be wiser. He had that day dined alone at his own table, and now sat gazing, without a wish, at the rich dessert that was spread before him—not only without a wish, but without a definite idea, for he drank deeply, with a determination to drown reflection, and now the lights were dancing before him with a dizzy glare, and half-imagined images flitted by, in quick succession, amongst which the pale and lifeless form of Ellen returned too often, until at last, by one of those unaccountable operations of the human mind, by which we sometimes feel impelled to do that which is most revolting to our feelings, he started from his seat, and determined that he would go and look upon the dead body. This resolution, once formed, was soon acted upon, for he had neither power nor patience to think, and in a few minutes he entered the hall of Mr. Eskdale, and called for Marston.

She came, and neither of them spoke, for Wentworth pointed to the stairs, and the woman, taking up a tall candle, walked silently before him, until they stopped at the door of what was once Ellen's chamber. The door was locked, and Marston tried to turn the key without making any noise, as if afraid to wake the slumberer within. They entered—four wax candles that stood burning night and day, two at each end of the coffin, gave a pale and solemn light to the chilly aspect of the room. Over the coffin there had been carefully drawn a cover of white muslin, which Marston slowly folded down as soon as Wentworth drew near; and he stood gazing on the lifeless figure, with the bewildered astonishment of one who has but a partial apprehension of some great and awful calamity.

The soft tresses of silky hair that were wont to wave and glitter in the light, agitated by the quick and playful movements of her who was so proud to wear them, were now combed out and laid in bands upon the forehead, as smooth and close as if no breath or motion had ever stirred them. The eyes from which the very soul of merriment had once beamed forth, were now for ever folded under their snowy lids, and the long lashes fell with a deep shadow on the cheek—the hollow cheek for which health and youth, and beauty had once contended, as for a treasure that was peculiarly their own—and then the mouth—where now was the exquisite play of the lips, that would puzzle the beholder with such rapid expression of mingled emotions—of pride—of laughter—of contempt—until all were lost in a smile, so beaming with the best affections of the soul, that those who felt its sweetness were apt to forget every thing beside? Those lips were now drawn out into long purple lines, between which the white teeth were visible, and the chin, and the nose, too, had become so pointed and prominent, that those who had well known Ellen Eskdale might now have looked upon, without recognizing, her face. And yet, in spite of all these fearful changes, there was beauty still—that beauty which every heart can feel, but which no words can describe—the beauty of eternal stillness—the beauty of death!

Wentworth gazed, and gazed, and neither he nor his companion spoke one word, until at last he lifted his rosy fingers, warm with the circling blood of life, and touched the cheek! The chill of horror that instantly ran through his veins, brought back his scattered senses, to suffer with redoubled intensity of feeling. He had pictured to himself, before he came, the eye, the lips, the forehead, the whole countenance; but the solid marble feeling, the cold resistance of that cheek, whose yielding softness he had known so well, was what no one had ever described to him, what he had never dreamed of.

That chilling touch had, in one instant, dispersed all his imaginary fortitude, and he stood beside the coffin, pale as its own lifeless occupant; weak and trembling as a child. At length, with uncertain steps, he gained the door; and though Marston tried to make him understand that the funeral would take place on the following day, he neither heard nor tried to hear, but hurried down the stairs, and through the hall, without any other member of the household knowing he had been there.

How dark and dreary was that long night to Harry Wentworth. Sleep came not to draw her misty curtain between him and the distressing realities of life—the still more terrible realities of death. If for one moment he closed his eyes in forgetfulness, the next they were wide open, vainly endeavoring to pierce into the abyss of darkness; and whenever he turned his face towards the vacant pillow, his distempered imagination presented a long white figure, stretched beside him, with Ellen's eyes, just as he had seen them in their last interview, fixed full upon his countenance, while every time his hand touched the cold bed-clothes, the remembrance of that icy cheek came back to him, bringing its own deathly chillness to his bursting heart.

How was the strong man brought low, and his boasted power subdued, beneath the mastery of ungovernable feeling. It was not altogether fear that held him in subjection—still less was it sorrow—but a terrible warfare of all that can agitate the soul, heightened it may be at times, (for who can fathom the depths of the human heart,) by a fearful looking-for of judgment.

At five o'clock on the following morning, the household of Harry Wentworth were alarmed by the ringing of their master's bell.

"It must be as I thought," said the old house-keeper, "he is breaking his heart for that dear young lady,"—and recollecting the efficacy of hartshorn in many former cases, when her own heart was broken, and well knowing that neither her master nor John would be able to find the nostrum, she took up the light, kept always burning in her room, and proceeded to the landing of the stairs, where she could distinctly hear the conversation which took place between the master and his man.

"Sir," said John "the roan has never eaten a handful of corn since the trotting match on Weston common."

"Then take Ronald: I don't care which, only mind you are there in time to let him breathe before we start. The hounds meet at Bexley. I shall breakfast at the Grange, and see that you are ready for me. But stop—give me a light, for this room is darker than ——"

"Break his heart!" said the house-keeper, and she turned again into her own chamber, where she was soon asleep in her own bed.

It was a noble and heart-stirring sight to those who care for such things, to see young Wentworth that day on his black hunter—a furious and high mettled animal, that few could manage: but it was the pride of his rider that he could manage anything—could bring anything into subjection. He forgot that little field of action, his own heart, and those eternal enemies, his own wild passions, and his own stubborn will. In fact he forgot every thing for a few hours at least, for the frost was all gone—the scent lay well—the ground was in the best possible condition, and Ronald outdid himself, to say nothing of the merits of the poor fox, who died like a Briton.

There was excitement in the chase that day, enough to wean a heart like Wentworth's from every thought of sorrow; and if sometimes the image of his lost treasure would present itself unbidden, it only served as a stimulus to fresh action—to urge his horse to a more desperate leap.

Thus passed those hours of boisterous hilarity, and forgetfulness of care. But moments of enjoyment must have a crisis, and mornings of felicity an afternoon.

Wentworth staid long upon the field, for there were the different properties of different animals to discuss; bets to decide, and a world of business to be gone through; so that when he turned his horse's head to the road leading towards the city, the darkness and haze of a dull afternoon, in the early part of February, was already beginning to render distant objects misty and undefined.

It so happened, that all the gentlemen whose destination was the same, had preceded him by some hours, so that he was left to pursue his solitary way, and ruminate in silence on the dregs of excitement; the most unsatisfactory aliment in the world. Gaily whistling up his spirits, he began, for want of better amusement, to think of some familiar air, by which he might beguile the time. "Gentle Zitella," had already passed his lips; but there is a power in sound to call up buried images, beyond what the utmost stretch of imagination can realize; and with that light and playful ditty, came back the vivid remembrance of her who had so often sung it with him; and he saw again the slender fingers, white as the ivory keys they touched, and the sparkle of the sunny eyes, and all the bright and rapid variations of her incomparable charms.

There was no bearing this;—stillness, like that of death, was all around him; and had not his horse, with something of his master's irritability of feeling, started at every fresh object upon the road, and thus with the application of whip and spur, supplied him with continual occupation, it is impossible to say to what height his impatience might have risen. It was too much for mortal man to endure—to be haunted night and day as by a spectre, and all this torment from one who would not willingly have cast a shadow on his path. It became necessary to call up all that was potent and dignified in his nature, for he was not the man to be made a fool of by such idle fantasies; so he discontinued his boyish occupation of lashing off all the young twigs within his reach, and sat bolt upright in his saddle, and felt himself a man and a gentleman.

In this style he was issuing from a bye-lane, which led out by a sudden angle into the great public road, when in an instant, his philosophy and himself had well nigh been dismounted, by Ronald giving a tremendous start; and Wentworth started too, for by that turn in the road, they had come at once upon the sight and sound of the quick stroke of a spade, upon the fresh earth of a new-made grave, in a little churchyard, that was separated by a high and thin hedge from the public road. The funeral procession was all gone—the clergyman had left the church—the clerk had just locked the door, and was carrying home the keys, and a troop of merry children were enjoying their last gambol amongst the graves, before the sexton should finish his work and turn them out of their favorite play ground.

"That's a cold lodging" said Wentworth, as soon as he recovered himself; while he pushed up his horse's head as near as he could bring it to the part of the hedge, beside where the sexton stood.—"That's a cold lodging for somebody, my good fellow; for whom are you doing that kind service?"

"Sir," said the man, looking up, and resting one hand upon the spade, while with the other he slowly raised his hat; "who lays here, did you mean, Sir?—It's a Miss Eskdale,—there's a monument in that church to old Sir Jonas Eskdale, and the family has buried here ever since his time."

Before the old man had finished speaking, Wentworth was again proceeding slowly on his way, but his head was now bent forward, and strongly, and violently, yet without aim, or object, his hands were clenching the reins of his bridle.

For some time he pursued his way, more like a statue than a living man, when another start of his horse induced him to look up, and he saw that he was falling in with a long line of mourning coaches; and now he could hear the hollow rumbling of the hearse, as it passed under the arch of the ancient gateway, and, when he looked down the first street into the city, its glimmering lights were intercepted at intervals by the nodding of the heavy plumes.

Wentworth would have given much, could he have entered by some other road, for to say nothing of his own internal struggle, he felt, in this rencontre, the want of the decency of external mourning.

In his scarlet coat, he had unwittingly joined the funeral procession, and his sleek and high mettled hunter was proudly rearing and prancing beside the hearse, which had just conveyed Ellen to her grave.

Before he could reach his own door, it was necessary to pass the house of Mr. Eskdale.

He looked up to the windows—the drawing-room was again lighted, and the shadows of female figures flitted to and fro.

Ah! how well could Wentworth picture to his mind the scene within. The blazing fire of a winter's evening—the many lights of paler lustre—the thick folds of damask curtains—the crimson furniture, that gave a glow of warmth and comfort to all around—the soft and flowery carpets, and the rich sofas inviting to luxurious repose. He thought of all these, and then of that little churchyard, where the night was closing in unheeded, and that solitary grave, on which a still and steady rain was falling, unfelt; and then, for the first time, the full conviction took possession of his soul, that Ellen was indeed no more—that through the whole of his after-life he should never gaze upon her face again. There might, and he believed there would be much to cheer and animate him on his future course, but Ellen would not be near to share it. Creatures as bright and beautiful might minister to his gratification—music might soothe him on his way; but Ellen's harp, and the far sweeter tones of Ellen's voice would be forever mute.

Wentworth passed on—his heart was not broken—he rushed with fresh ardour into the vortex of dissipation—he drank deeply of the cup of pleasure; but sometimes, before the cup was tasted, there would arise thoughts, that were almost intolerable, of that dismal church-yard, the hearse, the coffin, and the worms.

Oh! it needs religion to reconcile us even to the earthly part of death.

Of the family of the Eskdales, it is not necessary to say more than that, at the expiration of the usual time for seclusion, they entered the church, in which they maintained a warm and comfortable seat, dressed in a full costume of fashionable mourning; that many times during that day's service, the mother's face was shrouded in a white and delicately scented cambric handkerchief; and that once or twice, when the daughters lifted up their blue eyes, they were seen to be suffused with tears.

CHAPTER VI.

If any young reader shall have glanced over this picture, in search of highly coloured, or romantic scenery, without any regard to the general design of the painting, disappointment will be the probable issue, accompanied by a want of patience to bear with the author a little longer, while she gives a summary of her meaning, or, in the true style of fable writing, adds a moral to her tale.

The individual, whose short career has been described in these pages, may serve to represent a vast multitude of sentient and immortal beings, who pass from the cradle to the grave, without once enquiring for what purpose they have been sent to trace their little journey of experience upon this earth—with what provision they have set out upon that journey, and what will be the event of its termination.

The human mind, in its natural state, has, under all circumstances, powers of action and capabilities of enjoyment; and must necessarily be supplied with objects on which these powers may operate, and sources from whence these capabilities may extract pleasure.

How dreadful, then, must be the error of those parents who would forcibly compel their children to walk in the right way, by imposing upon them unnatural restraints; checking their innocent mirth, and violently uprooting, instead of properly directing, those desires which nature has implanted in their hearts. If this be the straight and narrow path which is recommended to us, no wonder that so few continue to walk therein.

In order that death may be divested of its terrors, it is not necessary that we should render life still more terrible. In order that we may think of the grave without shuddering and horror, it is not necessary that we should make the way that leads to it a howling wilderness;—in order that we may be willing to die, it is not necessary that we should hate to live.

The bountiful Creator of our being has supplied his creatures with sources of happiness, so various and so multiplied, that the meanest peasant may find them in his daily path, while, to the liberal and enlightened mind, earth, air, and ocean, teem with wonder and delight. How, then, can there be sin in opening the heart to those pleasures which the present state of existence affords. The great and important question is, in what measure, and in what manner we shall enjoy them.

If the body be permitted to gain the ascendancy—if we spend our money, our time and our energies, in ministering to the gratification of our senses; whether in gross indulgence, or in that which is more refined and voluptuous, well may we shudder to perceive in that body the symptoms of disease or age; when we know that it must pass away into a state which offers every thing humiliating and repulsive to the natural feelings. But if, on the other hand, our pleasures and pursuits have been such as to elevate and purify the mind, that mind, being itself immortal, will rejoice at the prospect of that day, when it shall burst the bonds of its prison-house, and leave behind the gross impediments of clay.

But how, asks the young reader, is it possible to attain this state of mental exaltation. My dear young friends, well may you hesitate, before you attempt so difficult an ascent, without the help of religion; but religion, vulgar, degraded, trampled-upon religion, is able to accomplish all this for you; and that, without the aid of science or philosophy: and religion has done as much for many, whose portion in this world was, to be despised and rejected of men; convincing them by the surest evidence, that the termination of life is not in itself an evil, nor the approach to it a season of dread. That death may be compelled to lay down his hideous sceptre,—to cease to be a king of terrors, and placing on his brow the diadem of peace, stretch forth his hand, in kindly welcome, to the shores of a long wished-for eternity.

As farther proof how much the body may be made subservient to the mind, we have only to refer to the history of some of the ancient philosophers, who knew not God; and yet were able to meet death with calmness and satisfaction, and plunge, without fear, into the abyss of uncertainty. If, then, the case of these wonderful beings, who shone like stars in the distant firmament; beautiful in their own lustre, but dimly disappearing before the glorious orb of day—if the case of these wonderful men supplies us with proof, how much the body may be brought into subjection to the mind; how much of firmness and fortitude may be attained; how much resignation of self and sensual enjoyment may be effected, by a steady and systematic cultivation of the intellectual powers, combined with a contempt for those luxuries and pleasures which afford gratification to the senses alone; what should be the expression of our joy, what the measure of our gratitude to him who has permitted us, in this our day, to add to the negative satisfaction of the stoic, the high hopes, and the glorious privileges which religion alone can offer.

Philosophy may destroy the burden of the body, but religion gives wings to the soul. Philosophy may enable us to look down upon earth with contempt, but religion teaches us to look up to heaven with hope. Philosophy may support us to the brink of the grave, but religion conducts us beyond. Philosophy unfolds a rich store of enjoyment, —religion makes it eternal. Happy is the heart where religion holds her throne, and philosophy her noble handmaid, ministers to her exaltation!

THE CURATE'S WIDOW.

Oh! amiable lovely death!—Shakspeare.

CHAPTER I.

In order to present the young reader with a contrast to the foregoing picture, it is almost necessary to enter into the humble and limited experience of the true christian, under similar, and even greater trials. Such a picture of private life offers nothing in the way of romantic interest; nothing to excite the passions; nothing to awaken in the soul one spark of poetic feeling; but if it should possess a charm of sufficient power to fix the attention of the reader, to excite a greater love of virtue, or awaken in the soul a spark of religious zeal, the Author will not have to lament that she has written in vain.

"How shall I build an altar,
  To the Author of my days;
With lips so prone to faulter,
  How shall I sound his praise?

Thy temples were too lowly,
  Oh! great Jerusalem;
The Lord of hosts too holy,
  Too pure, to dwell in them!

Then how shall I, the weakest,
  His servant hope to be?
I'll listen when thou speakest,
  Spirit of love to me!

I'll do thy holy bidding,
  With unrepining heart;
I'll bear thy gentle chiding,
  For merciful thou art.

I'll bring each angry feeling,
  A sacrifice to thee;
I'll ask thy heavenly healing
  Even for mine enemy.

So shall I build an altar,
  To the Author of my days;
With lips though prone to faulter,
  So shall I sound his praise."

Such were the words sung by Alice Bland, as she sat on a low bench at her own door, one beautiful sabbath evening; and the cheerful cadence was joined by the sweet voice of a little dark-haired boy, whom she pressed closely to her side; while their eyes met with an expression of such affection, as none but a mother and a child can know. And then they looked away again, over the green fields, far on to the village spire, and traced a little winding path that issued from a group of stately trees, with diligent search, as if for the appearance of some expected object, that was to bring additional enjoyment to their quiet and peaceful pleasures.

"He is coming, he is coming," said the child, and they both ran forward through the garden gate, and down the green lane, where they met a tall, sallow, and exhausted-looking young man, dressed in clerical costume, and wearing the still more imposing solemnity of his sacred office, as one who deeply felt its awful and almost overwhelming responsibility.

Never did plumed warrior, returning from the field of glory, meet a kinder welcome from his lady-love, than that with which Alice Bland greeted her returning lord—lord both of her heart and home. And he too had his full particpation of delight, as might be seen in his dark and often melancholy eyes, now lighted up with all the feelings of the husband, and the father, as he stooped to kiss his boy, the very emblem of himself;—he stooped, for he had lately discovered that to lift him from the ground, required an effort almost beyond his strength; especially after so long a walk, a day of such laborious duty, and on a sultry summer's evening: indeed the first greeting was hardly over, before he complained of the oppressive heat of the weather, took off his hat, and wiped his brow, that was pale and wrinkled with exhaustion and fatigue.

Alice placed his arm within hers, and led him gently up the lane, while the boy ran forward and threw open the garden gate, holding it back at the very widest, that his father and mother might pass through without hinderance.

Within the cottage all was peace and simple comfort. Their one domestic was enjoying the liberty of the sabbath amongst her own people, and Alice with her willing hands, had prepared the social tea, with cream, and fruit, and every thing that she thought would be most refreshing to the weary invalid. Little Marcus had gathered a plate of strawberries, of which he felt himself the proud proprietor, and these, with both his hands, he presented to his father, with that deference which his mother had taught him was due to those who were ill; and though his father told him again and again that ladies should be first attended to, the influence of the mother prevailed, and the ill-mannered boy persisted in the error of his ways.

Happy pair! this little point of etiquette was all that Marcus and Alice Bland ever found to contend about; for in duty, as well as in pleasure, their hands and hearts were united.

The social meal was prolonged by pleasant converse, and the frolic of the happy child, until the golden hues of sunset, and the lengthened shadows of the trees gave place to the sober livery of twilight.

Little Marcus had sung his evening hymn, and lisped his evening prayer, and the fond parents had both pressed their farewell kiss upon his cheek, when they sat down together, and in silence, as if listening to a boding voice, which of late had often whispered to their hearts, though neither had trusted their lips with a response. At last the husband spoke, and that melancholy sound seemed to Alice deep and impressive, as the tolling of the bell, to those who watch the motionless body of the dead.

"When I am gone," said Marcus, and he paused; for he was startled by the convulsive pressure of the hand that was clasped in his, but his wife made no reply, and again he spoke:—

"Alice, my beloved wife, there is an awful sentence pronounced upon us. We have long known it, why should we shrink from acknowledging to each other that we must part. Close, as the connection between soul and body, has been the union of my spirit with thine; but as it is appointed unto all that they should die, so is it appointed to the dearest that they should part. We are not as those who are sorrowing without hope; for we know, and believe and are persuaded, that we shall meet again; and that in all things excellent, and pure, and holy, we are bound together by ties which death cannot tear asunder. Look up my beloved, and tell me, though this separation must cut us off for ever from earthly hope, tell me that thou hast no repinings, no murmurings against the divine will."

And Alice answered in a firm and steady voice, "I have none;" and then they pursued the solemn subject, and branched out into its painful realities, with the faith and the confidence of sincere and humble christians. The father spoke tenderly of his child; and then the mother covered her face with her hands, and wept aloud; but her tears were tears of womanly feeling, not of despondency or doubt.

CHAPTER II.

Alice Bland was a plain and useful character, with few pretensions to gentility; but she possessed that rare and valuable tact, which preserved her from every offence against the laws of good breeding. Her husband was a scholar and a gentleman; but they were both of humble parentage; and had it not been for their unbounded affection for each other, their simple habits, and contentment in their lowly station, they would have found it extremely difficult to exist, upon the slender pittance which the curacy of the neighbouring parish afforded. But Alice was cheerful, active, and domestic, and made the best of every thing, even of herself, though without knowing it; for her appearance, dress, and manners, were as simple and unpretending, as well could be. And then she had such a warm welcome in her very look; indeed some people said it was her comfortable, and care-taking ways, that first won upon the poor invalid; for he was a lodger in her mother's house, long before they married, and Alice used to wait upon him like a sister, and truly he both deserved and needed it; for he was an orphan left almost destitute, was kind in his disposition, studious in his habits, constitutionally pensive, and pious upon principle.

It was scarcely possible for the relentless hand of death to cut asunder a closer, dearer or more tender thread than that which bound together this simple pair; and yet they saw every day that there was urgent need for preparation for that awful and tremendous event, which, after they had once spoken of it, became the theme of their serious and most confidential communion.

Marcus Bland was sinking fast away; but to him death had no terrors, and though his griefs were those of the husband and the father, his hopes were those of the Christian, pure, and elevated, and holy; bearing him above all considerations either earthly or perishable. But she, the vine, who had bound her tendrils round his branches, and interwoven her very existence with his, and the young sapling, how were they to endure the storms of winter, without the shelter of the parent stem. For them he mourned in secret; for them he prayed, that every rough blast might be turned away, that genial showers might descend, and that they might live and flourish in the sunshine of eternal glory. And Alice prayed also, both with her husband and in secret; still bearing nobly on, for the end was not yet, and she had all those hallowed duties to perform which keep alive the heart of woman.

"You are better to day," said she to her husband one afternoon, when he seemed to be recovering from the severest paroxyism of his disorder.

"I am better," said he, "but I want breath;" so Alice folded back the curtains of the bed, and opened the window, and they looked out together again upon the green fields, and the winding path, which he had so often trod when going forth on his pastoral duties.

"I want breath," continued he, "and voice, and energy, to tell you of the ineffable enjoyment of dying the death of the Christian. My heart is filled with the unspeakable love which we believe to be a part of the Divine essence; for which we have often prayed, and which is of such difficult attainment amidst the troubles and turmoils of life. Alice, thou shouldst have no tears for such an hour as this. Oh, cherish the remembrance of our parting scene, as the support and the consolation of thy future life; and when I am gone, think not of me as a man who was humble, and pious, and devout, but of one who lived and died in the love of Christ Jesus, and the faith which is built upon his resurrection: who, if he had any knowledge above that of the vilest sinner, owed that knowledge to the precepts of his heavenly Master; if he had any faith beyond that of the hypocrite, freely acknowledged that faith to be from above; and if he were at last supported through the bitterness of parting from the dearest of earthly companionships, knew it could only be by the interposition of divine mercy.

"Think of these things, my beloved wife, more than of me. The cup of which we have partaken together, has been sweet as the waters of paradise. Remember from whence that cup was filled, and believe that there are rivers of delight in store for those who faithfully fulfil their appointed task.

My last, my parting injunction is, to pray fervently; and to teach our child to pray. By forgetfulness of this duty, we often suffer estrangement from the Divine presence, and then, in our times of utmost need, when we would willingly return to this resource, it seems as if a veil had dropped between us and heaven. Pray, then, dear Alice, even when the refreshing dews are upon thy path, and there seems no immediate need for prayer."

Alice made no answer; but she pressed his hand as if to say, "My path must henceforth be through the desert," and then her husband went on.

"There is a strange fluttering at my heart, and I feel that death is near. Tremble not, I beseech thee, but raise my head, and let me die where it was my happiness to live. My poor boy! I would not have him near me, for he could not understand my situation, and might learn to be afraid of death. I have nothing to bequeath him but a father's blessing, and a father's kiss; thou shalt press it upon his cheek when I am gone —the last and the dearest." And then his words became inarticulate, and his breathing difficult; but Alice supported him to the very last, unaided, and alone; for to her it would have seemed like profanation, to call in the help of stranger-hands; and, having no fear of death, nor weak longing to escape from the presence of the dead, she remained alone in the chamber, through the solemn stillness of that hour which follows the mortal separation of soul and body; while the room seems filled with the atmosphere of death, and voices of etherial beings are whispering tidings from the land of spirits.

The first sound that startled her from that heavenly communion, was the voice of her child in the garden below. It became necessary to rouse herself, and descending into her little parlour, she caught up ber boy in her arms, and for the first time burst into an agony of tears.

How solitary was that long night to the heart of the widowed mother! Hour after hour she spent in the chamber of the deceased, watching that pale extended figure, until the white bed clothes seemed to tremble beneath the intensity of her gaze; and sometimes she started at a fancied heaving of the breast; but faith and love were strong within her, and sweeter to her was that silent vigil, than all which the busy world without could offer.

As the miser delights to count over every item of his hoarded treasure, so she recalled and dwelt upon each excellence of him, whose expiring lamp had, so far as regards the things of this world, left her in total darkness. But as she knew that another morning would dawn, and that the sun would return again; that light would dance upon the hills, and the voice of gladness be heard in the vallies, so she trusted that the sun of righteousness would arise, and shine upon the darkness of her benighted soul, and she trusted not in vain, for oil was poured upon the troubled waters, and her soul was filled as with an holy calm.

Tell us, ye sons of pleasure, ye daughters of dissipation, how it is that you endure the blasts of the desert, without the aid of religion—without the consolation of prayer.

Though Alice Bland forgot not for a single moment that the wheels of destruction had passed over her earthly hopes, she remembered also that she was poor; and that to the poor belong many duties, which the children of affluence and refinement think it inconsistent with the tenderness of wounded feelings to perform. To every arrangement for household comfort she attended with her wonted punctuality; and all things for the order and decency of the burial were of her contriving, without any omission of what was respectful and neighbourly.

The day before the funeral arrived, and Alice had not yet taken her child into the sacred chamber. She had herself been there since the first rising of the sun; and while the dew was yet glittering upon the leaves, she had gathered sprigs of thyme, and rosemary, to place within the coffin, and sweet-scented flowers to garnish the room; and now, when her silent breakfast was over, and she and the child and the one domestic had knelt down together, to pray for the blessing of their heavenly Father upon the transactions of another day, she led her child up stairs, and raising him in her arms, he rested with his rosy fingers upon the side of the coffin, and looked upon the face of the dead. He looked earnestly and long, and then directed an enquiring glance to his mother, as if he asked of her an explanation of the strange mystery; but he made no remark, though he turned again and again, as if fascinated by the beauty of that still pale countenance, from which every trace of anxiety and care had passed away. It is true, the raven hair retained its few silver threads, but it rested on a brow as serenely beautiful as the surface of the summer sea, when its waters sleep beneath a cloudless sky, and make no ripple on the shore. And the bright eyes were closed upon the world for ever, not as in weariness or disgust, but as if, to their inward vision, was revealed a light, compared with which all without was perfect darkness; and the pure lips were closed, from whence had flowed the eloquence of feeling, the force of truth, and the inspiration of that wisdom which is from above.

Little Marcus soon returned to his usual sports, but many times during that day he broke off suddenly, and went and leaned upon his mother's knee, and once he looked anxiously in her face, and said, "Was it my father?" But his happy little bosom bounded with fresh enjoyment, and his mother tried in vain to make him sensible of his irreparable loss.

In the midst of the preparation for the last solemn rites, Alice was not inactive; but seemed to be thinking of every one more than of herself; planning for their accommodation, and attending to their wants, yet all with a sweet mournful dignity, as if she bore about with her a sorrow too deep for common sympathy or condolence The most trying part of that day, was the quiet after the funeral, when the guests were gone, and she retired without an object to direct her steps. Extreme restlessness, that dreadful accompaniment of the last degree of mental suffering, took possession of her, and she wandered from room to room, as if hoping in every place to leave some portion of the load that weighed upon her, until at length she sought consolation in prayer, and remembering her husband's parting injunction, knelt down, and humbly and fervently petitioned, that to her cup of bitterness there might be added some drops of comfort. And her petition was not rejected; for sweet sleep stole over her wearied senses, and she awoke in the morning with fresh strength and courage to pursue her solitary way.

CHAPTER III.

How little is known of what the human heart may endure and struggle through, by those who slumber in the lap of indulgence! Death, it is true, with his grim visage, and aim that no earthly power can avert, will sometimes steal in upon their visions, but they can gather round them a band of graceful mourners, and having no active part to take in the ceremony of preparing for the grave, they are at liberty to sigh away their sorrows in costly weeds, and weep at will over the urn of the departed. But the luxury of weeping gracefully, nay, the rational privilege of mourning quietly, and without interruption, is too frequently denied to the poor. Wounded and weary, they must go forth again upon active service; they must engage in the bustling concerns of life, even when the light of life has been extinguished; they must arise and gird themselves for warfare, when their bosom's shield has been cleft asunder.

Thus it was that Alice Bland compelled herself, or was compelled by circumstances, to enter upon a serious consideration of her present melancholy and deserted situation; not in order the more fully to comprehend the extent and the depth of her affection, but that she might arrange and act upon some plan for the future maintenance of herself and her child. That she must leave her sweet cottage, was a truth upon which she never once attempted to close her eyes; because her doom was inevitable, and she had long known it: so she bestirred herself, and took an inventory of all her worldly possessions; every now and then laying aside something useful or comfortable for a sick neighbour, or some trifling memento for an humble friend.

With such occupations she busied herself during the day; and when the evening came, she went out with her presents, calling upon every one who had known and valued her husband's pastoral care, and saying some cheering words to them at parting, as if they were the mourners, and she the comforter. And truly she needed a comforter in her turn; for, by the time she reached her home again, she was like the bough that has scattered its last leaf upon the merciless wind. But the Comforter was near—the promised Comforter, and darkness was turned into light at his presence.

Days passed away, and Alice still lingered at the cottage, for she was in treaty for a situation with a distant relative, and waited his answer and decision, before she entered upon the last hard duty of advertising a public sale, and disposing of all her goods and household property upon the very spot where she had known so much happiness. The flower-beds which her husband had planted and weeded, were to be trodden down by the feet of strangers; and the shrubs which he had reared and cherished, were to become the property of another. All, except the bed on which he died, she was willing to part with; and the table on which he used to write, his chair, and a few simple things which possessed a sort of sanctity in her eyes. These she reserved for herself, and securing them in what was once her own chamber, rose early, and prepared for the long dreaded day.

Neighbours flocked in from all quarters, some from curiosity, and others in the hope of making a cheap bargain; but all peeped about, and were equally earnest and willing to try the strength of chairs, and rap their knuckles upon china, and feel the weight of carpets and counterpanes.

There was not a corner in the whole house free from their intrusion; and Alice, having resigned herself for that day entirely to the service of her friends, they were so charmed with her attention and activity, that they applied to her for information about almost every article. Alas! she could but too well remember where and when they had been purchased, what elegant taste had selected them, and whose beloved fingers had hallowed them with his touch. But no one guessed what was passing in her mind; and they plunged deeper and deeper into her house-economy, ploughing up her feelings as they went. And no one pitied her, for she never wept in public; and many remarked, as they went away, that Alice Bland was just the cheerful, active sort of person, to get through with a thing of this kind;—nothing could have been more satisfactorily managed, and the refreshments were excellent.

Thus they dropped off, at first in merry troops, then one by one, until all departed, and Alice stood alone at her own door, looking around upon a scene of desolation. But where was little Marcus all this while? His mother had given him his dinner in a basket, and sent him out early in the morning to play in a neighbour's field, where he was allowed to keep a goat, with strict orders not to return until he was sent for, nor to wander from the field, but to fill his basket with flowers, and amuse himself, as well as he could, with his shaggy favourite.

At first the boy was happy enough, and thought his mother had seldom done a kinder thing; but perpetual amusement is difficult to ensure, even in the company of a goat, and, before eleven, Marcus was glad to eat his dinner, wondering, all the while, what he should do next. Oh! the flowers! he would take home such beauties for his mother; but why was he to stay so long, and why did nobody come for him; he sat down and wondered exceedingly. His goat, too, was neither so playful nor so fond of him, as it was at first; and sure he thought it was not like his own dear mother to keep him there all day. Moreover, he believed it was growing very late, though the sun was still high over head: and then the thought came across his mind, that his mother had forgotten him, and, as a very reasonable consequence, he began to cry.

Long after this consummation, Alice came into the field, and found him weeping bitterly; his cheeks flushed and swollen, and his bright eyes glimmering through tears, which burst forth afresh at the sight of her who had been the cause of his grievance.

Alice again had to act the part of the comforter; and in fulfilling this holy duty, how often are we ourselves comforted!

The next morning Alice arose early, and, having despatched a hasty breakfast, assisted the young woman, who had been her helpmate in domestic duties, to pack up her small wardrobe; and having added all that she was able to spare from her own, paid her wages, and bid her farewell with the affectionate interest of a friend; walking with her as far as the garden-gate, and then holding out her hand again, she wished her happiness in her new situation, and hoped she would read her bible often, and be active and industrious, minding, above all things, to be faithful to the will of God.

The poor girl was unable to speak for her gathering tears, but carrying little Marcus in her arms to the gate, set him down beside his mother, and, placing in his hand a small basket, her parting present, kissed him fondly, and went silently away, her heart too full for expression.

"What shall we do now?" said Marcus, ooking after her.

"We must go too," said his mother, and she drew him gently into the house, and bid him gather up all his play things, and fill his basket with those which he liked best; and truly she could hardly have found him a more lasting occupation: for even when she had herself arranged all that she wished to take away, Marcus was not half satisfied with the selection he had made, but entreated his mother to wait one moment, while he emptied the basket upon the floor for the twentieth time.

"I will wait at any rate, until the cart arrives," said his mother, "and see, here it is coming up the lane. You must make haste, for all that we cannot carry, is to be taken away in the cart."

"Why must they be taken away at all? are they not ours?"

"Yes;—but we are going too."

"Going! where? and what for?"

"I cannot tell you now, my love. You must make haste, for the man will not like to wait."

In a few minutes the little furniture which Alice had reserved for herself, with some chests of household goods, were placed in the cart; and the man drove away, whistling as he went, and never looked back, nor thought of the mother and the child whom he had left so lonely in their deserted dwelling.

"Are you quite ready?" said Alice to her boy, as he made his appearance, looking sorrowfully round the empty room.

"It does not look like our own house now," said he.

"It is well it does not," thought his mother, as she led him by the hand, and closing the door, turned the key in the lock for the last time.

By how sudden, and yet simple a stroke, the flood-gates of memory may sometimes be thrown open.

Alice Bland had gone through the duties of the past week, with a resignation that was wonderful even to herself; but just as that familiar sound caught her ear—the turning of the key in her. own door—there came back upon her mind the overwhelming recollection of the many sabbaths, when she and her beloved husband had walked together to the house of God, holding sweet counsel as they went. And now she was going forth with her poor child, like Hagar into the wilderness, but oh! more desolate than Hagar, she was going a stranger into the wilderness of the world!

Close beside her, and half hid amongst the leaves of the rose-tree, the jessamine, and the clematis, was the rustic bench on which they used to sit through the twilight hour,—the only hour which their domestic economy allowed for indolence; and even then, they were accustomed to hallow this season of rest by conversing upon heavenly themes; encouraging each other to fresh exertion in the Christian warfare, numbering their blessings, and not unfrequently offering up hymns of thankfulness and praise to him who had filled their cup of happiness so full.

Alice looked around, and there was not a shrub nor flower, which had not its accompanying chain of recollections, closely interwoven with her heart of hearts. There was the bush of sweet brier growing beside the parlour window, when it used to offer up its welcome perfume after the summer shower; the evening primrose, now closely folded up, that would soon open out its delicate flowers, where there would be no eye to gaze upon its moonlight beauty; the bright laurel, that spread its deep shadow upon the walk; and the festoons of rustling ivy, "never sere."—All, all, were old familiar friends, and Alice was leaving them for ever!

Oh! bend my spirit to thy will, and strengthen me for thy service!" was the inward prayer of her heart to him, who alone knoweth the bitterness of the portion which he sometimes sees meet to set before his suffering creatures.

Alice and her boy passed through the garden-gate, closing it gently after them, and entered the green lane; and then, what a home sound there was in their voices, enclosed, as they were between the high hedges of hawthorn, whose white blossoms fell, like flakes of snow, upon the green herbage below, or sailed away a scented burthen upon the passing gale. Here she had been accustomed to talk of household comforts to him for whose sake all comforts were doubly valued: for here they used to catch the first glimpse of little Marcus throwing wide the gate, and here they used to see the smoke of their own chimney, and think and speak of the enjoyments of their own fireside.

"It is the Lord's will," said Alice, after she had looked round for the last time, and then she walked on in silence, until Marcus who had not before this moment been fully aware of the extent of his bereavements, stopped suddenly, and called out, "But the goat!"

"Oh! I had quite forgot to say anything about the goat," replied his mother, "but we shall have to call in the village to leave the key, and I will ask our neighbours if they will allow him to remain in the field; he will be much happier there, than in the town where we are going."

"And should not we be happier too? Let us stay, mother! do!" And he looked up into her face with such a pitiful and imploring countenance, that Alice felt it almost beyond her strength to combat this new difficulty.

"We must go, my love, or we shall be too late for the coach;" but it was not until after many and repeated assurances that they would travel very fast with four horses, and that a man would really blow a horn, that she succeeded in dragging the little obstinate away at a tolerable speed.

Having reached the public road, only a few minutes after the time which Alice had fixed in her own mind to be there, they could see at a great distance a cloud of dust, in the midst of which a heavy coach came clattering down the hill, and stopped within a yard of the place where they were standing; the outside passengers looking half smothered with heat, and choked with dust, and the horses panting, and blowing, and tossing the foam from their mouths.

"All's right," said the guard, as he slammed the door to, with such violence as made little Marcus start from his seat: and then the horses went off again at full speed, the harness rattled, and the driver cracked his whip, the heavy wheels grinding up the road as they went, and the dust arising in thick volumes, and settling upon every object both within and without.

Alice shrunk back into the corner of the coach, for the other side was occupied by a young lady and her brother, fresh from Cambridge, whose restless eye examined the face of the young widow, with as little delicacy as if it had been a new pattern for a waistcoat; while Marcus, as soon as the first shock of astonishment had gone off, composed himself to rest, and silently thrusting his hand into his mother's, and leaning his cheek upon her arm, fell into a quiet sleep from which she would have been sorry to awake him to the most distant participation in the agony which she was enduring.

Thankful for the protection of her weeds, the poor widow bent down her head, and fixed her eyes upon the countenance of her child, with feelings, which those only can imagine, who know what it is to shrink from the obtrusive glance of strangers, within the inner tabernacle of the soul, where one pure image is enshrined in the spotless garment of unchangeable and holy love.

CHAPTER IV.

If the kind reader will condescend to take another view of the desolate widow, it must be within the walls of an humble dwelling, one of an extensive row of houses which formed a narrow street in the outskirts of the metropolis.

Here Alice Bland had fixed herself on account of the cheapness of the accommodation; here she occupied two small rooms, from neither of which she could see a single blade of green grass, or space of sky sufficient for making any observation upon the weather; and here she had agreed with a fashionable milliner, to spend her morning, noon, and evening hours in arranging gay ribbons and many-coloured head dresses, and mimic flowers and feathers, to adorn the sunny brows of youth, or conceal the wrinkles of old age, to add lustre to the bloom of beauty, or beguile the eye of the beholder from the deep shadow of cankering care.

"Who can have a heart light enough to bear such 'blushing honours' as these upon her head?" said Alice, as she held a splendid turban in her hand; "and these silvery flowers, who can feel pure enough to wear them; and this richly worked handkerchief, who but an eastern prince, would purchase and use it?"

Could she have followed her specimens of handiwork to their place of exhibition, she might have seen the splendid turban mounted upon the dark and shrivelled forehead of one, who scowled upon the happiness of others, without the heart to enjoy, or the power to blast it. She might have seen the pure and spotless flowers, drooping over throbbing temples, where every vein was flushed, and contrasting their silvery light with the wild flashes of a restless eye, that glared with the lurid brightness of false and feverish excitement. And the delicate and costly handkerchief, she might have seen suspended in the red hand, that told its own tale, of "excessive turtle, and good living." She might have seen all these, and a thousand incongruities beside, which would have driven her home, even to her own comfortless apartment, with something very much akin to satisfaction, if not with real enjoyment. But Alice Bland knew little of the fashionable world, and fondly fancied that the mysterious beings for whom she was perpetually providing embellishments, the richest, gayest, and most costly, which her ingenuity could invent, must in themselves possess a charm, and a power of enjoyment, beyond what common natures were acquainted with; and consequently, she thought her own portion by comparison, more bitter than it really was. Possessed with this idea, she found it difficult at all times to guard against repining; especially when any trifling circumstance brought back a quickened remembrance of the sweet home she had lost; when she looked out from her little casement, and saw that the moon was high in the heavens; for even brick walls are beautiful by moonlight; and when the rays of the setting sun, reaching a certain angle in the opposite side of the street, slightly illuminated one pane of her window, and a small portion of her curtains; for then she knew that the same sun was tinging with golden beauty, the tops of the trees, and the village spire, upon which she had often gazed so fondly. But most of all when her beloved child came home from school weary and dispirited, and seemed to pine for the green fields, and the fresh air, to which he had been accustomed; then her spirits sunk within her, and she was almost ready to say, "my burthen is greater than I can bear!"

It was some weeks after her settlement in town, and during one of these fits of melancholy abstraction, that the sound of carriage wheels was heard rolling up to the widow's door, and a thundering knock soon followed. Alice looked out, half frightened, and saw by the elegance of the equipage, that its occupant must be of rank; but she had no time to make further observations, for a light figure sprung from the step as soon as the door was opened, and the carriage drove off immediately.

What was the astonishment of Alice, when she found that she was herself the object of this unexpected visit; and when the same light figure walked with easy condescension into her own apartment, her fine face adorned with smiles and graces, which disappeared the moment the door was closed, and they two were left alone.

Alice rose up to beg the lady would be seated; but she had already thrown herself into a chair, with evident petulance and chagrin, at the same time drawing off her glove from an exquisitely beautiful hand, and untying a close bonnet, which she threw back, and exhibited a countenance, from which the spirit of a ministering angel ought to have looked forth. Alas! how much the finest works of creation may be perverted from their original design! Fatigued with harassing and despicable cares, her young brow was already crossed with wrinkles; and her dark eye shot forth fierce flashes of jealousy, and revenge; while her lips, that looked as if formed only for cherub smiles, were distorted and compressed with rage and indignation.

"Audacious woman!" she at length began; then suddenly recollecting that she had in reality no just cause of grievance, she lowered her tone, and commenced upon another key.

"I have been directed to you, as the person whose ingenuity invented that exquisitely managed turban, which the Marchioness of ——— exhibited on Friday night, and which has forever established her celebrity in the fashionable world."

"I am that person, Ma'am, and I shall be happy to execute anything of the same kind for ———"

"For me! presumptuous wretch! do you suppose I would humble myself so far, as even to employ the same fingers which work for the Marchioness of ———? No! I would rather make my appearance in the world with that widow's cap of yours upon my head;" and then in an under tone she said, or rather sighed, "Heaven only knows what I would give to be entitled to wear it." While Alice discovering at the same time that she wore a wedding ring upon her finger, was so shocked and startled by the coincidence, that she could not help fearing some wild maniac had found her way to her obscure abode.

The lady however went on, more coolly, but with a tone and look of authority, which were but little calculated to produce the intended effect.

"I have come," said she, "to demand of you the only reparation which it is in your power to offer me. I have formed my plan; it is only for you to act upon it. The Marchioness will most probably apply to you again, for her beauty is not of the kind to maintain itself. I have purchased a gauze which is of the exact colour to antipathize with her complexion. Now I insist upon your making it up in time for the grand entertainment at Lady L——'s, and telling the Marchioness, who will undoubtedly call upon you, that you never saw anything half so becoming in your life. She has implicit faith in your good taste. You will lose nothing by it; for even if the joke should be discovered, you ensure me for life: and every one must allow, that by such an exchange, you lessen your labour at any rate."

"Let me assure you, Ma'am," said Alice, with great gravity, "that in making such an application to me, you have quite mistaken my character and principles."

"Character and principles! how you talk, woman! We never hear of such things, except when we are urged to do what is disagreeable to us."

"Then I make use of the plea upon your own ground; for it would be extremely disagreeable to me to do so mean a thing, as that which you propose to me, and what is more, I will not do it!"

"You are very blunt, my good woman; but I hear you have lived in the country, where it would be a thousand pities for talents such as yours to be buried. Think how much the patronage of a lady of rank may do for you. There is Mrs. B——, who was brought up to the same employment as yourself, now sporting her carriage."

"It is idle," replied Alice, "to waste your temptations upon me, for I am fixed in my determination. I have but one object in life beyond the fulfilment of my duty as a christian, and that is, to secure a maintenance for my child, and if possible, to place him, when he shall be a man, upon the same footing in society which his father held; but even to secure this darling object, I would not stoop to do that which would render me contemptible in my own eyes, and guilty before Heaven."

"Nonsense, nonsense! You make too serious a thing of a mere joke. Have you no love for a joke?"

"Not for a mean joke."

"Then you will not oblige me?" and the lady smiled with such syren sweetness, that Alice again examined the case, and enquired of her reason whether it were utterly incompatible with the feelings of an upright and generous heart; and her resolution was stronger than before.

Assured of this, the lady was obliged to commence another attack upon fresh ground, and casting down her eyes, declared that she would in her turn be serious; for notwithstanding a natural playfulness of temper, which sometimes carried her away, she was in reality a very wretched creature. "I was married," said she, "at the age of seventeen, to a wealthy old peer, whom I hate as cordially as I love his establishment and his purse. I cannot say more, without exposing secrets and betraying confidence; but there are reasons, why I would sacrifice my daily food and my nightly rest, to humble the Marchioness of——; in fact, she must be humbled, and if you will not serve me, some one else shall."

So saying, she looked at her watch, and hearing at the same time the sound of her carriage entering the narrow street, she rose and walked haughtily to the door; but not before she had tried, as a last resource, the offer of a bribe, which Alice rejected with more indignation than good breeding; assuring her at the same time that she would rather be the destitute widow, who is compelled to earn her daily portion with pain and labour, than the rich and titled lady who scruples not to enter the dwellings of the poor, to insult them with her passions, and disgust them with her folly.

"Is this a specimen of the envied and privileged class of society?" said Alice, as she looked out upon the gay livery and the prancing horses! "It is better to be a 'lone woman' in a desert, than such a pitiable wretch as this!" and she sat down more cheerfully resigned to her fate, than she had been before. Indeed the constant employment which her good taste and industry ensured her, served very much to while away the monotony of her life, and to keep alive the hope that burned within her breast and gave a charm and a zest to every occupation.

CHAPTER V.

It was not from innate skill in the art of beautifying, that Alice Bland was able to succeed so well in her new occupation; nor for anything innate, unless a naturally clear perception of the fitness of things, with a quick eye for the arrangement of colours and general effect, might be called so: for she had in her early years acquired a tolerably correct knowledge of this branch of business, so important to the great world of fashion, during many repeated visits to an aunt who was a milliner; and it had occurred to her in her forlorn situation, as being the most likely means of enabling her, not only to be independent herself, but to procure such instruction for her boy as might fit him for the future high calling, to which she was determined, if possible, to devote him.

That he might walk in his father's steps, was the first wish of her heart; for this she humbled herself, for this she toiled, and for this she endured all present privations cheerfully. Yet still there would sometimes flit across her mind, certain doubts as to the propriety of her calling; for she was rising in celebrity, consequently she was more frequently admitted behind the scenes; and ever since the visit of the unknown lady, she had been perplexed with apprehensions that she was, though in a remote way, ministering to evil passions, and selfish and contemptible gratifications. Still it was an occupation, constant and unremitting, and she found at the end of the first year, that her circumstances were materially improved.

Another year passed away, and she was able to place her boy at a higher school, where he made astonishing progress in his learning; and oh! the heart of the fond mother would bound with delight, whenever he came to her with a demand for a fresh supply of books, and when he told her with pride in his dark eyes and blushes on his cheeks, of his master's commendations.

Another year passed, and Alice became the private and confidential assistant of many ladies, some of whom would gladly have purchased, with a considerable sacrifice of their rank and riches, a renewal of their waning beauty. This was a kind of life that Alice, in her heart, despised; and she began to think seriously of entering upon one, which, though less profitable, would be more dignified; and her decision was more easily made after an interview which she had, about this time, with an unfortunate lady, who had been struggling for fifty years against the inroads of deformity, and disease.

Alice was sent for one evening, and shown, by a private passage, into a splendid apartment, in which she waited some time for the lady's orders to proceed to business. At last she was ushered into the presence, and found herself in a long dressing room, every inch of which was filled with perfumes and cosmetics, laces and ribbons, satins, and embroidery. At the farther end and almost buried in rich damask cushions, she beheld a lean and haggard figure, whose good pleasure, delicately hinted, was no other than this, that she wanted in plain words, to be made up for the evening; while two or three waiting women, hurrying to and fro, offered cordials and stimulants every moment.

Shocked and horrified at the unnatural spectacle, Alice remained speechless with astonishment, and recurring to the remembrance of him, who was still a sort of second conscience to her, she shrunk from the prostitution of her talents to so vile a purpose.

"You are ill, Ma'am, I fear," said Alice.

"No! no! I am going to the Duchess of B——'s. The foreign ambassadors are to be there, in short, every body in the world,—and—and—I have heard of your good taste and ingenuity. My women make a fool of me. Try what you can do. You shall not have to repent the waste of your time and trouble."

In vain did Alice protest that she had no skill,—that she was giving up her business,—that she never did any thing in this way. All would not do. The women went on, consulting her in every thing they did, until she was inadvertently drawn in, though scarcely to give more than a casting vote with regard to colours and ornaments.

The poor lady was miserably ill, and dreadfully deformed, but so skilfully was the whole affair managed, that when, with the help of two women, she rose up and walked across the floor, there was such a majestic rustling of silks, and such a graceful waving of feathers in the scented atmosphere, that you might almost at the first glance have mistaken for a gem, the worthless pebble concealed within its costly casket.

In constant attendance upon this miserable creature, was a fair young girl, the daughter of a poor relation; and it was thought by some, that Miss Salisbury paid dearly for her introduction to fashionable life, by the duty of supporting half the weight of her patroness; who, in sober truth, was not able to walk alone, and therefore used to lean languidly upon the arm of the poor girl, who looked about her in astonishment, wondering whether she was really happier than when she rambled in her father's green fields at home.

Miss Salisbury was now called for, and in the mean time, the lady viewed herself from head to foot in a tall mirror, and then, turning triumphantly to Alice, asked what she thought of her?

Never before in her whole life, had Alice been so puzzled how to answer conscientiously. She hesitated, and her silence was graciously construed into a tribute of admiration.

Miss Salisbury appeared, offering her ready arm, and the procession moved on.

"Stay one moment," said the lady, "you have forgot my fan."

The women flew back to the drawers and cabinets, and Alice, in the mean time, taking from her pocket a little testament, pressed it into the lady's extended hand with both her own, and hurrying down the private stairs, escaped from the house as if from the den of an enchantress.

"I will give up this disgusting business," said she to herself, as she walked across the wide square in which the house was situated. "I will disgrace *his* name no longer. The meanest office of servitude would be more dignified than this. But whither am I wandering?" for the scene she had just witnessed seemed to have made her insensible to the danger of being alone at that hour in the streets of London, and she now looked around and above her, and saw that the stars were shining as meekly upon that human hive, as upon the flowering hawthorn, that scattered its white blossoms in the green lane beside her once happy dwelling; and she thought the spangled heavens above, were like an ark of promise, that God will be equally near to those who call upon him in the crowded city, as in the quiet grove; in the haunts of man, as in the solitudes of the wilderness.

The path of the true christian is not always either peaceful or pleasant. He must be content to labour through the dust, and the drudgery of a bustling world; but even here he will find his happy times of refreshment, his sweet seasons of rest.

When Alice reached her home, her first object was to look at her sleeping child; to smooth his pillow, and to press upon his cheek a kiss so tender, that it could not have disturbed the dreams of a slumbering cherub.

"Poor child!" said she, "I am giving up thy only prospect of success, but thou shalt never feel the injury I have done thee. I will work doubly hard, and thou shalt yet be a scholar and a gentleman. Thy father's virtues shall guide and direct thee, and may a blessing be upon thy path!"

Alice gazed for a long time upon his spotless and beautiful cheek, over which the fringe of his long dark eye-lashes cast a deep and mournful shadow; and while she gazed, a cold feeling of apprehended danger stole upon her soul, making that precious object seem dearer than he had ever been before; and then tears of unutterable tenderness rushed into her eyes, and she soothed his slumbers with the followed simple words:—

THE WIDOW'S SONG TO HER CHILD

"Sweet be thy sleep, beloved one!
From fear and danger free,
The toils, the cares, of day are done,
And I return to thee

The pilgrim loves his native home,
Beyond the wide blue sea;
Though far his wandering steps may roam,
Yet not as I love thee.

The wild bird has her nestlings all,
High in the sheltering tree,
Her faithful mate to hear her call,
But I have only thee.

Oh! say not so; the hand that guides
The sailor o'er the sea,
That stills the storm, and stems the tides,
That hand is stretch'd o'er thee.

Beside thy couch of nightly sleep,
A guardian angel, see!
When tears thy midnight pillow steep,
Those tears are bless'd to thee.

Thy cares, thy griefs, alike are known,
How deep so e'er they be;
And number'd out before that throne,
Where mercy pleads for thee.

CHAPTER VI.

"These fields are not like our own fields," said Marcus to his mother, as they walked out one sabbath evening in the suburbs of the city. "Here the grass is worn away with trampling feet, and the birds are frightened from the hedges. When shall we go back again, mother, for I am tired of dust and noise? My head aches all day; and sometimes when I ought to be busy with my lessons, I am thinking of that pleasant home we had in the country."

Alice looked in his face while he was speaking, and saw, with speechless anxiety, what she had often feared before, that the confinement of their present situation, with the application and study that were necessary for his success at school, were robbing his cheek of its bloom, and casting a premature and unnatural shade upon his fair brow; and then she felt, and acknowledged for the first time, that it was indeed a hard thing to be poor. "But he shall not suffer," said she; and the very next day she went in search of lodgings at a little distance from the dust and the smoke of the city, where they might have the sight at least of a small plot of garden ground.

It was necessary to pay twice the sum for these lodgings which she had paid before; but she hesitated not one moment, though her means were considerably reduced, and a fearful uncertainty seemed to hang over her future prospects. Yet such is the power of an energetic mind, assisted by a right faith, that she was always ready to adopt upright and decisive measures; leaving the consequences in the hands of him who alone can know whether reward or chastisement will be most conducive to the good of his creatures: and in the mean time, prepared her mind either to rejoice in success or to submit patiently to disappointment.

There was but one evil in the wide range of human suffering, upon which she could not look with a firm and collected mind. Constant, and almost laborious exertion she had been accustomed to, through the whole of her past life; and therefore it added no weight to the cares which pressed heavily upon her, but rather took off the keen edge of sorrow, by furnishing a constant supply of objects, which, though trifling in themselves, demanded a portion of her interest and attention. But this was an evil which came upon her in her hours of melancholy musing, not like the shadow of a mighty cloud, for it seemed to have no termination, and that it would never pass away. Loneliness and labour, and privation, she could bear, and had borne cheerfully; but whenever she tried to look upon this overwhelming sorrow, it appeared to admit of no palliation; for this wound there was no balm, and the expression of her rebellious spirit, as it writhed beneath it, was, too often, "Spare me this!"

Alice Bland was now deprived of all means of encreasing her source of pecuniary subsistence; but she had laid by what to her was a considerable sum of money, during the last few years: which added to the allowance for the widows of poor clergymen, raised her above all fear of actual want. But so little was it in accordance with her disposition to give way to indolence for the present, or negligence of the future, that she set about with great perseverance and industry, to pursue some other mode of procuring an addition to her slender income. For this purpose, she entered into an engagement to supply a bazaar with fancy needlework, and late and early did she labour for the scanty pittance that was doled out to her,—a minute fraction of the whole value of the article; often, when her eyes and fingers were weary with her monotonous employment, rousing herself again by the hope of being able to take her boy for a few weeks into the country, when he should again be liberated at the midsummer holidays.

Marcus was now nearly twelve years old, and, in spite of the paleness of his complexion, you could hardly have found a more handsome or noble looking fellow. "So exactly like his father," said Alice, for she had no higher standard of manly excellence or beauty; but there were those, who, remembering his father with no such partial admiration, would have said the son bid fair for being a finer man in every respect; and that he was no worse for adding his mother's energy and decision, to his father's calmness and refinement.

Perhaps the reader may smile to find the term refinement applied to the child of a poor widow like Alice Bland; but refinement may, and does exist sometimes in the humble walks of life; and what is more surprising still, it is sometimes altogether wanting where there seems to have been every thing conducive to its cultivation and growth.

In talking of refinement, we are apt to think it belongs only to the higher classes of society; and is the result of what is called a finished education, and must necessarily be accompanied by polite accomplishments, and polished manners. But true refinement, (or rather delicacy of feeling, for the one implies a process, and the other a quality) is more the gift of nature than the production of art, and thus it may be found in the cottage and wanting in the drawing room; it may be disguised by the broad peculiarities of provincial dialect, and mimicked in vain by the mincing phraseology of the boarding school; it may exist under the coarse and toil-worn exterior of the peasant, beautifying all the tender offices of life, and giving to home charities, and domestic virtues, the charm of generous sympathy and high honour; and it may be sought for among all the artificial adornments of the fashionable and high born, and not found, where it is most wanted, in the interchange of kindness, the conferring of benefits, and the necessary and mutual dependance of man upon his brother man.

Alice Bland, and her interesting boy, were not unacquainted with this feeling. They had learned to watch each other's eyes, and to know when the least shadow of anxiety or care needed the gentle hand, or the kind word, to chase it away: and they knew also how to make great sacrifices, for they were all in all to each other; and they could each give up a darling object for the other's good, without a sigh or a tear; in short, without betraying by the slightest difference of look or manner that it was a sacrifice. And if, in all these little acts of self-resignation, Alice bore the palm, it was not from any want of affection in him who was the object of them, but merely because she was a woman; and we all know it is deeply implanted in the heart of woman, to love what she does love better than herself.

Thus they lived on, the mother and the child, mutually ministering to each other's enjoyment; and perhaps the absorbing interest which occupied their thoughts, made them a little too forgetful of the wide world without, and perhaps also, it left too little of the warmest and tenderest feelings of the heart for devotion to higher objects. However it might be, we know that these exclusive attachments are not permitted to exist long in this state of being, without a blight; and that, from whatever quarter the blight may come, it is directed by him who punishes in order that we may look to him for reward; who wounds, that we may ask for healing at his hands.

The summer came, the bright and joyful summer, and Alice and her son left behind them, without a sigh, the congregated thousands who pant in the heated atmosphere of the metropolis, during the sweet season of the springing of flowers in the green field, and the singing of birds in the waving and shadowy branches of the trees.

They left without a sigh, for they were going to renew their acquaintance with the face of nature; a face like that of an old friend, early known, and dearly loved, and mingled in fond recollections with all their favourite themes of thought and conversation.

A kind acquaintance resident in Kent, had engaged for them a small cottage in the most picturesque part of that country; and when the coach stopped at the door, they sprang from it as if they were expecting to meet a home welcome. Every thing around looked so green, so fresh, so cool and quiet, that their hearts were filled with gratitude, and they longed to offer thanks to some human being, who might be feeling like themselves. But no! there had been no kind hand busy with the work of preparation;—no living creature in that remote situation knew of their existence until the week preceding, nor cared for their comfort and accommodation, when they did know; and they soon found that thanks were only due to that Power, who spreadeth out the heavens as a canopy, and maketh the earth a garden, in which man may find all that can delight his senses, and fill his soul with admiration. Nor were they forgetful of the duty of acknowledging his mercies; for when the evening came, they knelt down together, and with united hearts offered up the tribute of their thankfulness and joy.

The next day they rambled free and uncontrolled, and day after day they spent in the same manner, Marcus amusing himself with collecting the flowers and plants with which he had long been endeavouring to make himself acquainted, and often sitting down with his pencil to sketch an old tree or village church, never dreaming how exquisitely all these little memorials of his enjoyments would one day become, to her who was ever at his side, watching him with maternal fondness, and dwelling with something of prophetic interest, upon every development of his clear and comprehensive mind.

"I should like to die in the country," he would often say; "that birds might sing over my grave, and green grass grow all around me. Mother, did you ever look into that little churchyard at the end of the street where we used to live in the city? Don't lay me there when I am dead, for I think I could not rest under those hot stones and dusty nettles." And then his mother's eyes would fill with tears, for she saw more clearly every day that one prevailing thought was giving an unnatural solemnity to his young mind, and throwing over his early years the deep shadows of premature decay.

Still they were happy—happy as those who sit down for one uninterrupted hour of cheerful, and intimate, and confidential converse, before a long, long separation. But the boy gathered no strength in the country, and the mother found there was more and more need for her to shelter under the shadow of the mighty Rock, for that life would soon be to her a weary land.

Oh! it needs religion to reconcile us to the thought of death!

CHAPTER VII.

It was not many weeks after the return of the widow with her son to the city that she found it necessary to call in medical advice; for he was evidently sinking fast; and though she had little faith that human skill could save him, she determined that nothing should be spared which might lessen the suffering of his last days.

His complaint was pronounced to be one under which he might linger for some time; but little encouragement was held out to hope for his ultimate recovery. The poor boy, however, was not destined to pine away the victim of protracted suffering. His disease made rapid progress, and he was soon so much an invalid, as to be compelled to keep his bed; and then his mother felt doubly thankful that she had removed him from the close and dismal apartments which they first occupied; for now they could look out upon the blue sky, and see the brightness of the morning sun upon the branches of a willow and a laburnum, which grew beside their window; where Alice had her little garden of mignionette in a narrow box, containing all her property in the wide realm of mother earth.

It was on the first day of September, that eventful day when the heart of the sportsman bounds with delight, as he gathers up his forces, and sets off with "slaughtering gun;" himself and his dogs uniting upon one common level, for one purpose, and with one feeling, to disturb the stillness of the deserted harvest fields, taint the pure air of a fine autumnal morning, and break in upon the peace of the most harmless and unprotected of earth's creatures: it was on this day that Alice Bland sat at the window of her quiet chamber, sometimes looking out upon the yellow leaves fluttering for a moment in the buoyant air, and then settling amongst their withered companions upon the bosom of that common parent, who offers a last refuge to the fallen, the faded, and the forlorn; and then turning her anxious gaze upon him of whom the autumn leaves were but too true an emblem.

He had been sleeping for some hours, and when he awoke, he asked his mother to come nearer. "Sit down beside me," said he, "upon my bed, and let me hold your hand. Dear mother, I have been thinking, that when I am gone, you will be left entirely alone."

Alice turned away her face, but she was able to answer with a clear voice, "There is no loneliness, my child, where God is."

"I know it mother; I know that God is every-where, and that he will not turn away from those who call upon his name; but there are times when we cling to a kind hand, and listen to a voice that is sweeter than music, and feel that we cannot bear to be alone. Who will meet you at the door when you come home? who will pray with you at night? and oh! my mother, when you are ill, or in sorrow, who will sit beside your bed, and watch you so tenderly as you are watching me?"

"My child," replied his mother, "we must not venture upon these minute enquiries, into what we are capable or not capable of enduring. Who could love as I have loved, and bear to lose what I must lose, if, when the account was closed, each individual item of the great sum of affection should be counted over, and its weight and value estimated after it was gone for ever. It is for those who suffer, and feel their own weakness, to endeavour so to journey along the pilgrimage of life, that their steps may neither be impeded by the stones and stumbling-blocks that lie scattered in their path; nor led astray by the flowers that grow by the wayside: and in order to do this, it is necessary to keep our eyes fixed stedfastly upon the star of promise, the only star that is never lost in clouds. Wounded and broken as I am, and lonely as I shall soon be, my heart is yet supported by faith; not the presumptuous faith that a miracle will be wrought in my favour; that I shall be preserved from sickness and sorrow, or that celestial spirits will be sent down to smooth my dying pillow; but the humble faith that he, in whom I put my trust, will so temper the feelings of my soul, that while I endure the common lot of humanity, I shall not feel as I have done, such entire dependence upon the sweet sympathies of kindred minds; but that, when I come to the last hours of my solitary life, I shall be supported above all weak longings, even for thy care and kindness, my beloved child; and sustained by the undying hope of entering into that realm of happiness, where I trust thy father is, and where thou wilt soon be."

"You are right, mother," replied her son; "we will talk of these things no more. God is all-sufficient;" and then he lifted up his hands, and his weak voice, and prayed earnestly that his mother might be made the peculiar care of her Almighty Father; that her earthly trials might not be long, and that they might soon meet, where there should be no more tears, and no more separation.

Three days after this conversation took place, Alice Bland was sitting, at the same hour, in the same chamber, and beside the same bed, on which a long extended figure lay, in the stillness of everlasting repose. The sweet calm of unbroken serenity was upon his features, and his white hands were stretched out in motionless and marble coldness by his side—his hands, on which the mother's eyes were fixed; for oh! how well could she remember the many days and nights, when those fingers, warm and pliant, and gentle, in their infantine tenderness, had played upon her cheek; how distinctly could she recall each varying expression of that fair countenance, as of a book, every line of which was engraven upon her heart, in characters indelible and clear, though the original page was sealed for ever.

But let not rude and unhallowed fingers attempt to lift the veil that is drawn over the sacred altar of a mother's love. This venerated shrine offers no wonderful exhibition to the gaze of the curious observer; but here, as to the altars of old, the weary, and the wounded, fly from the arrows of persecution for safety and protection. Here the tears of the penitent may flow in peace; here the frailties upon which the world would trample in disdain, may find a cloak; and here, the erring wanderer, who has made shipwreck of his hopes, may return to the welcome of a home.

Alice had no assistant in the work of preparation. All day she occupied that silent chamber, with the feeling of one who stands upon a small and solitary island, in the midst of the wide ocean, and will not step into his frail boat before the hour appointed for him to launch forth alone upon the boundless expanse of friendless and inhospitable waters. And when the night came, she had no weak fears, nor fantastic visions of wandering spirits; but drew closer in the darkness to the bed-side, until wearied nature sank under the long vigil, and sleep drew around her the curtain of forgetfulness.

It was but for a few brief days and nights that Alice could be permitted to sit and gaze upon her last earthly treasure; and oh! how solemn was the dawn of each succeeding morning as it rose upon the living and the dead! How silently the still evening closed around! Yet in that sweet hour, when the husbandman returns from the field of labour, when the cattle are driven down from the hills, and the sheep are gathered into the fold; when the weary bird flies back to the woods, and covers her nestlings with her brooding wings; when the mother smoothes the pillow of her child, and presses on its rosy cheek her farewell kiss; when all the softening influences of domestic peace and home affection are drawn around the heart; —even in that sweet hour, Alice uttered no lamentation, and the tears that chased each other down her cheeks, were not tears of repining: for she had not been one of those who leave the commencement of the great and important work until the time when there is urgent need for its full and entire completion; who enter the vineyard to feast upon the grapes, having never pruned the vines; who go forth into the harvest-field to reap, having never sown the precious seed. In the spring time of her life, in the morning of her days, she had diligently sought the true fountain; and now, when every other draught was turned to bitterness, she found and felt the efficacy of the waters of everlasting life.

A second time Alice Bland stood a deep

and solitary mourner by the side of the closing grave. Over her pale features was spread the calmness of resignation; and none of the surrounding throng of lookers on knew, or cared to know, with what feelings she turned away, when the last solemn rites were over, from that little churchyard—not the noisy space of ground allotted to the burial of the dead, which her son had so often spoken of with disgust and horror; but a quiet resting-place, one they had fixed upon together during their last walk into the country. Here she had stood beside the grave, not only the chief, but the sole mourner; and here she left with her buried treasure all the hopes and the affections which bound her to this troubled life.

From this now sacred spot of earth, Alice returned to her home.—Home! what is home? Surely there must be something more than a hired tenement to constitute a home; but Alice had in this wide world nothing more. Happy—happy is it for those who feel that their home is "an habitation not made with hands, eternal in the heavens!"

The Christian character is almost universally described as one which is, and must be, at variance with what is commonly denominated the world; consequently, the Christian church is called the church militant, and the Christian himself is often spoken of as one who is compelled to fight the good fight. All the good lessons which we learn from our infancy, our observations upon the world in general, the experience of every day, and the precepts of the holy scriptures, combine to teach us that the utmost stretch of faith, and perseverance, and watchfulness, and zeal, are necessary to protect us against the mastery of evil passions within, and the temptations of the world without. It is, however, graciously permitted to us, in almost every situation in life, to enjoy the consolation of human help; to have some star or stars in our own low sphere to light us on our way; some kind voice to cheer us on our pilgrimage; some home of welcome in the hearts we love, where the wounded may fly for healing, and the weary for repose.

How thankful, then, ought we to be for this mingling of earthly affections with heavenly; this lightening of the task of duty: this sweetening of the cup of self-denial! and how deep, how sincere, should be our pity for those unto whom this merciful dispensation is not extended, unto whom it is decreed, by the wisdom that erreth not, that they shall journey through the wilderness alone; unto whom the sentence has gone forth, "Behold! I will take away the desire of thine eyes as with a stroke!"

In this situation the Christian is most severely tried; for here no earthly encouragement is held out, and whatever is done must be done purely for the love of God, for the pleasure of obeying his law, and walking in his ways.

In order more fully to illustrate the nature of true resignation, and more clearly to exemplify what ought to be the state of the human mind under this trial, it will be necessary to trace the progress of the humble individual whose character has been here described, one step farther on her path of patience and fortitude. For this purpose let us look in upon the childless widow in her solitude. Let us imagine her on the day following that of the funeral, solitary, but not inactive; for Alice busied herself with examining each article of the personal property which her son had left; and though her eyes were sometimes so dimmed with tears that she could hardly read the different labels he had placed upon all his school prizes, and his memorials of affection and early companionship, she still went on, leaving out whatever she thought might be more valuable to others than to herself; though it was a hard thing to part even with his wardrobe, now that she was so desolate and forlorn. This duty, moreover, was faithfully gone through, and Alice sat down to spend the evening alone;—alone, and without employment: for when she laid down her bible, and would have taken up her work, the thought that she had now no longer any one to work for, seemed to paralyze her fingers, and throw a chain of icy coldness upon every effort to rouse herself for active exertion.

It was not long, however, that Alice permitted her spirit to sink under the pressure of unmitigated affliction. "It is the will of my heavenly Father," said she, "that I should bear my burden alone; and with his help I will not faint by the way; there must yet be some field of usefulness open for me, or my soul would be required of me. I will still labour in his vineyard, though my strength should be as that of the bruised reed; I will still worship at his altar, though my only offering should be a broken heart."

With such feelings, strengthened into resolution by earnest and continual prayer, Alice set about to prepare for a change in her occupations and her place of abode.—Having heard that a mistress was wanted for an infant school in a distant part of the country, she offered her services, and was appointed as a decent, useful looking woman, by those who thought they were conferring upon her a favour.

Here let us observe how little is known by those who flatter themselves they are dispensing favours—how very little is known of the misery which the necessity of being the object of them, sometimes inflicts upon the receiver: thus we complain of ingratitude, because our bounties are not seized with avidity, and acknowledged with delight; when in reality each act of beneficence, upon which we pride ourselves, has been gall and bitterness to those who were compelled by circumstances to accept it.

Alice had no natural inclination for the situation, nor for the line of life which she had chosen, and would rather have shrunk away from the arduous task which she had imposed upon herself; but it seemed more desirable to her to enter at once upon the field of active and imperative duties, than to leave her inclination time to wander, and make its own selection amongst those which were merely optional. She therefore, took her place amongst the little throng, and went diligently and faithfully through the whole process of instruction; while visiters flocked in to see, and ladies made their comments, and the wonders and praises of the new establishment spread far and wide.

It was no difficult thing to discover that Alice was a trusty servant, and, as such, she was valued and approved; but no one knew what her heart had suffered, or was then suffering; nor why when the school was closing, she would often single out a little dark-haired boy, whose pale complexion and soft shadowy eyelashes gave him an air of melancholy and languor, and often, walking home with him to his mother's door, would stand there until she saw him comfortably seated at his own fireside, and then turn away to take a long solitary ramble by the sea-shore.

Yet the character of Alice Bland was not one that was capable of remaining long unknown. Though unobtrusive in her charities, and limited in her means, she was so unbounded in her desire to be useful, that neither time nor opportunity seemed wanting; and it was a common reply with her, to the apologies of those who feared they might be making too great a claim upon her kindness, "Don't think of that. I am a lone woman. I have no ties at home, and therefore I am the more fit to be serviceable to others. To him who has given me health and strength, and a few kind feelings, I have to render an account; and blessed be his holy name, I am supported through every day by the consolations of his love. I am a weak instrument it is true; but then there is the more need that I should diligently watch, and earnestly embrace every opportunity of offering my mite. It is not the magnitude of our good actions by which we hope to be saved; it is the feelings from which they arise, and the spirit in which they are performed, that are the test of obedience."

In this spirit, the spirit of Christian love, the poor widow persevered in the path of duty. Filled with this spirit, she laid aside all weak lamentations and fruitless repinings. Encouraged by this spirit, she kept perpetually in view the blessed goal, where she already beheld, in imagination, the souls of her departed robed in white. Supported by this spirit, she became a prop to the feeble, and a comfort to the needy Inspired by this spirit, she journeyed patiently along the pilgrimage of life, and was enabled, at the end, to lay down the burden of the flesh, rejoicing with the gladness of the captive who leaves his prison-house.

MARRIAGE AS IT MAY BE.*

> Yes, he deserves to find himself deceived,
> Who seeks a heart in the unthinking man.
> Like shadows on a stream the forms of life
> Impress their characters on the smooth forehead,
> Nought sinks into the bosom's silent depth;
> Quick sensibility of pain and pleasure
> Moves the light fluids lightly; but no soul,
> Warmeth the inner frame.
>
> WALLENSTEIN.

IT is a common and popular plan, in writing what is called an autobiography, to account in some plausible manner for the way in which the pretended manuscript has fallen into the author's hands. On the present occasion, however, the picture that is presented to the public, offers so little either of the extraordinary or the marvellous, that it appears quite unnecessary to introduce it under any other character than that of a confidential communication from one lady to another.

Painful as it may be to bequeath to posterity a record of our own errors, the heart that is deeply interested in the well-being of society, will think the instruction of even one of the rising generation cheaply purchased by its own exposure.

To you, the friend of my early years, I submit this manuscript, with strict injunctions to keep it secret until I and mine shall have ceased to suffer the agonies of wounded feeling. You may not outlive us, or if you should, your judgment is now too mature, and your walk in life has ever been too circumspect for you to reap any advantage from my experience. But you have daughters: and may they read with charity, and wisely profit by the history which I am about to give, of that most lamentable of all calamities—most irreparable of all misfortunes, —an "ill assorted marriage."

You who have shared in the pleasures and pursuits of my youth, are aware that my life was unmarked by any incident of sufficient interest to strike the attention of an impartial reader; notwithstanding I was distinguished for my quickness at school, and regarded as a prodigy of genius at home. Early deprived of the blessing of maternal care, and left at the age of sixteen to the unrestrained indulgence of my own tastes and caprices, I set about with the most voracious appetite, to feast upon that species of literature that was most in unison with a sensitive and undisciplined mind, and most conducive to the growth of that morbid melancholy which has followed me through life; restraining the aspirations of hope, weighing down the energies of resolution, and damping the feeble fire of a lukewarm faith. In the spring-time of life, when the heart is most capable of enjoyment, I was consequently wretched. I was told reproachfully, that it was the absence of religion which made me so, and I began to "believe and tremble."

In my father's house we had no religious

* The writer of this story would be sorry to draw upon herself the suspicion of having placed a worthless individual in the situation of a Clergyman of the Church of England, for the purpose of throwing an air of disrespect over that particular religious body. With creeds she holds no controversy,—for parties professes no preference. Her apology must be, that in painting from private life, she has delineated no traits of character which she has not seen, nor delinquency of conduct with which she has not been acquainted.

exercises. The gay and the worldly-minded sought our society, and with these I was constantly associated; until I felt like a being who is carried away against his inclination by the mere press of a crowd, with which he holds neither sympat' y nor common feeling.

Amongst those who frequently sat at my father's table, was a young man of excellent disposition, whose light and easy manners won upon us all, and made him friends for the moment, with every description of character that happened to be brought in contact with his own. He was undergoing the process of preparation for the church, though still but a boy, when we first met; but he had read poetry, and been taught at high schools, and flirted with a young widow; and just for present pastime was very much at my service, either as a butt, a lover, or a convert. As a butt, I first tried him, and found him the liveliest, wittiest, and best tempered creature in the world; as a lover, I did not allow myself to ask what he might be; but as a convert,—I triumphed in the thought. Here was a field for my energies to work in. His good heart,—his habits of dissipation,—his deference for, and evidently growing attachment to myself,—what vain woman, building her eternal hopes upon the frail reeds of self-righteousness, could resist a temptation like this? It was too much for me.

For some time I was made happy in the confidence that I should obtain the reward of having saved a "soul from sin;" for my promising protege, though led away by gay companions, always came back to me in his hours of penitence, and a hopeful and interesting charge I had; until the hope, if not the interest, was somewhat abated, by my young friend proposing himself to me as my future husband.

I own I was a good deal surprised, that he who had always acknowledged such an immense inferiority on moral and religious grounds, should now esteem himself a fitting helpmate for me in the pilgrimage of life: but, forgiving the presumption of the boy in the flattery of the woman, I gently declined his proposals, pitied him, spoke of friendship, called myself his sister, and the thing went on as such things usually do.

All this while, however, my heart was ill at ease. I felt like one who goes into the field of battle, bearing the banner of his cause, without having learned to defend it. If we build our religion upon a false foundation, we make but a sorry edifice. Mine was a temple in which I found neither shelter nor repose, but rather a fantastic fabric, whose dizzy pinnacles threatened to fall and crush me in their ruins. Thus my days passed on. If I began to converse on religion, I often concluded by listening to love; and night invariably found me listless, weary, and unsatisfied. My pupil, too, began to exhibit points of character, of which I had not before suspected him. There was a degree of wounded pride with which he listened to my repeated refusals to become his wife, that frequently urged him on to the manly revenge of determined inebriation; while many of my enemies, and some of my friends, wondered at and blamed me, for my intimacy with a being so unrestrained and desperate. Still it was no easy thing to break entirely asunder the chain which linked us together, for all his best hopes both for this world and the next seemed bound up with me: and I had the vanity to believe, that in casting him off, I should most probably consign him to everlasting perdition.

Surrounded by dangers and quicksands on every hand, it never once occurred to me that I was pursuing a wrong course; but still I determined to struggle through, though I felt myself plunging deeper and deeper at every fruitless attempt; and when time and experience brought me to my senses, it was too late to extricate myself from the difficulties in which I was involved. In this manner years passed away.—My lover was confirmed in his habits of dissipation, and my friends had some of them become enemies, loud in their declamations against me, though I observed that whenever they had an opportunity of receiving his attentions, they were disposed to be any thing but uncharitable towards him.

Disappointed in all my hopes, and hemmed in by difficulties, I endeavoured to seek from the only true source, that help which I ought to have solicited at an earlier stage of my blind and foolish career. I believe I was sincere; but, if I recollect right, I prayed more earnestly that I might be extricated from my present perplexities, than assisted to bend down my spirit in meekness and resignation, to the trials and troubles which followed as natural and inevitable consequences of the course I had chosen for myself.

You remember the tale of my being likely to marry a gentleman at that time residing abroad. It occupied a good deal of our thoughts and feelings; but neither you nor any other of my friends knew the reasons which induced me to consent to such a step. As regards the individual, he did not interest me deeply, only as he was connected with my hopes of emancipation from the thraldom of evil. I believed and still believe him to be an amiable character; but there were circumstances connected with our separation which did not reflect much credit on his name. My friends, consequently, congratulated me, and said, I had had an escape; while others laughed and said, I had had a disappointment. I tried to bear it with an air of philosophy, but all my efforts were vain. As regards the man, the case was comparatively neither aggravated nor cruel, for such things occur every day; but from a Christian friend—from one in whose society I had hoped to find benefit and instruction, I felt the blow, and almost fancied that my God had forsaken me. I had been buoyed up with the prospect of a happy and lasting union with one who would be willing and able to direct my steps aright, with what he persuaded me was a call to serious and imperative duties, away from the temptations which had long beset my path; but now, my spirit was smitten down and prostrate in the midst of its own desolation.

I know not how it is, but there are times when affection wins upon us with tenfold power. I had been willing to leave my home connections, almost entirely for the sake of escaping from all associations with him whose destiny seemed to be mysteriously linked with my own; but he bore the alteration in my prospects so nobly, and then, when he found me left behind and neglected came forward so generously with the same offer of faithful and unalterable attachment which I had so often rejected, that while my spirit writhed under the recent smart, while I fancied myself shut out from all help, either human or divine, I was the more reckless what I sacrificed for the sake of helping others, and in an evil hour I promised to become his wife.

Never shall I forget that day. It was in the month of December. A slight sprinkling of half-melted snow lay on the ground. A shrewd friend was staying with me, whose quick eye seemed to pierce into the secret recesses of my heart. "All things pertaining" to that time are written upon my memory, with a depth and distinctness not to be described; for such was the agony to which my feelings were wrought, that I almost wondered how the common affairs of human life could go on, without any one taking note of my calamity. But so it was.

I will not here trouble you with a relation of what took place preparatory to my melancholy union with one whose joy was beyond bounds, nor how keenly I felt the altered looks and constrained behaviour of those whom I knew to be in their hearts despising me. Had they spoken freely, I could have borne it better; for then there would have been something like a respite in their silence; but from this mute but perfectly intelligible kind of reproach, the heart has no intervals of relief; and I rejoiced at the coming of that day, after which I should be able to say to my conscience, "the Rubicon is now passed," I have no longer the power to return. It came at last; and I set off with my young husband to spend the honey-moon amongst the lakes and mountains of Cumberland.

After deliberately taking what we firmly believe to be a wrong step, we not unfrequently endeavour to console ourselves, and to quiet the whisperings of self-reproach, by doing double duty immediately afterwards; and, in this way, I diligently set about to work that reformation in my husband's heart and character, which I had promised myself should be the happy termination of my Christian labours.

For a short time every thing went on pleasantly enough, for we had no one to interrupt our gravity; his mind seemed willingly to take the tone of mine; and it was not difficult under such circumstances to draw forth even from him the often repeated quotation about looking

"From Nature up to Nature's God."

The first sabbath that we spent was at a small town on the banks of one of the most picturesque lakes in this delightful country; and here, thought I, we shall be able to acknowledge the sweet influence of peace, to enjoy communion with our own and each other's hearts, and to worship in the house of God together.

Perhaps I need not own to you that the prospect of being the wife of a clergyman, was the most powerful reason for my consenting to become Mrs. Henry Wilton; and the gravity and apparent attention with which I now saw my husband conduct himself during the service was a great solace to my heart. I had always considered that his high office would impose a wholesome restraint upon him, and that the respect he was accustomed to evince for the observances of religion, would draw him away from all evil communications. Alas! I had never reflected, perhaps I had never observed, how frail, and worse than frail, are all outward observances, when the thoughts and feelings of an unsubdued nature are rioting within.

On our return from church we were met by a young man of no very promising aspect, who saluted my husband with the familiarity of a college acquaintance, and I had the mortification of hearing a cordial invitation for him to dine with us, as cordially accepted. Nay, he was even kind enough to join us in our ramble by the side of the lake, and when we called for a boat he very readily stepped in, and sat down beside us. It was not difficult to assign a character to my new acquaintance, a character more frequently found than admired; for although college slang was the only medium through which he condescended to convey his ideas, I understood enough and more than enough, even from what was to me an unknown tongue. He was the son of a London silk mercer, and bore about with him the certificate of his pedigree so clearly stamped upon his countenance, that you could scarcely look at him without picturing his father, the keen tradesman, glancing over his ledger, and his aunts and cousins running about from house to house, and from neighbour to neighbour, collecting receipts for sweet cakes, gravies, and home-made wines. Not but that

"A man's a man for a' that."

But the descendant of this noble house endeavoured to distinguish himself by talking about the *οιπγγοι*,* and swearing at waiters, and looking big at inns, for he was evidently unacquainted with any other kind of greatness. At such a time, and in such a place, I could scarcely have been brought into contact with a being more repulsive to me, and what made his society infinitely more intolerable was, to see my husband completely led out of his better self, sharing in the vulgar volubility of this heartless, mindless, mockery of a man.

Relieved by any thing which brought a change, I was glad to return to the inn, and here, while the pleasures of the table were prolonged, I was compelled to listen to often-

* For an unlearned writer to make use of a Greek word, may well be thought a piece of unpardonable presumption; but surely the same apology may be repeated —that of painting from private life—from the number of young men in the middle classes of society, who think that a college education entitles them to make use of this expression to distinguish themselves from the *common people*.

repeated and common-place enconiums on my husband's good taste, interrupted only by the good taste of the viands, and the different wines in which they both appeared deeply interested. In fact they were dining so much to their mutual satisfaction, that I felt no scruple in making my exit at a very early period of the entertainment, informing my husband as I passed him, that I should spend the evening upon the water.

"Take care of yourself," said he, with many of those endearing expressions which people are wont to use when their hearts are not entirely with you, "and we will join you in the course of half an hour."

There are few things that make a plain man look plainer than an expression about the face which reminds you of dinner and wine, and when I turned away from the door of the apartment, but more especially when on passing it again, I heard peals of laughter from within, I could not help wishing with a sigh, that it was possible to love my husband better.

The book which I selected for the companion of my rambles, was Milton's Paradise Lost, and in these delightful pages I lost myself for a while, carried away, as it were, from the realities of earth, up to a higher sphere of intellectual and pure enjoyment. From some inexplicable cause, however, as if the chain of imagination had snapped asunder, I suddenly awoke to the full consciousness of my own situation. Above me was an almost cloudless sky, with the sun gradually declining towards his golden couch, far in the west. Around me was the magnificence of nature; the summits of the mountains bathed in radiance; and nearer, the woods, and islands, and grassy slopes, clothed with summer's richest drapery; while all were reflected in the glassy mirror of the peaceful water, over which I was silently gliding; and in the midst of this region of repose and loveliness, what was I?

As a being created for immortality, and endued with feelings, and powers and capabilities of a high and intellectual nature, I dared not contemplate the yoke to which I had just submitted myself; and as a Christian, accountable to an unerring and Almighty Judge, the thought was still more dreadful. Despicable and disgusting pictures of the future presented themselves to my mind; degrading associations, low thoughts, and gloomy forebodings fell upon me with a deadly weight; until with the feeling that they were rapidly becoming more than I could bear, and glad of any thing that might divert me from myself, I told the boatman to row me back to the shore, almost unconscious of what I either said or did.

Here I was not met, as I had anticipated, and I sauntered on, solitary and musing, not unfrequently stopping to admire the flowery gardens, and the pretty cottages wreathed all over with garlands of beauty. The scent of innumerable roses, the freshness of the air, the exercise, the sight of happy and healthy faces, and the many social groups gathered together in the fond enjoyment of a day of rest, brought me back to something like a sense of pleasure; and I returned to the Inn just as the afternoon was waning into evening, quite disposed to make the best of every thing.

With this determination I opened the door of the dining-room, not doubting but I should find my husband overjoyed at my return.

May I ask you, my friend, if you have ever gone suddenly from the pure atmosphere of a summer's day, from the fanning of the breezes that play over the lake, and sport with the spray of the waterfall, and dance upon the tops of the mountains, and sleep in the valleys amongst bowers of rose-leaves; have you ever gone suddenly from the freshness of such enjoyment, into a dining-room that has not been opened for three hours after dinner? Now this was exactly what I did on the afternoon of a Sabbath day, after sailing on the lake, and reading Milton. And there sat my husband with a flushed and dizzy look—not certainly intoxicated—he would have been horror-struck at the thought, but with all that was most gross and despicable in his nature laid bare upon his brow. Not intoxicated certainly; but just so much deranged by the lowest kind of excitement, that he had almost entirely lost his self-possession, and that lively tact with which he could sometimes play off an assumed part; and thus, when he declared that he had been ten times down to the water to look for me, he betrayed himself by a knowing wink at his companion, which seemed to say, "This is the way to manage a wife."

Long and intimate association with evil has somewhat seared my natural feelings to that quick sense of transgression on the part of others, which I once had, yet not so entirely but that I have a vivid recollection of the intense agony I suffered from the repetition of this falsehood, trifling as it was in every respect, except that of its own base nature.

Of all that comes across our path in the rough and varied journey of life, there can be nothing more deadly and dissevering to the social affections which bind us to each other, than the first falsehood. When the trusting and unpractised youth goes forth into the world, fresh from the shelter of the paternal home, and strong in the early instilled principles of truth, perhaps he is consigned to the oversight, and protection of the avaricious, or the worldly-minded, and here he learns for the first time—learns with horror and dismay, that in order to maintain what is called a respectable standing in society, to combat with the difficulties, the competitions, and the tricks of trade, to obtain "that bread which perisheth," it is thought necessary by mankind in general, to deceive, evade, and circumvent, and too frequently to sacrifice entirely the fair principles of honest dealing. Let me ask, whether, after such daily contemplation of the lowest prostration of the human soul, he would not at times be willing to give all his acquired possessions to be able to return to the innocence of his early years, and to feel again the confidence with which he could once sit down and look around him in simplicity and peace, before his ear was startled by the first falsehood?

It is not so much the direct character of a lie to which I am now alluding, though hateful, and vile, and sinful in itself; it is its direful consequences, felt as they are, not only in the inner chambers, the secret recesses of the heart, but on through all the chain of human fellowship, to the extremest boundaries which separate man from the brute creation. Nor is the first falsehood a stain that can be soon wiped off; an error that can be easily redeemed. The best atonement we can make to each other, is a free acknowledgement of our transgression; but even after this, we see and feel that we are "fallen from our high estate," from the safe ground which we occupied in the affections of those around us.

Can the wife ever ask counsel again of the husband of her choice, after she has detected him in the first falsehood? Can the husband ever look again with perfect satisfaction upon the countenance of his wife, after the first falsehood has polluted her lip? Alas! no! A barrier has been broken down, and the waves of sin and sorrow roll in upon their paradise of domestic enjoyment.

When the mother looks into the face of her child and sees there, instead of the sweet open confidence of truth, the bright eye cast down with shame, and the rosy lip trembling beneath its burden of deceit, her heart faints within her, as she beholds for the first time "the trail of the serpent," amidst the loveliness of her own Eden. And oh! if she to whom belongs this holy name, could even dare to violate by falsehood the sancity of her high title, I could almost think, that not only the besom of destruction would sweep away the happy circle from her hearth, but that her guardian angel, thenceforth abandoning his trust, would bear the melancholy tidings up to the highest heaven, where the cherubs that wing their happy flight around the throne, would veil their faces and weep.

But to return to my story. I need hardly say that after the scene I have described, I had little satisfaction in rambling through the delightful country in which I had promised myself so much enjoyment; for it was easy to see that my husband was not exactly in his element, and that his heart went not along with me in my admiration of the beauties of nature, whether simple or sublime; we therefore cut short our sentimental tour, and turned our course towards our future home, where from the anxiety which he evinced to enter upon his pastoral duties, I felt confident I should see his character exhibited in a more favourable point of view. I did not then know that the opportunity of displaying a bombastic sort of eloquence upon which he prided himself, was the grand charm which these duties possessed; and that the soundness and safety of a favourite hunter, upon which he had made some tremendous bets, were of more importance to him than the study of cloud capped mountains, silvery lakes, rich verdant woods, and foaming waterfalls.

The home upon which I entered had every thing in its appearance both within and without, to invite a weary spirit to repose; and I sat down, well pleased to be mistress of a parsonage house. My husband, naturally kind-hearted, was delighted with my evident satisfaction, and in this frame of mind he readily agreed to a variety of rules, and stipulations, which I proposed to him for the future regulation of our domestic economy. Amongst these, I insisted upon our never visiting or receiving visiters on a Saturday; for in a situation high and important as his, I thought it necessary to have that day exclusively devoted to preparation for the Sabbath; and as all his occupations were painfully prolonged by indolence and procrastination, I found it difficult enough, even with my assistance, to accomplish the concoction of a sermon on the following day. It was completed however, grammatically arranged and put together, (for I cannot say that we composed it,) by one o'clock on Sunday morning, and at half past nine my husband crept down stairs in his slippers to a cold breakfast, which had been waiting for him more than an hour. His rings, his dress, were scrupulously selected and arranged, and his white bands lay smooth under his chin; but there was no smoothness on his brow, for he knew and felt that he was too late, and that every one was thinking him so; a feeling well calculated to ruffle the countenance, as well as the temper, prompting to a childish peevishness and petty revenge upon shoe-strings, hot coffee, grooms, horses, and wives. Of course we had no time for family prayer, a duty which we had decided the day before should never be interfered with by any other consideration. Nor indeed could I have well endured such a mockery in my lord and master's present state of mind; so we set off together with a spirited well-fed horse, enlivened all the way by rearing, prancing, driving, and slashing over a dirty high road. It was but a short distance to the village church, which stood embowered in a beautifully wooded valley, but the Rev. Henry Wilton esteemed it derogatory to his importance to be seen walking over the green fields, through which we might have passed by a cool, pleasant, and much shorter way.

On entering the church, where the congregation had already been waiting some time, I observed my husband slacking his pace, and assume an air of tenfold majesty, that was but little in keeping with his juvenile appearance, and the jocund air, and playful manner, which he seemed formed to wear

"Oh! wad some power the giftie gie us,
To see ourselves as others see us"—

thought I, as he ascended the steps of the pulpit; and then, when I tried to turn my attention to more serious things, there came, instead of the ridiculous, images that were still more repulsive, and texts of scripture presented themselves, burdened with deep and poignant reproof, such as "They made me keeper of the vineyards, but mine own vineyard have I not kept;" so that, although the service was got through with tolerably well, I felt that I, at any rate, had not been ministered unto, and hoped that others had been more favoured. Without having added one mite to that peace of mind which I so much needed, I turned away from the house of prayer, where, for any edification that I had received, there might as well have been the "tables of the money changers, and them that sold doves." However, it was a gratification to my natural vanity, to be the well-dressed wife of a clergyman, and I lifted high my head, taking care to bend it occasionally with graceful condescension to the poor and needy, as I passed them by.

(What a strange compound is our nature! when we do not acknowledge, nay, we hardly feel our own want of all rational, substantial, and healthy support, so long as we can wear the trappings of greatness, and the world does not look in and see the emptiness beneath.) And yet, we scarcely live through a single day, sometimes not through a single hour, without pointing at the abuses, the inconsistencies, the fallibilities, the abominations of that world, from which we are at the same time concealing our faults, even the most trifling, by every possible subterfuge, and evasion; sparing neither time nor trouble, cost nor comfort, pains nor patience, to accomplish our purpose. Nor do we ever kneel down in prayer, open our bibles, or converse on holy themes, without acknowledging the justice, the purity, and the omnipotence of that power, before whose all-seeing eye we dare deliberately to violate the laws which he has laid down for the merciful government of his creatures.

Amongst the numerous visiters who came on an early day to pay their compliments to the bride, were a Mr. and Mrs. Ormorand, whose appearance and manners were well calculated to excite a wish to cultivate their acquaintance. Mr. Ormorand was a gentleman without business, living genteelly upon a small income, which, with good management, was just sufficient to afford every rational gratification to an humble, yet philosophic mind, and Mrs. Ormorand was in all things a fitting wife for such a character.—In their society I found all that I most wanted at home, but I soon discovered that my husband's natural and undisguised antipathy to intellectual and scientific pursuits, in short, to any thing that required the least exercise of mind, was very likely to become something like hatred of the individuals who thus possessed the power of throwing him and his small attainments into shade. Not that he was altogether ignorant or illiterate. In many of the popular works of the day he was well versed, as well as in magazines and reviews belonging to the party for which, as a staunch supporter of church and state, he professed a sort of boisterous attachment. Besides, he had an excellent memory, and could spout pompous passages from plays; often, when I wished to talk seriously, going off as Othello, upsetting the chairs and tables in the thundering rant of King Riehard, and subsiding into the majestic madness of old Lear. But this was nothing for my private gratification, (still less was it in public,) and then, as to the wonders of the animal kingdom, the varieties of climate, the study of plants, minerals, and fossils, as well as the history of the creation in general, he was so thoroughly and blindly ignorant, that he had scarcely patience to listen with common civility when such were the subjects of conversation in his presence. I had, it is true, observed this peculiarity long before I married, but then he had such a lively and humorous manner of turning the discourse, such a burlesque way of appearing, if possible, more ignorant than he really was, that the importance of his deficiencies was lost in the entertainment they afforded. But two people confined to each other's company, hour after hour, and day after day, grow weary of their own jokes, and when this amusement was entirely vanished from our fire side, I felt a miserable blank which I would gladly have filled up, as far as I could, by the society of Mr. and Mrs. Ormorand. But this unfortunate partiality of mine for my literary and intellectual friends, was a constant source of strife and contention, not unfrequently terminating in deliberate and determined inebriety on the part of my husband. They were, besides, dissenters, and all dissenters were, in his opinion, low-bred people, so that it was almost an act of rebellion whenever I sought the comfort of their social circle.—Here, however, I was accustomed to meet with that enlargement of feeling which extends, in the fellowship of brotherly love, to all the community of Christ, that charity which, "hopeth all things," that philosophy which bows before religion, and brings forward the treasures of earth, ocean, and air, to magnify the glory of their Creator.

To deprive myself of the advantage of such associations was an act of greater self-denial than I felt equal to; but I paid dearly for my short-lived enjoyment.

In due time, however, the hunting season came, and then my husband had sufficient animal stimulus to supply him with good humour even for the Ormorands, and we went on peaceably for a while, each following the bent of our different inclinations. With the hunting season came its worst accompaniments, dinner parties, and drinking if not to actual brutality, yet to an excess that was far beyond my powers of toleration. On such occasions I was accustomed to shut myself up in my own chamber; but even here my senses were stunned, and my feelings shocked, by the shouts and the loud peals of vulgar laughter that issued from the dining-room.

How was it possible, after such days as these, to call in the domestics for evening prayer? and in the morning the aspect of things was so little better, that in time the custom was laid aside altogether; and we, who stood at the head of a clergyman's household, might truly have acknowledged to ourselves, and to each other, that we were not in a fit state to engage in the duty of family prayer.

Wounded, weary, and disappointed, I now sought the society of the Ormorands more for a sort of fascination which it possessed, than for any solid satisfaction which it afforded; indeed, had I weighed my feelings on returning home, I believe the balance would have been on the side of misery; the comparison was so dreadful, so heart-rending, so utterly devoid of all consolation. I had no pursuits; for, galled and fretted as I was, and bound up for life with a character so uncongenial, the mind loses the energy to pursue any thing, and stagnates in despair. There was but one hope for me. To pull down the religion I had built up for myself, and erect another edifice upon the true foundation: but this was going to the root of the matter in a way I had never dreamed of, and I still continued to recoil from my bitter portion, without studying or soliciting the means of rendering it more palatable. It seemed to me, in this state of mind, that no creature upon the face of the earth was so wretched as myself; and I often compared my situation, surrounded by comforts which I could not enjoy, to that of him who was doomed to perpetual thirst in the midst of water of which he was unable to drink.

If the mornings which took my husband to the field were the happiest of my life, the evenings of these days were the most miserable; for just at that hour (the grey twilight of a winter's evening) when those who enjoy domestic comforts gather in to the social circle, and draw around them the blessed influence of peace and love, I used to sit solitary and musing, waiting the tread of a tired hunter along the gravel walk beneath my window; and then the noisy entrance of a blustering man, calling with impatience for his dinner, to which he would sit down without either grace or gratitude; and when his keen appetite was a little abated, came the luxury of recounting his "glorious leaps," and magnificent exploits, added to that of drinking my health, with the health of any other person, man, woman, or child, who might "prove an excuse for the glass;" and then followed the deadly stupor of exhausted animal nature, with the heavy eyelids closed, and the whole face stiffened into the stupidity of sleep.

It is true I cannot pay myself the compliment of saying that I endeavoured to make the best of these opportunities to struggle against the disgust that was fast gaining upon the tardy growth of my affections, or to bring down my understanding to enquire whether my own internal pride of heart and want of charity, and neglect of duty, might not be as culpable in the sight of Heaven, as those grosser vices at which I felt so indignant. No! I made no such appeal to reason, no such inquiry of conscience, but have often sat for hours lost in a fruitless reverie, with no other sound to cheer me than the deep breathing of a weary huntsman, while my eyes were fixed upon the red embers of an unstirred fire—unstirred, because I was unwilling to break the repose of a sleep which, however annoying in itself, afforded me a respite from that which was still more so; and in these dreamy hours what retrospections came back upon my heart! bringing again the sweet picture of my father's house, the voices of my sisters when we were happy girls at home, the fields where we used to play, the books we read together, and more than these, the fresh buoyancy of feeling, never, never to be recalled.

How far my husband's character might have been improved by studious care and well-directed kindness, I am not able to say, for I acknowledge with shame and compunction that this was a trial which I never made. Having trusted to his promise as a lover, I was piqued and wounded by his failure as a husband, and disappointed in no small degree on discovering, that neither my influence, my wishes, nor my example, were sufficient to win him over to a change of heart. As if there could possibly be more potency in the charming of a weak-woman, than in the daily experience of the unsatisfactory nature of mere animal enjoyment, the force of early instruction, and the conviction of natural reason.

Of all those human infatuations which stand forth in glaring and palpable mockery of nature, and experience, and common sense, none can be more blind and fatally delusive, than that which leads a vain woman to believe, that by marrying a vicious man, she shall be able to turn him from the error of his ways. It is true he may promise well. Nay, he may sometimes even believe his own words. But let her look to the talent that has been committed to her care, to her own little garden of weeds and wandering plants, to the soil untilled, and the fruit unripened, and ask of her own heart, where is the proof of the watchfulness, labour, and skill, necessary for the cultivation of the wide desert that has been laid waste by the spoiler. While her own scanty harvest tells too truly of careless husbandry, it would be daring presumption to wish to increase her responsibility, and if she had indeed been faithful over that which was committed to her, she would shrink from the unequal yoke, the fellowship unholy, of him who had not learned to love the institutes of religion.

Mr. and Mrs. Ormorand possessed that true liberality of feeling which delights to unite different denominations of Christians in one sacred bond of social union, esteeming all equally who partake of the spirit of their Heavenly Master.

In their society I was accustomed to meet a Lady St. Lewis, the wealthy patroness of an active and popular party in the religious world. Accustomed to lead direct, she moved about with the majesty of a queen, and I own it was difficult for me to believe that true heartfelt humility could dwell beneath such an exterior. But my friends assured me that she was most devoted and persevering in her endeavours to do good, "and if," said they, "we look for so much energy and zeal without the least mixture of evil, we must extend our views beyond this world. It is for us to rejoice that we have amongst us a distinguished female, who accounts it no stigma upon her birth and station, to stand forward in the cause of religion."

Perhaps the strict sectarian views of this lady might be one reason why she always assumed a double share of hauteur in her communications with me, nor was it possible for me to remain uninfluenced by this pointed manner, so well calculated to establish between us a sort of precise, cold, good behaviour, which I should have been sorry indeed to infringe upon by the least touch of familiarity.

With my husband she held no intercourse. How would it now have been possible for beings so differently constituted, to meet on any common ground? Indeed they seldom met at all, except when he had good humour enough to come for me at night, and drive me home; and then the starched air, and impenetrably close shut lips of Lady St. Lewis, sufficiently indicated her sense of contamination to be dreaded from such society. She was of all persons the one in whose presence you would most dislike to be guilty of a breach of good manners, or to give cause, by any kind of failure on your part, for what you more than suspected would be internal triumph on hers. With these feelings I always met her, and was truly thankful when I could say "good night," without having had my husband's conduct as well as my own to answer for.

There came at last, however, a sudden termination to our slight and unsatisfactory intercourse. It was a memorable evening. Lady St. Lewis and I never met again.

We were seated, in our usual manner, around Mr. Ormorand's hospitable hearth, he who was properly the head of his family, expatiating upon that most interesting subject of discussion, (a subject which so few can treat with candour and coolness,) the difference of creeds, and the peculiarities of religious opinions: I, with my hands ever unoccupied, reclined upon a chair opposite the fire, and Lady St. Lewis was seated erect upon the sofa, stiff and strong in the dignity of a "well-grounded and orthodox belief;" while at her side was Miss Robinson, a young girl with meek brow and braided hair, who occupied the dubious and unenviable post of poor relation; an humble friend, an untiring responder, and a faithful supporter of her ladyship's arguments.

"I regard it," said Mr. Ormorand, "as a great blessing, a blessing for which we ought all to be unfailingly thankful, that in consideration to the weakness, the inconsistency, and the manifold wants of our nature, we are permitted to hold different shades of opinion, to adopt different modes of worsh.p, suited to the natural tone of our minds, and to meet at last where all these slight distinctions are merged into one bond of everlasting union.

"Let it be remembered," continued he, "amongst the mercies of which we daily partake, that we dwell in a land where our worship, whatever form it wears, may be lifted up in the face of mankind without fear, or shame, or danger, to that throne which our less privileged forefathers not unfrequently addressed, in secret and sorrow, from the abodes of infamy, within prison walls, and amidst the horrors of martyrdom."

Just at the close of this sentence we were all startled by a thundering knock at the door.

"Who can this be?" exclaimed Mrs. Ormorand. But I spoke not, for I knew too well. It was my husband. I heard his step coming with an uneven sledgy sound along the floor of the hall. One look was sufficient. With an elaborate attempt at more than common propriety, he addressed Mrs. Ormorand, and then turning to Lady St. Lewis, bowed so low that I began to fear he would never recover himself, but he did at last regain that erect posture which is so valuable a distinction between man and the brute; and having done this, he seated himself, with great complacency, beside me.

What can it be, which, on such occasions, seems to give tenfold intensity to the organs of sense and perception. In spite of my determination not to see anything, I beheld every body's eyes, and caught all the enquiring glances by which they appeared to ask of each other,—"What can be the matter?" And deaf as I would gladly have been, (deaf as the rocks to the drowning seaman,) I distinctly head Miss Robinson whisper to her aunt, "The man is intoxicated," while the indignant lady drew her neice closer to her elbow and shook the full folds of her dress, as she gathered it round her feet, away from all chance of contamination.

It seemed that others were. not quite so much alive to the true state of things as I was myself, for good Mrs. Ormorand, always endeavouring to set every one at ease, addressed my husband on the common topics of the weather, the roads, and the moon; while he, having just sense enough to perceive that he had made a breach in our conversaticn, begged we would proceed.

"Let me see," said he, with a sprightliness that intended to be very captivating, "I dare say you were talking about bible societies, or Sunday schools. Do you know Mrs. Ormorand, there is nothing I doat upon like Sunday schools."

"Perhaps," replied this excellent manager of mischances, "you will have the goodness to add to the collection I am just now making for our annual rewards."

"With all the pleasure in the world!" exclaimed he, who was nominally the patron of the institution.

Thinking the tide was now setting in more favourably, I ventured to raise my eyes, and saw him fumble a sovereign out of his purse, and present it to Mrs. Ormorand.

"So far so good," thought I; and my pulse beat slower. Encouraged by this appearance of sanity, Mr. Ormorand commenced again with the conversation which had been so suddenly interrupted, and addressing himself politely to my husband, "We have been endeavouring," said he, "to reconcile the slight differences in our religious belief, by considering the advantage which is thus afforded to the union of a variety of characters in one great cause; and you, Sir, I am sure, as a gentleman of liberal mind, as well as a warm supporter——

"A supporter, Sir," said my husband, springing upon his feet, and placing his hands upon the back of a chair, with all the mock majesty of a public speaker, while he thundered forth, with a voice which brought the domestics to the door to listen, "A supporter, Sir, of that church, Sir, whose institutions I venerate, whose laws I uphold, and whose unsullied purity I set forth: of that state, Sir whose king I obey, to whose loyal subjects I offer my right hand, and of whose aristocracy, I am happy to say, that I make one, Sir."

"Show me the man, Sir, whose heart does not glow with indignation when he hears a base calumny against the church, Sir, that church which has flourished through ages, in the unassailed and unassailable power of her saint-like sublimity. Show me this man, Sir, and I will strike him with my foot. Show me Sir, the traitor who dares to harbour in his soul, not only the remotest thought, but the smallest iota of an idea derogatory to the majesty, and the might, and the magnificence of his sovereign, and I will shed my best blood, Sir, in uprooting him from the earth. Show me again, Sir, the man, woman, or child, who is base enough to submit to the degradation of dissent from that most holy, most venerable, most mighty, most grand,—most—most—every thing of all institutions; and I will hiss, Sir, I will hiss as I do now;" and he actually pointed his finger full in the face of Lady St. Lewis, and prolonged the hissing sound until we had all time to grow stiff in the attitude of amazement.

To relate circumstantially what followed would be impossible. I had wondered until my astonishment was exhausted, I had felt until feeling was worn out, I had endured until the power of endurance was no more; I lost all susceptibility of impressions, and can recollect nothing after this scene except a confused call for carriages, in which lady St. Lewis and my husband both insisted upon being first. Her ladyship, however, gained the point in starting, but my worthy Nimrod soon drove past her with a yell of triumph, which made her coachman start upon his seat, and draw his horses off the road, as if to make way for a madman..

The week which followed this scene of absurdity was one of unbroken sullenness on the part of the offender, and of something very much of the same kind on mine, interrupted only by occasional tart and taunting allusions to the gross effrontery of such conduct.

When the morning of Saturday arrived, no change for the better had taken place, and it was with evident satisfaction that my husband informed me of an engagement he had made for that day, to dine with a neighbouring gentleman, who was more celebrated for his wine than his wisdom. Now was the time for me to exert my influence, if I had any, to lay aside all putulant airs, and to show by the sacrifice of my own wounded pride, how sincere was my desire to promote the interest of that cause, for which I had once been so solicitous, that the day before the Sabbath should be devoted to the services of religion. But no. I could not, at least, I would not, bring down my spirit to remind my husband of his duty; for it was impossible to do this without at the same time recalling the past days when I had been humble enough to make a favour of his concessions; and in the present state of my temper nothing could have been more galling than to make the acknowledgment, that such a being, so lost to common sense, and common decency, so prone to grovel in his own egregious folly, could possibly confer a favour upon me.

I saw him linger even beyond his usual time of trifling, I saw him come back into the house before he mounted his horse, and even turn again as he passed the window; but I made no answer either by look or sign to his evident desire to be recalled, and casting off the last weak longing after better things, he gave himself up to one desperate resolution, and set spurs into his high-mettled steed, the sound of whose galloping hoofs died away upon my ear, as I sat in silent self-condemnation, musing upon the opportunity I had thus perversely thrown away. In spite of the many times I told myself durmg the day that I had only done wha every other woman of spirit would do, my heart was ill at ease; and when I sat down to my solitary tea, I thought of the riotous board, where, at that very hour, my husband was drowning all recollection of the past, and what was still worse, all anticipation of the future. In vain I endeavoured to console myself by saying it would have been of no use even if I had endeavoured to detain him. Beneath the all-seeing eye of Omnipotence, how futile is this plea, when no attempt has been made, not a finger stirred, not a word spoken, at the very moment when a still small voice, was whispering "Now is the appointed time."

Oh! that we would be satisfied to fulfil our simple part, and to leave the event in His hands "with whom are the issues of life!"

Had I, in the hour of trial, submitted to the dictates of duty, I might even on this most miserable evening of my life, have found some drops of sweetness in my cup: for then I could have lifted up my heart in prayer with the consciousness of having done my best; and I too might have uttered the touching and impressive language "though he slay me yet will I trust in him." But now, with a smitten and writhing spirit, I applied myself to the painful task of preparing a sermon for the next day's service.

Hour after hour passed on, and the Sabbath came apace; but he who was to spread forth the tidings of the gospel to a listening people was still at his unhallowed revels. At deep midnight I opened my window and listened, and again, and again, until the grey dawn appeared in the east, and the birds stretched forth their buoyant wings, and all nature awoke in freshness, and beauty, and peace. At last I heard the sound of a horse, right welcome as it came before the domestics were abroad. I opened the door as gently as I could, and the brisk morning air brought a touch of gladness on its wings.

The worst confirmation of our fears is a relief to the agony of suspense, the torture of apprehension; and yet, when I saw my husband staggering home with all that disorder of look and manner which remains after such a day, or rather such a night as he had spent, and when I thought that in a few hours he must appear in public as a minister of a pure and holy religion, my heart sunk within me, and oh! what bitter self-upbraidings were mine, that I had done nothing, attempted nothing, to rescue him from such an exposure, to spare that church which I professed to venerate, the stain of such a disgrace.

If it be true that a man when intoxicated always exhibits his natural disposition, my husband must have been gifted with an uncommon share of obstinacy: for when in this state it was impossible to divert him, still less to force him, from any absurd determination he might take up. It was consequently vain for me to attempt to convince him that he would be unable to go through with the usual service of the day, and when I proposed to send over to a neighbouring clergyman and ask him to take his duty for the morning, he replied with indignation that he wanted no interference with his duties.

What could be done in such a case! Once I thought of sending for Mr. Ormorand, but knowing my husband's antipathy to him and his family I dared not even pronounce his name, lest it should occasion some terrible explosion of rage.

With that sickness of soul which makes the hand tremble, and the knees grow weak, and the brain reel with giddiness, I prepared to accompany my husband to church. But it was in vain. My resolution failed me, and while he was adjusting the reins, I stepped back into the house saying that I did not feel well enough to go.

Had the prayers of my heart that morning been offered up in the spirit of true humility, I have little doubt but they would have been heard and accepted. Most assuredly they were wrung out from a broken, if not from a contrite spirit: but even in the agony of my feelings I can well remember that I drew many conclusions about what certain individuals would think, and had much to combat with in my own mind, besides the overwhelming idea of the mockery which might, at that very time, be offered to the throne of mercy.

Absorbed in these gloomy reflections, I was seated with my eyes wandering over the garden, the fields, and the fair prospect before me, when, long before the usual time for leaving church, I saw my husband led home, leaning on the arm of Mr. Ormorand. I could not meet them at the door, but stood up to receive them in the room, where I had spent the last tedious and comfortless hour, like a culprit who awaits his final sentence.

"Tell me the worst," said I, seizing the hand of Mr. Ormorand, who told me nothing, but shook his head and answered gravely and evidently with great distress, "This will not do."

"Do not leave me," said I, for I felt utterly helpless, and destitute of all comfort; and, bursting into an agony of tears, I entreated him to tell me all the fearful truth, for nothing could be worse than my apprehensions.

The case was indeed bad enough, yet not so glaring, but that many of the congregation were left to believe that my husband had been taken ill. What added peculiar poignancy to my distress, was to discover that, from a kind and delicate regard to my feelings, and the shock they must have received on the evening of the terrible rupture with Lady St. Lewis, Mr. and Mrs. Ormorand, had left their usual place of worship, and attended our church that morning, with the generous intention of convincing me that they, at least, could look charitably upon my husband's conduct. But this was a breach of propriety, a violation of all moral and religious feeling, for which they could find no palliation; and it was evident, that the calm and well-regulated mind of Mr. Ormorand had been deeply shocked and wounded.

"This must never be repeated," said he, as we walked together in the garden. "It is worth any sacrifice of private peace to prevent"—he did not say what, but went on. "You must labour diligently and faithfully, and if your best endeavours cannot overcome this dreadful propensity, I entreat you then to apply all your energies, all your zeal, to induce your husband voluntarily to resign a situation, from which he must in time be expelled." And thus, with many strict charges respecting my own vigilance and care, he left me; and I turned into my own habitation on the noon of a smiling sabbath, when the cottager goes home from the house of prayer; and all who value the privileges of a Christian community, acknowledge with thankfulness and joy the welcome influence of a day of bodily rest, and spiritual refreshment. I turned in to my own habitation, to sit down with a husband, whose senses, half drowned by recent intoxication, were still dense and brutalized, and whose very countenance, retaining the mark of the beast, was flushed, and distorted with fever, and burning thirst.

Now, my friend, I believe you have had experience enough in the deceitfulness of the world, more especially have seen enough of that worst kind of deception by which we endeavour to impose upon ourselves, to lead you to join with me in deprecating the false delicacy by which women are accustomed to blind themselves to the true nature of vice. Thus we speak of a gentleman, being gay, being under the excitement of wine, being good-hearted, but a little dissipated, an enemy to no one but himself; and thus we marry the creatures whom we pity for such gentle errors, when we think we would not for the world unite ourselves to a vicious, a drunken, or a bad man. Not that I would in any way imply that, because of our own exemption from glaring vices, we should look with uncharitable eye upon those whose temptations may have been incalculably more powerful than ours; but oh! what weight, what dignity would be added to the character of woman, if, when speaking of mankind, she would raise her mind above that network of nonsense which is used in polished society, to throw a veil over those vices which cry aloud for our deepest, our most fervent, most persevering reprobation. I could draw a picture of what a gay man is in private life, but which of my fair sisters would not turn away her eyes, and say it was impossible that her Lothario should ever resemble that.

But enough of this. I wish not to expose my poor husband's transgressions more than is necessary for warning others from risking the same rash experiment, which plunged me into the deepest despair; and while I speak fairly of his character, I desire to treat my own with the same candour, and to prove that whatever his undisguised errors, or even sins might be, they were more than balanced by those which I endeavoured to conceal within my own heart; by the unpardonable presumption which led me on to undertake his conversion, having never made my own "calling and election sure;" by the rebellious and unsubdued pride in which I refused to fulfil the only conditions which could produce a favourable change; and by the contempt with which I looked down from my own fancied elevation upon his lost and fallen state.

Severely, deeply, as my feelings were harrowed by this last exposure, I still adopted no conciliatory measures, nor condescended to enter upon an impartial examination of the root of the evil.

The next morning, I will venture to say, did not rise upon any creature more wretched than myself. I awoke with an indistinct sense of something impending over me, something dreadful, that would happen, or had already happened, and scarcely could the severest calamity that words might describe have been so intolerable in its oppressiveness as that universal yet indefinite kind of desolation which was made sufficiently evident to my fully awakened thoughts.

"What am I, where am I, and what do I possess?" are three appalling questions which we not unfrequently ask ourselves on first awaking from a long and heavy sleep. I had no answer by which to allay the anguish of my heart, and when I arose, it was but to take up again the weary burden of the past day.

Under the pressure of affliction in which no one can partake, and which we imagine nothing can alleviate, we do not beguile the time by tracing our accustomed walks in grounds or gardens, but seek either the city or the solitude, the crowd or the wilderness; because in both situations we feel ourselves equally unobserved. In this state of mind I chose out for myself a melancholy retreat, where neither my husband nor my domestics were likely to find me. It was in a wild and untrimmed plantation, where the grounds of the parsonage were bounded by a brook that murmured perpetually over a gravelly bed. There was no beauty in this scene except what the little brook and the wild weeds gave it; yet here I used to sit on the moss-covered stem of a fallen tree, envying the very birds, and the insects that winged their flight around and above me. Even winter could not keep me from this spot, for I loved its withered grass, and bright green moss, and silvery lichen; but most of all, I loved to listen to the blast that roared amongst its leafless boughs.

Here I was one day indulging the full bent of my distempered fancy, until at last my thoughts broke forth in words.

"Everything in nature," said I, "has some purpose to fulfil, some power to exercise, some impulse to obey, but me. I alone, of all creation, live on from day to day, in a perpetual imprisonment of soul.—Why, why was I ever animated with human life, when the very worm has an existence more enviable than mine? The simplest denizen of air may 'flee away and be at rest;' the birds have their unwearied wings to bear them to a distant land: and the stream that murmurs idly at my feet, after meandering through a thousand meadows, finds a welcome in the bosom of the ocean at last."

I had scarcely uttered these words when my ear caught a rustling sound amongst the dead grass and fallen branches on the opposite side of the brook, and I saw the figure of an aged woman stooping down to fill a pitcher with water. The bank was so damp and slippery that it would have been difficult to find safe footing even for one more light and agile. After many fruitless attempts, she looked up, as if to see whether any one was near of whom she might ask assistance, and half ashamed of my tardy offer, I crossed the stream and stooped down myself for the water.

There was to me a strange novelty in doing even this act of common kindness, which pleased me for the moment, as it brought a change; and I insisted upon carrying the pitcher, if her home was not far distant.

"Oh! no," said she, with many apologies, "it is close by. Just at the skirt of the wood. You may see the smoke beside that old tree. But still it is too far for you to carry such a weight, and the way is not the cleanest." Here she hesitated; for there was evidently some other reason why she did not wish me to go with her, and this exciting my curiosity, I persevered with my burden, which, had it been imposed upon me, and not of my own choosing I should have thought intolerably heavy.

The cottage to which our path led, was beautifully situated, and at first I thought it presented a perfect picture; so apt are we to imagine that the cares and troubles, and perplexities of life must necessarily be shut out from such picturesque and secluded retreats. On a nearer inspection, however, I found an air of great poverty spread over the whole, and a slovenly appearance about the door, that might soon have been done away by a strong and willing hand.

At the entrance of a little plot of garden, the old woman stopped and took the pitcher from my hands, with many hearty thanks for the service I had done her.

"May I not go in with you?" said I.

"Oh! yes, ma'am if you please," but she stopped again, and looked distressed. "I have a poor lassie," said she (for they were north country people) "who is just now in some trouble, and will not be much pleased to see the face of a stranger, but I am sure you are a kind-hearted lady, and you may be able to say something that will comfort her."

We were standing but a few paces from the door, though screened from the small window, and while we hesitated about entering, I heard the following words sung in a sweet and plaintive voice by some one within, who appeared to be unconscious of a listener.

SONG.

"Listen! oh! listen! is Ronald returning?
Hear ye the sound of his step o'er the lea?

Come again, lost one, the bright fire is burning,
The hearth is swept clean in thy cottage for thee.

"Sad is the night, and the morning how dreary;
Dark is the sun-rise when Ronald's away;
Come again lov'd one, my bosom is weary,
Pining to welcome thee through the long day.

"Where is my joy if thy smile is not near me?
Where is my hope if thou wilt not return?
Vainly my bonny bairn's lisping would cheer me,
Vainly my mother's bright ingle would burn.

"Where are the sunbeams that danced on the mountain?
Where is the moonlight that slept in the vale?
Where is the sparkling foam of the fountain?
The music that sigh'd in the whispering gale?

"Where are the songs I have heard the birds singing?
When all was melody tun'd to mine ear?
Now every note a sad burden is bringing,
Warbling of spring-time, while winter is near.

"Where, bonny babe, is thy wandering father?
Close thy sweet eye-lids, and hush thee to rest,
Ask me no more, hapless thing; I would rather
Lull thee to sleep on this comfortless breast.

"Come again Ronald, the bright fire is burning,
Thy wife and thy mother are watching for thee;
Come again loved one, thy joyful returning
Brings beauty to nature, and gladness to me."

"Oh! that's her way," said the old woman. "When she's left alone it lightens her poor heart to sing these dismal ditties, if she thinks no one can hear her. But come in, my good lady, you must not stand here in the cold."

The sound of our steps at the door brought the young woman in an instant from the fireside, where she had been sitting with her baby in her arms. There was at first a bright flash of expectation in her looks, which faded away on seeing who we were, and though she welcomed us in with civility and kindness, I saw her often turn away to wipe off the tears that were continually gathering in her eyes. At last she retired into an inner room, and I was left at liberty to ask her mother what was the cause of her distress.

"It's a long story," said the old woman, "and one that is too common for you to listen to; but the shortest and the worst part of it is, that my poor Jenny has a drunken husband. He was a bonny Scotch lad when we first knew him, and even now he has the kindest heart; but oh! these sad ways of his will bring us all to ruin!" and she, too, wept, without any attempt at concealment.

"And yet," continued she, "it is not so much the loss of worldly comfort, though that is going fast; but there's his own soul to think about, poor fellow, and the bairns that should be looking up to him, and Jenny's health—she's pining away daily, and the more I talk to her of heaven, the more she frets about her husband and her children. You should have seen her when she married. The sweetest face—the lightest foot—you never heard the lark carol on a May morning with a gayer heart than hers."

"Oh! my dear Lady, it needs faith," and she fixed her eyes intently on my face,—"it needs faith to bear these things day after day, and yet to say in our nightly prayers, 'thy will be done.'"

"I have lived to the age of threescore years, and my life has been none of the smoothest. Sometimes I have known poverty, and sometimes comfort, but I have always had need enough to lean upon the only arm that was able to support me; yet, I can truly say, without any wish to complain more than is necessary, that to console my poor daughter, and to keep her thoughts steady to the true point, is the hardest task I have ever had yet. Perhaps you have never known trouble, ma'am. Perhaps you have never been disappointed, nor found yourself bound up as it were with the tares, when you thought you should have stood among the wheat. If so, you will be tired of hearing me talk about what you do not (and I pray you never may) understand. But sometimes it is a relief to tell our troubles to a stranger, for it seems almost as if a new face would bring some new consolation.

"I am not tired of hearing you, indeed," said I, "go on, and tell me all about your daughter."

There's little to be said of her, poor thing, more than may be said of many who have no one to speak for them. She was brought up in a careful way, and yet married just for love, without, as she often says now, so much as asking a blessing upon what she did; and then she reproaches herself, and says she deserved this, and more; not in the way of complaining, you would never hear her do that; and if she does but hint at her husband's fault, she takes care to tell of his kindness too, and says that, though his sins look more than her own, they are not half so great, or so many. And though he grows worse and worse, and what with wanting money, and drowning his right senses, his temper is not what it used to be, still she never tires of trying to please him, but keeps the house neat, and makes every meal ready as if he were here, even while she believes in her heart he will not come; yet she says, he shall not find any difference if he does. And now she'll come, and get out the tea and please herself with thinking how comfortable everything is for him, and she'll wait, and wait, and scarcely eat a morsel herself, and look so sick and faint, that my heart aches to see her.

Oh! if we had no consolation beyond ourselves, I think we should both die before the end of another day! But we are not, I hope we are not, without some hold of better things. We pray diligently, and sometimes our prayers are blest to us, and we rise up, if not in the expectation that they will be answered in the way we wish, yet in perfect trust that we shall be wisely and mercifully dealt with, and that the very burden of which we are complaining, is exactly the trial we are most in need of. Sometimes we feel this in such a lively manner, that it almost grows into gladness; and we look on beyond this little spot of earth, this little speck of time, and are satisfied that we know not what is best for us, and then we speak to each other words of cheering, and read our Bible, and see how the Lord led his people through the wilderness.

Oh! my dear lady, miserable as we may appear to you, we would not exchange these seasons of blessed confidence for all that a wealthier or seemingly happier station could afford.

Perhaps you have never been brought to this. Perhaps you have been brought to it by an easier way. I have no right to ask questions of you, but there is something in your face which tells me that all is not sweetness of which you have to drink. Whatever your trials may be, I think they cannot well be greater than my poor daughter's. Remember, when you go home, that there is consolation even for these; and, so saying, she bid me good day, for I had already risen to depart.

On returning home after this scene I was much struck by a sense of my own deficiency in all that I had found here exemplified; in patient submission, in watchfulness, and confiding trust, in short, in the three Christian graces, faith, hope and charity. And yet I had dared to think my portion hard. And so unquestionably it was to me; but I had chosen my own lot; I had taken up my own burden, I had filled my own cup with bitterness; and since to my natural feelings that lot was most wretched, that burden most grevious to be borne, and that cup most unpalatable; there was urgent need for me to look beyond my present blighted and gloomy prospects, to that region of blessedness, where there is neither blight nor gloom.

"But what," exclaimed I, giving way to my cheerless meditations, "what is there in this wide world for me! This poor woman doats upon her husband with all the enthusiasm of youth, and the very love which tortures her heart, at the same time keeps it from the stagnation of despair."

In the midst of my gloomy reflections I was startled by the sound of carriage wheels at the door, and looking out, I saw my husband, extremely pale, dressed in a loose gown and supported, or rather carried into the house by a medical gentleman who lived near us.

He had gone out that day with the intention of compelling a young horse to take a desperate leap, and the consequences were such as might have been anticipated. The beast was obstinate, the man furious; at last after a dreadful conflict, both horse and rider had rolled together down a steep bank, and, had not a poor man been passing at the time, in all probability my husband would have been unable to extricate himself. He had paid dearly for his exploit by many severe contusions, but he had a good-natured way of making the best of that which was undeniably bad, and he now looked cheerful, and affected to be much less hurt than he really was.

There is nothing wins upon our kindness more than suffering patiently endured; and when my husband saw my real concern, and my willingness to serve and assist him, his joy and gratitude were beyond bounds.

"Be always thus," said he, "and you may make of me what you please."

"Be always ill," thought I, "and it will be no effort to me to do my duty."

It is peculiar to weak and flippant characters to imagine that every new impression they receive will be deep, and lasting, and influential upon their future conduct. The surface of their animal existence is so often and so easily stirred, that they have no time to ascertain what lies beneath, and thus are incapable of reasoning from analogy, of judging rationally of their own feelings or motives, and of drawing conclusions from the force of established habit, the power of association, and the impossibility of acting rightly merely from occasional efforts of the natural will.

Any one who had but slightly studied human nature, would have thought my husband, during his confinement to a quiet chamber, in a state of mind which promised great amendment of life. Even I was fain to build upon the earnestness of his promises, made in the warmth of awakened feeling; and thus the moments we spent together while he was ill and helpless, were amongst the happiest of my life; for I had then an object in view, towards the attainment of which I seemed to be making some progress. Nor was it an unpleasing task, to reason with one who now was glad to listen; to plead with one who heard me in a subdued and gentle spirit. But my hour of trial was not yet come, and often after this I was compelled to return to the cottage of the poor woman, to take a fresh lesson for my own private walk, to gather fresh strength for the performance of my own duties.

It was with deep and heartfelt regret I observed in my repeated visits, that disease was making rapid progress in the once healthy frame of the young woman. The kind of melancholy which I endured, and which I fancied so intolerable, made no inroads upon my constitution; but hers was a torture of the heart, a strife between love and sorrow, which no human constitution can long sustain.

Often, as I had entered the cottage, I had never yet found the wandering husband at home; until one evening, when nature was again assuming the freshness of spring, I was surprised to see the figure of a man seated beside the poor invalid. At first I hesitated, but Jenny's voice called me in with such a gladsome tone, that I could not turn away without once witnessing her joy.

"He is here!" she whispered to me as I stood beside her. "He is here!" she repeated, with a look of happiness that I never can forget.

Ronald was indeed a fine looking man, whose strongly marked countenance indicated a strong character. At first I thought him handsome; but when he spoke there was a thirsty kind of irregularity about his features, which had no doubt been brought on by his dreadfully debasing habits. Jenny, however, seemed to be unconscious that he exhibited any other aspect than that of perfect beauty; for she leaned with her thin white hand upon his arm, and looked up into his face, as if she read there all that was written in her book of life.

This little act of kindness on his part (his merely staying with her one evening when her mother was absent,) was worth, in her estimation, all that the world could offer of riches, rank, or splendour; and her gentle eyes were lighted up with something of the brilliancy they had worn in former days, and her hollow cheek was tinged with a feverish hue of crimson beauty. Oh! how different from the rich glow that had once distinguished her as the pride of village maidens!

It was with difficulty I persuaded Ronald to keep his place at the fire, when I sat down beside them. He would gladly have gone away, like one who feels that much charity is needed to tolerate his presence; but Jenny and I both did our best to detain him, and when she asked me to read to them a chapter in the Bible, saying she was sure that Ronald would like to hear me read, he felt compelled in common civility to remain.

Half afraid of venturing too far in the presence of one with whose character I was in a great measure unacquainted, I chose the parable of the Prodigal Son, and my heart melted as I went through those touching passages which describe the return of the penitent.

On looking up I saw that Jenny had covered her face with her handkerchief, while with the other hand trembling like an aspen leaf, she still grasped the arm of her husband, who bent down his head over a rosy child, seated on his knee, and stroked its glossy ringlets, tied and untied the strings of its frock, and pressed its cheek to his breast, as if glad to do any thing that might relieve him from the misery of sitting quietly beneath the scrutiny of searching eyes.

"Is there any thing," thought I, "that a stranger's voice may say to add weight to that of conscience?" and I offered up an inward prayer that my humble endeavours might not be made in vain. I know not how it was, but I found strength and power on that occasion to utter words that sounded daring to a strong man, and a stranger; but he bore them well: and when I took my leave, even offered to attend me home, as darkness was fast coming on. I accepted his offer, and we talked by the way of the hope there was in store for the penitent; of the efficacy of prayer; and of the mercy that fails not even in the latest hour. And then, last of all, we talked about poor Jenny; and though I could not say (for I did not believe) that even his altered life would now save her, yet I urged upon him many times before we separated, the satisfaction he would afterwards feel in having cheered her last moments, and watched her gentle spirit depart in peace.

It was wonderful to me, that after the exertions I had been able to make with those whose feelings and habits were comparatively strange to me, I should find any difficulty in performing the same duties at home: but so it was. Ronald was a man of strong and deep character, with whom the words that fell unanswered upon his ear were often graven on his heart; nor was it from carelessness about the ruin which his habits brought upon his family, that he had so long persisted in the evil of his ways. So far from this, the very anguish of his self upbraidings sometimes drove him away from home, and in this manner his desperation served to increase its own violence.

The case with my husband was essentially different. His was a mere animal propensity—over which a variable and volatile spirit had little power. It was not to drown the anguish of a tortured mind that he swallowed the fatal draught, but solely for the sake of the excitement and the love of what he called "good company." In his often-repeated fits of penitence there was no want of sincerity for the time; but nothing could give constancy and firmness to his resolutions. Thus, on recovering from the long confinement to which his accident had subjected him, he rushed again into the world with fresh interest, and sat down to the jovial board, determined to drink *but little!*

Still there was a radical change in my feelings towards him, and the views which I entertained of his character no longer plunged me into moodiness and despair. During his illness I had reaped the blessed fruits of continued exertion for another's good; and though I could not be said to love him beyond the common kindness we feel for those who share our lot in life, I had learned to look charitably even upon him. When I endeavoured calmly to weigh and estimate his character, thousands of instances occurred to my recollection in which I might have acted a more Christian part towards him, and with these considerations came fresh pity and forgiveness for his faults.

"But what?" said I, one day, to Mr. Ormorand, when we had been speaking with kindness and commiseration of the absent—"What can I do to save him?"

"My dear friend," replied Mr. Ormorand, "you must do your best: I never heard that we were commanded to save each other. Happy is it for us that the salvation of our own souls is all that is strictly required of us. But remember that, in order to make sure of this great object, it is necessary that we watch over each other for good; that we do not 'darken counsel' by calculating too much upon the end, but persevere faithfully and diligently in rendering our appointed service. Your endeavours to save your husband from disgrace and ruin may not be attended with the reward you desire; but are there not other rewards in the hand of Omnipotence, far, far beyond what your most earnest endeavours can deserve? Is there not 'that peace of mind which passeth all understanding' never denied to the humble and persevering suppliant? Are there not the promises of the gospel to support the pilgrim on his way? Is there not the unbounded ocean of everlasting mercy, into which the tears of our weak nature may flow? Oh! do not despair, even though the desire of your eyes should be denied! You know that in this world is not our rest, and that none can drink of the cup of life without tasting its unpalatable dregs. Yours may be all centred in one drop of inexpressible bitterness! But is not the rest more sweet than falls to the lot of many? I know what you will answer me: you will say, 'let the axe fall anywhere but here. Let my outward portion be one of poverty and suffering, but leave me a home where my spirit may dwell in peace. Let the blight come in the tempest, so that my fireside comforts remain unscathed. Let the lightning strike my bark upon the ocean, so that it spare my summer bower!' And I, who know the strength of these feelings, not from their anguish, but their blessedness, preach to you, it may seem, in mockery of that which I have never experienced, but still with a heart that bleeds for your calamity; and still with boldness; for I know that the events of this transitory life are not as they appear to our contracted vision; that there is the working of a mighty and mysterious Power around and above us, striking out waters from the barren rock; upon which we have lain prostrate in our despair, bringing forth flowers and fruits in the wilderness, where we have stretched our wearied limbs to die; and raising up joy and beauty from the ashes of our ruined hopes!

"Let us look, my friend, away from this one point of misery, and number the blessings that are beyond. Have you not the means of assisting and cherishing the poor? Employ yourself diligently in the service of others, and your home—at least your heart—will no longer be desolate. Not administering outward comforts merely, but conveying instruction to the ignorant; and thus, while bearing a blessing to the needy, you will often be blessed yourself.

"I recommend these pursuits especially to you, because I believe them to be amongst the means afforded by Divine Providence for beguiling the mind from melancholy and fruitless brooding over its own secret and selfish sorrows. Beyond these are those spiritual helps, which I need not point out to you, but which I pray fervently may prove the unfailing support of your soul."

It was not long after this conversation took place that I was summoned to attend the last moments of poor Jenny; and here, if I had doubted the efficacy of that faith, which my worthy friend had so earnestly recommended to me, I should have seen a lively and striking instance of its power to support the feeble spirit.

The exhausted sufferer was still able to speak; and, as if aware that time with her was short, she laid her hand upon my arm, as I stood beside her, and looking imploringly in my face, entreated me, in the simple language of her heart, to put my trust solely and entirely in Him, who knows what is best for his frail creatures; "for," continued she, in a cheerful and animated tone, "it is this that has supported me; it is this that will support you."

The aged mother sat by the bed, with more of peace in her countenance than I had seen there before; and Ronald, poor Ronald, now smitten to his inmost soul, covered his face with both his hands, and sobbed aloud, in the bitterness of unspeakable anguish; sometimes, as he was able to raise up his head, catching Jenny's eye turned towards him with such looks of tenderness and love, that the fountains of his tears burst forth again, and he wept like a child, without concealment or shame.

"Oh! may those tears be blessed!" said the dying woman. "Think not of me, Ronald, when I am gone. I was but like a flower in your path, love, that withered at noon-day. But think of the flowers of paradise, and the burden that must be borne, and the battle that must be fought, before we can enter where they bloom for ever. Keep on, keep on, the strife will soon be over; it is worth all to gain the prize!" and, so saying, her gentle soul departed.

From this time Ronald was an altered man; not but that he had sometimes hard conflicts before he could compel himself patiently to endure the gnawing worm of self-reproach; but what with the vigilant care of a Christian mother, and the winning helplessness of his poor children, and, above all, with that mercy, whose unfailing fountains refresh the soul of the penitent, he was enabled to keep on a steady course, without any after breach of regularity of life or conduct.

Not so, my poor husband. I have now watched over him for years. I have seen him dismissed from his high station, and returned thanks that he was no longer permitted to disgrace the ministry of the church. I have descended with him into the most private and secluded walk of life; and though I have found in that walk much to reconcile its roughness, and smooth down its thorns, I still lift up my voice from a weary and wounded spirit, (and oh! that I could speak more powerfully) to warn the trifling, the thoughtless, and the rash, from that most lamentable of all calamities—most irreparable of all misfortunes—"an ill-assorted marriage."

PICTURES

OF

PRIVATE LIFE.

SECOND SERIES.

BY MRS. ELLIS,

AUTHOR OF "WIVES OF ENGLAND," ETC

"Would you judge of the lawfulness or unlawfulness of pleasure, take this rule: whatever weakens your reason, impairs the tenderness of your conscience, obscures your sense of God, or takes off the relish of spiritual things;—in short, whatever increases the strength and authority of your body over your mind, that thing is sin to you, however innocent it may be in itself."

AUTHOR'S EDITION,

COMPLETE IN ONE VOLUME.

New-York;

EDWARD WALKER 114 FULTON-STREET.

PREFACE.

Though well aware that to erase, even from a popular volume, every sentence against which an objection can be brought, must be to leave the author in the predicament of the complaisant artist who effaced his painting in his endeavours to please the public, in striking out every part which did not obtain entire approbation; yet is there one feature in the Pictures of Private Life which has been hinted at by more than one Review, of too important a nature to be passed over without serious consideration.

It has been said of the First Series of this work that the religious sentiments it contains are not sufficiently *decided.*

If by *decided* is meant *sectarian*, I freely acknowledge that I have, both in the first and second volume, studiously avoided every sentiment, and every mode of expression, not common to Christians of every denomination, deeming the fundamental principles of religion all-sufficient for my purpose. Had that purpose been confined to the narrow circle of domestic life, I should doubtless have made many additions from my own peculiar views of what may be most expedient, useful and salutary under certain circumstances of birth and education. But these views, had they even agreed with one particular party, and obtained from that party the recommendation of being more *decided*, would have been of little service to the community at large, and might possibly in some cases have prevented the introduction of more important truth upon which all communities agree.

It must also be remembered that my object is rather moral than religious. To higher teachers I leave the definition of what religion is; my humbler and more befitting task is to show what we should be without its supporting and purifying influence; to point out the different paths which conduct us to or from this blessed goal; and, if possible, to spare the idle and the thoughtless the cost of learning by their own experience what fatal consequences attend upon the choice of an erroneous course.

I cannot commit the present volume to the good-will of the public, without one word of a lighter nature to the gossips who sit around the Christmas fire—to those whose busy hands are ever ready to direct the arrow for which they have not bent the bow. By such, a great deal has been said in reference to my last volume on the subject of personality—a subject on which I beg leave to assure them that I have been more guilty of inadvertency than design; and that many likenesses have been pointed out to me, with the coincidence of names and initials, of which I was altogether unconscious at the time of writing.

That an author should draw a likeness without knowing it, will scarcely be believed by those who are not acquainted with the process of thought by which an abstract idea is derived. But to use the parallel of painting, as best adapted to the purpose, let us suppose an artist employed in representing a personification of melancholy. He gives himself up for a while to the abstract idea. But his business is to convey it to others, and imagination quickly produces the figure to which memory has (unconsciously to him) given the features of the person from whom he has possibly derived his first or most forcible impressions of melancholy. While absorbed in the single idea derived from these impressions, he pursues his work without recognizing the likeness, until others more discriminating are kind enough to point it out; and, then, if the representation should by chance be of any temperament, quality, or passion, more despicable than melancholy, woe to the poor painter!

There is no teacher like experience; there is no proper regret for the past but that which produces amendment for the future. I now offer to the public a volume containing many characters, all so carefully selected, watched and guarded, that, but for the mere circumstance of their humanity and consequent participation in human infirmities, I could almost defy the scrutiny of the most penetrating eye to detect a resemblance, unless it be to my friends' friends, and surely I shall not be considered accountable for that.

To those who have been more active than judicious in distributing the likenesses of the last volume, I would recommend that they look for themselves alone in this, and that they confine their search to the examples that are most praiseworthy. If they succeed, how happy will it be for them and me!—How much happier, than should they choose out the most exceptionable characters, fix them upon individuals of their acquaintance, and blame the writer for the consequences.

CONTENTS.

PICTURES OF PRIVATE LIFE.

MISANTHROPY.

> And none did love him, though to hall and bower
> He gathered revellers from far and near,
> He knew them flatterers of the festal hour;
> The heartless parasites of present cheer,
> Yea! none did love him—not his leman's dear.
>
> CHILDE HAROLD.

CHAPTER I.

As the Rev. Charles Forester, rector of the parish of Haughton, was turning down the brow of the hill which overlooked his own quiet dwelling in the valley, he was met by his sister, Mrs. Percival, who, laying hold of the rein of his bridle, playfully cried out, "A boon! a boon!"

"What is your pleasure, fair dame?" asked the rector.

"To-morrow is the day," replied the lady, "appointed for certain rural sports, such as fishing, boating, and the like: and we desire the company of your daughter Agnes, who always adds double pleasure to whatever party she may honour with her presence."

Mr. Forester shook his head. "I do not like your parties upon water; Agnes may sit in damp shoes, to say the least of the danger;" and he hit his pony a smart stroke upon the neck, which made him quickly disentangle his rein, and start off at a brisk trot.

Mrs. Percival walked off also in the opposite direction, knowing, by long acquaintance with the habits and feelings of lordly man, that the less she said to urge her suit, the more likely was her brother's heart to relent.

It was not long before he was again at her side.

"I have been thinking," said he, "that the poor child has but little entertainment at home, and that, if she does really add so much pleasure to the party, she might as well go. But mind, sister; in the article of clothing, I depend upon you, as understanding these things better than myself; and if she should catch cold—"

"Thank you! thank you!" interrupted Mrs. Percival; "I will gladly bear all the punishment you may think fit to inflict upon me, if we should catch cold."

The morning was beautiful when the merry group set off. Agnes, who had not yet learned the painful lesson, that when boys go forth to enjoy themselves, girls must stay at home, took the place, prepared for her comfort and safety with cloaks, cushions, and wrappers, which she pushed aside as soon as her father and Mrs. Percival had concluded their many charges to the old, experienced watermen, and were fairly out of sight. Close beside her sat her cousin Arnold Percival, a tall, commanding-looking youth, some years older than herself, whose right to the privileged seat no one disputed; and at the farthest possible distance, stripped to his shirt sleeves, and tugging at the oar, was his younger brother, Walter. These two boys (or young men, as they were more likely to have called themselves,) were each born to an inheritance as different as the dispositions which they carried along with them. Arnold was heir to an entailed estate, which would, at some future time, afford him the possession of an almost princely fortune: Walter had no other dependance than upon a clear head and ready hand. Gladly would Arnold have shared half his wealth with Walter; but Walter, since he was not born with a title to it, scrupled to receive the slightest pecuniary obligation from his brother. Perhaps, had their hearts been laid open, pride would have been found the only quality in which they resembled each other; but Arnold's pride was of an open domineering character, while his brother's was so deep and hidden, as to be scarcely discernible in his outward actions. Arnold's characteristics, as a boy, were indolence and indifference; the one arising partly from constitution, partly from the knowledge that he should never be called upon for exertion; the other from a general distrust of kindness, and latent suspicion that his money, not himself, was the object of attraction. Walter would have been enthusiastic almost to madness, had it not been for the common sense and correct feeling which kept all the exuberance of his mind in check: thus he was accustomed to pursue his favorite employments in secret, to rise early, and sit up late, to labour and endure, with a pertinacity that was almost certain to ensure success. What his favourite employments were, and what the degree of mental power he was capable of exercising, few people suspected, and none knew; for he was careless at school, and made little progress in the beaten track of learning. Arnold was more successful in his aquirements, as he was solicitous that nothing should be wanting to complete the dignified and imposing character to which he aspired. Every one might discover, at the first glance, that Arnold was the gentleman; and it needed as little penetration to see that Walter would one day be the man of upright and steady usefulness, of strict punctuality, promptness, and integrity in the common affairs of life. Arnold never called a servant or ordered a horse, but they were ready on the instant. Walter hated that any one should do for him what he was able to do for himself; but when he did require service from his mother's domestics, he could obtain it as readily for love, as his brother could for fear. Arnold held no communication with what Walter was accustomed to call the *useful* classes of society; but Walter listened to their complaints, redressed their grievances as far as he was able, and showed them respect by a thousand little acts of consideration, richly worth their cost. Arnold's face was of a handsome, proud, and melancholy cast, finely moulded, but cold and inanimate; and the glance of his beautiful dark eye was generally directed to distant objects, or wandered on in listless and dreamy vacuity; while Walter, much below his brother in stature, was equally inferior to him in all that could strike the attention of the superficial observer. His eyes were blue and clear, and usually concentrated in their look, as if the faculties of his mind were fixed upon some powerful image, or strong focus of light, revealed only to his inward vision; his lips were thin, firm, and compressed, and all his movements decided, prompt, and energetic; he had, besides, in very early life, an uncommon flow of animal spirits, so that, before he began to think deeply, he played with more vivacity than any other boy. At the time of the fishing party, the change in his character had but just appeared. Some rude attempts at mechanism, closely concealed in the remotest corner of his private closet, bore testimony to earnest and grave thought; but he had too much of the boy about him still to sit long at any employment and he now laughed, shouted, and rowed with unrivalled strength and determination.

It was a glorious day. The sun shone out in cloudless light; the boat glided swiftly over the waters; the trees bent down their feathery boughs as if to soothe the rippling stream that foamed and fretted against the rocky shores, and the birds sung sweetly in the distance, until startled from the branches, they winged their rapid flight away from this region of peace and beauty. All things above, around and beneath, wore the garb of nature's holiday; and even Arnold, charmed out of himself, sent forth his deep-toned voice in a wild and melancholy song. At length they reached the basin or broad space in the river, where their sport was to begin. Lightly every foot sprang from the boat, and Agnes, no less eager than the rest, seizing the line which Walter had prepared, took her place beside a drooping birch and waited for her prey.

Arnold, alone, of all the party, declined to enter into their amusement. Striding from rock to rock, he quickly disappeared from their sight, and winding round a high point which jutted out into the stream, seated himself like an eagle upon it height, exalted, in his own ideas, to as great a superiority over the merry creatures he had left, as this solitary rock was above the shallow waters rippling at its base. On his difficult and circuitous path he had gathered handfuls of fern and wild flowers, each little group a picture of woodland beauty, enough to send the spirit up to Heaven in the incense of gratitude; and now the misanthrope amused himself by casting them one by one into the stream below, moralizing as they dropped from his fingers and fluttered in the summer wind upon the emptiness and worthless of all things. Wearied as man must naturally be with that system of reasoning which tends to establish the non-existence of useful ends, and wise purposes in the creation, Arnold at last descended from his height and joined the party below. Some were reclining in laughing indolence upon the rocks; some pursuing their amusement in solitary silence; and others exulting in the triumph of a first bite; while Walter was busily employed in leading Agnes away from the deceitful and slippery shore, to some safer standing-place, arranging her tackle, and doing every thing for her except draw out her luckless victims.

Arnold looked upon his brother and his fair cousin with the same sneer of contempt with which he had first regarded the group of idlers and the patient solitaries farther up the stream. He made no remark; but his countenance and his character were so well known to all, that they bore along with them an influence more readily felt than explained.

Agnes laid down the line and said she was weary; Walter took it up and walked off with an air that showed his will, if not his power, to catch every fish in the river; the idlers rose and wondered when the party would think it time to eat; the solitaries gave up their fruitless task and gathered round their friends; while Agnes, ever the first to perceive and turn away the dark spirit of discontent, ran for the baskets of provisions, and began to place around upon the rocks the welcome viands which Mrs. Percival had prepared; and fortunate it was for her endeavors to maintain good humor and good will, that they were backed by the keen and healthy appetites of the whole group. Even Arnold could eat; and Walter, after being summoned by the shrill notes of the bugle, came wandering up from his retreat.

Agnes had chosen for the place of refreshment a sort of picturesque cave or hollow by the side of the stream, where they were shaded from the sun by the branches of the feathery birch, and lulled by the ripple of the water at their feet.

"Is it not happiness to be!" exclaimed the delighted girl as Arnold took his wonted place beside her; but there was no answer in his face to any voice that spoke of happiness, and she appealed to Walter the last of a row of boys seated on the opposite side of their sylvan temple. He answered from his clear blue eyes with such a look as the wounded and weary, the deceived and the deceitful, try in vain to assume; a look that lasts but seldom beyond the days of our childhood; a look that reminds us of a higher and purer state of existence, and tells more of what we might be than what we are.

The feast was ended, the songs sung, and all were ready to renew their sport.

"Are you weary?" asked one.

"Weary? never!" exclaimed Walter, and he bounded forth again like a young fawn upon the dewy plain. Arnold and Agnes were left alone to their meditations, for Agnes knew that her grave cousin was no favourite with the boys; "and therefore," said she to herself, "as no one wishes for his company, I will stay with him, that he may not be left entirely alone."

"So you really like the sport of fishing," said Arnold.

"Oh! yes," replied Agnes, "I like to look into the bosom of the clear water where it is shaded from the sun, and to see the rocks and pebbles and wild weeds on the shore. As for the fishing, I don't care much about that, only it makes an object."

"What a pity," said her cousin, "that you cannot find a better object. I was thinking, as I looked down upon you from the rock, that amongst all the savage wonders of creation, man was the only animal who had refinement enough in his cruelty to make one living creature a bait for the destruction of another. The tiger, the cat, and all that relentless tribe, are accustomed to sport with their victims before they devour them; but when we see the lion catch the butterfly and hang it out as a lure for the birds of the air, that he in his turn may prey upon them, then may we truly say that the lion in his nature is noble and generous as man. I watched you this morning for hours, as I sat alone; but with most amazement my eye dwelt upon the figure of a fair young girl, who snatched out in triumph the poor inhabitants of the stream, and left them on the sandy shore to pant away, in lingering agonies, the miserable remnant of their lives."

Agnes bent down her head, and blushed in silence. At last, after many fruitless attempts to smile, sne said, "You are too severe, Arnold, upon a small matter; yet now that I think of it seriously, I cannot say much in its defence, and therefore I will never do the like again."

At this instant, a loud splash was heard in the water, and a general cry arose from the party. "Walter, poor Walter, has fallen in!"

Arnold did not stay to hear more. He was an excellent swinner, and from the first impulse of a naturally kind heart, he leaped into the stream. The hollows amongst the rocks were so deep and deceitful, that it was some time before he he succeeded in finding and dragging his brother to the shore. Agnes was at his side in a moment, chafing his temples, his hands, and his feet, but apparently without avail.

"Let us carry him," said she, "to the nearest house; and directly all the boys offered their services, for Walter was the pride and the joy, of every heart, the prince of comrades, the king of good fellowship and glee.

Arnold took upon himself to direct who should assist and who should not, walking at the head of the party, and pointing out a cottage at a short distance from the river. Here he stood over his brother in a calm and collected manner, ordering such means to be tried as he believed to be most rational and efficacious; but no sooner did the glow of life return to the cheeks of Walter and joy to the watchful eyes around him, than Arnold withdrew from the group, and only returned to reassure himself of his brother's safety, and recommend to the boys who had excitement enough for one day at least, that they should seek the boatmen and make the best of their way homeward. "And for you, Agnes," said he, "I give you your choice: "If you prefer remaining with my brother, you shall; if not, I shall endeavor to supply your place." On which Agnes decided at once to stay, and Arnold walked off with the rest.

When Walter had fully recovered the possession of his facuties, his gratitude was beyond bounds. Starting from the bed upon which he had been laid, he dressed himself in a grotesque suit of clothes belonging to the cottager's son, and then placing a chair beside the fire for Agnes, assured her over and over again, that he was perfectly well, and that she alone was in danger of suffering. All her kindness and care only redoubled his protestations that he felt nothing but health and gladness, and when the carriage sent for them by Mrs. Percival, arrived at the door, he assisted his gentle cousin with as much alacrity and politeness as if his recent exploit in the water had been nothing but a dream. The time before they reached home was spent in mutual congratulations that things had been no worse: for "Oh!" said Walter, "it might have been you dear Agnes, instead of me!"

CHAPTER II.

PERHAPS the kind reader will not unwillingly pass on with me over the space of a few short and uneventful years, supposing by a slight effort of the mind, that according to the usual course of time, the old will have grown more grey, the young more grave; that a few venerable heads will have been laid in the quiet tomb, and a few warm hearts have awakened to the conviction that life is not altogether a garden of flowers, that the sun of human happiness does not always shine, and that the pictures of imagination to maintain any claim to truth, must, like the world which they flatteringly represent, have their revolutions of night and day.

In the next place, let us look in upon the parlour of Mrs. Percival, where a comely matron with whom time has had none but gentle dealings, plies her quick needle, ever and anon glancing round to ascertain the perfect and systematical adjustment of books, pictures, and vases of summer flowers, with which her elegant apartment is profusely adorned. At the opposite side of the table, a pale girl dressed in deep mourning is bending over a half-finished drawing. A girl—no! when she raises her head, and fixes her grave and earnest eyes upon the countenance of her aunt, you see at once, that Agnes Forester is no longer a girl. But why that "sable stole," and meekly braided hair,—and why the absence of all those ornaments with which her doating father used to delight to see his child adorned? The fact, that Mr. Forester had been called away to his long home, must account for one part of the change, and the melancholy truth that he had left behind him but a scanty pittance for his daughter, now thrown actually upon the kindness and protection of her aunt, must account for the other. The anguish of the first grief which ever assailed her heart, had given to the once happy face of Agnes a tinge of melancholy, while certain difficulties arising out of her present situation with a feeling of dependance, and a strong desire to adapt herself in every way to what a strict sense of propriety might require, added a gravity to her look and general deportment somewhat beyond her years. Her aunt, too, though of a disposition naturally kind, frank and generous, had just that prompt decided matter-of-fact way of speaking, which, accompanied with a vein of dry sarcastic humour, has a direct and powerful tendency to seal up the fountains of a young and tender heart. To magnify small grievances, and brood over half conceived anxieties, and "weep we scarce know why," are amongst the weaknesses of youth, while our portion is yet so pleasant, our summer so bright, and our hopes so little scathed, that we can afford this expenditure of feeling without any adequate cause. But when watched with critical inspection, and coolly questioned as to the direct origin of our tears, we learn not to cease to weep,—alas, no! but to weep only in private, and to wear for the public a mask, whose unmeaning and impenetrable aspec bids defiance to that scrutiny which time and experience have not yet prepared us to bear. Thus Agnes Forester, in the presence of her aunt, was a correct, amiable, and well-behaved young lady, but little more; for the full tide of her warm feelings was only permitted to flow without restraint in secret and solitude.

"Which of your cousins do you like best!" asked Mrs. Percival, all on a sudden, and fixing upon her neice a look, sharp as the needle she had just drawn from her work, while Agnes, startled no doubt by the abruptness of the question, blushed the deepest crimson.

"Why do you hesitate, child?" continued the aunt, "as if I had plunged you into a metaphysical dilemma."

"It is a subject I never thought of before," said Agnes, "and it requires time to decide upon.

"But which could you best spare? for, as they are both likely to leave me soon, I am constantly weighing and balancing the losses I shall sustain."

"Both likely to leave you!" said Agnes, looking up.

"Yes, both. You know Arnold must go to college; and Walter, poor fellow! will be obliged to pursue some employment that will afford him a maintenance for the future."

"I knew," said Agnes, "that Arnold was constantly talking of college, but I did not understand that he really meant to go."

"I hope he does," replied the mother. "He wants knowledge of men and manners; he wants association with the world, to give him a better opinion of it. But this is nothing to my purpose; I want to know which of them you could best spare. I have weighed the matter myself, and drawn my own conclusions; and now I ask you, just to know whether you agree with me."

Agnes leaned back in her chair; and while playing with her pencil, and fixing her eyes upon the fire, gave her mind up to itself, more than she was wont to do in the presence of her aunt.

"Why, Arnold," said she at last, "is more my companion; he rides and walks with me more than Walter does."

"And yet Walter trains your horse, and takes care of your dog, and feeds your birds, and does ten times more for you."

That's very true, and I should be ungrateful, indeed if I did not miss him sadly; but if he went out into the world, I should have the happiness of knowing that he would always make friends, and obtain good will from every living thing around him. While for Arnold I should feel such dreadful anxiety, lest his character should not be properly estimated. Besides, wno would he find to love, or to love him, amongst the multitude; or who would ever dive into, and discover, the excellent qualities that lie buried in his heart.

"And pray, may I ask what those excellent qualities are?"

"Oh! a deep, mysterious, Byron-like sort of virtue."

"I am equally in the dark," replied the aunt, "with regard to the virtues of the noble poet. Perhaps you will enlighten me."

"A wild, recklessness, disinterestedness, a —— something, I hardly know how to give it a name."

"And the names you have chosen, my dear niece, are so little adapted to my preconceived notions of moral excellence, that I confess I hardly understand you. But, passing over his wildness and recklessness, as qualities which I as a mother, am not capable of appreciating, let me ask in what way he has ever shown his disinterestedness?"

"Oh! in a thousand ways, dear aunt, if you did but know him better. Was it not he who saved his brother from a watery grave?"

"And would not your Newfoundland dog have done the same?"

"I cannot talk with you," said Agnes, half vexed and half amused, "you turn everything to ridicule."

"Ah! do not mistake me, replied her aunt; nor think that a mother can turn to ridicule the melancholy infatuation of her own child, and of one whom she loves dearly as her own. I thought you had been better taught, Agnes Forester, than to call that virtue which glitters only in the distempered dream of a delirious poet. Depend upon it, there is little virtue in those characters which separate themselves from the chain of human sympathy, and cannot stoop and bend, and devote themselves to the general good of society."

"There!" exclaimed Arnold, as he entered just in time to catch the closing sentence, "there spoke the spirit of one who deserves a crown of glory from that society which she idolizes. Of glory such as nothing but the flash of the meteor, and the glimmer of the glow-worm, and the sparkle of the sun-beam on the wave, can rival in stability and weight. Are you, my fair cousin, taking lessons in my mother's system of popularity? Allow me to add my voice to hers. First, then, as a dutiful son, I take up her earnest injunction, that you stoop, and bend, and devote yourself to the good of society· and the better to ensure this laudable end, you shall move amongst mankind upon the principle of the serpent, for ever coiling, winding, and unfolding, so as to elude the attacks of all enemies, and pierce with poisoned fang, under the shield of friendship. In the 'game of life,' that weary clog which we call a heart, must be cast off and left behind. You will need nothing of your own, but laughter for the merry and sighs for the sad, good principles for the pious and good wishes for the poor. Add to which, you must be ever ready to lend a spark to the rising star, and a hand to extinguish the falling; you must watch the signs of the times, and take the tone of the leader, whatever that leader may be. You must have no feeling but what serves to animate and beautify your face, no prejudices but those of the friends who surround you; no spleen, but when you are wanted to fight their battles; no revenge but for their wrongs; no hatred but for their enemies. With such qualifications you may fairly mix in that whirlpool of base passions, falsehood, and weariness which is called society. Believe me, dear Agnes, there is nothing to repay you for the trial, unless you are longing to exchange your beauty for vile paint, your fair brow for wrinkles, your smiles for deceitful blandishments, and your warm heart for a heap of ashes. The kindness which welcomes you into what is called the 'bosom of society,' is nothing better than a snare to beguile you into an exposure of your thoughts and feelings, that the vultures who prey upon the peace of their human victims, may thrust their ravenous beaks into your heart's core. The flattery which hails your approach, is only to lure you on to fresh antics for the sport of the multitude; and the generosity which heaps honours and favours on your head, has its tenfold reward in the chains which it is thus enabled to throw around your feet."

"And yet," observed Mrs. Percival, coolly, "this society which you vilify, is made up of creatures very much resembling ourselves. You, I suppose, as being most important, personate one of the vultures who prey with their naughty beaks. Agnes is amongst the generous, who throw chains—and since there is nothing better left for me, I must be of the multitude who laugh;" and, so saying, she left the dignified orator to enlighten his fair cousin yet further upon the never-ending source of eloquence, the follies and abuses of society.

CHAPTER III.

From that unfortunate disunion of feeling which too frequently separated Arnold Percival from all intimate and heartfelt communion with his mother, she was accustomed to seek relief in the clear, constant, and rational character of her son Walter; and now, with a letter in her hand, which she had just received for him, she entered the apartment that was considered exclusively his own; not an elegant dressing-room, rich in decorations and perfumery, where the interesting occupant lounges at ease upon luxurious sofas, or sits as it were "corporeally amalgamated with the downy cushions," glancing over the well-penned, or rather well-printed page of a new and fashionable novel;

but a wide, low, half-furnished chamber, with a north aspect, where, before a large table, spread over with papers and plans, rough-drawings, estimates, and valuations, the young engineer was accustomed to spend half the day, and sometimes half the night.

"I have brought you a letter," said Mrs. Percival, handing it to him; and Walter, taking out his penknife, cut round the wax with as much exactness as if he had been a collector of seals. With lips compressed, and eye steady and sedate, he glanced over its contents, and then presented it to his mother.

It was the letter he had long been anxiously expecting, and came to inform him that a situation for which he had applied some time ago, was now open to him.

"This is just what you wished for," said Mrs. Percival, returning the letter; and she would have congratulated her son on the success of his application, but for a sudden difficulty she felt in accompanying her words with that cheerfulness of look and manner, without which congratulations can be of little value. And Walter, too, kept his eyes closely fixed upon the elevation of a bridge which lay before him, while he expatiated upon his good fortune, as if he wished to make himself desire it more than he really did.

"And when?—" asked Mrs. Percival; but she could say no more, for she felt then in losing this excellent son, the repose of her heart in its domestic sphere would be gone—the charm of happiness which bound her to her own fire-side would be broken.

"I suppose," said Walter, rising, and affectionately taking his mother's hand, "I suppose it must be soon. When a hard task has to be accomplished, the more speedily we commence with it the better. Were I to wait until I really felt in my heart that I was willing to leave you, I should be here for ever: and yet I would gladly have been allowed more time." And he fell into a sort of reverie, in which he recounted, as if thinking aloud, the many things he wished to have accomplished before his departure from home. These services, upon which his heart had been fixed, related chiefly to his mother and her affairs; but the account wound up with the training of a new pony, so as to make it gentle enough for Agnes to ride.

"I think said Mrs. Percival, looking out of the window, "you need feel no anxiety about the pony; Arnold's young horse seems to suit Agnes so well. See! see! how she reins it in." But Walter was, or at least appeared to be, busy again at his work, from which he was not the man to be beguiled by the ambling of a high-mettled steed; and such was his dislike to see a woman brought into any sort of difficulty or danger, without a good and sufficient reason, that he neither saw, nor wished to see, how skilfully Agnes could manage Arnold's horse.

The road which the equestrians had chosen was particularly suited to the taste and feelings of the misanthrope; for it led them to the brow of a bold promontory, where they were surrounded by scenes of rugged and lonely grandeur, amidst which man in his civilized and social state, could hardly find a resting place. Here, when the storm was raging, and the breakers dashed against the white rocks, and curled in foaming eddies far up into the echoing caves, Arnold would often come, and stand a silent and delighted spectator of the warring elements. But now the sun had risen upon a clear and smiling day, and the wind was so still that the leaves scarce fluttered on the topmost boughs, and therefore Arnold had asked his cousin Agnes to join him in his ride; and she, with that submissive gentleness with which women are sometimes too apt to bow to lofty and commanding spirits, had laid aside her pencil and her books, and equipped herself for a morning's excursion—perhaps not unwillingly; for to say nothing of the interesting companion which Arnold could make himself when he chose to condescend, riding itself was a perfect delight to her; and the fresh air that swept over the high promontory, at whose base the mighty ocean was slumbering, the cry of innumerable sea-birds perched upon the ledges of the cliffs, or stretching their white wings, and sailing away—away over the blue depth of silent waters, the sunbeams dancing on the pebbly shore, now revealing the minute and exquisite workmanship of nature in the feathery sea-weed and the sparkling shells, and then lighting up the bold outlines of stupendous rocks, and throwing back their shadows far and deep—all combined to give life, and joy, and animation, to one who was peculiarly formed for that happiness which derives a perpetual supply from the grandeur, and beauty, and harmony, of the creation.

Arnold, too, was wont to feel a lighter and more genial spirit stirring within him, when away from the haunts of man; nor was Agnes the less happy that hers was the only companionship which his reserved and gloomy nature could brook.

"He hates mankind, but he does not hate me; to others he is sullen and unsocial, but to me generous and kind; the chords which produce nothing but harsh and discordant sounds for the vulgar ear, are turned to melody for mine;" was the frequent language of her heart, which bounded with triumphant gladness at the thought; and, with the happiness of one who rejoices over a secret treasure, fully sensible of its intrinsic worth, though aware that others are not capable of estimating its value, she uttered many a cordial response to the fitful and capricious revealings of that heart, which exposed its internal workings to no eye but hers.

After standing for some time upon a commanding height, which overlooked the sea, Arnold proposed that they should leave their horses at a small inn, frequented chiefly by fishermen, and situated in a deep ravine which opened through precipitous cliffs down to the only landing place in their immediate neighbourhood. Here, in a little sandy creek, lay Arnold's own boat, in which, not only when the waves were calm as now, but sometimes when it needed a steady brain and adventurous spirit to tempt their awakened fury, he was accustomed to work his passage through the breakers, and then resting on his oars would dream away hours of solitary musing. With stout and manly efforts, he now pushed off from the shore, and Agnes, to whom the air and exercise of the morning had given more than her wonted share of freshness and beauty, seated herself like his good genius beside him.

"Look Arnold," said she, clasping her hands with enthusiasm, "look at the white rocks now! Hark! to the cry of the sea birds, and the roar of the surf in those hollow caves. And then the clear depth beneath us!—Behold what a world is below! Masses of stupendous magnitude like the cliffs above, down, down to an immeasurable depth! Think if we should strike upon some of their rugged and frightful pinnacles which are barely discernible through the deceitful water; if a gale should arise, or a whirlpool draw us in with its devouring strength!"—

"Then we should die together!" said Arnold, and Agnes looked up into his face to see if there was more in his words than 'met the ear.'

Accustomed to behold him on all occasions with eyes cold and averted, she now blushed to find, that for the first time in her life, they were fixed upon her with tenderness and deep interest; for such was the high tone of his reserved and stately character, and such more especially had been his uniformly respectful delicacy towards herself, that she had never before been reminded by look or word, of the probability that he could be more to her than a brother.

How mighty and mysterious are the influences of association, which strike the multitudinous keys of thought and feeling, sometimes ringing a thousand changes upon a single word or an unexpected look!

For some time Agnes remained in silent musing, her head turned away from Arnold, and her hand drooping down, so as just to touch the sparkling waters that rippled against the side of the boat. Her eye wandered over the wide scene of splendour and beauty that was spread before her, and apparently her mind went along with it into the clefts and fissures of the rocks, where the sea-weed lay in dark and heavy masses, or high up to the promontory's brow, or far into the horizon, where a few white sails were seen like aerial beings winging their flight to a distant, it might be, to a happier land. Alas! no! her thoughts had now little to do with the loveliness of nature. Her imagination was in the land of visions, conjuring up strange pictures of the future, in which the only actors that appeared in her air-built castles were herself, and that mysterious and unfathomable being who seemed formed to be the ruler of her destiny.

"Here," said Arnold, replacing his oars and folding his arms, "here is loneliness enough. Ah! give me the inhospitable desert, where I may breathe and move in freedom; or the wide waste of boundless ocean, where upon its restless bosom 'I still may ride and sleep.'"

"And here," said Agnes, "would it be your happiness to be alone?"

"No, not alone. If any mortal mixture of earth's mould could be found, whose sense of enjoyment was like my own; and not of enjoyment only, but of wrong, and injury, and weariness, and oppression.—No, Agnes, there is not, there cannot be a creature constituted like myself."

"But is it necessary that the people with whom we live should have feelings and prejudices like our own?"

"Ah! there you touch the root of my malady. I cannot live with *people*. If I hold any companionship, it must be with one being, and one only, and if that being could not look upon human nature with sentiments like mine—if she brought with her a bright eye, a rosy cheek, and a heart warm and social as your own; how *then* could she endure my moodiness, or sacrifice the bloom of her life to the premature winter of mine?"

"She would endeavor," said Agnes, laying her hand upon his arm, "to make the misanthrope less moody. She would tell him that the wide universe, even in whose deserts are fountains of delight, was created by a Being wise and merciful, who has allowed to the creatures of his formation just happiness enough in this life to make them wish for eternity, and just sufficient suffering and trial to fit them for everlasting enjoyment. That it is not only in the sunbeams and the ocean, and the free air of the wilderness, that we feel his goodness; but in the power and might of human intellect, in the unshackled intercourse of mind, and in the kindly affections of relationship and home."

"And how would you teach this to me?"

"To those who can feel, there are many ways of teaching. But, come, it is time to return."

CHAPTER IV.

WHEN the equestrians reached Mrs. Percival's door, Walter appeared as usual, as if by a kind of magic which brought him always to the very spot where Agnes wished to dismount, and at the very moment when she wanted a helping hand, and was happy to find a cheerful welcome back. To-day however, she only answered by a slight inclination of her head, and scarcely a single smile to Walter's congratulations on her safe return; nor did she appear either surprised or deeply interested, when he said, in a quiet and unobtrusive manner, as they walked together into the house, "I am going to leave you, Agnes."

"Going to leave us! When?"

"To-morrow, I believe."

"What, so soon!"

"But all this was said with such a careless and wandering eye, that Walter, whose heart had been full enough before, turned suddenly away from his unfeeling cousin and scarely exchanged another word with her during the rest of the day.

It is true her behaviour appeared unfeeling to one who was looking, on this occasion at least, for a little sympathy—a little kindness in return for all that he had lavished upon her but it is fortunate for the human heart that it cannot feel at all points at the same time; and Agnes had seen a sort of vision that morning, which left her little interest for the realities around her.

The evening of the same day was spent by Walter and his mother in all the bustle of preparation, in which he appeared to take an unusually active part, hurrying from room to room with a firm and determined step, as if the very violence with which he trod the floors at the same time trampled down some painful and almost uncontrolable feeling. The mighty business of packing was at last nearly completed; unloaded shelves and empty drawers were again examined, and one thing only was wanted—a piece of music, which Agnes had copied for him, and which was still amongst her own, beneath the piano in the drawing-room. His strong hand trembled when he touched the door; but he did open it at last; and there, half shrouded in the muslin drapery of the window, stood his cousin and his brother, with the pale moonbeams shining on them through the fringe of jessamine, which formed a canopy above, and sent forth its delicious odours through the casement, now thrown open to admit the sweet scents and sounds of summer's twilight hour.

The two friends, who looked so much like lovers, were carrying on an earnest conversation in low murmurs, which was hardly interrupted by Walter's entrance. Quick as thought, he turned over all the music, and then, snatching up the piece he wanted, stumbled over an ottoman, and hurried out of the room, humming a merry tune as he went.

Whether Agnes had never been told that her cousin would leave early in the morning, or whether, after being told, she had really forgotten it, does not appear very decided. When she retired to rest that night, however, she had no definite idea that, to see him again before his departure, it would be necessary to shake off her slumbers long before the usual hour; nor, indeed, if she had been told, would this have been easily accomplished; for sleep was long that night in visiting her eyelids—such lively and varied images gathered round her, amongst which her cousin Arnold bore no insignificant part. Every development of his mysterious character was examined, admired, and dwelt upon. Looks, words, and circumstances, were recalled; comparisons were drawn; disjointed things were united; qualities the most opposite to each other were reconciled and mingled; and then all were woven together into that frail and fantastic garment which imagination throws over the future, beautifying, in the distance, that which, on a nearer approach, may prove to be nothing better than a waste or a ruin.

With the first dawn of the morning, Walter arose and looked out upon the dewy lawn. "Here they will wander in the cool evening," thought he, "when I am panting in the dust of the city. But it matters not.

I will never eat the bread of idleness; and when I can assist my mother, she will be better able to afford a home for Agnes;—perhaps Agnes will not need one then," was the thought which followed; and there is no knowing where his meditations might have carried him, had not his mother tapped gently at his door, and asked some kind question about his comfort. It was evident that the night had not been to her a season of rest; and, with tearful eyes she now called her son to join her at that melancholy place of meeting—an early breakfast-table, before a painful separation and a long journey. Together they left the room; but Walter stood behind for one moment, as they passed his cousin's door, to hear if there was any sound within; but he never trusted himself with her name, and Mrs. Percival was too much absorbed in her own griefs to recollect that any thing could aggravate his.

As for Arnold, there was no reason why he should disturb himself in the morning, for he had visited his brother in his own chamber the night before, and very properly taken leave of him there. So, Walter sat down with his mother, and tried to drink her scalding tea, and to swallow the food which she continually pressed upon his plate. His watch lay beside him on the table, and he would have given something just then to know what length of time was required for a young lady to dress. One quarter after another passed away, and Walter grew alternately hot and cold, red and white, hurt and irritated; and yet, no sound was heard upon the stairs. At last, when the half hour which he had allowed himself had fairly expired, he took up the watch, and returned it to his pocket, with the air of one who has "decidedly given the matter up;" and having done this, he had more thoughts to spare for his mother, and consequently took leave of her with the warmth and tenderness of one whose heart was almost exclusively her own.

Something after this he seemed to have forgotten, and although the domestics would any of them have run up stairs or down in an instant, esteeming it a privilege to serve him, he either could not or would not explain exactly what he had left behind; but hurrying back to his own room, strode along the passage with such a tremendous tread as would, he thought, have been enough to awaken the "seven sleepers of Christendom." But no—it would not do. Young ladies can sometimes sleep very soundly when their cousins are going away; and Walter, when he looked back to the house, and up to the second row of windows, saw no white handkerchief waving as a farewell sign.

There are few things in life more hateful than the first conviction we feel of our own ingratitude to those who we know will be deeply pained by our neglect.

Before Agnes had quite finished the duties of her toilet, at a late hour that morning, the thought struck her that it was possible Walter might be gone; and that, even if he were not, she had much to atone for in her unkindness the day before; for she had not done him the slightest service, nor even made him the offer of any. And then she excused herself by thinking that her aunt was one who never wished for help; and Walter, too, was of the same independent spirit; besides, he had not been so pleasant lately as he used to be. He had grown more cold and distant, and she hardly knew whether her company was agreeable to him or not. But she would go directly and look for him in the garden, and ask him if there was any thing she could do.

On her descent to the garden with this laudable resolution, Agnes was met by a boy bringing home her dog.

"Where have you been, Peter?" said she, "and who told you to take my dog?"

"Mr. Walter, ma'am," replied the boy, "gave me strict orders to exercise him every day. He chose to walk two miles with him himself this morning, on purpose, as he said, to play with the poor animal for the last time, and to show me how to make him take to the water, and then to rub his coat, and all how I am to manage him; for, as he said, just as the coach was driving up, 'the poor fellow perhaps would miss him more than some others would.'"

This reproach, simple as it was, and altogether unintentional, struck Agnes to the heart; and she retired to her own room to pour out the bitter and burning tears of self condemnation.

The coach which Walter had chosen as the most suitable vehicle for himself and his sorrows, was one much celebrated for its rapid and furious progress; and though often inclined to pity the poor horses, he was upon the whole well pleased with the speed with which he passed through the air; the dangerous swing of the carriage, the shrill notes of the bugle, and the wonder and acclamation with which the arrival of such a vehicle is always hailed by the untiring rabble, supplying the stimulus which he wanted from without, to relieve that which was somewhat too intense within.

It was a close and sultry evening when this gallopping phenomenon reached the suburbs of the metropolis, whirling along in an increased vortex of dust and impurity, the horses foaming and panting in the heated atmosphere, the coachman stunning the ears of his fellow travellers with oaths and rude jests, the busy multitude through which they now passed evincing their metropolitan indifference by the apathy with which they looked up from amongst their heaps of withered vegetables, or peeped from the still more disgusting appendages to the entrance of the slaughterers' dens, wiping their wrinkled brows with well-worn aprons, and kicking the lean dogs that came to smell (for, alas! they might not taste) their dainty viands. Then the rattle of carts and carriages, and, beyond in the distance, the unceasing and interminable din of this human hive! What a situation for the heart-sick traveller, whose senses had been awakened in childhood to the music of summer birds, the murmuring of pure waters, the green pastures and flowery meadows, the scent of hay fields, and all the sweet sounds and sights that fill up the treasury of nature.

Could Walter have looked back to the scenes of his childhood,—to the favourite haunts of his maturer years, he would have seen, at the very same hour which first found him a weary and comfortless inhabitant of the city, a little boat pushed off from a rocky shore against which the idle waves were gently heaving with a regular and lulling sound, while all beyond was bright and silent as a sea of glass. The shadows of the majestic cliffs fell far over the sleeping waters, while here and there, a bold fragment of rock caught the last tinge of golden sunset, and the western sky was lighted up with such refulgence, that the waving tendrils of wild plants which grew upon the brow of the precipice were shaped out in clear and distinct outline. It was almost profanation to disturb the stillness of such a scene even with the splashing oar; so Arnold rested from his labours, and Agnes, bending over the side of the boat, seemed to watch the feathers of the sea-bird as they sailed past her on the surface of the gliding current.

"Poor Walter!" said she, at last, with an involuntary sigh.

"I should say happy Walter," observed Arnold. "Who would not rather bid adieu to breaking hearts, than live for ever with those 'who cannot bless them—whom they cannot bless.' It is happier to feel that there is a chain which binds you to some human fellowship, even though that chain should be strained to its utmost stretch: than to stand alone as I do, and to know that in your moments of weakness, you can have no support beyond yourself."

"Ah! now," said Agnes, "you speak as I would always have you speak. Why, why should you be oppressed with this miserable loneliness, when the world has so many warm hearts for those who will but seek and value them?"

"But none for me, Agnes. It is my destiny to be for ever pining for something which I cannot find in this weary life; something more constant and sincere than the general character of society affords; something deeper and more durable than that all-prevailing and palpable mockery which you call friendship."

"The ties of relationship," said Agnes, "when rightly estimated, afford us much of strength and consolation in seasons of trial and difficulty. Have you not a mother, whose devotedness to her children is most exemplary, and a brother——"

"My mother," replied Arnold, "has no longer that affection for me which constituted the happiness of my childhood. The melancholy fact is, that I have worn it out by my morose and sullen temper. My brother, too, whether from the difference which he feels in our circumstances, or from some other inexplicable cause, has become reserved and distant towards me, so that you, Agnes, are the only being upon earth to whom I can open my heart, or communicate the feelings most intimately connected with it."

"Shall I tell you," replied Agnes, "why others cannot, or rather do not, share in that intimacy which I enjoy? It is because your character is never unveiled before them. It would be unreasonable to expect that any one should love us because of the mere circumstance of our existence, or even for some latent feeling of regard which lies dormant at the bottom of our hearts, unknown to any being but ourselves. There must be a mutual understanding, occasionally an unreserved exposure of the inner mind, accompanied by innumerable little acts of kindness and consideration to constitue the happiness and the durabilty of all earthly attachments. Your heart is bound up within too narrow a compass; all its best feelings which might shoot up and flourish, and bring forth fruits of gladness, and beauty, and benefit to mankind, return without having found an object, and fall back upon itself with deadly and oppressive weight. Oh! be to others what you are to me, and they will—they must"—"love you," she would have added, and the time was when she could have spoken these words with the same earnest gravity, and without one thought of shame; but now her cheek was spread over with a burning blush, and her eyes looked away from him whom she was addressing, and she found out again that it was time to return home, for the moon was just rising over the silvery waters, and the distant line of coast grew indistinct in the dimness of summer twilight.

CHAPTER V.

Although the departure of Walter Percival was felt as a severe loss by every member of his mother's household, she herself was the only inconsolable sufferer; and much she wondered that Agnes, who had shared so largely in his kindness, and, she suspected, in his love, should go about her usual occupations as cheerfully as if no inroad had been made upon her sphere of enjoyment. It is true, she sometimes bemoaned his absence, and exclaimed, "How much I miss poor Walter!" but her looks were not exactly suited to her words, and Mrs. Percival was little gratified to hear her favourite son perpetually spoken of as "poor Walter!"

"There must oe, and there is, a reason," said the sage lady to herself, "why Agnes is so callous to all other feelings. Well did the poet say,

'The course of true love never did run smooth.'

for here is my poor niece wasting her young affections upon this statue of a man, who will never make her any other return than in cold civilities, and long stories about his own dark destiny; and blindly overlooking, slighting, and forgetting the kindest and most generous heart that ever warmed a human bosom."

It is possible that Agnes Forrester was not quite so blind as her wise aunt suspected; for a woman's heart does not always go along with her judgment, but will sometimes strike off in an oblique direction, leaving the intellectual faculties to wonder at its eccentric movements. Besides which, the all-powerful influence of society has so fettered us with the chains of false delicacy, that we are not, on any account, to suspect the designs of a gentleman until an offer of marriage has really and *bona fide* passed his lips: and Agnes, like many other girls of her age, and in her circumstances, was glad to lay hold of the plea for continuing her intimacy with Arnold. "For I have yet no right," said she, with a sigh, "to suppose that he values me in any other way than as the playmate of his youth; and if he ever should, it will be time enough to take into account his capability for making a good husband, when he offers himself as one."

Now there was something in this last homely expression that always brought a chill along with it, when applied to her cousin Arnold; and yet what must all their sailing, dreaming, and moon-gazing come to, but either this or nothing.

"Oh! that I could ask counsel of my aunt," said she; but Arnold was at that instant by her side, and she asked counsel only of her own heart.

"Has my mother told you," asked he, "that I am really going to try my fortune at college?"

"She has; and I only wonder that I never heard it from yourself."

"It is so impossible for me to believe any one interested in my fate," replied the misanthrope, "that if any thing extraordinary were to happen to me, which I must reveal, I believe I should tell it to the winds and waves."

Agnes bent down her head, and the deep shadow of her long, dark eye-lashes concealed the glistening of her tears.

"I wonder," said she at last, "what earthly token, what pledge or proof, in word or deed, would be sufficient to convince you that you were dear to any human heart?"

"I never feel so near that blessed truth," answered he, "as when I am in your presence; but one hour of solitary musing always undeceives me, and I am lonely and desolate again."

"Oh! do not indulge in these unsocial and unprofitable musings," said Agnes, forgetting, in her earnest warmth, all that had so lately occupied her thoughts: "you are not lonely—you never shall be desolate!"

Arnold began to think his hour was at hand; and, had he been subject to sudden impulses, the spell which bound his gentle cousin to him with more than sisterly affection would, probably, have been broken, then and there, by a full disclosure of his hopes and wishes. But he knew her firm character too well to risk any thing by rash confidence; and therefore they sailed together again upon the quiet sea, and Agnes scrupled not to be still like a shadow by his side.

"Let us go out, for the last time, in my trim boat upon the ocean," said Arnold, the day before he was to leave home; for it is one of the characteristics of a melancholy temperament, that when any sort of pleasure does by accident occur, it shall be supposed to be for the *last time;* and Agnes heard the mournful and prophetic tone in which these words were uttered with as sad a countenance as even Arnold himself could desire.

It was a clear autumnal day. The yellow fields and variegated woods were clothed in more than real beauty to the youthful and romantic wanderers, and every sight and sound in the wide realm of nature was sanctified by the idea of being seen, heard, and felt together for the *last time*.

How scornfully can those who are hackneyed in the sayings and doings of busy life look down from the citadel of the world and laugh at the loves and the follies of their early years: but is there not more of bitterness than mirth in such laughter? and would they not give all the wealth of the peopled city to see again, with eyes that were lighted from within, and to walk once more in the sunshine of their own hearts? It is not thus with the happy few who are reaping the reward of a well-spent life. They can look back with as little of contempt as regret upon the enjoyments of youth, that live in recollection like the roses of summer, when the cold snows are sleeping on the ground—faded and fallen, it is true, yet fair and faithful pledges that the blessings which have been may yet be again: that the power which first created can still renew; and that every particle of our past or present happiness is an emanation from that source which is able to fill the future with eternal joy.

It was not easy for the two friends to converse on any light or trivial topic, and all the subjects which had lately afforded them the deepest interest, on this day appeared to be accompanied with too close a relation to their own individual feelings to be either safe or pleasant ground to touch upon. Consequently, they rode on in almost unbroken silence, yet each occupied by the same train of reflections, thinking, as it were, into each other's minds, feeling simultaneously, and understanding without words.

Arrived at Arnold's favourite point of observation, they stood upon the bold promontory, and gazed once more upon the wide expanse of waters. "Without a mark, without a bound," it lay before them like the ocean of infinity, on which their thoughts were floating. Arnold's tall and commanding figure stood upon a point of projecting rock, and Agnes, in her gentler character, held her wonted station, like a sister spirit, at his side. There is no human sentimentalist who would not have pronounced these two beings to have been created for each other's happiness; but there is much to be done in the world, besides looking, thinking, or even feeling in unison with those we love; and life is altogether a very different scene from a sea-view on a sunny day.

Lightly upon the glassy surface of the ocean did Arnold's little boat glide off from the rocky shore; and when he rested upon his oars, there was such solemn beauty and stillness all around, that Agnes was less disposed than ever to interrupt the harmony by any words of her own. Still she had had much to say to her cousin before he left his home, and how could she answer to her conscience if she wasted this last opportunity?

We have not yet said that Agnes Forester was beautiful, but there was something more than beauty in every change and movement of her expressive countenance. Even in its repose there was more to be learned, admired, and felt, than in the most loquacious efforts of many of her sex; and, now, when her heart was labouring with a burden of disinterested anxiety and love, Arnold could not choose but gaze upon her face, to read there what her lips seemed unable to utter. At last she spoke, and the very tenderness of her expression showed how far were her thoughts from dwelling upon herself.

"I have often wished, dear Arnold, for the power of conveying my sentiments to you without the use of words, and never more so than at this moment; when I seem to have no proper language to express the deep and earnest desire which I feel for your happiness. Not merely for your successful studies, your satisfactory allotment in life, or any consideration confined to your temporal good; but that you may shake off that heavy stupor which paralyzes the faculties of your mind, and stand forth amongst your fellow men as good and noble as the best."

"It is my fate, Agnes. It was born with me, and will haunt me to the grave."

"But what is it that makes our fate? It s indeed our fate (if you choose to give it that name) to be born in one particular nation, with a certain form and complexion, and not improbably with some peculiar tendency of constitution, both mental and bodily; but are all our reasoning faculties, with the power to choose and adopt our own habits, to go for nothing, while we float down the stream of time as weak and worthless as the weeds upon this wave? And, above all, is the grand working of an Almighty power pledged to assist our feeble efforts, not to be called in to promote the great end of our being, to complete our preparation for a higher and happier state of existence?"

"I hear your voice," said Arnold, "like the music of an angel's lyre. It charms me with strains in which I cannot join. It tells me of joys which never, never can be mine."

"Oh! do not speak to me in poetry. I have given myself up too much to ideal happiness. This may possibly be the *last time* that we shall ever share together that happy confidence which has been the blessing of my life; and none can hear those boding words with more true sadness of heart than I do now."

For a few moments Agnes turned away her face, it might be to conceal her tears, but she quickly resumed—"I have often thought it would be an excellent plan for friends about to separate, each to impress upon the mind of the other, as their parting charge, what they most wished them to bear in mind when absent."

"Tell this to me," said Arnold, "and depend upon my faithfulness."

"I have no scruple," replied Agnes, "in saying, that you can in no way add to my happiness more effectually than by endeavouring, consistently with the designs of Providence, to promote your own."

Arnold looked disappointed; and when Agnes appealed to him for this last duty towards herself, he coldly replied, that he knew of no fault she had to correct; and as to any thing that would merely make him happy, he hoped he never should be selfish enough to wish for that.

"This plan of mine," said Agnes with a

sigh, "does not appear to answer; for, if I guess right, we are both mutually disappointed in the result. You, because I have asked almost the only thing you would not do to please me; and I, because your answer convinces me that you do not love me: for, since we are all imperfect creatures, I have no idea of that love which does not seek to improve its object: and how can this be done, when there is wilful blindness to each other's defects?"

"Think anything but that," said Arnold, affectionately taking her hand. "Agnes Forester, you have seen me as I am. My naked soul has been revealed to you without disguise; for I would scorn to purchase what I most desire by false pretensions, of any kind whatever. Yet I know, and have long known, that for any one to see me thus and love me, would be impossible. And when I tell you that all the affection I am capable of feeling is centred in you, that you are the good angel that must decide my destiny, and that I should long since have disclosed these, my real sentiments, but for the cowardly dread of breaking the spell which has been the only comfort of my life, I await your answer without fear; for those who hope nothing, escape the anguish of disappointment. Yet speak to me, dear Agnes, for I would hear the last fatal sound, like the closing of the prison-door upon the criminal, rather than my darkness should be again disturbed by such faint and distant gleams of forbidden happiness, as even I at times have conjured up."

A deep blush, like the crimson glow of evening, when it suddenly bursts forth upon every cloud and wave, and headland of the western shore, had risen to the face of Agnes while Arnold was speaking. Thrice she strove to answer; but the tears that fell one after another from her downcast eyes seemed to be flowing with too full a tide for words. At last she mastered her rebellious heart, and replied,—"Arnold, I have long loved you with what I believed to be the affection of a sister. What that affection might have become it would be fruitless now to conjecture; for you compel me to express my full conviction, that with one whose sentiments and feelings are like your own, there could be no real happiness."

"You are right," exclaimed Arnold with bitterness. "It would be worse than folly to unite yourself to misery. In this world, where truth and sincerity of feeling are without worth or value, no man should ask a woman to share his fortune, without he could offer her a light heart and sunny brow, and a home of unceasing merriment and joy. You are right, Agnes Forester, to ask yourself where would be the gain. I should be a dull companion for a winter's evening, and you know it well."

"Hear me again," said Agnes, as she appealed to him through her tears, that now were falling without control. "You wrong me, Arnold, if you think it is for myself only that I am speaking. You compel me to say more than woman should say; to tell you, that I am unable to imagine any gratification to my natural feelings, so great as that of cheering your hours of moodiness and sorrow; and that I would rather share your fortune, were it humble as my own, than be set apart for the brightest destiny that ever fell to the lot of mortals. But in this world we live not for the enjoyment of the present moment only, and marriage is a holy and enduring bond; and woe betide the woman who enters into it with base or selfish views. Either you must be aware that the sentiments you entertain of human life, and the duty of man to his fellow-man, are widely at variance with what I believe to be right, or my words have hitherto strongly belied my thoughts. I know not how far a blind and idolatrous love might in time carry me on towards conformity with your views, or how it might soothe me into a dangerous and luxurious repose in the midst of that enjoyment which I am unable to think of anywhere but with you; but I am not blind now; I wish not to make an idol even of you; I cannot conscientiously say I believe that, in the present state of your mind, you could assist me to correct my own. I am far from the presumption of taking charge both of your soul and mine; and I know that I must answer at the last day for the decision of this moment."

"Ah! make me what you will," exclaimed Arnold. "If this be all the barrier betwixt us, you shall mould me to your wishes."

Agnes shook her head. "It is easy," replied she, "to say that we are willing to be moulded by those we love; but would it not be safer and wiser to submit to the moulding of Him who first created us; for we know not that those whom we most admire are able to form a correct notion of what is fitted to our individual good; but we do know that a wise Providence has placed us here for his own gracious purposes; and that he will require us to render an account of how these purposes have been fulfilled. A vain woman may persuade herself that she has power to change the character of the man who loves her; but I am not yet to learn that the change which is wrought merely for the sake of a fellow-creature can neither be lasting nor sincere."

"Agnes," said Arnold, "you are a sage, cold reasoner; you know not what it is to love."

"How is it possible to convince you that I do?" sighed Agnes; and after musing for a while, with her eyes fixed upon the distant horizon, she resumed—"If it is so easy to change the heart, and to adopt new habits of thinking and feeling, this may surely be done, as well before a bond is entered into as after. I therefore give you twelve months from this time to approximate to the character which I most desire you should be. All the assistance that my limited knowledge and unlimited affection can afford, shall be at your command; and oh! if the day should ever come!"—but she checked her enthusiasm, and turned away from those earnest eyes, that reminded her she might possibly say, as well as hope too much.

"You are not satisfied," said Agnes to her moody companion, after they had both been silent for some time.

"I am bound to be satisfied," said he; "but, nevertheless, I think the man who is worth trying is worth trusting."

"I do trust you, Arnold, as I would trust no other man. You have now the opportunity of deceiving me, but I know you will not use it unfairly; and I rely as implicitly upon your candour and sincerity in this instance, as I ever did before. But let us clearly understand each other ere we separate. It seems to be on the important subject of duty, that our sentiments differ so widely. I maintain, that a life of usefulness alone can be a life of happiness, and that every human being has the power of being useful in some way or other according to his circumstances and natural capability."

"With the former part of your statement I fully agree,—that none can be happy who are useless and inactive; but to my own case I cannot apply the latter, for I believe there will ever be a blight upon all my endeavours to serve my fellow-creatures."

"And with you it is very probable that such an idea should exist, for your endeavours have hitherto been made more in the way of sudden efforts or convulsions arising from the impulse of the moment, than from that steady and systematic application of energy and zeal, which is necessary to ensure any beneficial result. And even here, I find my views are essentially different from yours; for I cannot believe any one to be exempt from the duty of loving and serving his fellow-creatures, even if, as you say, a blight should be upon all his endeavours; because that duty is one which we owe to a Being of infinitely higher authority than man, and is strictly enjoined in the Holy Scriptures as a test of our obedience and faith.

"I have often thought, it is by looking too much to the effect of good endeavours, by expecting too immediate an evidence of our usefulness on earth, that many well-meaning people are discouraged and thrown back into stupor and despondency; forgetting that He, who has appointed our task, has bestowed a blessing upon the performance of it, by making us happy in the use of the means, while

He reserves to himself the mystery of the end. Thus there can be no disappointment attendant upon the service of the humble Christian; because, whatever he may have sacrificed, or lost, or suffered, he has still been faithful to his Heavenly Master, and in that faithfulness itself, not in its effect upon others, is the only sure and lasting happiness which this world can afford."

Arnold was now silent, and Agnes, surprised at having been carried away into a style of speaking so different from her usual manner, endeavoured to atone for having occupied the time too much with her own words, by saying no more until they reached the shore. Here her favourite dog awaited her return, and glad to break through the cold solemnity which had somehow or other stolen over her companion and herself, she stooped down to receive his caresses with more than her wonted warmth.

"Happy fellow!" exclaimed Arnold, with a look of scorn, "you have no probation to endure. It is better to be a dog than a man."

"Is it better," answered Agnes, "to have had nothing committed to your care, than to return your talent and receive ten?"

CHAPTER VI.

There are few things in life that make a woman more serious than the necessity of deciding whether she will accept or reject the hand which is most agreeable to her in the world. Until this important crisis in her fate arrives, she appears to be but a passive recipient of flattering attentions; but in one hour, perhaps, one moment, she has to dispossess her mind of all its vain illusions, and to act simply and decidedly for herself, without support or assistance from any earthly creature. All must be completed, too, in so short a time, for the least hesitation, the least delay, is construed into a tacit consent, and the lover triumphs accordingly. Who then shall withhold the meed of admiration from her who refuses from principle the man whom she is most inclined to love; voluntarily pronouncing her own sentence, cutting off her own hopes of that domestic enjoyment which is dearest to a woman's heart?

Agnes Forester had been accustomed even from childhood to habits of serious thought, and the circumstance of having no mother to watch over her early years, by throwing her upon her own resources, had confirmed this habit, and made it the most striking feature of a character, otherwise natural, cheerful, and energetic.

On the day of Arnold's departure, she was more serious than usual, and fearing that Mrs. Percival might attribute her want of lively spirits entirely to the loss of her cousin's company, she determined, that before she slept that night, her aunt should be in possession of the confidence to which she was so fully entitled.

With generous minds confidence does not often form a subject of regret. Mrs. Percival was always most amiable when trusted, and Agnes, when she retired to rest, felt, not only that an important duty had been discharged, but almost as if she had found, for the first time, a firm and substantial friend. There was now no mystery between the aunt and niece; and, though Mrs. Percival sometimes sighed over the little interest which the name of Walter excited, she could not but admire and commend her niece for the decision which she had made.

Agnes was not a girl to sing love songs to the moon. Perhaps no one could be capable of a deeper or more lasting attachment; but her life was filled up with active duties, and she had neither time nor inclination to sit down and brood over selfish or imaginary sorrows. Those who give themselves up to the absorbing influence of what is called love, might think that she knew little of the tender passion, when we say, that she went on with the accustomed pursuits, read the same books, applied herself to the pencil and her music, and visited the poor with apparently the same interest as before; but the deepest feelings are not the most conspicuous in our daily walk, and here is the great virtue of cultivating habits of industrious and useful occupation, that we fall into them without an effort, when the mind has most need of being beguiled away from its own secret cares.

Who can read these tender and touching lines beginning —

> Yes, there are real mourners,—

without feeling that the simple child of nature, whom the poet so ably describes, was enduring the fulness of earthly affliction, and that in its most refined and exquisite form. And yet he tells us that

> "Attention through the day her duties claim'd,
> And to be useful, as resign'd, she aim'd;
> Neatly she dress'd, nor vainly seem'd to expect
> Pity for tears, or pardon for neglect."

The first letter from Arnold Percival, after he reached the place of his destination, was filled with an account of the disagreeables of his journey, descriptions of the cold welcomes, or rather the absence of all welcome which awaited his arrival, and the unfriendly faces and strange habits of all around him. The next was more cheerful, for it spoke of having found a friend at last. "One who rails at human life by the hour, 'sans intermission.' His name is George Randall, of good family and prepossessing manners (at least to me;) but you shall see him in the winter, when he has promised to return with me. There is some mystery about his early years which always gives him pain when enquired into; but it is not difficult for me to read, in the workings of his proud and sensitive mind, the effects of injustice and injury from his fellow men—from those who are either tyrants or slaves, just as they are placed above or below the central line of independence, where strength and weakness meet, and beyond which no man is to be trusted."—

"Hey day!" said Mrs. Percival, who was reading the letter, "it is well that we antiquated people are not required to understand the logic of the present times. Let us pass on to something more intelligible."

—"Tell Agnes that she must call up all her philosophy, for she will now have two combatants instead of one; and Randall, who knows the world, will be able to bring facts to support my opinions."

Mrs. Percival handed the open letter to her niece, who glanced over it with apparent indifference, yet with that keen searching which none can understand so well as those who look for some kind mention, some afterthought 'some trivial fond record,' to be seen, felt and valued, by no one but themselves. But, no! this casual mention of her name was all the remembrance it contained, and Agnes felt it was not thus she was treasuring the recollection of Arnold.

Some time elapsed after this before she heard again from her cousin, and the next letter effectually damped the ardour of delight with which she broke the seal, for it spoke in no measured terms of unpleasant affairs, disagreements and hatreds, in which Randall had proved himself a noble fellow and a staunch friend.

"Alas!" sighed Mrs. Percival, "I fear his nobility is nothing better than pride, and his friendship self-interest."

"We will not judge him yet," interrupted Agnes, while her countenance expressed that peculiar kind of anxiety which nothing but such painful suspicions could possibly give rise to. "Arnold," she continued, "will never make a friend of the man whose opinions materially differ from his own; and who but himself can think as he does and act nobly."

The winter came, and with it the two collegians to the remote village of Houghton. They were now bound together in the closest intimacy, by that kind of fellowship which may not improperly be called a defensive league against the whole human race. Arnold, confident that the appearance and manners of his friend, if they did not always inspire admiration, must invariably obtain respect, was proud to present him to his mother and cousin, who regarded the handsome stranger with curiosity not unmingled with suspicion. He was indeed a handsome man, according to the usual application of the word. His features so finely and regularly moulded, that the beholder looked again and again for that repose and satisfaction, which fine features alone are unable to afford. The restless wandering of his eye would have been sufficient of itself to rouse the fears of a phisiognomist, but there was besides a ready-made smile of unparalleled sweetness which he wore on all occasions, exciting a doubt whether it had first been assumed for the sake of displaying an exquisite set of teeth, or for the still more dangerous purpose of disguising some secret passion or impulse, whose frequent recurrence had rendered the disguise habitual.

It was impossible to read such a countenance, all bland and smiling as it was; and Agnes turned away from the cold marble study to gaze with renewed satisfaction upon the nobler brow and more intelligible expression of her cousin Arnold; who was too much above the least practice of deceit himself to detect a false smile, or even a false word in others. Thus he was often deceived, and every fresh instance of misplaced confidence increased the bitterness with which he thought, and spoke of the actions of mankind in general.

Whether it was that the company of this associate, by throwing his best qualities into contrast, rendered them more conspicuous, or that the mental perceptions of her cousin had become more vivid during his short absence, certain it was that Agnes never had admired him so much as now. She even fancied that he had grown kinder and more cordial, and her own welcome was in danger of being more warm than was warranted by the circumstances attendant upon his departure. It is possible that Arnold was glad to feel again the comfort of a home, for, in spite of his cold exterior, he had in reality an affectionate and generous heart, that yearned for all those social sympathies which his perverted notions of what was really estimable, perpetually induced him to trample upon as worthless. And thus, like the heroes of a popular poet, he made his own wilderness at the same time that he mourned over its desolation.

The day of Arnold's return was one of those which make us gather into the very centre of whatever household comfort can be found—dark, cold and pitiless without. But Mrs. Percival's hospitality was like an enchanted circle, within which, whoever entered found full indemnity for past suffering. The countenance of Randall, however, handsome though it was, did not harmonize with the domestic scene. No, not though he praised the viands of every description, and smiled indiscriminately upon furniture and faces. The evening closed in with an increased howling of the blast abroad, which made the warm glow of fire and lamps within more welcome. The curtains were let down, the sofa drawn forward, and piles of dry wood blazed and crackled on the hearth. Still, conversation became commonplace, and at last it flagged altogether. Mrs. Percival ordered coffee, and Randall sipped and smiled, but without cheerfulness. Agnes next bethought her of a portfolio of engravings, mixed with a few of her own drawings, which Arnold had been wont to commend. Upon these the stranger bestowed unbounded admiration, but they were soon turned over, and the leaden extinguisher of dullness fell upon the party again.

Thus may one strange countenance, or rather one strange heart, untouched by the social sympathies of life, uninfluenced by home associations and dear remembrances of early affection and enjoyment, cast a damp upon the genial hour; like the fabled spectres of old, whose presence, although unmarked by any thing unnatural in themselves, was said to make the lights of the festival burn blue.

There is no cheerfulness like the cheerfulness of the heart. That honest, open daring to be innocently happy, which shows itself in the clear brow and sunny eye, connecting, as with the links of a bright and living chain, fond thoughts and early loves, unshaken truth, unblighted hope, remembrances of home, and early companionship, with the intense and heartfelt pleasures of the present hour. Why,—why within the book of beauty is this fair page so seldom found?

An over estimate of the attractions of Randall had induced Arnold so far to violate his constitutional reserve, as to warn his friend against cultivating an attachment to his cousin; "for," said he, with embarrassment quite unusual to him, "I believe her hand—her affections—at least"——

"Say no more," interrupted Randall, whose dreams were not of matrimonial bondages, "your cousin's heart would be safe from me, were she enchanting as Calypso, or fair as the fairest of her nymphs."

There was indeed no need of such a warning, for Agnes and Randall seemed mutually repulsive to each other; so true it is that simple virtue has no more attraction for a base and artificial character, than that character has in return for virtue itself. With such feelings, it was distressing to Agnes to find herself on the following morning tete-a-tete with her cousin, because she knew that the first question might reduce her to the necessity of giving pain, where she would so much more gladly give pleasure. Arnold, too, was at a loss how to commence the enquiry which he was determined to make; at last, stooping down to caress the once envied favourite, he said, with a significant smile, "Love me, love my dog."

"I hope the adage does not apply to friend as well as dog," replied Agnes, plunging at once into the difficulty which she knew must be encountered.

"It does, with tenfold force."

"To try, at any rate, is all the proof which can, in common fairness, be required; and if you will give me time, I will try to like your friend."

"I should have thought the feeling might have come without an effort. What have you to allege to his disadvantage?"

"You speak as if I entertained a prejudice against him, for prejudice it must be, and that of a very unwarrantable kind, where nothing is known. I only acknowledge an absence of love, and for this I can give you no better reason than that I do not understand him."

"He is clear as the day."

"Not to me; for I have no sympathy with him: and it requires a long time to understand those characters to which we cannot apply the key of sympathy."

Arnold was disappointed, for he knew the warmth of his cousin's heart, and her freedom from caprice, too well, to suppose that she would willingly withhold either sympathy or love from any one. Pleased, however, to observe that his mother had been favouring the stranger with her company in a ramble through the grounds, he sought an opportunity of ascertaining whether her perceptions had been equally dull.

After many stout efforts to bring down his pride to the level of asking a question, he did at last enquire plainly and decidedly how Mrs. Percival liked his friend: to which his mother, never more puzzled to give a decided answer, coolly replied, "He has handsome teeth."

"Out upon the woman!" said Arnold to himself. "They are all as perverse as their first mother:" and he ordered his horses, and rode for the remainder of the day with his new friend, whose various good qualities the fair and foolish sex were evidently unable to understand or appreciate.

Women, when entirely divested of passion and prejudice, are better judges of character than men; because, from the facility with which they throw off selfishness, they are able to identify themselves as it were with others; entering into their circumctances and motives, and diving into the deep recesses from whence arise the springs of action. If, therefore, women are not remarkable for understanding clearly, nor consequently for acting wisely, it is because their feelings are so powerful and vivid that they seldom listen to a story, witness a fact, or experience any of the common vicissitudes of life, without having the faculty of judgment, which they undoubtedly possess equally with men, tossed to and fro, and sometimes finally dethroned by the stirring passions of the moment, such as hope, fear, pity, love, or indignation.

CHAPTER VII.

A WEEK of uninterrupted social intercourse was scarcely gone, before the aunt and niece had both discovered that Arnold's new friend was in every way ill-adapted to correct the faults of his disposition.

"I cannot tell why he has chosen him," said Agnes, with some impatience. "I should have thought he would rather have fixed upon a straightforward, blunt, and independent man; one who, if I may use the words of Shakspeare, 'would tell truth and shame the devil.'"

"Do you not perceive," replied Mrs. Percival, "that straightforward, blunt, independent characters, by bolting at once upon the truth, must frequently infringe upon the imaginary dignity of those who shroud themselves in haughty reserve?"

"But this man has a cringing servile manner; peeping askance from beneath his eye-lashes to make observations when your attention is turned away, yet never openly and fairly looking any one in the face."

"You must not find fault with that, when he takes so much care to utter grand sentiments (whatever he may feel) always dressed up with a spice of nobility and daring."

"Arnold, too, is kind and generous; but this man is cold and immoveable as marble, except when animated by hatred or revenge. Only think how his countenance changed, how his brow contracted, and his eye flashed, when they talked over the insults and injuries they had received from the party at college."

"And yet I dare say," continued Mrs. Percival, "there are few of that party who bear in mind the circumstance of their existence; so much do characters of this description magnify their own importance, in the malevolence and hatred which they suppose themselves to excite. Would they but apply the same magnifier to benevolence and love, the deception might be worth cherishing. For my own part, I always think that we must in some measure deserve the hatred of mankind before we obtain it; or else have distinguished ourselves so decidedly as to call forth the most powerful feelings of envy, that dreadful passion, which, like hatred, delights to drag every thing to light that is capable of being tortured to the disadvantage of another. Now few who complain of the unkindness of their fellow-creatures will grant that they have deserved it; and still fewer can prove that they are distinguished enough to be the objects of envy. But come, let us endeavour to dismiss these harsh thoughts, for see, the two friends are approaching with faces more grave than usual!"

As soon as they entered, Arnold placed an open letter in his mother's hand, announcing the serious and alarming illness of the old gentleman (a stranger to them) who preceded Arnold in the entail, and whose death would place in his possession a splendid establishment, and almost princely fortune.

Agnes felt a strange tremor steal over her as her aunt was reading, and for a long time she dared not raise her eyes to Arnold's face; but when she did look up, he was seated in a musing attitude, his eyes directed to the distant woods or the sloping lawn, with neither cloud nor sunshine on his brow, nor any change of feature indicating the least emotion of soul.

"I wonder," said he at last, "whether this man will leave any one to mourn his loss. Whether one tear of real sorrow will be shed upon his grave, or whether, all like me, will be watching for what they can seize and appropriate as their own. What a world is this, where one cannot possess, without robbing another; where one cannot be made rich without a hundred being poor!"

"You can hardly call that robbery which

is awarded to you by the law of the land, without wrong or injustice on your part," said Mrs. Percival; "still less can you say that that man has lost his wealth, who is called away from it by death."

"But the herd of dependents, and poor relations who have been hangers-on upon his bounty, how they will hate to see my face, to say nothing of the little admiration I shall have for theirs; and then the trouble of doing justice to this person and the other, of satisfying all claims, and standing in a conspicuous situation before men, to be pecked at by the very daws of office; to be flattered, followed, and caressed, and, worse than all—oh! Agnes! to be fallen in love with by young ladies!"

Agnes rose, and playfully dropping her lowest curtsey, hoped she never should offend in that way.

"Well," continued Arnold, evidently endeavouring to shake off the slight appearance of excitement into which he had been betrayed; "it will be time enough to lament over these evils, even the last and greatest, when the old gentleman has really paid the debt of nature. You and I, Randall, have other things to think of. Let me see—how long is our respite from classic lore?"

"You will hardly return to college under present circumstances?" said Mrs. Percival.

"What circumstances can possibly affect me," replied Arnold, "so as to tear me from the shrine of *Alma Mater?* Besides there are other reasons. The vulgar herd would toss their antlers, and say they had driven us from our ground."

Time flew on, but still no further tidings of importance reached the village of Houghton; and Agnes, on the day before her cousin's departure, willingly mounted her horse to enjoy a ride with him once more. Randall had set off in company with them, but, not relishing the situation of third, turned round to enjoy a better sea-view from a distant point of land, and Agnes perceived, with heightened colour, that she was alone with Arnold.

"You see, Agnes," said he, addressing her in a kind and familiar tone, "I begin to approximate: I have made a friend."

"Ah! you compel me," replied Agnes, "to say what, in your ear, will sound harsh and ungenerous. You have indeed found a companion, but, are you more happy for his society?"

"I have more courage to brave the ills of life."

"Have you more patience to endure them? for, after all, since we cannot overcome what you call the ills of life, patience to bear them is what we most need."

"I hate patience!" exclaimed Arnold; "it was made for beasts of burden."

"I believe there never was a really great character," replied Agnes calmly, "without patience; most assuredly there never was a true Christian without it."

"But to argue in your favorite style, from scripture truths: Did not Job loose all that he had, while he sat bemoaning himself amongst the pots? Was anything left to him except his wife, who, if one may judge by her advice, was no great treasure; and were not his bosom friends let loose to worry him in his last extremity?"

"You forget that all these circumstances form but a series of trials by which his patience was proved; that in the end he was made a wealthy and happy man again, and that in the mean time he was reaping a harvest of wisdom from the fountain of all true knowledge; as we no doubt may do, if not immediately from the voice of an Almighty teacher, yet, remotely, by the same power operating through the medium of that discipline which is dealt out to us in our afflictions."

"I have always thought," observed Arnold, dropping the argument for the sake of his favourite theme, "that this specimen of friendship is the most perfect of any that we have on record. How exquisitely true to nature is the conduct of his friends, first making a show of sympathy by sitting in silence upon the ground, and then falling upon him with their pitiless reproaches, until the very dregs of bitterness were wrung out from his soul in those memorable and touching exclamations—'No doubt ye are the people, and wisdom shall die with you. Miserable comforters are ye all. How long will ye vex my soul, and break me in pieces with words? Suffer me that I may speak, and after that I have spoken, mock on!'

"Commend me to an honest enemy. There is something clear, definite and intelligible in the hatred that seeks to wound you at every point; and consequently you may arm yourselves against it: but the love that insinuates itself into your very bosom, there to tear up and examine all the materials of which you are compounded, to drag to light your hidden stores, and expel per force whatever is repugnant to its own nature; there can be no defence against such an enemy as this, for at every effort to expel the intruder or resist its ravages, it turns tender and tells you it is all for love.

"Who but a friend ever assumes the right of choosing what shall make you happy, and of inflicting it upon you? Who lays bare your own heart before you, at the very moment when you are least inclined to witness such a spectacle, but a friend? Have you committed any act of misdemeanor under the consciousness of which you are agonizing in secret, who breaks in upon your solitude with the story of your shame, but a friend? Is your character (unknown to you) stained with the very foible for which you have chastised another, who retorts upon you but a friend? Are your finances suddenly and totally expended, or is your lady-love just married to another, who steps in with the pleasing intelligence but a friend? Is the anguish of ingratitude rankling in your heart's core and thrilling through every artery and nerve, who has plunged the poisoned dagger but a friend? In short, look around upon the miseries of human life, and see whether the hardest portion has not invariably been dealt out by those who have assumed the prostituted name of friend. Ah! the emptiness, the shallow void, the utter worthlessness of that mockery which men call friendship! It is a game fit only for children to play at, when they seek for something less productive than blowing bubbles in the air. Yet why call 't unproductive when it is operating every day through all classes of society, when it is the grand engine of deception by which men, and women too, impose upon each other; for all falsehood flows from this polluted stream, and no man was ever yet betrayed to an enemy, who had not first trusted in a friend. 'My friends are false!' has been the burden of the deepest groans of wretchedness since the world first began, and the only cry which escaped the lips of Cæsar in his dying agony was, '*Et tu Brute!*'"

"And yet," replied Agnes, "you boast that you have found a friend."

"I boast not. I only say that I have found the thing so called. The proof is yet to come. At present he is tractable and civil, as all new friends are."

"But, according to your own rule, you ought to hold yourself ever upon your guard against deception."

"I do. And shall doubtless shake him off when he begins to take liberties."

"Oh! Arnold," said Agnes, looking at him through her tears, "when will you learn to value that which is truly estimable, before that which merely affords you momentary pleasure?"

"I value Agnes Forester before all the world. How can I better prove the correctness of my judgment."

Agnes blushed, and smiled, and for one moment,—one dangerous moment, there flitted across her mind the natural and womanly question whether it would not be worth risking all things, and uniting herself with Arnold's fate for good or for evil; so that she might ever be near the altar of his heart, to watch and extinguish its unhallowed fires.

"No, no," said she to herself, "It will not do; I have no confidence in my own power. I might live with him and love him, until I choose rather to think unjustly than to think differently, until I preferred falling with him frankness, that she was not happy, he answered her with bitter lamentations over his own inability to make her so.

"My love," said he, "blights wherever it falls. I am like the Indian tree, beneath which the birds that have flown for shelter lie dead."

Ida was terrified.—"Let us return to England," said she; and they set off on the morrow.

Arnold had few agreeable associations connected with the idea of returning. The world was all alike to him, whether at home or abroad. He expected no happy faces to look out for his arrival; and when Bella Dunhill threw open the park-gate without one enquiring glance into the carriage, he placed the rude indifference of this ungrateful woman to the account of human nature, and execrated the whole race with redoubled spleen.

Ida felt more in her proper element, although that element was a new one, as the rightful mistress of the noble dwelling, which the good taste of Mrs. Percival and Agnes had invested with an air of comfort as well as elegance.

For Arnold's worthy mother, as the first kind looking person she had met with for a long time, she gave way to a sudden burst of almost childish affection, which Mrs. Percival, from being unable to comprehend anything irrational, mistaking for affectation, did not receive so warmly as she otherwise would have done; and the young heart of the stranger was chilled again.

"Marion," said she one day, after a passionate burst of tears, addressing a simple-hearted domestic, who had accompanied her from Scotland, and whom, for that reason, she chose to have usually about her person, "what shall I do for somebody to love me?"

"Suppose you were to try to love somebody yourself," replied the woman.

"I do love somebody—I love my husband."

"I should hardly have thought that."

"Why not?"

"Because, if I must be so bold, I thought that along with love there went a great deal of kindness, and trying to please, and that sort of thing, that would just find you employment, and keep you alive in this dull place, and make all things seem quite different to you."

Ida, struck with what the woman said, remained musing for some time after upon the possibility of making her present lot more cheerful. During the reverie, her fingers had been turning over the leaves of her album; and when she awoke to a fresh sense of her real situation, she observed that the following lines had been recently added to her collection:

Away, away, I heed thee not!
  Tell me no more thy mournful tale:
I have no pity for thy lot,
  No ear to listen to thy wail.

Weep not; thy tears are like the rain
  That falls upon a senseless stone;
I may not, will not weep again,
  My sighs are hushed, my tears are gone.

Smile on some brow more calm than mine,
  Press on some fairer cheek thy kiss;
I have no joy no blend with thine,
  No love to answer love like this.

Touch not the harp; I will not hear
  One tone that tells of former days:
Sing to the waves that murmur near;
  Pour on the winds thy charmed lays.

Where is my heart? Go ask the wind
  That wanders through yon ruined tower,
If e'er its piercing search can find
  The hearth that blaz'd in festive hour.

No! lost is every trace of mirth,
  And hush'd is every festive sound;
The very breeze which fann'd that hearth
  Hath strewn its ashes o'er the ground.

But still the glorious beams of day
  Shine brightly on the castle wall:
On bastion worn, and turret grey,
  The silver streams of moonlight fall.

Fresh glittering ivy weaves a wreath
  Of shining beauty round its brow:
The mouldering ruin stands beneath,
  Unconscious, cold as I am now.

These verses were in Arnold's hand-writing. "No, no," said Ida, "the case is hopeless;" and she covered her face with out a well of water; a wide wilderness without a place of rest!"

On the following day, Mrs. Percival and her niece went at an early hour to pay their respects to the lord of the castle, and Agnes scrupled not to lend her aid and advice in the arrangement of his domestic affairs, and the establishment of order and comfort; for she carried about with her own feelings so little of self, that much of the false delicacy which is encouraged in her sex was absent from her mind. Thus the castle of Houghton was nothing more to her than the residence of her cousin Arnold; and thus she could form plans for his happiness, entirely independent of her own.

"We have been thinking," said Mrs. Percival to her son, on his return from riding, "that you must give a public entertainment, in order to establish yourself on a proper footing with your neighbours of all classes. It is well for the rich and the poor sometimes to partake of the same hospitality, in order that they may be reminded of their close alliance, and mutual dependence upon each other."

Arnold mused for some time, and then replied with indifference, "These things I leave to the management of ladies, who have ingenuity enough (if that were the only quality required) to rule the world. Make of me what you please. Show me off as a puppet or a monster, provided I am neither required to dance on wires, nor roar for the entertainment of the multitude."

In the mean time all went on smoothly, and even cheerfully, except, that Randall, who seemed incapable of the feeling of trust, kept continually feeding the mind of Arnold with suspicions that were foreign to his nature; and which, operating upon a character like his, were calculated to produce the worst possible result.

On one unfortunate occasion, a purse of sovereigns was not found in the place where it was supposed to have been deposited; and Randall cast an evil eye upon a faithful old servant of the name of Wallis, who had been left in charge with the two young Percivals by their dying father, and who had loved them as his own sons.

"Impossible!" said Arnold: "the old man has been like a parent to me; I would trust him with anything I have; and that under any temptation."

The fortress of long-continued confidence not being easily shaken, the subject was dropped for this time; but Randall tried it again and again, and that in the most wily and insinuating manner, until Arnold, ever too indolent to defend his own opinions, began to give way, and, wearied out by the perseverance of his friend, an ungracious consent was at last wrung from him, that a strong box in the possession of Wallis should be opened and examined. This outrage was committed in the absence of the old man, and there, unfortunately for him, the exact sum that was missing lay carefully concealed in a private drawer.

When Wallis returned home that evening, he was struck with the cold looks and colder welcome of his fellow-servants.

"What is the matter?" said he. "Has anything befallen our good master?" But no one answered him, and he hastened to assure himself, by delivering a packet, for which he had been sent out early in the day.

Arnold started at the sight of his old friend; for his honest and trustworthy countenance brought fresh conviction with it that Wallis had, indeed, been deeply wronged; but he received the packet with unaltered manner, and while pondering, with his usual indolence, upon the best method of atoning for the past, the old man left the room, and rejoined his companions, who, by this time, having yielded to their impressions in his favour, had determined, with one voice, to let him know the worst.

Wallis heard them without a word; but he drew himself up to an unusual height, as he stood erect in the midst of the group, and a deep flush of indignation rushed into his cheeks, to leave them more pale and haggard than before.

"It is time that I were gone!" said he,

when the dark story, with all its exaggerations, was concluded. "This night—this very night—I will seek another roof to shelter my head, where, if I cannot sleep so softly, I shall at least be treated like an honest man!" And so saying, he left the servants' hall, and walked away from the castle with the speed and the determination of his younger years.

The next day, Arnold missed his faithful domestic; and for many succeeding days he watched the opening door, with a degree of anxiety almost beyond his powers of concealment; but nothing could bring down his haughty spirit to make enquiries respecting the consequences of his own injustice; and though he never for a long time went abroad without looking for his well-known figure at every turning of the road, he was not once heard to utter his name: and, such is the barrier which pride and reserve establish against social intercourse, that no individual amongst the household at the castle dared intrude so far upon the confidence of their master as to hint at the melancholy fate of his much-injured servant.

This sad affair, however, had no sooner reached the ear of Agnes Forester, than she set out in search of the old man, to hear from himself the story of his wrongs. He had found shelter for his wounded spirit in a lowly dwelling, where, as he said, he was at least free from the suspicion of taking what was not his own, and where (his wife being dead, and his children settled in the western world) he hoped to end his solitary days in peace.

"I blame no one," he said to Agnes, "but the stroke has fallen here;" and he laid his hand upon his heart, and sighed heavily.

"Your master himself did not suspect you," observed Agnes, kindly; "all will surely be well again."

"I have carried him, Miss Forester, when an infant, in my arms," said the old man. "I taught him to ride, and to hold a gun, and to shoot an arrow at a mark: indeed, there is hardly any thing which belongs to a gentleman, except, perhaps, his learning and foppery, which I did not teach him. And to come to this at last!—To have my locks broken in the sight of the very scullion and stable-boy! But I will not talk of it, for it makes me feel prouder than a Christian ought to feel. I shall not be long for this world now, and pride, you know, is not for another."

"My cousin Arnold," observed Agnes, "is too just and too generous to be long under the influence of ill advisers. He will see his error, and all may yet be well."

"You remind me," said the old man, "of the words of the Rev. John Fletcher, of Madeley; and he stood up before Agnes, and earnestly fixed his eyes upon her face, while he repeated the following passage, with that precision and emphasis which is peculiar to those who are unskilled in the rules of rhetoric, and unaccustomed to the sound of flowing sentences:

"'See that crystal vessel. Its brightness and brittleness represent the shining and delicate nature of true virtue. If I let it fall and break it, what avails it to say, 'I never broke it before—I dropped it but once—I am extremely sorry for my carelessness—I will set the pieces together, and never break it again?' Will these excuses and resolutions prevent the vessel from being broken—broken for ever?' Now, this is the case with my heart; nor could all the kindness it is in your power to offer, wipe away the remembrance of the past, or undo what has already been done."

Still Agnes urged upon Wallis the probability of his being reinstated in his master's good opinion: the old man proudly replied, "You forget, Miss Forester, it is I who have to forgive; and I do forgive from the bottom of my heart. At the same time, I maintain that the honest man, who faithfully serves his master, though filling the lowest station amongst mankind, is as much entitled to an unsullied name, as the monarch who sits upon a throne. But I said I would not talk of these things, for they make a strange feeling rise up in my heart—a feeling that must be overcome before I can enter into that rest which is prepared for the faithful."

The preparations for the entertainment, which Mrs. Percival had devised as the only means of introducing her son to that circle in which he now held so conspicuous a station, were carried on by herself, Agnes, and Randall, without any participation on the part of Arnold, who carefully avoided those apartments where the greatest revolutions were in operation, and who, when the dreaded day at last arrived, had many serious thoughts of escaping entirely from the scene of action. But in proportion as he hated to be made a subject for the comments of the multitude, he endeavoured to avoid that singularity which must inevitably draw down this calamity upon his head, and therefore he resigned himself as well as he was able to his impending fate. With an air of indifference, not altogether ungracious, he received his guests; and if they did not feel the welcome of which he politely assured them, the fault was not in his words. Mrs. Percival, always on the alert, supplied by the frankness and cordiality of her looks and manners what was wanting in her son; Agnes faithfully performed her part, although with less activity and freedom; and Randall liberally bestowed his smiles upon those who sought only a momentary gratification.

"And this is what men call happiness!" said Arnold, as he turned away from a lively group, after music and dancing had begun; and persuading himself that no one would observe his absence, or heed it if they did, he escaped through an open green-house, that was studded all over with coloured lamps, and walked forth to enjoy the calmness of a dewy evening.

"Where is Arnold?" whispered Mrs. Percival, in consternation to Agnes, who had taken note of his departure with that quickness of perception from which a beloved object escapes not amidst a crowd, however dense,—to which one individual voice is audible amongst a thousand—one face and form perceptible when all others are obscure.

Randall was summoned to a short and secret council, but he knew nothing of his friend, and there was now no time for consultation.

"We must do the best we can," said Agnes, and this laudable determination was so ably supported, that many who had not at first been struck with her beauty, returned home to pronounce Miss Forester the most charming girl they had ever beheld; so much is the countenance improved by that genuine good humour which is founded upon good feeling.

Having once escaped from the busy throng to the uninterrupted indulgence of his own thoughts, Arnold felt little inclination to re join the company; and the din of many feet, with the confused sounds of music and revelry, only drove him farther from that merriment, in whieh it was so difficult for him to participate; until at last his morbid feelings were so worked upon, that he believed it impossible for him to return, and pacing to and fro upon the lawn before the windows, he gave himself up to a sort of nervous sensation, which it would be in vain to describe to those who have never been preyed upon by moodiness and despair, while surrounded by the gay, the thoughtless and the happy;—a sensation which approaches nearer to the nature of insanity, than any other that we endure in a state of liberty and freedom of will;—a sensation which so completely distorts the mental vision, that we behold every thing through the medium of self-torture;—a sensation which, in the present instance, almost persuaded the misanthrope that he was expelled by the contempt of his fellow-creatures from all participation in their enjoyment; that the strange lacqueys who thronged his hall were placed there as spies upon his private actions, and that a company of triumphant revellers had taken possession of his castle for the purpose of making a mockery of him and his wretchedness.

There is something so selfish in the nature of melancholy, that its victims invariably suppose themselves singled out for a peculiar fate, as if the laws which regulate the universe had been devised for their especial torture. Thus, while disclaiming the remotest idea of their own importance, and pronouncing themselves blanks in the creation, let them but pursue the course of their own murmurings, and they will go on to tell you that they are treated as if they were nobody—trampled upon by their fellow men—unloved, unsought, unvalued, their kindness returned with ingratitude, their trust betrayed, their affections abused, shipwrecked in all their adventures, disappointed in all their schemes, a blight upon their very name, and their foreheads stamped with the firebrand of destruction. But they heed it not! No! they are above complaint, for they despise the world more deeply than they feel its injustice.

Now do not such harangues as these prove beyond a doubt that such individuals esteem themselves a vast deal too good for the lot that has fallen upon them?—that they believe their fellow creatures to be very much in the dark as to their real merits;—that they are piqued and galled by the mistake, and burn with rage to revenge it? And worse than all, do they not secretly indulge the vain and presumptuous idea, that an Almighty Father has not extended towards them that mercy and justice which are shown in his government of the world in general? And thus, when they complain that the course of human events is so directed as to produce upon themselves the worst possible effects, are they not, by arraigning the wisdom and goodness of an Omnipotent Creator, blaspheming a holy name, and charging God foolishly?

"I am like no other creature in the universe," said Arnold, as he paused before a sparkling fountain that sent up its silvery waters in the moon light, to fall with a lulling and monotonous sound into the clear basin below, where the lights from the castle windows were glancing on its rippled surface. "Each particle of spray from these musical waters falls back again into the bosom from whence it flows, shining forth for one brilliant moment, and then returning to supply the parent stream. The gale that whispers through the trees, raising the white foliage of the mournful willows, and making the feathery aspen tremble at its presence, although no man knoweth whence it cometh nor whither it goeth, hath yet its purpose and its bound appointed, whether to bear along with it the scent of citron-groves, or the breath of the deadly pestilence; and the silent moon, so lonely and companionless in her beauty, that the bereaved and the desolate look up to her for that sympathy which they seek in vain elsewhere—the moon can shed her welcome smiles upon a distant world, gladdening the heart of the weary traveller as he journeys through the wilderness, and lighting the mysterious pathway of the mariner along the mighty deep. It is man alone, of all existing creatures, who lives on without an object worthy of one heart-ache in a thousand which his birthright costs him: and I, of all men the most companionless, stand here a mere excrescence upon the surface of creation, without an aim, a purpose, or a wish."

These melancholy meditations were interrupted by the sound of carriages rolling up to the door to bear away their precious burdens from the festive scene; and Arnold, by a mighty effort, compelled himself to reappear before his guests in time to receive their parting adieus. The sounds of revelry now died away upon the ear, the tread of separate feet became more distinctly audible; and, when the apartments, lately so brilliant and gay, began to look cold and deserted, Mrs. Percival thought it high time to commence an animated attack upon her son, which she did by describing, in no measured terms, the perplexity to which his absence had subjected her; and Randall, too, threw in his suspicions, more warily expressed, that many of the guests had retired at an early hour, in high dudgeon at the disappearance of the master of the house. "To say nothing of my conscience," he added with a smile, "which you have laden with falsehoods innumerable; for I was compelled to invent a story of your sudden indisposition, and force it down with asseverations, all chargeable to your account."

"Mr. Randall's detail of the consequences of your absence," said Agnes, gravely, "is serious indeed. The early departure of your guests I should hardly have called a grievance, for at this hour of night it is time for the body to repose, and the mind to reflect; but for any one to say they have been compelled to utter a falsehood, is to speak of a severe infliction, such as I am not prepared to believe we are ever subjected to in this world."

One of Randall's fierce looks, shot askance from under his contracted brow, made the colour rush into the face of Agnes, who quailed not for an instant, but, fixing upon him, her clear and beautiful eyes, bold with the heart's best courage, the countenance of the stranger gave way before her, and he looked around with restless impatience to find some object which might vary the scene, and relieve his mortifying embarrassment. At last he touched the harp, upon which he was a skilful performer, and played a light and lively air.

"I am not disposed for music to-night," said Arnold, in a subdued tone: "when the chords of the heart are unstrung, there can be no answering harmony within."

There was something in his voice and manner that night so mild and mournful, and he had borne with such calm patience the reproaches of his mother and his friend, that Agnes, who from the first had felt more grieved than angry, could not choose but pity him from her very soul; and, when the party separated, she accompanied her 'good night' to him with a look which plunged him into a long deep reverie, as he sat silent and alone, with both his hands pressed firmly upon his forehead. At last he arose, as if awaking from a dream, and looked round upon the dying lamps, whose varied hues afforded a striking emblem of faded splendour. Garlands of flowers, fallen and withered in the heated atmosphere, were drooping from the columns, around which they had been entwined; and the silence which pervaded all things was more sad and solemn, when contrasted with the merry sounds to which it had succeeded.

"Oh! Agnes Forester," exclaimed Arnold, "thy light step should ever walk these stately halls, to remind me that my home is not a sepulchre, in which lie buried the fond affections that are said to sweeten life. Thy smile should still be before me, to direct my journey through the wilderness. Thy heart should be mine and mine only, to teach me that there is yet a blessing upon this barren earth—a blessing even for me!"

CHAPTER IX.

Agnes Forester, although perfectly feminine in all her habits of thinking and acting, was not wont to be long blinded by her affections to that clear sense of right and wrong which she endeavoured to make the strict and invariable rule of her conduct: she therefore sought an early opportunity of pleading with Arnold on behalf of his old servant; and, though repeatedly repulsed by the unwonted severity of his manner whenever this subject was touched upon, she returned to it again, with the fondly cherished hope of eventually inducing her cousin to act consistently with his better feelings. By the most cautious and well-timed infringement upon his prejudices, she had prevailed upon him to become the frequent companion of her visits to the poor, and while she strove with unceasing assiduity to excite in his mind an interest in their welfare, she was often deeply pained and disappointed to find that her own company and converse had been the only attraction which had led him to their humble dwellings.

"I cannot imagine the satisfaction," she would often observe, "of living in the world without becoming acquainted with the circumstances of the poor but useful classes of society by whom we are surrounded; for while ignorant of the nature of their wants, it is impossible to take the right method of relieving them. Besides, since the customs of the world have denied to them the liberty of intruding upon our society, it is a duty which we owe to them to make some advances towards a better acquaintance."

"I would say to any other woman than yourself," replied Arnold, "that there is also something very attractive in being welcomed as the Lady Bountiful of the parish, and followed by the blessings of the poor wherever you go."

"For my own part," said Agnes, with some warmth, "I never hear the blessings of the poor, without shame and remorse that I have not done more to deserve them; nor can I suppose any one gratified by such incense, unless they are egregiously vain; nor entitled to receive it unless they have obeyed the injunction, which we regard too little, of selling all and giving to the poor. But see," said she, pausing, and looking out towards the sea, where the narrow valley sloped away in a kind of heath, upon which a few lean horses and a fettered donkey cropped the scanty herbage; "what smoke is that rising from amongst the furze and brambles? Let us walk that way, for I am curious to know why it should be ascending there in so regular a column."

Arnold and Agnes directed their steps to the wild and rugged piece of ground, where, close beside the rising smoke, they found a woman diligently employed with her netting-tackle, which she plied with wonderful dexterity. The labour of her hands, and the tenour of her thoughts seemed to proceed with the same determined course, for she did not condescend to look up at the approach of the strangers, nor vouchsafe a reply until they had often repeated the question of what she was about, and where was the place of her abode.

"Here," said she at last, impatiently, as if wearied out with their impertinent intrusion; and they saw that a deep hollow, somewhat like a grave, on the side of which she was seated, was littered with straw, and partly covered over with the branches of trees, fern, and other materials heaped together, so as to form a sort of thatch for one half of her habitation.

"But you surely do not live in this place night and day!" exclaimed Agnes.

"I live here always, except when I go to the town to sell fish."

"And are you not afraid?"

"I am afraid of nothing," replied the woman, her harsh and rugged features relaxing into a mournful misrepresentation of a smile; 'nothing that belongs to the earth, the sea, or, the heavens. I am afraid of nothing but the people who ought to be Christians, and the wrongs and the injuries they have done, and are still doing to me and mine."

Arnold now came forward, and asked her if she had any parents? "No!" Had she a husband? "She had once, but he had left her." Had she any children? and she pointed to a little grizzly urchin who was cowering amongst the bushes, and who, on perceiving himself the object of attention, scrambled away as fast as he could, with limbs all twisted and deformed, and scarcely able to bear the burden of his body.

"I had three sons," continued the woman, "but two of them are dead—one of hunger, and one of disease; and that monster that you see there was once as fair and straight a child as any mother's eye might look upon; but what with poverty and starvation, and the persuasion of neighbours, I was prevailed upon to send him to work in the factory, where he was beaten and abused until he lost the very shape of man. I had a daughter too, but they took her away to the Sunday-schools, where fine ladies put such notions into her head that she never owns me now."

"Have you no relief from the parish?" asked Agnes, but she soon repented having put the question, for the woman rose up and shaking her clenched hand, repeated her words with the rage of a maniac, declaring that while breath was left her, she would live in the free air, for which she had to thank nobody; and that when her last hour should come, she had only to lie down where she slept every night, and her boy would heap the earth upon her, and no parish overseer would then grudge the money for her burial, or sell her body to the doctor to pay his fee.

There was something so unnatural in thus making a grave her daily habitation, and in the expressions and gestures of the poor wretch altogether, that Agnes would gladly have turned away, but Arnold, more interested than he had ever been before by the distresses of the poor, still plied her with questions which only tended to call forth a deep sense of injury, either real or imaginary, and a wild and passionate thirst for revenge.

"The poor creature is certainly mad," whispered Agnes at last, drawing Arnold away from the spot. "You only increase her malady by talking to her."

"It is the most rational madness I have met with for a long time," observed Arnold. "I am determined to befriend this woman, if it were only for the true estimate she has formed of human life."

"It would be well indeed to find her an abode where she might be protected from such hardship and danger as she must necessarily be exposed to here, but I doubt whether her case is not beyond the reach of your kindness, for the most charitable conclusion which I can draw from her conduct is, that of decided insanity. And with many assurances from Arnold that it was the very excess of her sanity, or rather the extreme acuteness of her mental perceptions which made her incomprehensible to others, the two cousins separated after their walk, the one to muse upon the misery of living in the midst of mankind, and the other to make serious and matter-of-fact inquiries into the former character of this strange woman. Nor was it without heartfelt pain and anxiety, that Agnes learned from authentic sources, what had been the depraved and licentious nature of her past life. All, however, agreed that her mind at the present time, was strongly tinctured with insanity, the consequences of her own ungoverned passions, and the distresses and privations to which they had reduced her.

Bella Dunhill was indeed a well known character, not only for the singularity of her present mode of life, but for the stormy temper and bad morals which had separated her from her husband and all her early friends. Even the poor child, of whose ill treatment in the manufactory, she so incessantly complained, was said to have received his greatest injuries at home during his mother's fits of inebriation. But there were many who believed the frightful distortion of his limbs had come upon him, not from any bodily hurts but solely as a judgment upon his sinful parent; and such was the repulsive nature of her conduct, connected, perhaps, with a superstitious horror of her present mysterious way of living, that the dreary spot of ground where she and her little urchin burrowed, was shunned by the villagers towards the close of day, and the name of Bella Dunhill was used to frighten fretful children into silence.

All the information on this subject which Agnes could depend upon, she communicated to her cousin on the following day; but his resolution was taken: a lodge at the entrance of his park was vacant, and Bella Dunhill and her crippled boy were to become its future occupants. His lately kindled zeal to do good was, however, a little damped, by the ungracious manner in which his proposition was received by the woman herself, leaving it doubtful whether she would eventually accept his offer or not: but Arnold, pardoning her on the score of past injuries having soured her temper, the keys were left in her hands, and one moonlight night, not long after, she bade adieu to the sea-shore; and gathering up from different hiding places, her store of provisions, which amounted altogether, to a more plentiful board than might be found in many ceiled houses, she bestowed them carefully in the lodge, and Clym, (alias Clement,) was seen the next morning, dragging his limbs across the road to throw open the park gates for his master's carriage.

"You see, Agnes," said Arnold, with triumph in his looks, "that I am not quite so indifferent to the sufferings of the destitute as you have sometimes supposed."

"Arnold," replied his cousin, "it is the greatest trial of my life to think differently from you on matters of importance; and yet, how often am I compelled to blame what you esteem your best actions, so little are our feelings influenced by the same rule."

"It is a stern duty, Agnes, that you impose upon yourself; for it seems to extend to every thing I have the misfortune to say or do. But come, let me hear what objections you have to bring forward against my protecting this poor woman."

"I have no objection certainly to your protecting her, for no one could be more desolate and forlorn; but that she should be singled out to fill a place of respectability and trust, is, in my opinion, furnishing a bad precedent to others. Her past conduct, which I believe to have been very licentious, ought not to be regarded too severely if there were any evidence of an amendment of character; but I think you will hardly persuade even yourself that her present behaviour and conversation bespeak her to be a person worthy of confidence and respect."

"In this case, however, as well as in all others, you have unquestionably a right to act as you judge best; and, as the thing is done, I will trouble you no more about the consequences. Perhaps I intrude too often with my quaint opinions upon your sphere of action."

"Dear Agnes," interrupted Arnold, "when did I receive your admonitions with impatience? When did I conceal anything from you? When did I shrink from your severest reproofs?"

"Never," replied Agnes; "you are very good, to bear with me as you do. The reason why I wished to re-assure myself of your forbearance was, because I had another subject to lay before your attention in a way that I feel convinced will be most unpleasing."

"Pour on—I can endure."

"With regard to your old servant Wallis, I have never yet spoken so fully and decidedly as I feel in my conscience that I ought."

Arnold's brow lowered, but Agnes went on:—"I hear that the lost money was found in a situation where it must unquestionably have been placed by your own hand."

"It was," replied Arnold.

"Then let me ask, my dear cousin, why justice has not been done to the poor injured man?"

"He has been informed that the mistake was discovered, and, of course, might use any means he thought proper for the re-establishment of his character."

"I should have thought that the individual who committed the wrong, would have been the one to look to for the re-establishment of that character, especially as he holds a high and influential station in the world; while the injured man is poor, unprotected, and almost without a friend. Your conduct in this instance reminds me of what I have heard stated, that whenever an act of moral injustice is glaringly committed, the aggressor is the last to be reconciled to the injured party; as if he were the person who had something to forgive."

"I have at different times sent him considerable sums of money, all which have been returned."

"You must have known, Arnold, that the wounds of a noble spirit were not to be healed by money."

"Then you propose, as an atonement for the past, that I should call together all my domestics, and placing Wallis in the midst, should address him in a melting speech; and when all hearts were softened, and all faces drowned in tears, should kneel down and receive his pardon and his blessing. This, Agnes, would be a scene to your taste, much more than to mine."

"Arnold," said his cousin, looking more grave than before, "I am not prepared to answer you with sarcasms on such a subject as this. You and I stand in a serious relation towards each other. We have often had occasion to speak of the propriety, the utility, and the wisdom of different things, but I feel it my bounden duty in this instance to appeal to a higher test, and to ask whether you are acting consistently with the will of God? Whether you do not feel it impossible to offer up your secret prayers while this load is upon your soul, and whether a proper humiliation before the throne of mercy would not enable you cheerfully and promptly to discharge this important duty?"

"You have chosen the right word," replied Arnold, "for it is under a system of perpetual *humiliation* that you hope to wear me down to what I ought to be. But your method will not answer—you may harden what you cannot subdue."

"And where is the humiliation, even before mankind, of acting nobly? No one presumes to call himself infallible. We are all liable to err; and is not an error freely and fully acknowledged infinitely less degrading than one which is obstinately persisted in?"

"I cannot oblige you in this instance, Agnes. I hate to be the puppet of a show, and to hear the comments of weak voices upon what I may choose to say or do."

"Then try to divest yourself of these foolish thoughts about your fellow-creatures, and imagine for an instant that you are alone in the world, standing before the presence of your Creator, deeply implicated in an act of disobedience to his holy will."

"Are we not told that there is no act of disobedience too deep or daring to be forgiven?"

"But when did we ever hear of forgiveness while the sin was persisted in? And is not every hour that you live without doing what justice you can to this poor man, a convincing proof that you prefer the gratification of a mean and slavish pride, to the noble independence of daring to do what is right?"

"Then, Agnes, you shall do this noble deed for me. You shall proclaim to my household, that I have been base and ungrateful enough to heap disgrace and shame upon the hoary head of a trusty servant. You shall tell them also, that their master is too great a coward to acknowledge his fault before them; that he hides himself from their very looks, and employs the voice of a woman to speak for him."

"If there is really no other way of setting the matter right, I will, for the sake of the old man, (and with your permission,) give my own version of the case to your domestics, nor need you tremble for the dignity of your character in my hands. But, Arnold, this is only my last resource;—dear Arnold, is there not something due from yourself? Is there not something due to her ——"

Agnes could proceed no farther. The subject was too near her heart, and tears of more than common anguish fell thick and fast, while she bent down her head with a vain effort to conceal them; for Arnold had unconsciously pronounced his doom—and hers. On this one subject her thoughts had lingered, with the fond hope that, if he yielded to her arguments, she should then feel justified in giving way to such anticipations of the future, as were perpetually forcing themselves upon her affectionate heart: "but if (she had said to herself that very morning) Arnold cannot be made to see this glaring case as I do, it will be proof indisputable, that in the great consideration of moral good and evil, we never can be united by that participation of feeling which is the foundation of all human happiness."

For many months, Agnes Forester had been remarked upon as being more grave and thoughtful than could be accounted for by her age or circumstances; but now her gravity assumed an air of sadness, which her aunt, shrewdly guessing at the cause, endeavoured by the most delicate attentions to soothe; and Agnes, perceiving her kind wishes, succeeded in forcing herself to converse and smile with a cheerfulness which repaid Mrs. Percival for all her solicitude. Still her energy gave way—her health declined—the colour faded from her cheek, and Arnold, who seldom observed the minutiæ of common life, could not, with all his incredulity, blind himself to the conviction that he was, or had been, deeply and tenderly beloved. But that any woman should refuse, from principle, the man who would otherwise have been her choice, was to him so far beyond belief, that he bestowed little regard upon their frequent difference of opinion, so long as he could enjoy such clear and indubitable evidence of his cousin's attachment to him. For her encreased sadness, he could assign no cause, but strove to beguile her secret cares by more than wonted kindness and solicitude, until Agnes was often compelled to depart abruptly from his presence with tears that were altogether inexplicable to him.

In this manner time glided away, and on a bright and cloudless morning, when autumn had again spread her yellow curtain over the face of nature, Agnes begged her cousin would accompany her on a visit to a poor man whom she had promised to see that morning. They walked together to the door of the cottage, where Arnold, at the request of his cousin, placed himself on a low bench within a sort of porch, while she entered an inner apartment, in which the object of her kind interest was seated by the fire.

It was a well-known voice that bade her welcome, in tones of the most heartfelt gladness; and, Agnes, after asking many questions about the health and comfort of the invalid, sat down beside old Wallis, who affectionately took her hand, and pressed it closely with his time-worn fingers.

"You see, I grow weaker every day," said he, without the least symptom of regret, either in his countenance or voice.

"I do, indeed, perceive an alteration," said Agnes, and the old man went on. "I have been thinking to day, Miss Forester, that pride has been all along my besetting sin—pride in a good name; and though he who robbed me of mine, ought certainly to have known me better; I have no doubt but this affliction was permitted to fall upon me, in order that I might arrive at a better knowledge of my own heart; for affliction is a searching thing, and we sometimes learn in adversity, what we never so much as thought of while all went well with us. It was wrong, very wrong, in me, Miss Forester, to rebel as I did against the stroke; and when I said in my towering pride, that I forgave him, I felt an unchristian triumph in the thought that I was heaping coals of fire upon his head. But now I see differently. I see that he was in error, but we are all liable to err. I can now say, indeed, that I forgive him from my soul, and only wish that I could see his face, and see it once more looking kindly on me before I die."

"Perhaps he will visit you," said Agnes.

"I wish he would," sighed the old man, and he went on recalling the pleasant days when Arnold was a boy. "And, Walter, dear Walter, where is he?"

Agnes felt almost ashamed of the little information she could give about her cousin Walter, and rising from her seat, with an affectionate farewell to her poor friend, rejoined Arnold, who was turning over the leaves of a book with all the noble affectation of being totally unmoved by what he must have heard.

"Agnes," said he, sternly, as soon as they had left the cottage, "I did not expect this from you. I did not anticipate the risk of being betrayed into a scene. Henceforth you must perform your errands of charity alone."

"Be it so!" said Agnes, and she felt that another link was broken from the chain which had once bound them together. "Be it so!" she repeated, but do not be harsh with me to-day, Arnold."

"Is there any charm in this day more than another, that I should not enjoy the liberty of speaking freely what I think and feel?"

"Speak, but speak gently; for it was on this day twelve months ago, that I agreed upon that time for the decision of my future fate, and to-morrow, we shall stand in a different relation towards each other."

Arnold said no more; for there was something in the firm and mournful tone of her voice, which, connected with her previous sadness, had startled his philosophy, and plunged him into the most gloomy forebodings; and they arrived again at Mrs. Percival's door without either of them having relieved their minds of the heaviest burden they had ever borne.

It happened that Mrs. Percival had an engagement from home that evening; in consequence of which Arnold and his cousin were left alone to extract what happiness they could from such an interview. In vain did Agnes attempt to converse on common topics; it seemed as if her very speech had failed her, for often, when she would have made some casual observation, the words died away upon her lips, and blushes alone were left to tell their meaning—perhaps the very meaning she would least have wished to reveal. At last Arnold, encouraged by her embarrassment, took her hand, and said, with a look which belied his words, "Then it is really your intention to renounce me, Agnes?"

"Say, rather, that you renounce me," she replied; "for no other words can justify the anguish of this moment!"

"Why, dear Agnes, should you endure that anguish which is so entirely self-imposed?"

"You mistake me, Arnold; the suffering which I endure is not self-imposed. You think meanly of me indeed, if you think that I am grieving merely because I cannot be the companion of your future life. You may find many better qualified to supply my place, nor am I so romantic as to think that I shall never love again; but you must know little of the strength of early and long cherished affection, if you do not understand the agony of seeing it thus mournfully cast away."

"Agnes, you cannot call it cast away, when it is treasured as the greatest blessing of my life."

"Did I not tell you that my resolution was fixed?—Did I not allow you twelve months before I should act upon that resolution?—And what is the result?"

"That I am the same blighted branch I was then. But am I accountable for my own desolation? Is it for me to give showers and sunshine, or to put forth blossoms and fruit without the blessing of heaven?"

"The blessings of heaven are so mysteriously dispensed by that wisdom which cannot err, and that mercy which cannot fail, that man, in his narrow sphere of knowledge, is unable to say whether, in possession or privation, they are most bountifully bestowed. But I cannot argue with you to-night Arnold; we should but trace the same circle of ideas through which we have passed so many times with so little satisfaction. All I can now feel—all I can now say is, that you and I must henceforth be to each other friends, and friends only."

"You cannot mean it," said Arnold, starting up—"you cannot be so cruel!"

"Perhaps you think I cannot be so firm; but I will prove my words. Only you must come to me, Arnold, in your seasons of affliction; you must come to me always for those services which you cannot ask of another; you must come to me for every thing but that intimate communion of feeling which you and I must now endeavour to find elsewhere."

Arnold was at last convinced; and, pacing to and fro in the apartment, he resigned himself entirely to despair. At last he stopped suddenly, and, fixing his eyes upon the face of Agnes, who was now pale and silent as a marble statue, he appealed for the last time to her love and pity.

"Then you leave me, Agnes, for ever!" said he, in a voice whose piercing tones were mingled both with anguish and reproach. "You extinguish the lamp of the benighted traveller; you tear away the last rose from the withered wreath; you dash down the cup of healing from the lips of him who has no other. You will go forth into the world with a thousand sources of enjoyment of which I know nothing. The hearts and the homes of the happy are ever open to receive you; the smiles of the good and the blessings of the poor await you on every hand; but for me there is now neither love, hope, nor consolation in the wide wilderness of life!"

He ceased, and Agnes made no reply. She had grown still paler while he was speaking—her very lips had lost their ruby colour—with a gentle but determined step she passed away from his presence—and Arnold was alone.

CHAPTER X.

It was late on the following day when Randall made his appearance with a message from Arnold, stating that he was under the necessity of going to London for a few days, and, having many arrangements to make before setting out, had commissioned his friend with his adieus to the ladies.

"No one," observed Mrs. Percival (with the air of one who pays a compliment,) "could be better calculated to take off the pain of an adieu."

Randall bowed, scarcely knowing whether he was flattered or not, but deeming it the best policy to appear so.

Agnes, who knew little of the world, and had never disappointed a lover before, felt anxious and alarmed when she heard of her cousin's abrupt departure, half fearing he might rush upon some desperate act that would endanger his safety and happiness; and, vainly wishing that he had but left her one line to explain his intentions, she retired to her own room to ponder in secret upon that cruel separation which had deprived her of all right to enquire into his private actions. There was besides another subject of serious importance which now occupied her deep and earnest consideration; nor was it until long after the hour of night that she shook off her meditations and prepared herself for repose; but the clear brow reflected in the mirror by the light of a fading lamp, wore that night an aspect more calm than it had done for many months before; and her countenance, though pale and thoughtful, was stamped with the firm and sedate character of a well-supported resolution.

The next morning she sought an interview with her aunt before the cares or occupations of the day should have dissipated her thoughts; and with calm voice and collected manner she spoke of the necessity there was for her to seek some other place of abode, where her mind might be more at peace.

"You know, dear aunt," said she, "that I am not addicted to sentimental melancholy, nor would I indulge my feelings at the expense of duty. I have no fear of being betrayed into a weakness inconsistent with my present purpose; but I do fear for my health and the equanimity of my spirits, which I would gladly preserve for future usefulness."

Mrs. Percival, startled by this unexpected proposal, into something more than her wonted tenderness, with tears besought her niece to think well before she decided.

"I have thought, and I hope, thought well," replied Agnes, "for I become more and more confirmed in my decision; and that not on my own account alone."

"And what shall we do without you, dear Agnes, Arnold and I together? and where will you go?"

"That is the most serious part of the matter; for you know I am poor. But surely we may hear of some kind lady, who wants an humble friend as an agreeable companion. I could hardly offer myself at present."

"No! no! you must not think of it. Neither Arnold nor Walter would forgive me, should I give my sanction to such a scheme."

"Ah! you have named the right person!" exclaimed Agnes. "A friend in the hour of need has my cousin Walter ever been to me; and if he can be brought to approve my plan, he will soon see it executed." And taking a pen, she sat down to explain the case as well as she could, without touching harshly upon the faults of Arnold, for nothing else, she thought, but a clear and simple statement could enable Walter to judge of the propriety of her plan.

Mrs. Percival had permitted her niece to write with full confidence that her son would put an immediate stop to her intended proceedings. What, then, was her surprise, when she herself received an answer, by return of post to the following effect.

That Walter, highly approving of his cousin's intentions had applied, on the instant, to Lady Forbes, a distant relative of his mother's, whose delicate health and peculiar habits disqualified her for taking that place in society which her character and manners were fitted to adorn. That his proposal was eagerly embraced; and that he should return with his brother, for the purpose of accompanying Agnes to town.

The prospect of so soon beholding her son almost reconciled Mrs. Percival to the idea of losing a companion, who, since the real cares and perplexities of life had established a closer intimacy between them, had been to her most dear and valuable; and still, at intervals, her tears would flow, upon the thought how soon these treasures would both be gone. "And what shall I do," she would then say, "to beguile the moodiness of poor Arnold?"

But she never gave way to this kind of lamentation without regret; for there came across the countenance of Agnes such a look of distress, as made her each time determine that she would be wiser for the future. So sad it is to hear the name of one we love connected with tones of tenderness and pity, for the very pain that we ourselves have inflicted.

It was a great relief to all parties when the cheerful face of Walter Percival again appeared at Houghton; whether he busied himself with the many alterations and improvements at the castle, which his brother allowed him to set agoing, or entered, with an interest peculiar to kind and social characters, into his mother's sphere of domestic comfort at home. But chiefly to Agnes, circumstanced as she then was, his social and open manner, accompanied by the most delicate respect for her feelings, shown in a tenderness that was less expressed than understood, were more welcome for the extreme need she now felt of such sympathy and support.

Let none, who would add to the happiness of their fellow-creatures, be above those little attentions from which the proud and the selfish excuse themselves, by saying they are too trifling for their regard. Is not human life made up of trifles; and what being possessed in any degree of susceptibility of feeling, has not been soothed by kind attentions, or pained by the want of them? No! despise them as we will, it is the impulse of nature which compels us to recall the little services of our absent friends, as the dearest pledges of their affection. Who has not felt himself (perhaps it would be wiser to say herself) as it were in a land of strangers, when surrounded only by those, who, paying no regard to her individual tastes and feelings in the minute circumstances of life, perpetually crossed her inclination, and jarred upon her prejudices, by addressing her on topics the most repugnant—offering her gifts of which she could make no use—helping her to food which she was not in the habit of tasting—proposing conveyances for which her health was entirely unfitted—choosing, for her gratification, enjoyments for which she had no relish;—and thus inflicting upon her the greatest annoyances of life, without the least idea that she was not made happy? And we some of us well know, that there have been those so stripped, so destitute of all human sympathy, that a voice in the multitude amongst whom they believed themselves to be alone, suddenly touching their individual feelings by some reference, however simple, to things which they had sought or shunned, approved or rejected, in former days, has filled their eyes with tears, and their hearts with gratitude, that any one should be remembering them at the time when they felt themselves most desolate and forlorn.

Lady Forbes had charged Walter, if possible, to take his cousin back with him, promising that nothing should be wanting to make her residence in town agreeable, and that she should be treated with the greatest liberality, as money was no object with her.

This lady was born in India, where, at a very early age, she married Sir William Forbes, her senior by thirty years, at whose death she was left in the possession of more wealth than wisdom to enjoy it. She had been the mother of several children, who had died in infancy, all except one daughter, sent over soon after her birth to benefit by the air of Scotland amongst her father's relations. Whether from a want of felicity in her matrimonial connection, or from a combination of uncongenial circumstances which attended the formation of her character, the unfortunate mother had suffered a naturally amiable temper to become completely soured; and having, at the same time, given way to a general mistrust of her fellow-creatures, she had consequently few friends in India to regret her departure for England, and still fewer to welcome her to the shores of that country where she now bemoaned her sad and isolated existence, without the energy or even the desire to make it more happy, by being more active and useful. Companions she had tried in numbers almost incredible, but, in her opinion, they had all treated her ungenerously, some dishonestly; and she had parted from every one with mutual dislike. She was now entirely alone—a situation of all others the most dreadful to her; and, from Walter's description of his cousin, she caught at the proposition with such avidity, that she considered herself extremely ill-used when informed that she must wait a few weeks before Agnes Forester could possibly appear in town.

The appointed day, however, came at last; and Agnes, weary and somewhat dispirited, alighted from a hackney-coach with her cousin Walter, who wished, for the first time in his life, that he could have driven her up to the door in his own carriage, if only to inspire the domestics with a little more respect for her who, in his opinion, deserved the richest honours of an admiring world.

Lady Forbes was a handsome woman, of that indescribable age about which you feel sorry that any one should make exact enquiries. Dark, indolent, and perfectly eastern in all her habits. To have appeared entirely in character she should have worn a crimson or yellow turban, and slaves should have been crouching at her feet, or fanning her with the gorgeous feathers of some Indian bird. As it was, the turban and the slaves alone were wanting—for she reclined on a couch with all the luxurious indolence of a more sunny clime, and her apartment was furnished with a degree of costly elegance that would scarcely have dishonoured a sultana. Her dark eyes half hid beneath their languid lids, and long shadowy lashes, were slowly raised on the entrance of Agnes, and she stretched forth a delicate white hand that dropped listlessly by her side after her effort to perform a welcome, as if weighed down with its burden of rings and glittering gems.

Agnes felt all that uncomfortable sensation with which we open out from the wrappings of a journey in the presence of those whose toilette has been more recent, and who appear never to have known the touch of vulgar dust; she therefore begged permission, as soon as Walter had departed, to retire at an early hour. Her lodging-room, that citadel of a woman's comfort, was prepared with the greatest taste and elegance, so that she almost dreaded to unfold her simple wardrobe in such charmed precincts; but weariness does much to overcome the influence of finery, and, though the visions which flitted before her mind, as she tossed upon the downy bed which vainly invited her to repose, were many and strange, her thoughts were at lest composed and settled, for she had not applied in vain to the fountain of all consolation, whose healing waters were ever ready for her utmost need.

One great difficulty amongst many, which attend what is called a *situation*, is the doubt about the actual occupations of the day, which every one must feel at first, from not knowing what is expected, what will please, or what will disappoint; nor can any thing be altogether more pitiable than the fate of her who goes forth into the world to be agreeable for hire. She may possibly have been tenderly nurtured in a pleasant home—her wishes gratified—her tastes consulted—her feelings indulged—the idol of a partial circle to which her very failings have endeared her. But the stroke of affliction has fallen, her father's finances are suddenly reduced, or his life (the prop of his family) is taken away; and, with either of these sad events, and the breaking up of the whole establishment, have come the usual falling away of summer friends, the settlement of the sons in trade, and the daughters in *situations.* The one individual whom we have singled out may have besides her own secret sorrows—strange comments made upon her character which none dared utter before—the cold treatment of a friend—a lover estranged—in short, the breaking-in of the floods of adversity upon her little garden of homefelt delight: but she forgets for a while her own cares in the dispersion of her family, and prepares to share the general wreck. A *situation* is found. "How fortunate!" exclaim those who must otherwise have opened their doors to receive her. A morbid invalid is in want of perpetual entertainment, and the broken-hearted girl must bid adieu to her native place—to every tree, and hill, and grove—to all the associations of early life, and the tenderness of close relationship. With probably tenfold the refinement of those amongst whom her lot is cast, she goes to dwell in a land of strangers, where she must have neither hopes, passions, nor remembrances which may not be made subservient to the purpose of pleasing her, who feels, whenever her spirits begin to flag, that she is not receiving the worth of the money which she pays for her companion to keep her in good humour.

Men may complain that they have to labour with head and hand to obtain their daily bread; and dreadful indeed is the vortex into which absolute men of business are plunged!—deadening to the intellectual faculties, and oppressive to the spirit that would gladly flee away and be at rest: but men have their hearts, their passions, their feelings to themselves; they have only to calculate and look for money: while women are taxed for their powers of pleasing, of loving, serving, and suffering for others; in short, for just what it is impossible that money should purchase—for the flowers of existence that sweeten life only when they grow spontaneously.

Deal then gently with your homeless sisters—ye who possess the power to buy amusement! And remember, that she from whom you are perpetually demanding sympathy, has once enjoyed, and still may want that sympathy herself; that the fount from whence you would draw unceasing gratification, must sometimes need supply; and that the lamp from which you would borrow light, may not always have the blessed oil to spare.

Agnes Forester had none of these gloomy associations to embitter her present lot. Her choice had been a voluntary one, made in the same spirit in which we apply a wholesome but unpalatable restorative, and as such she had no disposition to murmur at the duties which consequently fell upon her. These duties were certainly of a very mysterious character; but a willing mind can mostly find employment sufficient even for an able hand.

A careless observer would have pronounced Lady Forbes to be the victim of morbid sensibility. Agnes soon discovered that selfishness was the root of her malady—indolence the incubus that clenched her feelings in its leaden grasp—and mistrust the demon which guarded them against the entrance of any good.

Still she was a lovely woman, possessed of many graces both natural and acquired; and her entire helplessness, the effect of habits long indulged, rendered her an object rather of pity than dislike.

All the mental powers which Agnes could command, concentrated and directed to one purpose, were unable for some time to devise any mode of acting likely to be serviceable in such a case; but the effort which she made was of the greatest possible benefit to herself, drawing away her thoughts from the tree of forbidden fruit, and feeding them with safe and wholesome sustenance. At her first initiation into office, she was entrusted with enormous bunches of keys, for Lady Forbes was tormented with the idea that her worldly substance was perpetually prayed upon by thieves; and, as she had too little energy to make herself acquainted with the real value and extent of her household possessions, and trusted no one, it was impossible that her mistake should be rectified.

"One thing I must beg of your ladyship," said Agnes, after a few days' residence beneath the same roof had strengthened her courage to speak freely—"that I may be treated with implicit confidence. If we hold ourselves above all falsehood and duplicity, I believe we shall be as little inclined to suspect those with whom we associate, as to associate with those whom we suspect. If your ladyship is really unable to trust me entirely in your domestic affairs, I am sorry for it; not only because I shall then be reduced to the inconvenience of choosing another situation, but because I shall be convinced that you can never know what it is to possess a real friend."

Lady Forbes looked astonished, a little angry, and a great deal more alarmed. Whether her house was really about to be turned out of the windows, she could not tell; but, certainly, none of her companions had ever spoken to her in this style before; and, judging from present appearances, it seemed but too probable that if her house should go, she would go along with it. "A *companion!*" she repeated to herself; but finding that Agnes waited for an answer, she replied, at last, that she had certainly no reason to doubt the sincerity of Miss Forester:—and in this humour the two ladies sat together without interruption during the rest of the morning; for Lady Forbes never went out except on the sunniest day,—saw nobody, and partook of no amusement but that which has been commemorated as the choice of a certain poet—reclining on a couch, and perpetually reading novels. Happy was it for her companion that no voice could travel over the magic lines with sufficient speed to keep alive her ladyship's spirits: Agnes was, therefore, left at liberty to pursue her own thoughts; and a long train of unprofitable musing would doubtless have been the consequence, had she not roused herself into action by reflecting, that although the stipulation between Lady Forbes and herself might require nothing further, she had a more serious duty to perform, a higher covenant to fulfil.

"Am I my brother's keeper?" is an answer we are ever prone to make when the daily duties which we owe to our fellow-creatures present themselves at an unwelcome season, or in a character too irksome for our indolence. No one has ever felt the power of a holy affection, without desiring to render to the beloved object a service the most devoted, and sometimes the most sacred. But is this all? Alas! the dearest to our hearts are not always near us; and are we, therefore, to drag on a life of indifference and unconcern with those amongst whom Providence has seen meet to place us? Shall we not, rather, have to render an account in strict reference to them, of our daily walk and conversation, in which the answer, "Am I my brother's keeper?" will be as impotent a sound as when it echoed from the lips of the first murderer.

Agnes Forester felt that nothing could be accomplished, without interesting the feelings of her new friend—feelings which had so long been dormant, that it required the greatest delicacy and the most assiduous attention to draw them forth, without any appearance of impertinent intrusion upon her private affairs. But there is one key which seldom fails to open the human heart, if properly applied—the key of sympathy; and Agnes had so long cultivated a deep interest in the feelings of others, particularly in the sufferings which she had any hope of alleviating, that she could enter into the minutest circumstances of those around her, without either affectation or pretence; and thus she enjoyed many opportunities of soothing and supporting, which others equally willing might seek in vain by every means to obtain.

Lady Forbes had never been so fortunate as to meet with this quality in any of her former companions; and it was much to her own surprise, that she found herself, at a late hour one evening, telling Agnes of her early marriage with one who had regarded her only as a lovely child, nor sought in her society one intellectual gratification; and the lonely, wearisome, and monotonous life which she had consequently led. It is true she had not unfrequently related this story before, but she had never found a listener who appeared to feel with her and for her. Those who have lived alone in a busy and stirring world can best tell what it is for the first time to awaken real sympathy—not the simper of mere politeness, or the sigh that responds from lips unacquainted with sincerity, but the deep, earnest sympathy of a feeling heart. This was the happiness of which Lady Forbes tasted for the first time; and when she parted from Agnes that night, it was with the warm pressure of the hand—that silent earnest of future good understanding.

Confidence once established, the way opened, and the work begun, Agnes went on with cheerful perseverance; and, although there were many objections to the graver books which she strove at times to introduce, and many excuses for the few faults which she ventured to point out at first in her ladyship's domestic economy, and then in her habits of acting and thinking, she evidently gained ground; and succeeded finally in obtaining that confidence and respect, without which, she could have done nothing.

It was with the greatest satisfaction that Walter found his cousin, now fully established on the footing of a tried and valued friend, rather than a mere companion. "But Agnes makes every one love and respect her," said he, with a sigh, which none but himself could rightly interpret; and he resolved to call more frequently, since the manners of Lady Forbes began to be less forbidding. She would even join with social good humour in the society of the two cousins, and sometimes rallied Agnes on the attentions of her faithful knight. "Poor Walter!" Agnes would reply, with calm brow and unblushing cheek. "We have been brought up together from our infancy, and to me he has ever been like a kind and affectionate brother." Why would it have been impossible for her to answer in the same words, and the same manner, had the name of Arnold been substituted for that of Walter?

Before one month had passed away, Agnes believed herself to be in possession of the entire confidence of Lady Forbes; and so essential had she become to her happiness, that she was regarded as the very support of her life,—referred to in all doubts, appealed to in all difficulties, and entreated oftener than the day, never to leave her. In vain did Agnes argue, that a proper reliance upon that support which is promised to the needy, with the use of right reason in the common emergencies of life, would effectually prevent that servile dependance which places us too much in the power of our fellow-creatures. Lady Forbes had only advanced one step from the centre of selfishness, and that step was to throw her burdens upon Agnes, who thought, acted, and spoke for her,—in short, was trusted so far, as to open and read her letters.

It happened one day, that she had broken the seal of a letter at the request of her friend, and stood for some moments in silence before she began to read. Lady Forbes looked up, wondering that she did not proceed, and catching a glimpse of the hand writing, uttered a loud shriek, sprang to the side of Agnes, and, snatching the letter from her hand, demanded in a hurried manner, whether she had seen any of the contents.

"I saw the name of mother," replied Agnes, "and I blush to think that this is the first intimation I have had, that Lady Forbes has a daughter still living."

For a proper explanation of this mysterious letter, it will be necessary to go back to the circumstances which had transpired at Houghton Castle.

CHAPTER XI.

ARNOLD Percival had seldom been so much roused as when he first learned the determination of his cousin Agnes. The degradation, the annoyance, to which she might be exposed, rushed upon his mind with aggravated horrors; indeed the scheme was altogether so hateful to him, that silent as he usually was, as to anything connected with his inner feelings, he found it difficult on this occasion to be quiet; and what is worse than all besides to an enraged man, he had no one to reproach,—nothing of which he could complain; for she who was the source and root of his provocation, bore too sacred a name for him to sully it with a breath of blame, and the act itself, though humiliating in the eye of the world, wore no impress but that of a noble and independent character. Feeling that he had no just grounds for his indignation, he shunned the society of his mother, whose quick perceptions and unscrupulous freedom, would neither permit him to be silent, nor tolerate his vindication of a wrong cause. In this temper he had little disposition to do the honours of his house to a friend of Randall's who dined at the castle that day; and retiring from table at an early hour, with the best apology his ingenuity could invent, he took his wonted stroll about the grounds and garden, after the departure of the daylight had secured him from the observations of impertinence. The same lovely picture of quiet and repose lay stretched before him in the light of a cloudless moon,—the same scene unchanged by the stormy passions which struggled for the empire of his heart. In vain he asked for sympathy from nature, who answered him in silence and beauty, while his soul was a stranger to repose; and he felt as if the solemn majesty of night was speaking to his troubled spirit in the language of reproach.

After passing to and fro, until wearied with his own fruitless repinings, he turned towards the door, and would have entered, but the sounds of uncongenial mirth issuing from the dining-room, checked his purpose, and leaning against the wall, he fell again into a deep and silent reverie. Few persons can be so much absorbed by meditation, as to be insensible to the sound of their own names; and Arnold, who had before been deaf to the conversation within, now found that he could distinctly hear the following words spoken with that freedom and emphasis which belong to the excitement of wine.

"Bored to death, my good fellow. Nothing but the idea that he is incapable of managing his own affairs, would induce me to listen for another day to the eternal story of his wrongs, sufferings, and sorrows."

"But what say you of his horses, his tables, and his wine? for these are the temptations to hold by a friend."

"His horses are good, but he never hunts; his table is more indebted to the liberality of his house-keeper than himself; and of what value are his wines to me, when he never drinks? In fact, you never saw such a moping owl out of the liberty of a church-yard. A slight metamorphosis would make him into a cypress tree, standing by the side of a grave. But the best joke is yet to come.—I forgot to tell you of his pride ——"

"Proud, is he?"

"Aye, as the son of the morning. Lately, however, he has evinced symptoms of being in love with a poor portionless cousin, whom he thought to make the lady of his castle; but she, forsooth, entertaining some romantic notions about duty and that sort of thing, would none of him, but shot off to a situation in town—a governess, milliner, or compounder of sweet-meats, I know not which; leaving the broken-hearted lover to sigh away his sorrows to the winds that howl around his dreary castle."

"Are my horses ready for a journey?" said Arnold to the first domestic who appeared in the entrance-hall. "Tell Collins I shall set off to-morrow morning for the north;" and so saying he walked up stairs to his own apartment with a firm and determined step, that startled Collins from his evening slumbers. What a pity that the fillip which his energies had just received did not spur him on to something more important than a journey he knew not whither. But we measure the magnitude of our resolves more by the effort they cost us, than by the effect they are likely to produce; and thus we not unfrequently expend the whole force of our minds in accomplishing some puny purpose, which would scarcely have required one previous thought in the well-regulated conduct of a rational being.

The man who will not use his energies in the common affairs of life, though he may fancy himself possessed of powers which would, under certain circumstances, render him grand and terrific; yet these circumstances never happening to occur, he floats upon the stream of time as weak and worthless as any other bubble. The most important test of what mankind have agreed to designate by the word character, is the usefulness by which a track is left upon the map of life, to mark out the course of a certain individual, and direct posterity to the same goal. Arnold Percival could have given no better account of the purpose of his present journey, in preparing for which he raised his whole household, and made himself as busy as he could be about anything, than that he hoped to drive away reflection, and by flying from place to place, to leave himself behind. And had he been asked what trace would be left of him after his death, he would have answered, with gloomy satisfaction, "A nameless tomb:" as if men were sent upon the earth for no more glorious purpose than that of mingling again with its perishable dust.

There is nothing like expeditious travelling, for lulling the senses to sleep, for deadening the perceptions that are too keen, and softening down the impressions that are too vivid. It seems to supply a constant conductor to the overcharged feelings, which are consequently relieved without an explosion.

"We are certainly going to Johnny Groat's house," said Collins to the coachman, who complained that one of his horses had been lame for the last three stages, and would be unable to proceed much farther.

"I have never heard of any bounds to this northern expedition," Collins still muttered to himself. 'On to the north,' is the only answer I get; but I suppose the sea will stop us some time, and that before long, if we travel at this rate."

The fact was, Arnold himself had no fixed purpose in his journey. The mighty effort of setting off had cost too much for him to be capable of resolving again so soon, and had not the lame horse decided the matter, they might, as Collins surmised, have paid their respects to Johnny Groat, or rather his descendants, in their family mansion. The small inn at which their rapid course terminated, was by no means destitute of comfort, and Collins congratulated himself on his good fortune in having escaped a highland bog.

Arnold was the least satisfied of any of the party, horses included; and when he entered the inn room fitted up for the reception of the higher class of travellers, it was not with the best possible grace that he saluted a young man in the dress of a sportsman, who had already obtained possession, and who looked up only for a moment from the lock of his gun, about which he was busy both with head and hand. His weary dogs were sleeping at full length by the fire, and stirred not at the approach of Arnold, who felt it rather too great an imposition on his good humour to be compelled to endure the company of both man and dogs. The gun at last being thoroughly examined and repaired, Kenneth Frazer began, with perfect urbanity and freedom, to converse on the common topics of the game, and the game season.

"Let the gentleman come to the fire," said he, rousing his sleepy animals. "Sad dogs these of mine, sir—but there's no making gentlemen of brutes."

"Can you reverse the rule," said Arnold, "and answer as fully?"

"I fear not," replied Kenneth, with such a good-humoured, happy countenance, that the gloomy misanthrope felt almost ashamed of his remark, and changing the subject, he then told his companion the reason of his unwelcome detention, and how much he apprehended from the annoyances of his present situation.

"I have been thinking," said Kenneth, that your Southern habits would ill accord with the wild mountain life that we lead here; nor do I know, if I should ask you to go with me to my mother's house to-night, whether I should not be subjecting you to scenes and circumstances equally at variance with your taste; but if you will trust yourself to the warm welcome of a highland home, I have a good mother, who will make you as happy as she can."

Arnold, at the same time that he was half tempted to accept this invitation, forced himself to decline it, with many protestations that he could not be guilty of such an unwarrantable intrusion.

"Guilty or not guilty," said Kenneth, "I will order your horses, and if you will promise to ride a moderate pace, I will be your escort through the glen, which leads us to my mother's house by a nearer way than the public road."

In half an hour the travellers were welcomed at the door of a spacious and venerable hall, half covered with wreaths of luxuriant ivy, and spangled over with the white stars of the rambling rose. A group of happy, healthy looking girls gathered round their brother, casting, ever and anon, shy glances at the stranger, who was more cordially greeted by the mother, a respectable and matronly dame. But Kenneth pushed on, with anxious and enquiring glance, as if he had not yet seen all nor half his mother's household. At last exclaiming with impatience, "Where is Ida?" he was answered in a tone of regret by many voices at once, that she had left home in the morning on a visit to a friend, and would not return until the following day.

"Sad news is that for any guest of ours;" replied Kenneth, "for, good girls as you all are, there is no happiness like the sight of Ida amongst you. I believe I have brought a very fine gentleman home with me," he continued in a lower tone, when Arnold had left the room, "for he travels with four horses and an equipage fit for a prince: but, never mind that, I dare say he will be hungry in due time, as well as meaner people; and there can be no doubt about my mother's larder. Still one cannot eat always, and how to entertain him is the question, without Ida."

Arnold now returned, and really well pleased with the comfortable aspect of all things around him, thanked his host most cordially for the unexpected improvement in his circumstances. A plentiful repast was soon spread before him, and Mrs. Frazer reminding him of his own mother in her genuine hospitality, certain thoughts of home in this far-off country, made his heart for a moment glow with gratitude, that he had found a welcome so entirely unsought and unmerited.

If a man be capable of cheerfulness, it will surely be, when, after long travelling through strange places, with nothing to cheer him by the way but inn-welcomes, (with which the poet Shenstone, no doubt for want of better, was so well pleased,) he becomes, unexpectedly, the recipient of genuine kindness, and is plunged at once into the very centre of home comforts. Arnold felt all this, and along with it, a transient touch of happiness that lighted up his brow and made him one of the handsomest of men.

"What a pity Ida is not here!" whispered Catherine to her brother: but a sudden thought had just flashed across his mind, and he did not wish for her quite as much as he had done at first.

Weariness and excitement rendered sleep too desirable for either the stranger or the sportsman to sit up late that night; and Arnold sunk to rest with a faint notion that he might possibly be happy if he lived amongst the mountains of Scotland.

The next morning the name of Ida was upon every lip again, until Arnold, little accustomed to be curious, began really to ponder in his own mind who this Ida could be. The girls could not be persuaded to walk, because they expected Ida every moment;

they could neither play nor sing because Ida was not there to join them; in short, nothing could be accomplished or enjoyed without Ida; and who this all-absorbing creature was, Arnold was quite too dignified to ask. Had there been no hope of seeing her his curiosity might possibly have got the better of his pride, but the expectations of the party now ran high, and even he condescended at intervals to direct his gaze to the point of sight from whence the blessed vision was to issue.

She came at last. A young happy-looking girl, mounted on a spirited pony, rushed past the windows, with a merry smile and a nod of recognition to her friends, who answered her well-known greeting with acclamations of delight.

"Is this all?" said Arnold to himself. "A wild highland lassie, when I had been dreaming of Ida of Athens and all the other poetical Idas." But Ida herself was now led in by Kenneth, who introduced her to the stranger by her christian name, as if that alone were a sufficient distinction.

She was indeed a beautiful girl; with eyes which the memory never loses after they have once been seen and felt—eyes of that peculiar character, that, to say they were brown, grey, or azure, would be to libel their pure and spiritual expression, which strikes the heart with a sensation, independent of the mere qualities of shape and colour—eyes that seem, not so brilliant in themselves, as lighted from within by a radiance so bright as to beautify every thing they gaze upon.

These eyes were turned upon Arnold with more than common interest, for the arrival of a stranger of distinction in that remote district, was an event of rare occurrence; and when we connect such eyes with a form of perfect symmetry, bright, but varying complexion, regular features, and a snowy forehead, half hid by a profusion of auburn curls, which the playful wind had woven into wild and fantastic wreaths, there can be little wonder that such a vision of youth and beauty soon dispelled the feeling of disappointment which had begun to darken the brow of the beholder.

All was now changed within the hospitable home of the Frazers. Good humour, mirth and gaiety, reigned throughout. Every heart seemed lightened, and even the Misanthrope forgot for a while to rail against mankind. In conversation Ida was more expert than profound; but the family with whom she had been tenderly nurtured, were so accustomed to attach importance to her simplest words and actions, that every thing she uttered seemed to have a peculiar meaning, and every thing she did, a peculiar grace.

Gentle reader, hast thou ever been thus cherished? Hast thou ever dwelt in the centre of a circle of partial admirers, where thy voice was a sound commanding instant attention, thy smile the awakening of joyous laughter, and the expression of thy slightest wish the signal for immediate gratification; where thy countenance was watched with the tender anxiety of unceasing affection—where thy mere playfulness was hailed as the very soul of wit, and where all thy faults were regarded as interesting peculiarities? Hast thou then gone forth from the genial atmosphere of this garden enclosed, to learn, amongst impartial strangers, the real value of thy boasted endowments? To speak where no one cared to listen—to smile and behold the blank faces of those who shared not in thy joy; and, worse than all, to weep where thy tears were unheeded? Yet murmur not, for such is the lesson we all, soon or late, must learn; and such are amongst the painful means made use of to teach us that self is not intended as the object of our idolatry; that we are each as travellers bound upon a pilgrimage, at the end of which we shall have to give an account to a gracious Master, of the services we have rendered or neglected to our brethren by the way. Well may we tremble then to find that we have been receivers only, partaking of the wine and the oil which others have ministered unto us, while we have not so much as touched their burdens with one of our fingers!

The beautiful creature, upon whom Arnold gazed with increasing admiration, lived like a butterfly in a bower of roses, never dreaming of aught but enjoyment. The evil propensities incident to human nature had never been called into action in her young heart; her will had never been crossed, her vanity mortified, nor her caprice rebuked; and therefore she believed what every one told her—that she was no less amiable than lovely. "Amiable she must be," thought the kind but injudicious friends by whom she was surrounded, "for she never sees a countenance overcast with gloom, but she endeavours to chase away the clouds." They forgot the possibility that this might be solely for her own sake, because her own gaiety was damped by the gloom of another.

With the light, easy confidence of one who is unacquainted with ridicule or reproof, she soon commenced a spirited warfare against the moodiness of Arnold; and, finding herself foiled by his grave arguments, seized her guitar, and, with an arch smile, that but for her beauty would have been provokingly triumphant, struck into a light air, accompanied by the following words:

Oh! tell not to me—I am happpy and young—
Of the cold winds that blight, and the storms that destroy;
Of the hours when the chords of the heart are unstrung,
And may not be tuned to the music of joy.

I know not such hours, for my heart has no chord
That will not respond to the rapture of bliss;
My song has no echo, my lips have no word
To tell of a moment less happy than this.

I feel not, I heed not, the canker and blight
That fall on the children of sorrow and gloom!
My life is a day of unclouded delight,
In a gay sunny garden of odour and bloom.

My forehead is graced with a garland so fair,
That no dark-boding frown ever lingers beneath.
Then touch not my flowers too rudely, nor tear
One sweet-scented blossom away from my wreath.

And say not the tempest is howling around,
Nor point to the clouds that may gather afar,
But fly from my bright world, where roses abound,
Away to some lonely and desolate star.

CHAPTER XII.

"Kenneth," said Ida, "I am bent on conquest. I am eighteen, and have never had what the world calls a lover. Do you think I could captivate a man of sense?—Not of sense exactly, but a grave man—a gloomy man—a——"

"Just such a man as ——"

"Spare my blushes!" she exclaimed, laughing, and playfully laying across his eyes a hand so exquisitely white and beautiful, that few men would have wished for its removal. Kenneth sat under its pressure with patience, if not with philosophy; and she went on.

"Mention no names, but tell me what you think of my power."

"Of your beauty you will not allow me to judge, nor of your good sense, since I may not even guess at the object of your choice; but of your power to blind, I am at this instant a living witness—and blindness, they say, is a great help in cultivating the tender passion."

"Then, I release you at once, lest you should become a victim to it; for it is a man of sense, you know, that my ambition points at."

"Thank you, Ida. Then I am to understand that you are serious?"

"No, I am never serious; but—"

"But I see that you have placed a white rose, with the best possible effect, amongst your hair—that you have arranged your dress with more than common attention—and that there is a bright sparkle in your eye, that tells of anticipated triumph."

"And what objection have you to my scheme?"

"Nay, Ida, you must first tell me the merits of it."

"Oh! a little change, and the pleasure of laughing at a grave man all day."

"Are you so weary of us, then: or have you so little love and kindness shown you here, that you wish to throw yourself upon the untried feelings of a stranger?"

"Don't talk to me so gravely, Kenneth.

I will not stay to hear you: I have promised to ride with Mr. Percival this morning—will you see that my pony is ready?"

As her light form flitted from before the eyes of Kenneth, a sad thought crossed his mind—more sad than the first blight to the spring-blossoms—the first frost of autumn—the first cloud that passes over the moon when the midnight tempest is gathering. It was the first injurious suspicion of her he loved—the first idea he had ever entertained that Ida was less noble and affectionate than he had fondly deemed her.

Ida's graceful form and girlish beauty were well displayed when mounted on a spirited pony, which she reined in with incomparable dexterity, while her eyes were lighted up with animation; and her luxuriant hair, which possessed the rare quality of curling naturally, lost none of its beauty, by waving in the fresh gale of an autumnal morning.

Arnold, delighted with the gay picture, which presented such a perfect contrast to his own dark imaginings, lost himself in strange visions of what some would have called happiness.

"Ida," said he, suddenly breaking the chain of reflection, and starting at the idea of his own familiarity. There was something in his voice which invariably commanded attention; and when his fair companion turned her face, he apologized for the freedom he had used, saying he had found the name of Ida associated with so much love and happiness, that he had neglected to enquire for any other.

"Then Ida let it be," said she, with the frankness, if not quite with the innocence, of a child: "It is the name I bear from all who love me, and cannot be unwelcome from you."

Arnold, like all proud and reserved persons, was charmed with the openness which spared his dignity the cost of making advances; and the ride was prolonged that morning, over purple heath and mossy dell, until the party at home began to wonder whether the English gentleman and Ida had heard the hour appointed for dinner. Indeed, a general dulness prevailing over the establishment, made the time seem longer to those at home than it really was. The family group had seen the two equestrians set off; each cherishing some secret cause of disappointment, scarcely acknowledged to themselves, still less to each other Catherine had ordered her pony, too, and Ida knew that she loved riding as well as any one; but Ida had mentioned herself only whenever she spoke of that morning's excursion with their visitor. Margaret was just going to show Mr. Percival her greenhouse, when Ida called him back, telling him it was time to set off. Rosa had given up the hat she wanted herself, because Ida complained that her own was not becoming; and Kenneth, poor Kenneth! had never seen any other gentleman than himself riding with Ida before: but he had nothing to complain of: and therefore he took his gun, whistled up his dogs, patted them with more cordiality than ever, and comforted himself with the love of the dumb creatures, in which nobody could rival him.

At a late hour Ida returned with her companion, hope in her eye, and triumph on her brow. Absorbed entirely in herself and her own gratification, she acted the part too often acted by young ladies; and while affecting to be so amiable as to notice everybody, showed each individual, too plainly, how absent they had been from her thoughts. To Mrs. Frazer she expressed unusual surprise and concern that dinner should have had to wait. Of Catherine, who had had no one to ride with her, she asked if she had tried her pony that morning; of Margaret, who had lately suffered from a sprained ankle, she inquired whether she had been to the brow of the hill; of Rose, who had risen with a bad head-ache, why she looked so dull; and when dinner was nearly over, she found out, with regret, that Kenneth was not present.

It is by such absurdities as these that women incur the ridicule of men and the malice of each other. The naked exposure of selfishness and vanity, which Madame de Genlis has exhibited in her "Palace of Truth," is surely less disgusting than this attempt at deception, which conceals the real state of the case from no one but the pretender.

"But Ida was so lovely, so young, so happy; she had been so long their favourite, it would be so sad for an unkind word to reach her ear, or for the breath of blame to obscure even for a moment, the sunshine of her life." So reasoned this generous but ill-judging family; and then, "she was like an orphan, too, cast upon their care by a heartless and cruel mother. No, Ida could not have a fault; she must be loved and cherished, and tenderly treated." So they put the best construction they could upon all her actions; and if mankind in general would have treated her as kindly, she might have passed through the world like a creature in a dream. But many a hard hand is stretched forth to tear away the curtain of self-deception; and even Ida, in her turn, was compelled to look into

"That naked sepulchre, the human heart."

There can be no need to trace the progress of that sort of delusion which is commonly called an attachment, where the vanity of each party is fed by the preference of the other, and where self-love is kept alive by the hope of future gratification. Many mornings like that lately described came and went. The two equestrians were never weary of ambling over the heathy hill, or through the winding glen; and Ida was as lovely each day as the preceding. Once, only once, had Arnold seen a touch of sadness on her brow. She was talking of her mother, and a pearly tear stood on her eyelashes, until he wondered how it could be possible for any of her kith and kin, up or down to the remotest branch or root of relationship, to neglect to claim the privilege of being one of Ida's kindred. This one tear, with the heavy drooping of the eyelids, the gentle fall of the voice, and the graceful bending of the head, melted away the last link in the chain of his philosophy; and he found himself by the side of a girl of eighteen, to whose real character he was a comparative stranger, her acknowledged lover, and her future husband!—a situation no less surprising to himself than to others.

All was consternation in the apartments of the fair sisters, when Ida told her tale of wonder; and although it was accompanied by many fits of hysterical weeping, she had no answer for the often-repeated question—"Then why don't you refuse him at once, if the thought of leaving us makes you so unhappy?"—But young ladies are not always unhappy when they weep:—and Ida was well pleased at the bottom of her heart with this crisis in her affairs.

The letter which had produced so unexpected a revolution, in the usually quiescent Lady Forbes, was one from her daughter, announcing this important event; accompanied by another from Arnold; who, when he found that the lady with whom Agnes resided was no other than the mother of Ida, would almost have sacrificed his new-found treasure to have been excused the task of writing it. "But I have plunged into the gulf," said he, "and there is no receding. The gulf!" he repeated,—and shuddered as if cold waters were closing over him.

As soon as Lady Forbes had a little recovered from the repeated fits of compunction, which, on the discovery of her secret, had threatened to overwhelm her, she endeavoured to apologize to Agnes for her unnatural conduct by a train of ill-formed excuses, which, to such a character as that she was addressing, only made the case appear more unnatural still.

"I was afraid of the trouble," said she—"I felt that I had no strength, no nerves to cope with the boisterous spirits of a child—I could not do my duty to her—she was placed with the best sort of people in the world, and my remittances have been most liberal and punctual. She has had the first masters—the most finished education while she lived in the City of Edinburgh, and every advantage in the way of health and happiness in the country. But I see you cannot forgive me, Agnes—you will never love me again. Nay, do not turn away, nor look so sorrowful—I would rather make you angry than make you weep. Dear Agnes, why are you so pale?"

"The evening is cold, and I feel the draught from the door."

"Sit down beside me, then, and give me one of your long lectures. You do not say a word to me now, Agnes—now that you find me out to be more sinful than you ever thought me before.'

"Lady Forbes," said Agnes, rising, and speaking in such a hollow mournful tone, accompanied by such a look of anguish that her ladyship was awed into silence—"my lecture for this night shall be comprised in a few words. Remember that those with whom you live may sometimes have griefs which are altogether unconnected with yourself. I do not feel like myself to-night, but I hope to be quite recovered in the morning; and if I never trouble you in this way again, may I claim it as my reward that I shall never be questioned respecting my behaviour at this time?"

Lady Forbes held out her hand with tears in her eyes. Agnes took it affectionately, and pressed upon her forehead a kiss of peace, saying, in a low but solemn voice, "My dear friend, I have often prayed for you;—will you this night offer up a petition for one who is more needy than yourself?"

How Agnes spent that night will be best understood by those who have known the pressure of grief under which no earthly friend could comfort or relieve them. In the morning she was able to appear, as she had anticipated, herself again; and, after hearing repeated a long list of excuses from Lady Forbes, she combated her reasoning, or rather her want of reasoning, with arguments which will suggest themselves too readily to the mind of every judicious, or even kindly feeling woman, to need repetition here.

Perhaps the grand error in her ladyship's conduct was one in which we too frequently indulge—the justifying her deeds unto herself after she had let slip the first and most fitting opportunity of acting rightly. On her arrival in England there certainly had been something to allege in her behalf in her impaired constitution, and real inability to take any active part in life. Even the idea of beholding her child overwhelmed her with nervous apprehensions, and the accounts she received at stated intervals from her late husband's relations of little Ida's health and happiness, led her in time to persuade herself that it was a duty to allow her to remain in Scotland. Thus years passed on, and she grew more and more nervous at the thought of seeing her daughter, in proportion as she felt ashamed of not having earlier sought an interview; and she vainly endeavoured to console herself with the idea that her error, persisted in for a few months longer, would add little to the culpability of years. No sooner, however, had she become intimately acquainted with Agnes Forester, than a sort of second conscience seemed to be set upon her; and the neglect of her daughter, which she had before regarded more as her misfortune than her fault, arose before the quickened sight of her newly-awakened mind in the character of a crime—a crime too deep to be disclosed—which, although it haunted her every day like a frightful spectre, she fondly hoped would remain invisible to every one but herself. The shock being once over, it was a relief, however, to have it disclosed, and she sat languidly pleading with her companion in favour of the past, never dreaming that a greater trial was yet to come.

Agnes Forester was not one to let remorse alone suffice either for herself or others. "Let us say no more on this subject," said she, "at present, but talk of the future. You will, of course, take the earliest opportunity of seeing your daughter now?"

Lady Forbes looked aghast; and her love for her late favourite, seemed, like the courage of Acres, to be oozing out at the ends of her fingers.

"At all events," Agnes proceeded, "these letters must be answered. Have you any objection to the match?"

"Every objection in the world," replied her ladyship.—"Ida is quite too young—she has never been properly introduced. She cannot know how to govern a household;—besides, I shall inevitably become a grandmother. No, no—the thing is out of all reason."

"Your last objection," observed Agnes, coolly, "will hardly do to allege; and the others are such as a very little reasoning may easily set aside. For instance, was not your ladyship married at an earlier age? Will not your daughter be very properly introduced under the protection of a husband? and is she not more likely to have learned to govern a household while residing with a domestic family in Scotland than had she been trained up in town?"

"Well, well," answered the lady, peevishly "I see every body is against me—answer them as you like."

"As *I* like!" said Agnes, with such a sigh as would have affected any heart that was not too closely coiled around its own centre. "I will answer them favourably with your permission," she proceeded; and Lady Forbes sighed too, before she yielded her reluctant consent.

Not many weeks after this time, Arnold was again a guest beneath the hospitable roof of Mrs. Frazer, where some wished that his horse had never been lame, or that it had been lame again a few stages earlier in his journey.

Ida had grown graver in his absences, at least she had fits of gravity, or rather sadness, and would sometimes give way to violent weeping, which was succeeded by laughter almost as violent; but she was delighted with her wedding-dresses, and unquestionably happy while fitting them on. Her eyes had lost none of their lustre, but those who studied her countenance, when they were bent down, involuntarily yielded to sensations of pity; when, suddenly she would look up again with laughing gaiety, as if she had been playing tricks with their sympathy.

What is it?—what can it be, that makes us gaze upon some of the fairest works of creation, through the mist of tears? Our hearts overflowing towards them with floods of tenderness, and while some mournful voice seems to whisper it will not always be thus, we long to stretch out our arms to shield them from the threatening storm; and offering the bosom already torn, to receive the poisoned arrow which may be meant for them.

One of these fair flowers, inspiring the beholder with prophetic sadness, was Ida—the cherished—the beloved: and when she took her place for the last evening of her life, in the midst of the family circle of which she had been the central gem, they sung without the sweet accompaniment of her voice, their last farewell in the following simple words:—

FAREWELL TO IDA.

Adieu! adieu! beloved one!
  A mournful strain we breathe;
The fairest blossom of the spring
  Is falling from our wreath.

Our gem will soon be snatch'd away,
  The gem so proudly worn;
The chord of sweetest melody
  From our silent harp be torn.

Then fare thee well, beloved one!
  We cannot give thee more
Than a blessing on thy parting steps,
  When our happy dream is o'er.

Have we not shared one blessed home,
  In childhood's sunny hours?
'Tis idle now to answer us,
  That home will still be ours.

We shall want thy merry smile, Ida,
  To fill our hearts with glee;
We shall miss thee at the close of day,
  When the dew lies on the lea.

We seek thee in the forest glen,
  Beside the wimpling burn;
And ask the forest birds to say
  When Ida will return;

We shall gather all the wild flowers
  Which Ida used to love,
And place them in our bosoms,
  Our fond regret to prove.

We shall mark the spot so faithfully,
  Where thy fav'rite roses grow;
Nor lose it from our memory,
  Beneath the deepest snow;

We shall sing our winter songs again
  Around the evening fire;

But the sweetest sounds without thee,
Will be like a broken lyre.

Still, still thou canst not leave us, Ida;
When summer woods are green,
Thy gentle form by burn and brae,
In fancy will be seen.

Thy cheek in many a sweet flower,
Thy brow in silent eve,
When heavenly dews all silently
Their misty mantle weave.

And wilt thou not in sunny hours,
Sweet Ida, long to be
Once more among the green hills,
Like a happy bird and free;

Can aught be dear to Ida's heart,
Which nature hath not nurs'd?
Can aught in after life be worth
The best love and the first?

Then take from those who love, thee, Ida,
A blessing on thy way;
A blessing on thy parting steps,
And on thy bridal day.

And fare thee well, beloved one!
A long and sad adieu!
Thou may'st seek the wide world over
And find no friends more true.

CHAPTER XIII.

The happy couple! (alas! that pleasant words should ever lose their original meaning by frequent misapplication)—The happy couple set off on their journey southward; Arnold, well pleased to have escaped a fit of hysterics, to which he had lately discovered that Ida was particularly liable. Now if there was one kind of convulsion of the human frame more repugnant to his taste than all others, it was an hysterical convulsion. It argued an uncollected mind; an undignified character; a general derangement of those faculties which operate to maintain self-possession;—in short, Agnes Forester was never guilty of hysterics.

These considerations produced a reverie; and if there was one kind of stagnation of the human frame more repugnant to the taste of Ida than all others, it was the stagnation of reverie;—it argued a wandering of the mind from things present, which in certain cases, was intolerable—affections dormant, or else preoccupied—interest unawakened, or never to be awakened again; and in short, Kenneth Frazer was a stranger to reverie.

Arriving at these conclusions by the same process of thought, and, almost at the same instant, the married pair looked at each other, but spoke not;—they had nothing to say. Each wanted to be amused—to receive—but not to give. Oh! the dullness of that long journey! And long, indeed, it seemed likely to be, for neither party had a will of their own; both so obliging that they would not—could not choose where their travel was to end. Ida, when appealed to, had no wish; Arnold had no wish but to gratify her; and, Collins began to fear with greater reason than before, that their journey would be terminated only by the Land's End.

In process of time, however, there arose such pertinent remarks as these, accompanied by smiles that were not of the heart: "How pleasant it is," observed one, "when persons will decide." "There is nothing," replied the other, "which annoys me so much as indecision."

"Name any place you would like to see, either in England or abroad, and we will soon be there," said Arnold. "All are alike to me."

"You know I have seen nothing," sweetly replied the bride. "Any tour that you would have the goodness to propose would be gratifying to me."

"I said all places were alike to me. I should have made an exception of London," observed Arnold, with a sigh.

"How unfortunate that London should be the very place I had set my heart upon!" replied Ida, and she, too, sighed.

It will be easily perceived, that these two individuals had married on a wrong foundation. They had each been accustomed to the constant subserviency, and the frequent homage of all around them; expecting and receiving their gratifications from the hands of others. Self was the centre around which their separate interests revolved, with a perpetual monotony of motion; and woe unto that self when the centripetal machine was not supplied from without.

Against remaining in London, Arnold was decided; and having a more determined will than his fair bride, she was allowed to make another choice, in consequence of which, they set off to spend the winter in the south of France.

Agnes Forester had consulted with her cousin Walter, as she did in all her emergencies, when she first heard of this extraordinary match; and they had agreed, that let the consequences be what they might, they were both from their relative circumstances highly improper persons to interfere; one from pecuniary considerations, and the other from considerations of a more delicate nature. The apprehensions of Lady Forbes were lulled to rest, by hearing that the married pair had passed through London without allowing her an opportunity of seeing them; an opportunity which Walter was also well pleased to have escaped. All three seemed to think a storm had happily passed over, and Agnes tried to look unhurt. Faithful in the performance of her daily duties, she went on with her routine of wonted occupations, from which, nothing short of entire inability could divert her, and this inability she did not allow herself to think of unless its claims were imperative.

Lady Forbes had suffered herself to become the victim of suspicion, making frequent use of that self-preserving argument, that, "as there are so many impostors, it is better not to give at all."

"You have, it is true, been sometimes deceived," observed Agnes, in the midst of one of her often repeated attempts to extend her ladyship's bounty; but there is still sufficient penury and want that is undeniable."

"And so there would be, were I to give away my last farthing. Behold with what a population of paupers our streets are filled!"

"That is one of my objections to living in a large city," said Agnes; "for, do as much as we will, the heart is still oppressed by the sight of spectacles of wretchedness and vice, which are but too apt to weigh down that lively sense of a gracious providence, which it is so desirable to bear about with us. Still, as it is God's world and not ours, we may surely leave to him the government of all that is beyond the reach of our private resources. As well might the husbandman say, 'I have ploughed and sown, but the rains have sometimes descended to deluge my lands; I will, therefore, cultivate my fields no more,'—as we withhold our hands from the needy, because our bounty has sometimes fallen upon the unworthy. Man reasons better, where he reasons in favour of his own interests, and therefore keeping back nothing which belongs to his own department, the husbandman ploughs and sows again, trusting to God to give the increase.

"I would not willingly hear this miserable plea brought forward by any one whom I esteem, because I believe it is generally made use of by the indolent and the avaricious, to spare themselves the trouble and the expense of charity. We know that there is selfishness and dishonesty enough in the world to induce the unprincipled to take advantage of our credulity. Our Saviour knew this, when he addressed the young man who had been endeavouring to justify himself by the fulfilment of many duties in these clear and imperative words; 'Sell all and give to the poor.' And whatever may be the depravity of mankind, it remains no less incumbent upon us to share our plenty with the needy, but at the same time, to spare no pains so to distribute our bounty that it may flow in the channels most likely to lead to good. After all we are but blind and feeble instruments, and may sometimes defeat our own purposes; but if we have done our little part, according to the best of our fallible judgment, and if we have done it with perseverance, patience, humility, and prayer, we shall be happier than those can ever be who remain inactive in the field of labour, neither scattering seed in due season, nor reaping in time of harvest."

A greater proof could scarcely have been given of the natural goodness of temper and disposition which Lady Forbes possessed, than her willingness to hear the truth from Agnes, however humiliating it might be. She had long been dissatisfied with every thing around her, secretly believing the root of the evil to be in herself; and so weary of life under existing circumstances, that she would almost have caught at any thing that held out a hope of change. Harassed with such feelings, she was the more ready to listen to what she called the long lectures of her companion; especially as Agnes never failed to accompany even her severest comments, by every kind attention, and proof of tender attachment, which arose from the genuine impulse of her affectionate heart.

While contemplating the character of Lady Forbes, over which long indulgence of injurious habits had obtained a lamentable ascendency, it is true, Agnes was, at times, but too much inclined to despair; but, checking all calculations about the future, she went on with her arduous duties, cheered by the reflection that while man is but required to use such means as are placed in his power, with God all things are possible; and that whatever end he may appoint to our labours, he has bestowed upon the service that is willingly and faithfully performed, a blessing which never yet was known to fail.

"It may be so ordered," she would sometimes say to herself, "that I shall see this interesting woman grow still more useless and unhappy. Shall I therefore look up to my heavenly Father and say, 'I behold no fruit of my labours. I will cease from the task which thou hast appointed me?' No! not so long as his glorious sun shines over me, his blessings fall upon my path, and the strength of his gracious arm supports me!"

Disappointed in not finding that interest and excitement which one of the party, at least, had anticipated in the novelty of travelling, Arnold Percival and his fair bride settled themselves down for a while in an old chateau, which happened to strike their attention, from its beautiful and picturesque situation. Here they again sat in waiting for amusement—that capricious nymph who seldom comes when especially invited, but delighting to glide in and out at pleasure amongst the different scenes of life, sometimes exhibits her "soncie face," where it is least befitting, "mang better fowk:" always making herself the most welcome as well as the most frequent guest where the room is supplied with occupants of more importance, and she is not expected to take the chief seat.

Arnold was no less surprised than grieved to find that Ida had not brought her good spirits, her gleesome look, and merry laugh, from Scotland with her. He had overlooked the impossibility of transplanting, along with the beautiful flower, the genial atmosphere in which its early bloom had been cherished: and poor Ida felt as if she had now nothing in the wide world to live for. Self had hitherto been her object, but when that object was ministered to on every hand, watched, admired, and nurtured with the tenderest care, self-love was a very different thing from what it now was, dwelling alone, and supporting, without aid, its solitary existence. She was then like the queen of a garden of roses—fairest of the fair; now a lone flower, rearing its head in the midst of the desert, with no beauty to reflect its own.

Constantly supplied with all that love and kindness could offer, she had never done anything in her turn to discharge the debt, but sometimes to raise a laugh, or join a song, or play a lively air; she had now no other resources upon which to draw, and these were no sooner tried than given up as hopeless; for the merry tones of her voice died away, with no response but the wild echoes of a dilapidated mansion; the mournful songs she had been used to sing brought tears into her eyes; and Arnold was unable to endure the sound of lively music. On one occasion he detected her in tears, and when she complained to him, with her natural frankness, that she was not happy, he answered her with bitter lamentations over his own inability to make her so.

"My love," said he, "blights wherever it falls. I am like the Indian tree, beneath which the birds that have flown for shelter lie dead."

Ida was terrified.—"Let us return to England," said she; and they set off on the morrow.

Arnold had few agreeable associations connected with the idea of returning. The world was all alike to him, whether at home or abroad. He expected no happy faces to look out for his arrival; and when Bella Dunhill threw open the park-gate without one enquiring glance into the carriage, he placed the rude indifference of this ungrateful woman to the account of human nature, and execrated the whole race with redoubled spleen.

Ida felt more in her proper element, although that element was a new one, as the rightful mistress of the noble dwelling, which the good taste of Mrs. Percival and Agnes had invested with an air of comfort as well as elegance.

For Arnold's worthy mother, as the first kind looking person she had met with for a long time, she gave way to a sudden burst of almost childish affection, which Mrs. Percival, from being unable to comprehend anything irrational, mistaking for affectation, did not receive so warmly as she otherwise would have done; and the young heart of the stranger was chilled again.

"Marion," said she one day, after a passionate burst of tears, addressing a simple-hearted domestic, who had accompanied her from Scotland, and whom, for that reason, she chose to have usually about her person, "what shall I do for somebody to love me?"

"Suppose you were to try to love somebody yourself," replied the woman.

"I do love somebody—I love my husband."

"I should hardly have thought that."

"Why not?"

"Because, if I must be so bold, I thought that along with love there went a great deal of kindness, and trying to please, and that sort of thing, that would just find you employment, and keep you alive in this dull place, and make all things seem quite different to you."

Ida, struck with what the woman said, remained musing for some time after upon the possibility of making her present lot more cheerful. During the reverie, her fingers had been turning over the leaves of her album; and when she awoke to a fresh sense of her real situation, she observed that the following lines had been recently added to her collection:

Away, away, I heed thee not!
  Tell me no more thy mournful tale:
I have no pity for thy lot,
  No ear to listen to thy wail.

Weep not; thy tears are like the rain
  That falls upon a senseless stone;
I may not, will not weep again,
  My sighs are hushed, my tears are gone.

Smile on some brow more calm than mine,
  Press on some fairer cheek thy kiss;
I have no joy no blend with thine,
  No love to answer love like this.

Touch not the harp; I will not hear
  One tone that tells of former days:
Sing to the waves that murmur near;
  Pour on the winds thy charmed lays.

Where is my heart? Go ask the wind
  That wanders through yon ruined tower,
If e'er its piercing search can find
  The hearth that blaz'd in festive hour.

No! lost is every trace of mirth,
  And hush'd is every festive sound;
The very breeze which fann'd that hearth
  Hath strewn its ashes o'er the ground.

But still the glorious beams of day
  Shine brightly on the castle wall:
On bastion worn, and turret grey,
  The silver streams of moonlight fall.

Fresh glittering ivy weaves a wreath
  Of shining beauty round its brow:
The mouldering ruin stands beneath,
  Unconscious, cold as I am now.

These verses were in Arnold's hand-writing. "No, no," said Ida, "the case is hopeless;" and she covered her face with both her hands, and burst into an agony of tears.

Men may drag on existence without an object; women hardly can: for they have the activity of feeling as well as thought to keep down. Ida was capable of loving, but altogether ignorant of the duties which belong to love, and without which, the tenderest love of the fairest object is worth nothing: for it has so pleased the Disposer of human affairs, that every connexion by which the chain of mortal fellowship is held together, should have its relative duties. Friendship has many—too many for the generality of mankind to fulfil—but love has more: and the woman who expects to retain her husband's affections by merely loving him, will find herself as much mistaken, as if she had calculated upon maintaining her life by the mere act of breathing.

Light, childish, unsophisticated, the creature of impulse, tossed about by every sudden and varying emotion, it was impossible for Ida to understand the character of Arnold Percival; and the mystery which to her involved his habits and feelings, rendered him, in time, an object of vague and unaccountable fear: so that she felt more disturbed in his presence, than lonely in his absence. With head, heart, and hand equally unoccupied, she, at length, became subject to fits of listless inactivity, which were only broken in upon by occasional visits of kindness from Mrs. Percival. These visits, however, were productive of little gratification on either side; for never, since their first interview, had Ida been herself in the presence of her mother-in-law, who, in her turn, was unable to understand the pretty idle wife her son had brought with him—apparently without any motive, but that of caging her in his castle; for his own happiness was evidently not increased; and his frequent absence from her society, and neglect when present, rendered her an object of compassion even to strangers.

In this way, the domestic affairs of Houghton went on, or rather remained, until a change was perceptible in the behaviour of Ida, which the domestics rejoiced in, as a proof that she was beginning to feel more at home. But Marion always shook her head at their congratulations, and started when she heard the snatches of wild Scottish songs which her mistress amused herself with singing. Arnold alone perceived no change, except what he thought a slight improvement in her spirits. He had, however, been compelled to see, that often when he left his room, Marion would be hovering about as if she sought an opportunity of speaking with him privately on some subject, evidently not of immediate import, or she would have spoken sooner. At last, he was tired of meeting her meaning looks, and asked if she wanted to speak with him. After ascertaining that the doors around them were closed, Marion stepped up so close to his ear, that he thought it best to retreat into his private room, in order to avoid the necessity of a nearer approach. Here Marion felt at liberty to speak, but liberty seemed to be all that she had gained, for no intelligible words for some time passed her lips.

"I wanted to know, sir," said she—"if I am not making too bold—if—if you have ever—"

"Go on."

"I wished to know, sir, if you had observed any thing particular about my lady's manner lately?"

"Your lady's manners are not to be talked over by her servants. What do you mean, Marion?"

"I said manner, if you please, sir—and that, as I take it, means something different. But, dear me, sir, you must not be too nice about words now!" And the good woman wiped her eyes with her apron.

"What can you mean, Marion? I believe your lady is in excellent health, and her spirits have certainly been better lately."

"Better! do you call it? Oh! sir, it's the nerves. She told me it was all nerves, and hysterics, when she used to go on so strangely in France, while you were out of the way. I wish we were back again in Scotland!" and Marion sobbed aloud.

"Speak your meaning plainly, my good woman," said Arnold, kindly, "and tell me the worst!"

"Well, then, I have great reason to believe that my dear young mistress is losing her senses!"

"Leave me alone," said Arnold, in an altered tone; and the woman went her way.

CHAPTER XIV.

It was, indeed, as the simple-hearted Marion had suspected, the reasoning faculties of Ida never having been subjected to the slightest discipline, had given way, under the total change which had taken place in her habits and circumstances. It is impossible to say how much the progress of this malady might have been accelerated by constitutional tendency; but certainly nothing could have been more uncongenial to such a character than the life she had lately led.

Arnold had no other resource under this undeniable affliction, than to shut himself up, and brood over the fatality which, as he believed, attended him through every circumstance of life; while Mrs. Percival wrote to her niece, urging her, if possible, to come down immediately.

"What can be the matter?" exclaimed Lady Forbes, observing the pale and horror-struck countenance of Agnes, as she read the letter. "Is it of Ida that you learn tidings?" the terrified lady continued; for she was in constant anticipation of a day of retribution for her neglect.

"It is," said Agnes.

"Let me hear the worst. Tell me if my daughter is dead."

"She is not dead; but now, if ever her mother is called upon to show her sense of the holy duties which belong to that sacred name —"

"She is ill, then? But you know I cannot nurse her—it is impossible."

"Dear Lady Forbes, I have received a request from my aunt, which I cannot refuse to comply with. I am under the necessity of leaving town immediately—let me entreat you to say that you will go along with me."

"If my daughter is really ill, I should only add to the trouble of the household. Do you think there is danger?"

"Not of death."

"Then why should you urge my going? I can be of no possible service to her."

"Still I cannot, will not, leave you. Go with me—for your own sake, if not for the sake of your child."

"But you tell me she is not in danger. It would be wiser for me to wait until she recovers her usual health, for our first interview must unavoidably be a painful and agitating one."

"Lady Forbes, there are other calamities besides death. You have learned many things lately—have you learned how to bear to hear the truth?"

"Speak on."

"May He who alone can support us in our utmost need strengthen you for the trial, when I tell you that your daughter has lately evinced symptoms of an unsettled state of mind, which have greatly alarmed those around her."

Lady Forbes arose from the couch on which she had been reclining, more like a spectre than a living woman, "It was her father's malady," said she, in a firm voice—"Agnes, I will go with you!"

The shock which Agnes in her heart believed her friend was capable of bearing, and bearing well, had produced the desired effect; but so strange to the character of Lady Forbes was the manner which accompanied her sudden resolution, that Agnes, desirous of some protection and support, pressed her cousin Walter to accompany them in their melancholy journey. Few words were spoken by the way; and when the carriage passed through the avenue of elms, Agnes felt as if the weight of present sorrow had almost obliterated the past.

"In my own wisdom," said she, "I should

have chosen this affliction for any one rather than Arnold but well is it for us that we are not left to choose either for ourselves or others."

"It would be an ungracious office," observed Walter, "to choose afflictions for our fellow-creatures." And he sighed to think how probable it was that Agnes would have chosen for him not only his brother's affliction, but his wife.

Mrs. Percival was at the door, waiting to receive the mournful party; and Arnold forced himself to appear immediately after they had alighted, well knowing that every moment of delay and expectation would add difficulty to the effort.

There was no change in his countenance. It was always sad enough for sorrow; and a stranger would not have known that fresh floods had recently been added to the "tide of his griefs." Lady Forbes, for the first time in her life, forgot herself; at least, she forgot all those little personal sufferings and perplexities with which she was wont to annoy, and be annoyed; but her heart was too much subdued by remorse, to allow her to take any interest in the scenes or circumstances around her.

While the company were thus collected, pondering individually upon the best means of acting or remaining inactive, the door was thrown open, and the object of their intense solicitude stood before them. She was dressed with elegance, if not with studied care. Her beautiful hair, which she persisted in wearing short and unconfined, waving in rich profusion over her forehead and temples; while her eyes, rendered doubly brilliant by the unnatural excitement of her mind, flashed and wandered from one object to another, with a strange and alarming scrutiny. A varying hectic flush upon her cheek betrayed the feverish state of her fluttering pulse; but there was, beyond this and the flashing eye, little indication of any deeper cause of interest than arises from the charm of youth and innocence, combined with exquisite loveliness. It seemed as though the lamp of reason, instead of being extinguished, now burned with a bright but uncertain flame—for one moment revealing the clear truth, and then confusing light with shadow, until the whole became indistinct and unintelligible.

As the fair sufferer advanced to greet her unknown guests, Arnold escaped from the apartment, and Walter stepping forward in a kind and cordial manner, introduced himself and Agnes, and then endeavoured to engage the attention of Ida, by enquiries about the grounds, the garden, the prospect, or any thing he could think of, to divert her observation from Lady Forbes, until a more suitable opportunity for making known their relationship. It mattered not to him whether her answers were to or from the purpose; his object would be gained, if he could render her familiar with the presence of her new friends, and confident that they were such. But the countenance of Lady Forbes had first struck her attention, and she was not so easily beguiled from the interest which suddenly filled her heart.

"This lady," said she, placing her hand within that of her unknown parent—"you have not introduced. My name is Ida—at least it was when I was happy, and lived in Scotland."

"My name is Ida too," answered Lady Forbes; at which her daughter smiled incredulously, and went on.

"I know not who you are, but I hope you will stay with me, it is so lonely in this strange place. You seem to be in sorrow," she continued, seeing that the lady's tears fell fast: "I sometimes am in sorrow too; and if you will pity me, I will pity you—surely, that is fair. I used to think, that if any one cared for me, it was enough; but now I am going to care for others, and make them happy if I can. Ladies, would you like music?" And she began to sing and play a wild Scottish air; but, turning again to Lady Forbes, she asked, in a grave and anxious manner, why she wept. "Has any one been unkind to you? or have you been unkind to any one?"

Lady Forbes bowed assent.

"Then, shall I tell you what is the best thing you can do?—Be as kind as you can in future."

"I will," said Lady Forbes; and, with an almost bursting heart, she pressed upon the fair cheek of her daughter a mother's kiss.

Agnes, finding that kind of confidence established which, under their present melancholy circumstances, was all she had left to desire, walked out to seek a yet more painful interview with her cousin Arnold, who was wandering alone, scarcely knowing where he went. Forgetting every thing but his recent griefs, she drew her hand within his arm, and spoke to him with the freedom and familiarity of their early days, before any feelings of a more exclusive nature had taught them to lay aside the privileges of friendship.

"Was it not a happy circumstance," said she, "that we prevailed upon Lady Forbes to come down with us? She is really an amiable and interesting woman, and I hope will remain with you, and be a comfort to you."

"She can be no comfort to me, Agnes. You speak of happiness and comfort, as if they were words that could find a meaning in the language of man."

"I speak of the happiness and comfort that are left to us, as we speak of the flowers that remain after the storm has laid bare the forest."

"It is for you, Agnes, to gather those flowers: for you they are spared—for you they bloom and flourish. It is for me to sit under the leafless boughs, and listen to the blast of desolation."

"Have you consulted a physician?" asked Agnes, well knowing the labyrinth into which this figurative mode of speech would lead.

Arnold replied that he had not. Indeed, it was the first time he had thought of one.

"Of whose skill do you entertain the best opinion?" enquired Agnes.

He had little opinion of the skill of any.

Agnes had well nigh lost her patience; but, knowing that her cousin cared not what was done, so long as he was not required to act, she told him that, with his permission, she would send off for one immediately, as, whatever their doubts might be, they were not justified in neglecting the only means that were at their command.

"Do exactly as you think best," said Arnold: "do as much, and as quickly as you can, for I am sure you will do right. Fill my house with doctors, nurses, quacks, and old women—employ my servants—spend my money—travel with my horses: only spare me, Agnes, for I have already enough to bear!"

"Oh! that I had been wiser—that I had been more attentive to my duty—that I could recall my early life!" sighed Lady Forbes, as she laid her head upon her pillow: and Arnold, too, as he sat alone by the light of a dim lamp at the hour of midnight, retracing, in imagination, the path of life, to find out some cruel fatality,—some early deviation, for which he might blame his destiny, and not himself,—went on, and on, until he reached the days of early boyhood; and the fresh flow of childish tenderness seemed to rush upon his heart again. "Oh! that I could return!" he, too, exclaimed. But the difference in these two individuals was, that in one case, the remorse attendant upon the past produced that sound, deep, and rational repentance, which operates upon the future; while, in the other, the unwonted occupation of retrospection and self-examination was accompanied by nothing but the agony of despair.

"Oh! that I had been wiser," is the natural expression of the soul, when first awakened to a sorrowful conviction of what has been lost, sacrificed, and suffered, or has still to be endured from its own blindness, folly, or perverseness.

"Oh! that I had been wiser," is the exclamation of the merchant, when he has neglected to insure his property, and the storm has swept away his possessions; of the husbandman, when he has sown in the wrong season, and the floods have deluged his fields; of the builder, when he has laid the corner stone upon a sandy foundation, and the edifice begins to shake; of the traveller, when he has rejected his guide, and finds himself bewildered at the fall of night; of the mariner, when he has disobeyed the orders of the pilot, and is wrecked upon an unknown shore. Does not the merchant then make haste to insure what is still left? does not the husbandman long for the coming of another spring, that he may scatter his grain in due time? does not the builder search diligently for the rock upon which his tottering edifice may be rebuilt? does not the traveller bespeak for the coming morrow, a guide, from whom he resolves that nothing shall separate him? and does not the mariner, escaped from shipwreck, submit himself gratefully to the guidance of the pilot during all his future wanderings on the sea?

It is in the great and paramount consideration of eternal life that we are satisfied to lose the prize of our high calling, while expending fruitless lamentations over the irrevocable past. The past—that unfathomable ocean, into which the river of time is insensibly gliding. The past—that unsearchable abyss from which we vainly endeavour to snatch the perishable idols of our hearts' secret worship. The past—that mysterious vortex that has swallowed up all we have been, thought, felt, acted, or endured; and from which it is no less impossible to recover a fallen kingdom, or a ruined world; than a faded rose-leaf, or an idle thought.

With the awful and irrevocable past, what then can we finite creatures have to do, but to gather wisdom, and perhaps to gather it with tears? Yet here we sit on the verge of the gulf of eternity, brooding in our grief, and too often calling that a godly sorrow, which worketh no amendment. It is with the no less awful present that our business lies. Here is our field of action. Here is all that is left to us by which we can prove the depth and sincerity of our regret. The wasted moments of the precious future as they are incessantly becoming ours, will rise like a cloud of witnesses to the courts of Heaven, bearing fearful testimony to the barrenness of our remorse, and the emptiness of our repentance.

Nor is it always permitted us to prove before mankind, that we have reaped wisdom from the past. The merchant may not be always able to send merchandise again upon the sea; the husbandman may have no grain remaining in his garners; the occupation of the builder may be taken away; the traveller may have reached the end of his journey; and the mariner be disabled for future service on the ocean: but the affairs of human life are so regulated that we cannot live a day—seldom an hour—without an opportunity of acting, speaking, or thinking, wisely or unwisely, with a good or evil motive, for a purpose which is either right or wrong; and, therefore, none can excuse themselves on the ground that they would have done better had they been tried again. So long as we inhale the breath of existence, we are always in a state of trial. There is no situation so humble, there are no circumstances so limited, as to exempt us from the duty of Christians; and he who takes note of the sparrow falling to the ground, will assuredly not overlook the moral progress or declension of an accountable and immortal spirit.

What would an earthly master think of the servant who should answer his reproofs with the constant and unavailing cry, 'Oh! that I had been wiser.' So far as it evinced his conviction of past error, the answer might be well; but that conviction alone would be of very little value to the master who was expecting faithful and important service; and few there are, who would bear with it—fewer still, who would try that unprofitable servant as we are tried with fresh offers of pardon, mercy, and support, if he would but turn again into the path of duty, and walk in the way which had been graciously pointed out for his good.

Under the first pangs of a stricken conscience, we exclaim, "Oh! that I had been wiser!" but woe unto the undying soul, that bears along with it no other language to the great tribunal on the day of judgment; that has no other plea to lay before the majesty on high, for the abuse of means that were abundantly afforded, the perversion of feelings that were bestowed for a benefit and a blessing to mankind, the misapplication of powers that were capable of ripening into a harvest of usefulness, and the neglect of countless opportunities of conviction, repentance, and amendment, which infinite wisdom had adapted to its imperfect and finite state, and which infinite mercy had continued to hold out even when rejected again and again.

'Oh! that I had been wiser!' should be hailed as the first expression of that infant wisdom which is to be cherished and cultivated for future profit. But let none rest here, believing they are to be saved by merely uttering this feeble cry. It is true it may be accompanied with tears of unutterable anguish, with humiliation that weighs down the spirit to the lowest depths, with remorse that burns with incessant and unquenchable fire; but while the wide future remains unoccupied by a single wise resolution, and the present is empty of all proof of reformation, our tears will be as fruitless in working out the great end of our being, as the raindrops on the flinty rock; our humiliation, as destitute of benefit to ourselves or others, as the scattering of the withered leaves upon the autumn floods; and our remorse as unavailing as the moan of the criminal led out for execution.

CHAPTER XV.

"I AM sorry to trouble you about any affairs of my own," said Walter one day to his brother; "but, since it is always pleasant to have an opportunity of helping a poor man through the world, I think I may venture to lay my case before you."

Arnold made no reply, except by a slight inclination of the head; and Walter went on to state, in a business-like manner, how he was about to become a candidate for the office of engineer in a projected work of great extent, in the immediate neighbourhood of his brother's property; and how his brother might assist him, by using his powerful interest to obtain for him the desired appointment.

"That is the very scheme," replied Arnold, that you yourself laid out some years ago."

"It is."

"And will you allow others to carry off the credit of devising what you seem willing to fall in with in a secondary way?"

"There can surely be little less credit in making a useful discovery to-day, than yesterday. As I never communicated my views to these persons, they are as fully entitled to the approbation of their fellow-creatures as I can be. The improvement of the country was their object, as well as mine; and had I endeavoured to put my plans in execution, I should doubtless have been stimulated, as most men are, by motives of private interest. All I now desire at their hands is, to be allowed to help forward the work as their engineer."

"There is nothing on earth so disagreeable as puffing off the abilities of one's own relations."

"I would thank no man to puff mine. All that I request of you is to mention my name."

"As a meritorious person, fully qualified, I suppose?"

"If to understand the business for which I was educated, and to which I have devoted many years of study and labour be meritorious, you may. Of greater qualifications I do not boast; but were I conscious of less, I would not offer myself. I see, however, that you are not disposed to take an active part in the matter. Will you oblige me by a decided answer, whether you choose to assist me, or not?"

Arnold still hesitated; and before he could arrive at a conclusion, Walter had bid him good morning, and ridden off to make a more successful application elsewhere.

By timely thought, promptness, and unremitting endeavours, his object was gained, and he once more became a happy and welcome resident beneath his mother's roof. But neither the addition of his cheering society, nor any thing else that happened, or could happen, brought any alleviation to the gloom and weariness of the misanthrope. Unfortunately for him, the power of suffering was not diminished by his incapacity to enjoy. With the perceptions of his mind alive only to impressions of pain, he looked round upon the world as upon a universal desert, where the sun might scorch, and the winds pierce, but where no flower could ever bloom, nor murmuring waters send forth the glad tidings of refreshment and repose.

Not such were the feelings of the mother, who now watched over the second infancy of her benighted child. What visitations of agonizing remorse were hers, as she looked upon her blighted flower, and pressed upon her bosom the fair cheek that should have earlier known that resting-place. But hers was a lively grief, which brought along with it a quick, animated sense of present things, and intense desires for the future; so that her soul knew no repose but in the consolations of prayer. Indeed, where else can any soul oppressed with the burdens of humanity repose, but in that humble dependence upon an Almighty Power—that constant reference of its cares and sorrows to Him who knoweth its infirmities—that unceasing appeal to infinite mercy for fresh supplies of strength, and patience, and support, which may not unfitly be called perpetual prayer? Who, even of those who have lived through what is called a life of enjoyment, can say that they have found repose elsewhere? Gaiety, excitement, nay, even "a wild, delirious joy," they may have found: but what are all these, when compared with repose?

There is no writer who has left upon record so touching and so true a testimony to the vanity and the weariness of mere human enjoyments, as he who had the means of obtaining, and the power of appreciating, beyond what ever before or since has fallen to the lot of man. And yet he tells us, that in the midst of all, he said, in his heart, "Of laughter it is mad, and of mirth what doeth it?"

"My mother!" were the tender and familiar words with which poor Ida now often startled her weeping parent. It pleased her childish fancy to utter them, and served as an affecting memento to remind Lady Forbes of what she ought to have been, and still might be. Nor was the lamp of reason so nearly extinguished in the mind of her lovely charge, but that she could appreciate the kind offices and faithful duties which her mother became daily more solicitous to fulfil—more happy to perform. Ida had her intervals of reflection, in which her mind, set free from the petty incumbrances and toils of life, seemed to perceive with more than wonted acuteness, and to weigh with a truer balance than it had ever done before. She would then speak clearly and decidedly on questions of importance, as if her feelings had been awakened to a new moral sense; when suddenly a wild bewilderment of thought would come, like the confusion of a dream over a fair and sunny picture. But she was always gentle, harmless, and lovely, even under her darkest visitations, gathering wild flowers, and loving sunshine, and sweet perfumes—pressing her mother to partake in all her innocent enjoyments—connecting, by some mysterious chain of feeling, all things sweet and happy with Scotland, and the life she had led there; and yet invariably looking sad, and lowering the tone of her voice to the deepest melancholy, when she spoke of any person, place, or thing she had known in that beloved land.

While time passed on in this manner with the mother and the daughter, the one, 'queen of a fantastic realm,' the other, a weak but willing pilgrim, just commencing the career of duty; Arnold Percival resigned himself completely to the evil influence of indolence and melancholy; loving nothing so much as solitary wanderings far from the busy world which he professed to hate. The greater part of each day he still spent upon the ocean, or gazing over its wide expanse from a favourite station on the rocky and projecting cliff, while at night, he often took a solitary ramble to whatever spot chance might direct his uncertain steps. It was at the close of a sombre day—

'When autumn winds were at their evening songs,'

that he walked forth as usual with often repeated but fruitless efforts to forget himself. Lost in deep reverie, he found himself at last beside his mother's garden. The gate opened with the pressure of his hand, and without aim or object, he wound his well-known way amongst the shrubs as if old habits were leading him whithersoever they would. In a few moments more, he was gazing upon the bright fire blazing in his mother's parlour, through a screen of jessamine not yet faded, by which he was concealed from the observation of those within. His mother was seated by the fire, with her perpetual knitting in her hand, while her face, lighted up with an expression of lively satisfaction, was turned to Walter, who appeared to be reading aloud from a book which must have been a favourite with Agnes, for she, too, raised her eyes so often, and with such deep interest, that Walter could not choose but look from his book as often, to participate in her enjoyment.

There was nothing in the situation of these three individuals to make them happier than human beings generally may be, nor in that of Arnold to render him more wretched than most of us at many seasons of our lives have been; and yet his morbid imagination immediately transformed the scene within into that of the garden of Eden, and himself into the enemy of all happiness, whom the poet has so ably described as unable to look on, without the stirrings of the deadliest of human passions.

Envy is a feeling so odions in itself, with so few redeeming accompaniments, that none will own its baneful influence; although an impartial investigator might too often detect its lurking venom, mingled with the cup of life. Arnold Percival would have repelled with indignation the charge of envying either man or woman their good fortune, and yet he was not only unable to participate in the enjoyment of others, but the mere contemplation of it added fresh bitterness to his secret repinings.

"Every one can find happiness on earth but me," he murmured to himself, as he stood riveted to the same spot, and gazing on the same scene. "Every one can partake of social endearment; every one can draw around some centre of enjoyment but me. From the loved and the lovely I must dwell apart, with the cancer of despair in my bosom, and the poisoned arrow of destruction in my heart."

What a wonderful and inexhaustible fund the melancholy mind can draw upon for materials to build up its own wretchedness!

While Arnold Percival was observing from without the internal movements of his mother's establishment, she herself rose up, and after ringing the bell, a servant who came in, unconsciously closed the shutters in the face of the misanthrope, who immediately gave himself up to the absurd idea, that he was violently shut out from the presence of the happy group. As he turned to retrace his steps, the rustling of the withered leaves that lay scattered in his path, gave notice to his cousin's dog that a strange foot was near, and, before he had time to make himself known, he was beset and annoyed by the loud barking of the watchful animal.

"The very dog," said he to himself, "that I have seen crouching at her feet with tenderness and love, grows furious at the sight of me. He walked on, but thick clouds had now overcast the moon; a hollow wind which had all day been moaning amongst the "sere and yellow" leaves, rushed along with the gathering darkness, and it was with difficulty that he reached the nearest cottage before the bursting of a tempest which threatened to cut off his farther progress for the night. The place in which he had found such timely shelter was a porch, where he had once, on a very different occasion, seated himself before; and, had not the darkness prevented his making any local observations, he would, probably, have risked the fury of the raging elements, rather than have remained in safety under the cover of that particular roof.

"It is a fearful night," said an aged voice within. "We are better in this low cottage, Mary, than in the high towers of a castle, when such a storm is howling."

"It is not all who live in castles, that are either safe or happy," was answered by a female.

"I fear not," said the old man, with a deep sigh, "I fear not!"

"And yet they may be as happy as they deserve," observed the woman. "Who that has never loved any one, or been kind to any one, can either expect or deserve happiness themselves?"

"Mary, we judge blindly, when we judge one another. It is wiser and more profitable to look into our own hearts, to read the words of eternal life, and to pray." And so saying, he commenced his evening service, and after reading aloud a chapter of the bible with more solemnity than fluency, he poured forth the genuine feelings of his soul in a simple but affecting prayer. He had never, since an important event in his life had first placed him in a situation of serious trust, omitted morning and evening to offer up a petition for the welfare and right guidance of his young master, and he performed his holy duty as faithfully, as tenderly, and with as much fervent zeal, now that that ungrateful master had suspected, wronged, and finally dismissed him from his service.

"And this man can pray for me!" said Arnold, as he leaned his head against the cold, stony wall, and closed his eyes upon every thing but the remembrance of his early years, and those bright visions of departed innocence which memory sometimes conjures up, making fresh tears burst forth from eyes that have almost forgotten how to weep, and quickening the fainting soul with renewed agony, but not with renovated life.

The simple inhabitants of the cottage retired to rest; the storm passed over, and the misanthrope went forth again, in the dark and lonely night, to trace his way to a home, to him more dark and lonely still. On turning to close the gate at the lodge gently, and without noise, he saw a light in Bella Dunhill's house, which suddenly disappeared, but not before he had perceived that other persons besides the wonted inhabitants were up and stirring at that unseasonable hour. His first impulse was to give a thundering knock at the door; but, on second thoughts, he determined to tap gently at the shutter. The door was quickly unbolted, and Bella herself looked out stealthily, saying, in a sort of whisper, "Roger, is it you?"

"It is I," replied Arnold; and, thrusting back the astonished woman, before she had time to prevent his entrance, he stood in the midst of a gang of desperate poachers, who had long made her house their place of secret rendezvous.

Arnold was a stranger to the sensation of fear; and when he had stimulus enough to act upon, he could act with firmness and judgment. He had no weapons to defend himself, nor was any violence offered—not even when he snatched a blazing brand from the half-extinguished fire, and held it to the faces of the men, as they rushed past him to effect their escape. By this means he recognized many of his own labourers and dependents, and observed that Bella Dunhill, immediately on his entrance had laid her hand upon a loaded pistol, which she grasped with such a fierce and threatening look, that he scrupled not to select her from the number of her faithless friends, who had one and all deserted her to her fate, as a fitting example to those who might be disposed to tempt his future vengeance.

The stimulus of this scene, with the prompt and active exertion it had called forth, made the misanthrope for a short time forget himself; and could he have drawn rational deductions from what he had seen, heard, and felt, that night, he might thenceforth have been "a wiser and a better man." He might have learned, from the scene in his mother's parlour, that there is such a thing as enjoyment, even upon earth: he might have learned from the prayer of the discarded servant, that whatever human nature may be in its perverted state, there is a power that can subdue, temper, and refine its faculties, until they are capable of all that we admire as generous and noble: he might have learned, from the conduct of the ungrateful woman whom he had befriended, that none can be worthy of respect or confidence who are insensible to the kindly feelings which a Divine Being has bestowed as a blessing upon his creatures, or averse to the principles which He has laid down for their especial benefit: and, finally, from the effect of his own exertions, he might have learned, that man is only in a natural and healthy condition when using the powers with which he has been gifted, and that, in order to add happiness to health, he must use them for the purposes which are most in unison with the Divine will.

To him whose mind is accustomed to observe, contemplate and adore, what lessons of instruction may be gathered from the past: to him whose feelings are tuned to the melody of nature, what harmonious music is in the wide universe around! What faith may be built upon the often-repeated instances which memory recalls, in which the heart, panting after some ideal good, has been mercifully spared the anguish of possessing—what hope from the visitations of unexpected light which have broken in upon our darkness—what charity from the many wrong calculations, false steps, and fatal deviations, which we ourselves have made!

CHAPTER XVI.

Agnes Forester was now less constant in her attendance upon her friends at the castle, although still ready to offer her services whenever and in whatever way they might be required; yet, having seen with unspeakable satisfaction, that Lady Forbes was gradually becoming an altered character—that the melancholy situation of her daughter, by rousing her dormant energies, and exciting a deep interest in her feelings, had combined, with causes of a higher nature, to produce that change for which she herself had so ardently laboured, watched, and prayed—she now deemed it as unnecessary as unwise to obtrude her services more than for the common purposes of kindness and civility, which enhance the enjoyment of social life. With Arnold she was now perfectly at ease; at least, as much so as her naturally affectionate heart could be while contemplating his perverted feelings, and gradually deteriorating character;—deteriorating, because it is the inevitable consequence of every fault, as well as every vice, long and inveterately indulged in, to spread its baneful influence over other faculties of the mind, just as a poisonous weed, at first too insignificant to mar the beauty of the garden, will, in time, extend itself, so as to prevent the growth of either flowers or fruit.

Agnes, after having once learned to consider her cousin Arnold as the husband of another, never afterwards entertained an idea that could have interfered, in the remotest manner, with that sacred connexion. She had no wandering and undisciplined thoughts to startle her with their impropriety, nor morbid feelings with which to brood over the past, until the present should become irksome and intolerable: he was now her cousin Arnold, and no more; and she could read his countenance, and listen to his voice, with as much composure as to that of any other person.

With a mind so tempered, she refused not still to be the occasional companion of his walks, his rides, even to the very cliff and the sea shore, where they had wandered in other days, nor was there anything in his manner to awake the scruples of the most delicate mind. It is probable that, in the general desolation of his heart, the warmest and tenderest sentiment he had ever entertained, had been chilled, and withered, and finally had perished under the universal blight; but over some characters, habit is more powerful than impulse· and we often continue to serve, and suffer from those we love, long after the life of our affection has been extinguished. In this manner, Arnold was accustomed to bear with Agnes when she thought it right to remark upon his conduct, as he would have borne with no one else; and she seldom failed to thank him both by words and looks for the kind forbearance he had shown her.

"There is nothing," said she, one day, during a long ramble by the sea-shore, "which I dislike so much, as the mere act of finding fault, when accompanied by that peevish and uncharitable spirit which too often prompts us to say to those who are smarting under the consequences of their own folly or misconduct, 'You should not have acted thus, you knew what it would lead to—it is all your own fault.' But it sometimes becomes necessary, that we should retrace the errors both of ourselves and others, in order that we may not fall into the presumptuous absurdity of self-exculpation, *nor charge God foolishly.*"

"Reason as you like, Agnes," replied the misanthrope, "you never will convince me that the cup of life has not been prepared for me with peculiar and especial bitterness."

"Think, for one moment, Arnold, of what you are saying. You are accusing the Almighty of injustice and malevolence."

"I presume not to penetrate into the designs of Providence, nor to say, even if my existence should be overshadowed with tenfold gloom, that such a destiny would be inconsistent with that wisdom which I am not able to comprehend."

"But your feelings belie your words, and while you *feel* that divine mercy is not united with divine wisdom, you cannot love your Heavenly Father as you ought."

"Was I not born with a constitutional tendency to sadness?"

"Precisely in the same way as a thief may say, that he is born with a constitutional tendency to take what is not his own. Philosophers may dispute the question, whether we inherit or acquire our mental faculties? whether they are developed in prominences upon the skull, or exist only in operations of mind apart from matter? I am no philosopher, and, therefore, I leave these difficult points to those who feel better qualified to unravel the mystery of our being, not without fervent desires after that state of existence, where, I trust, we shall be better prepared to receive and understand the truth.

"Looking at human nature through the medium of my own dull senses, and I would humbly hope with the assistance of some better light, I am disposed to think, that the tendency of which you speak, whether originating in bodily conformation, or early bias of the mind, has been appointed by Providence as your especial temptation or means of discipline; the difficulty to which you may find countless promises to apply,—the enemy against which you are to arm yourself with the weapons of Christian warfare. Few persons, I believe, have arrived at the conclusion of even a well-spent life, without being able to confess that their course has been beset by one evil propensity above all others. Misanthropy has been yours, arising out of what you call constitutional melancholy; and until you can prove that you have made systematical resistance against it, by perseverance, patience, and prayer, I can never join with you in thinking, that you have been harshly dealt with, or that God has not been merciful to you as well as to the rest of his creatures."

"And yet, when I recall my past life, I see nothing but a series of disappointments attendant upon all I have ever hoped or desired. From the brotherhood of man, I selected one friend—and one only ——"

"For what did you select him?—Not for his noble independent character, but for his servile pretence to sentiments and feelings like your own. You might persuade yourself, that this apparent resemblance was sympathy, that connecting chain of kindred interests and associations; but, he who finds his friend resemble him only in the worst parts of his own character, may certainly suspect that he has made a wrong choice, and with nothing more substantial to calculate upon, may certainly anticipate deception and final disappointment. With regard to your misplaced charity and kindness, the same arguments would very justly apply, and I regret that you should not have made the experiment elsewhere."

"Agnes, you are a cool reasoner, and a strict judge. What have you to say to that melancholy circumstance which has sealed my doom, and made me for life the most miserable of men?"

"My dear cousin, I would not willingly speak on this subject, but in words of the deepest tenderness and sympathy; yet since we have entered upon it in the spirit of impartial discussion, and since there is no alternative but to throw the blame either upon you as an accountable being, or upon that which you call destiny, but which must eventually be referred to the Author of our being; I scruple not to say, that in contracting this alliance, you were guilty of the greatest imprudence of your life. Far be it from me to touch with too much freedom a character whose every feature has now become sacred to us through suffering. I have never met with any one more lovely, seldom with one more calculated to inspire affection; but look into your own heart, and ask what sympathy could possibly exist between two beings so differently constituted, or how it was possible that you could minister to each other's happiness?

"Marriage, like all other social engagements, is not merely an appropriation to ourselves of what we desire to possess. It is a mutual compact, in which much must be contributed on both sides to render it productive of real satisfaction. It is not my wish to lift the veil which is very properly drawn over the secrets of domestic life, nor to pronounce upon what might have been conceded, palliated, or reconciled; the grand error was in the first determination you made to unite yourself to one whose disposition, tastes, and habits, were so totally different from your own, that I should suppose it almost impossible for any circumstance to occur in which you would think or feel together."

"And yet you, who were the monitress of my early years, never gave me one word of warning, when you saw me risking the happiness of my whole life upon one fatal cast!"

"Arnold, you cannot surely need to be reminded how ineffectual my warnings hitherto had been, and how impracticable I had ever found it, even in the most trivial instances, to change your ill-chosen mode of thinking and acting. Besides, so distant as I then was—so ignorant of the circumstances by which you were influenced—what right had I to interfere? I was astonished, it is true; yet I knew not then how rashly you were acting. But let us leave the past, dear Arnold, to be visited only when we are disposed to doubt the good providence of God, and would say, in the presumption of our hearts, 'I have not merited this stroke.'"

"Then, upon what subject, may I ask, would you please to expatiate, with such a companion by your side? Tell me what the future has in store for me! Look at my household gods, and say if they rule not with the sceptre of destruction?"

Agnes was, indeed, at a loss: whether she stretched her prophetic view over the future, or looked with more scrutinizing eye upon the present. To the gloomy and determined misanthrope the one was as barren in prospect as the other was sterile, cold, and unfruitful in possession.

"You make me no reply," said Arnold—"you do well to be silent. You have known me too long to mock my ear with the words of consolation."

"I have, indeed, lost the power to light again the little beacon of hope which you have so often extinguished—and, with that power, the presumptuous thought that I might, in some way, assist to pilot you through the storms of life: but remember, that the beacon fire which is lighted by a human hand is, at best but an emanation from the fountain of eternal light, which no tempest of this nether world is able to extinguish, and which may shine upon the bosom of the stormy ocean, or the brink of the quiet grave—that the warning voice of man is but like the cry of the shipwrecked seaman amongst the rocks and shoals, while the arm of Omnipotence is able to roll back the fury of the foaming waves, to stay the lightning, and hush the pealing thunder, and lead forth the despairing seaman into the harbour of everlasting rest!"

Years passed on, and the misanthrope remained unchanged, except that a deeper gloom was added to his despondency—a more intolerable sense of wretchedness to his despair. As the fresh glow of early life subsided, one kindly feeling after another ceased to warm his heart, until the last and longest cherished, the pleasure he had ever found in the companionship of his best friend, was gone for ever.

Agnes had become the happy wife of Walter Percival, whose active and energetic character was well calculated to assist and forward all his plans of usefulness. Together they supported the declining health of a devoted mother, whose unfailing cheerfulness fully repaid their assiduity and care: together they visited the fatherless and the widow in their affliction, watching over the feeble, comforting the forlorn, and directing the blind and erring wanderer how to obtain an entrance into the strait and narrow way: and having lived for others more than for themselves, they were permitted to partake together of that cup of earthly enjoyment which never was, and never will be, held out to those who would snatch it with unhallowed hands—who would demand, as a right, what is only granted as a boon—who would stand unbidden at the marriage feast—who would ask for the ten talents, after having lost the one.

Years passed on, and Lady Forbes was still faithful to her trust, watching, with maternal solicitude over the mental darkness of her benighted child.

"I have much to atone for," she would often say, when Agnes remonstrated with her upon her too constant and unremitting attention. "Time is fleeting, and silvery hairs are warning me that I have not much to lose. Spare me not, Agnes, for I would not spare myself. I know that nothing I can now do will obliterate the past; but when I reflect upon the mercy and forbearance of a Divine Providence, who bore with my selfish idolatry so long, and at last set before me a higher duty and a better hope, I am not willing that one hour should pass by in which I may be found to have forgotten the mighty debt I owe. You yourself have taught me that we are unable to purchase heaven by our good actions; but all the efforts of the longest life to obey the Divine will are due from us, in gratitude for the countless mercies we have received. Of my life, one half, at least has been wasted: you, who have ever been my best monitor, should not hinder me in laying my offering of autumn fruits upon the altar."

"You will not take my mother away," said Ida, pressing the hand of Lady Forbes upon her burning brow; "no earthly power should separate a mother from her child.

This was one of the lucid intervals in which the poor sufferer enjoyed the luxury of weeping; and her tears fell thick and fast, as she told, in broken accents, how her young heart had often pined for a mother's love.

"They were kind to me in Scotland," she continued—"kind to soothe, and flatter, and caress me—but a mother might have been kinder still: she might have told me when I did wrong, and I should not have resented it from her. No! no! we will not be separated—we will live together, and I will try to be less selfish than I have been. My own dear mother! my best friend! what can I do now to serve you?"

"You shall sing to us, Ida."

"I will sing to you a hymn that Kenneth Frazer taught me—yet not a hymn exactly, but something that calls back my better thoughts, when I am forgetting to be grateful."

The spring flowers know their time to bloom;
  The summer dews to fall;
The stormy winds to rise and come
  At winter's dreary call;

The nightingale knows when to sing
  Her midnight melody:
The stranger bird to stretch her wing
  Far o'er the distant sea.

The silent stars know when to raise
  Their shining lights on high;
The moon to shed her silver rays
  From out the azure sky;

The sun his chariot wheels to roll
  Toward the golden west;
The tides to flow from pole to pole;
  The foaming waves to rest.

Thus wide creation owns a power
  Supreme o'er earth and seas,
That portions out some fitting hour
  For all his will decrees.

Then while of nature's works the prime
  Man boasts his nobler call,
Shall he, ungrateful, own no time
  To thank the Lord of all?

THE PAINS OF PLEASING.

> Defend me, therefore, common sense—say I,
> From reveries so airy, from the toil
> Of dropping buckets into empty wells,
> And growing old in drawing nothing up!
>
> COWPER.

CHAPTER I.

"Do you think the good lady of this house will ask us to sit down, Charlotte?"

"I think she ought," was the reply, as two fair damsels took their stand upon the clean stone step of a plain brick dwelling.

They had been engaged the whole morning in collecting subscriptions for the Bible Society, and had not yet found their reward. Amongst the inhabitants of the small country town in which their circuit lay, some had regarded them with suspicion, some had attacked them with reproaches, and few had offered them a seat; until, wearied with their task, they determined to take advantage of the first tolerable-looking mansion for that rest which even virtuous exertions require.

"This long delay promises but a cold welcome," said one of the young ladies, as the slow movements of slippered feet were heard along the passage.

With much apparent difficulty the key was turned, and the door being partially opened by a wrinkled hand, an old woman, whose years might have entitled her to a place of rest in this world, at least, but who was evidently still tortured with household anxieties, stood before them, as if to impede their entrance.

"Does Mrs. Irvine live here?" asked one of the ladies.

The woman made no reply; but turning deliberately round, opened the door of a small parlour, wide enough for them to enter.

"Nothing but old women," thought the damsels, as they observed the figure of a person little inferior in years to their silent conductress, seated by the fire. There was nothing peculiar in her dress or countenance, and when she begged them to be seated, it was as much with the indifference of one who has grown familiar with the world in its most ordinary character, as one who has acquired the ease and complacency of fashionable life. She was, however, too well bred to ask her visitors the purpose of their coming; and after a few common-place remarks, they sat and whispered together, or rather talked over, in an under tone, the adventures of the morning, as if no one had been present.

"What had we best do with the money from Mary Staines?" asked one.

"Give it to the treasurer at once," was the reply.

"I think not. It would certainly be more just; but don't you think it would offend dear Mr. Drawnover.

"Mr. Drawnover has nothing to do with it, that I know of; and yet it might be dangerous to displease him, he seems disposed to be so liberal."

Difficulties seemed to increase around these sapient agents of reformation; and so warm were they in the contest between justice and the liberal Mr. Drawnover, as not to notice the change which had taken place in the whole aspect of the old lady, their sole auditor; until, arriving at the crisis of their dispute, one of them positively asserted that her plan would be the most equitable. The old woman then rose from her chair, and, fixing a keen look upon the other, laid her withered hand upon her arm, and exclaimed, "And can you hesitate?"

An electric shock would scarcely have occasioned greater convulsions in the form of the fair disputant.

"Listen to me!" continued the ancient dame, drawing her youthful companion to the window. "Behold yon sun, the great source of light and life! Were he to consult the inclinations of man, where, think you, would he shine? When the city dame walked forth, she would beg that the splendour of his beams might be turned away, in mercy to her lily skin; while, at the same time, the husbandman would implore the blessing of his rays, to ripen the harvest of his hope; and the sportsman would curse his mid-day heat; while the prayer of the aged and infirm would arise from the abodes of wretchedness, that some portion of his warmth and brightness might illuminate their humble dwellings: but yon glorious luminary, drawn by the hand of mercy, and directed by the councils of wisdom, goes on his heavenly way undeviating, giving beauty and gladness to the earth—to the industrious labourer, the morning light—to the flowers and fruits, the mid-day heat—to the worn and the weary, the calm of evening—and to the wide realm of nature the repose of night!

"You wonder at my earnestness and warmth. Look upon me; and if your youthful eyes shrink not from a sight so abject, contemplate the being before you. I have spent a long life in the service of my fellow-creatures, adapting myself to their various moods and temperaments, labouring to make myself beloved—and my reward has been a lonely and desolate old age. Not one of all those to whose happiness or amusement I have contributed would now seek me in this lowly habitation, to soothe my hours of weariness or pain. I had friends—I had fortune—I had all that renders life desirable, and have been assailed by few of its most trying calamities; yet has disappointment been my daily portion, and sorrow the companion of my path. Tears more than time have worn these furrows on my cheek—I am not so old as I am wretched!"

A long pause ensued, during which the sufferer appeared to be struggling with some mental agony. Restless, but silent, she sat with both her hands pressed violently upon her forehead, and her head bent forward as if beneath the weight of severe affliction. It seemed as though the floodgates of memory were thrown open, and the deluge that poured in brought nothing along with it but

"Wrecks, and the salt surf weeds of bitterness."

It was strange to behold one who had so nearly finished her course—one who had approached the confines of eternity—thus agitated by the recollection of former years. It was not, however, with fruitless effort that she endeavoured to regain her former composure. She cleared her voice, and smoothed her forehead, and, rising from the posture of humiliation, in a calm and collected manner resumed the thread of her discourse.

"I said that I had spent a long life in the service of my fellow-creatures. Well might I quote the memorable words of the dying Cardinal, and say, 'That had I served my God half as sincerely as I have served my friends, He would not have left me thus.' I said that I had served my fellow-creatures; but what was my motive? If kind offices, and willing gifts, and charity, and good will—if patient suffering, and unmurmuring submission, may entitle me to the name of Christian, I, indeed, have been a follower of Christ. But, let me ask again, what was my motive? With kind services I sought to purchase friends, amongst whom I might live, the centre of a charmed circle—friends, whose partial love might screen my faults and foibles, even from my own observation; with gifts I conciliated those whom my humour sometimes offended; with charity I bought the poor, that my step might be welcome in the cottage of the needy, and my countenance hailed as the harbinger of joy. To every creature in the universe my heart naturally overflowed with benevolence. I was patient, too, by nature, and never hesitated to suffer in the cause of another, when certain that suffering would be known and appreciated. To submit, without resistance, was a part of my creed—and verily, I had my reward; for all that I did and endured (and truly there was enough of both) was without any reference to a higher object than that of making myself beloved: and I am the more willing to lay my own errors before the world, because the character at which I aimed is one that too frequently passes under the designation of *amiable*, and, as such, is held up to admiration, while concealing, beneath a cloak of loveliness, a selfish and ignoble mind.

"Should either of my fair friends be running heedlessly upon the shoals where I have suffered shipwreck, it may be worth her while to listen for a few hours to the detail of circumstances tending to the developement of those feelings which have made me what I am—feelings, which have been a constant source of disappointment and humiliation for threescore years—feelings, which still pursue me to the brink of the grave, and occupy that place in my heart where higher thoughts should reign supreme.

"Raise not your expectations to the heights of romantic interest: mine has been the common lot of mortals—my character unmarked by any extraordinary traits. The narrative to which I call your attention is that of a mis-spent, but, in great measure, an inoffensive life, displaying none of the extremes of vice or virtue, good fortune or calamity. Perhaps, were I inclined to look with partial eye upon the past, I might be able to recount no trifling number of actions commendable in themselves, and which, had they originated in a love of God, and devotedness to his service, might have been held as memorials in my favour, but which, having nothing for their object, save the transient applause of fickle friends, have passed away from my remembrance with the worthless stimulus by which they were excited.

"Alas! my young friends, it is only that heaven-born benevolence, which regards all human creatures as the children of one Universal Father, that can prompt us to true Christian charity and love. It is only by first desiring to serve God, that we can ever effectually serve mankind.

"But I detain you, and the hour is late. Come to me to-morrow evening, if you are at leisure, and have no more agreeable employment, and you shall listen to the story of an old woman."

CHAPTER II.

Faithful to the appointed hour, on the following day the two young ladies seated themselves at the fireside of their venerable friend, who commenced her simple narrative without farther introduction.

I was born to that station in life which entitled me to all the indulgences and advantages that a reasonable mind could desire. My mother died early, and my father, being fully engaged with the business of a bank, in which he was an active partner, an older sister and myself were sent, during the usual term of education, to a fashionable boarding-school, and afterwards left to the uncontrouled formation of our own tastes, and the regulation of our own conduct. For my sister this was all sufficient, as her regular, methodical, and even temperament secured her against any temptation to deviate from the customs most approved in society. At first, I thought that her immoveable stability of character arose solely from apathy of feeling; but I learned in time, to respect the substantial reasons she was able to give for everything she did; and after experience taught me that she had all along been acting upon principle. She had not, it is true, the most conciliating manners to those around her; and often, when I would gladly have made her my guide and support, I fancied myself driven away from her confidence and affection. Still she was so exemplary in her daily walk and conversation, that she was exactly fitted to be held up as an example to others, and, in this way, was often forced upon my notice in the most injudicious manner, along with reproaches liberally bestowed upon myself.

Thus is the baneful poison of envy not unfrequently administered to the infant mind—fatal to happiness, and destructive to every kindly feeling. Thus I inwardly resolved, that if I could not be so much respected as my sister, I would be more beloved: nor was I long in accomplishing my purpose, for alas! it is not merit alone that ensures the attachment of our fellow-creatures.

Naturally quick sighted and versatile, I first made observations upon the tastes and prejudices of those around me, and then, as I felt my way, fell in with their peculiar sentiments, until I often found that I had really adopted what I had intended only tacitly to assume. I was not, certainly, daring enough openly to assert my acquiescence in that which I did not believe; but, there are many ways of appearing to agree with those who converse with us, without directly telling a falsehood.

No sooner were my sister and myself of age to be introduced, than having the reputation of fortune and some beauty, our house was thronged with visitors. For our countenance and protection under these novel circumstances my father had arranged with a widowed sister, Mrs. Morris, who had long been struggling to maintain her daughter and herself upon the scanty remnant of a clergyman's stipend, and they came accordingly to live near us, not a little gratified by the opportunity of partaking in the amusement of our parties.

At first, I advanced warily upon the slippery and adventurous path I had chosen, for I had much to learn, without which it was impossible to make successful advances; but my faculties being always awake and watchful, it was surprising how soon I was able to throw in my well-timed observations upon the common topics of conversation. This, however, was not so much my field of triumph as the cultivation of private intimacies; for, I may say for myself, that I had naturally a kind and affectionate heart, and that the sympathy and interest which I so fluently expressed, was real. Nor was it less sincere than unbounded, for in my varied experience, I imbibed no prejudice, but could feel for all—the high and the low, the wise and the weak, the good and the evil.

On first turning my attention to religion, I was much surprised, that the blessed hope held forth to all mankind on equal terms, instead of being a bond of holy fellowship and love, should so often, under false pretences, be made the root of envy, malice, and all uncharitableness! Of this, I had ample opportunity of making frequent and mournful observations, for the circle of my acquaintance included sectarians of almost every description, who seriously and earnestly warned me against the danger of each other's society. "There must," thought I, "be something strange in that institution, whose members disagree amongst themselves;" and I had one friend, who ventured to insinuate, that the fault was in religion itself, and not in the misconceptions which man had formed of it; the mingling of his own pride, passion, and prejudice, with its holy injunctions, and the resistance of his rebellious heart to the over-ruling influence of a merciful and gracious Providence.

Amongst my intimate and confidential friends, I could claim a methodist, a quaker, a unitarian, and a calvinist; all characters whom I esteemed superior to myself, and well calculated to instruct my mind, and direct my judgment. With each of these, I endeavoured to make my creed agree as nearly as possible. I attended their places of worship, read their books, and listened to their arguments, invariably arriving at the final conviction, that a great deal might be said for all. But though I was satisfied with this conclusion, my friends were not. With the most sweeping condemnation they attacked all doctrines but their own, and some of the most unsatisfactory moments of my life were spent in listening to the abuses and sarcasms which these professors of Christianity levelled against each other. But more distressing still to me, were the less obtrusive lamentations expressed in a milder spirit with which they would sometimes bemoan the errors of those who looked upon the great truths of religion with views and feelings different from their own. To those who spoke thus mildly, I was disposed to give more heed, and used on such occasions to retire to my own chamber, with a heart tortured by accumulating doubts and apprehensions.

"If," thought I, "it is impossible that any creed but one can save us, it is high time for me to settle my own faith," and in order to do this without partiality or bias, I read the scriptures with my separate friends, listening attentively to their different interpretations of particular passages, until my brain was nearly turned, and my spirits were more oppressed than before. Oh! if I had but simplified my views—if I had but dared to shake off the bondage of the world, and looked for instruction to Him who is able to teach as never man taught,—I might now in my old age have opened the bible as a book of consolation, with feelings undisturbed by the conflicting opinions of man, which still attach to every page upon which I cast my eye, as memory recalls the various translations, constructions, and arguments, that were forced upon my attention along with my first searching of the scriptures of truth.

Finding it impossible to reconcile my own ideas of religion to the various and contending opinions of others, I secretly resolved to leave this great and weighty consideration to a later period of my life, when my judgment would be more matured; and while carefully observing the line of right and wrong in my moral conduct, hearing all the arguments of all parties, and keeping my mind unwarped by prejudice, and open to conviction, I could not, I thought, be deviating very far from the right path; and must in time gather wisdom. As if nothing more was required to constitute my claim to eternal happiness. Surely the simple question why Jesus Christ was sent into the world, might have roused me from this dangerous dream of slothful security. But the "aim of my existence" was not here—Christ was not the master whom I had chosen; the world was the tyrant who ruled my life, and the hardness of his yoke, and the weight of his burden, I had hardly yet begun to feel.

Sometimes, it is true, I thought it would be more noble boldly to assert the independence of mind; and I had myself some favourite notions, which I more than once stood forth to defend; but such ebullitions of feeling seemed to make me enemies, and I found it would not do.

I recollect one evening in particular, when the conviction of the smallness of the part I was acting forced itself upon me with mortifying truth. At the house of a gentleman, who took an active part in all popular affairs, a large party had been collected, previous to an evening lecture on the subject of slavery. It was my fate to be seated beside a very handsome gentleman, just returned from the West Indies, who was insinuating his plausible arguments, wherever he could find a sufficient want of good sense and good feeling to make room for their admittance. Seeing he was likely to be the star of the evening, I accommodated my lens accordingly, to receive the beams of this western luminary. I was a good listener, than which a greater recommendation cannot well be found to the general suffrage of society; for since by far the greater part of mankind (to say nothing of woman) are better pleased to talk than be silent, one-half, at least, in all companies must remain dumb and disappointed. I had, I believe, an attentive, interested look, that made many an unfortunate proser, who had worn out his audience until one after another had gone off to join the general buzz, turn to me, with his unfinished history of himself or his doings still quivering on his lips: and let none plume themselves upon the quality of patience, unless they can say, like me, that on such occasions they have invariably heard the story out.

In the present instance, I had nothing to do but to ask a few grave questions on the subject of slavery, as if I really wanted to be informed by a judicious, impartial, and enlightened observer, before I made up my mighty mind; and a pair of brilliant eyes were beaming upon me, and before the whole assembly I was seen to be engaged in earnest conversation with the gentleman from the West Indies. He spoke so long and loud, and looked so animated and handsome, that other listeners joined our circle of interest, which at last extended itself so as to include all the party except one; and other pretty ladies besides myself peeped from beneath their shining ringlets, and asked if it was really true that the slaves were so well dressed, and did not actually feed on odious beans?

"True, beyond all doubt," replied the gentleman, "that they are often dressed in a manner that would excite the envy of many a poor English girl. Could one of your peasants behold the active, healthy-looking men and women, whose labour may well be called play, when compared with that of your population of paupers; could he behold them seated through the sultry hours of the day under the shade of magnificent trees, whose Indian foliage spreads a cool shadow on the verdant earth, there enjoying their plentiful repast of wholesome rice, flavoured with delicious vegetables; could he behold them returning to their habitations, where hunger and poverty are never permitted to threaten their security, he would rather petition that he and his family might share the fate of the negro, than that the negro should be exposed to that penury under which he is groaning."

"But the cart-whip!" sighed a gentle lady.

"The whip, my dear madam, is more a threat than a real infliction, and, I scruple not to say, has been more heard of in England than in the country where it is said to resound with such frightful severity."

"But the separation of near connexions, and the breaking up of families!" said a fair bride.

With a smile worthy the demon of Faust, the handsome gentleman replied by ill-timed sarcasms upon the exaggerated happiness of domestic life, questioning whether many a wise man would not rather be well rid of his Zantippe, than doomed to the discord of her temper through life.

This remark was ill suited to the taste of English ladies; and I was amongst a very small minority who laughed, and seemed to think the joke a good one.

"There is one question," said my sister, with earnest gravity, "which I have always thought sufficient to quiet the idle speculations of those who are not compelled to regard the subject in a political point of view—Is slavery compatible with the principles of Christianity?"

Here the gentleman forgot himself again, and asked, with a look of derision, whether Christianity was ever intended for a class of beings acknowledged to be but one step above the brutes?—at which, the minority became smaller, and even I scarcely ventured a look of approbation.

The pause which followed allowed my sister time to speak again, which she did with a degree of warmth and indignation startling almost to herself.

"For those who have to govern the state," said she, "it may be essential to the present condition of man, that a portion of apparent evil should be mixed with good, in order to force into operation those wholesome regulations which are designed to correct old abuses and long-established errors—in the same way that medicines of poisonous quality are sometimes administered to the sick, before the constitution can be fitted for natural food: but, when those whose sphere of action is within the limits of social and domestic life can listen with pleasure to sarcasms levelled against the institutions which secure to them the possession of all they most value or enjoy, we may safely conclude, that the ladies of England are not yet sufficiently enlightened · and therefore I propose, as the evening is far advanced, that we should prepare to listen to sounder reasoning, and arguments more fitted for a Christian community."

With this the company rose, and a gentleman who had sat apart from the rest attentively turning over a bundle of papers which he held in his hand, walked across the room, and, offering his arm to my sister, said, with a look of benignity, "I am happy to have found a sister-spirit in a strange land."

I now found he was the lecturer; and, when the West Indian paid the same compliment to me, I held down my head with very shame and vexation, at being thus identified with what I believed in my heart was the wrong cause.

"Who is that dogmatical young lady?" asked my companion, with a scowling brow.

I could not, dared not say she was my sister, but, drawing my shawl around me, complained loudly of the evening air, as if I had not heard his question.

Before the lecture concluded, I was more ashamed than ever of my new friend. He had come for the express purpose of disturbing the meeting; and, after the ridiculous bombast of every attack upon the patient and dignified speaker, he directed his triumphant eyes to me with such pointed certainty of applause, that I would gladly have exchanged my conspicuous situation with that of the lowest door-keeper in the apartment. Unmoved by these repeated vociferations from the midst of the assembly, the lecturer went on with his cool statement of facts, and his earnest appeals to common sense; as little shaken by each momentary commotion, as the sturdy oak of the forest by the pelting of the passing shower: and, before the expiration of one hour, the brave supporter of the West India interest had made good his exit, leaving the field to the undisputed possession of an abler power.

CHAPTER III.

"How very much I should like to ascend in a balloon!" said one amongst a group of young ladies who sat around my father's fire. Her courage being called in question, we appealed to each other on the score of individual daring, until, as the enthusiasm spread, we one and all declared that, if ever the temptation should be offered us, we would mount without a shadow of hesitation.

I was then a young and credulous looker-on upon the ways of the world, and did not know how very little the idle bravado of a private circle has to do with the real business of life. My cousin, Jane Morris, a strict judge of the conduct of others (whatever she might be of her own,) was amongst the number; and, when her earnest protestations joined the rest, I thought the experiment must surely be worth trying.

About twelve months after this, I was visiting in a distant county, when a celebrated aeronaut announced his intention of ascending from that privileged spot. He was known to the family with whom I was then a guest, and spent the day preceding his exploit with us. Ever too ready to catch the tone and manners of those by whom I was surrounded, I looked upon this person as nothing less than a hero; and, when he spoke of happier men who were honoured with the company of ladies in their aerial adventures, I turned to him and asked whether he had not a friend or sister courageous enough to share his dangers.

"No," said he, with a sigh, "I am alone in the world."

There was something in his look and the tone of his voice, which interested me deeply. A new feeling flashed across my mind. I hesitated—the countenance of my host wore an approving smile, and I offered myself as his companion in the exhibition of the following day. A burst of applause, worthy a more noble effort, immediately followed, and for a few hours of my life, I believed myself to be a heroine.

I will not describe the enthusiam which

supported me through these hours, because I esteem such bewilderment of mind no better than a dizzy dream; neither will I tell you how much more beautiful this world of ours appears to the distant and elevated beholder, than to those whose nearer inspection penetrates into the minutiæ of ordinary existence: it is more consonant to my purpose to say, how frequently I recalled the conversation of the little party before alluded to, and with what triumph I thought of returning home, the object of their wonder, envy, and admiration. For I should then have been exalted above the world; I should have dared to do what other women only dream of, I should have voluntarily risked my life. "For what?" would have been a very natural question, and one to which I was ill prepared with a reply; but I thought of no such strict investigation. I had been urged on by the approbation of every one around me; I was animated and cheered by my companion, and, I knew that kind welcomes and applause awaited my return to earth.

My wild adventure was attended with no accident. Safe again upon terra firma, I was hailed with a momentary interest, so rapturous while it lasted, as to make me feel like a creature from another world; and in a few days, I had the more mundane but not less exciting gratification, of seeing my own name in the public journals associated with magnanimity, beauty, and grace.

With these accumulated honours fresh on my brow, I returned home, where my glory was soon robbed of its lustre by the cold, reproachful looks of my sister, and the open ridicule of my cousin Jane. In vain I reminded her of what she herself had said. She scarcely recollected the circumstance at all—certainly, nothing on her part that could have given sanction to so extraordinary step.

"Do you mean to say that, had you been in my place, you would not have gone?"

"Most assuredly not."

"That you would not have enjoyed it?"

"Perhaps, I might, in a private way; but as a public exhibition, with a strange gentleman!—I assure you there are very unpleasant things said about it, and I have heard the gentleman's character called in question."

"He was known and respected by the family, with whom I was a visitor."

"By a family of unitarians, it is not improbable that he might. I would choose my associates amongst those who were better able to direct my conduct; and then, if I had not sufficient judgment to keep me from going astray, I should, at least, acquire ballast enough to keep me down."

This conversation was interrupted by the entrance of my father, who kindly welcomed me home, but who, when we were left alone, took the first opportunity of expressing his sorrow for what I had done. "Not," he added, "that there is any moral culpability in the act itself; but, when a young lady chooses to be eccentric, she raises up many enemies, and loses much of that safe and quiet standing in the world which is essential to woman's happiness."

Deeply as I was pained by this gentle and delicate reproof, I could not still believe that my distant friends, but more especially the public papers, could be so much mistaken in the real merits of the case. I thought the good people at home were narrow-minded, ill-informed, and did not know exactly what they were talking about; so I took my work, and went out with this confidence to spend the evening where I had ever been a welcome guest, at the house of an old quaker gentleman, whose active and inquisitive mind led him to take more interest in the affairs of the busy world, than was quite consistent with his secluded habits, and advanced age. Amongst his few faults, was that of loving too dearly to listen to a well-told story, and many a pleasant hour had I sat by his side, telling of the characteristic sayings and doing of his neighbourhood. Here I had never found the .east diminution of cordial hospitality; here even on the present occasion, the same kind greeting awaited me; and "here," I thought, "I can expatiate at large upon my recent elevation." The daughters, who draw so beautifully, will listen while I tell of my bird's-eye view, and the old gentleman will be delighted to hear how the world looks from a balloon." But somehow or other, no one introduced the all-absorbing subject, and, although I ventured more than once to hint at my late travels, and excursions to different places, no one "took up the wonderous tale," but conversation became heavy, and a perceptible sensation of something lurking in the back ground, made me wish myself away; and when I heard whisperings about a fire being lighted in a little private study, belonging to my venerable friend, I felt almost as if the hour of doom were at hand. It was an easy doom, however, compared with what the solemn preparations had led me to expect, for nothing could exceed the kindness of the lecture which I listened to that night, from one whose charity knew no bounds. But I was distressed to find, that here, even in my strong hold, I could no longer be looked upon as a fitting companion for young girls, whose characters were unformed, and when I returned to the quiet sitting-room, I felt in the presence of the simple, rational, and happy circle around the fire, as if I bore the stigma of a crime, for what my heart told me was nothing more than an indiscretion.

One slight circumstance was yet to stamp my condemnation with a deeper impression. The two sons of this worthy family were of those opposite extremes of character, which are not unfrequently found in the society to which they belonged. The elder was enlightened, serious, and philosophic; the younger irrational, absurd, and vulgar. With the elder, I had long been on terms of the most cordial intimacy; the younger I always shunned, as an antidote to every thing that was interesting or agreeable. On the occasion, the elder apologized for not going home with me as usual, saying, that his brother would be glad to be my companion; and the younger stepped forward, quite delighted to walk home with a spirited girl, who had been up in a balloon—saying, all the way, how much he hated tame, quiet women, like his sisters, who did nothing but knit; how much he admired ladies who had the courage to act independently; and how he would never marry any one who did not hunt.

On the following day, I appeared in a large party, rather crest-fallen, it is true, but still with faint hopes that some liberal minds existed capable of appreciating the magnitude of mine: but I found these liberal minds only in the idle and the dissipated, who flocked around me, as if my late exploit had established me on the footing of a kindred spirit; and I returned home, to wonder what that conduct would be that was approved by all. Had I but made the same earnest enquiry about the nature of that conduct which obtains the approbation of Him who has laid down his law for the regulation of our lives, I should not have sunk to rest with such a heavy heart, nor awoke on the morrow with such faint and uncertain views of the course I ought to pursue.

"What is the object of my life?" is a question so necessary and natural to all who know themselves to be accountable beings—who cannot, for one moment, stay the process of thought, nor live for a single day without wishing, hoping, or taking some steps towards attaining—that it seems almost incredible that any mind should exist unawakened by this important and alarming query.

"What is the object of my life? From what am I expecting success, or fearing disappointment?" Whatever may be the nature of this object, it will undoubtedly prove our greatest blessing, or our greatest curse; and if, on mature investigation, we are compelled to make the humbling acknowledgment, that we have no such object—that we are living on, from day to day, like the beasts which perish, eating, drinking, and sleeping, without any other aim or purpose—we ought, at least, to lay aside the pride of human nature, and not think that we are hardly dealt with, if we perish everlastingly. But since there are few who would be willing to pass this sentence upon themselves, (let us hope few upon whom it could be justly passed,) does it not argue ignorance of our real state to say that we have no object? and does it not behove every one to make diligent inquiry what that object is; since, however it may be hidden from the eyes of man, there will come a day when the secrets of all hearts will be laid open—when the smothered fires that have long burned on the altars of the false god will blaze forth, and when the hidden worshippers will have to stand or fall by the idol they have chosen.

Lost in a labyrinth of fruitless speculations, I could not, dared not, acknowledge to my own heart what my object was—but I knew too well what it was not. I knew it was not the service of my God, nor the promotion of His glory; and though, in my secret soul, I pined for something more substantial than I had yet found to rest upon, I never resolutely turned my thoughts to that which would have been my shield of safety in the hour of danger—my rock of defence in the pilgrimage of the desert—my home of rest after the toils of life.

Finding the stability of my character a little shaken, in the estimation of some of the more grave and scrupulous amongst my friends, I redoubled my exertions, in a private way, to win by kindness what I could not command by respect. I was ingenious in all kinds of fancy work, painting, trimming, cutting, and carving; and countless were the hours that I spent, labouring early and late, for albums, and bazaars, wedding presents, and birth presents; often denying myself necessary reading, exercise, and relaxation, to finish a cap for the baby of one dear friend—to stipple through the widespread leaves of a moss-rose for another—and to invent, sprig, spot, and spangle for all. At first, I thought to make a merit of my services by telling of the quantity of work I had done; but I soon found, that what was done for all lost its value in the estimation of each, and that to please one effectually, I must be silent as to what I had done for another. I was consequently deprived of the only reward I really merited—praise for my industry; and while accumulated labours crowded upon me, I could not even complain of want of time.

"Only just this little etching for me," said one, when I told how my sight was failing.—"When my cap is finished, I will ask you for no more," said another.—"I have promised my friend one of your sweetest drawings," said a third. And so on; for my exertions were by no means confined to the circle of my own associates; beyond them was the wider circle of theirs; so that, had the supply been increased a hundred fold, it would still have been unequal to the demand. But then my work was so exquisite—my drawings so beautiful—my inventions so inimitable—I was such a dear, good creature—so useful in all their difficulties—so necessary to all their enjoyments: and so, in good truth, I believe I was. Yet, all the while, my own album lay open, and unfilled; for, knowing too well the cost of contributing, I could not press my own suit beyond a simple request, and therefore I found none who had time to make me a work-bag, nor was there an eye in our whole community that was sharp enough to see to sprig an apron for me.

"Well, well," thought I, "it is of little consequence; now I will

'Wait till the days of trial come—
The dark days of trouble and wo—'

and then it will be my turn to receive."

In addition to the many difficulties and disadvantages which I have mentioned as belonging to such a varied and wide circle of intimate friends, I ought certainly not to omit one which I esteem the greatest, as being most dangerous to that uprightness of conduct, and open rectitude of mind, without which no character can be worthy our esteem or admiration.

Amongst my friends, were some who cordially disliked each other; and to these it was often my misery to listen, while they heaped invectives, sarcasms, and abuses upon the absent party. Nor was my silent listening sufficient to satisfy their spleen. I must take their part. I must say that they were right, and the other party wrong. It is an uncommon case upon which something cannot be said on both sides; and if there was but one palliating circumstance in the conduct of those present, and one act of glaring culpability in that of the absent, I sought out and dwelt upon them with all the warmth that friendship could require. The persons accused would then tell their story, to which I endeavoured to listen with the same impartiality, and during which I usually acted the same part—a part which might have been safe and well, had not my name, in some subsequent burst of anger, been made use of as that of a convert and ally, and thus a double and deceitful character assigned to me; nor could I possibly, in such circumstances, have steered clear of such imputations, without I had possessed more tact than the most artificial of women, and more wisdom than the wisest of men.

I had, I believe, in my early youth, high notions of candour and sincerity, openness of dealing, and independence of mind; but the service of the world is mournfully destructive to noble sentiments and generosity of heart.

I well remember, on one occasion, hearing a friend of mine much spoken against by a family at whose house she was in the habit of visiting; and, believing herself to be a welcome guest, she had kindly offered to assist the young ladies in their knowledge of one of the continental languages; and this kindness was rewarded by the most cutting sarcasms thrown out against her talents and acquirements. She was one whom I esteemed highly, but I had not the courage singly to oppose the tide; besides, there were things said to which I could offer no opposition, such as the frequency of her visits, and the vexation with which they heard the announcement of her name. I, therefore, thought I could not do less, in common justice to my friend, than apprize her of her real situation with regard to this family, which I did, by merely warning her against seeking their acquaintance, without any of the more mortifying parts of the story. Having done this, and not liking to do it secretly, I sent a note immediately, to inform one of the young ladies of the part I had acted. The most violent burst of indignation against me followed: I was called a spy, a meddler, a false friend, a deceitful enemy; and, finally, the despised person, whose company carried disgust along with it, was apologized to, invited, and treated with tenfold favour.

Those who live on vanity must not unreasonably expect to die of mortification. This simple event threw me into the deepest depression of mind, and, for a while, I believed I was, in reality, all this harsh family had called me. Instead of sinking under a cloud of melancholy which mystified my sense of right and wrong, I ought to have gathered wisdom from the past, by learning that, had I openly dared to take the part of one whom I esteemed an injured person, it would have relieved me from the painful necessity of hearing insinuations or abuses which out of consideration to me, would most probably have been discontinued; but that, not having taken this part, I had no title to the name of a true friend, and no right to make such a communication as that title alone could justify.

This was but one circumstance out of many of the same nature, too tedious for me to relate, or for you to listen to; and, amongst the number, must not be forgotten those in which I myself, from hearing one party only, imbibed some degree of prejudice, and acted accordingly.

Oh! my young friends, it was a wearisome and heartless service in which I was engaged. It was a hard and toilsome journey that led me through the wilderness of life!

CHAPTER IV.

To act the part of a true friend requires more conscientious feeling than to fill with credit and complacency any other station or capacity in social life; because, in all others, the duties are more generally acknowledged, more evident, and more imperative: but in friendship, it is the heart only that decides what shall be done, or suffered, stimulated, or subdued, encouraged or repelled; yet of all the little niceties of private intercourse, conscience takes cognizance; and those who presumptuously assume the sacred name of friend, without appealing to her tribunal, will find their punishment in disappointment and remorse. An agreeable, kind, or prudent friend, it is not difficult to find; but a *true* friend is a pearl of inestimable value, rarely met with, and not always prized according to its worth; for a true friend must often administer the bitter draught of reproof, as well as the cup of consolation—and who amongst us is able to drink of this draught, and bless the hand by which it is presented? We may perhaps, after the lapse of time, recall the anxious solicitude of those who sought to correct our errors, and wish, in our moments of self-condemnation, that we had them near us to point out the way of amendment; but, alas! our petulance, at the very time when affection had wrought them up to the most painful effort which a kind heart is capable of making, has driven them from our side, and we find, too late, that we have no longer a true friend.

A friend must be intimately acquainted with your character, and have just enthusiasm enough in her attachment to render the meanest parts of it most disgusting to her, whatever they may be to others; she must have forbearance enough to tolerate your peculiar views and sentiments with sufficient dignity to support her own; she must watch over you for good, and study to protect you from evil; she must commend without exciting your vanity, and condemn without bitterness or reproach; she must be sparing of ridicule except when used to correct slight errors, or like the stroke of the staff upon the ice to ascertain its strength, and give confidence for farther trial; she must be willing to receive as well as to give, keeping no account of obligations; she must never permit a misunderstanding to remain unexplained, or an accidental want of kindness unatoned for: and, while the most trifling personal services are willingly performed, she must above all things seek to ennoble and exalt your mind, sacrificing the pleasures of the present moment if necessary to your everlasting happiness, and faithfully commending you in her prayers to the guidance and protection of him who is alone able to prepare you for the habitations of eternal rest.

If, after all that I have said, I should be able to add that in the course of my experience with the world, it was my happiness to find one true friend, you will rightly esteem me amongst the most privileged of human beings. That this friend was of my own sex it is scarcely necessary to say, since whatever may exist in the dreams of the enthusiast, I believe that a true, ardent, and lasting friendship between young men and young women is seldom to be found in real life; and who that is capable of estimating the influence of each character upon the other in their social intercourse, can withhold their regret that these attachments should so invariably be destroyed by the false delicacy, and all other kinds of falsehood that prevail in the world. Yet such is the tone and character of society in its present state, that men will be jealous, and women will coquette, even in friendship; and, while this is the case, the three grand ingredients of friendship, candour, confidence, and stability, must be wanting to render their intercourse either refined or durable.

The first time I ever beheld Helen Grahame was at the house of a widow lady, where other idlers besides myself were loitering away a winter's morning, by the help of that most empty of all devices, that men, or rather women, have adopted for the purpose of killing time—the amusement of making calls. The cold season had but just set in, and the drawing-room being yet uncheered by a fire, we were seated snug and warm around a social hearth in a sitting-room, where a little girl of ten years old was preparing for her drawing lesson.

"Take your papers to the farthest table," said the mother. "I dare say Miss Grahame will not mind us, she is always so abstracted," she continued in an under tone, when the door opened, and a tall thin figure entered, muffled in well-worn furs which had evidently seen better days. Miss Grahame hesitated when she saw how the apartment was occupied.

"The morning is so cold," said the lady of the house, "that we cannot leave the fire. Will you permit us to remain, Miss Grahame, if we promise not to interfere?"

The artist bowed such an assent as implied a want of ability to refuse, yet not ungraciously, for her look, her voice, her whole manner were gracious in the extreme; and, at the same time, so dignified and condescending that when she applied herself to the business of the day, I could not help thinking that her native element would be found in a very different sphere. The contour of her beautiful profile, (for her face was so thin that you could not study it in any other way,) the intelligence of her deep dark eyes, and the gracefulness of all her movements, interested me deeply; but when I heard the hollow cough which frequently interrupted her instructions, saw the long thin fingers with which she held her pencil, and caught the stolen glance which she more than once directed to the distant fire, my interest gave place to sympathy, and I longed to offer her some token by which she might know it to be sincere. My anxiety was in some measure relieved, when I saw the child, with an expression of unaffected solicitude, look up into her face, and say, "Are you better this morning, Miss Grahame?" At which she drew her left hand over the shoulder of her pupil, and, bending towards her so near as to touch the rosy cheek with her own, from whence the roses had for ever fled, pursued her occupation without any other remark than what related to the subject with which they were engaged.

"I have brought my portfolio," said she, "this morning, in order that you may make your choice; for I well know how hard a task it is to copy what is not suited to our own taste."

"Ah! have you?" said the child, and clapped her hands with exultation.

"Stay, stay, my love," said Miss Grahame —"you must first finish this tree, before you begin with any thing else."

With a look of disappointment the little pupil resumed her pencil, and laboured diligently until the tree was completed, but not without regretting that it was so full of foliage, and asking more than once if it would not look better without the lowest branch.

"Now, now!" she exclaimed, after the last rough touch upon the stem—"now I shall see all your beautiful drawings!"

"You will be disappointed, my love," said Miss Grahame, with a faint smile, as she looked round, evidently afraid lest the raptures of the young enthusiast should awaken interest elsewhere. But I was the only one who heard or noticed what was going on. The rest of the party were too busy with the events of a late extraordinary marriage to hear any voice but their own; and Miss Grahame spoke in so low a tone that it was with difficulty I could catch her passing remarks upon the drawings which the delighted child was turning over.

"But this beautiful house," said the girl; "you must not take it from me, but tell me where this charming place can be."

"That is the place where I was born," said Miss Grahame, with an altered voice. "I cannot talk to you about that drawing, I hardly know whether it is good or bad."

"And why do you not live there now?" asked the child, still detaining the picture.

"It was sold, my love."

"And did you get all the money? it must have been sold for a great deal; you must be very rich. If I were you I would not teach drawing, nor wear that shabby fur."

I could not forbear a stolen glance, to see with what philosophy Miss Grahame bore this questioning. I expected to behold her countenance flushed with indignation, as mine was for her; but knowing that no unamiable feeling was mingled with the artless familiarity of her young friend, she answered, with a placid and benignant smile, "The money is not mine, my love, it was given to those who had a better right to it. But come, we must not trifle away our time; and since you consider money so valuable, I am sure you would not like your mamma to pay me for spending half an hour with you in idle talk."

"Oh! yes I should, for I like to talk with you best; and I never see you, except in these short lessons, and you will not stay a moment when they are over."

"You know I have others to attend to; and I assure you it is harder to me than to you, when I chide you for talking to me," said Miss Grahame, pressing a kiss upon her brow. "It is not a fault of which I can accuse many; but we both know it would be very wrong in me to receive money for what I have not done."

When the first set of callers rose to depart, I found an opportunity of addressing the young student and her interesting instructress; but I almost repented of my purpose, when I observed the patient look of resignation with which Miss Grahame endured my advances, until convinced that I was really interested, and then her countenance wore the double charm of intelligence and gratitude.

Having spoken of some paintings she had at home, I said I should esteem it a great privilege if she would allow me to call and look over her private collection.

Miss Grahame blushed, and I thought, for an instant, looked distressed; but she immediately presented me with her address; and hoping that I would not raise my expectations too high, begged I would spare her an evening hour, as she could not make sure of being disengaged at any other time.

I went accordingly on the following day, and found the Miss Grahame, whom I had imagined born to tread the marble courts of kings, a solitary occupant of lodgings, that were neither commodious nor situated in a genteel neighbourhood. She was seated close beside a pale lamp, with her eyes thickly shaded, so as to strengthen her sight, for a beautifully fine drawing, which she was under the necessity of executing by that distressing light. On my entrance, she laid aside her shade, and welcomed me with a grace that would have done honour to a nobler habitation. The walls of her small apartment were crowded with pictures, some in elegant frames, some without any. Three portraits were amongst the most highly adorned; two of an elderly gentleman and lady, the other of a young man, whose striking likeness to herself immediately arrested my attention. Narrow as was the space allotted to a diversity of subjects, they were extremely well arranged; and everything around bore marks of elegance, of taste, order, and regularity. But oh! what poverty; never, never, shall I forget that little room! and Helen Grahame, with the figure and bearing of a queen, seated there in loneliness and penury. "She must be a wretched woman," thought I, and doubtless something of the same kind was legible on my countenance; for she smiled, and asked me with great simplicity, how I liked her little den.

"We learn a great deal in passing through the world," she added: "I should once have thought it impossible to be happy in such a place as this."

"And are you happy?" I exclaimed.

"Oh! yes, quite contented in my present lot, finding perpetual pleasure in my books, and my daily occupations, and very, very thankful that I am able to maintain myself, to assist one whom I love, and to burden nobody. Sometimes, it is true, my spirits fail me with my failing health; but God is gracious to the feeble, and my trust is in him."

As she said this, a peaceful smile passed over her features, like sunshine through a wintry cloud. And then, as if unwilling to occupy my time with what was foreign to the purpose of my visit, she unfolded a large portfolio of drawings, and spread them before me, without either vanity or affectation, saying, in a voice of peculiar sweetness, whose tones my ear will never lose, "I hear, Miss Irvine, that you draw beautifully. May I tell you one thing, amongst the many that I have learned by experience? These performances of my early years have passed through a severe ordeal; they have been exhibited in splendid drawing-rooms, when my father was a wealthy man, and passed from one fair hand to another, to receive the most extravagant encomiums that flattery could bestow. During the last two years they have been shown about as pattern-cards, to prove that I am really worth my pay. I need hardly say, that in one case the encomiums have been as much too profuse as the criticisms and condemnations in the other; indeed, scarcely anything was ever said in their favour when they were exhibited merely as works of art, the production of a lady's hand, which has not been unsaid since a price was set upon them."

"And how," I asked, "were you able to bear the change? were you not overwhelmed with disappointment and chagrin?"

My friend looked really amused when she replied, "As I knew at first they were not above mediocrity, I set down for nothing all the praises that went beyond that; and by treating all the disparaging remarks they are now subjected to in the same way, I am able to balance the two accounts, and think them moderate still. We must all have a standard of our own, if we wish to enjoy a moment's peace. The world is a capricious tyrant, ruling us by so many different laws, that unless we think, judge, and determine for ourselves, there is not only great danger that our thoughts, judgments, and determinations in matters of minor importance, will become weak and confused, but that we shall lose sight of that clear undeviating line which separates good from evil."

"Speaking of the world in general, I fully agree with you," said I; "but with regard to our particular friends, surely their opinions may sometimes be adopted in preference to our own."

"Our friends," she replied, "are in this sense only parts of a whole, and though our affectionate partiality may separate them in idea from the rest of the world, they undoubtedly partake of the same tastes, feelings, and prejudices of which that world is composed. Besides, since we are all responsible beings, both here and hereafter, naturally and reasonably suffering what no one can suffer for us,—the consequence of our daily errors; it is necessary that we should look well to our steps, and not trust too much to the guidance of the various travellers upon the path of life, who frequently, more willing than able to conduct us through its mazes, would lead us hither and thither, from this side to that, round by one way and then by another, until the evening would overtake us in the wilderness, and we should have to answer to the good master who had sent us with directions of his own, that we had not deemed them sufficient, that we had listened to those who were themselves bewildered, and thus had lost our way.

"But I entreat you to pardon me; I am actually preaching a sermon, when I had meant only to show you my drawings."

The fair speaker then rose, and after ringing the bell, pressed me to partake of her usually solitary tea.

From this time I found in Helen Grahame, all I could desire in a friend; and many were the hours of social enjoyment that I spent in what she first called her little den; and where I soon found it possible to forget everything except the high tone of feeling which influenced her character; the noble generosity ever warming her heart, and the happiness which attends a close and familiar intercourse with refined and elevated minds. Never did I see this admirable woman distressed by paltry cares and vexations, though few could have more to contend with; nor weighed down by the humiliations of mortified vanity, though few had experienced a more total change of fortune. She had not made the world her idol even in the day of prosperity, when its smile was upon her; and therefore her spirit was not daunted by its frowns, nor her feelings soured by its unkindness.

CHAPTER V.

Not many evenings after the first I ever spent with Helen Grahame, I joined a mixed party where a gentleman was present who struck me forcibly by his resemblance, not only to the portrait I have mentioned, but to my friend herself.

"Who is that gentleman with dark hair?" I asked of a lady who sat near me.

"Oh! that," she replied, lowering her voice, and her brow at the same time, as if the fact was not fit to be spoken aloud, "that is young Grahame; have you never heard of Grahame, of Stapleton-lodge?"

"No; what is there to hear of him?"

"Nothing good, I assure you. The spendthrift has wasted his father's property, some say, broken his heart; and now, do you know, he drinks dreadfully. Indeed, I am surprised that any one should think of inviting him to an evening party."

"I understand he is a delightful companion, when quite himself," observed another lady. "But drunkenness is such an odious vice, one never can forget it."

My cousin, Jane, who liked nothing better than a conference held upon the follies and vices of mankind, now joined us, and with bitter invectives expressed her horror that so shocking a creature should be asked to meet us.

Grahame, who was an extremely handsome man, had now risen, and joined a group of ladies, who, whatever they might say or think of him, when absent, looked evidently well pleased with his presence. From them he arrived by a chain of communication at the part of the room where we were seated. He had the most independent, yet most insinuating manner of pleasing I ever remember to have seen, so that, while you were actually fascinated by his conversation, you felt almost piqued that he had taken so little pains to render it flattering or agreeable: and, while many were severe upon his character, all the young, and not a few of the old, were won by his address.

"Now," thought I, "My cousin Jane will show her just abhorrence of his conduct; and when he took a vacant place between us, I turned to observe the indignation of her countenance, and listened for the well-merited reproofs which I felt convinced she would bestow upon him."

"It is a long time," said he, "since I had the happiness of seeing Miss Morris."

My cousin bowed not ungraciously, and said, it was, indeed, a long time since they had met.

"The last time," he continued, "was on the day of that romantic excursion, when the storm overtook us half way up the mountain, and you were the only woman who had the courage to stand with me upon that tremendous precipice, and watch the lightning playing at our feet."

"When I borrowed a cloak of the shepherd's wife, and put on the shepherd's hat and looked——"

"As you ought to look,—the genius of the valley below, protecting it from the fury of the tempest. Do you not think it is worth all the tame pleasures of domestic life, now and then to spend a day like this amongst the hills, with nothing but the purple heather beneath our feet, and the blue heavens above our heads?"

"I do."

"Then, why are we so sparing of an enjoyment which may at any time be ours? What say you to a party on the river to Heaton Grove, where I understand the woods are delightful? Will you go?"

"With all my heart."

And thus the conversation went on, to my utter amazement, until interrupted by some common-place remark from me, which seemed to break the charm; for Grahame immediately turned, and addressing me in a grave and earnest manner, said, "I have not the pleasure of having been introduced to you; but as you are the lady who has kindly visited my poor sister, I know you will pardon me, when I say that I have made my way from the farthest extremity of the room, by slow advances, and circuitous march, for the purpose of thanking you."

"What I have done solely for my own gratification," I replied, "cannot surely entitle me to your thanks."

"But I have heard of such a thing as being thankful for favours yet to come; and I am living in the hope that your first visit may not be your last. Poor Helen was once the idol of that society from which she is now excluded.—And for what? Because she teaches to the children of these people the accomplishments by which society is enlivened and adorned."

"What a marked difference is shewn by the world in its treatment of men and women."

"Your remark is but too just, Miss Irvine. Only think of me for one moment (I ask no more)—a spendthrift, who has ruined his father—a man without any honourable means of existing—to say nothing of my present habits, which are well known to every one here; yet so long as I can wear broadcloth, and drink wine, and tell a good story, and talk of the hounds I once kept, there will still be gentlemen so liberal as to invite me to their dinners, and ladies so generous as to dance with me, laugh with me, and plan parties of pleasure of which I am to be one; while my sister, the noblest, the most dignified, the purest minded of women, pines in her solitude, unheeded, and may not join the circles which she is only too good to adorn, because, forsooth! she prefers maintaining herself by her own exertions, to that worst of all slavery, dependence on the great. Will you, Miss Irvine, visit my poor sister sometimes? Will you cheer her loneliness, and make her feel that she is not altogether desolate?"

"She cannot be desolate while she has a brother so kindly interested for her happiness."

"Ah! I find you do not know me. I owe your patience in listening to me to your ignorance of who I am."

"Are not others equally patient who know you better?"

"And thus," said he, in a lower tone, "they prove themselves to be pretenders to a greater love of virtue than they really feel. We who are called men of the world, acquire great knowledge of the human heart. We hear the cry that is set up for the cause of virtue; we come into the presence of virtuous women, where charity, indeed, would seem to prevail; for, how few! how very few! appear to remember our transgressions against us, or turn a deaf ear to the flattery of profane lips. Yet this charity, I have good reason to believe, is of rather an evanescent nature, and does not always accompany the ladies to their own fire-sides; where, if my Ariel tells me right, they not unfrequently vilify the character of him upon whom they have so lately bestowed their sweetest smiles. Is it not so, Miss Irvine?"

"No, no; you are too severe. Women are misguided in their judgment of men, by the artificial rules established in society, which confuse their sense of right and wrong; and where they *know* one man to be addicted to vices which they abhor, they have so much reason to *suspect* others, that it would be almost impossible for them to fix a definite line by which to mark their approbation or contempt."

"It is my turn now to complain of your severity," said Grahame, laughing, "Then you *know* my conduct to be bad, but you *suspect* that of so many others to be no better, that you will not single me out as the object of your especial abhorrence."

"I think nothing that I have heard of your conduct so bad," I replied, "as the coolness and indifference with which you speak of it yourself."

"Thank you, Miss Irvine: you might have told me to begone in gentler words."

As he said this he rose, and turning for an instant towards me, our eyes met.

The woman who would not flirt, who would not please where she ought not—in short, who would act prudently and conscientiously, should be very careful of her eyes. The eye is the mirror of the soul, into which nature teaches us to look, in order that we may read the truth. While the lips are closed in secrecy, the eye will often betray what the heart is most solicitous to conceal;

and she who would pronounce a repulse, must be ever watchful of a wandering glance. The eye, that wonder-working miracle of intelligence, is capable of unveiling, in an instant, the pretensions of the most accomplished hypocrite; of giving bitterness to jest, and sweetness to reproof; of unsaying what the lips have said; of freezing the fountain that was flowing fresh and warm from the heart, and of melting into tenderness the flinty bosom that was steeled against the voice of pity.

What was written in my eyes on that memorable occasion, it is impossible for me to say; but Grahame seated himself beside me, and I saw and heard him only for the remainder of the evening.

It was not long before I repeated my visit to Helen, whose character I found more interesting the nearer I was permitted to approach towards that intimacy which I have ever looked upon as the greatest temporal blessing of my life. There was at this time a cloud upon her brow, and something of abstraction in her manner, which I was unable to understand, not knowing the anxiety that was preying upon her susceptible mind, and undermining her naturally delicate constitution. We were conversing on subjects which excited her to energy and warmth, but I observed that she often paused suddenly, and turned her head in the attitude of listening when the wind rushed past the windows, or when a step was heard pacing along the quiet street below. At last there was a loud knock at the door, and Helen started up with hope and gladness in her eye, exclaiming, "It is my brother."

I enquired if he had been long from home? —"Oh no! only at a dinner party."

She then continued, in a low and hurried manner, "You do not know (Heaven grant you never may!) what it is to doubt."—Her words were interrupted by the entrance of her brother, and she turned to receive him, with a smile that might almost have wooed a spirit from the bowers of bliss. Would that it could have kept a sinner from the haunts of vice!

Grahame had torn himself away at an early hour from the convivial board; and his sister, aware of the struggle such an effort must have cost him, devoted herself to his amusement with a degree of vivacity and animation, stimulated by the real happiness of feeling that he was again safely and securely at her side, and that one hour of temptation had passed over without its victim.

I know not how far my own conversation contributed to the enjoyment of this evening; but it was one over which memory still lingers, and from which time has not yet effaced the nearest approach I ever remember to have made to earthly happiness.

Grahame was a man who possessed a sort of mastery over the minds of others—a power which he was best pleased to exercise, in turning serious things to ridicule, unveiling false pretensions, and lowering the standard of human intellect: when, therefore, he chose to lay down his offensive weapons, and to enter unarmed into the social intercourse of life, his looks, words, and most trifling acts of kindness, possessed a tenfold charm, arising partly from the warm, sincere, and earnest feeling, which accompanied them. With this feeling, his intercourse with his sister was invariably marked; and, while he professed himself incapable of loving any other creature in the world, my vanity was piqued at finding myself so totally excluded; and that fatal yearning of the heart was awakened in mine, to appropriate to itself some secret treasure, to erect some altar even to an unknown God,

> "For pilgrim dreams at midnight hour to visit,
> And weep, and worship there."

Nor was I long in discovering, that in an affection pure, deep, and ardent, I, as that sister's friend, might possibly become a partaker; and, without calculation of the consequences, I tried with fresh energy, my powers of pleasing. What was the motive which impelled me onward, I scarcely know. It might be a vain and foolish ambition, to obtain the affections of one who was said to be incapable of loving. Whatever it was, I unquestionably had my reward: whatever it was, the moving-spring bore no proportion to the importance which I attached to the object; for when I first listened to professions of attachment, humble, deep, and unchangeable, from this man of pride and poverty, I felt as if I had gained the world.

Let no woman, who would not steep her bread in bitterness, and her pillow in tears—who would not have her brow overshadowed with grey hairs, her cheeks blanched by a premature and deadly paleness, her eye too dim for tears, her voice too faint for prayer, and her step too feeble for the burden of the day—be led on by pity, admiration, vanity, or any other power or impulse to love "the man whom she esteems not." There are other afflictions in this world which break the natural heart, and bow down the aspiring spirit, and quench the buoyant hopes of youth—but none can be like unto this; for it poisons the very springs of tenderness and affection, and pursues us like a merciless enemy, even into the sanctuary; where, amidst holy thoughts, and fervent supplications, there falls upon the soul a cold and heavy sense of lonelinesss, an aching want of one who is not near to bow the knee, and sue with us for pardon and salvation.

To love with ardour and constancy one "whom we esteem not," some hold to be impossible; and so unquestionably it is to a well-regulated and rightly-influenced mind; but, amongst the multitudinous mass of human beings, how many minds are not thus regulated and influenced—how many are divided between earth and heaven, loving the things of this world, yet longing after another! It is to that such this warning must apply; for such was I, at the time of my intimacy with the brother of Ellen Grahame, who, shut out from all confidential intercourse, except with his sister, loved me the better, that I dared to break through the shackles of society for her sake and his. I had, it is true, my share of suffering to endure, for both:—my friendship for Helen was laughed at as an affectation of romance; she was called the "picturesque young woman," and I the lady patronness; but when my intimacy with her brother was suspected, nothing could exceed the horror of some of my friends, especially my cousin Jane, who, for her part, would never encourage the advances of a man whose character she did not approve.

I was not naturally ill-natured, nor was it any gratification to me to make a tart reply; but I could not help reminding her of the evening when she and this desperate character were engaged in such close and earnest conversation.

"But you must remember," she replied, "that I purposely left my seat and went to another part of the room."

"Yes, my dear cousin, when his attention was absorbed by another lady, yet not until you had agreed to join him in a party of pleasure."

Experience, always allowed to be an able and powerful teacher, is most instructive in what relates to our intercourse with what is called the world, because the daily and hourly occurrence of familiar events, all tending to the developement of character, places the human mind in its infinite varieties, perpetually under our observation.

Before twenty years had rolled over my head, I had become a proficient in the art of pleasing; and so habitual the practice of it was, that my labours of love were by no means confined to my own sphere in society; and so difficult did I find it to turn a deaf ear to the complaints of poverty or suffering, that my purse was first drained, and then my ingenuity put to the rack for expedients to relieve, assist, or comfort. But the greatest trial to my patience was in the constant visitations of persons, in whose affairs I had no interest, but whom I was still unable to part from without an invitation to come again. Thus it not unfrequently happened, when I had commenced a favourite book, set apart an evening for a particular friend, or planned an agreeable excursion, in stepped a very distant relation, the widow of an inn-keeper, who remembered my mother when a bride, and had brought her work, and her eldest son, to spend a long day with me. Or, in the noon-tide heat of summer, there would come a bevy of young women, dressed in red, from my father's farm, saying, (though the fact had escaped my memory) that I had kindly invited them the last time I was there. Add to which, there were dabblers in the fine arts, who came to see my bust of Apollo, my pictures, medallions, and all sorts of niceties, which I had studiously collected for the gratification of my visitors—flower-fanciers, who came to see my carnations—young girls who had no pianos at home, and came to practise upon mine—sons and daughters of my very dear friends, to whom I had offered to teach Italian—in short, the labours of Hercules were nothing to mine; and to the labour was added no trifling accompaniment of vexation—such as, my best engravings lent out to copy, and sent home with a blot of ink upon the best face—my Roman head returned without a nose—and the most valuable books of my library not returned at all. But I was patient and long suffering; and the praises of my goodness, the thanks for my bounty, the flattery of my talents, and the insatiable love of pleasing, spurred me on, until I ceased to have a moment that could be called my own; and the prime minister himself could hardly have his waking thoughts and nightly dreams more full than mine were of floating visions of indefinite good and certain evil.

It is not to be supposed, that in the science of winning hearts my studies were confined to my own sex only. I had my complement of lovers; and since I could not marry, I pitied them all. Indeed, my refusals, wrung from me by necessity, were couched in such gentle words, and accompanied by so much tenderness and compassion, that I believe the attachments which they pronounced unchangeable would really have proved so, had their termination rested with me. It was so harrowing to my feelings to occasion a moment's pain to any one, that I shrunk with horror from inflicting what they told me would be nothing less than death upon those who loved me so devotedly. But experience here, as in many other cases, taught me to be more sparing of my sympathy; for I soon found, that from this death my admirers were blessed with a very speedy resurrection. One who had sat down, with loaded pistols on the table, ready to shoot himself at a certain hour, was married in three weeks; another, whom I had driven into banishment to the wilds of America, did certainly emigrate, with a companion more willing to share his fate; and a third, who had declared his determination to drown his passion in the din of war, entered into the tobacco trade, and became a stout and wealthy man. Thus I was relieved from the torturing anxiety I felt for the lives and happiness of my lovers, and the remorse which must have been mine, had I found myself really the destroyer of either.

CHAPTER VI.

There is nothing more wonderful in the construction of the human mind than its capability of suffering. I never loved but once, and that attachment cost me more than all the other troubles of my life. So far as it might aid my purpose, I should be willing to recall that season of trial, to dive into the abyss of memory and bring up the bitter weeds which overspread and choaked the natural springs of hope and energy in my heart; but there is no language capable of conveying an idea of what the heart that has felt alone can understand. We may speak of the ordinary calamities of life, because we usually address ourselves to those who have experienced the same; but there are sufferings of which it is as vain to attempt a description, as to tell of the impression made by a dream, of which we may indeed relate the facts and circumstances, but that which constituted the vividness, the life, the essence of the vision, must be ours, and ours only.

In referring to this part of my life I am able to recollect nothing but what bore some relation to the moving spring of all my thoughts and actions. I am not aware that I neglected any of the various claims upon my attention, which I had myself established; but I know that I performed my wonted routine of occupations with more heaviness and languor, and that, although I had long neglected the duty of prayer for myself, I then learned to pray earnestly and diligently for another.

It has been said by an able and popular writer, that even if prayer had never been enjoined as a duty, we should still have applied to it as a necessary resource from the very weakness of nature. It was in this way, despairing, helpless, and utterly destitute of power in myself, that I offered up petitions for the better guidance of one whose happiness was of more importance to me than my own. I had heard of gracious and almost miraculous answers to prayer, and for some time deceived myself with the presumptuous hope that I, who had hitherto neglected to lay hold of this blessed privilege, might just kneel down and pray for any particular good which I chose to specify, and that my prayer would be granted. But my presumption had its cure—and, in my own condemnation, I had cause to bless the mercy and justice of Him by whom it was appointed.

Helen Grahame was fully aware of the attachment which existed between her brother and myself, and often thanked me with tears of gratitude for having cheered him with the happy thought that, when she was gone, he would have one friend left behind. Nor were her tears those of gratitude alone—she sometimes spared from her own hard lot the most tender sympathy for mine—that I should have fixed my affections upon one whose character and circumstances were so ill-calculated to increase my happiness.

"Grahame has a kind and generous heart," she would say, "but you must never marry him until ——" and then her voice would falter between hope and despair. "The sister who was born beneath the same roof with him, upon whom he has a natural claim, has no right, even if she had the inclination, to cast him off; but to continue a connexion of this kind is very different from establishing a new one. Be kind to my brother, I beseech you, for your regard may help to save him. Show him that you think him worth your solicitude, but on no account, I entreat you, enter into any sort of engagement with him, nor sacrifice one iota of your own respectability, even in the opinion of the world, for his sake. Such a sacrifice would be unspeakably calamitous to you, and could be of little service to him; for such are the necessary laws instituted for the protection of the female character, that, should a woman descend but one step from her proper station to draw up a man who has fallen below his, she is not only unable to assist him who will not assist himself, but becomes inevitably involved in his degradation."

I was sitting with Helen late one evening, my sister having agreed to call for me on her return from a party, when my friend disclosed to me more than she had ever done before of her past life and change of fortune.

"I do not like to dwell much upon this theme," she said, "for when I speak of my parents and the home I once enjoyed, I feel my failing health too keenly, and the want of those comforts which a weakly frame is apt to make us pine for. The natural heart is affected by natural things, and human tenderness ever accompanies human weakness; thus, while I weep too often when I think of my own mother, and turn too fondly to her past kindness when treated harshly by strangers, my desire is to think more and more of that Parent whose arm is still near to support me, of that home where the weary may find everlasting rest, and of those comforts which are mercifully provided for the helpless and the needy."

I replied, that we did well to look to the rest that was eternal, for this world had little to offer.

"I believe," she continued, "that the true Christian may enjoy a degree of peace, which almost deserves the name of rest, even in this life. It is not so much the fault of the world as of our own hearts, that we are so tossed about by contending interests, and worn by paltry cares and vexations. If we first love God, and then the creatures he has formed after his own image, we shall be able to regard the world, of which they form a part, without either attaching to it the importance that is felt only by servile minds, or the contempt which is assumed along with a pretence to superior wisdom; but if we first love the world, we shall find neither time nor ability to devote our thoughts to the author of it; and, however faithful our service may be, we must still look to the world for our reward, and to a jealous God for our punishment.

"Let me warn you, my dear friend, against too great a sacrifice for the sake of pleasing. It is an amiable desire which leads you on, but you must have learned by this time the utter impossibility of gratifying all the wishes of all your friends; and there is an economy of time and thought which is necessary in order that we may husband our powers for more useful purposes. Nothing can look more like virtue at first sight, than to spend all your time, your thoughts and talents, in the service of others; but may not these valuable faculties and possessions be frittered away in things of very trifling importance, when they might, with just the same degree of kind and generous feeling, be more beneficially employed?"

The evening was now growing late, and, as hour after hour passed on, Helen became more grave and silent, until her cheerfulness entirely gave way, and she could speak on no theme but one.

"My friend," said she, "you are with me now for the first time in my hour of weakness —the midnight hour—when my brother has not returned!"

She was pacing to and fro in her narrow apartment, and I had no consolation to offer, except a few empty words of hope that he would soon be here.

"He will, I doubt not," she answered— "but how?"

I had never beheld him except as a man of dignity and refinement, and was unable to picture him, even to my imagination, in any other character.

"We are all that are left of a fallen family," she went on, "the last of a blighted name; but this would be nothing if my poor brother could but lay down his head at night with the blessing of Heaven upon his slumbers.

The midnight hour was now passed, and Helen was still pacing to and fro with weary and irregular steps. Her hollow cheeks had grown more pale and haggard, from the want of natural repose; and her dark eyes more bright and flashing, with the fever burning in her veins. Her long raven locks had been thrown back from her forehead, as if to lighten the burden of her brain; and it might be with a slight touch of impatience, arising from her disorder, and the many, many times she had paced the floor at the same hour of night, when no eye was upon her save that which seeth in darkness as at noon-day.

Oh! were it possible for man to penetrate the recesses of woman's heart, to know all her fervent love, her deep anxiety, her burning hopes, her aching fears, her devotedness, her zeal, her forgetfulness of self, he would surely sometimes tear himself away from that fellowship which is not of the heart, to mitigate her anguish, and snatch her from a premature but lingering death!

The brother of this incomparable woman came at last—and how? We heard the tread of many feet, and one rude laugh, before the bell was wrung with a violence that made us start; for Helen had been so careful that all the inmates of the house should be asleep, and unconscious of what might pass, that we had spoken softly and seldom for the last hour. She now took up the lamp in silence, and beckoned me to follow. I did so, and received it from her hand when we had reached the door, which she unbolted as quickly, and with as little noise as possible. I had seen her a few moments before, languid, weary, and almost helpless as a child; but she now stood in a commanding attitude before the jovial crew, who controlled their boisterous mirth at her presence, while she received her brother, reeling from their arms, steadied him along the passage, and up stairs, without a word, except to tell me to bar the door and remain below; and if my sister should call, to go quietly, without waiting to see her again.

Awed into obedience by her firmness, dignity, and self-possession, I did as she directed; but when all again was silent and secure, I lost my presence of mind, and throwing myself upon a couch, gave way to the natural horror occasioned by the spectacle I had just witnessed of the man I most admired and loved—lost, degraded and brutalized.

The woman who continues to love the man whom she has seen intoxicated, proves, beyond a doubt, one of these two facts—either that she has no true sense of what constitutes the dignity of the human mind, or that her love is love indeed.

It was not long before Helen returned, still pale; but now that her faint hopes were over, and she had nothing more to fear, calm, patient and resigned, with the active assiduity of an affectionate nurse, she stirred the fire, and made ready some refreshment, as if he for whom she prepared it was worthy of her tenderest care; nor was I forgotten in her solicitude for him. While waiting for the boiling of the water, she turned towards me, and holding out her hand—"My poor friend,"—she was beginning to say,—but we both knew it was no time for words; and the next moment I felt her tears upon my cheek.

"When will you be able to find rest for yourself?" said I.

She smiled, but made me no answer.

"Dear Helen, you cannot drag on life in this manner."

"I have existed in this manner for two years," said she; "you see I have a great deal of strength left;" and so saying, she took up the coffee, and smiled as she passed me, with such a look of love and pity as I imagine ministering angels wear, when they go forth upon their errands of mercy.

Soon after this I heard the sound of carriage wheels, and, in a few moments, was listening to my sister and my cousin, relating the various amusements, literary and intellectual of the past evening. "How differently the same evening may be spent!" thought I, and was silent.

Had the brother of my friend been a man of generally depraved conduct, or dissolute manners, the fatal spell which bound me to him could never have existed, or must have been broken on the first discovery that such was his real character. But he was at this time the victim of one vice only, into which he plunged in a sort of desperation, brought on by his altered circumstances, and his want of right principle to bear them with fortitude; and this vice had not yet been long enough in operation to produce the natural and inevitable consequence of vitiating the whole heart, of extinguishing every hope, and expelling every laudable desire. He had his seasons of penitence, of which I was not unfrequently a witness;—his visitations of agony and remorse, in which he would appeal to his sister and to me for that encouragement which I, at least, was unable to offer. But Helen had looked upon the vicissitudes of life with a deeper sense of the merciful dealings of providence than I had. As we journeyed through the wilderness together, she was to me like a blessed messenger, who brought tidings of wells of water when I was faint and despairing.

"You see," she would often say, "my brother has not yet lost his love of virtue. To you I need not point out the delicacy and tenderness of his regard for those whom he is able to respect."

"While this remains," I replied, "there is hope."

"There is hope to the very last," she answered. "There was hope for the thief upon the cross, when he appealed to the crucified Jesus; and there is hope for the sinner in his dying hour. I own my spirit faints within me at every fresh instance of ingratitude and alienation of the heart from God; but I know that he continues to be merciful, and that when we are weak and powerless to assist each other, he has often his own wise and gracious means, inscrutable to the understanding of man, by which he calls back ms wandering sheep, and appoints his servants at the eleventh hour."

With this melancholy attachment, kept alive by alternate hope and fear, still praying upon my heart, I dragged on a comfortless existence; but so great was my proficiency in the art of managing my countenance, my voice, and my whole demeanour, that I could still laugh with the merry, sigh with the sad, argue with the contentious, sentimentalize with the poetical, reason with the profound, and trifle with the gay; indeed I could accomplish all the business of life (for of mine this was the business) without betraying the real state of my heart and affection. There was one thing, however, I could not do—I could not sit down with a confidential friend, and talk over in perfect openness and freedom, some of the topics which had been wont to interest me most. Here I was at fault; and consequently some of my friends thought me less agreeable than formerly; and no wonder; for to be generally pleasing in society, it is necessary that the heart should be free from absorbing care; and what cause can be so productive of care, perplexity, and distraction of thought, as an unfortunate and ill placed attachment?

Oh! guard against this enemy, my young friends, as you would against one that is able to destroy the happiness of the soul, both here and hereafter; and let your defence be a rightly governed mind, and your protection the overshadowing love of your heavenly Father; for this enemy is one which sometimes comes in the morning of life, like a scathing wind upon the blossoms of spring; and the mind that was just putting forth in hope and gladness, shrinks back, and contracts within the narrow precints of despair—becomes fettered with heavy bonds, that cannot be broken, and laden with a weight that no after circumstance can remove. It may seem childish or romantic to dwell thus upon the continuance of a passion, proverbial for its lightness and buoyancy; but there are hearts from which, though the cause may be forgotten, its melancholy effects will never be effaced.

As I was one day sitting under the dispensation of a long story, told for the twentieth time by an old foxhunter, a note from Helen Grahame was put into my hand. I affected to receive it with perfect indifference, and folded it in my fingers, with my head turned towards the sapient narrator for full five minutes longer. At last, after helping him to laugh, as I had often done before, at what he called a capital joke put upon the village schoolmaster, I took an opportunity of escaping, and opening the note in my own chamber, read as follows:

"Come to me as soon as possible, and bring a physician with you, for my brother is dangerously ill."

A slight line was drawn through this, and another sentence hastily added:—Come alone: the physician must not find you here."

With trembling steps I hurried on to see my friend, and share in her anxiety, however deep its cause might be. I found her watching beside her brother, whose flushed countenance, burning hand, and wandering eye, bespoke an alarming state of irritation. A dangerous fever was pronounced to be his malady; and all the little consolation I enjoyed, and which Helen was too generous to deny me, was that of providing, out of the liberal allowance with which my father indulged his children, those comforts and necessaries that would otherwise have been beyond the reach of my poor friend.

"I am not so ignorant of the nature of true affection," she said, "as to deny you this gratification; especially as my own recources, depending upon my daily labours, are now cut off. I once enjoyed the happiness of giving; and from what I remember of it, I know that you are more blest than I in receiving."

The fear of exciting suspicion prevented

my being often present with Helen in her distress, but my thoughts were with her always in that little darkened chamber, while my tears and prayers upon my sleepless pillow bore witness alone to the agony that wrung my heart. Prayers, such as I had never breathed before, seemed now the only language in which I could unburden my griefs; and while comparatively reckless of my own eternal safety, I entreated for one who was now unable to ask for himself, that he might be restored to life—to life,—indeed, to all that constitutes the vitality of our existence;—to "the means of grace, and to the hope of glory."

"I prayed (for I was not naturally selfish) that this might be accomplished, even if I myself were struck out of the account, and if it should be effected without any instrumentality or participation of mine.

Well may it be said of the human heart, that it is deceitful above all things, when it can deceive us even in prayer. I thought, at the time, that I should not only be satisfied, but happy, if my prayer was granted. I was tried, and the weight of my disinterested zeal found wanting.

In the course of a few weeks my friend was restored to peace of mind, and her brother to the full possession of his mental powers, though still much reduced and enfeebled. Helen told me almost in an ecstacy of joy, that he had often requested her to read particular passages from the Bible to him during his illness. She had sometimes feared this might be only the wandering of delirium; but we both now observed that his conversation, though he spoke seldom, was much altered.

I was left alone with him for a short time one evening, when he addressed me very seriously, requesting that I would not question him as to the state of his mind and feelings.

"I cannot bear it now," he added. "I have passed through a great deal besides the agony of disease; and I would not willingly have my thoughts interrupted."

My friend and I now rejoiced in secret and alone, and the gratitude with which I returned thanks to the Giver of all good, the Reclaimer of the wandering, the Redeemer of the lost, filled my heart with a happiness as new, as it was perfect in its mastery over all my former doubts and fears. In the wide field of minute and trifling things, where women, and women only, find food for sweet and bitter fancy, we ranged together, culling the flowers, and expatiating on the sweets, of the enjoyment of which we fondly imagined that nothing could now deprive us.

CHAPTER VII.

Grahame was restored to health, and to a better government of his mind and conduct. I still continued my short but frequent visits; for debility, and the want of any useful employment, with a distaste for the company of his former associates, kept him a close prisoner: I therefore made sure of finding him—and finding him all that I could desire he should be. Was it so? Alas! while the cup of joy which my friend partook of was filled without alloy, there were certain drops of bitterness in mine, which I could neither describe to another, nor reconcile to myself. While the feelings of Grahame towards his sister were animated with fresh warmth and gratitude, there was something in his behaviour, imperceptible it might be to one who did not love, but oh! how changed to me! It might be nothing more than an alteration in the cadence of the voice, every tone of which had established in my heart its own distinct and peculiar echo; or the averted eye, which told too plainly, what no one else could understand—the chain of sympathy broken, and broken for ever. But I had nothing to complain of. I could not tell the friend of my soul that her brother's voice was changed, and that he did not look at me as he was wont: nor was the change so marked as to entitle me to ask for an explanation.

There was nothing I could do but pity myself, and be silent.

It was not long before my friend told me that her brother's altered views had stimulated him to seek some regular employment, by which he might become a more useful member of society. I thought he might have first mentioned this to me; and when I found that my father was the person he had chosen to consult respecting his future proceedings, I felt doubly pained at being thus completely excluded from his confidence. Still as there never had existed between us any kind of engagement, beyond what was implied in a mutual acknowledgement of regard, I could not, in common delicacy, demand what I had never before doubted was my right.

My father communicated to my sister and myself together the first intelligence I heard, that he had agreed to find employment for Grahame in the bank; "for," said he, (and I inwardly blessed him for the words) "I firmly believe him to be an altered man; and his talents for business, if he will but use them, no one can doubt."

I felt my face beginning to tell its burning secret, but I had a ready way of extricating myself from all such emergencies; and after tying up a drooping rose, which had suddenly attracted my attention in the adjoining green-house, I returned when my cheeks were cooler, and assured my father that Helen Grahame's description of her brother was so favourable, that I did not think those who trusted him now would find him unworthy.

"I wish it may be so," observed my cousin Jane. "I should be very careful how I trusted him."

My sister spoke more kindly, and begged my father, if he thought it would be any support to his better resolutions, to extend his confidence so far as sometimes to invite him to the house.

My hand trembled as I gathered up another rose, and I almost forgot the cloud which had lately overshadowed me, in the happiness of this moment.

The altered character of Grahame justifying the confidence of my father and the hopes of my sister, he was admitted occasionally into our family circle on terms of social intercourse. At first, I felt solicitous to conceal the degree of intimacy which had once been ours; but my apprehensions of detection were quieted in the manner I should last have desired. Had any thing of this nature been betrayed, it would have been on my part only; and I must have been miserably deficient in female delicacy and tact, had I not been willing also to forget what no longer appeared worthy of being remembered.

Once, and once only, was the subject alluded to between us. I had completed a gift, which he had himself asked of me, in days which I will not call happier, but in days when I believe I was less wretched. This gift I presented to him one day, when we were alone. He received it, I thought, with some emotion; and, addressing me once more by my name, (that sound so full of meaning,) "Caroline," said he, "I am unworthy of this. My love has been shaken by a tempest. If it has now neither leaves, nor flowers, nor fruit to offer you, blame me not. I owe you much, and I feel that I am not ungrateful."

"Name it not," said I. "To see you changed in heart and conduct is all I ever asked as my reward. Continue thus, and I shall be"—the happiest of women, I would have said—but my heroism forsook me, and I turned away to hide my tears.

"Caroline," said he, and he laid his hand upon my arm for the last time, with a look which owed its tenderness to pity—"amongst the heavy burdens which have lately rested on my conscience, is the stern duty of telling you —"

"Say no more," said I.

"Thank you, for wishing to spare me."

"It was myself I wished to spare," I added; and he paused for a moment.

"You need not tell me, Grahame, that you love me no longer. It is sufficiently evident to one who can think and feel."

"But I must tell you the cause. With the change of my heart, my views of moral excellence are changed; and, while I no longer admire that generosity and kindness which owe their existence to the impulse of the moment, I feel that I can love only where there is consistency of character, and stability of principle."

How strange is the capability of the human mind for receiving impressions from what does not appear at the time to strike the attention. It must be, that the faculty of perception is quickened anew by the touch of some vital part, or that the flood-gates of the mind, thrown open by one tremendous burst, loose particles and broken fragments are borne in along with the impetuous current. Whatever the philosophy of this mental phenomenon may be, I can remember even now, the day, the hour, the state of the atmosphere, when these words were spoken—the room, the pictures, the furniture within—the flowers, the birds, the sunshine without. And yet, so absorbing was the theme to which the words related, that I stood fixed to the spot like a statue, long after the speaker had departed, and left me alone—alone, indeed! for I was lost in a grief that admitted no fellowship—a grief, under which, even had it been possible to find, I could not have sought, communion—a grief which I neither looked for consolation to soothe, nor anguish to embitter—a grief "sufficing unto itself in its terrible individuality." This was the man for whom I had prayed, and wept, and suffered. My supplications had been that his heart might be changed: his heart was changed, and I had no right to complain.

In my desire to administer comforts and indulgences to one who had enjoyed, in early life, a more than common share, I had practised a degree of economy, at variance with my usual habits; and when idle comments were made upon my lately acquired propensity to spare every unnecessary expense, I felt a secret exultation burning in my cheeks, and lighting up my eye with more happiness than I could have derived from any merely selfish gratification. But this secret spring of enjoyment was destined to be dried up, like many others with which I had been wont to refresh myself in the wilderness of life. Grahame could now economize; and he, too, had his hidden purpose, for which he toiled and hoarded. A calculation as accurate as could be made, of all that I had spent upon him was entered into, at his desire, by his sister, and the supposed amount laid before me in genuine and current coin. I resisted with all the spirit that was left me, and denied the correctness of the sum—but all in vain. There was something cool and imperative in his manner, that awed me into obedience, and I received the money with that sickness of soul which attends most frequently upon its resignation. Nothing, however, could have induced me to spend this sum upon myself. It was hid in a secret receptacle, where it might have remained until this day, had not an opportunity occurred of sending it forth through a more worthy channel.

The health of Helen Grahame was failing rapidly; and when the summer came with its wonted respite from the toils of education, it appeared highly necessary that some plan should be adopted, to restore her wasted powers, and enable her to renew her accustomed labours. Her thoughts were so far removed from all false delicacy and paltry pride, that she could accept a kindness with the grace and dignity of one who gives; and when I pressed upon her the advice of her physician, and my own scheme for removing her to the south of England, she answered me with tears of gratitude, as she would wish to be answered in similar circumstances herself.

"It was once," she said, "the happiness of my life to be generous and bountiful. It is now my part to receive; and I thank my God that I have one friend, who is both able and willing to assist me. We are dependent creatures, bound to each other by innumerable obligations, which constitute the strength and durability of social fellowship. It may appear to those who think superficially, more noble to be above receiving assistance; but, were all too proud to receive, the duty of giving freely and cheerfully would find no room to operate; and if none were willing to be helped, how should we exercise the Christian graces of kindness and charity? I have struggled hard that I might not cumber the ground, nor encroach upon the bounty of others. Were it probable that you would ever feel the want of what is now ministering to my necessities, believe me, I would rather die than prolong my life, at the expense of injuring you: but you tell me, and I cannot doubt your word, that you are well able to assist me; and I will not deny you the happiness of binding up the broken reed."

My kind father, ever too indulgent to his children, and not averse to my project, added more than was sufficient to my hoarded store; and if, when I set off with my precious charge to the southern coast, the pulsation of my heart was not in tune with perfect happiness, the fault was not in my friend, nor in the animating sense of satisfaction which attends upon our kindest and most disinterested actions. Often, as we proceeded slowly on our journey, was the countenance of that friend turned towards me with looks of inexpressible tenderness, while she pressed my hand, but spoke not; for there was even between us one subject, one of intense and mutual interest, now seemingly forbidden. I, at least, could find no words sufficient for my feelings, and Helen struggled long with hers, before she could convey an idea of them to me. Nor was it possible, even then, that her sympathy could be equal to my need. Hers was a gentle spirit, heavenward bound, passing through the vale of tears, with no desire but to point out the celestial city to other wanderers by the way, and to gather in the nearest and dearest beneath the shelter of the sacred walls. I was a dweller in the wilderness, lighting up my lone cave, spreading forth my store, and preparing rest for the weary traveller: but the traveller had passed on, and the desert was more dreary, the cave more lonely than before. I knew that he had gone forth to seek a "better land," and that all who seek may find; yet was I unable to bless his parting footsteps, for I was left behind. No! it was impossible that Helen Grahame should wholly sympathize with me. Those who live for heaven cannot feel with those who live for earth.

I, who had prayed that the wanderer might be reclaimed in any way, on any terms, and had added in the fervour of the moment, even without my instrumentality or participation, now found that my prayer was granted, and acknowledged that I was not happy. Yes, I was almost happy, when I felt the play of the gentle breezes, and met the pleased and animated look of my friend after the first view of the wide ocean had burst upon us, as we descended into a peaceful valley, where the green slopes and the rich luxuriance of foliage, bespoke a mild and genial atmosphere, such as the wasted and the weary delight to breathe.

We were not long in fixing upon a low myrtle-wreathed cottage for our temporary residence, where, if the roses were not fair to me, the woodbine lovely, and the jessamine sweet, they were all I could desire for Helen. In her enjoyment I sought and found my own, and so well was I versed in the art of appearing what I was not, that this excellent and guileless creature knew little of the sadness with which I sometimes looked around upon that world of nature, where her purer eye beheld enough of beauty, glory, and magnificence, to fill the anthems of celestial praise, and inspire with undying melody the harps of the archangels.

After my friend had retired to rest, came my hour of melancholy, when no eye was upon me but that of the great Father of the universe, whom I was not serving: when no step was near, and yet I marked in the wide expanse before me the foot-prints of a God, at whose shrine I was not offering up my heart: when the blue skies, the shining stars, and the silent vault of Heaven were above me, and I was not bowing before the majesty of their creator, nor acknowledging his empire in my soul.

For a short time, the invalid revived, and

we spoke of the future, as those converse who expect to share a long life together; but this transient hope soon failed us, and I was at a loss how to carry on our conversation beyond the present hour. Helen assisted me; for death was no new subject of contemplation to her, and whether she spoke of this world or the next, her heart was full of hope and trust.

We were seated together one sunny morning, with the door of our cottage thrown open to admit the refreshing breezes that waved the light sprigs of jessamine, and mingled its perfume with the clustering rose, when Helen asked me if I did not wonder at her apparent indifference about her worldly concerns.

"You see me here," said she, "almost pennyless, my strength failing, and the time fast approaching, when, unless something unexpected should occur, I must return to arduous duties, which I am rapidly becoming less able to perform."

I replied, it was, indeed, a most perplexing situation.

"And yet I do not fear," she continued. "There is sometimes a veil mercifully drawn over what we are unable to look upon. I pretend to no prophetic vision; but have we not heard of instances in which the mother has been permitted to forget her child, so that the thought of its orphan helplessness did not imbitter her dying hour? Is it not the same merciful hand that is now closing my eyes to the mysterious future, in order that I may trust more entirely to my Heavenly Father. My friend," she continued, stretching out to me her emaciated hand, "you who have supplied to me all the tender offices of a sister,—I know not whether the happy hours we have lately spent together are ordained to be the last and the sweetest; but as I have always wished to be a faithful monitress to you, so now I would leave, if we must indeed be torn asunder, my parting charge upon your heart. Endeavour to live more to yourself, or rather, more to your God; and while, as a practical Christian, you neglect none of the duties enjoined us towards our fellow-creatures, hold yourself more separate from the world. Your hour of trial has not yet come, and, oh! that it never may! I have no quarrel with the world, nor would complain of its unkindness; but as a master, it is a cruel tyrant, and its service wretched slavery."

My friend paused, after uttering these words, and we both looked out in silence towards the blue sea, where a few white sails were passing to and fro, and the waves just ruffled by the summer gale, fell upon the shore with a distant and monotonous sound.

Our musings were interrupted by the rapid approach of a well known step. In an instant, Grahame stood before us, and unconscious of the critical stage of his sister's malady, gave utterance at once to the glad tidings he had brought.

"Helen," he exclaimed, "I am an independent man! I can now repay your kindness. My uncle in Scotland is dead, and I am proved to be his heir. My own Helen, let me hear you say how happy we shall once more be together."

Helen had started from her seat, on the first appearance of her brother. Her hands and eyes were raised to Heaven, and one burst of gratitude had passed her lips, when a sudden flush of crimson rushed into her cheeks, spreading with a rapid and burning glow over her temples and forehead, while she sunk back, supported only by her brother's arms. For one moment, her countenance was lighted up with a faint smile. It was the last effort of expiring nature, and my first, my only friend, was no more.

She was buried in a quiet church-yard in that sequestered valley, where the early blighted, the feeble, and the failing, still resort; but where the genial airs too often sought in vain, visit none more lovely, or more worthy to be loved. We left her lowly grave to the solitude of that woodland scene to the sprinkling of wild flowers, the song of summer birds, and the unceasing murmur of the ocean waves. We left her grave, where we had wept together, and returned again to the busy and tumultuous world.

There was nothing on the journey to cheer or revive my drooping spirits. Grahame neither sought, nor offered consolation. He was deeply affected—perhaps, too deeply, to think of me; for had there not occurred one short interval of notice, the nature of which rendered it infinitely worse than none, I should scarcely have supposed him to be conscious of my presence. We were pursuing our melancholy way in silence, when he suddenly addressed me in a very serious manner on the subject of economy, a prelude which introduced once more the return of the sum of money I had expended upon my lost friend. In vain I attempted to remonstrate; I could not find one word to express my sense of the cruelty of denying me this last poor consolation. The money was placed in my hand, and I grasped it unconsciously, without once glancing at the sum, while he went on, hinting at the need I might one day feel of that bounty which I bestowed too profusely. His words conveyed no meaning to my ear at the time; I only felt that he spoke daggers; but after circumstances convinced me that he was acting the friendly part of preparing me for a calamity which he had good cause to apprehend. This short communication over, we fell again into our former silence. I wept, but my tears were not all for the departed; and in this unsocial manner, the journey was completed. Weary and dispirited, leaning on an arm that supported me because I was a necessary burden, I reached my father's door. The night was far advanced, but all seemed bustle and unsettlement within.

"Have you had company?" I asked.

"No," was the ready reply of my cousin Jane, accompanied with a look of meaning, which, exhausted as I was, I longed to understand. More assiduous than usual in her attentions, she followed me to my own chamber, where my sister was waiting to receive me, and her embrace being also more warm than usual, I felt certain that some influence was at work, with which I was unacquainted. Some secret spring of excitement had evidently been opened—of excitement that was not altogether joy, for there were traces of recent tears, which, when I asked for my father, flowed afresh.

"What is the matter?" said I. "What can have happened amongst you? I see both smiles and tears. Tell me, that I may share in one or both."

The mystery was soon unravelled. My father's affairs had, for some time, been advancing towards a fearful crisis. Grahame had made this discovery, and, unable to extricate or assist him, had done what he could, in the way of lightening his burdens, by offering his hand to my sister, for whom he had lately entertained the highest admiration. This intelligence was communicated to me; and the latter part of it, as if I were altogether unconcerned, and would, of course, rejoice in my sister's good fortune; for the death of Grahame's uncle, added to his own continued stability of conduct, rendered the match in every way desirable. Did I rejoice? Ask those who have striven, from the cradle to the grave, to divest their hearts of selfishness, to inure themselves to torture, and to live only on the happiness of others—ask them whether the natural glow of human feeling is ever totally extinguished—and you will be able to imagine whether I could rejoice.

After adding to the intelligence, which I thought sufficient already, that, in anticipation of the sudden winding-up of my father's affairs, it had been concluded to fix the following day for my sister's marriage, I was left alone, with many kind wishes that I might sleep well, and arise refreshed from the fatigues of my journey.

The vulgar adage, that "misfortunes never come singly," has often given rise to thankfulness in my heart, that thus we are spared a degree of suffering which might otherwise be intolerable. It is impossible to feel, with equal poignancy, two calamities at once; and, consequently, while two strokes fell upon me, I endured only the agony of one.

The wedding-day passed over as such things usually do. My father appeared at breakfast in the morning, hurried over his part of the ceremony, and often turned, when he felt that enquiring eyes were upon him. My dresses had been prepared for me; and I acted my automaton part, without any clear perception of what was passing. I was to accompany my sister as her bride's-maid; and, when I begged to be allowed to remain with my father, was told, that my aunt and cousin were much more fitting helps, and that my duty was to support my sister, and sustain her spirits. "And who is to support me?" said I, in the bitterness of my heart; but I neither resisted, nor complained; and the bridal party set off (the newspapers said, in high glee) for a tour on the continent.

CHAPTER VIII.

During my six months' residence on the continent, dark passages in the annals of our family occurred. The alteration in my father's circumstances, the falling away of trusted friends, and the dishonour thrown upon his name, were calamities which he met with apparent fortitude, but at the expense of his life. Beneath the skies of Italy, this melancholy event was communicated to his children, who were then too distant to return, with any hope of being able to perform the last sad duties of affection: nor was it, until wearied with our continental rambles, and wishing for more settled habits, that we bid adieu to the shores of France, and sailed for our native country; where a home, supplied with all the comforts, and embellished with many of the elegances of life, was prepared for our reception—a home that was no home to me; for there is something in dependence upon others, in being an useless attachment to a family of which you are not by right a member, which drives the heart out of doors, however comfortably the person may be provided for. During the season of visiting and receiving visitors, I was, however, very much at ease on the score of usefulness, for the entertainment of promiscuous guests was decidedly my sphere of excellence. My sister felt this and valued me accordingly; for, whenever I forgot my duty, grew silent, and fell back by a sudden transition of thought into the aching void of my own bosom, I was reprimanded, stirred up, and requested to be more entertaining, until my situation sometimes reminded me of that of the caged inhabitant of the wilds, when poked out and made to roar and play tricks for the edification of the insatiate mob.

My powers of pleasing, seldom exercised in vain, again obtained for me that popularity I had once enjoyed, and with it those racking demands upon my time and talents which had frittered them away before. If less interested than formerly in the business of making friends, I was, perhaps, more patient and complying, from a painful and humiliating sense of my altered and helpless situation: and thus with the increase of my intimate associates, my expenses were increased also; for there were tender-hearted creatures who wept at parting, and would not be pacified without a promise of correspondence; young gentlemen who did everything but offer me their hands, and, amongst the rest, wrote for a letter of advice every week, protesting that I was the only person who had power to influence their lives; besides the whole community to supply with keepsakes, tokens of affection, and what not. Resources I had none, and my brother's liberality was the last I would willingly have encroached upon; so that notwithstanding the comforts of his home, which I was often pressed to regard as my own, I lost all fortitude to behold my three letters every morning, to draw upon him for the constant hire of carriages and other expenses attendant upon the social life I was leading, and determined to seek a residence where I could economise and live more privately.

I had, or believed I had, innumerable friends, and I now resolved to favour them with some of those long visits which they had so often solicited. What I am about to relate of these friends may appear to militate against that benevolence and good-will which long experience has taught me to believe does really exist amongst mankind, and which it would be both unjust and ungrateful in me to attach with doubt or suspicion. It is my firm conviction that a great deal of personal kindness may be found in the world, and those who complain of the contrary have, surely, never looked for it in a right spirit. For my own part I have little doubt that more than one family would willingly have taken upon themselves the entire charge of my maintenance, that many would have freely ministered to my necessities, out of their own means, that all were kinder to me than I deserved, and that the distressing circumstances in which I was involved, were not owing so much to any fault of theirs as to my own mistaken views of human life, and that which ought to be our chief object in journeying through it.

One of the greatest inconveniences arising from a multitude of friends, is that of being the recipient of advice from them all; so that a soul of adamant alone can remain unshaken in its determination, while subject to the influence of opinions so various and contending. On the present occasion, as well as on all others, in which I was called upon to act, my friends poured in upon my attention their different sentiments respecting the steps I was about to take. I listened, consulted, and listened again. Each night undid what the day had done, and the comments of the morning undermined the convictions of the night. But there were moving springs within my own heart, which my friends were unable to take into account. Independently of pecuniary considerations, there were melancholy associations attached to my sister's home, which I should have been sorry, had any one possessed the penetration to discover.

That woman must have an undisciplined mind, indeed, who can harbour for the husband of another, one thought that militates against her happiness; but I own, I could not contemplate the domestic scene at my sister's fire-side, without being made doubly sensible of my own forlorn and unprotected situation. I could not feel that Grahame was my brother. I could not attain the art which the Greek philosopher esteemed more highly than that of memory—the art of forgetting.

People reason superficially, when they talk about the prudence or imprudence of our actions. They see the surface only, and know not what lies beneath, which we, who have been plunged into deep waters, may be struggling to escape from. They perceive not the bright vision in the distance, which lures us on—they feel not the thorns under our feet, nor know the hidden snares of a path where flowers have been scattered.

With a heavy heart, I left my sister, to try my fortune on the precarious footing of that affection which had risen up, and been nurtured under the sun of prosperity. My first attempt was made upon the heart of a very early friend, to whom I had written, stating the pleasure I intended doing myself and her. She received me with kindness, it is true, but wishing to be quite candid, told me, when it was too late, that I had fixed upon the very time when she was unavoidably most engaged. However, she would make no stranger of me. I begged she would not, and assured her, I had no objection to be left alone.

This lady was a rigid disciplinarian; I believe a good woman, but certainly one who would never heal a broken heart. Her pleasure, (I will not say her pride,) was in rectifying abuses, dragging hidden things to light, and making the world go her own way. I had thought her severe even when we shared the gladsome days of girlish glee together; but an unusually plain person, and forbidding manners having repelled many of her associates, her temper had become soured by the absence of those mutual kind offices which sweeten life, and soften down its rugged passages.

Miss Sharpe was sparing in all personal indulgences, and strenuously recommended others to be the same; a piece of advice which she assisted them to adopt by excluding all temptations from her domestic establishment. Still she was kind; and, in the midst of her hard fare and home-dealing, would press upon me the welcome of the heart, and urge my remaining with her, for reasons peculiar to herself; because she had great hopes of being able to do me good, by beating off all the superfluities of my character, and reducing me to the measure of that narrow space, which she took good care I should not forget was allotted to me in the creation.

I have often thought the power of sympathy extended far beyond the opportunity of expressing it, else why that mysterious attraction between individuals who know little of each other's real character. Even within the guarded circle of Miss Sharpe's associates I found some to whom I could confide my thoughts, and many more who trusted theirs to me; but in these moments of social intercourse I was watched with such a scrutinizing eye, that the pleasure was hardly worth the price paid for it;—I sometimes talked too much, at other times too little, always said something that would have been better unsaid; and so invariably acted unbecomingly, that I was tempted to call in question the real regard of my friend, for one whose conduct and manners afforded her so little satisfaction. I was then told it was wounded vanity that made me doubt her affection; that I had lived so much on flattery I could not bear to hear the truth, and that my friend had always thought me exceedingly vain. I could not but wonder why this wholesome intelligence had never been communicated to me before. Alas! the season of adversity is too often made choice of for the telling of home truths, and the correction of faults that were willingly borne with in our prosperous days. How is it that the world performs so much more faithfully its stern duties to the poor than to the rich? That those who have not one worldly wish ungratified, feel themselves called upon to preach patience and humility to the fallen, while they fail to whisper a word of censure to those who are above them? Would not a slight effort of moral courage sometimes turn the bitter and unwelcome tide into channels where it is more needed?—a slight touch of Christian charity withdraw it from the low places already deluged by the waters of affliction?

Although Miss Sharpe professed to love candour above every thing, I observed that few people were candid with her; and therefore determined to try the experiment of returning the compliment. It was always painful to me to dwell upon the failings of my friends, either to themselves or to others; so I ventured warily, and with great delicacy, to hint at the beauty of gentleness of manners; but no sooner was the hint understood, than a storm burst forth for which I was little prepared, and, in the rage of the moment, harsh things were said that would have driven a spirit, even more subdued than mine, to seek shelter elsewhere. I believe my friend was sorry afterwards that she had compelled me to leave her before the work of reformation was completed. I have no doubt that her endeavours were kindly intended to promote my good, but her remedies were too severe for my constitution, and I left her with the conviction more than ever impressed upon my mind, that it is impossible to love those who will not let us have a single fault—just as impossible as to thank the doctor who declares his determination to follow up the application of probe, caustic, and bitter draught, until every constitutional malady, even the lameness with which we were born, shall be removed.

My next experiment was made upon a safer, though less rocky foundation. Mrs. Frank Burton was a lady whom I had formerly known as a lively, handsome, and almost fascinating country belle; with bright black hair, dark eyes, round face, and never fading bloom. She had been a celebrated horsewoman, a loud random talker, and something of a coquette; and I felt a good deal of curiosity to know what sort of figure she would make when adorned with matronly honours. There was but one kind of character which Mrs. Burton could be—a saucy affectionate wife, a foolishly indulgent mother, and a warm-hearted, active, bustling, hospitable, mistress of a house. Her easy doating husband, well satisfied to have secured a treasure for which so many sighed in vain, smiled with ineffable complacency at her boisterous volubility, and would hardly have purchased the entire possession, either of his dignity or his repose, with the sacrifice of her pretty pets, and becoming frowns, which he well knew would soon give place to smiles more lovely, and endearments more winning.

Mrs. Burton was not the woman to wait until her guest had been shown up stairs before she yielded to the impulse of hospitality. The farthest gate between two prodigious jaw bones at the extremity of an avenue of poplars was thrown open, the groom was in readiness for the horse, and the master and mistress both stood upon the step before the door, smiling their hearty welcome; while alternately wrapped in the wide folds of the matron's skirts, or peeping past her apron, where three little merry looking creatures with cherry cheeks, and pouting lips for ever moistened by the honey dew of their mother's confectionary. My friend received me with an embrace so warm and cordial, that I trembled for the derangement of her yellow head-dress, and the profusion of laces and ribbons freshly distributed over her stout and comely person. But I soon found she was used to this kind of thing, and would care little for the destruction of her best wreath of red roses, if the work of mischief were but wrought by an impulse of affection; nor was she so far removed from the stage of infancy, but that a kind kiss would alleviate, if it did not entirely remove all her grievances, and make peace for the most daring offender.

I was soon asked into a spacious and handsome dining-room, where two or three lazy pointers were kicked up from the hearth rug, and an old favourite cat encouraged to remain. Here a hundred kind questions were asked me, which I was not allowed time to answer, wine and the richest of all rich cakes pressed upon me, and the dear baby sent for to see the lady, and try whether he would be quiet in her arms! but this experiment proving decidedly to the disadvantage of the little rebel, he was snatched away, and I was then hurried up stairs, where innumerable empty drawers, closets, and shelves were exposed for my accommodation, and other preparations for a long visit, made sufficiently apparent to destroy all doubts, could any have existed, of the reality of my welcome; and a long visit I inwardly determined it should be when my kind hostess had left me, and I looked out upon the park-like green before the house, where dogs and children gambolled in unconstrained enjoyment. On turning round, my senses were forcibly saluted by that which proved to be an omen of good things to come. Such a dinner! none but stout gentlemen with white napkins tucked into their button-holes, should sit down to such a meal as was spread before us every day at one o'clock. The afternoon was the thing we did not know what to do with: for Mrs. Burton having enforced by example as well as precept, the necessity of tasting every dish, was neither so lively nor so good humoured, as in the earlier part of the day; and consequently the children were very naughty children indeed. One had to be chastised, another forbid to play, and the frequent slaps, scoldings, and natural explosions of juvenile rebellion, drove the quiet husband out of doors, a circumstance which neither added to, nor took away from our enjoyment.

After such fatiguing afternoons, an early tea was generally thought the most desirable consummation, and then the board was again covered with such a profusion of sweets, niceties, relishes, and temptations to eat, that I could but wonder how the children, whose inordinate demands it wonld have been deemed the height of cruelty to refuse, could possibly retain their glowing cheeks and fine healthy complexion; but constant exercise in the open air is a wonder-working power, and these little revellers rushed forth again into the garden, the orchard, and the fields, determined to wander far and wide from home, because they knew the hour would not be long in coming, when they would be severally hunted, caught, and put to bed, he who was the best runner, last of course.

It was with regret I discovered, even on the first day of my visit, that Mrs. Burton was not a woman to sit down with on the stillness of evening. I had calculated upon reading a great deal to beguile the monotony of my life in the country, and for this purpose, had brought my own books, not expecting much from the library of Mr. Frank Burton: but my friend so often interrupted me with exclamations foreign to the subject, was so exceedingly inattentive when I read aloud, and yawned so desperately when I was silent for ten minutes, that I found even here, where one would have almost felt at liberty to do or to be any thing, it was necessary I should set aside my own gratification and endeavour to be more generally agreeable. Mrs. Burton, with all her kindness, was a plain spoken woman, and scrupled not to tell me she was disappointed that I did not let her more into what had been going on in the world since we parted. "Tell me," said she, "some droll stories about those odd people, the Prinkets. By the bye, has the old maid with the pink nose had an offer yet? Or did any one ever come at the bottom of that mystery about the coachman? And the poor little man that used to peep out of his high window whenever the dogs barked? But, never mind now, I have a whole boiling of preserves to tie down before the folks come. Only just think! and then I have to dress. Let me give you a hint this afternoon, Cary, to make the best of yourself. I have a beau for you." And she left the room with a knowing wink that spoke great things for my future settlement.

For my own part, I was far from being solicitous about any beau that this good woman might provide for me, although few people could be more in want than I was of a settled home; for I was entirely without resources, except what my brother's bounty supplied, and moving about from place to place, involved me either in a great deal of expense, or a great deal of meanness. To please my friend, however, as a duty I owed in return for her hospitality, I dressed myself in the manner which I doubted not she would think most becoming, with a variety of colours, and the display of my most costly ornaments; and her raptures on my first entering the drawing room, where she was still busy arranging the furniture and dusting the mantel-piece, fully repaid me for the violence I had done to my natural taste.

The guests arrived at an early hour, while the afternoon sun was yet shining hot upon the flower-beds. I stood at the window watching them alight, and, when a spruce young man rode up on a high-mettled hunter, my friend gave me a smart pinch upon the arm, before she turned round to receive the first motley group of visitors. I thought this evening would surely be the dullest of my life, and had almost resigned every hope of exerting myself to any purpose, when perceiving the great deference paid to my appearance, I began to increase in self-importance, and this sensation being by no means an unpleasant one, my good humour increased also, and I benevolently resolved to turn that importance to the advantage of the company. At this gracious moment, my promised beau made his appearance. He looked at me and scarcely at any thing else; nor was I averse to look again when I heard him announced as Mr. Burton, of whom I had often heard, as the eldest brother of the family, and the wealthy proprietor of a handsome estate, much in want of a lady wife to grace his establishment. From him my attention was quickly diverted by the face of my worthy little friend, twitched all over into meaning, while she presented me to her brother, for there was no opportunity of saying audibly, "This is the lady I have so often recommended."

The brother was a decided improvement upon Mr. Frank Burton. He really had some notion of books, and had made himself so well acquainted with the history of his own estate that he could talk about Roman roads and the Roman method of constructing walls.

Alas! that refinement should spoil half our pleasures, while it makes us but a poor recompense by purifying the other half until they are too exquisite to last!

Spurred on by the vanity of being the star of this evening, I laid aside all the refinement I could spare without loathing myself, and was 'hale fellow well met,' with all the stout matrons, country damsels, old squires and young bucks, who drank their dozen cups of tea, eat their proportion of plum-cake, talked scandal, and played cards at Mrs. Burton's party. It was, for aught I know, a pleasant evening to all the other guests—to me it was not.

On the following morning, while my friend was occupied as usual in her domestic turmoils, greatly increased on this occasion by the eating and drinking of the preceding day, I was seated alone, and, while lost in a kind of reverie composed of floating pictures of my own future fate, and indefinite speculations as to the real character of this Mr. Burton, how he would be likely to acquit himself at the head of his own table, and many other strange thoughts for a stranger as I was then,—the man himself appeared, and accosted me with the familiarity of an old acquaintance. He said his man had brought along with him a capital lady's nag, and if I was fond of riding it should be saddled immediately. I looked out, the sun was bright, the atmosphere fresh and invigorating; I consented, and we set off for a long morning's ride.

The man who wishes to make interest with a woman, does well to lend her a good horse and accompany her through green lanes and woody slopes, where the trampling of the hoofs is scarcely heard upon the soft turf. Whatever affords us real pleasure we are disposed to like, and the transition from the animal to its master is not so great but that a kind and grateful heart may sometimes be induced to make it.

Mr. Burton and I soon discovered that a summer's morning was not the best time for riding, and his sister's early tea afforded us a much more interesting opportunity of ambling through the lanes; sometimes while the lengthened shadows lay in cool relief upon the ground, and, sometimes, when the moon was shining through the silvery mists of twilight. How often did I wish, during these excursions, that my kind companion would be willing to remain silent, and just keep a little way behind, or that I could close my eyes to his plebeian person, and my ears to his coarse brogue. With what satisfaction could I then have looked from the hill where he took me to obtain a distant view of the domain which he was proud to call his, and with what fondness might I have caressed the faithful animal which he was pleased to call mine.

When a man gives you his horse it has a serious sound; and the woman who does not wish an offer of himself to follow, would do well to ride no more. It would certainly have been one of the last of my wishes that Mr. Burton should present his large hand to me, and yet I rode out with him again and again, helping out his few ideas with so many of my own, and supplying him with words when at a loss, as if from the very sympathy of my mind, that we did vastly well together, and he at least was perfectly satisfied; for my habitual mode of appearing pleased left him little room to doubt that I was so with him. I was living too amongst those who looked upon him as a sort of superior being, and I sometimes questioned whether I should not be more fastidious than wise to throw away an opportunity of making what his sister was pleased to call a '*fine catch.*'

Amongst the many arts which I had learned in my intercourse with the world, was that of warding off, or bringing on an offer of marriage, with so much tact and delicacy, that none but the most penetrating, or the most ill-natured could accuse me of design. On the present occasion however, I had to contend with so strong a determination to that fatal point, that I found I must either give up my pleasant ambling altogether, involve myself in a very disagreeable dilemma, or leave the hospitable roof of the Burtons, where I was at least sure of a heartfelt and genuine welcome: nor was it until I resolved upon this last alternative, that I felt the strong hold these cheerful and unpretending people had upon my regard. By adopting their habits, and laying before them my more extensive knowledge of facts and persons (and they wanted nothing more) I had become a general favourite, and had good reason to believe that the early and late parties of Mrs. Frank Burton had never been so brilliant before.

I had not at first quite understood what people of vulgar and empty minds are most in want of for amusement, but I was perfectly initiated now, and could peck at the imperfections of my superiors, laugh at round backs and crooked noses, wonder whether those who were better dressed than myself had paid their Christmas bills, set down all methodists for hypocrites, interlard my conversation with a little country slang, and, finally, fill up the chapter of folly by *ridiculing what I did not understand.*

Thus had my time been spent; and, because thus spending it, had obtained for me unbounded admiration, I felt some regret at taking leave of my friend Mrs. Burton, and receiving the tenderest adieus of her wealthy brother, which, however, he kindly promised with a look intended to be expressive, should not be for ever.

CHAPTER IX.

From tne hospitable home of the Burtons I made a sudden and almost startling transition to the residence of my most aristocratic friend—perhaps I ought rather to say my acquaintance, for Mrs. Arundel had never possessed enough of the milk of human kindness to sweeten our ntercourse into friendship. She was, however, a very desirable sort of person to keep on good terms with, for those who wished to catch, now and then, a glimpse at what is called good society, and were willing to sacrifice the warm comfort of the heart for this uncertain privilege.

Mr. Arundel was pleased to send his carriage to accommodate me, for which I should have been more thankful could he have compelled his coachman to look pleased: but there is something in the services which the domestics of the wealthy render to their poor friends and poor relations, which makes them, to the receiver, any thing but agreeable obligations. On alighting at the door of my new domicile, I was greeted with no kindly welcome. A pert looking woman showed me up stairs to my own room, where I was left to myself with the consoling information that the bell would ring for dinner in the course of an hour. Dinner! I had ridden ten miles after having partaken of an early tea. But there was no need to expose my late barbarism. I had only to prepare for one of Mrs. Burton's hot suppers, and, like many other extreme cases about which so much wonder and alarm is expressed, there would be little difference except in name.

Before half an hour had expired, Mrs. Arundel was graciously pleased to send her own woman to assist me in performing the duties of my toilet, thus conveying the first intimation that she was conscious of my arrival; nor was it with gratitude at all proportioned to the favour that I accepted the services of Mrs. James, whose little sharp eyes seemed to flash and peep about, penetrating through my ill-stocked wardrobe with most unfeeling scrutiny. "To spy out the nakedness of the land," has this woman come, thought I, but I submitted myself to the magic of her pliant fingers, as the only chance I had of appearing in such a manner as would not make me wish myself up stairs again after I had been seated at table.

Once during this tedious operation I opened my lips, and ventured to ask if Mrs.

Arundel had any visitors at present staying in the house.

"Oh! yes," replied the woman, with a look suited to the importance of her information. "Lady Moira and Sir Charles have been here some time."

Aching, as I was, from head to foot with curiosity, no less than with the various twitchings and maltreatment of my tormentor, I still could not bring myself to ask who these illustrious visitors were; whether the gentleman was young or old; nor whether his relationship to the lady was filial or connubial. The woman looked so impertinently solicitous to enlighten my ignorance, that I determined to receive no further information from her, and drawing down a curl to hide the worst part of my forehead, where an embryo wrinkle was threatening to mar its polished smoothness, and casting one lingering look of satisfaction towards the mirror, I followed her to receive my long-expected welcome, in the dressing-room of Mrs. Arundel.

"Only think, my dear!" she exclaimed, after an embrace, which I could well have done without; "Lady Moira and Sir Charles here! Well, I dare say they will not frighten you away. You will find them the best people in the world to do with, if you can but be natural and easy with them—so happy together, it is really quite delightful to see a mother and son so united. I often wish Arundel would take a lesson of politeness from Sir Charles. There is nothing so captivating in private life."

I ventured to remark that Mr. Arundel had once been admired for his politeness.

"Ah! a fiddle-faddling way that he has, which nobody cares for. That is not what I mean. I mean something that makes you feel handsome, and good-humoured, and as if every one liked you, without a word being said directly to the point, and when you know that it is not so."

"Sir Charles must be very clever."

"No, not so clever either in the way of reading, or politics, or any thing of that kind; but just the sort of man to make a woman happy;" and she sighed.

All this while my friend was studying in a tall mirror, her face, her figure, her attitudes, all that could be studied without the counterpart upon whom these charms were to be played off. Sometimes her head was tossed backwards so as to create a sudden trembling and glittering amongst the glossy curls—sometimes a scarf was carefully placed as if in the act of falling or just caught up by the soft and snowy arm—and sometimes a glance was thrown over the graceful shoulder to ascertain whether the Grecian bend of the back was made sufficiently evident to all admirers. I thought my labours at the toilet that day had been unparalleled, but they were nothing to those of my friend, and she was a married woman!

"What can be the meaning of this munificence of charms?" thought I: "The husband has always been represented to me as the very personification of insignificance; and surely married ladies are not solicitous to charm elsewhere."

Sir Charles Moira, young, handsome, accomplished, and graceful, was insignificant too; every one was insignificant when compared with Lady Moira. She was still beautiful, though in the meridian of life. Her dress was that of a mourner, though not of the deepest shade; but it needed no peculiar costume to indicate that the widow's grief had not outlived her weeds. A profusion of light flowing hair mingled with the sable honours of her brow; and when she smiled, it was with the gracious condescension of one who is so rich in happiness, and liberal of favours, that she can dispense them to all without suffering any diminution. There was something in her whole appearance so incomparably magnificent, that when she first entered the room I could not help comparing her to a richly-freighted vessel in full sail, and myself, with the rest of the company, to little boats and small craft, thrown back upon the foam of the receding waves.

I had never heard of Lady Moira before this day. Her sphere of existence had been, and must ever be distinct from mine; yet such is the mysterious influence of that which mankind have agreed to call good-breeding, that in an instant I was awed into admiration, and employed my mind almost entirely in wishing everything unsaid and undone that would not give pleasure to Lady Moira. She had evidently found other minds equally subvervient. Her wishes had been anticipated, her will obeyed on the slightest intimation. Adulation had been perpetually breathed into her ear; and to obviate the doubts that might sometimes arise respecting her sanctification in the world to come, she was dignified with her apotheosis in this.

Sir Charles, the most skilful and accomplished flatterer, had practised upon his mother's credulity since the days of infancy, and she had bountifully repaid him in the same coin; so that whatever either might require of the other (and they sometimes required a great deal) was brought about by such circumlocution and studied sweetness, that it might truly be said, "the paltry prize was hardly worth the cost."

With this interesting couple I now plied my ready skill to please, by arts adapted to their taste; but I soon found, that however I might congratulate myself upon the success of my endeavours, I was not at all congratulated by Mrs. Arundel, who had never dreamed of finding in her poor friend a delightful companion, a charming girl, a dear entertaining creature, as I was perpetually called, with even warmer encomiums upon the agreeable addition of my society to their previously happy little circle.

It is a severe test of love to find our friends decidedly preferred before us, just when we had been hoping to obtain favour; and Mrs. Arundel could not conceal from observation, that the green-eyed monster may shoot his envenomed dart, even where connubial felicity is not concerned. Paying as little regard as I possibly could to the frequent splenetic insinuations with which this monster inspired the lady of the house, I was enjoying a season of almost uninterrupted triumph, when, on one ever-memorable day, my newly-acquired honours were brought low, and miserably soiled in the dust.

Lady Moira was a charming performer on the harp, with which, however, she was but seldom pleased to throw her audience into ecstacies; but she had graciously chosen out one morning a favourite Italian air, which Sir Charles accompanied with his voice, while I acted the enraptured with all my might, when a bustle was heard in the hall, a loud voice, alas! too easily recognised, and Mrs. Burton accompanied by her brother, were ushered in, as having called to see Miss Irvine. In vain had the servant opened the door of another apartment; Mrs. Burton had heard music, and music she declared was her passion.

With my wonted self-possession, never more severely put to the test than on this occasion, I advanced to meet the unwelcome intruders, hoping, by a closer encounter to quiet the exclamations of this boisterous little woman. But no; she had been completely broiled; the horses' fetlocks buried in dust all the way—did not think it had been so far, or would not have come only to see about a loin of veal; "for people tell me," said she, "the butchers here keep better veal than down yonder, where we live. Tom rode so fast, too,—in haste poor fellow." She added in an under-tone, with a nod and a wink; "and then this habit; do you know, Cary, I have never had a habit on since little Peter was born—bless the boy!" And then she applied her handkerchief to her face, and untied her bonnet, exhaling all the while long and audible breathings, which must, I thought, extend to the other side of the room where Lady Moira and Sir Charles were seated, vainly endeavouring to look absorbed in the Italian music.

Mrs. Arundel had now her hour of triumph; and I marked the inward satisfaction with which she smiled at my dilemma; while, determined that I should not escape without smarting to the very bone, she entered into a lively conversation with Mrs. Burton, in which the honest-hearted woman did not detect the snare, but rattled on with long histories about her poultry, and the poultry of her neighbours, her children, and all the odd things that were constantly happening in her establishment.

My swain had the good sense to be silent while he sat behind the door with his hat held between his knees, in his bare red hand, gloveless, and swollen with the summer's heat.

"I thought I heard music," Mrs. Burton exclaimed. "Pray go on, ma'am; pray go on, sir," to Lady Moira and Sir Charles. "There's nothing I delight in like music. Law, Cary, do you know what has happened to Burton's fiddle?" and she indulged herself for one moment with a sort of internal chuckle, the constant prelude to her favourite stories, of which, in all companies I was apprehensive.

"Well, you must know, I was reaching up for a pot of orange-jam, (Frank always likes orange-jam at his tea; and little Peter, bless the boy! has just begun to eat marmalade;) —well, as I was saying about the jam, my foot slipped, and plump I went down into the fiddle! It was well I was no worse; but I believe if I had broke my leg I must have laughed, as I walked out with the fiddle on my foot like a patten." And she showed us how long and loud she could laugh, even at the remembrance of the catastrophe.

Lady Moira and Sir Charles, after exchanging glances, now left the room, and to my unspeakable relief Mrs. Arundel quickly followed. Mrs. Burton then rose, and making some excuse about shopping, departed also, leaving my smirking beau as he thought, master of the field.

Seeing from the expression of his face, what was likely to be the business in hand, and thinking the sooner it was brought forward and discussed the better, I sat very silent, during the infliction of a formal offer of marriage from this man, who seemed very much disposed to doubt his senses, when it was followed up by an answer as formal and decided from me.

"Why, what can have changed you?" he exclaimed, when I persisted in my refusal. "I am sure you must have understood my meaning, when you rode about with me in the lanes down yonder."

"I understood that you were kind enough to lend me a horse."

"Oh, yes! and I will always be kind to you, Miss Cary."

Finding it would not do to speak of kindness, and hating to be thus reminded of my past folly, while the music Sir Charles had just been singing lay open before me, I repeated my unsavoury words, with an emphasis so strongly marked with impatience and contempt, that my quondam admirer lost his temper, and with it the little propriety of conduct which alone had rendered him tolerable.

"I see what you are aiming at," said he, with the most insulting rudeness: "Sir Charles has a pretty income, to be sure, but what is that to people who live as he does? I'll tell you what, Miss; you'll not soon meet with another man to lay an estate like mine before you, all in a ring fence, with plenty of game for your dainty appetite; but you'll rue the day yet, when you see another Mrs. Burton, which you shall before you've made sure of Sir Charles;" and so saying he walked off, closing the door after him, with a thundering sound that brought the domestics startled and tittering from the servants' hall.

The scene being now completely over, I felt really glad that it had been no worse, conscious as I was that the inconsistency of my late behaviour deserved, if possible, a punishment more severe: nor could I behold from my window Mrs. Burton and her brother trotting out of town in high dudgeon, with the butcher's boy and loin of veal a very little way behind, while neither of their heads were turned to give a parting nod, without feeling that I had richly merited to lose my place in their regard.

It is almost impossible to lose the love we once possessed, without a melancholy sense that something has been taken away from us, although it might not, while it lasted, be of any real value. Mrs. Burton was a warm-hearted, well-meaning creature, and had loved me better, perhaps, than many whose affection I had been more solicitous to obtain. She was now, in all probability, struck off from my list of friends, offended, perhaps wounded. She must think me ungrateful, and I had the misery of reflecting that she might think so with perfect truth. Every loss we experience makes us pause and examine what is left; and I turned upon my own heart to see what stores I had yet to draw upon for satisfaction. Under present circumstances, I had indeed no wish to call Mrs. Burton back, but this simple affair, so laughable to others, plunged me into a train of gloomy reflections, against the sadness of which I was unprovided with any kind of antidote.

I had now been living for a long time amongst those who thought religion an unnecessary burden to take up, so long as life could be made pleasant without it; and as I made it my business to fall in with the sentiments of those around me, I was but too ready to treat religion with as little regard as they did. The inevitable consequence was, that my mind was more empty than ever of any kind of consolation, that I was less prepared for the rough accidents of life, and, worst of all, that I was rapidly receding from that heavenly goal to which the only hope that never fails us is directed.

The circumstance which had cost me the loss of an old friend, was never alluded to by Lady Moira or Sir Charles: so much does politeness wear the character of real kindness; but Mrs. Arundel was unsparing in her ridicule, and quoted poor Mrs. Burton on every possible occasion, wondering oftener than the day where I could have gathered up such people; while I could call to mind, without much difficulty, the time when such people were not entirely excluded from her own sphere of existence.

To my new friends I felt unspeakable gratitude for their forbearance; and had it not been for the fascination of their society, I should have wisely left my present abode, where it was in vain to flatter myself that I was wished for by the lady of the house. I was besides in considerable difficulty about where to go next, and the fact of seeing no shelter for our heads in any other place, has a great tendency to reconcile our remaining where we are.

Impossible as it was, on first entering the house of Mr. Arundel, to believe that the master of it, or rather he who should have been the master, could ever be an object of interest, I found, during a very short stay, that pity has the power to metamorphose the character, and invest even the person with attractions that were never dreamed of before. This spell was put in force. Long and intimately as I had been acquainted with the world, and low as I had bent myself beneath its influence, I had not acquired all its bad habits, most certainly not that of trampling on the fallen. My delight was often to take part with the weak, whether the strife in which they were engaged was right or wrong; and in this spirit I never failed to throw in a word on behalf of the helpless husband, when I thought him in danger of being borne down by his wife's authority. I believe the little gentleman had never experienced so much consideration before, and his unbounded thankfulness was expressed by

'Nods, and becks, and wreathed smiles,'

which were carefully watched and registered by one who seemed determined to torment herself, as well as others. I even went so far as to enter into close conference with him about his plants, his hot-house, and all his hobbies, upon which he had never been able to persuade his wife to ride, but which, now that she saw me earnestly engaged with, she appeared to think most interesting subjects of consideration; expressing her indignation in no gentle terms, that so much should be planned and undertaken without consulting her.

I was glad to find the worthy man rising in importance, though at the expense of my own comfort; and he was glad to find, for the first time in his life, that however Mrs.

Arundel might slight or undervalue his attentions, he still had the power to pique her by bestowing them elsewhere.

I had lately observed, that in the midst of some of Lady Moira's warmest expressions of regard, her countenance had lowered on the approach of her son, and that he too, in the absence of his mother, was much more solicitous to please, and more evidently pleased. He had a friend, daring and dissipated, whose unscrupulous frankness let me into the secret of Lady Moira's terrors lest her son should form a connexion with any one unequal to himself in rank. Confusion was now thickening around me. Contending interests seemed ready to burst in a storm upon my head. What was to be done? I had no adviser, and my own heart had too often been a treacherous counselor, to be trusted to with any confidence that it would lead me right, or even extricate me from present difficulties; for this was more specifically my object than to act with a single eye to what was right. Sir Charles had become more pointed in his attentions and Lady Moira, in the same proportion, more cold and haughty. She was even closeted in close consultation with Mrs. Arundel and that woman's case is hopeless when she has none but men to take her part. Every day I made some faint determination that I would leave these troubled spirits, but my determinations served no other purpose than to draw forth from Sir Charles his deep regrets, and deeper sighs, and protestations as earnest as words could make them, that it was impossible to be happy without me. At last the storm burst. The jealousy of Mrs. Arundel was wrought up to the crisis of explosion, on finding that I had one day been two hours in the conservatory with her husband. I was abruptly dismissed, with a slight imputation on my character, and the married couple were better pleased with themselves and each other than they had ever been before. I was the luckless scape-goat, who had been played upon for their own purposes; and having no one to defend my cause, I bore the blame, as the unprotected mostly do. I had, however, some satisfaction in thinking that Mr. and Mrs. Arundel were more united than I had found them. The husband well pleased that he had sufficient power to torment his wife with jealousy, the wife convinced by the late fears she had entertained of losing the affections of her husband, that those affections were worth retaining.

CHAPTER X.

FORTUNATELY for me, before the wrath of Mrs. Arundel had reached its height, I received a very pressing invitation from a worthy family of methodists, who lived in some degree of affluence in a pleasant situation, not many miles distant. To them I went with all my humiliations on my head, and with my thoughts disturbed and confused by the late cruel occurrences which had driven me to take advantage of their hospitality. But they were simple-hearted, quiet people, who did not examine the human mind, or any thing else very deeply, and so long as I appeared comfortable, and spoke cheerfully, they had no apprehensions about what I might be feeling.

Susan Penrose, the only daughter, possessed more penetration than her parents, and perceiving that I was not quite so happy as a Christian ought to be, undertook with all the candour of her guileless heart, and the zeal of her profession, to make me happier by making me better. Susan's character was one which it was impossible to know without respecting. She had not enjoyed a liberal education, but religion had done all for her that was wanted—had refined her feelings, and elevated her thoughts, supplying her with that dignity which unfailing rectitude imparts, and that grace which is acquired in the constant performance of virtuous actions. I could not live beneath the same roof with this estimable being, without feeling fearfully conscious of my own littleness, and I wished, earnestly wished, that I could shake off the fetters by which I was bound, and walk as she did, free in the light of the glorious gospel. It is true my thoughts were sometimes diverted from the seriousness of this family, by speculations about what this person and the other might think of their quaint habits and homely ways; nor was Sir Charles Moira the last whose image I conjured up to place in idea beside me, whenever any thing occurred particularly unlike the customs of the fashionable world; but it was not my wont to criticise on my own behalf, and I had seen too much of general society to be forcibly struck with what is commonly called absurdity, but which might frequently be more justly explained as something foreign to our own prejudices and peculiar views, derived from a limited circle of beings as absurd in their turn to others, as others are to them.

An intimate acquaintance with the different classes of mankind, and the various circumstances which develope human character, does much, and ought to do more to make us sparing of that ridicule which frequently arises from our ignorance, and might more properly be turned against ourselves. Those who have often seen the wise act foolishly, and the fool more wise in his generation than the man of boasted learning, who know the influence of circumstances and situation in forming the character, who feel the humbling truth that virtue too often retains its high standing in the world from the mere absence of temptation, who have been accustomed to examine their own hearts, and have learned in this examination, that just so far as they have been tried they have yielded, will feel little inclination to laugh at follies which are common to all; as little as to set up the senseless boast, that had they been in certain situations they would have acted differently from others; and still less to triumph over those who have been tried and proved in a furnace, the fury of which they themselves have never felt.

In the family of Mr. Penrose, I saw the influence of religion in its simplest and most substantial form, ungraced by factitious ornaments, unadorned by that drapery which recommends it to general beholders, but at the same time conceals its real and unblemished beauty.

Weary of my past life, disappointed, perplexed and troubled, how did I long, while kneeling by the side of Susan Penrose, that I could enter into the spirit of her prayers, and offer up my soul as I knew she was offering up hers.

"Perhaps I shall become like these happy people in time," thought I; and I joined in their religious exercises, and listened to their long discourses with so much gravity and interest, half felt and half assumed, that they began to speak of me and treat me like one of their own community, and I was both proud and pleased to be thus recognized, for never in my life had I seen more clearly the beauty of holiness. Would that my vision had not again been obscured!

I was seated one day with Susan beneath a veranda which shaded the door and the front windows, enjoying the softness of the autumn breeze that played through the interstices of the clustering vine, when strange feet, and voices more strange in such a place were heard advancing along the garden, and two sportsmen issued from the shrubbery walk.

It was Sir Charles and his friend Jeffreys. I believe I had not properly concealed the foolish pleasure I felt on seeing them, for Susan told me afterwards with great simplicity, she had no idea they had been such intimate friends, or indeed that I could be intimate with such. The fact was, that although I offered to the religious habits of this family all I could offer, my entire approbation, I had been, while residing under their roof, extremely dull; and the appearance of the two strangers brought back such vivid remembrance of lively hours enjoyed elsewhere, that I was almost delighted to behold them again, and asked with apparent interest, a multitude of questions on subjects which Susan, who sat by, had never before suspected could occupy my thoughts. Once or twice I saw her grave face turned towards me with an expression of perfect amazement, while I rattled on with these idle creatures, chiding them occasionally for their extravagance, but laughing all the while, as ladies will laugh sometimes when they ought not.

Sir Charles, escaped from maternal influence, was more easy and delightful than I had ever seen him before, and Jeffreys was always entertaining and good-humoured. How was it that Susan never smiled at his jokes?—she must be the most insensible of women. And why had she put on that close cap? and why had she chosen this morning, of all others, to look less refined than usual? The case was an easy one to understand. I was now looking through a different atmosphere; for my atmosphere always took its peculiar tone of colouring from those who ruled my thoughts for the time being. I had not the power to see any object in a clear and steady point of view; but, borrowing lights and shades from all the fluctuating circumstances of life, my ideas, even of right and wrong, were unsettled and confused.

"Well, this is Arcadia indeed!" said Sir Charles, as he took his seat beside me, and I had the mortification of seeing Jeffreys edge himself in beside Susan with a look too plainly indicating his intention to quiz the fair methodist. But it was impossible to make game of Susan. Her calm dignity preserved her from insult, and, when she rose and walked into the house, I felt ashamed of being identified with those whose impertinence had driven her away. I soon forgot, however, in the light pleasantry of my companions, that there was anything in the world worth thinking of but sunshine, good-humour, and Sir Charles: and, when the sportsmen rose to wish me good morning, I listened with more satisfaction than wisdom to the gentle tone, the half-whisper, which assured me they should seek the bowers of Arcadia again.

"Were these your companions at Mr. Arundel's?" asked Susan, as we sat together again in the afternoon.

I answered with triumph, that Sir Charles was staying in the house all the time, thinking the enviable situation I had lately enjoyed was the subject of Susan's thoughts.

"I wonder you were not weary," she observed, and my triumph was at an end.

The next visit of the sportsmen was later in the day. Dark clouds were gathering around, and the wind, blowing in fitful gusts, had driven us all to seek shelter within doors. We were quietly seated together in a parlour by no means resembling Mr. Arundel's drawing-room, good Mrs. Penrose carefully darning her husband's stockings, when the two gentlemen, running to escape the first pelting of a thunder-storm, rushed into the hall with boisterous mirth.

"Your friends are come again," said Susan; and, under present circumstances, I really felt less hope than fear that her words were true.

Again every thing was transfigured before my eyes. The parlour in an instant became more gloomy, the carpet more gray, the few books that lay about more soiled and more ultra-religious, and certainly Mrs. Penrose was more fat and lame than she had ever been before. I saw no longer with my own eyes, nor heard with my own ears; but, identifying myself as it were with the intruders, their senses became the medium through which every impression reached me. Just in the same way that, after having passionately admired some book, we take it up to read again with a friend whose tone of feeling is essentially different from our own. When, behold! the book is not the same. It has faults we never perceived before, and those passages which we know our friend will condemn, stand forth in such glaring and conspicuous light, that we lay the whole aside with disappointment and disgust, made deeper by the conviction that, since nothing can enforce the belief that the book has actually changed its character, we must submit to the mortification of believing our own judgment to be in fault.

The storm which had driven the sportsmen to make so unceremonious an advance upon the hospitality of my friends, still kept them prisoners, and, what was worse, imprisoned the master of the house, who threw towards me many an enquiring look, which seemed to say, "Whom have we here?" But the afternoon was such as would have reconciled a man, less kind-hearted than Mr. Penrose, to the presence of guests even more objectionable than Sir Charles and his companion, and, as evening drew on, they were pressed to remain for the night if the storm should not abate.

It requires a prodigious share of effrontery to carry on, without flagging, light senseless conversation in the presence of a grave, matter of fact man of sense, especially if that man be the master of the house in which the scene of your folly is laid. Under almost any other circumstances I should have rejoiced at the casualty which detained Sir Charles as my companion for a whole evening; but, clever as I was at reconciling incongruities, it was utterly impossible to make the present time glide smoothly on; for, while the thunder rolled above our heads, the solemn and becoming gravity of my serious friends was strangely broken in upon by the ill-timed jokes of Jeffreys, and the vivacity of Sir Charles. I could not keep my place with both parties, brought as they now were into close contact; and, such was my weakness, that the reverence I had hitherto felt for the sedate habits of this family, gave way, and more than once I was startled in my merriment by the flash of the lightning, and the deep sighs, almost amounting to groans, of the master and mistress of the house.

The time at last arrived for evening prayer. Mr. Penrose was not the man to apologize for the custom of worshipping his Maker at morn and evening, and, opening his well-worn Bible, he began to read, with a loud nasal cadence that brought the blush of shame into my face. Yes, such is the littleness of vanity, and the excess of human folly, that I dared to feel ashamed that night, when a pious man, at the head of a well-ordered family, called together his household, and read aloud, from the book of consolation, the glad tidings of a Saviour sent into a sinful world. I felt ashamed when he knelt down and poured forth a fervent prayer from the earnest simplicity of his heart, while I ought to have been reminded by the thunder rolling around us in tremendous peals, that the God who graciously directed us to seek his throne by prayer, is too mighty to be insulted with impunity.

Our visitors were evidently strangers to such a scene. Sir Charles possessed too high a sense of propriety not to make some show of conformity; but Jeffreys, who cared for nothing but the indulgence of his own humour, watched the entrance of the uncouth domestics, one after another, with no small entertainment—holding a newspaper in his hand during the whole of the simple and appropriate service. At last a hymn was sung, and, to my utter confusion, Jeffreys raised his voice amongst the rest, louder and louder, with long-drawn notes of drawling discord, that made Susan, who stood near me, close her lips and sing no more.

One look, and only one, I ventured to direct towards that part of the room from whence these extraordinary sounds were issuing. The performer stood with his head thrown back, his mouth wide open, and his hands spread forth in mockery of the extreme of sanctimonious fervour. Sir Charles looked also—Jeffreys caught his eye, and an explosion of laughter followed. The hymn ceased; Mr. Penrose desired his servants to remain;—in their presence he wished to show his just indignation at such conduct.

"Young men," said he, in a commanding tone, "the manner in which you have chosen to abuse my hospitality I regard as an insult to religion more than to myself, and as such you must feel that it entitles you to the severest reproof. I made you welcome to my home, not from respect, but compassion; because I would not drive the vilest miscreant from my door in such a storm. In the same way you are welcome to shelter your heads for the night; but, from this time henceforth, remember that nothing but a change of heart can make you welcome to my house again.

Sir Charles advanced with many smooth apologies, for I believe he was really sorry, but it would not do. "Say no more, sir, don't trouble yourself," was all that Mr. Penrose would answer, except to add, that the night was now advancing, and they would find their chambers ready. They were not, however, quite humble enough for that; but while the rain was yet pouring in torrents, wished us good night, and went their way.

I soon escaped to my own room, but not to sleep. Even had my reflections been of a more imposing nature, I should have been kept awake by the long and loud altercation of Susan and her father in the room below. She was earnestly pleading with him, and I guessed too well that I was myself the unworthy subject of her solicitude. At last I heard him say distinctly, as he crossed the hall to the stairs—

"If these are the companions that Miss Irvine must draw after her, I care not how soon she leaves my house."

It was long after midnight when Susan left the parlour. Her gentle step paused at my door. She opened it almost without a sound, and, shading her candle with her hand, came and stood beside my bed.

"Are you not asleep, Caroline," said she, "it is very late, or rather early."

"No; I cannot sleep to-night; but pray what keeps you up?"

"I am in a great deal of trouble," said she, and the tears fell fast down her cheeks —"trouble on your account."

"Ah! Susan, you think I am a sad wicked creature."

"It is not that altogether," said she, hesitating, and looking more and more distressed. "I have been thinking for three hours what I ought to do, and praying that I may simply do what is right."

"Then discharge your duty, Susan, if it relates to me; and depend upon my not taking it amiss."

"There is no rule safer than that of doing as we would be done by, and it is in this way that I now tell you, I think—I have reason to believe it would be better for you to go away. Now, what do you think of me for saying such a cruel thing?"

"That you are a good honest-hearted creature, Susan, as I always thought you;" said I, holding out my arms to her while we mingled our tears together.

"You and I, Susan, are not fitted to live together in this world. Would that I could feel sure I should join your habitation in the next! You know not the temptations which beset my path. Pray for me sometimes when I am gone."

"I will remember you in my supplications," she replied, "every day, and oftener than the day." And after strenuously urging me to be more decided, and more consistent, she then knelt down beside me, commending me to the care and protection of Him "who seeth not as man seeth," and "with whom is no variablenes nor shadow of turning."

CHAPTER XI.

I HAD now no resource but to throw myself upon the kindness of my Aunt Morris, and my cousin Jane. They had often invited me to pay them a visit, and though I entertained no doubt of the welcome I should receive, certain remembrances made me shrink from the discipline with which I knew this welcome would be embittered. There were, however, some considerations connected with money matters, which made it expedient for me to see them, and I determined accordingly. Jane Morris was my agent in the sale of a variety of specimens of fancy work, drawings, and other articles of taste, which had formerly been so rapturously admired by my friends, and so often begged and borrowed, that I could not doubt they would soon be bought.

Had my aunt still resided in my native

place, I should have felt it almost impossible to visit her, now when my own circumstances were so completely changed. But she had removed to some distance, though still within reach of those whose intimacy I had once enjoyed, and who had thus an opportunity of extending their kindness to me in the way that would have been most agreeable, and certainly at a time when it was much needed.

I had often been told in happier days, when surrounded with all the comforts of life, that I could never want the means of subsistence; that I had a fortune in my head and even in my hands. The truth of these assurances had now been put to the test, and many an anxious and enquiring look did I cast towards my cousin Jane, before I could bring myself to ask what money she had in hand for me.

"Money!" was her hopeless reply, with a tone of astonishment, the very emptiness of which sent a sudden quivering through my nerves, and an aching through my heart—"Money! I believe I have five shillings for a little cap, but really you must take your things away, for I am quite tired of showing them about, and as to the drawings, I cannot get them off on any terms! People say they are badly coloured, and quite out of perspective. For my own part, I do not understand such matters, and therefore cannot give an opinion."

"And pray whose opinion do you give?"

"Mr. Blundell's, the Morrisons', and Miss Green's."

"Miss Green's?"

"Yes; they tell me she laughed very much in Miller's shop the other day, at a house, which she said stood on one corner. You may possibly remember the piece. It has cattle in the fore-ground."

I did remember the piece; and I remembered also that Miss Green had once attempted to beg it of me by earnest entreaties which I had great difficulty in refusing; but when I heard that Mr. Blundell, a man who took the lead in all matters of taste, was her companion, and had doubtless set the laugh agoing, I did not wonder that she, who had no judgment of her own, should have been willing to follow.

Oh! ye who love to sport with ridicule, and think it pleasant pastime to murder with the shafts of criticism, how often is your cruel aim directed to the stricken deer, and your envenomed arrow sent into the bosom that was galled before!

How little can be known by you, whose days are spent in luxury and idleness, of what is felt by those who depend upon the mercy of your smiles for the very sustenance of life! You can take up the productions of the pen or pencil, find out each petty fault,—laugh, sneer, and cast aside, while the author or the artist: whose genius has been exhausted, and whose sensibility tortured for your amusement, waits for his daily bread. You can open the little volume, dedicated by the lowly to the great, and stretched at ease on a voluptuous couch, can peer amongst the pages, to draw forth with "critical inspection," and examine with anatomical scrutiny the sentiments that have been wrung out from a breaking heart. You can expatiate with all the dignity of a judge, who pronounces sentence of death against a criminal, upon the want of light and sweetness in the picture of some lonely wretch whose life is all shade and bitterness, and who, in attempting to imitate the fair face of nature, has not derived his resources from the exuberance of a pampered fancy, but from half extinguished recollections of beauty and harmony, which the discord of worldly strife, and the harshness of penury, are fast obliterating from his weary and distempered mind. You can luxuriate in the realms of art, light as the butterfly amongst the flowers of summer: but how unlike this happy and harmless insect tasting of innumerable sweets, while it depreciates and poisons none. Before you the works of imagination are spread forth to be contemned and trampled upon. Pause then, for one moment, in your merciless career, and reflect that such are often the productions of those whose labour is carried on at the midnight hour, when you are in your downy beds, and ceases not for the throbbing of the heart that is torn with unkindness, nor the aching of eyes that are blinded with tears.

My agent was but too faithful in her report. The efforts of my genius had been miserably depreciated in value, and what was of infinitely more consequence to me, had not been sold. Not that the kind companions of my early years had ceased to be kind, or would not willingly have given me the stated price of all my worthless trifles; but it makes a wonderful difference, whether at hing is exhibited as a matter of taste, or as an article of sale. Many will value as a gift what they would not buy at any cost, however small; not at all because they grudge the money, but because, while receiving a gift (that not being always a matter of choice) their own judgment is not implicated, but the giver being solely responsible for all deficiency of merit, they can say to their criticising friends, "I know it has many faults, but I value it for her sake, poor thing!" and thus save their credit; but for the appalling question, "And pray how much might you give for this splendid concern?" they are provided with no saving reply, but must suffer an imputation upon their good taste, in having chosen to make such a purchase.

No one can thoroughly know the world and its odd ways without they have been poor. A thousand secrets are laid open to the eyes of the needy which the children of affluence will not believe of themselves; and the rude key of penury unlocks the laboratory of the human mind, where a view may be obtained of the various particles of which it is compounded before they are refined, amalgamated, and sent forth for the ornament of polished circles. It is almost worth enduring a little reduction of our means for the knowledge which is thus obtained; but then it is the loss of caste that reveals the truth; and who, from the poor Indian, owning no property beneath the sun but his Braminical thread, to the philosopher who professes to despise all worldly possessions, would not rather endure every other earthly loss than this.

The discipline I was subjected to beneath the sheltering roof of my aunt Morris was like hard labour, and strong bitters, used to correct the evils of too much indulgence. For some days I bore it well, thinking the "pelting of the pitiless storm" would surely cease in time; instead of which it rather gathered and accumulated upon me, until I found my temper had imbibed the bitterness of which I was constantly partaking.

Gentle ladies, have you a cousin Jane? If not, your gentleness has never been fully put to the test. Have you a friend who takes the liberty of a near connexion, or familiar acquaintance, to tell you every disagreeable thing which every body has said about you, and that not at all on her own behalf, so that you cannot retort or repel the injury? While she has no part nor lot in the matter, but just thinks it right to tell you so much that, in time, you are induced to believe all old friends are changed, and all new ones are false. Perhaps the most distressing part of the information laid before me, was what had been said by my sister. Jane Morris had lately been staying with her, and reported that she had made many remarks about my expences, did not at all approve of my way of living,—should be truly glad if I had a settled home, and wished I would consent to live with them, where I should be more free from unpleasant remarks.

"Never!" I exclaimed with warmth quite unusual to me. "I will live any where but with them. I will advertise for a situation."

My aunt peeped over her spectacles, and thought I had better advertise for a husband.

"They have heard," continued my tormentor "all about your affair with the Burtons. Mrs. Arundel tell every body, and how you tried to captivate Sir Charles."

"And how I failed?"

"Not exactly that; for I find he followed you to the methodist's, where he found you amongst such low people that he had little inclination to go again."

"Did Sir Charles tell his own story?"

"I am not quite sure of that. I think it was a friend of his who told Mr. Grahame that they were sent out of the house because they laughed at prayers, and that you cried, but I am sure you don't mind any thing about what people say."

"Oh! no, not the least."

"I am sure you cannot think seriously of so young a man, especially after you have so lately been attached to Mr. Burton."

"Attached to Mr. Burton!"

"Yes; good Mrs. Burton says she never saw any one more attached than you were to him until living amongst high people changed you: that no one ever was more changed than you were when she called upon you: that you minced your words and sailed about as if you had been a duchess. But you don't mind poor Mrs. Burton."

"Oh, no, I don't mind any thing just now," said I, forcing a laugh.

"That's very fortunate. I am glad you are in good spirits, I want to talk to you a little about money; and that is rather a heavy subject to those who have none."

"Pray go on. It makes no sort of difference."

"Well, there is a great deal said about your expenses, and the presents that you make; though, to be sure, the cambric handkerchiefs you gave old Mrs. Armstrong all proved to be cotton; and the amethyst in Miss Green's broach, which they say looks very well by candle light, is not real. And your correspondents, I understand, are enough to ruin a nabob. Mrs. Arundel says her husband had to pay five pounds for your letters, though you only stayed with them six weeks: and the house-keeper thinks you are sadly too fond of good living for a person in your situation."

I was beginning to breathe when the reports were only charged with what housekeepers said about good living; but the attack came upon me again with unabated fury, until I really believed myself driven to the lowest pit of degradation in the opinion of all whom I had once esteemed, and who had once esteemed me. Had I reasoned coolly I should have come to the conclusion, that my friends thought no worse of me than that I was very foolish, a sentence we so often pronounce upon others, in so many different ways, that I had no right to think myself harshly dealt with because some of its varieties had now reached my own ear.

That there are such people as my cousin Jane, I think all who have reached the age of thirty, and many much younger, will allow:—people who want the moral courage to attack with their own weapons, but wound with tenfold force by borrowing darts, and poison to dip them in, from others. What their object can be, is difficult to understand. If they really mean to do us good by laying bare the truth, they must be ignorant that such truths are only calculated to stir up envy, malice, hatred, revenge, and all those evil passions, by which the peace of society is destroyed: converting friends into enemies, and darkening the hours of social intercourse with the shadow of mistrust. If they mean to make us wicked, and, consequently, miserable, they can scarcely adopt a plan more sure. And yet this contemptible system of irritation is what some would make a merit of by calling it *speaking the truth.* But truth is of too celestial an essence to be thus violated. As the most precious coin, when used as a bribe for base purposes, is most extensive in its baneful influence, so truth, unsanctified by virtue, may be made more fatal even than falsehood to security and happiness.

I could not remain long with my aunt and cousin. The constant recital of petty facts, all tending to humiliation, overthrew the equanimity of my mind. The catalogue I well knew, was filled up with things no worse than are said and done every day, and might, by a philosopher, have been set aside as unworthy of a moment's consideration. But I was no philosopher, I was living upon the good will of society, and they were gall and bitterness to me.

Where now in the wide world was I to go? Stirred up to indignation by the tittle-tattle of my cousin, I had written a hasty and insulting letter to my sister, declining any further advance of money from that quarter; and, under the influence of the same feeling, I had lately passed Miss Green, from whom I had received a pressing invitation, without any sign of recognition. In short, I was rapidly becoming the victim of the most unamiable of passions; for no other reason than because the senseless gossip of an idle woman had conveyed to my ear the unkind and uncharitable remarks made upon myself, which we are making upon each other every day.

Where in the wide world was I to go, and how was I to find bread? I, who had a multitude of friends, was without a home. I, who had a fortune in my fingers, found nothing in my purse, and my cousin Jane was constantly reminding me that my things would not sell.

"Perhaps not," I replied, "amongst these spiteful people who are determined to crush me; but I will try my fate with strangers. There is a world elsewhere?" and, so saying, I proudly withdrew myself, and prepared for my departure, no one could conjecture to what place.

The London coach took me away from my aunt's door, and set me down in a narrow bustling street of the metropolis, in the very heart of the city, where an early friend, whose mind would once have done honour to the most refined and elevated sphere, now dragged on her existence as the wife of a tradesman, in the midst of perpetual toil and confusion. I had known her, when a young woman, mild, delicate, and gentle. Her home was not the most comfortable, and she had married young, hoping (surely this is hoping against hope) that with the change would come some little improvement in her circumstances. Her husband was a kind, rational, and worthy man, worn down with the burden of an unprofitable business, a sickly wife, and nine children. With these people it was my intention to lodge, and to support myself by painting.

It was on a Saturday evening, about the middle of October, that I sought out their humble dwelling; and, after winding along many streets, in a drizzling rain, which I thought might just as well have spared itself and me a month longer, I saw the name of Wilson in large gilt letters over the door of a shop, where many busy feet were passing to and fro. Mr Wilson, adorned with his apron, had just time to stretch his head over the counter and ask me to walk forward into the parlour where I should find his wife.

"Take away that barrow," he called out, in a loud authoritative tone to the shopman, who, with alternate skip and strut, hastened to remove the obstacles, and threw open a door, through which I groped my way along a passage, directed to the parlour only by the screams and uproar of nine children undergoing the agony of a Saturday-night's wash. My heart failed me; but the rival discord of the shop prevented my return. While I hesitated, the parlour door was suddenly thrown open by one of the little rebels, hoping to escape his share in the general purification; and the scene within was thus revealed to my wondering vision.

It was ten years since I had seen my friend—ten married years. Nine children, three attacks of hooping cough, four of measles, scarlet fever, croop, and one cripple had done much to make Mrs. Wilson exceedingly unlike the fair girl I had once known her; but living in a dark street in London, poverty and underselling had done more. Oh! who can say they do not wish for money, so long as young helpless girls will marry before they have had much more experience than the dolls they have just laid aside—so long as men who have not wherewith to clothe and feed themselves, will link their hard fate with those who are not used to hardship. At first all may go smoothly on. New furniture looks well, and kind, pitying relations, make presents that show upon the table and the mantle-piece. They are both young, guileless, and confiding; and affection in the young is more potent while it lasts, than the old will believe; but even love may be drawn upon too often for draughts too large; and Cupid, and the poor man's banker, make the same complaint. The first child is welcomed by the nurse, and the young mother, and sometimes the father is beguiled of his pressing cares by its happy smiles. A second finds a welcome, because two are little more trouble than one; and a third, because they hope it will be the last; but they have no nursery, and it is very difficult to find a welcome for the fourth. The wife loses her health and her spirits. Her cheek grows hollow, her eye dim, and she is evidently sinking under her accumulating cares; but an underselling tradesman has just settled near them, and they cannot afford to hire more help. The doctor is called in; he looks with compassion on that gentle drooping form, and recommends quiet, with frequent reclining on the sofa. Alas! there is no sofa; and if there were, how should that wife recline—how should she find rest, whose ears are stunned with perpetual discord, who is constantly called upon to appease the anger of the turbulent, to soothe the fretful, to gather up the bruised, and to forget herself. *Perchance* the husband loves her still, all changed as she is, and thinks kindly of her, for he can do no more; but the hardship of her lot is not much alleviated by his thoughts. Oh! who does not wish for money when they see the children of such people wanting that education which their parents have enjoyed, and consequently falling into a lower grade of society, without either the dignity of their father or the refinement of their mother; strangers even to the decency of manners and conduct without which we ought not to be contented.

With such a family as this I was now come to eat my bread. I could not expect a welcome, but I found one; for the poor are not the last to fulfil the duties of hospitality, nor the worn and the harassed the most unwilling to show that they can exert themselves yet farther for a friend.

Mrs. Wilson was on her knees in the midst of her noisy group when I entered. She started up at the sight of a stranger, and it was some time before she discovered, by the flickering light of the fire, who that stranger was; she was herself so changed, that but for a peculiar smile which played for a moment on her lips, and which had once been familiar to her face, I should scarcely have known her.

I told her I was come to be her lodger, She thought I was jesting; nor was it until I had convinced her of my meaning by repeated assurances, that she acknowledged, by a silent tear, how sorry she was to be unable to offer me a home on any other terms.

"You are weary," she said—"I will just put the children to bed, and then you shall have tea."

I asked if, in the mean time, I might go up stairs to my own room.

Poor Mrs. Wilson looked confounded; she had forgot, while offering me a welcome, that, on the birth of her last child, she had resigned the privilege of keeping what is called a spare room, and that it was impossible any apartment under her roof should be exclusively my own. She might have recollected too, if this had not been enough, that long before this fearful encroachment upon comfort, she had laid aside all pretensions to neatness and regularity, and that, even in what was now called the best, instead of the spare room, every drawer was stuffed, and every shelf crowded with different articles of clothing, concealed from the depredations of the small fry, who ranged at large, and intruded with their busy fingers wherever they were not prevented by lock and bolt.

"Stay one moment," said my friend, and I was left in the dark while she ran upstairs. Half the little tribe escaped on the departure of their mother. Of the remaining half I could only make friends with one, while the others shrieked and rolled about the floor, until they woke the baby in the cradle, and I had more than I could well manage to still its cries.

Mrs. Wilson now called to me from the top of the stairs, and I ascended with the cheering hope of finding quiet at last; but, woeful to relate, a low wide bed, made to contain three at least, stood close beside the one prepared for me, and the poor mother told me, with many apologies, and much embarrassment, that she could not offer me any other room, nor find room for her children elsewhere.

"Don't mention it," said I, "it is of no sort of consequence;" and she left me to attend to her duties below.

It was, indeed, a heart-sickening scene upon which I cast my eyes;—carpets torn and soiled, spread out to look their longest and widest, and the bed adorned with shabby finery which had no doubt been splendid in the first days of wedlock; but all things the reverse of comfortable, dwindled into insignificance when compared with what I anticipated of the wide bed, with its three inmates, and the consequent disturbance of my morning hours.

My meditations were interrupted by the little trio themselves appearing, so clean and merry, that I could not find in my heart to wish them elsewhere, especially after I had asked myself what right I had to come into their sleeping-room and wish them out of it.

The next day was one of as much repose as this family were ever permitted to enjoy; but late going to bed, late rising, all the children to dress and keep clean in their Sunday-clothes, with only one servant, made it seem not much like repose to me. It was, indeed, no day of rest. The father dressed his eldest boy in tight jacket and blue cap, and walked off with him to church; the servant followed, and the mother cooked and nursed alternately all the morning, adorned herself in a little finery for the afternoon, and nursed again. I had no occupation but that of making myself a favourite with the children, which I did so effectually that I never could shake off their turbulent familiarity again. When I went up stairs half a dozen were dragging at my skirts; and when I came down, they jumped upon me from the banisters. I complained, but Mrs. Wilson never took my part; she smiled, and was glad, poor woman, to see them happy and not at her expense.

This, however, was not the way in which I must spend my time. I said that my object in coming to town was to make painting my profession, and I was then permitted to lock the door of my chamber for the day, with many charges to shut up my valuables for the night.

CHAPTER XII.

My picture proceeded slowly, for I had nothing to copy, and was not quite so skilful a performer as false friends and flattery had once induced me to believe. Still it did proceed. There was a visible line of demarkation between the heavens and the earth, and an old castle with a group of trees were beninning to emerge from chaos. My hopes rose with the clothing of the foliage, but not quite in proportion to the cost of the ultramarine which I spent upon the sky. It was worth a great deal to me, under present circumstances, to have an object from which I could derive a ray of hope, however small, and more and more rays were daily emanating from my picture. Bright visions of future aggrandizement rose upon me. Generosity stood forth in distant perspective, and I began to calculate upon the precise time when, after receiving the reward of my labours, I should place in the hands of Mrs. Wilson at least twice the sum upon which we had agreed for a month's lodging. My temper grew sweeter as my spirits were enlivened. I forgave my cousin Jane; I played at bo-peep with my companions in the morning, rose early to catch a view of my performance in the first light of day, and even permitted a little fellow, whom I had singled out as my favourite, to remain in the room with me while I was at work, provided he sat still upon the floor, and did not touch.

Like all favourites, he used his prerogative at first with moderation. On the second day I was obliged to enforce the law of not touching; on the third I had to insist upon his being quiet; and on the fourth was compelled to make a new law, that, if he rose from the floor, he should be dismissed altogether. It was a dull thing to sit still upon the floor, which nothing but the idea of its being a privilege could have reconciled; but little Jemmy was permitted to have a long piece of string, and he made the most of that.

My picture was nearly completed, and really, when there was no other to compare it with, looked, I thought, very tolerable. A few strong touches were yet to be given, bold and productive of great effect. I advanced —retreated—applied the finishing stroke, and retreated again; when crash went the whole fabric in hopeless and irrevocable ruin on the floor, overwhelming, amongst disjointed fragments, the mischievous author of it, whose busy fingers, after tying the string to the foot of the easel, had pulled it away with a sudden jerk.

That a painting never falls to the ground without the freshly smeared surface being downwards is just as worthy of remark, as that the fall of bread and butter is attended with the same fatality; a fact, the truth of which every school-boy will stand forward to attest. My picture was no exception to the general rule; and Mrs. Wilson's carpet being of too frail a texture to be ever shaken, the case was a desperate one indeed. There was nothing for me to do, but to commence my labours afresh. Little Jemmy was dismissed now and for ever. My spirits sunk, my temper failed me on the slightest provocation, and nothing but the idea that I was eating bread which I had no right to call my own, could have supported me through the wearisome task of completing another picture.

Another, however, was completed in time, and I set off on a tour of observation through the streets of London, to see what place would be most likely to receive so precious a deposit. I was not long in fixing, and with my last five shillings in my pocket, hired a hackney coach, and went forth to make my fortune in a flourishing establishment at the West End.

Finding everything here conducted on a magnificent scale, and thinking my best plan would consequently be to assume a character of importance, I asked for some costly engravings, and looking at them with the air of one who is very much disposed to purchase, but has some trifling reason for not purchasing just now, I took out my purse, concealing the empty end, and paid three shillings for a worthless article, as if money was so plentiful with me, that I could afford to throw it away.

After spending some time in this manner, I caught the quick eye of one who held a place of authority in the establishment; and who seeing a well-dressed lady disposed to trifle away her time and money, thought I must be worthy of his most polite attentions, while stretching himself forward with an ineffable smile, he laid before me rich costly books in splendid bindings, and pictures—ah! how unlike to mine!

A group of gentlemen were lounging in one corner of the shop, reading the newspapers, and turning over the trifles of the day. One glance at the idle party made me retreat to the farthest distance to transact my business with Mr. Bond. I know not what I said, nor how I made my meaning understood; but he must have been well acquainted with such meaning to understand it all. I can only recollect a dreadful sense of suffocation in my throat, and the fall of the man's countenance when he opened out my picture, and held it this way and that, to receive some flattering light by which one touch of merit might be revealed. "Ten guineas" was marked upon it as the price, but he chose to read "ten shillings," declaring it was quite too much. "Indeed we have no sale whatever for such things as these," he added, returning it to me, and glancing impatiently towards more profitable customers.

I still waited, for I was too much stupified to move. Whether Mr. Bond for once felt a touch of pity I know not, but he took up the picture, which I had let drop beside me on the floor, and condescended to point out some of its defects.

"It wants," said he, flourishing his hand

over it, with an air that implied its want of everything but paint,—"it wants sweetness —it wants repose."

"It may well want repose," I exclaimed. "If you knew where it had been painted—"

"That is no concern of ours, ma'am— None in the world. The public have nothing to do with that." And he spread forth his hands, as if in the act of driving me out, advancing every step that I receded, and opening the door most willingly for my exit.

"You had better take the painting, ma'am; we can do nothing with it here."

"You can burn it, I suppose," said I, and turned away.

I scarcely knew where I was going. Every object swam before my eyes, and I felt as lonely in that crowded street as if I had been a pilgrim wandering across the great desert. It is under this kind of bewilderment amongst the busy multitudes of the thickly peopled city, that the last attack of cruelty is generally made upon the miserable—an attack upon his purse; but the lightness of mine would have greatly mitigated the pain of losing it; and fearless of anything being added to my sufferings, I was pursuing my uncertain way, when suddenly my sleeve was touched, and a young man from the shop, almost breathless with haste, asked me to step back, saying that a gentleman had purchased the painting.

"Who is the gentleman?" I asked. The young man did not know, but said he had been standing by while I was talking with his master, and had heard all we said.

"Whoever he may be, I must thank him," I exclaimed; and when Mr. Bond with great formality laid the ten guineas before me, I begged to be permitted to see my benefactor, if possible.

With my heart overflowing with gratitude, I followed him into an adjoining room, where Sir Charles Moira advanced to meet me with his blandest smiles.

How was it that I could be thankful no more, that I longed to return the money, and would willingly have been pennyless again? It seemed as if money, of which I was always in want, was perpetually to be the bane of my happiness; and that my necessities were never to be relieved without my difficulties at the same time being increased.

I made one effort to express my thanks—thanks which I did not feel. I tried, for one moment, to be nothing but what I really was—the poor woman receiving the price of her honest labours; but I could not so far forget my former self. The remembrance of Lady Moira rose before me in overwhelming majesty. I was once more Caroline Irvine, with all her vanity, and all her littleness, and had accepted the offer of Sir Charles to escort me home, before I reflected what a home was mine.

Ah! would we but reserve our shame and our embarrassment for that which is really disgraceful and perplexing, what burning blushes, what bitter tears we might be spared!

I had none but a straightforward path to pursue. A few words of candid explanation would have revealed my simple story, and made it the last wish of Sir Charles to continue my acquaintance; but the best (I would have persuaded myself the only) time for explanation was now over; and we were pursuing our way together, I knew not to what place, nor cared, so long as it was not to that little shop, through which we must have entered had he taken me to my present home.

The morning was fine, and when my companion proposed that we should see some of the wonders of the place, I had little inclination to refuse, because I should thus enjoy a few more hours of his society, and put off that most dreaded, the hour of return. From one exhibition we passed on to another. Conversation never flagged. Sir Charles was more delightful than ever, and I rattled on with that desperate gaiety which is but a poor substitute for wretchedness.

There is no liberty like that of a vast city —no security from observation like that of being one of the multitude. Sir Charles had now nothing to fear from his lady mother, and I was a hundred miles distant from my cousin Jane. These hours, which I vainly tried to persuade myself were happy, flew swiftly on, and my behaviour had rendered it more difficult for me each succeeding moment to speak the whole truth. My companion had been too polite to hint at the affair of the picture, and I had ever since the morning, acted the lady so completely, that he must either have doubted the pecuniary dilemma which his own eyes had witnessed, or despised me for my affectation and inconsistency from the bottom of his heart. Most probably he did the latter. Indeed, had he done otherwise than despise me, he would not have attempted as he did, to lead me on from one place to another, until the day was far spent, beguiling the time with professions of admiration more ardent than are ever inspired by respect.

Women would do well to judge by this rule, of the estimation in which they are held by those whose right province is to protect them from harm and danger. It is impossible that a gentleman should be ignorant of those niceties of conduct, by which the purity and dignity of woman's character is preserved; and if he do but whisper a proposition for her to sacrifice the very smallest of these for any purpose whatever, even for his own sake, the case is a clear and decided one, that he thinks meanly of her to suppose that she will listen to his request, and that his regard for her is not such as to make him solicitous to maintain the beauty of her unsullied name.

The sum of my folly was now nearly completed, and I gravely insisted upon returning home alone.

"Alone! impossible!"

"Be kind enough to order me a coach, and I shall go very safely."

"But not alone," he repeated with a look that startled me, and I walked on again in silence, pondering on my dilemma. We were approaching one of the theatres—a celebrated performer was to delight the world that night. Carriages were rolling up, delivering their precious burdens, and then making way for others. Ladies richly dressed stepped forth, emerging from the darkness of a November evening, into the brilliant light of the theatre. Sir Charles, without a word of parley led me in. I knew not at first where he was taking me, and when I discovered, my remonstrances were too feeble to induce him to return; and, in a few moments I was seated beside him in the broad glare of a thousand lights. I had now time to think, and with a full sense of my situation, there rushed upon my mind such an overwhelming conviction of the absurdity and imprudence of my conduct through this day, that I neither listened to the music, nor heeded the spirited performance which called forth from lighter hearts than mine, unbounded applause.

My past life had been an idle one, vanity its moving spring, and folly its ruling star; but I had never completely sacrificed my self-respect till now; and many were the tears I dashed away from my eyes this night to look at the brilliant scenes, and the brighter beauties of the stage, which my gay companion whispered in my ear, were less lovely than myself.

I believe half the sins that stain the record of woman's life owe their origin to criminal weakness, rather than criminal design. I use the harsh word criminal, because that weakness deserves no better name, which is encouraged and yielded to without any appeal to an higher power for the support which is mercifully promised to the feeble. The falsehood that is told from fear, wears less the appearance of depravity than that which is told solely with a wish to deceive; but the falsehood that is wrung from terror is just as likely to be supported by other falsehoods, and to draw after it an equal train of guilt and shame. So, the slightest error knowingly persisted in, and followed up by its natural and inevitable consequences may become morally as culpable as the grossest vice. How watchful, then, should all weak creatures be of the first false step, never risking the slightest deviation under the presumptuous hope that they may have strength to return.

It was my weakness rather than my depravity which made me shrink from disclosing to Sir Charles the exact state of my circumstances and situation. This weakness had first plunged me into difficulties from which I had not sufficient rectitude and moral courage to extricate myself. At every step I had become more involved, and each succeeding moment now found me more wretched than the last.

The scene closed, the curtain fell, and rude voices from the galleries had vociferated their last applause, when I rose to depart. Silent, speechless, and sad, I leaned upon the arm of Sir Charles, who no doubt attributed the change in my manner to the prospect of being so soon deprived of the irresistible fascination of his society. His voice became more gentle, his behaviour more tender, and his looks more meaning, everything that could be done he did to mitigate the pain of losing him; and I found, when it was too late to save myself from his contempt, the necessity of making some exertion to preserve the little independence I had left.

Springing into the coach he had sent for, I insisted upon being alone; but he was at my side in a moment, and the driver waited for his orders. I remonstrated, but I had voluntarily given up my own dignity, and a lady has nothing else to defend her. It is in vain attempting to persuade the man for whom she has made this sacrifice, that he has not unlimited power over her heart. There is no alternative, but either to submit to his society and his civilities whenever he chooses to impose them upon her, or to pique his vanity, and irritate his temper by obstina.e rudeness, and then he may revenge himself upon her reputation, by representing her folly in such a light that the world will give it a harsher name.

No! there is no way for a woman to escape more wretchedness than any female heart can bear, but by walking humbly before her God, and trusting solely to his guidance through the mazes of her difficult path, where the snares of the world, and the deceitfulness of her own fancy would be perpetually leading her astray, had not that warning beacon been lighted, by which alone we are able to perceive and shun

"The thousand paths that slope the way to sin."

The vanity of Sir Charles was beyond the reach of attack: his temper was immoveable, and the driver still waited for his orders.

"To the City," I said, in too low a tone for him to hear, and Sir Charles was obliged to repeat my words.

"To what part of it?"

I named a street adjoining that in which my friends lived, somewhat broader and less filled with trade, and then shrinking back into a corner of the carriage, listened in sullen silence, to the most flattering asseverations, which now delighted me no more.

Arrived at the street I had mentioned, I was asked for the name and the number, and whether they were on the door.

I stretched my head out of the window as if to look for the place, and then told the man in plain words, so that he might hear and Sir Charles might not, that it was a grocer's shop I wanted, and the name Wilson.

It was quickly found. A thundering knock awoke my host and half his children. Young cries were heard above, and the moving of heavy bolts below. At last the door was opened by Mr. Wilson, in his night-cap. Sir Charles kissed my hand, and I sprang out of the coach.

"Surely," thought I, when my head was once more laid upon my pillow, "the mortifications of this day are enough to cure me of folly for the rest of my life."

I forgot that past folly, knowingly persisted in, is sin, and that sin is not removed by the agonies of mortified vanity.

I could not sleep. What a long season is the night to those whose hearts are oppressed with misery, and who endure that misery without the consolation of prayer. I did not pray. Had any decided calamity fallen upon me, I should have thought of no other resource; but, like many others suffering under a load of accumulated cares, I thought my petty anxieties and griefs were not subjects to be laid before the eye of Omnipotence. A feverish tide of troubled thought was rushing through my soul, where hope had forsaken her last resting place, and frightful apprehensions contended for the empire she had just resigned. Not one of all the fair pictures of imagination now seemed tangible and true, but dark visions of futurity opened upon me through the mist of tears.

If religion be the blessed messenger sent down upon earth to still the sighs of the sorrowing when the footsteps of time or death have trampled down their earthly treasures, to calm the waters of affliction, and bind up the broken-hearted; not less is her holy influence needed to smoothe the ruffled mind, which petty cares have made their prey, to quiet the rapid and tumultuous throbbings of the heart, and to direct the wandering wishes which find no certain gratification in this troubled world, to one whose pleasures are unfading, and whose rest is eternal.

CHAPTER XIII.

On the following morning I awoke with many serious thoughts, but still without any fixed determination to pursue a more decided path. My attention was absorbed by present difficulties, which I vainly tortured my ingenuity to find expedients to escape from. Indeed my whole life was a system of expedients, not to attain any laudable object, but to help me on the winding and circuitous way, by which I hoped to arrive at the universal good-will of society.

I was pondering in my own chamber upon the propriety of returning the price of my picture to Sir Charles, whose charity (for I could not attribute to him any other motive in his purchase,) was not exactly what I wished to profit by; and against the return of this money I was setting the discharge of the debt I owed to Mrs. Wilson; weighing the difficulties, and comparing evils, when a letter was brought to me from my sister. Well remembering the insulting nature of my last to her, I opened it with nervous terror, soon quieted by the kind and delicate manner in which a very eligible situation was proposed to me, and a supply of the ever needful conveyed, without the slightest allusion to the past. I was now great again, for all human greatness is by comparison. I returned the ten guineas in a blank cover, made presents to the little Wilsons, prepared for my journey, and took leave of my poor friend, with that rapidity of execution with which we escape from the misery that we cannot relieve.

I was met at the distance of one stage from my future residence by a gentleman's servant, whose kind and respectful behaviour was a sure and pleasant omen of domestic comfort. It was late in the afternoon when I first saw the lights of Mr. Morton's habitation glimmering through the leafless trees, as we wound along the side of a hill, and descended by a gentle declivity into a thickly wooded valley, where the bright line of a narrow and meandering river was here and there seen glancing through the mist. At the door I was received with a cordial welcome by a matronly-looking woman, who might be either housekeeper or nurse, and who in either situation had obtained sufficient knowledge of the domestic affairs of the family, to be able to satisfy the demands of my curiosity.

Mr. Morton was a widower, within the last year deprived of a wife whom he had almost idolized, since whose death he had but rarely been seen to smile. He was a man of fastidious tastes, and secluded habits, not lavish of his affections, but when he did love, it was with tenderness unspeakable; and all that he now seemed capable of feeling was expended upon an only child, whose extremely delicate constitution rendered her an object of painful solicitude.

"You will think Mr. Morton cold and forbidding at first," said my informer, who was kindly disposed to let me into every secret; "but there never was a more devoted husband, a kinder father, or a better master; and if you can but attach yourself to the poor child, and win her affection, you will be sure of his."

Although the worthy woman possibly meant nothing more than her master's good will, when she spoke of his affection, I thought this was going too far, and changed the subject by asking some questions about the child, when I was shocked to learn that there was every probability of her remaining an invalid for life.

"She was a sweet young creature," said Mrs. Woods; "none can help loving her who have seen her suffer. Oh! what a comfort you will be, ma'am, to this family! For though we may nurse and do all that we can, Miss Eleanor is now able to converse like a woman, and wants better society than such as me. Indeed we sometimes think she is too sensible, and that having such busy thoughts and quick feelings, makes her health more delicate. But oh! ma'am, you will be a comfort to her. I know you will." And so saying, Mrs. Woods left me to enjoy without interruption, and for the first time in my life, the hope of being really and properly useful.

The apartment into which I had been shown was called Miss Eleanor's study; but it wore more decidedly the character of a sick room, and though a few well-chosen books lay on the table, couches, cushions, and various inventions for the alleviation of suffering, bore testimony to the melancholy truth, that if this were the path to science, it was not strewn with flowers. A few appropriate pictures adorned the walls, such as simple cottage scenery, a girl drawing water at a well, a child at play, a favourite dog, a bird let loose. One large painting hung above the fire, concealed by a curtain, which I ventured to raise. It was the figure of a Madonna, beautifully executed, not with the unmeaning countenance by which most artists have chosen to disgrace this holy character, but with the clear forehead and intelligent eyes of one who could think as well as feel. I saw at once the departed mother, whose sacred silence subdued my lighter feelings, and I inwardly resolved that the reverence with which her pictured form inspired me should be my safeguard and protection while cherishing her orphan child.

Forcibly impressed as my mind already was with what I had heard and seen, I was yet more deeply interested on entering the room where the poor invalid lay. Her father was bending over her couch, and rose not until I approached, when he regarded me with an earnest and scrutinizing eye, as if to ascertain whether I were such a person as his daughter would find it possible to like.

"You have undertaken a wearisome task," said the child, holding out her hand to me, "but if you can bear with me and my impatience, every one else, I am sure, will try to make you comfortable."

"And will not you, my love?" asked the father.

"I will do my best," said she—"but there is very little that I can do."

"You can tell me freely all you want," said I.

"Ah! that I am sure I will!" she exclaimed; "you look so kind I know I shall be able to tell you every thing. But are you strong? are you healthy? are you quite able to keep awake sometimes in the night? Poor Mrs. Woods sleeps so soundly, I do not like to disturb her, and the night is so long when nobody speaks to me. It is a sad thing, Miss Irvine, that sickness makes us selfish."

"It has so pleased the disposer of our lives," I replied, "that no situation shall be without its peculiar trials. During sickness when we are exempt from any of the temptations of the world, and are almost compelled from our very weakness to seek for divine support, we might possibly grow self-righteous, had not this temptation been permitted, to convince us that we are still subject to the most despicable of human frailties."

Mr. Morton looked attentively at me, as if to discern the spirit which had prompted this speech; but the unsophisticated child, satisfied that none but a good woman could talk so well, asked me if I were not too weary to sleep beside her that night. She evidently wished it, and I could not refuse. Her father now left us, and we entered into many arrangements respecting personal comfort, and were soon as familiar and cordial as if we had been acquainted for years. Mrs. Woods would willingly have retained her place for that night, but the sudden preference poor Eleanor entertained for me, rendered me more than willing to share whatever disturbance she might endure.

The enjoyment of sleep I could not even anticipate. Strange visions of the past and future flitted before my mind, nor was the present less strange to me that it was rich in promises of peace and comfort. To be regarded with affection by this suffering child, it might be with esteem by her father, and to contribute to the happiness of both, was a harvest of enjoyment I was all unworthy to reap. I looked back into my past life, and tried to blame my luckless fate for half the culpability to which my burning tears bore witness. I had few deliberate and determined sins to charge my conscience with. The world had certainly dealt unfairly with me. I felt nothing but kindness and good will towards the whole human race, and only wished I could prove by self-sacrifice, how inexhaustible was that kindness, how unfailing that good-will. Every subterfuge that human frailty could lay hold of I tried that night, to convince myself that I had no need to be unhappy, but it would not do. Conviction came not so readily as my tears, and I wished myself a child again, that I might offer up to heaven an unsophisticated mind, and bow before the throne of mercy in perfect simplicity and singleness of heart. It is true there was no moral stain upon my character. I had laboured hard to promote the happiness of others, and religious sentiments were familiar to my lips; but how stood my trembling soul in the presence of its Creator? I could weep at midnight over my thorny and bewildered path, but I never, either at midnight or noon-day, breathed an humble prayer that I might be solely guided by his will. I never formed an earnest resolution that I would serve Him and Him only. I never seriously endeavoured to lay hold of those promises by which the burden of past transgression is made more tolerable, nor looked with steadiness towards that star whose inextinguishable light would have led me safely through the storms of life.

Unacquainted with the importance of living for one object only, some may be disposed to think that I distressed myself more than was necessary, so long as what the world calls guilt was not stamped upon my conscience; but are we not told in the record of eternal truth, that those who are not for the righteous cause are against it? And though I could freely and fluently recommend religion to others as an ultimate good, where was the evidence of my own espousal.

While pondering in my own mind upon a world of dark and troubled thoughts, my attention was arrested by the sweet voice of my companion, repeating, in a low and gentle tone, the following words:—

In the still watches of the solemn night,
  While chilly dews are falling thick and damp,
And countless stars shed forth their feeble light,
  The silent mourner trims her cheerless lamp.

Alone she watches through the midnight hour,
  Alone she breathes the melancholy sigh,
Alone she droops like some neglected flower,
  Unseen the tears that dim her sleepless eye.

Alone! There is no loneliness with God,
  No darkness that he cannot turn to light;
No flinty rock, from whence his gracious rod
  May not bring forth fresh waters, pure and bright.

There is no wilderness whose desert caves
  Are hid from his all-penetrating eye;
Nor rolls that ocean, whose tumultuous waves
  May not be silenced when the Lord is nigh.

There is no bark upon the trackless main,
  No pilgrim lone, whose path he cannot see
Peace! then, poor mourner, trim thy lamp again,
  The eye that knows no slumber, watches thee.

These words were followed by a sigh so deep and heavy, that I roused myself from my fruitless meditations to ask, whether my young friend was in pain.

"Not so much in pain, as weary," she replied. "I am afraid I have disturbed you, but the night is very long, and my mother used to teach me to repeat verses and hymns when I could not rest. You must not pay any regard to me, but try to sleep again."

I replied, that I had not yet slept.

"Ah! I dare say you have been thinking of your home."

"I have no home, my love."

"No home! Then you must sometimes be very sad. But still you have a home for your thoughts. Some secret resting place of which no one can deprive you."

Poor child! she little knew in what a barren wilderness my thoughts were ranging, nor how long it was since they had found a resting place.

I made no answer, and the invalid, somewhat excited by fever, went on with her conversation, asking with perfect simplicity, many close questions which I had no choice but to answer, yet to answer which, fully and candidly, would have deprived me for ever of her esteem. Towards morning, however, she slept soundly, and awoke without much recollection of what had passed in the night.

I had now a severe ordeal to pass through in the presence of Morton, whose commanding countenanee, reserved manners, and strict scrutinizing eye, rendered him a truly alarming person, when brought into close contact with one who felt no certainty of his approbation. I soon found that the society of this man would either render me more contemptible, by driving me to the practice of deceit, or more worthy, by inspiring the desire to merit his respect, which it was easy to discover could be obtained in no other way, than by a steady, consistent, and rational course of action. The mind of Morton was not so expansive as his character was dignified, and his tastes refined and exclusive. Had he seen more of the world, he might have been more liberal, but his sentiments would have been less pure. What would I not have given for a full and complete conviction, that he thought he had acted wisely in choosing me for the companion of his child? I vain I sought to win his favour by every artifice which I deemed too remote for detection. Artifice had no effect upon a character so firm and sterling. What I failed to accomplish in this way, was, however, in time effected by my simple and unstudied services to his child; who sometimes gave her father such glowing descriptions of my unremitting kindness, that he rewarded me with a smile too expressive of entire confidence, for me ever to forget.

It was, indeed, as the kind nurse had told me; no one could witness the sufferings of Eleanor Morton without loving her. She was not impatient, but so perfectly guileless, that she concealed nothing, and after having permitted herself to speak as she thought too freely of her own distressing feelings, she would sometimes shed, over what she called her weakness and ingratitude, tears more agonizing than pain alone had been able to wring from her. With no one was she so completely undisguised in her moments of suffering, as with me.

"Mrs. Woods," said she, "pities me too much, and I cannot tell my father all that I feel, lest I should distress him. It is quite different with us all now that you are come, Miss Irvine. Are you not happy to have made us so cheerful again? Even my father is quite an altered man. I thought this morning, when he looked at you, that he smiled as he used to smile upon my mother. And do you know he talks of inviting company to the house again, for he says it is not good for you to lead so secluded a life.

I replied, that my wish was only to be useful, and that I felt no want of society.

"Well, don't say anything about it, for I am quite sure it will do him good, as well as you, to have some one now and then to converse with out of our own family. I dare say you will take all the trouble off his hands, and will not let him feel the want of my mother, who used to be so easy and pleasant in conversation, that entertaining company has appeared quite impossible to my poor father, since he was alone."

I could not help feeling a secret glow of exultation at the idea that I should now be able to exhibit my character to Morton, in what I considered its most pleasing light. The guests arrived. I had dressed myself with studied care; and my spirits rose, with the prospect of once more having a fair field, in which to exercise my powers of pleasing. Knowing, too well, the trial of patience it must be to Morton to carry on the empty common-place of desultory conversation, I endeavoured to relieve his difficulty, by doubling and redoubling my natural vivacity; and whatever his guests might think of my proper station in his establishment, I was fully convinced of their perfect satisfaction in finding so lively and entertaining a person, for that day, at the head of it.

More than once I detected the steady eyes of Morton fixed upon me, when his lips were silent, and there was an earnest meaning in his gaze, which made the colour rush into my face—I knew not why. At last he left the room, and for so long a time, that I began to think seriously of my little invalid friend; and apologizing to the company for the necessity of attending to duties which I had too long forgotten, I ran hastily up stairs to pay my first visit to Eleanor since the arrival of the guests.

Her father was bending over her couch in the same attitude in which I had first seen him. They had been conversing, but their voices dropped when I opened the door; and when Morton rose for me to take my proper place, he pressed his handkerchief to his eyes with more emotion than he was wont to betray, and hastily left the room.

"Come near to me, my friend," said Eleanor, stretching out her hand. "You have been a long time away. I am afraid my father thinks you have neglected me; and there is so much mirth below, he does not know how to bear it. My mother was a very gentle woman, such as you are in the nursery with me. But are you always the same, Miss Irvine?"

"I am always sorry when I have given pain," said I.

"Perhaps you are too anxious to give pleasure," continued the child. "And that I am sure would give my father pain in any one he loved."

I was almost comforted with the close of this sentence, for there was a certain refinement and devotion in the character of Morton, that made his esteem the highest object of my ambition. But his love!—I had never dared to think of his love before.

"We heard of you," the child went on, "long before we saw you; that you were a very charming woman, a sort of idol in society. Now, my father is worth pleasing, but you cannot please him and all the world beside. He will explain to you better than I can, how it makes a person little and contemptible to be always studying to please, and how there is but one Being in the universe whose favour is worth the constant trouble of obtaining. Do not think me impertinent, Miss Irvine, for speaking to you in this manner; I am only an ignorant child, but I lie here upon this weary bed, pondering upon many grave and serious things, which, if I could enjoy exercise, and play like other children, I should most likely never dream of. Tell me, my dear friend, that you are not offended."

"No, no," I replied, "I am distressed, but not offended. You shall be my kind and faithful monitress, Eleanor, for your Heavenly Father makes up to you for the privations he inflicts, by a clearer sense of what is right, than I have ever enjoyed."

"But may you not enjoy the same? May not all who wish to be directed find a guide?"

"Yes, Eleanor, but to wish earnestly and with true sincerity of heart is the difficulty."

"And to wish always is another difficulty. For sometimes when I am quite at ease, and kind friends are doing more than enough, I do wish from the bottom of my heart, that I may never be impatient again; but when my pain returns, and no one is at liberty to stay with me, or perhaps when they do not understand my meaning, I scarcely wish at all; and then you may be sure I am very impatient, and very wicked. I think the only way is to wish as much and as often as we can, and to pray God not to forget us, in our moments of weakness, when we are but too likely to forget him.

More than twelve months had now passed since I first became an inmate with this family, and the time I spent with Morton and his interesting child, was certainly the most useful, as it was the happiest of my life. Amongst the select circle of their intimate associates, was a lady whom I never could compel myself to like so well as my judgment convinced me that I ought. Had Miss Evelyn ever been addicted to the levities of youth, she was past the age for those levities to interfere with the dignity of a character even less intellectual than hers; and the speculations of idle gossips who sport with great characters as well as small, had fixed upon her as the future mother of my helpless charge. Mother! I almost shuddered when I thought of this woman as the mother of poor Eleanor. She was, however, in high favour with the father, and a frequent visitor at his house; where her masculine understanding, deep knowledge of books, and fearless conversation on subjects usually beyond the aim and compass of her sex, threw me and my shallow attainments, so far into the back-ground, that had it not been for the kind regard of Morton, not unfrequently shown me, by little personal attentions in the midst of her luminous harangues, I should have felt more disturbed by her presence than was at all reasonable, so long as these kind attentions were continued. It was enough for me that while Miss Evelyn was quoting learned authors, and arguing about the construction of a Greek sentence, my personal comfort was not forgotten. It was more than enough; for what woman's heart is not made to glow with more intense delight by these proofs of tenderness and regard, than by the most flattering tribute of mere admiration.

With the lapse of time, Morton gradually recovered the serenity of his mind, and could even enjoy a social evening spent in society congenial to his taste. Miss Evelyn had joined a select party, gathered round his fire one winter's day, when the conversation turned upon the internal evidence of the Holy Scriptures, and Morton took up the arguments of those who would overthrow the Christian scheme altogether. It might be evident to others that he was doing this merely for the sake of proving afresh the weakness of these arguments, but to me it was not; and finding him on the weaker side, and Miss Evelyn on the stronger, and choosing rather to support him, than to defend the truth, I threw all my force into the rising scale, convincing those who heard me, that I was ready to advocate the cause of right or wrong, just as caprice might dictate, but that I should never be a very able defender of either.

Argument has a much greater tendency to convince those who speak, than those who hear; and I was just beginning to be fully confirmed in the truth of the absurdities I was uttering, when Morton suddenly broke the thread of our discourse by acknowledging himself foiled by the superior dexterity of Miss Evelyn, "or rather," he added, "by the superiority of that cause, which I only attacked for the pleasure of hearing it defended by a woman."

Every eye was now turned towards me, and Miss Evelyn was not too dignified to triumph over a fallen enemy. I tried to look at ease, and to put on an appearance of having been at play rather than in earnest; but a sensation of intense littleness prevented the expansion of a smile, and I rejoiced almost for the first time in my life, as soon as I found myself forgotten.

When the guests were gone, I looked .o Morton for consolation; but I looked in vain. His eye was turned towards me with an expression of melancholy tenderness which I did not understand, and for several succeeding days, his behaviour was equally inexplicable. I sometimes detected him gazing silently upon my face, and could not, when I turned away, help feeling that I was still the object of his earnest attention. Sometimes, after conversing in a tone unusually familiar, he abruptly left the room; and at other times, his voice was so mournful, and his countenance so dejected, that I longed to participate in his secret cares, and if possible, to chase them away. All kinds of caprice and inconsistency were so foreign to his nature, that I was entirely at a loss what construction to put upon this change, and had it not evidently been a case of deeper intricacy than ought to be communicated to a child, I should have referred my anxiety to Eleanor. So far as I could venture with propriety, I did, and learned from her that she too thought something must have disturbed her father's mind. "More especially," she added, "because he yesterday gave orders for the removal of the curtain which concealed my mother's picture; and after gazing on her face, for a long time, he said, in a melancholy voice, 'Eleanor, we need all the helps we can lay hold of in this troublesome world. May not the holy calm of this countenance sometimes help to preserve you and me from evil? If guardian spirits are permitted to attend us through the pilgrimage of life, surely your mother will be mine and yours. And as I had no thoughts concealed from her while living, so I desire that those eyes may be constantly before me to remind me of my duty now.'"

It was not many days before the mystery was unravelled. I found upon my table, on retiring for the night, a letter directed for me, in Morton's hand-writing. I took it up —a sudden thought flashed across my mind, bright as the beams of the rising sun to the bewildered traveller. "It must be so—then why this melancholy—this deep conflict of feeling?" All was accounted for by the idea that a parent has much to take into consideration. I gave the reins to my imagination, and for one short moment, was happy. I was grateful, too, and bowed my knee to return thanks, that at last I had found a home, a protector, and a guide.

"All-unworthy as I am, he shall not find his confidence misplaced. I will cherish his poor child, and in loving her and him, I shall learn in time to love all things holy.

An important fact was yet to be ascertained. The seal was unbroken, and my ecstacy was of such short duration, that I had scarcely strength enough remaining to unfold the paper. The first ill omen I perceived was a sum of money which fell at my feet unheeded. The letter was a long one, kindly and delicately worded. I remember every sentence, every thought, every syllable, at which I looked and looked again, to ascertain whether it would bear a different construction. The concluding paragraph ran thus:

"How ungrateful is the duty of offering you, in return for all your kindness to me and mine, this painful proof of my entire confidence. I know that I am depriving myself of a companion, who has both the power and the wish to soothe me, and that no one on earth can now supply your place. I feel as none but a parent can feel, that I am depriving my helpless child of the tender solicitude of a mother, and when she appeals to me only for those services which you have been accustomed to perform, what answer shall I make? All these considerations I have weighed day after day, and often at deep midnight, when you were not near me to beguile my thoughts, I have watched you with the eye of a husband and a father, and my solemn conviction is that we must part. Not that you have omitted to fill up the measure of sympathy and kindness with all that an amiable heart could supply, but because the mother of my child must be religious as well as amiable; the wife of my bosom must be united to her God.

"To a woman of your delicacy I need say no more, than that you are too charming, and might become too dear. What I have already said has been wrung from my heart with more agony than I had thought myself capable of feeling again. Farewell! and if the assistance of a true and faithful friend can ever be of service to you in any future difficulty, remember one who never can forget you."

As if in mercy to me, Eleanor was permitted to sleep soundly that night. In the morning I learned that Morton had gone out early, saying that he should not return until the evening of the following day. I could not misconstrue his meaning. He wished not to meet me again. While sending me forth from his home, he had done what he could to smoothe my way. He had told the domestics that circumstances had occurred to induce me to leave his family immediately. The great difficulty was with poor Eleanor. For her he had left a note, and when I returned, after having placed it in her hand, I found that she had buried her face in the pillow, and that her tender frame was almost convulsed with the violence of her grief; but while trying to comfort her, I was enabled, in some measure, to forget my own. I sat with her all that day, and towards evening we could both converse more calmly.

"My father has not told me," said she, "why you are going to leave us, nor do I seek to know, for, had it been right that I should, he would not have concealed it from me. I almost wish you had never come; and yet it will be pleasant to think sometimes when I am suffering, that you would gladly be near me. May God be good to you, as you have been to me. I will pray for you in the long night, when I cannot sleep; and if ever time hangs heavily upon you, if friends are unkind, or you are tossed about without a home, think, if it be any consolation to you, that you are remembered in the supplications of a poor child."

Eleanor talked and wept until wearied nature was worn out. I told her that I had concluded to set off with the first dawn of the morning. Before she sighed her last farewell, her strength was so much exhausted that I could perceive the poignancy of her grief was gone; and before I stole out of her chamber, I had the satisfaction of feeling her breathe quietly, and regularly, as I stooped down to gaze once more upon her calm and beautiful face.

It was through the dull haze of a winter's morning that I turned to look again into that peaceful valley. I saw the light from the window I had called my own—I saw it for the last time glimmering through the trees. The river was still gliding on—all nature was the same as when I first beheld that scene. Another spring would clothe those trees in verdant beauty, but no bright hope of renovated gladness shone upon my path, for mine was the winter of the soul.

THE END.

A

VOICE FROM THE VINTAGE,

ON

THE FORCE OF EXAMPLE:

ADDRESSED

TO THOSE WHO THINK AND FEEL.

BY MRS. ELLIS,

AUTHOR OF "THE WIVES OF ENGLAND," ETC., ETC., ETC.

AUTHOR'S EDITION,

COMPLETE IN ONE VOLUME.

New-York;

EDWARD WALKER 114 FULTON-STREET.

A VOICE FROM THE VINTAGE.

CHAPTER I.

PECULIARITIES OF INTEMPERANCE AS A VICE.

If the physician, on taking charge of an invalid, should simply employ himself in laying down rules for the preservation of perfect health, it is evident that his advice would be of but little service in the removal of any existing disease under which his patient might be laboring. His rules might be excellent, his theory correct; but how would such a patient benefit by either? His malady would require the application of some direct and practical remedy, before he could be in a situation to take advantage of any method, however excellent, for the preservation of perfect health.

It is thus with the moral, as well as the physical maladies of mankind. It would be a comparatively easy and pleasant task to lay down rules for the preservation of sobriety, order, and happiness, provided they had never been interrupted; but when evil habits have once gained the ascendancy, and the moral harmony of society has been destroyed, there must be a corrective employed to check what is evil, before any incentive can efficiently operate in promoting what is good.

Although the *exceeding sinfulness of sin* precludes all idea of there being in the Divine sight, any degree or modification in the nature of sin itself; yet with regard to particular vices as they come under human observation, there are certain points of distinction which demand particular attention, and require appropriate treatment, as we see by the variety of regulations instituted for the well-being of society, and the still greater variety of systems of moral discipline brought into exercise for the purpose of controlling the evil tendencies of our common nature.

None who have ever been truly awakened to a sense of the all-sufficient power of religious influence upon the human heart, will be liable to suppose, that any mode or system of moral discipline, simply as such, can be effectual in its operation upon the life and character, so as, ultimately, to secure the salvation of the soul; but as a child is carefully taught that truth and kindness are good, and falsehood and cruelty evil, long before it knows any thing of the religion of the Bible; so, in the case of every particular vice which has been known in the world, it may fairly be said to be better that it should be given up, than continued; provided only, it cannot be overcome except by the substitution of another. It is no small point gained, when an immortal being, a fellow-traveller in the journey of life, is prevailed upon to cease to do evil in any one respect. He is, at least, in a better condition for learning to do well, than while persisting in his former course.

If a child, a servant, or any one under our care, has been accustomed to tell falsehoods, we rejoice over the first symptoms of their having learned to fear a lie, even though their conduct should evince no other indication of a moral change. We do not say, "Let him return to the evil of his ways, for it is of no use his leading a stricter life in this respect, unless he becomes altogether a changed character." We do not say this, because we know that the well-being of society, and the good of every individual connected with him, require that he should give up this particular habit, and if for no other reason, we think it sufficient that it should be given up for this—that the tendency of all evil is to contaminate, and that no vice can exist alone, but if indulged will necessarily extend itself, and pollute whatever it comes in contact with, by this means producing innumerable poisonous fruits from one deleterious root. Thus the state of society is proportionally improved every time a vicious habit is wholly given up; and if this be true of vice in general, how eminently is it the case with that if intemperance; because there is no other, which, on the one hand, is so countenanced by the customs of the world, and which, on the other, spreads its baneful influence to so fearful and deadly an extent.

Intemperance is the only vice in the dark catalogue of man's offences against the will, and the word, of his Maker, which directly assails the citadel of human reason, and by destroying the power to choose betwixt good and evil, renders the being whose similitude was originally divine, no longer a moral agent, but a mere idiot in purpose, and animal in action. The man who is habitually intemperate consequently makes a voluntary surrender of all control over his own conduct, and lives for the greater portion of his time deprived of that highest attribute of man—his rational faculties. It is, however, a fact, deserving our most serious consideration, that in this state he is more alive, than under ordinary circumstances, to the impulse of feeling, and of passion; so that while on the one hand he has less reason to instruct him how to act, on the other he has more restlessness and impetuosity to force him into action.

It has been calculated that of persons thus degraded, there are at the present time existing in Great Britain more than six hundred thousand, of whom sixty thousand die annually, the wretched victims of this appalling vice.

Such, then, is the peculiarity of intemperance, that while all other vices leave the mind untouched and the conscience at liberty to detect and warn of their commission, this alone subdues the reasoning powers, so that they have no capability of resistance; and while all other vices are such from their earliest commencement, this alone only begins to be a vice at that precise point when the clearness of the mind, and the activity of the conscience, begin to fail; and thus it progresses, according to the generally received opinion, by increasing in culpability in the exact proportion by which mental capability and moral power are diminished.

What an extraordinary measurement of guilt is this for an enlightened world to make! In all other cases a man's culpability is measured precisely by the ability he has to detect evil, and the power he possesses to withstand temptation. In this alone he is first encouraged by society, and this is while his natural powers remain unimpaired. No blame attaches to him then. He is a fit companion for wise and good men: but no sooner does his reason give way than he is first slightly censured by society, then shunned, then despised, and finally abhorred; just according to the progressive stages by which he has become less capable of understanding what is right, and controlling his own inclinations to what is wrong.

It is another striking feature in the character of intemperance as a vice, that it commences not only under the sanction of the low, but under that of what is called the best society; not only under the sanction of the world, but under that of religious professors, who believe themselves called out of darkness into light. It begins with the first welcome which kind and Christian friends assemble to give to a young immortal being, just ushered into a state of probation, by which it is to be fitted for eternity; and it extends through all the most social and cheering, as well as through many of the most lasting and sacred associations we form on earth; until at last, when the tie is broken, and the grave receives our lost and loved, the solemn scene is closed, and the mourner's heart is soothed, by the commencement of intemperance.

I say the *commencement*, for who can tell at what draught, what portion of a draught, what drop, for it must really come to this—who can say, then, at what drop of the potent cup sobriety ceases, and intemperance begins? The intemperate man himself cannot tell, for it has justly been observed, that "instead of feeling that he is taking too much, his only impression is, that he has not had enough." Who then shall warn him? Even if he were in a condition to listen to remonstrance, who should be his judge? If it be perfectly innocent, nay right, in the first instance to partake of this beverage, say to the extent of two thousand drops; if all sorts of persons, up to the highest scale of religious scrupulosity, take this quantity, and more, and deem it right to take it, even to double or treble it as occasion may demand, it must be strong evidence that quantity, as regards a few thousand drops, can be of little consequence. Still there is, there must be a precise point at which mankind ought to stop, or why is the unanimous voice of society lifted up against the intemperate? But why, above all, are we told that no drunkard can *enter the kingdom of Heaven?*

Ask this question of a hundred persons, and they will in all probability each give you a different account of the measurement by which they ascertain at what point intemperance begins; because there are all the different habits and constitutions of mankind to be taken into account, as well as all the different degrees of potency in the intoxicating draught, according to its name and quality. Of twenty persons seated at the same table, and regaling themselves with the same wine, it is more than probable that the fatal drop at which intemperance begins, would not be in the same glass with any two among them. Who then shall decide this momentous question? for it is momentous, since eternal condemnation depends upon it. Let us reduce the number of persons, and see whether by this means the case will be more clear. We will suppose, then, that three persons sit down to table to take their wine, or whatever it may be, in what is called an innocent and social way. Out of this small number, it is possible that one may commit a deadly sin without taking more than the others. Yet to him it is sin, simply because the drop of transition between good and evil, from the peculiar constitution of his bodily frame, occurs in his glass at an earlier stage than it does with the others. These three men, consequently, rise from that table according to the opinion of the world in a totally different moral state, for one has been guilty of a degrading vice, and the others are perfectly innocent. Yet all have done the same thing. Who then, I would ask again, is to decide in such a case? I repeat, it cannot be the guilty man himself, because that very line which constitutes the minute transition between a state of innocence and a state of sin, is the same at which he ceased to be able clearly to distinguish between one and the other.

It is impossible, then, that this question should ever be decided, unless every one who indulges in the use of such beverage would take the trouble to calculate the exact distance between the extremes of sobriety and intoxication, not only computed by every variety of liquid in which alcohol is contained, but by every variety of bodily sensation which he may be liable to experience. This calculation will bring him to one particular point, which may not improperly be called the point of transition, at which positive evil begins, and beyond which it is a positive sin to go. Who, then, I ask again, shall fix this point? It must of necessity be left to the calculations of the man whose inclination in the hour of temptation is *not* to see it, whose desire is to step over it, and whose perceptions at that time are so clouded and obscured, that he could not ascertain it if he would.

Here, then, we see a marked difference betwixt intemperance and every other vice. Theft, for instance, is as much theft at the beginning as it is at the end; and if a case should occur in which there was any doubt about the act being really such, reason might immediately be applied to as unimpaired; nor would any other of the faculties of the mind have suffered in the slightest degree from the commission of a dishonest deed. Neither are there any degrees of theft openly countenanced by the world, and by religious society. We will not say that there are not tricks in trade, and dishonest practices which exist to the discredit of our country and our profession, but they are chiefly done in secret, and acknowledged, at least in the pulpit, to be wrong.

Another characteristic of intemperance is, that it often begins in what are considered the happiest and most social moments of a person's life. It begins when the hospitable board is spread, and when friend meets friend; when the winter's fire is blazing; when the summer's ramble is finished; on the eve of parting, when moments glide away with the preciousness of hours; when hearts warm towards each other; when broken confidence is restored; when the father welcomes back his son; and when the young and trusting bride first enters her new home. All these, and tens of thousands of associations, all as tender, and some of them more dear, are interwoven with our recollections of the tempting draught, which of itself demands no borrowed sweets.

How different from this are all other vices! Injurious to society in the first instance, as well as in the last, selfish in their own nature, and avowedly abhorred, they no sooner appear in their naked form, than a check is put upon them by the united voice of society. The thief is not welcomed into the bosom of kind families after he has been known to steal a *little*. The miser, whose evil propensities are, next to intemperance, the most insidious in their nature, is spurned and hated before his failing has become a vice. And so it is with all who sin in other ways. They are acknowledged to be dangerous as companions, and injurious as citizens, in the commencement of their guilt. It is only by denying a knowledge of their actual conduct, that they are supported and countenanced even by their friends. So *far as they are acknowledged* to be guilty, they are condemned, though having sinned but a *little;* while the victim of intemperance alone carries with him the sanction of society long after the commencement of his career; nay, he drinks of the very same bowl with the religious professor until he has lost the power to refrain.

The victim of intemperance may have originally sat down to the same cheering draught as the religious man. He may have been his friend. But it so happens that his constitution of body is different. With him the transition point occurs at an earlier period than with the other. He passes this without being aware of his danger, and his mastery over himself is lost. What horror then seizes the religious man, not against himself for having partaken with his friend, but against that friend for having gone too far. Had he begun with him to commit a little theft, or to tell a slight falsehood, and his friend had gone too far, he would have blamed himself for the remainder of his life for being accessory to the downfall of that friend; but here he starts back, considers himself, and is considered by others, as perfectly innocent; while his friend, who has committed nothing but a *little more* of the very same act, is shunned as degraded, and denounced as guilty.

The voice of society is most injurious, and unfair, with regard to intemperate persons. They are classed together as belonging to the lowest grade of human beings, frequenters of vicious haunts, and perpetrators of every abomination. It is a melancholy truth that such for the most part they *become;* but it is equally true, that many, if not most of them, have been thinned out from the ranks of honest and of honorable men, whose principles and habits were precisely the same as their own, in the first instance, but whose bodily constitution, and whose powers of self-mastery, were stronger, and who thus happened to remain on the safe side of the transition line.

I would not, for an instant, be supposed to doubt the efficacy of constant watchfulness, under the influence of religious principle; and, above every other consideration, the all-sufficient power of that Divine assistance, which alone can be expected in answer to fervent and heartfelt prayer. I would not insinuate a doubt that thousands have not been prevented by this means from going too far, even under the critical circumstances already described. But I speak of people generally—of society as it is constituted—of things as they *are;* and I speak under the conviction, that, notwithstanding all the efforts of ministers of religion, and of zealous and devoted friends to the promotion of the Gospel of Christ, some additional effort is required, and some other means are necessary, in order to rescue from destruction the thousands who now fill the ranks of intemperance, and the thousands beyond these, who, from cultivating the same habits, are following unconsciously in the same fatal course.

There is another important point of difference betwixt the victims of intemperance and those who are addicted to any other vice. The dishonest man begins his guilty course with a meanness of purpose, and a degradation of soul, which mark him out as a stain upon the society of which he forms a part. The miser cherishes, along with his thirst for gold, a hardness, a grudging, and sometimes a hatred against his fellow-beings. And so it is throughout the whole catalogue of evil, which marks the downward progress of degraded and guilty men. They are guilty and polluted even before the vices to which they addict themselves are committed. They are guilty before the world, and obnoxious to the open censure of society, just in proportion as they have harbored a thought, a conception, or a design, inimical to its well-being, and destructive of its peace. But the intemperate man begins his career with no such malevolent feeling. He begins it, most frequently, without a wrong intention at all; and is often—alas! too often—the kindest of the kind, the favorite guest, the beloved companion of those who cheerfully accompany him along the first stage of his dangerous career. It is, however, the most lamentable feature in his case, that although he may thus begin with a noble, generous, and affectionate heart, he invariably *becomes* mean, selfish, and even cruel.

An impartial observation of the world will, I believe, support me, when I repeat, that the habitually intemperate are, for the most part, persons who have been originally social, benevolent, and tender-hearted, lovers of their fellow-men, of cordial meetings, and of those gatherings together of congenial spirits, which it would be impossible for a harder and less feeling nature so fully to enjoy. They are persons who, from excessive sensibility to pain and pleasure, are liable to be too much elated by the one, and depressed by the other, for their own peace—persons to whom enjoyment is too intense, and suffering too wretched, to be experienced with equanimity of mind—to whom a social hour with chosen friends is absolute felicity, and a wounded spirit death.

To such the intoxicating draught has ever been the strongest temptation, because, while on the one hand, it seemed for the moment to heighten every pleasure, on the other it has, for a season equally transient, the power of smoothing off the edge of every pain.

Again, we all know the force with which certain bodily diseases operate upon the mind; we know that the sensation of perfect health is enlivening to the mental faculties, and even cheering to the soul. In this state we can form and execute plans of which we should have been incapable under certain kinds of sickness, even had the power of action been unimpaired. Thus the mind is in a great degree dependent upon the body, and especially those functions of the body, with which nervous sensation is most intimately connected. In a state of nervous disorder, the powers of perception, judgment, and decision, are so far deranged, that even conscience ceases to exercise a just and lawful influence, and ideas are conceived, and actions performed, under a total incapacity for clearly distinguishing right from wrong.

Inebriation, from the effect it produces upon the stomach and the brain, has a more instantaneous influence upon the nervous system, and consequently upon the mind, than any other disease. There are of course, degrees of this influence, beginning first with the slightly pleasurable sensation which some persons experience after drinking a single glass of wine, and extending to the last and fatal draught of the poor outcast from respectable society. It is often asked, why does not the drunkard stop? and he is sometimes most severely blamed for taking too much, by those who take only a little less. But how should he stop, when his mind has lost its healthy tone in consequence of the particular state of his body?—when he ceases to be capable of distinguishing betwixt good and evil, and cares not for any consequences that may come upon him? How should he stop? It is a mockery of common sense, and an insult to common feeling, to suppose that of himself, and unaided, he should have the power to do so. At that critical moment he has not even the *wish* to stop. So far from it, his inclination is on the opposite side, and the whole force of his animal nature, with an excess of bodily appetite, are increasing on the side of evil, in the same proportion that his mental capabilities, his conscience, and his power of self-mastery, are becoming weaker on the side of good.

And this is the man of whom the world judges so hardly, because he has passed unconsciously the forbidden line—because he has never been able to ascertain exactly where it was—and, most probably, because from some natural constitution of body, the same draught which was safely drunk by another, was one of fearful peril to him.

The original construction of the bodily frame has much to do with the diseases to which we are liable through the whole of our lives. There are hereditary tendencies which the skill of the physician, the care of the parent, and the advice of the friend are strenuously exerted to correct. In no case are hereditary tendencies more striking than in the children of intemperate parents. It is true the very excess, and consequent ruin of one generation, not unfrequently tend to place certain individuals of the next more scrupulously upon their guard against the same lamentable fate, and ultimate safety often depends upon an early apprehension of danger. But there is in the bodily constitution of such families a peculiar liability which ought to render them the objects of the tenderest sympathy, and the most watchful care to others. There is in their very nature, if once excited, an aching want of that stimulus, which even a very slight degree of intoxication supplies; and when once this want is gratified, it increases to such a degree, as to resemble a consuming fire, whose torment nothing can alleviate, but constant libations of the same deadly draught.

Now it is quite impossible we should know, when mixing in general society, where and when we may meet with individuals of this constitutional tendency; for even with children of the most respectable parents, it sometimes prevails to an alarming extent. Perhaps we sit down to table with twenty persons, and among them is one of those to whom the cup of which others are drinking, as they believe innocently, is the cup of poison and of death. Perhaps that one is a father's hope, or the only child of a widowed mother, or the beloved and betrothed of a young and trusting heart, about to become the father of a family, the head of a household, and himself in his turn an example and a guide to others. His friends drink with him. They all partake in safety, but within his bosom the latent elements of destruction are set on fire, and he plunges headlong into shame, and misery, and ruin. To a certain extent his friends have gone along with him. They have even pressed and encouraged him to partake; but no sooner do they perceive that he has overstepped a certain dubious and almost imperceptible limit—or in other words, that his bodily frame has not been able to sustain what they have borne uninjured—than they turn from him, and acknowledge him no more as a companion and a friend. They are, in fact, ashamed to be seen with him. He loses caste among them, becomes a marked man, and is finally left to perish as an object of disgust and loathing, too gross to be reclaimed, and too low for pity.

Nor is it with those who are constitutionally liable alone that this bodily tendency exists. The habit of intemperance itself creates it; and thousands who have begun their ruinous career simply out of compliance with the usages of society, and not a few who have done so under medical advice, have acquired, for certain kinds of stimulants, and sometimes for all, an habitual craving, which they have ultimately sacrificed every other consideration to gratify. How do we know then, in mixing with society, but that we are sitting down to table with some individual who has just arrived at the turning point in this career?—one who has just begun to suspect his own danger, who is hanging, as the weak always do, upon the example of others, and looking especially to religious people, to see what sanction they may give to an indulgence for which he is ever in search of an excuse? How do we know, among the many with whom we associate, and whose private history is untold to us—how do we know whose eyes may be fixed upon us, with anxious hope that we shall go along with them in the course they are so desirous to pursue, though they would still wish to pursue it without condemnation or guilt. Now, if these eyes should be beaming from a young and trusting heart, unconscious of the whole extent of the danger, and fondly believing that safety dwells with us, but more especially if they beam from the fair countenance of woman—oh, if at the same moment we could look upon the misery and the guilt that would ensue to the being thus regarding us, and thus plunging into perdition from our example, what should we say to the Christian man or woman, who could esteem a trifling act of self-denial—of mere bodily privation—as too great a sacrifice to be made on such an occasion!

"Oh, but!" the indignant exclamation is, "we do not meet with persons of this kind in respectable society. *We* do not sit down with such at table. The haunts of vice are where they resort. *We* can have nothing to do with their excesses." From whence then has come that degraded figure, with his tattered garments, yet with the air of gentility still about him? From whence has come that wretched female, shrinking from the public gaze, as if the remembrance of her childhood, and the honored roof beneath which her girlish footsteps trod, was yet too strong for that burning fire to consume, or that fatal flood to drown? Among the six hundred thousand victims of intemperance now in existence, are there not many such as these?—many who have known what it was to be respectably brought up, who had better thoughts, and purer feelings, in their youth, and who shrunk, as we do now, with horror and disgust from the contemplation of a figure presenting such a wreck of humanity as theirs?

But acknowledging that these six hundred thousand persons are already lost—that their doom is sealed—that they are beyond the reach of our influence, and beneath even our charity to pity as we pass them by—acknowledging what is a well-authenticated fact, that sixty thousand of these die annually—what shall we say of the sixty thousand who will, during the course of this year, come forward to supply their place in the ranks of intemperance? Let us pause a moment to contemplate the awful fact, that unless rescued from destruction by some extraordinary interposition of Divine Providence, there will be sixty thousand persons entered upon the list of intemperance during the present year, and that an equal number, before twelve months have passed, will have died the death of those of whom it is clearly stated, that none can enter the kingdom of heaven!

Yet, after all, the actual death of these persons, violent, and distressing, and hopeless as such deaths generally are—their actual death must not be considered as by any means the extent of the evil of intemperance in any single case. I have already stated, that although intemperance often begins with unconsciousness of evil, in connection with social feeling, and benevolence of heart, and often, too, with high intellectual advantages, it almost invariably ends in every species of degradation to which human nature is liable—in falsehood, meanness, profanity, and every description of vice. Thus there is a bad atmosphere surrounding each one of these individuals, which taints, and often poisons, the moral feelings of those who breathe within it. Besides which, every one who feels himself to have overstepped what the world considers as the bounds of propriety, feels an interest in drawing others down along with him into the same gulf. His influence is consequently exerted over the unwary, the trusting, and the weak, and often exerted in such a manner, that his death, awful as that might be, would still be a blessing, by comparison, to those he would leave behind.

And what shall we say in additicn to all this, of the sum of misery by which our land is deluged, of the thousands of widows, and tens of thousands of orphans, the broken-hearted women and the destitute children, the household happiness destroyed, and the golden promises blighted, for which we have to blame the drinking habits of our country, habits which are still sanctioned in the commencement by the respectable, and even the religious part of the community? What shall we say of the waste of precious hours, which has been computed at the rate of "fifty millions per annum, lost to this country merely from the waste of time, and consequent loss of labor, owing to habits of intemperance?" What shall we say to the "loss of useful lives and valuable property from the same cause, on the land by fires, and other casualties, and on the sea by shipwrecks?" What shall we say to all these facts, for they are such—and British women, however high their station, or refined their sensibilities, ought to know that they are so—facts written on the page of eternity, for which time, the very time in which we live, will have to render its long and fearful account.

But let us not be discouraged by dwelling too long upon some of the dark pictures which this view of human life presents. Even this melancholy page has its bright side, to which we turn with gratitude and hope; for is it not our privilege to live in a state of society among which has sprung up an association of love, whose banner is a refuge for the destitute under which all may unite—the rich and the poor, the strong and the weak—for the purpose of arresting the fearful progress of intemperance, and encouraging those who, under bodily suffering and mental depression, are struggling to escape from the fatal grasp of this gigantic and tyrant foe? Yes, it is an unspeakable privilege to live at the same time that such an association is gaining ground on every hand, enlisting numbers, and gathering strength, as we fervently believe, under the blessing of Divine Providence, from the same source as that which inspired the Apostle, when he pledged himself to act upon the principle which has ever become the basis of this association for the removal of intemperance—"*Wherefore, said he, if meat cause my brother to offend, I will eat no flesh while the world standeth, lest I make my brother to offend.*"

"Occasions for displaying the same generous disregard of selfish considerations, for the benefit of others, frequently occur; and instances of such disinterestedness are not so rare in the Christian world as to be matters of wonder. But perhaps never, until the present age, has this principle been made the motto of a great action of philanthropy; never before did thousands unite together for the moral benefit of their fellow-men, by means of an express abridgment of their own liberty of indulgence. And, after all that has been pointed out as distinguishing this remarkable period, perhaps nothing is more worthy of being regarded as its distinction, in a moral point of view, than this—that multitudes have abandoned—not for a time, but for life—a customary, innocent, moderate gratification, which did them personally no harm, on the single ground that others abused it to harm—that 'this liberty of theirs was a stumbling-block to the weak.' In this way an attempt has been made to begin the removal of a great mass of crime and wretchedness; the removal of which once seemed so hopeless, that the boldest enthusiast hardly dared to dream of it—which had so entrenched itself in the passions of men, in their habits, in their laws, in their interests, that it laughed defiance at all opposition. Against that evil, this principle of disinterestedness has been brought to bear; and the evil has begun to give way. An illustrious exemplification of the strength there is in Christian affection!"

CHAPTER II.

INTEMPERANCE AS IT OPERATES UPON INDIVIDUAL CHARACTER.

INTEMPERANCE, as it operates upon individuals, consists in the degree or extent of a certain act, and not in the act itself. All persons allow that intemperance is a destructive and loathsome vice, and we are expressly told in the Scriptures that no drunkard can enter the kingdom of God; yet at the same time it is maintained by religious persons of every denomination, and to them we trust it is so, that drinking a small quantity of intoxicating liquid is perfectly right. We will suppose, then, that drinking a hundred thousand drops of this liquid is a sin of the deadliest character, since it excludes from the blessedness of heaven, and that drinking ten thousand drops is not only right in itself, but an act which may with propriety be associated with many of our observances of religious duty. I repeat, then, there must be between these two extremes a portion, a measure, nay even a drop at which propriety ceases, and impropriety begins; and however delicate may be the shades of difference towards this blending point, it is of the utmost importance to religious professors, and indeed to all who love their fellow-men, that they should be able to say exactly where the line is, and to show it to others, before they venture to set an example to the world by venturing upon a course, which, if pursued too far, must inevitably end in ruin and death, and which can only be entered upon with perfect safety by ascertaining what has never yet been discovered, exactly where the point of danger is.

What, for instance, should we think of the wisdom of that man, who should go blindfold up an elevated plain, knowing that from its summit, a slippery and uncertain point, whose locality he had no means of determining, his course would tend downwards with accelerated speed, and that thousands and tens of thousands had perished by arriving at this point sooner than they had anticipated. What should we think if his object in choosing to venture on this path was not any actual necessity, but a mere momentary gratification, to feel the coolness of the turf beneath his feet, or the scent of sweet flowers by the way? We should scarcely point out such a man as an example of the influence of common sense upon his conduct, much less should we wish to follow in his steps; for though the point of danger might be distant to him, it might, from its irregular and uneven nature, be very near to us.

Yet we see every day, and sometimes oftener than the day, well-educated, enlightened, benevolent, and even religious persons, sit down to the cheering glass of social entertainment, and while they take that, and perhaps another, and it may be a third, they talk of subjects refined, sublime, and elevated, and take sweet counsel together, and feel themselves spiritually as well as corporeally refreshed. They retire from the table to look out upon the moving world around. They behold the poor outcast from society, the victim of intemperance, and their delicacy is wounded by the sight, and they shrink with horror from his degradation and his shame. Yet that man's crisis of danger occurred perhaps only a very little earlier than theirs. He began the same course in precisely the same way. He had no more intention, and no more fear, of passing the summit of the hill than they have now; but owing to his bodily conformation, of which he was not aware until he made the experiment, owing to the peculiar nature of the draught of which he partook, to the manner or the place in which it was presented to him, but more probably than all, to the apparent safety of such men as those who are now turning from the repulsive spectacle that his emaciated frame presents, he overstepped the line of safety before he was aware, and perished on the side of misery and guilt.

If a religious parent has a son addicted to the vice of gambling, he does not sit down with him to what is called an innocent game, that is, to play without money. He does not resort with him to the billiard table, even though betting should be scrupulously forbidden there. No, the very thought of the amusement, simply considered as such, becomes abhorrent to his feelings; and comparing the vast amount of mischief which has been done by this means, with the small amount of good, he banishes entirely from his house both the cards and the dice, that he may avoid all future injury to his son by putting from him even the appearance of evil.

It is upon the same principle that few

religious people in the present day will take into their hands a pack of cards, though all must be aware that there is nothing absolutely wrong in the painted paper, nor even in the game itself, beyond its loss of time. Yet from all appearance of evil in this particular form, they think themselves called upon to abstain, not only because of the crime and the misery to which gaming has led, but because the very nature of it is opposed to the spirit of the Gospel. From appearing to have any connection whatever with what has been applied to purposes so base, they very properly shrink with horror; but from appearing to be connected with what has been the cause of another species of iniquity still wider in its extent, and more insidious it its nature, they feel no repulsion whatever.

But to return to the consideration of intemperance as it operates individually. It is a remarkable fact, that all persons begin this habit of indulgence innocently, or in other words, without the least intention of becoming intemperate. Whatever their situation may be now, time was when they sat around the social bowl, as unconcious of evil as you are at this moment. By degrees, however, the potent draught became pleasant to them, so pleasant that they ventured nearer to the point of danger; and then, as has already been stated, the nearer thy approached, the more careless they grew whether they overstepped the line or not. If, in such a situation, a human being could retain the full possession of his senses, he would know that the further he advanced in such a course the greater his danger would be; but the very opposite of this being the fact, and the perceptions of the intemperate man becoming more dim in the exact proportion as his danger increases, his case is one which claims, for this very reason, our especial sympathy and peculiar care. We should never forget, then, that the nearer the evil of drinking wine or any other intoxicating beverage approaches to sin, the less the mind perceives it, the less in short it is capable of understanding what sin is, so that by the time the point of danger is passed, there remains little ability to perceive that it is so, and then a little further and a little further still, and neither power nor inclination is left to return.

It may very properly be argued that the individual who has once been guilty of this breach of decorum and propriety, must know that the intoxicating draught is dangerous to him, whatever it may be to others. Unquestionably he does, and he feels, after having once fallen, more certain that he will never fall again. He thinks he shall now know where to stop for the remainder of his life, and he begins again very cautiously at first, congratulating himself, after a great many successful efforts, upon having so often stopped on the right side of the point of danger. As his confidence increases however, he ventures further, for he has acquired a taste for the indulgence, and he likes the stimulus it gives to his animal frame, and the elasticity it imparts to his spirits. He likes too the feeling that he is not bound, or shackled; that he is able to associate on equal terms with other men, and can and dare do as he pleases. In this mood then he passes again the point of danger, and finds again, on returning to his senses, the folly and the sin he has committed. Still, however, he is not cast down. He has no more idea that he shall ever become an irreclaimably intemperate man, than you have that the drunkard's grave will be yours. He is quite sure that he can stop when he likes. Society of the best kind, and friends of the most respectable order, all tell him that he can, and he is but too willing to believe it. With this assurance they place before him the temptation. They invite him to partake, and if he should by any strange misapplication of their kindness go too far, they wash their hands of his guilt—it is *his*, and not theirs.*

It is strange that sympathizing, benevolent, and well-disposed persons should be able to look upon individuals in this state—should see their weakness and their temptation, and yet never once think there is any thing due from them towards a brother or a sister having just arrived at such a crisis of their fate. Indeed we are all perhaps too backward in offering advice or warning. We have much to say, and often say it harshly, and with little charitable feeling, when the case is decided; but the time to speak, and to speak urgently—to speak kindly too, as brothers or sisters in weakness, and fellow travellers on the same path—the time to speak with prayer and supplication—to speak with the Bible in our hands, the eye of a righteous God above us, and the grave, that long home to which we are all hastening, beneath our feet—the time to speak thus, is while the victim still lingers, before offering himself up to that idol whose garlands of vine leaves are the badge of death.

But suppose the friends of the poor tempted one *do* warn him of his danger. Suppose they deal faithfully and affectionately with him, and point out clearly to him the rock on which he is in danger of being wrecked. Suppose he sees that danger too, and is brought to feel it as he ought, and promises and purposes with all sincerity of heart to avoid it for the rest of his life. What follows? He mixes in society with the friends who have warned him, and with others, who believe themselves to be, and who probaby are, perfectly safe. Every board is supplied with the tempting draught. The hospitality of the world requires that he, as well as others, should be pressed to partake. Why should he not? He has no more intention of partaking to excess than the most prudent person present. So far from this, he is determined, resolute, and certain that he will not exceed the limits of propriety. He therefore joins his friends on equal terms; and who shall say, if they are innocent, that he is not? It is true, his crisis of danger has approached nearer to him, while theirs remains as distant as before. It is true his power of self-mastery is considerably decreased. It is true his bodily inclination is opposed to his will. Yet so long as other men, and good men too, nay, even delicate, correct, and kind-feeling women, are partaking of what is more agreeable, and quite as necessary to him as to them, who is there so ignorant of human nature, as to expect that such a man, unaided, should be able to stop exactly at the point where innocence ceases, and where guilt begins? Again, I repeat, it is a mockery of common sense to look for such a result, and it is cruelty to require it.

No; such are the usages of society, that an individual in the state here described is almost sure to plunge deeper and deeper into the vice of intemperance, until in time he grows a little too bad for

* The extent and variety of temptation to which individuals are thus exposed, is forcibly shown in an important and valuable work by John Dunlop, Esq., on "the Drinking Usages" of our country, a work which ought to be in the hands of every patriot Englishman.

tha, society to countenance or endure. His early friends, those who set out with him in the same career, then begin to look coldly upon him. They wish he would not claim them as friends, at least in public. He next falls out of employment; he is not eligible for any place of trust; he begins to hang about, and his former acquaintance endeavor to walk past him without catching his eye. At last he becomes low,—his coat is threadbare; his hat is brown; he is a doomed man; his best friends forsake him; the good point him out as a warning to the bad; he is a terror to women, and a laughing-stock to children,—and such are the tender mercies of the world in which we live!

It makes the heart ache to think how much has been said *against*—how little *for*—the victim of intemperance. We see the degradation, the shame, and the misery into which he has fallen; but who is the witness of his moments of penitence, his heart-struggles, his faint but still persevering resolves—faint, because he has no longer the moral power to save himself—persevering, because he is not yet altogether lost? If there be one spectacle on earth more affecting than all others, it is that of a human being mastered by temptation, yet conscious that the vice to which he yields is a cruel tyrant, from whose giant grasp he still struggles to be free. The writer of these pages has been appealed to again and again by the victim of intemperance, to say whether there was still hope—whether the door of mercy was closed—whether resistance to the enemy was still possible—whether the poor sufferer must inevitably be an outcast forever? Not in one instance only, but in many, has this been her experience; not from the ignorant, and the utterly depraved, but from the highly gifted, the enlightened, and the refined. She answered the appeal in every instance by dwelling upon the efficacy of prayer; but at that time there was scarcely power to pray, and neither courage nor resolution to make the attempt. It is a subject of bitter regret at this moment, that she was then unacquainted with the principle upon which the total abstinence society subsists, that she did not say with promptness and cheerfulness in her self-denial, "Let us make an agreement together that we will taste no more this poisonous cup; it is pleasant to me as well as to you, but it is not necessary to health or cheerfulness; let us, therefore, make the experiment of abstaining from it altogether, and what you suffer, I will suffer too." By this means it is probable that others—perhaps a whole household, might have been brought to join us; and how different the case would then have been from what it was, while the intoxicating draught was constantly brought out, while it was pressed upon all, and while every one partook of the refreshment it was supposed to afford!

I repeat, there is nothing more affecting than the contemplation of the victim of intemperance, while the conscience still remains alive to better things, and before the soul is utterly degraded. In this situation, it appears as if the whole world, parents, friends, associates, even the wise and the good, were in league against them. Nor is this all. Those bodily powers which to the thief and the murderer are still left free and unimpaired, to the intemperate man are no longer under his own command. His whole frame is debilitated, his nerves are shattered, and that excruciating agony, which is the result of an excited imagination, operating in conjunction with a disordered brain, so takes possession of him, that the hours of the long day, and the longer night, are only to be endured by having recourse to draughts of greater potency, and more frequent repetition.

It frequently happens, that some severe or trying illness is sent to arrest this more dangerous disease in its destructive course. The patient then has time to think. He has time to pray too, if he uses his privileges aright; and there is every reason to believe that many who rise up from such a bed of suffering, do go forth into the world again disposed to be both wiser and better men. And what, we ask again, is the result? In this debilitated state the physician recommends that what are called strengthening beverages should be taken in moderation. Kind friends are offering them on every hand; and when the patient goes into society again, he goes as a sober man, and therefore he may take them with safety—as a man reclaimed from drunkenness, and therefore he may begin to drink again!

Need we further trace out this mournful history, as repulsive as it is melancholy to contemplate. Such it cannot be denied has been the fate of thousands, of tens of thousands, and such is the experience of many at this time. We will, however, take a different view of the same subject, and suppose the case of an intemperate man, who makes the same effort to abstain at an earlier stage of his career, and in a different manner. He is one who feels himself convicted of sinful excess, and who feels also that nothing but total abstinence will save him from its woful consequences. He therefore binds himself singly, not only by a firm resolve, but also by a vow, to taste nothing that can possibly produce the effect of intoxication. Do any of his friends—those sincere well-wishers, who shudder at the prospect of what he might bring upon himself—do any of these connect themselves with him in this resolve, and say that, in the path of safety and of self-denial, they will walk by his side? No. He makes his resolution unaided and alone; and that very act which is so necessary, as the only means of rescuing him from ultimate ruin, becomes, in consequence of no one joining him in it, a badge of disgraceful distinction. In fact, he is a marked man; and when he goes into society, it is not to do as others do, but to confess by the rule he has laid down for himself, that he is weaker than they are, and that he has already been guilty of folly and of sin.

By abstaining only when there is urgent need to do so—only after excess has been committed—only when the individual who practices this needful caution is so weak as not to be trusted with the common usages of society, he is stamped at once with the stigma of intemperance, and his disgrace is more than he can bear. It may be said that he *ought to bear it,* and that on him alone ought to rest the consequences of his past folly; but I would ask —Do men bear it? No; and no good has ever yet been effected by arguing upon, or endeavoring to enforce, what is contrary to the principles that are in human nature—principles that have regulated the actions of mankind from the beginning of the world, and that will regulate them to the end. These principles may be brought under a better influence, and made to act in unison with those of the Gospel of Christ; but they are not rendered extinct, and never can be in our present state of existence.

It is too much then to expect of man, in his natural and unregenerate state, that he should be *willing*—nay, that he should be *able*—to mix with society as it is now constituted on such terms; but for a woman it would be still worse. What! shall I declare openly, when others sip their pleasant and refreshing beverage, that I dare not drink even moderately of the same draught!—that I have once gone too far, or am liable to do so again! The very case is revolting to human nature; and those who make this argument the burden of their low witticisms upon the advocates for total abstinence, know little of the purity of motive, the deep feeling, the generous impulse, and the disinterested benevolence upon which such persons act.

From the causes already described, more than from any other, those who have felt themselves to be in danger, and would gladly escape from their enemy, begin again in the same course, in compliance with the usages of society, and very naturally fall again into the same excess. The history of intemperance has been almost universally a history of successive alternations between sinning and repenting, between seasons of compunction accompanied with fresh resolves, and the same course of unintentional declension which has led to the same end; with this difference, that the power to will and the wish to act have been weaker after every fall. It has been altogether like the case of a man with a naturally weak brain, who should walk on a pleasant and tempting path by the side of a precipice overhanging a dangerous flood He falls in, as might be expected, but recovers himself, and tries the same path again. The experiment is repeated, and the same consequences follow; his companions and friends, who are stronger than himself, calling out to him to take more care for the future, not to go too near, but never recommending him not to try the path at all. At length he resolves to walk no more so near the edge of danger; and though the safer and more distant path is rough and uninteresting, and none walk in it but such as are avowedly in danger from their natural weakness, he tries it for a while. The flowery and pleasant path, however, is still the resort of his friends and associates, some of whom invite him back, while many laugh at his inability to do as they are doing, and thus he is induced to make the experiment once more, when his natural powers being now impaired by the many accidents he has brought upon himself, he falls again, with less capacity than ever to struggle against the devouring flood. He now sinks lower and deeper among the foaming waves, while from those who still walk in safety on the edge of the precipice, from the very same individuals who lured him back, expressions of anger and contempt burst forth, with, perhaps, occasionally the faint wailings of compassion, or the fainter lamentations of affectionate regret. And do none cry out to him, "Try yet once more, and we will walk with you on that uninviting path?" Is there no band of brothers ready to come forward for his sake? Are there no sisters, linked hand in hand, to promise they will never leave his side, but cheer him on, so as, if possible, to make it a pastime and a joy to walk with them even there? Is there no mother's voice to cry, "My son! my son! for thy sake will I never, as I have done, tread again that dangerous cliff—to me it might be safe, but since thy precious life is thus endangered, what are its flowers, its fragrance, or its grassy turf to me, in comparison with the safety of my child?" No; they all pass on—some with cruel mockery, others, it is true, with grief—but the victim is consigned to his fate, and the kindest only—let him alone.

On looking at the subject in this point of view, we see at once the beauty and the efficacy of the principle upon which temperance societies are established. If a society for the suppression of this vice were to consist exclusively of those who had been addicted to it, there would be disgrace and repulsion in the very name. Few, except persons altogether lost to shame, would have the courage to enrol their names in such a list; and the less shame was left, the deeper would be the stigma upon a community of such individuals. The thing, indeed, would be morally impossible, as much so, as for a few dishonest men to associate themselves together, and to say, "We will form a society for the suppression of theft, by inviting all who have gone too far in that vice to join us."

But the Temperance Society is based on a more rational, a more firm, and a more lasting foundation. Men, and women, too, who have never had to fear temptation for themselves, and these to the extent of hundreds of thousands, have linked themselves together by union of purpose for the general good, and have bound themselves, not by a vow, but by a public pledge, which may at any time be withdrawn, that while members of that society they will not partake of what, though innocent to them, has been the cause of an incalculable amount of crime and misery to their fellow-beings.

Convinced of the important fact, that when the turning point in a man's life has come, when he wishes to cease to do evil, and to learn to do well, the kindest service his friends can do him is to endeavor to raise his moral standing, it must necessarily be the object of this Society to render it respectable, so that no man may be degraded among his fellow-men by joining it. That so noble and benevolent an object should be in any way defeated by the backwardness, nay, the opposition of any among the enlightened and benevolent classes of the community, is one of the wonders of our day. "Yet still they have come from the east and from the west, both men and women, who were without hope in the world, and many of whom are now sitting clothed and in their right mind, giving thanks in the house of God, and offering up their prayers with the multitude, whose privilege it is to call upon His name. And still, notwithstanding all that has been thought, and felt, and done against this Society, thousands and thousands of helpless creatures have been reclaimed; from outcasts, have become blessings—from burdens, are helpers—from the shame, have come to be the joy of heart-broken friends. 'This is the Lord's doing, and it is marvellous in our eyes.' It is going on; and say what we may, what need not be denied of some doubtful procedures, of some unwise speeches, of some injudicious measures, of some even apparently rescued who have sunk back; still there remains ample room to believe the reform so far complete, that the next generation will know almost nothing of the curse which has burdened the past."

CHAPTER III.

MODERATION.

If between the two extremes of perfect innocence and actual sin, there is in the act of drinking intoxicating beverages a medium line at which the one ceases, and the other begins; there must also be between that point and the extreme of innocence, another line at which safety ceases, and danger begins. We will, for the present, suppose this line to be fixed half-way, though some of us are inclined to think it might be fixed upon the act altogether. Now as the line of sin seldom occurs at the same point with any two individuals, and even differs with the same individuals at different times, according to the capability of the body for sustaining such stimulus, without exhibiting any outward sign of derangement; as it differs also according to the nature of the liquid partaken of, and as some maintain, according to the circumstances under which it is taken, and as danger always commences at a certain distance from actual sin, it must be extremely difficult, nay, impossible to say exactly, where the line of danger is, or I should rather say, where it is not.

Here, then, we see again the peculiar nature of a vice which consists only in an increased *degree* of what is no vice at all; and hence arises the necessity of adopting a mode of treatment, with regard to our fellow-beings laboring under this particular temptation, which no other circumstances require.

Much has been said on the subject of intoxicating beverages not being necessary for our habitual use, and many able works, to which I would refer the reader, have been written to prove that they are not only unnecessary, but actually injurious. It is not my business to enter upon this subject here, further than simply to ask—Why are they taken? They are taken by most persons because it is customary to take them; by some, because they are considered essential to health; and by others, because they are agreeable in themselves, or in the feelings they produce. With all persons, however, they have a peculiar tendency to obtain power and mastery, because it is their nature to stimulate for a time, and consequently to produce exhaustion afterwards; according to that law in the human constitution which Dr. Farre describes, when he says, that "the circulation always falls off in a greater degree than it is forced." Hence the languor and weariness after fever, and faintness and want of stimulus occurring periodically with those who are accustomed to resort to the excitement of wine for the refreshment either of mind or body.

There is also another law in our nature which renders excitement extremely delightful. Indeed one would be almost tempted to think that, to a large proportion of the individuals who mix in general society, it was the one thing needful to their existence. There can be little doubt but that this law has been originally laid down in wisdom, and in mercy, to urge us on to action, and to prevent our wearying in the pursuit of what is good; but how has it been perverted from its original design! We seek the world over for stimulus to create the sensation we delight in, instead of being satisfied to enjoy, along with every act of duty, that natural excitement which it has been so wisely intended to produce.

But the stimulus to which we most habitually, and, according to the generally received opinion, most lawfully resort, is wine. We feel a little faint about the middle of the day, and we take it then. We are thus strengthened, and enabled to go out and make our calls, or to attend to our duties in any other way. We can even visit the poor, and we really do feel more vigor, more ability, and more courage to admonish them of their extravagance and excess, particularly in the way of *intemperance,* immediately after what we call the necessary stimulus has been taken. We come back, however, exceedingly tired, and did not the dinner table present us with a fresh supply, we believe we should scarcely be able to get through the day. Our fathers and brothers, however, are surely not subject to this faintness about the hour of noon? No;—but they come home reasonably, and absolutely tired, and they, too, must have their strength restored by the same invigorating draughts.

If such then be the condition, and such the habits, of persons in perfect health, and easy circumstances, what must be the measure of relief required from the same medicine by the millions who are ill at ease, who are suffering either from mental anxiety, or bodily pain, or perhaps from both? The human frame, even *with* the advantage of this wholesome and *necessary* stimulus, is subject to a variety of diseases, and uncomfortable sensations, which we are not only anxious to remove ourselves, but which our kind friends are anxious to remove for us; and artificial stimulus is thus resorted to, not to cure these diseases, for that it cannot do—not to remedy these uncomfortable sensations, for they come again—but to make us *feel them less.*

I would here beg to claim the particular attention of the reader—for here the subject assumes a most serious and important aspect—and I would ask the question candidly and kindly, are those diseases of the body, and those uncomfortable sensations to which I have alluded, really remedied, or lastingly alleviated, by intoxicating liquids; or is the body only brought into such a condition as to be made more easy under their infliction, and more careless about them altogether? are they not in reality superseded by other sensations of a pleasurable nature, so as to be no longer felt or regarded? We know that a very slight degree of pain may be so soothed by gentle friction, and by other means of a similar nature, as for a time scarcely to be felt, and certainly not cared for; while a greater degree of suffering is often alleviated by inflicting other kinds of pain upon different parts of the body. If, then, the whole of our bodily sensations could be just so far, and so agreeably, put in operation, that we should be wholly occupied with a lively and pervading sense of indefinite pleasure, it is but reasonable to suppose that we should be rendered by this means not only insensible to, but wholly unconscious of, a moderate degree of pain in any particular part. This, then, is precisely the manner in which intoxicating stimulants operate upon the bodily frame, except only in those very few and partial cases where they are really calculated to do good, in all of which, other and safer medicines might be substituted in their stead.

In reasoning on this important subject, however, I must confess I am one of those who do not consider the question of health as so deeply involved, as that of moral responsibility. But the case has now been tried for a sufficient length of time, even in this country, to prove that without any kind of intoxicating beverage, a state of health as good—nay, even better, may be enjoyed. Happily for our cause, there are hundreds and thousands of witnesses now ready to attest the fact, that they never were so well as since they totally abstained; while on the other hand, those who declare themselves incapable of doing without such stimulus, almost invariably show by an exhibition of some, or many maladies, that they do very badly with it.

If, then, it is the frequent and almost invariable tendency of those who take a little wine to make them comfortable, to take a little and a little more, as the body under its various ailments may seem to require, what must be done when the mind with its long catalogue of deeper maladies becomes disturbed ? What must be done as it becomes a prey to all those gnawing anxieties which mix themselves in with the under-current of daily life, especially in the present state of society ? Why, the sudden intelligence of an unexpected loss, will often induce a man to gratify himself with this kind of imaginary strength ; while the necessity of dismissing a servant not less frequently sends the mistress of a house for refreshment to her sideboard. And yet we are told there is no danger—no danger at all in all this. I repeat, that, not knowing exactly where the line of danger is, it is and must be a perilous experiment to all ; and nothing can tend more forcibly to substantiate this truth, than the fact that all men, and all women too, who are now the degraded victims of intemperance, began and went on precisely in this manner, not one among them intending, or believing it possible at first, that they should ever exceed the limits prescribed by safety or decorum.

But what is it which makes this wine, or this liquid, which soothes away our pain, so desirable ? Is it not a pleasurable sensation throughout the whole animal frame—a little warmth—a little comfort—a little energy—a little confidence—a little satisfaction in ourselves—a *very little* of all these, so little that we could not define their combined operation, except by saying, we *feel better than before ?* And yet this very feeling, innocent as it may appear in itself, is in reality a *degree* of intoxication. The same sensation thrilling through the frame, is what, by advancing a few steps further in the same course, would become muscular distortion—the same pleasant glow would become restless fever—the same sense of comfort would be ecstatic folly—the same energy would be madness—the same confidence would be incapability of shame; and the same self-satisfaction would be the same glorious exultation of the intemperate in his own disgrace.

It is painful—it is repulsive to enter into these minute descriptions on a subject which it would be a privilege to be enabled to forget, and to forget forever. But it is due to that subject, that it should be fairly treated, and it is due to the honored friends of the temperance cause, that their views and their principles should be clearly understood. Let us regard it then in another light.

We have, most probably, all witnessed the effect of nitrous oxide upon the human system ; or, if any have not, I may speak of it as that kind of gas which, when inhaled, produces the effect of immoderate laughter, with extraordinary excitement of the animal frame and spirits, so that the person thus stimulated exhibits the most ridiculous behavior. Now suppose the same individual, who had made this exhibition of himself in the evening, was to come the next day to transact any serious business with you, having inhaled only a very *small portion of the same gas*, only just enough to make him feel more comfortable than he did before, would you not consider him less sane, less rational, and less safe in every way, than if he had not breathed the gas at all? Unquestionably you would; and in exactly the same proportion as it made him feel more comfortable, you would be convinced it had disqualified him for the occupations, the reflections, and the duties of a man. I do not say that he would be *wholly* disqualified. Far from it. He himself would be more lively, more ready, and more confident of himself in every way. But would he in reality be more competent, and more deserving of the confidence of others? Most assuredly not; and you see in an instant in this case, that a perfectly wise man would not trust himself to breathe, though but in a small quantity, what was capable of confusing, and even maddening, his brain.

Again, let us ask of the Christian philanthropist whether, if he had committed to him the sovereignty of some newly-discovered island, for the government of whose inhabitants he had to make laws, which should influence the character and welfare of those people through successive ages; if also they had hitherto lived in total ignorance of the use and properties of intoxicating liquids—Let us ask whether, thus situated, and taking into account all the good, and all the evil, already done in other countries by the introduction of such knowledge, he would deem it benevolent or wise to introduce such indulgences among the people over whom he ruled, and for whose virtue and happiness here and hereafter, he was necessarily so deeply responsible?

Surely there are few who would not answer to this question, "No. Let my people go on in their ignorance of this incentive to passion and to vice. It is enough for me to govern them aright, without inventing a new enemy to their welfare in this artificial and extraordinary means of excitement; and lest my own example in using such means myself, even in moderation, should induce them to use it to excess, I will cheerfully endure the inconvenience of removing what is to me an innocent enjoyment, esteeming it a privilege to do so for the sake of those who are weaker and more ignorant than myself."

If, then, such would be the language, and such the decision of every sincere well-wisher to the human race, should not the same feeling operate at least as powerfully in a country already suffering from this fatal knowledge, in all its domestic, social, and political interests? And though, happily for us, it is not left to any single individual to make laws for our government in this or any other respect, it is surely not too much to ask,—why the same principle which would induce the absolute sovereign to give up his own use of so dangerous an indulgence for the sake of his people, does not operate with the enlightened Christian, so as to call forth the exercise of his influence to the utmost extent in the same benevolent cause?

Once more let us try the subject in a different point of view. There is much talk in the present day of the wonderful effects of mesmerism; and, without entering into the merits or demerits of the question at large, we will suppose, for an instant, that all the cases we read of are substantiated by sufficient proof. If, however, while we believed this mysterious agency to have been the means of removing or suspending certain maladies, we knew beyond a doubt that it had been the cause of death to many, of madness to more, and of misery to all upon whom it operated to excess; if no one either could tell exactly how far its operation was safe, but all could perceive that it had a peculiar tendency to lead people on in their exercise of it, from one step to another, until reason was finally overthrown, and folly and vice unscrupulously committed under its influence; should any of us in our senses, seeing and knowing all this, be willing to introduce the practice of mesmerism into our families, even when exercised to a very trifling extent? Should we desire to make it a part of our social enjoyments? or should we not rather, considering the immense amount of evil it was capable of doing in proportion to its good—*seeing too that the good was to the body, and the evil to the mind*—should we not rather dismiss the system altogether from our own practice, as unworthy the countenance of prudent and responsible beings?

Yes, already we are startled at the practice of this strange art in our hospitals; and although guiltless of having produced any deterioration in the morals or the happiness of the people, already we look with suspicion and fear upon that strong mysterious sleep to which its subjects are consigned, though no instance has yet occurred of its iron chains being riveted for more than a certain length of time, depending entirely upon the will of the operator. Such, indeed, is the character of mesmerism, with all its acknowledged harmlessness, that I much question whether the practice of it as a social amusement, even to a moderate extent, would be deemed a justifiable indulgence among rational and serious people; yet thousands upon thousands of such individuals allow themselves to partake every day, and in their most pleasurable and unguarded moments, of an indulgence far more difficult to limit in degree, and immeasurably beyond all that is yet known of mesmerism in the danger of its results.

It is true, that on the plea of health, of comfort, but more especially of habit, wine has already obtained dominion over our land, while mesmerism is but a stranger to our shores, and justly a suspected one; but if on the ground of its being likely to do more harm than good, and particularly *moral* harm opposed to *physical* good, we discountenance the one, how, on the same ground, can we find a pretence for cherishing the other? The very fact that intoxicating drinks *can* only in their highest use do good to the body, while they have proved themselves most fatally deleterious to the mind, ought of itself to be sufficient to make the Christian philanthropist pause, in order to weigh the subject carefully, impartially, and with reference to the divine law, which teaches us that the soul of man is above all calculation precious in the sight of his Maker.

One of the most potent arguments in favor of the use of wine, as it has operated practically upon society, and especially upon young men of hopeful talent, is, that some of our most popular writers, as well as our most distinguished men of genius, have been addicted to the use of it, in a measure far exceeding the bounds of moderation. It is a lamentable fact, that such has been the case; but whatever may be the fascination which popular applause has thrown around the public career of such men, we need only look into their private lives, to see how far they were in reality from being objects worthy either of envy or of imitation.

No; these are not the men whom after-ages regard as the benefactors of their race; and even if they were, what dark and gloomy chronicle shall tell of the numbers now without a name, of equal or superior genius to them, but with less ability to exercise that genius, not in consequence, but in spite of, such habits of excess? And, after all, it is the *number* of men of talent which makes a nation great and wise. It is not here and there a genius flashing in a century of ignorance. I repeat, such men are not the pillars we depend upon for the intellectual and moral dignity of our nation. Startling, brilliant, and eccentric, their course resembles only that of the fiery comet—a blaze in the heavens—a wonder to the eyes of men. Yet how different from the milder planet, or the fixed and constant star, to which the traveller turns with trusting heart, and by which the mariner steers his trackless course along the mighty deep!

It is to men of deep thought, of patient labor, and, above all, of steady mind, that society owes the greatest blessing, which it is the privilege of enlightened intellect to impart; and, in order to preserve that steadiness of purpose, that fixedness of resolve, and that supremacy of the mind over the body, which are essential to the efficient working out of any great and lasting good, it has always been found necessary to lead a temperate and abstemious life, both as regards bodily indulgence and animal excitement.

And if this is necessary for superior minds, in order to their beneficial exercise for the good of the community at large, it is at least equally so for common minds, as a means of preserving them from those follies and inconsistencies which are sufficiently called forth by the ordinary course of social and worldly affairs. It would seem, however, that the generality of mankind are so fortified against the evils, perplexities, and dangers of this life, by the wisdom of the serpent and the harmlessness of the dove, that they can afford to risk the consequences of perpetually adding to the stimulus which incites to sensation and to action, just so much as they take away from the calm judgment that is so often needed to control our feelings, and to teach us how to act aright. Hence an endless catalogue of evils, arising from the miscalculations, oversights in business, hasty conclusions, intemperate expressions, weakness under temptation, and general subserviency of principle to inclination, among men; while among women the sad consequences of the telltale tongue, the sudden impulse, and the wilful act, have been scarcely less calamitous. To women, especially, the excitement of society alone is often enough, and too much for the equanimity of minds over which there has been exercised no habitual control; and after the accustomed means of increasing that excitement have been freely, though not according to the opinion of the world *too* freely used, how many through the long, dull, weary, morning hours, have to look back with shame to the confused and busy scenes of the previous evening, among which the dim, but certain witness of their own folly stands forth conspicuous, as if to warn them against ever venturing upon the same unguarded course again!

But it would require volumes to detail even the most familiar instances arising from this practice as it prevails in society, impregnating with its poison the secret springs of feeling, and stimulating to all those little acts, thoughts, looks, and words, which constitute the *beginnings* of evil, and which may justly be compared to sparks applied to a long train of mischief, including the practice of every kind of selfishness, duplicity, and too often bad faith. Would that peculiar look, for instance, have been given—would that word have passed the fair speaker's lips—would that strange eccentric act have been committed, had no artificial stimulus been used? Oh, woman! reckless woman! how often has thy character received a bias, and thy whole life a shade, from the consequences of some rash purpose conceived without a thought of harm, and acted upon from the sudden impulse of a moment! How often has the friend of thy bosom been wounded, the love of years destroyed, and shipwreck made of happiness and peace, from the mere indulgence of a transient inclination too impetuous for reason to control! And yet under circumstances of peculiar temptation from the excitement incident to society, woman is the first to place herself in peril by voluntarily adding to the stimulus, of which she has already more than her natural prudence can restrain.

Thus, then, we venture to trifle with the immortal mind; thus we presumptuously dare to ruffle the calm of that bright mirror which ought to reflect the image of Divinity!

But there is another view of this subject which has proved a very conclusive one with me, and no doubt with many others. After a person has partaken even sparingly of intoxicating stimulus, I cannot believe that he is in so suitable a condition to pray as he was before; and yet the habitual frame of the Christian's mind should be such, as that he may be ready at any hour, or at any moment, to offer up those secret appeals for Divine sanction, guidance, and support, without which we cannot expect to be kept in safety, in our going out, or coming in—when we begin the day, or when we lie down to sleep at night. Besides which, there are all those momentary little occurrences of daily life by which we are surprised into evil more frequently than by obvious temptations—those sudden questions which we sometimes cannot answer without a secret prayer that our lips may be kept from speaking guile—those trials of temper, and those tests of principle, against which we have need to fortify ourselves by watchfulness as well as by prayer. And how is it possible we should be so constantly and entirely on our guard as we might otherwise be, while under the influence even of the slightest degree of this kind of stimulus?

There are but few persons, I should suppose, who would think of preparing themselves for the duties of public worship by the use of wine; yet, if there be one situation in which we are less in danger from temptation than all others, it may reasonably be said to be when Christian friends go up to the house of God in company. He to whom the secrets of all hearts are laid bare—He knows that even here the busy mind has enough to do to call in its wandering thoughts, and keep them fixed upon the words of the preacher, or upon the supreme object of adoration. But if here, when surrounded with all that can remind us by association and habit of the solemn purpose for which a serious, and apparently united, community of immortal beings are met—if even here, while the truths of the Gospel are laid before us, while prayer and praise are ascending from the multitude around, we are unable to control the faculties of the mind so as to bring them under subjection to the solemn requirements of the great duty of public worship, what must be the difficulty of exercising a suitable control over our thoughts and actions when not reminded of these things, when surrounded by worldly or thoughtless companions, when associated with the world in its stirring, importunate, and necessary avocations, or when mixing, so far as Christians can mix, with its pleasures and amusements.

In addition to the duties of public worship, there are those of private devotion—there is the reading of the sacred Scriptures, the prayer of the family, and the prayer of the closet; and how often must these be attended to at a time when the bodily frame is exhausted, and when, consequently, temptation is strong upon those who are addicted to such habits, to supply with momentary stimulus the enfeebled energies of the mind. What then, I ask, and I would ask it kindly and solemnly, is the nature of those prayers which are offered up under such stimulus? are they not often mere words, compiled from a set of familiar phrases, with which the heart has no living or present sympathy? And though to the mere formal hearer tney may exhibit no perceptible deficiency, He to whom they are addressed knows well that they have little to do with that worship, which he has expressly declared to be acceptable only when offered *in spirit and in truth.*

There are social and convivial meetings often held at the houses of religious people; and far be it from me to wish that it should be otherwise. Far be it from me to attempt to throw a shadow over what I am happy in believing is the brightest aspect of human life—the path along which the Christian walks humbly with his God. Individually I have perhaps rather too strong a tendency to think that religious people should, above all others, understand the science of rational enjoyment, and exhibit before the world the important truth, that even earthly happiness may be innocently, cordially, and thoroughly enjoyed. In this very enjoyment, however, there is excitement enough for the safety of what ought to be the habitual frame of the Christian's mind, in the meeting of friends, in the freedom of social converse, and, above all, in the exhilarating and delightful sensation of uniting, heart to heart, and hand to hand, with those whom we love and admire, in one great, one common, and one glorious cause.

There is sufficient excitement, too, occasioned by the general advocacy of this cause, by the public meetings, and the thrilling eloquence so often heard on these occasions—there is excitement enough in all this, and sometimes too much, for the even balance cf the Christian's feelings and temper, without the addition of artificial stimulus applied to the animal frame, which at best produces only a transient accession of energy, to be followed by a lassitude and exhaustion unknown to those who never use such stimulus.

I am, however, one of those who believe, that, in the sight of God, our habitual and secret feelings are of as much importance as the energy we carry with us into public effort. I believe that the ranks of the blessed in an eternity of happiness will be filled up, not by those who have merely moved others in a righteous cause, but by the meek and humble followers of a crucified Saviour, whose consistent walk on earth has been in conformity with his precepts, and under the guidance of his Spirit. It is not what we *do*, but what we *are*, that we must be judged by in the great day of account; and it is therefore the Christian's duty to examine every motive, to watch every act, and to control every impulse, so that his private as well as his public life shall be acceptable in the Divine sight.

Were this not the case—were it lawful

or expedient for the Christian to throw the whole energy of his mind and body into one great public effort, and to leave nothing for his private hours, for his family, or for the religion of his closet, but nervous irritation, weariness, or senseless sleep, I should be willing to allow that the use of stimulants might be favorable to such a course of action. Indeed, I am but too well assured, that many extraordinary instances of oratorical power, many startling flashes of brilliant genius, and many single efforts, almost supernatural in their force and their effect, have been produced under the influence of this kind of excitement. But who has followed the individuals, from whom such extraordinary action emanated, home to their families or their closets? or, having so followed them, who would pronounce upon their condition there as being that of happy men—of men whose daily and hourly conduct constituted one continued homage to the purity, the holiness, and the benignity of their Creator?

No. I appeal to common sense, to experience, and to observation of the world in general, whether the individuals thus occasionally wrought upon by artificial stimulus for a particular and transitory purpose, are not, of all mankind, the least enviable in their private experience and habits, the most irritable in their feelings, and the most weary of life and its accumulated ills?

Just in proportion then as the religious professor allows himself to approach to this extreme, his private life and the secret history of his religious character become stamped with an impress fearfully at variance with the calm purity, the clear intelligence, and the high spiritual enjoyment which constitute the Christian's happiest foretaste of the blessedness of the heavenly kingdom.

Such observations, however, belong only to the theory of this dangerous practice. Facts, awful facts, attested by ministers of every religious denomination, are not wanting to assure us, that of the causes of religious declension now prevailing in the world, the drinking usages of our enlightened country have been the most fatal in their consequences.

The author of "Anti-Bacchus," himself, a minister of religion, and one who has spent no small amount of time and talent in the investigation of this subject, has the following passage in his valuable work, and I know not how I can more appropriately close this chapter.

"Let us look round our congregations, and enumerate those opening buds of promise which have been withered and blasted, and let us inquire also into the influence which destroyed our hopes, and the peace and respectability of the offenders, and we shall find that in ninety-nine cases out of a hundred, these drinks have been the remote or proximate cause. I have seen the youthful professor, whose zeal, talent, respectability, and consistent piety, have promised much to the church and the world, led on from moderate to immoderate draughts, in the end become a tippler, dismissed from the church, disowned by his friends, himself a nuisance to society, and his family in rags. I have seen the generous tradesman, by whose zeal for the Gospel, and at whose expense too the ministers of religion have been introduced into a destitute village, and eventually a house erected for God, and a flourishing church formed, himself excluding himself by his love of strong drink. Would to God these instances were solitary! But, alas! they are not. Almost every church and every minister have to weep over spiritual hopes blasted, and Christianity outraged by these drinks.

"We must here also observe, that if but one member of the church had backslidden, if but one angel of the church had fallen, or but one hopeful convert had been lost, through the use of alcoholic drinks, the thought that only *one* had been betrayed and corrupted, ought to make us resolve to abstain. The consideration that what had destroyed *one* might injure *many*, would, were not our hearts more than usually hard, prompt us to vow never to touch or taste again. But we have not to tell of *one*, but of *many*, that have been ruined. The hopeful ministers of the sanctuary who have fallen are not a few. And as to members and young people of the highest promise, who have been lost to the church through this practice, these might be counted by thousands."

Such are the words of one of the most zealous advocates of total abstinence; and I give them in preference to my own, because I should be sorry to presume upon any right I may have, as a private individual, to interfere with the habits, or question the judgment of those, who, thinking differently from myself in this respect, faithfully fill the high station of ministers of the Gospel. Of them, and of religious professors in general, all I ask is, that they would give the subject their cordial and serious consideration, while they ask how many the force of their example might possibly preserve from the fatal consequences of this insidious habit. The question has now become one which can no longer be put from us as unworthy of examination, without a dereliction of duty. With the result of such examination I have nothing to do. *Let every one be fully persuaded in his own mind,* remembering that *full persuasion* can only be the result of serious, persevering, and *impartial* inquiry.

CHAPTER IV.

TOTAL ABSTINENCE.

If the brilliant career of some of our most distinguished men has been suddenly arrested by intemperance, and if the private career of others has from the same cause been overspread by a premature and total darkness, if, too, we have to lament the obvious and lamentable fall of pillars in the church of God, what must be the amount of genius dimmed, and religious hope extinguished, of which the world has taken no account, and which can be computed only by Him, without whose knowledge not so much as a sparrow falls to the ground!

I speak still of a *moderate* use of those stimulants which at once excite and soothe. I speak of cases in which just so much is taken as to lull the mind into a sort of agreeable repose, or into the still more agreeable belief that it is actually employed, when in reality it is not, or at least not to any practical or useful purpose. For this, after all, is the most delusive tendency both of alcohol and laudanum, to create, when taken in moderation, a pleasing sensation of activity in the nervous system, while thought flows on in so mixed and uncertain a current, as seldom to prompt to any definite purpose, or continued action—in that dreamy, after-dinner state, so little removed from mere animal existence. And hence, as this state becomes habitual, that weakness of resolution, indolence, and inability for prompt and energetic effort, which mark the characters of those who indulge in the frequent use of intoxicating drinks. With such persons, even while they seldom or never exceed the bounds of what the world calls moderation, what a fearful proportion of their lives is spent in this kind of half-existence—in merely dreaming that they live; and if the claims of society, business, or public usefulness demand from them at certain seasons a degree of extra exertion, how abundantly do they afterwards indemnify themselves for their loss of ease, by applying fresh stimulants to relieve the weariness under which they necessarily suffer!

By what means persons of this description are secured against ultimate excess and ruin, it would be difficult to say. With them, all is left to chance, to bodily constitution, and to habit. The consequence is, that from among their ranks, intemperance selects its most sure and most willing victims. It is worthy of observation, too, that at no stage of life are mankind exempt from the liability of falling under this temptation. I remember, when a girl, hearing a gentleman—and he certainly *was* a gentleman of the old English school, a man of enlightened mind, too, on almost every subject except the most important one—I remember hearing this man boast that he had been the means of making his neighbor a drunkard. He used to tell, also, at the same time, how this neighbor, in early youth an honest, upright man, retained the strictest morals, and the most complete self-mastery, especially in this respect, until the age of thirty; when, as a married man, and the father of a family, he fell into the snare of the tempter, never to escape until the hand of death removed him from the commission of sin, to the endurance of its consequences.

It needs, however, considerable experience of human life, and a somewhat lengthened observation of the changes which take place in individuals and families, to be able to trace out the reality of the curse of intemperance in its gradual operation upon the hearts and the lives of our fellow-creatures. In short, we must be able to look back to what the drunkard was, to see from whence he has fallen; and by that far-off eminence to compute the extent of his loss, and the depth of his degradation. The young, and those who have little knowledge of the world, are not able to do this; yet such is the force of habit, that we generally find the young more willing than the old, or even the middle-aged, to come forward and join the ranks of those who entirely avoid these drinks. It is not to them, however, that we can look for those strong convictions of the reality of the evil, which naturally impress the minds of persons who have been in a manner *compelled* to trace out the private history of the victim of intemperance. They can know nothing of the youth of early promise which once dawned upon yon poor outcast from society—how, fondly cherished by a doting mother, he grew up the pride of all the household—how the light of superior intellect adorned his mind, while beauty beamed upon his brow, and wit and humor woke the ready laugh which ever welcomed him among his friends. It is for those only who have been intimately associated with this child of hope, really to feel the heart-sickening spectacle of his gradual fall—his beauty faded, his intellect impaired, his wit become profane or low, or quenched in childish tears—not one of all his admiring and convivial friends who would now acknowledge him. Not one, did we say? No, not one among his companions of the midnight revel, or the jovial board. But though all have forsaken or disowned him, in the lone chamber of his widowed mother, tears are falling still, while prayers are breathing forth the very soul of that fond woman whose love is strong as death; and, strange to say, she who has suffered most, and been most humbled by his degradation, is the last, the very last, to cast him off. She who admired him most in his young beauty, who laid her hand so proudly on the golden curls which graced his noble brow, she looks upon him with a mother's fondness still, and would fold him to her bosom—oh, how fondly!—yet. She, however, is no philosopher, knows little of the wants of human nature, or the discipline required to bring it back from disease and wretchedness to a healthy and honorable state; and thus when the prodigal comes back, as he does occasionally, to share the scanty pittance refused to him elsewhere, she places thoughtlessly before him the tempting draught, in her blind and foolish ignorance deeming it necessary, when taken in moderation, for the restoration of his wasted strength. Thus it is easy to perceive that such a mother can exercise no beneficial influence over her infatuated son; and if not the mother, with all her tenderness and untiring affection, who, then, is to be looked to for assistance in the hour of need?

It is in fact this blind and persevering determination to advocate the use of a *moderate* quantity, which produces nearly all the excess now existing in the world. It has been justly said, that no one was ever yet allured into the ranks of intemperance by its actual victims, after they had obviously become such. Far more calculated to warn and to deter, is the wretched and disgusting spectacle the drunkard exhibits to the world; and if the choice were now submitted to the young beginner, whether he would lose a right hand or a right eye, or consign himself to such a fate, most assuredly he would prefer the former, so opposed is the last stage of intemperance to every thing we esteem as desirable of imitation: it is besides so generally considered by the world as being easy to retreat, after having once gone too far, that the young beginner never discovers how this situation can possibly be his, until it has actually become so.

We are all too much in the habit of looking upon the sins of intemperance as belonging only to its extreme stage of degradation; but did men sin no more under its influence than they do in this helpless and abject state, the evil itself would be lessened by an amazing amount. It is not excess to which the ruffian yields himself when he contemplates a deed of horror. That would disqualify his arm for the fatal blow. No, it is what is considered moderation which stimulates to the practice, not only of open and daring crime, but of all those acts of deception employed to betray the innocent and the unwary to their own destruction. It is the moderate draught which fires the passions of the revengeful and the malignant—in short, which gives the moving impulse to that vast machinery of guilt, which scatters misery and ruin amongst our fellow-creatures, which desolates their homes, shuts them out from Christian fellowship, and lowers our whole country in the scale of moral worth. It is this moderate portion which invariably makes bad men worse—need we inquire, whether it ever yet was known to make good men better?

Great and glorious, then, as the results of the temperance movement have been in reclaiming those who appeared to be irretrievably lost to their friends and to society, its most beneficial operation, and that to which we look for the greatest good, is its power to arrest the downward progress of the moderate, before they shall have lost caste among their fellow-men. In order to do this, it is necessary that there should be some powerful and immediate check against so much as tasting the dangerous draught. This check has been tried by a mere promise to a friend for a stated period, and has often proved sufficient for the time, though the opposite cases in which it has failed, may be reckoned as a thousand to one; for, until the temperance principle was made known, it never seemed to occur to such friends, that their part, and a very important one in the work of reformation, was to join with the tempted in totally abstaining.

And here let us observe, that it is one of the peculiar and striking features of intemperance as a vice, that its victims often loathe the very monster on whose polluted altars they are offering up their lives; nay, they even loathe themselves, and hate and despise the tyranny whose badge of cruel servitude they wear. In this state the struggles of the wretched victim to escape, are sometimes most painful and heart-rending to the confidential friend to whom they are disclosed. Sometimes prayer is resorted to, sometimes penance. Every device which a wounded spirit can suggest, except the only sure and effectual one, is by turns adopted and renounced; and still, though torn and lacerated by a thousand agonies, which the untempted can never know, until within the last few years, these miserable and isolated beings cried to their fellow-creatures for help in vain. Sometimes, by the mercy of God, they have been enabled to maintain through life a station of respectability at the cost of a lingering struggle almost too painful for nature to endure; and sometimes at an advanced age, as bodily infirmities have increased, the enemy at last has conquered them.

How little have such individuals known that the very moderation which they continued to practise as lessening their difficulty, was in reality the cause of all their suffering! One prompt and decided effort to put away the perilous thing *entirely*, and *for ever*, would have placed them immediately on the side of safety, where temptation would soon have ceased altogether to assail their peace. But, instead of such an effort, their whole lives have been a continued conflict, often carried on in weakness and distress; one perpetual sacrifice made at the expense of cheerfulness and social feeling; one act of painful self-denial, having every hour to be renewed, and consequently never bringing its appropriate reward of gratitude and joy. In justice to ourselves, then, it is but right that we should adopt a mode of acting prudently, at once more safe, and infinitely less irksome and destructive to our happiness. As an act of duty to God, it is highly essential that we should make a more entire and less grudging sacrifice; while as an act of benevolence to our fellow-creatures, it is not less important that we should show them how practicable it is, cheerfully, promptly, and wholly to abstain.

While speaking of the extreme pain and difficulty of partial abstinence, when opposed to inclination, a circumstance has been brought to my recollection which affected me powerfully at the time, though it failed to convince me of the unkindness and inconsistency of my own conduct. It was on the occasion of some visiters arriving at my father's house, when all the family except myself were absent. The customary duties of hospitality consequently devolved upon me, and with other refreshments, as a matter of course, I ordered wine to be placed upon the table. Seated in the same room at that time was one of the greatest sufferers from habitual and constitutional intemperance, it has ever been my lot to know—a sufferer both from the force of the temptation, and the remorse and loss of character it occasioned him to endure. He was a clergyman, and an eminent scholar, perfectly sane and sober then, having bound himself by a promise that he would scrupulously abstain for a stated period. When my guests had refreshed themselves, we walked out into the garden, leaving this individual, as I distinctly recollect, seated opposite the table, with his eyes fixed intently upon the wine; and he told me afterwards, that no language could describe the agony he endured while I was pouring out the tempting draught, and urging it upon my friends; but more especially when he was in the room alone with it before him. It is scarcely necessary to add, that he indemnified himself only too deeply for this privation, so soon as the term of his promised abstinence expired.

The advocates of total abstinence are accused of going too far in discouraging the use of intoxicating beverages altogether. But, surely, such charges can only come from persons ignorant of human nature, of the power of association, and of the force of the temptations to which that nature is exposed. I would appeal to individual experience, whether partaking even in a very limited degree of a stimulating beverage does not create an inclination for more? whether taking a glass of wine one day does not make more necessary the next? and whether, when such stimulants are resorted to as a means of restoring strength, they do not require to be continued, and even increased, for the same purpose? If, however, the strength was really increased by such means, the use of it would soon cease to be necessary—no one wishing to be strong beyond a certain point;—instead of which the demand is still kept up, for that very end which it thus appears plainly can never be answered by such means.

Another case in point at this moment occurs to me, which I am induced to record, because I know it to be a fact. A lady of my acquaintance, and I have it upon her authority, whose mind was seriously impressed with the importance of personal abstinence, struggled on for some time in the manner I have described, without being able to make a sufficient effort for the effectual carrying out of her purpose. Thus, she was often an abstainer for a week or a month, hoping she might keep up the habit, without really resolving to do so. While she remained in this state, it happened that on those days when she partook, with her friends, even of the smallest quantity, such was the force of habit, and such the power of association, that she invariably went to her store-room immediately after they were gone, and poured out for herself a glass of the wine she had just tasted; nor was she exempt from the same weakness for two or three days afterwards.

Dr. Johnson is often quoted as high authority in favor of the safety of abstinence, when compared with moderation. When asked by Hannah More, at a dinner party one day, to take a little wine, he replied, "I cannot take a *little*, and therefore *I never take any.* Abstinence is as easy to me as temperance would be difficult."

But the temperance society, in its far-stretching benevolence, embraces principles of higher obligation than this. "Abstain," said an assembly of ministers of the Gospel to a brother whom intoxicating drink was destroying. "Oh," said he, "how could I endure to be singular, to be ridiculed and scorned in whatever company I might appear!" "Abstain," said a worthy brother; "*I will abstain too, and keep you in countenance.*" This was a Temperance Society before the name was known.*

I have spoken of the situation of those who abstain because they have already fallen under temptation, and I have endeavored to show how their marked, degraded, and solitary lot is more than a sensitive and delicate mind can endure. But I have omitted to observe in its proper place, that there exists an additional reason why their unaided efforts should be so difficult to maintain, in the peculiarly morbid and susceptible feelings of those who are conscious of holding a questionable position among their fellow-beings,—in short, of having lost something of their respectability and high standing in the opinion of the world. Those upon whom the breath of censure has never breathed, whose character, in its unsullied purity and firm rectitude, has never been assailed, are fearless of the consequences of making an eccentric movement in a generous or noble cause. Any idle or narrow-minded suspicion attaching itself to them, they are prepared utterly to despise. It cannot harm them by its probability, and consequently they regard it not. But the former case is widely different from this, and therefore it is far more difficult for the tempted than the untempted man, in mixing with society, to bear, as he must, the vulgar and unfeeling insinuation that he abstains because he has not self-government enough to prevent his falling into excess. Again and again has this low-minded remark been made to the writer of these pages, without producing any other sensation than one of regret, that her friends should be so ignorant of the deep and spirit-stirring principle upon which the temperance cause depends; but had the same remarks been made to some of her acquaintance—some whom she would gladly ask the wings of more than earthly love to shield, what agony would this ill-timed observation have caused to thrill almost equally through her heart and theirs!

And what an absurdity is this insinuation, even when most harmless! As a method of reasoning amounting to precisely the same thing, as if we should say to a friend who had subscribed to the support of a blind asylum—"I am sorry to find by your name being on the list, that you are anticipating blindness. I never knew before that you were afflicted with weak eyes."

Enough then must already be known by those who have paid the least attention to the subject, to show that individuals now under temptation are not likely to save themselves, and that if any thing effectual remains to be done to save them, it must be by the combined and benevolent efforts of the sober part of the community. There must in fact be a decided barrier formed against the first step in the downward career of intemperance, and that must be by a society of persons stronger than themselves. "It would be

* Address of the Baptist Total Abstinence Society in Newcastle.

too much," observes the enlightened Thomas Spencer, "to expect one individual philanthropist to work out the reformation of the drunkard; nor is it probable that an individual drunkard would have courage to stand alone as an abstainer, amidst the jeers of his companions. But if a society were formed of benevolent men, for the express purpose; and if the enslaved victims could be encouraged by the influence of example to break off their yoke, and burst their bonds, then then would philanthropy have a cheering prospect of enlarged success; and then might the master evil of intemperance be gradually destroyed. *Such a society has been formed—it is the Total Abstinence Society.*"

That such a society, opposed as it is to the strong habits and stronger inclinations of mankind, has not only been formed, but has prospered beyond the most sanguine expectations, both in this and other countries, we have abundant proof. I quote from a record of what has been done in America, as well as what has been effected nearer home. I quote from the Eighth Report of the American Temperance Society, where it is stated that at that time in America more than 8000 temperance societies had been formed, containing it was thought more than 1,500,000 members, more than 4000 distilleries had been stopped, and more than 8000 merchants had ceased to sell ardent spirits, and many of them had ceased to sell any kind of intoxicating liquors; also upwards of 1200 vessels then sailed from American ports, in which no intoxicating liquors were used.

The next statement I shall transcribe is one of a still more cheering nature, inasmuch as it touches the patriot hearts of Britain, by approaching more closely her beloved shores. It is contained in the excellent summary of temperance proceedings conveyed by the first address of the National Society, which I would earnestly recommend to the attention of every reader.

"At the 'Great National Banquet' which lately took place in Dublin, Lord Morpeth, after giving particulars of the return of outrages reported in the constabulary office, by which it appeared, that since 1836 they had diminished one third, proceeded to remark, that 'of the heaviest offences, such as homicides, outrages upon the person, assaults with attempt to murder, aggravated assaults, cutting and maiming, there were

In 1837, ...	12,096
1838, ...	11,058
1839, ...	1,077
1840, ...	173

Facts like these require no comment; the mere abstinence from one article of beverage has done more in two or three years to diminish crime, than could ever be accomplished by all the powers of legislature, the activity of police, and the horrors of military force. But it is not in the diminution of crime alone, that we see the cheering and happy fruits of the temperance reformation in Ireland. The returns of the savings bank prove that improvidence has diminished, while domestic comfort, intelligence, and wealth have rapidly increased.

"The depositors in the savings bank were, in July, August, and September, 1838, 7,264; 1839, 7,433; 1840, 8,953; 1841, 9,585; while in 1842, the increase is still greater: and it is stated, that at one of the branches of these valuable institutions, the pressure of depositors was so great, that the committee had to open the bank another evening in the week.

We find, too, that this prudent provision for future wants has not prevented a large and rapid increase of present domestic comfort and home enjoyment, for in the report of the Waterford Temperance Society, it is stated, that 'In the city and suburbs there are at least one hundred thousand pounds' worth of value in the cottages of the laboring classes, in clothes and furniture, over and above what they possessed two years ago, besides a considerable increase of lodgments in the savings bank, made principally by the working classes. The healthy state of the city during this inclement year, and the last report of the fever hospital, speak loudly in favor of the cause. We may add a recent testimony from the same quarter, which appears in a letter from the mayor of Waterford, addressed to the vice-president of the Waterford Total Abstinence Society, and dated the 21st of October, 1842.

'My Dear Sir—

'My period of magisterial office, now on the eve of closing, has afforded me many opportunities of judging of the working of the temperance system, and of estimating the advantages it confers on the community at large.

'The fact is notorious, that since the temperance movement, *the actual amount of crime in this city has been considerably diminished, and that comfort, happiness, and plenty supply the place of wretchedness and destitution, once unhappily so prevalent.* I say the fact is notorious, because the diminished duties of the magistrates, and of the judges of assizes, amply testify to its truth, *and in my professional capacity as a medical man, I can fully bear out the advantages of the total abstinence system.* In the Leper Hospital, (general infirmary of the city,) over the medical and surgical departments of which I preside, as senior medical officer, the number of casualties admitted has recently diminished. In particular, I may mention, that formerly we had constant applications for the admission of women seriously injured by their brutal husbands when in a state of intoxication; I feel gratified in being able to state that *not a single instance has presented itself this current year.* This single fact speaks volumes in favor of the domestic happiness conferred by temperance. Some pledge-breakers have been brought before me, but it must be a matter of pride and of congratulation to every lover of morality and good order, to observe that the system has been so generally and steadily adhered to, and that a people so notorious for intemperate habits, should now be proverbial for the very reverse; but bright as is the dawn, I believe that it is only the harbinger of a brighter day, for I am far from thinking that we now witness the entire extent of the boon which the temperance system is capable of conferring. The rising generation, I anticipate, will be benefited by it even more largely than the present; and I trust that the temperance pledge will be handed down to distant ages, the memorial of the moral regeneration of the country.

'I have the honor to be, my dear sir,

'Your obedient, humble servant,

'Thomas L. Mackesey,

'Mayor of Waterford.'

"Sir B. Morris and Captain Newport, two of the magistrates who attended the total abstinence meeting when the above letter was read, most fully confirmed the statements it contained. We might proceed to prove, from the increased number of reading-rooms and schools, and from the rapid extension of mechanics' institutes, that the intellectual elevation of the people is keeping pace with their moral and physical improvement. Indeed, the whole picture which Ireland now presents of the delightful proofs of temperance reformation, may well rouse the feeling of astonishment, that more should be required to induce any individual to support by his example so simple and effectual a means of securing such an amount of public and private good."

But notwithstanding all these encouraging facts, and the strong evidence they bring along with them that the principles of total abstinence are peculiarly adapted to the wants of the people at large, one thing is still wanting to the furtherance of this benevolent institution; and strange to say, it is the co-operation of the higher classes, and especially of the religious part of the community. Happily for this cause it has prospered, and we trust, with the Divine blessing, will continue to prosper, even should such co-operation still be withheld; nor can we fear its failure while the comparatively few individuals of this class, who have already given it their sanction, remain to be its able, zealous, and consistent advocates.

Nor is it the least encouraging feature in the aspect of this interesting subject, that those who have embraced the principles of total abstinence—those who have formed themselves into a consistent and organized body, purely for the good of their fellow-creatures, have been chiefly individuals in the lower walks of life—hard-working men, and industrious women, who could ill afford to lose one of their accustomed means of indulgence, and, perhaps, had no other to give up. Had the case been otherwise—had enlightened men and influential women come forward in the first instance to recommend this system to others, by adopting it themselves, it is probable we should have felt less confidence in the great moral power which is now at work. It is probable we should have trusted more to our political economists, our public speakers, and our ministers of religion, and when they failed in the consistency of their example, the working classes might have failed with them. We might have thought, too, that the prospect was a mere chimera which would not stand the test of time. But as the subject now presents itself to our consideration, it bears an impress more than human; for what but the Spirit of God could have put it into the hearts of hundreds of thousands among the poorest and most ignorant members of the human family, to conceive a project at once so vast in its extent, so pure in its operation, yet so rich in its benevolence and love?

CHAPTER V.

PUBLIC OBJECTIONS TO JOINING THE TEMPERANCE SOCIETY.

We must, however, still speak with regret of that want of co-operation in the temperance reformation, which prevails among the higher classes of society, as well as among religious professors generally; and we do this chiefly on the ground of the desirableness of rendering the temperance society itself as respectable as it can be made in the opinion of the world. Were the victims rescued from intemperance, by the same means, and at the same time converted to the religion of Christ Jesus, they would know that to endure the scorn, and the persecution of men, was a part of the discipline to which, as faithful followers of their blessed Master, they ought to be willing to submit. But in the ranks of intemperance we have to do with human beings upon whom this wrong knowledge has never operated, and we must, consequently, adapt our means to the condition of man in such a state. We must consider, too, what is in human nature—what are its tendencies, and how they are generally found to operate, in order that we may not require of it efforts beyond its power to maintain. We must, consequently, not expect that a number of men, whom the vice of intemperance has already consigned to the deepest degradation, will arise of themselves and unite into a distinct body, thus tacitly declaring before the world who and what they have been. Yet, even if so great a miracle as this should be effected, what then would become of that still greater number who have not yet wholly fallen—who are still struggling against temptation, and whose situation at once inspires us with more of pity, and of hope. These, of all persons, would be the last to join such a degraded and stigmatized society as one composed exclusively of reformed drunkards; and it is for such as these—the tempted, the wavering, and the still-respected and beloved, that I would implore the consideration of those individuals among the enlightened portion of the community, who have hitherto stood aloof from the question altogether, or who have treated it with contempt. But more earnestly still I would implore the exercise of Christian benevolence in this cause, on the part of those who preach the glad tidings of peace on earth, and good will towards men. "If your name had not been tnere," said a reformed drunkard to his minister, "I never should have been a member of a temperance society."

There must be some powerfully operating reason why individuals, who esteem it not only a duty but a privilege to come forward in every other good cause, should be so backward in this. It cannot surely be unwillingness to submit to a mere personal privation; for were this the case, it would show at once that their own personal indulgence was esteemed of more importance, than the saving of their fellow creatures from one of the greatest of calamities. Oh! but their health—they have tried it, and it did not agree with them. They had a cough, or a fit of rheumatism, or a weakness of the throat, during the short time they abstained! Kind, Christian friends, warm-hearted, devoted, and zealous laborers for the good of the community! how often have the most delicate and feeble among you gone forth on errands of mercy, in the summer's heat, and in the winter's cold? gone forth, too, at times when, had a physician been consulted, he would have pronounced the act a dangerous, or at least an injurious one. How often has the faithful minister stood up to preach, or visited the poor and comfortless abodes of his people, at the risk of a headache, a sore throat, or damp feet? How often has the father of a family called together his household for evening worship, when, as a mere matter of personal benefit, he would have been better laid upon a couch of rest? How often has the tender mother, shrouding herself from the angry storm, penetrated into the chambers of the sick, to dispense to them more than the bread of this life? Do not mock us then with the assertion that you are willing, but afraid. We are incapable of believing it, when we witness daily on your part such noble acts of magnanimity, of faith, and love. No, you are not willing, and the only justifiable reason that can be assigned for your unwillingness is, that you are not yet fully persuaded in your own minds that the thing itself is good. Here, then, occurs a very important question—are you in a state of *willingness* to be *persuaded?* Are you making it a subject of prayer, that, if really your duty, you may see that it is so? Are you doing this, or are you putting the thought far from you, as not worthy to be entertained by one whose office is to instruct, admonish, and exhort; but not to exemplify a personal instance of self-denial, practised entirely upon the strength of that love which sent a Saviour into the world, and which remains to be the surest test by which his disciples are known on earth.

But in addition to the ministers, and other direct advocates of religious truth, there is a vast proportion of the respectable part of the community who care for none of these things; yet whose influence, if thrown into the scale of temperance, instead of accumulating, as it does at present, on the opposite side, would at once afford the most decided and efficient help to those who are now sorely tempted, wavering, and about to fall. If, for instance, in any of our large towns, men of importance and wealth—men who take a leading part both in business and society—men who originate and forward great public measures, and who at the same time enjoy the sociability of rational and agreeable amusements—if such men would, in any considerable number, give their names and their advocacy to the temperance cause, they would raise at once a glorious banner of encouragement and of hope, under whose protection the tempted and weak of all classes, but more especially young men, who are most frequently assailed by this insidious and malignant enemy, would bind themselves, by hundreds and by thousands, to abstain. It would then be no stigma either to youth or age. It would cease to be either singular or disgraceful; and he, over whom his mother's heart was yearning—with whom his father had pleaded in vain, would then be able to pass over to the side of safety, without any other individual knowing that he had ever been otherwise than safe.

And how many parents at this very time would give the whole of their worldly possessions to purchase the protection and attractiveness of such a society for their sons! But let me ask them a serious question. Fathers! have you come forward and signed your names by way of laying the first stone in this great bulwark to preserve your family, and your country? Mothers! I dare not ask of you. Let shame and confusion cover us, that we should have seen all that is transpiring more or less remotely in connection with every British home, that we should have marked the growing curse upon our own household hearth, and yet should so long have refused to deny ourselves the tempting draught, which we knew was one of death to those we loved. Yes, I must ask of you, kind-hearted mothers of England, why in this instance you are guilty of a cruelty so great? Would you not strip from your delicate limbs the garment of pride to clothe that beloved one? Would you not share with him your last morsel of bread, even if it left you famishing? Would you not give him the draught of water brought to cool your burning fever? And will you—can you—dare you persist in a system of self-indulgence, which, though innocent to you, may endanger both his temporal and eternal happiness?

I repeat, there must be some powerful cause which such individuals do not tell, operating in such cases against their acting a more decided and a more generous part. There must be some cause. Can it be their own love of the indulgence? If so, it is high time it was given up, for their safety as well as for that of others. Indeed it is chiefly in cases like these, that we are made to see the entire reasonableness of the system of total abstinence; for if the indulgence be easily resigned, a very slight consideration of the subject in connection with our duty to others, will be sufficient to induce us to give it up. While, if it be difficult to resign, it becomes clear that we are ourselves in danger, and our motives for self-denial are thus increased a hundred fold.

So far as I have been able to discover in mixing with society, one of the most openly avowed and most frequent objections to joining the ranks of total abstinence, is that already alluded to, a regard for personal health, originating in the mistaken but popular belief, that such stimulants are necessary for its preservation. It is, however, a curious fact, that persons who argue in this manner as regards themselves, are invariably such as suffer from some malady, either real or imaginary, and sometimes from an accumulation of maladies, which they still persist in asserting that they use stimulating beverages for the sole purpose of preventing. Now if such persons drank wine, or beer, or spirits, or all three, and at the same time were in perfect health, I confess they would be formidable enemies to the temperance cause; but with them it is always "*my*" gout, "*my*" rheumatism, "*my*" want of digestion, or "*my*" general debility, on account of which this potent medicine is taken, but which, by their own showing, it has hitherto proved wholly insufficient to remove.

Without entering generally upon the question of health, a question which has been circumstantially examined by judges more able than myself, and in relation to which many important and interesting facts are now laid before the public, tending clearly to prove, that, instead of suffering from total abstinence, most persons by whom it has been fairly tried, have experienced not only no injury to their health, but considerable benefit; I may, perhaps, be allowed to add a few words on the subject of my own experience, which may possibly derive additional weight from the circumstance of my having been, for many years of my life, an obstinate disbeliever in the efficacy of temperance principles to effect any lasting or extensive good; while of all respectable societies, that for the promotion of total abstinence—that which I now esteem it an honor and a privilege to advocate, would have been most repulsive to my feelings to join. Indeed, such was my contempt for the system altogether, that I often pronounced it to be a mockery of common sense, and at the same time frequently asserted my belief, that nothing could be more likely than the restraint of a public pledge to create an immediate inclination to break it.

For two years—years I may say of total ignorance on this point, during which I took no pains to make myself better informed, I treated the subject with the utmost contempt whenever it was brought under my notice. By degrees, however, it began to wear a different aspect before the world in general, and facts were too powerful in its favor to be disputed. By degrees it began also to assume with me somewhat more of a personal character. I could not see how I was right while indulging in what was so fearfully destructive to others, and to some whom I had known and loved. Yet such was the force of habit; such my willingness to believe what doctors told me, that wine was necessary to my health, at that time far from good; and such, also, was my dependence upon stimulants, for increasing the strength of which I often felt miserably in want, that three years more elapsed before I had the resolution to free myself practically, entirely, and I now trust, forever, from the slavery of this dangerous habit.

Four years of total abstinence from every thing of an intoxicating nature, it has now been my happy lot to experience; and if the improvement in my health and spirits, and the increase of my strength during that time, be any proof in favor of the practice, I am one of those who ought especially to thank God for the present, and take courage for the future.

Like many other women, and especially those who are exempt from the necessity of active exertion, I was, while in the habit of taking wine for my health, subject to almost constant suffering from a mysterious kind of sinking, which rendered me at times wholly unfit either for mental or bodily effort, but which I always found to be removed by a glass of wine. My spirits, too, partook of the malady, for I was equally subject to fits of depression, which also were relieved, in some degree, by the same remedies. During the four years in which I have now entirely abstained from the use of such remedies, I have been a total stranger to these distressing sensations of sinking and exhaustion; and I say this with thankfulness, because I consider such ailments infinitely more trying than absolute pain. That time of the day at which it is frequently recommended to take a glass of wine and a biscuit, I now spend as pleasantly as any other portion of the four and twenty hours, without either; and when fatigued by wholesome exercise, which is a totally different thing from the exhaustion above alluded to, I want nothing more than rest or food, and have not a symptom remaining of what I used to experience when I felt occasionally as if my life was ebbing away. Thus I am fully persuaded, in my own mind, and by my own experience, confirming as it does the testimony of many able and important judges, that the very medicine we take in this manner to give us strength, does in reality produce an increase of faintness, lassitude, and general debility.

Perhaps I may be allowed further to add, that the four years of abstinence I have already passed, have been marked by no ordinary degree of vicissitude, and something more than an average share of mental and bodily exertion; but whether at home or abroad, in health or in sickness, in joy or in sorrow, I have never really felt the want of the stimulants above alluded to; and I am now led into this lengthened detail of my own experience, purely from the hope, that, by adding facts to arguments, and facts in which I cannot be mistaken, I may encourage others to make the same experiment. It is true that any little ailment I may still retain, even the slightest ache or pain, is always attributed by some of my friends to a want of the stimulus of wine; but still I believe there are few ladies whose health, for all purposes of exertion as well as enjoyment, would bear any comparison with mine.

So much then for the constitution of woman, in one instance out of the many in which the experiment of total abstinence has been tried with success; nor has the constitution of man been found less capable of bearing this privation. Indeed, my personal testimony ought not to pass unsupported by that of one, who, before temperance societies were thought of, and in a distant and a different clime, was first led to the adoption of temperance principles, purely from regard to the safety of the semi-barbarous people over whose habits, in a moral point of view, his example powerfully operated. He was then convinced, that if others who had less power of self-restraint than himself, could not use this indulgence without excess, it was right for him, as a minister of religion, to give it up altogether. On returning to England, however, he adopted, under medical advice, the habits of society in this respect, until the temperance question was presented to his mind in all its serious importance; and it is under a system of total abstinence, not recommended by his medical advisers, that, after a lingering and distressing illness, he now enjoys the blessing of renovated health.

It is not, however, on the question of health alone, that I am prepared to sympathize with the weak of my own sex who may be anxious, but afraid, to make the experiment; for I know that it is the sensitive but often wounded *mind* of woman, which, more than her feeble body, places her under the power of this temptation. I know that it is too frequently her difficult part to live in one world of interest, and to act in another; I know that in society she is often imperatively called upon to be agreeable, when the power to be so is wanting; and I know, too, there are passages in human life which to her are like the falling of a deep cold wave upon the heart, from which it sweeps away all other thoughts and feelings. I know also it sometimes happens, that all this has to be concealed beneath a smooth and smiling brow; that the thoughts thus scattered have to be called back for practical and immediate use; while a manner disengaged, a frank and cordial greeting to indifferent friends, and a free and cheerful tone given to general conversation, are the contributions she is expected to pay to society—the duties in which she must not fail. I speak not of distinguished individuals—theirs is even a heavier tax than this. I speak of what we are all subject to, in such cases, for instance, as that of visiting at the house of a friend who has invited a party to meet us. It is possible that, before the arrival of the party, a temporary indisposition may have disqualified us from entertaining others; or a letter with tidings sad to us, may have been put into our hands; or a thousand things may have happened, any one of which may have been sufficient to sink the heart of woman.

Now in this simple and familiar instance, I believe we shall all be able to recognise one out of many cases, in which women are peculiarly liable to have recourse to artificial stimulus in order to support them, as they think, *creditably*, before their friends; and if in such a case as this they yield to the temptation of taking only a single glass beyond what is consistent with their safety, how often, amidst the variable lights and shadows of human experience, must their safety be endangered from the same cause!

I speak then of this, as well as of many other trials which beset the path of woman, feelingly and experimentally; and still I would say—fear not. One single effort conscientiously and promptly made, will enable you to pass through all the duties of social intercourse better without such stimulants, than with them. I will not pretend to say, as some do, that the effort is easily made. We forget the weakness of human nature when we call it easy; but I will say, that the difficulty is all in anticipation, and in the lengthened dragging out of a half-formed purpose. Two years of trial I myself endured in this manner, before my resolution was fully carried out; but no sooner was an entire surrender made of inclination to a sense of duty, than all temptation vanished, all trial was at an end; while the act of totally abstaining became so perfectly easy, as to call forth no other feelings than those of gratitude and joy, that I was thus enabled, for the sake of others, to share in the self-denials of the tempted, and the privations of the poor.

After all, however, there is a point beyond which no subject should be pressed, when it touches upon the health of others. For ourselves we may judge and act; but for no other human being of competent mind have we a right to lay down the law, because no less various than the minds and the characters of mankind, are the bodly ailments under which they suffer, and the remedies which they consequently require. Medical advice too must often be consulted, and when it is, the rules of the temperance society fully recognise its right to be obeyed. But still I would ask for this view of the subject, as for that of religious duty, a candid, serious, and impartial consideration; and more especially where the experiment is made, that it should be made fairly. If your abstinence is not entire, the experiment is far indeed from being a fair one; for so long as the habit of taking even a little is kept up, the inclination to take more is kept up also, and consequently the trial and the difficulty remain. If also, during the time that you abstain, you sit up late at night, neglect to take exercise in the open air, or in any other manner fail to adopt the most rational and obvious means of preserving health, it cannot be said that the experiment is a fair one; more especially when, as is too frequently the case, every malady occurring during this period is charged upon the newly formed habit of total abstinence.

Here, then, I must leave the subject of health to the private consideration of the candid and benevolent reader, trusting that those who are not accustomed to set the question of health in opposition to the exercise of their mental and bodily energies in the furtherance of other charitable objects, will, at least, have the fairness not to draw back from this, under the apprehension of any little risk they may incur in the way of mere personal comfort or convenience.

There are, however, other startling objections besides that of health, brought forward against the temperance movement, and especially by religious professors, who are in the habit of questioning the desirableness of supporting it, because it does not make people religious. But, can any thing be more at variance with the practice and sentiments of the most enlightened part of mankind on other subjects, than this far-fetched and untenable argument. Why, the support of good government, and the administration of laws, do not make people religious; yet, who doubts the benefit they confer upon society? Teaching people to read does not make them religious; yet, few in the present day are prepared to question the advantages of education. It is a fact too evident to need assertion, that the habitually intemperate man is not in a condition either to read his Bible, or to pray; and that owing to his selfish indulgence, and the consequent destitution of his family, the wives and children of such persons are, in vast numbers, too ragged and forlorn to be able to attend any place of public worship, or, in the case of the latter, any means of instruction. It is something then, and the serious and charitable portion of the community know it to be something, to put the drunkard in a situation to be *able* to read his Bible and to pray—to be *able* to listen to, and understand those truths upon which his happiness hereafter depends—to be able also, in addition to this, to provide for his wife and family, so that they too may receive the benefit of instruction, and join in the privileges of public worship. More than this, the temperance society makes no pretension to do. By the universal suffrage of its members, a law is passed among themselves for the physical and moral benefit of the whole body; and if, as we are well assured, there is a vast and cheering number from among the reclaimed, who have not rested satisfied with a mere physical and moral reformation, but have afterwards been brought to a saving knowledge of the truths of the Gospel, we claim for the temperance society no further merit in this great work, than that of having first restored to them the healthy action of their mental powers, so that they might listen to instruction *clothed* and in their *right minds*.

We presume not to suppose that in the resources of Divine mercy there are not means of sufficient potency to reclaim the most abject and abandoned of human beings, without the instrumentality of his fellow-man; nor do we dispute that if the words of the faithful minister *could reach* the *ear* and the *understanding* of the victim of intemperance, he would stand, as to the means of conversion, on the same footing with the victims of every other vice. But the difference between him and others, and that which places him beyond the pale of religious influence, is the fact that he cannot hear,—that his understanding is incapacitated, and, consequently, that his heart is sealed. What, then, is to be done? You must first awake the sleeping man, before you can make him understand that his life is in danger; and this is precisely what the temperance society professes, hopes, and trusts to effect.

"We can appeal to clergymen of the Church of England," says the address already quoted, "who have made extensive inquiries of their brother clergymen, as to the number of persons who have been reclaimed from drunkenness under their ministry, and it is confidently asserted as the result of that inquiry, that not one clergymen in twenty, after all their years of labor in the pulpit and in the parish, can point to a single instance of a person in ordinary health being reclaimed from this particular sin.* And yet the Total Abstinence Society can point to thousands of instances in which, in a few short years, by the blessing of God on the temperance pledge, the temptation has been overcome, and the victim reclaimed. But more than this, not a few of those who have been thus raised from the lowest depths of sin and degradation—who were not long since to be found in the haunts of vice, blaspheming the sacred name, are now to be seen at their places of worship, offering up their humble and sincere thanksgiving and praise to Him

* This statement is taken from "*An Address of a Clergyman to his Brother Clergymen*," published by the Church of England Total Abstinence Society, Tract, No. 5.

who in His mercy has been pleased to bless so simple a means, in bringing them first to reflection, then to attend upon religious worship, and finally to repentance and saving faith in a compassionate Redeemer."

But beyond the objection already stated, it is often said, that "we find nothing about total abstinence in the Bible." The truth of this assertion is freely acknowledged, as well as that the Bible contains nothing about public schools, particular modes of worship, or Bible societies; but if it contains nothing about total abstinence, it contains much about temperance, and much about excess; and if the one cannot be ensured, and the other avoided, without total abstinence, there is nothing said in the Bible to prevent this simple and harmless alternative being resorted to.

I must here be allowed, instead of offering any observations of my own, to quote from a sermon by the Rev. W. H. Turner, vicar of Banwell, a short and most satisfactory statement of what are the sentiments prevailing generally on this part of the subject among the members of the temperance society.

"I am well aware of the specious objection which has been raised, that as drunkenness was a sin known at the time of our Saviour's incarnation, and he set no example of total abstinence, that consequently his example is against us: nay, more, that if it is now insisted on as a point of Christian obligation, it would be imputing to Christ and his apostles a failure in their duty.

"In meeting this objection, I do not wish to dwell upon the fact, that the wines of Judea were widely different from the intoxicating liquors now causing so much sin and misery in our land. I would merely ask those who thus argue in consequence of Christ's having used wine, whether it can be doubted, that in the many changes of human society, circumstances may not arise which might make what is a most innocent habit at one period, a very dangerous, inexpedient, and sinful one at another? It was never intended that Christ's example *in things indifferent* (or not in themselves sinful) should be thus applied—it is the spirit rather than the letter of it we must use. His example, in the letter, applies only to the age in which he lived; in its spirit, to every situation in which man can be placed in this the period of his earthly trial. Now drunkenness in Judea was not the great stumbling-block to the Gospel, as it is at this moment in England; it was a sin there comparatively little known, while here it is the leading, besetting, and almost overwhelming one.

"But it will not be denied, I think, that the Apostle Paul must have known the mind, as well as what had been the practice of his divine Master; and do we find him urging that, because Christ ate or drank any particular article, that he had therefore a right to use it under all circumstances, or that it might not even be sinful in him to do so? Quite the reverse; while regarding such things as neither good nor evil in themselves, he is guided by the effect which his using them may produce on the eternal interests of his fellow-men. And such is the application we make of the Saviour's conduct, believing that we cannot have a better judge, or a more experienced commentator on all his actions, than St. Paul.

"The great principle which our Saviour gives us, and which his whole example enforces, as to our conduct towards our fellow-creatures, is to love them as ourselves. To bring His example in things indifferent, so as in any way to militate against this principle, must be wrong."

CHAPTER VI.

PRIVATE OBJECTIONS, AND GENERAL ENCOURAGEMENTS.

HAVING glanced slightly at some of the most serious objections to total abstinence, and such as will be found in many of the temperance publications more ably and more fully refuted, we will turn our attention to those of a less serious nature, though one can hardly help suspecting that the real root of the matter lies in some of these. I will, therefore, call them private objections, because, though powerful in their operation upon individual conduct, they are not frequently brought forward in public, nor made grounds of objection, except in the private intercourse of life. To examine these objections in detail, however, would be to collect together some of the most irrational modes of reasoning, and some of the most partial and unfounded statements, which have ever been laid before the world. A few only of these I will therefore point out, not as being worthy of refutation, but simply as proofs of the unfair and superficial manner in which the subject is too frequently treated, even by persons who professedly hold the welfare of society, and the good of their fellow-creatures at heart.

"What!" exclaim the lovers of what is called good cheer, and the advocates of the rights of the people, "would you deny the poor man his beer? Do penance as you like yourselves, but never attempt to deprive a free-born English laborer of the roast beef and brown ale of his country." Did the English laborer always manage to get his roast beef along with his brown ale, less would perhaps be said on the subject; but, unfortunately, in too many cases, the beef is wholly wanting. The advocates of total abstinence therefore reply, "we *deny* the poor laborer nothing. He is a free agent when he takes the temperance pledge, and is quite at liberty to withdraw his name whenever he wishes to discontinue the practice. But we invite him, and we do this with the most cordial desire to promote his welfare—we invite him to exchange his beer for bread, for decent clothing, and for a comfortable and respectable home, all which he has sacrificed for beer alone. We invite him to give up one article of diet, and that not an essential one, in order that he may purchase a sufficiency of wholesome food to satisfy the hunger of himself, his wife, and his children—in order that he may provide for his family a home, give them the advantages of education, and lay up a store for seasons of sickness, or of old age."

Again, it is said—"Why take up the subject of intemperance in particular? Why be so mightily concerned about that, when so many other kinds of reformation are needed?" I am not aware that the advocates of temperance are singularly negligent of the wants of their fellow-creatures in other respects; and even if they should throw more of their energy and influence into this cause than any other, it might surely be permitted them, as well as others, according to the bent of their own minds, or their own views of personal duty, to choose the field of usefulness in which to labor. In every branch of science and philosophy, as well as in all arts and manufactures, men are not quarrelled with, or considered more foolish on other points, because they give their time and attention chiefly to one object of pursuit or investigation; and why should it not be the same in that higher philosophy which has the moral good of mankind in view? Why should certain individuals not give the energy of their minds, and the weight of their influence, to the support of schools, asylums, or any other charitable institution whatever, without being accused of absurdity, because they do not give an equal share of attention to every other benevolent institution in the world? It would indeed require that the mind of man should be supernatural in its vastness and its power, to divide his attention equally among all the charitable institutions existing in the present day, without reducing the operation of his benevolence to little more than the mere bestowment of a passing thought upon each.

Then there is another very important objection, and one which must be treated with more gravity, inasmuch as it arises from the fact that the temperance society is joined in by persons of all religious denominations, and even by those of no religion at all; and if they meet together in this society for the purpose of being less irrational, less disorderly, and less vicious—why not? If a mighty river should overflow its banks, and threaten to inundate the land, should we refuse to lend a helping hand to construct an embankment for the purpose of keeping back the desolating waters, because here and there a man without religion, or whose religion differed from our own, was engaged in the great work? Most assuredly we should not; and if not in a case of physical calamity, how much less ought we to hesitate on the same grounds in stemming that destructive tide of moral evil which has long been waging deadly war against our domestic, social, and national prosperity?—more especially since it seems impossible that our religious sentiments should in the slightest degree be compromised by pledging ourselves, with whoever might choose to join us, simply to the advance of temperance and sobriety.

There is, however, an objection raised by some against this very pledge, which is called a vow, in consequence of which those who sign it are supposed to be under a sort of bondage, in itself neither rational, agreeable, nor altogether right. But I must here quote again on the subject from the societies' address, as conveying the sentiments of many rather than of one. It is here observed, that "such objectors do not scruple to sign an agreement for their own pecuniary advantage, in the shape of a lease, a deed, or a bill, &c. Why, then, should they object to sign an agreement for their own moral or physical advantage, or from the higher motive of benefiting others? There are, no doubt, many individuals who could abstain without signing any agreement, and who may therefore, apart from any scruple, consider it of no importance: let such remember, however, that they abstain, not so much for their own sakes as for the sake of others, and that the signing of a pledge has proved of infinite importance to the poor drunkard, and been the blessed means of reclaiming thousands, whose every previous effort to reform *without signing* had failed; why then should they object to encourage by their example that which can do them no harm, but which has been, and may still be of immense benefit to a poor fallen or falling brother? Let us view the matter in the generous spirit of the great apostle, who declared, '*To the weak became I as weak, that I might gain the weak; I am made all things to all men, that I might by all means save some.*' Would that this disinterested and benevolent spirit dwelt in every heart, and our appeal on behalf of the suffering victims of intemperance would surely be answered by discontinuing the custom which constantly *sows the seed* from which all their miseries spring."

An exclusive regard for our own individual benefit is natural to all human beings, and if not pursued at the expense of injury to others, the principle is certainly good as far as it goes; because, to use the words of the old adage, "if every one would mend one," the world would soon be better than it is. Thus we cannot but rejoice to observe that the system of total abstinence from intoxicating beverages is gradually progressing among individuals; that there is now no difficulty in refusing to take wine in company, and that, say what men will, the *habits* of the friends of abstinence are obtaining countenance and credit from society in general. No one can fail to be convinced of this, who looks back to the state of society in England twenty or thirty years ago; and while we are well aware that a large proportion of the families by whom intemperance is now discouraged where it was once allowed, would disdain the thought of associating themselves with a society of total abstainers, the fact is very evident that the moving of this great question throughout this and other countries, and the awakening of public attention to so important a subject, has had much to do with the increased regard for moderation prevailing in respectable families, and the diminution of intemperance among the people at large.

Good, however, as all this unquestionably is, it has nothing whatever to do with the establishment of a respectable society, under the encouragement of which the weak and the tempted may find safety without disgrace; and those who practise only upon themselves, and weigh carefully all their own feelings, whether for or against the system as it operates upon their own health and comfort, know little of the enjoyment of those far-stretching views of benevolence which embrace the good of the whole human family, and which glance over every little symptom of personal inconvenience, as not worthy of being thought of for a moment, in connection with so vast and important a scheme for the advancement of their fellow-beings in the scale of virtue and of happiness.

But again, as regards the pledge, it should always be remembered, that it is only considered binding so long as the name of the individual remains enrolled among those of other members of the society; that those who thus subscribe their names to a compact entered into by individuals for the benefit of the whole body, may withdraw them whenever they think fit; and the fact that many persons do so is surely sufficient evidence of perfect liberty of choice and free agency being allowed to all.

Those who have paid the least attention to the subject, must see that to the tempted the pledge is necessary, because it is a means exactly calculated to operate as a check at the only moment when a check can be availing—at the moment when the weak are hesitating whether or not they will take just a *little;* and if those who object to the pledge would be kind enough to propose any more agreeable plan by which the same kind of check could be brought into operation in an equally efficacious manner, I do not think the friends of the Total Abstinence Society are so wedded to their own system as not to be willing to exchange it for a better.

It has frequently happened, in consequence of the fallibility of human reason, that the first system adopted for the prevention of any particular kind of evil, or the promotion of any good, has not been by any means the best. Indeed, the very defects of the system in its early operation have awakened a spirit of opposition, which in its turn has originated another and a better system for carrying out the same object. Thus we have some of us looked long and earnestly to the avowed opponents of the total abstinence scheme of reformation, for some other—some nobler, and, at the same time, more effectual device, for accomplishing the same great end; but while all agree that the object is good, and all desire that the absolute drunkard should be reclaimed, not one of these enlightened individuals has yet favored us with a better scheme than our own; and until they do so, we must be satisfied to go on upon our present plan, by no means discouraged by what we already see and know of its results.

Often as the motives of human beings are mistaken in their transactions one with another, often as the actions of the benevolent are misunderstood, and a mean or selfish character assigned to feelings the most noble and disinterested, never have such motives, actions, or feelings, been more grossly misrepresented, than in reference to the temperance pledge. Oh! could such cavillers be made to believe me when I say, there are sensations of thrilling interest connected with the signing of this pledge, which heroes well might envy, and rich men give their gold to buy. Why, on that very page, disfigured by the unskilled lettering of a ploughman's hand, there are tears of such intense and exquisite delight, as unsophisticated Nature weeps when her emotions are too strong for smiles.

Upon that page, perhaps, the fond and faithful wife is gazing, heedless of the passing crowd. Her thoughts go back to the dark ruined home she has just left without a hope, and to her poor babes, who, weak with hunger, wept themselves to sleep. With borrowed cloak to hide her destitution, she stole out at the dark hour, and mixing in the crowd, found place among her fellows in poverty and distress, who came at least to *hear* of a strange but simple plan for calling back such wanderers as her husband long had been. And now she listens most intently, for the language is all such as comes home to her experience, and is level with her understanding. The speaker must have known her case. He tells of hope! but no—that never can be hers! If *he* were here—perhaps—and then a deep, deep sigh bursts from her lips; but she listens still, and more intently, to the speaker's moving words, until her heart becomes too full; and she looks round to see if any among her neighbors—for of friends she has none left—are there to profit by those words of touching truth. What ails the woman? Whom has she seen among the crowd? Her cheek is flushed with burning crimson, and her eyes are bright with living fire. It is—it must be him! She cannot be mistaken in her husband's form, still beautiful to her. Far back among the crowd he stands with folded arms, his gaze intent upon the speaker's face. No smile of thoughtless folly flits across his brow, but a deep earnestness is stamped on every feature as he gazes on. But what is that which moves him now? A simple tale of woman's truth. The wife beholds him dash the tear-drop from his eye. A gathering mist is in her own, but she forgets it all; nothing is present with her but that other self—that life in which alone she lives. Alas! it is all over: the speaker ceases, and the company breaks up. The wife waits anxiously the moment when her husband shall withdraw, thinking to join him at the door; yet, fearing to intrude too hastily upon his softened feelings, she stands patiently resigned, with folded arms upon her breast, pushed here and there by the receding crowd, no one of whom takes note of her or hers. Still there is something to be done beside the platform where the speaker stands, and numbers gather to the spot. A book is opened—a pen is offered—a kind and friendly voice invites the company to sign. Make way! the figure of a man advances from behind. Make way! for wonder glances forth from every eye. Behind that figure is a female form—a shadow—a pale faded thing, so feeble that she cannot stand, but leans upon his shoulder with one clasping arm. "There! I have signed!" exclaimed the man; "and now, my wife, come home, and let us pray to-night." Stop but one moment. What a hand is hers! so thin, so trembling; yet she grasps that pen as if it were a rod of iron, to inscribe deep words of mercy in the rock forever. They pass away together—that penniless and friendless pair, strong in each other's truth, rich in each other's love. Weeks glide away—months—or perhaps a year; and they are seen together now, so happy! with their rosy children, standing at their cottage door—their blazing fire and clean swept hearth, and plenteous table spread within.

Such are the scenes which cheer on every hand the laborer in the temperance cause, and if this passing sketch convey a slight idea of the interest excited by such scenes, what must be that of entering into the details of family and individual history, where all things temporal and eternal are at stake, and all hang as it were upon the transcript of a single name?

Nor is the situation of the drunkard's wife, sad though it be, the only one which claims our sympathy on these occasions. The little hungry and neglected child of an intemperate mother will sometimes come alone to sign; the old man with gray hairs, whose sons have all gone down before him, with this curse upon them, to untimely graves. And if nothing else affected us in such cases, one would suppose it might be enough to touch a heart of common mould, to think only of the poverty and destitution of those who thus come forward to make a voluntary surrender of what has become to them their only means of bodily enjoyment. *We* can go home to our abundance, to the cheering hearth, the social board, and to all those delicate and varied substitutes for gratifying pampered appetite, which custom has sanctioned, or ingenuity devised. *We* have all these, but the poor have nothing—more especially the intemperate poor; and, therefore, when they have signed the pledge, they have made what to them was the greatest possible sacrifice which duty could require; because, in proportion as they had previously given themselves up to the destructive habit of existing upon stimulants alone, their homes had become stripped of every other source of comfort or indulgence, and that which was in reality their ruin, had, in all probability, come to be applied to, in order to make them forget that they had nothing else.

What an effort then is this! what a sacrifice for a poor ignorant man or woman to make! and what a privilege to be enabled to assist them, by making the same sacrifice ourselves, in kind, though by no means in degree! Indeed, there is something in looking upon an assembly of persons of this description—in marking the tearful eyes and faded cheeks of those who are struggling against temptation, either to themselves or others, as against a mighty foe; there is something, too, in visiting their destitute and comfortless abodes, and giving them a word of encouragement, from our own experience, in favor of making the experiment at least; there is something in passing the senseless drunkard reeling home, and thinking that *we* have ceased to be one of the number who help on his way to ruin; there is something in these thoughts and feelings so far beyond the common interests which pervade the mere etiquette of polished society, that if any one should ask me what they could have recourse to as a means of excitement to supply the want of wine, I should recommend them to try the excitement of joining heart and hand in the promotion of the temperance cause.

Persons deeply impressed with the importance of these subjects of profound interest, which are necessarily involved in the temperance question, are not likely to have their attention diverted from the main points of discussion, by any little inaccuracies of style or diction which occur in the public advocacy of the cause. Hence it is possible they may think less than some others do, of the particular manner in which that advocacy is maintained. It may naturally be supposed, however, to constitute rather an important objection with the refined and fastidious, when not thus seriously impressed, that many public speakers on the temperance question are illiterate, and some of them injudicious men.

It is, however, a hard—I had almost said a cruel case, when respectable and enlightened individuals stand aloof from the cause for this reason—because if they and their associates of the same class would come forward in its support, there would no longer be any need to trust the management of temperance matters so much to the hands of ignorant or illiterate men. The absurdities of which they complain would then be done away with: the evils would be remedied; the objectors themselves teaching us a more excellent way of influencing the people at large.

It seems strange, however, that the charge of absurdity should so often be brought forward against the temperate class. In my own ignorance, I should have supposed that rather attached to the opposite party, and that we gave our countenance to absurdity more effectually, by joining in the habit of drinking wine, than in uniting ourselves with those who abstain from such things altogether. I should have thought too, in the same ignorance, that had we sought the world over for instances of absurdity, those which result from intoxication could not have been exceeded in any of its different stages, from the first of excitement, to the last of imbecility—from the buffoon at a country fair, to the gentleman who leaves his wine at a late hour to make himself agreeable in the drawing room to the ladies. I should have thought that to partake, even in a slight degree, of that which produced this absurdity in others, had been something like an approach to absurdity in ourselves. But the world is unquestionably a wise world, and these are enlightened times ; and the opinions of individuals must bow before those of the many.

Again, respectable persons, and especially those who have much depending upon the orderly and systematic operations of laborers and work-people, are very fond of saying that total abstinence is a *good thing for the poor,* and as such they often give it the advantage of their countenance to a certain extent. Even this acknowledgment is good, so far as it goes, and even this countenance is of use, for the poor are not so much accustomed to look to the rich for sympathy and encouragement, as to depend entirely upon them for their support ; and in the temperance reformation more especially, they have learned a new lesson of reliance upon themselves. It would not seem very wonderful however, if the poor under such circumstances should sometimes retort upon us, and say—"If you who enjoy all the luxuries of life and have no need to labor, cannot live without your wine, how can you expect a hard-working man who has nothing else, to live without his beer ?"

And this has been said many times, and would unquestionably be repeated much oftener than it is, did not some noble instances present themselves to our view, of wealthy and influential persons who have come forward practically and heartily to join in the cause, on the same footing as the poor, or at least so far as circumstances would allow their situation to be the same ; nor am I aware that they have lost any thing of their importance, or their good influence in other respects, from such association. What they have gained in peace of mind, satisfaction, and happiness, can never be fully understood or appreciated by those who have only gone along with them to the extent of countenancing total abstinence as an *excellent thing for the poor.*

But there is another objection which I speak of last, not because it is least important, quite the contrary ; for I believe it to be beyond all comparison more influential than any other, or than all others put together, in its practical influence upon individual conduct. It may safely be said to rule paramount in its widespreading power to deter both men or women of all classes,—the *old and the young,* the rich and the poor, the good and the evil, from signing their names to the temperance pledge. Indeed this single ground of objection is of such overwhelming potency, that vast numbers who have the self-denial, and who are now most scrupulous abstainers, would shrink from the bare idea of connecting themselves with a temperance society.

The fact is, they consider it *low,* and in that one word, we read the sad and irretrievable doom of all those poor tempted ones, who would willingly sign the temperance pledge, if any considerable number of the ladies or gentlemen of their acquaintance had done so.

In hearing this objection brought forward, which we do almost every day, and in detecting its secret influence, which we do still more frequently, I have often wondered, as in the case of absurdity, what could be more *low,* than the drinking practices of our country. It is true that in these, at least in their excess, the delicate and respectable part of the community do not immediately join ; but the miserable and degrading practices themselves are evident to us almost at every step in walking the streets of our large towns ; while often in the summer's evening's ramble, those village sounds, which poetry has ever loved to describe, are broken into discord by the mingling of insane laughter, and anger even more insane.

Now one would certainly have thought, in the first view of the case, that a delicate-minded Christian lady, for instance, would scarcely, even on the ground of vulgarity, have chosen to regale herself with the same kind of stimulus which she knew to have produced these rude revels, and these inhuman sounds. But truly the science of refinement is a mysterious and profound one, and it needs the schooling of a lifetime to teach a common mind, how total abstinence from every thing which can intoxicate, is essentially less low than to give our countenance, by the influence of habit, to the very practice which is associated with more vulgarity than any other now existing among mankind.

But granting the reasonableness of throwing the stigma of vulgarity on the side of abstinence, there is a material difference betwixt joining with the low for the purpose of raising their moral character, and joining with them in the use of that which must necessarily make them lower still. The most fastidious of Christian ladies would scarcely hesitate to enter a village church because a great proportion of the congregation there consisted of the poor. No, she would rather welcome and encourage their attendance, as a means of rendering them more enlightened, and consequently, more refined; and if, in the one case, we believe that the influence of religion will effect this change, in the other, we have reason to believe that the influence of total abstinence will at least effect a moral and physical amendment.

There is a class of individuals, and I have the privilege of being associated with one, who speak of every kind of wickedness as being merely in "bad taste," and consequently, not worthy of their attention either in one way or another. Now, although this may be a very comfortable way of passing over much that is painful in the aspect of this life, for my own part, I envy not the drawing-room distinction of being ignorant that there is such a thing as vice existing in the world. But knowing what we do know, seeing what we must see, unless our physical as well as moral perceptions were strangely obscured, can we stand aloof and refuse to lend a helping hand to those who are perishing, because it is not polite or fashionable or approved in the higher circles, to attempt to save them?

No one knows better than myself the pain of choosing such a theme as that which occupies these pages, and if it had not been sufficiently repugnant to my own feelings, there are kind friends who would have made it so by their harsh and uncharitable remarks, as if it had been a thing of mere pastime to write about the poor drunkard and his degradation. I would not, however, *willingly* exchange my humbling part for that which they take in this matter; for happier, far happier is the thought of doing nothing to accelerate the ruin of those who, from this fatal cause, are falling too rapidly around us, than of having thrown the weight of our influence, just so far as it had weight, on the side of an enemy already too powerful for the weak to conquer, or the tempted to resist.

To these, as well as all other objectors to the operation of the temperance pledge, I would say one word in conclusion: you cannot stop the progress of this cause; perhaps you would not if you could; why then attempt to wound its advocates? The enemy, perchance, is far from you. He may not yet have reached your family or breathed a blight upon your name. But if the time should ever come when you or yours should fall beneath his power, who then will be the friends whose pity you will ask—whose protection you will claim? Will they not be those who have formed themselves into a society for the purpose of arresting the progress of this desolating vice, and of saving the victim of intemperance when he could not save himself?

www.ingramcontent.com/pod-product-compliance
Lightning Source LLC
LaVergne TN
LVHW021318110826
845150LV00003B/612

* 9 7 8 1 4 2 5 5 5 6 5 3 2 *